THE
EASTERN
EUROPE
COLLECTION

THE
POLITICAL EVOLUTION
OF THE
HUNGARIAN NATION

ecil
areus

C. M. Knatchbull-Hugessen Brabourne

ARNO PRESS & THE NEW YORK TIMES

New York - 1971

Reprint Edition 1971 by Arno Press Inc.

Reprinted from a microfilm copy in
The Library of Congress

LC# 79-135843

ISBN 0-405-02785-0

The Eastern Europe Collection

ISBN for complete set: 0-405-02730-3

Manufactured in the United States of America

The Political Evolution

of the

Hungarian Nation

The
Political Evolution
of the
Hungarian Nation

BY

THE HON. C. M. KNATCHBULL-HUGESSEN.

IN TWO VOLUMES
VOL. I

LONDON
THE NATIONAL REVIEW OFFICE
23 RYDER STREET, ST. JAMES'S
1908

TO

AN 'AUSTRO-HUNGARIAN'

MY WIFE

PREFACE

THIS book in no sense claims to be a history. Within the compass of two volumes it is hardly possible to do more than give a general view of the gradual development of a nation which can boast a thousand years of constitutional existence. The greater part of the first volume should be regarded merely as an introduction to the succeeding pages which deal with Hungary's political *renaissance*, with the events of 1848, with the juridical relations of Hungary to Austria, and with the circumstances which attended the creation of the dualism of to-day. The last two chapters are intended to facilitate the comprehension of certain problems which are of more than local interest. If, as I hope will soon be the case, one of the historical authorities of Hungary (my indebtedness to whose works has b.en inadequately acknowledged in the limited space available for footnotes) finds time to write an exhaustive history of his country for the special benefit of English readers, my labours will be sufficiently rewarded if the present work receives mention as a serious attempt to lift a corner of the veil which ignorance of the Hungarian language necessarily interposes between the British public and the only reliable sources of information as to the growth and nature of the political institutions of the Magyars.

C. M. K.-H.

Hungaria . . . cum Partibus adnexis Regnum liberum, et relate ad totam legalem Regiminis formam (huc intellectis quibusvis Dicasteriis suis) independens, id est nulli alteri Regno aut populo obnoxium, sed propriam habens Consistentiam et Constitutionem, proinde a legitime coronato haereditario Rege suo, adeoque etiam a Sua Majestate Sacratissima, successoribusque ejus Hungariae Regibus, propriis Legibus et Consuetudinibus, non vero ad normam aliarum Provinciarum . . . regendum et gubernandum.—LAW x. 1790-91.

Rex habet superiorem, Deum. Item Legem per quam factus est Rex. Item Curiam suam.—BRACTON.

The Political Evolution of the Hungarian Nation

CHAPTER I

"LET not vanity deceive us ; it is the fact that Europe is scarcely aware of our existence, and that many an African settlement is better known than our country, which foreigners regard as a productive but uncivilised colony of Austria." These words are almost as true to-day as when they were spoken by Deák more than sixty-five years ago. There are many educated people in England who believe that Austria is a homogeneous nation speaking a mysterious " Austrian " language ; while Hungary, to whom "a venerable monarch, rendered wise by experience and benevolent by misfortune," has conceded some measure of local autonomy in order to satisfy the unreasonable demands of a turbulent population, is occupied by a gipsy race which justifies its existence by its ability to provide weird music for the postprandial delectation of cosmopolitan plutocrats. The better informed, who derive their knowledge of Hungarian history solely from prejudiced German and Austrian sources, are hypnotised by the legend that nothing but affection for the aged Emperor prevents the disruption of the polyglot congeries known as the Austrian Empire, and see in every act of assertion of Hungary's historic rights a parallel to the act of a maniac who, from motives of conceit or revenge, would amuse himself with lucifer matches in a powder-magazine. Even the Press will, from time to time, speak of the Golden Bull, the Pragmatic Sanction, and the Compromise of 1867, each in turn, as having conferred a Constitution on Hungary. Little wonder, therefore, that the position of affairs in the Dual Monarchy and the justification of Hungary's attitude with regard to certain questions are so misunderstood, a reasonable comprehension being impossible without some knowledge of the gradual development of political institutions which are as old as, or older than, the British Constitution.

As Guizot says, " l'histoire est essentiellement successive . . . un peuple a beau renier son passé, il n'est pas en son pouvoir de l'anéantir ni de s'y soustraire absolument, et bientôt surviennent des situations, des nécessités, qui le ramènent dans les voies où il a marché pendant des siècles," and this is perhaps more true of Hungary than of any other nation. The Hungarian Constitution, which has been obscured at intervals, violated at times, and suspended for a period, only to prove its indestructibility, is the product of no charter or fundamental statute, but is the result of a slow process of development, of a combination of statute and customary law which finds its nearest parallel in Great Britain. It is remarkable that two such different races should have proceeded on such similar lines as the Anglo-Saxon and the Asiatic people, which, both as regards language and primitive institutions, introduced an entirely new element into Europe. The four blows with the sword directed, at his coronation, to the four cardinal points, by every Hungarian king down to Francis Joseph are an emblem and a recognition of the fact that the Magyar people has had to maintain itself by force of arms against the unceasing attacks of alien neighbours ; and the fact that a few thousand wanderers from Asia were able to preserve their individuality and institutions in the midst of an ocean of Slavs, Germans, and Turks, and obtained comparatively quickly a position of equality with members of the European family, argues the possession of exceptional military and political qualities, of exceptional cohesiveness, of a stoical capacity for endurance, and of a rooted confidence in themselves and in their future which no vicissitudes of fortune have been able to destroy. The alien jargon first heard by European ears twelve hundred years ago has maintained its existence in spite of the competition of German and Slav dialects, of deliberate discouragement and temporary neglect, and has developed into a language which, for fulness and expressiveness, for the purpose of science as well as of poetry, is the equal if not the superior of the majority of European tongues. Palacky, the great Czech historian, expressed the opinion that "the invasion and definitive establishment of the Magyars is one of the most important events in the world's history. Slavdom never received a more fatal blow during its existence of several thousand years. It extended in the ninth century from the borders of Holstein to the Peloponnesus . . . . and the Magyar by driving a wedge into the heart of the state in process of formation destroyed it, and therewith all the hopes of the Slavs." A people which has rendered such services to the cause of European equilibrium, which stood for centuries as the *antemurale clypeusque Christianitatis* between the Turk and the Western nations, and has shown such vitality and persistency in the past, is the chief defensive force to be reckoned with in the future should, as some fear, a graver danger arise to the balance of power in Eastern Europe than was ever presented by the spectre of Panslavism.

Research and speculation as to the origin of the Hungarian race has on the whole been singularly barren of positive results, and the conflict of opinion as to whether the Magyars were Ugro-Finns who acquired certain Turkish customs, or Turks who adopted Ugro-Finnish habits, is probably of little interest to English readers. The very origin of the names Hungarian and Magyar is uncertain. Jordanes, who wrote in Constantinople about the year 550, refers to the Hunugurs as one of the Hun tribes inhabiting Scythia or the great Sarmatian plain in the neighbourhood of the Volga ; and Theophanes in his *Chronographia* of even earlier date speaks of Muagyer, possibly the primitive form of the name Magyar, as king of the Huns.[1] The earliest Hungarian writers[2] agree as to the Hunnish origin of the race, and the anonymous scribe or secretary of King Béla III. states that it migrated to Pannonia, having heard that that country formerly belonged to Attila, the ancestor of Árpád.[3] On the other hand, the Emperor Constantine Porphyrogenitus,[4] who presumably had access to the best contemporary sources of information, says that the migration westward was the result of attacks by a neighbouring tribe, the Patzinakites (Bessenyők), which necessitated the discovery of a new habitation. Professor Vámbéry[5] believes that the Hungarians were Turko-Tartars, and both Arab and Greek writers, including the two emperors Constantine and Leo VI.,[6] agree in regarding them as a branch of the Turkish race. Further, the oldest proper names Árpád and Zoltán are undoubtedly of Turkish origin. One thing seems sure, namely, that the earliest

[1] Marczali, "A Vezérek Kora," in *A Magyar Nemzet Története*, i. 8, Budapest, 1898.

[2] (a) "Anonymus de gestis Hungarorum," *circa* 1250, in Endlicher's *Hungaricarum rerum Monumenta* ; (b) Kézai, court priest of László IV., *circa* 1282, *Gesta Hunnorum et Hungarorum*, Endlicher, p. 83 ; (c) *The Vienna Illustrated Chronicle*, written in 1358 by a Minorite friar, Mark. Comparison of (b) and (c) shows that both were derived from an earlier source unknown to Anonymus.

[3] Anonymus, ch. v.

[4] *De Administrando Imperio*, ch. xxxvii., *circa* 950, in Marczali's *A Magyar Történet Kútfőinek Kézikönyve*. (*Enchiridion Fontium*), Budapest, 1901.

[5] *A Magyarok Eredete*, 2nd ed., Budapest, 1882, 24 *sqq*. 197-199. *A Török Faj*, Budapest, 1885, p. 95.

[6] *On Military Tactics*, ch. xli., *circa* 890. *Enchiridion Fontium*, p. 14.

definite home was in the neighbourhood of the modern
Uralsk and Samara, abandoned, in or about the year 700,
in favour of Lebedia, the district between Astrakhan and
Stavropol, where a stay of about a century was made
prior to the final migration westward. From Lebedia,
according to Constantine (ch. xxxviii.), part of the tribes
went towards Persia, in which statement he is supported by
the Pressburg *Chronicle* of the fifteenth century,[1] which
says that some of Nimrod's posterity—the Hungarians—
"inhabited a district of Persia and resembled the Huns
in figure and complexion, but differed from them somewhat in speech, only however to the extent to which
Saxons differ from Thuringians ;" and it is a fact that
there are Persian elements in the Hungarian language.
The spilling of blood at the taking of an oath referred to
by the anonymous writer[2] curiously recalls the Parthian
custom,[3] and a fourteenth century account[4] of Hungarian
military tactics exactly corresponds with the classical
description of Parthian methods.

One of the most interesting theories is that mentioned
by Pauler,[5] who identifies the Hungarians with the
Bashkirs, believing them to have retained the original
Bashkir language, while those of their fellow-tribesmen
who did not take part in the exodus lost it. The theory
depends to a considerable extent on the degree of trust-
worthiness attributable to the account which a Dominican
friar[6] gives of his wanderings in 1235, who alleges that
he found between the Caucasus and the Volga a people

---

[1] *Chronica minora*, ed. Flórián, p. 2.   [2] Endlicher, *o.c. p.* 8.

[3] Tacitus, *Annals*, xii. 47 : "Mos est regibus quotiens in societatem coeant
implicare dextras pollicesque inter se vincire, nodoque praestringere : mox
ubi sanguis in artus se extremos suffuderit, levi ictu cruorem eliciunt atque
invicem lambunt. Id foedus arcanum habetur quasi mutuo cruore sacratum."

[4] Matteo Villani, *Croniche*, vi. 54. *Enchiridion Fontium*, p. 225 *sqq.* : "La
loro guerra non è in potere mantenere campo, ma di correre e fugire e
cacciare saettando le loro saette, e di rivolgersi e di ritornare alla battaglia."

[5] *A Magyar Nemzet Története Szt. Istvdnig*, p. 241 *sqq.* Budapest, 1900.

[6] *De facto Ungariae Magnae a Fratre Ricardo inventae*, Endlicher, p. 252.

"whose language was completely Magyar," who knew that the Magyars were of like origin with themselves, and that they had gone westward, but were ignorant of their actual habitation. Vámbéry[1] does not believe in Brother Julian's description, and says that it is full of geographical inaccuracies; but it is curious that the *Chronicon Dubnicense*[2] of 1358 describes Scythia as divided into three kingdoms, one of which is Bascardia; that Arab writers refer to the Magyars as Badzsgerd; and that when in 1848 Cossacks from the Ural came to Hungary they invariably called the Hungarians Bashkirs.[3] It need scarcely be said that the early chronicles, though to some extent confirmed by outside sources of information, have no claim to be considered as containing more than a grain or two of historical truth[4]; they are, however, interesting as showing the views entertained by the Hungarians of the thirteenth and fourteenth centuries as to their origin and early history, and the nature of the family legends from which such opinions were undoubtedly derived.

As regards the early organisation of the tribes, we are perhaps on more solid ground, as our information is derived from a period when feudalism was firmly established in Europe, and if our authorities had merely drawn on their imagination for a description of the primitive political system of the Magyars, it is not likely that they would have given us a picture so widely different from that presented by the contemporary institutions of other countries. It appears that the nation consisted of

[1] *A Magyarok Eredete*, p. 112.   See also *A Török Faj*, p. 610 *sqq.*
[2] Ed. Flórián, p. 9.
[3] Marczali, "A Vezérek Kora," in *A Mag. Nem. Tört.* i. p. 34, citing Reclus, *Géographie Universelle*.   Count Eugene Zichy, as the result of his travels and investigations in the Caucasus, Siberia, the desert of Gobi, and elsewhere, believes that the Magyars originally came from North China and settled near the Volga and the Caspian in the second or third century A.D.; also that they kept quite distinct, ethnically, from Turks and Finns, but that they were undoubtedly influenced by the customs and language of both races.
[4] See Hunfalvy Pál., *Magyarország Ethnographiája*, Budapest, 1876, 283.

seven tribes, the names of which have been preserved by the Emperor Constantine,[1] and one hundred and eight families ;[2] the tribes, each under its own voyvode,[3] or military leader, being separate entities for all purposes, united only by the tie of common origin and language, and by the necessity of holding together for attack and defence, and "having no fortified camps like the Romans, but living as scattered tribes and families for grazing purposes until the day of battle."[4] There was no king or archon ; but apparently at an early date two common officials were elected by the tribes in general meeting— the kadar[5] or karkhasz,[6] and the gyula or gyűlasz[6]— both judicial officers, and identical with the Rectors referred to by the anonymous scribe as having been appointed for the purpose of "settling the disputes of litigants in accordance with customary law." From their decisions an appeal lay to the general assembly of the tribes,[5] which could not only revoke an unsatisfactory decision or excessive sentence, but "could, depose the erring Rector and captains at pleasure " ; from which perhaps we may conclude that Constantine, who states that the gyűlasz was superior to the karkhasz, was mistaken in supposing that there were two judges ; for gyűlasz looks suspiciously like *gyűlés*, the Hungarian word for the general meeting to which, as we have seen, an appeal lay. Verbóczy,[7] the codifier of the Magyar customary law (1514), says that "in old days, while the Hungarians still lived under tribal organisation, the exclusive power of making laws and statutes was vested in the people," which, according to a chronicle[5] already quoted, was summoned together by a herald

---

[1] *De Administrando Imperio*, ch. xl., one of them Μεγέρη, query Magyar ; Hungarian writers of the seventeenth century use the form Magyari for Magyar. Marczali, "A Vezérek Kora," in *A Mag. Nem. Tört.* i. 46 *n*.

[2] Kézai, Endlicher, p. 88.   [3] *De Admin. Imp.* ch. xxxviii.

[4] Leo, ch. lii.   [5] *Chronicon Dubnicense*, A.D. 1358, ed. Flórián, p. 9.

[6] *De Admin. Imp.* ch. xl.

[7] *Tripartitum opus juris incliti regni Hungariae*, ii. 3.

crying, "Hear the voice of God and of the entire community. Every man is to appear armed in such and such a place, and punctually at such and such an hour, to hear the commands and the considered will of the people"; and he who failed to obey the summons without valid reason was cut in two, or sent on a forlorn hope (*ire in desperatas causas*), or reduced to slavery.

When the great westward migration was decided upon in or about the year 890, necessitating a closer union and unity of leadership, the tribes under their seven captains held a general meeting at Etelköz (*i.e.* the parts near the Etel or Volga), elected Árpád, son of Álmos, their chief, and arrived at a compact[1] which, if in fact made, may be looked upon as the foundation of the Hungarian Constitution. It was resolved :

(i) That so long as those present or their descendants should live, their chief should always be chosen from the family of Árpád.

(ii) That whatever property their united efforts might obtain, no one of them should be excluded from participation therein.

(iii) That as they had freely chosen Árpád as their chief, neither they nor their descendants should ever be excluded from the king's council, or deprived of their right to share in the government of the country.[2]

(iv) That if any of their descendants should be unfaithful to the chief, and stir up strife between him and his relations, the offender's blood should be shed, even as blood was shed in the ceremony of taking the oath of fidelity to Árpád.

---

[1] Anonymus, Endlicher's *Monumenta*, p. 7. The 6th clause is added by Michael Horváth, *Magyarország Történelme* (revised edition, Pest, 1863) i. 21, *n.*, on the doubtful authority of the Szekler *Chronicle*.

[2] This is Horváth's translation, perhaps hardly justified by the original, "nunquam a concilio ducis et honore regni privarentur."

(v) That if Árpád or any successor should break the conditions of the compact, he should be for ever accursed.

(vi) That he who refused to attend the meetings of the tribes should be cut in twain.

With regard to the controversy as to the authenticity of this document, it should be remarked that though the original does not exist, there is a copy extant which was made in the latter half of the thirteenth century, and that it contains a balder, more unadorned statement than might be expected from the pen of one disposed to glorify the past and exaggerate the importance of the early political institutions of his nation. Further, there is its non-feudal character, the absence of any reference to a graduated hierarchy, which one might expect to find in the work of a mediæval forger. Be that as it may, the fact is unquestionable that members of Árpád's family ruled in Hungary for over four hundred years ; that the institution of the congregation of the tribes summoned for judicial purposes and for the decision of all matters of general interest, if not for the discharge of true legislative functions, existed long before the exodus from Lebedia, and continued till the establishment of monarchy by St. Stephen.

When Árpád and the seven tribal captains, each at the head of 30,750 men,[1] to whom an eighth tribe of Bolgars or Kuns attached themselves,[2] set out in quest of their new home, the northern part of the old province of Pannonia was occupied by the descendants of King Svatopluk, the founder of the great Moravian kingdom, while the district between the Tisza and the Danube and the mountains of Transylvania were inhabited by sparse bands of nomad Gepidæ, Avars, and mixed Slav tribes,[3]

---

[1] Petri Ransani Epitome, *Chronica minora,* ed. Flórián, p. 179.
[2] Pauler, *o.c.* p. 14.
[3] Csuday, *Die Geschichte der Ungarn,* 2nd ed. p. 36.

incapable of serious resistance to a relentless invader. How far the occupation was effected by force of arms, and how far it amounted to no more than the seizure of vacant districts is unknown ; in any case, by the end of the ninth century the Magyars were firmly established, roughly within the limits of their present territory. Tradition [1] says that as soon as the occupation was effective Árpád held a general meeting of the tribes at Pusztaszer, near the modern Szegedin, " and there he and his nobles arranged all the customary laws of the kingdom, and the rights thereof, and the conditions of obedience to the chief and his officials, and what punishment should be apportioned to each crime committed. There also the chief made grants of land, together with all the inhabitants thereof, to the nobles who accompanied him, and the place where all these matters were arranged the Hungarians called Scerii, for there the whole business of the kingdom was settled." [2]   This is, at all events in one respect, inaccurate, for it is certain that there was no private ownership before St. Stephen's time, all land belonging to the tribe and reverting to it on the death of the temporary occupant. Further, it is obviously improbable that any cut-and-dried organisation or system of laws was arrived at, offhand, by a predatory race, which, for a century after its appearance west of the Carpathians, was occupied in making itself a terror to all central and western Europe. Its first object of attack was Moravia, of which " it entirely extirpated the inhabitants [3] in 892," and between that date and 955, when an end was put to their incursions by the battle of Augsburg, the Magyars swarmed across Germany, the north of Italy, Provence, Burgundy, Aquitaine, and the Lowlands. It is known that fortified camps were established in numerous districts, the governorship of

---

[1] Anonymus, ch. xl.
[2] " Scerii, Puszta-szer, szerződni," to make a compact.
[3] Constantine, *De Admin. Imp.* ch. xli.

which was hereditary till monarchy was established, and it is possible that the anonymous writer, in speaking of grants of land, referred to the forts and to the land adjacent thereto enjoyed by the governors in virtue of their office. Beyond such organisation for purposes of defence, it is improbable that any great alteration was made in the system, or want of system, which had existed in the old home, and in fact continued unchanged for a century or more in Transylvania.[1] Chiefs of the house of Árpád continued to be elected, and the kadar, karkhasz, or karkhan, to perform his judicial functions,[2] until, with the cessation of warlike enterprises and the consequent slackening of the loose ties which bound the tribes together, the population scattered, and it became impossible for a single judge to perform his duties effectively. The only court of appeal and political authority was the nation in arms, which no doubt found justice and preponderance of logic to be on the side of the party whose supporters shouted loudest and presented the more threatening appearance.

With the introduction of Christianity the picture changes. St. Stephen is generally credited with having effected the conversion of his people, but it is a mistake to suppose that he had only to say the word to induce the acceptance of the new doctrines. On the contrary, conversion was a slow and, to many of the converts, a painful process. Bishop Piligrin, of Passau, is inclined to claim, in his letter of 974 to Benedict VI.,[3] the credit for having converted the barbarians; but his emissaries, by their own showing, baptized no more than five thousand converts, and Géza, the father of St. Stephen, " the first of the Hungarians to believe in Christ," [4] was probably a

---

[1] Herczegh, *Magyar Jogtörténet,* p. 102, 9.

[2] Pauler, *o.c.* p. 25. The third law of St. Ladislaus, cl. 2, A.D. 1092, mentions a judge, " Sarchas nomine " ? Karkhasz.

[3] Endlicher, *Monumenta,* p. 131 *sqq.*

[4] Petri Ransani Epitome, *Chronica minora,* p. 181.

more effective missionary, as he did not hesitate to have recourse "armorum terroribus,"[1] and many noble Hungarians, "baptismum fidemque respuentes," were reduced to a menial position.[2] Seventy years later King Béla summoned to his council two representatives, "possessed of the gift of eloquence,"[3] from every village, who proceeded to justify their reputation by the form in which they couched their request that they might be allowed to revert to their pagan habits. "Let us stone the bishops, eviscerate the priests, throttle the acolytes, hang the tithe collectors, demolish the churches, and break the bells."[4] Béla asked for four days in which to consider the matter, and while the first representatives of the elective principle in Hungary sang songs abusive of the faith, to the great satisfaction of the common people,[5] collected a large force which dispersed the demonstrators, and put an end to the last open protest of any importance against compulsory conversion.

Compulsion was, no doubt, fully justified by considerations of expedience. Stephen was aware that there could be no future for Hungary unless it joined the family of Christian nations—an alien and pagan race would always be fair game for Christian, and especially for German, aggression. Christian Europe was purely monarchical, and the first king of Hungary could expect no fixity of tenure unless he qualified himself for alliances, matrimonial and otherwise, with established reigning houses by the adoption of the current religion. The opposition came from those who identified Christianity with foreign interference of Pope or Emperor, implying the loss of national individuality, if not of independence, and disliked the idea of opening the door to immigrants, bearers of western civilisa-

[1] *Chronicon Dubnicense*, p. 34.
[2] "Ad turpia servitia sunt detrusi"; see also Bonfini, *Rerum Hungaricarum Decades*, Leipzig, 1771. Dec. ii. bk. 1. (1st edition, 1568).
[3] "Facundiam habentes," *Chron. Dub.* p. 70.   [4] *Ibid.* p. 72.
[5] Horváth, *Magyarország Története*, i. 176.

tion whom Stephen was anxious to encourage.[1] It was
fortunate for Hungary that both Pope and Emperor were
so fully occupied during the eleventh century—the one
with his claim to the disposal of the imperial crown, the
other with his desire to control the election to the Holy
See—that neither had time to turn his full attention to
the new Magyar kingdom, which thus was enabled to
consolidate and establish itself on a firm basis. Stephen's
first step was to secure himself from the interference of
German bishops, who claimed ecclesiastical jurisdiction
over his kingdom, which nominally formed part of the
dioceses of Passau and Salzburg, and from that of the
Holy Roman Empire, the emperor of which considered
himself the feudal head of Europe, and as such the sole
dispenser of royal titles. This he did by applying to
Pope Sylvester for sanction for the assumption of the
crown of Hungary, who, glad of the opportunity of
preventing the royal convert and his subjects from joining
the Eastern Church, treated him with exceptional consideration, granted his request, confirmed him in his title,
and, declaring that Stephen was a very apostle for having
turned so many souls to Christ, gave him authority to
have the cross borne before him as a symbol of apostolic
rank.[2] Thus fortified, Stephen was able to set about the
consolidation of his kingdom without fear of foreign inter-

[1] "In hospitibus et adventitiis tanta inest utilitas . . . diversas linguas et
consuetudines diversaque documenta et arma secum ducunt quæ omnia regiam
ornant et magnificant aulam . . . unius linguæ uniusque moris regnum imbecille et fragile est."—St. Stephen's "Institutio Morum," written for his son's
benefit, § 6, in Marczali's *Enchiridion Fontium*, p. 65.

[2] Bishop Hartvig, "Vita S. Stephani Regis," twelfth century, in Endlicher's
Monumenta, p. 173. The authenticity of Sylvester's letter has been disputed,
but the fact remains that every king and one queen of Hungary has been
styled "Apostolic Majesty." Fessler, *Geschichte der Ungarn*, calls it a "Kunst-
werk des XVII. Jahrhunderts." See Szalay, *Magyarország Története*, Leipzig,
1852, i. 71, *sqq.* Bryce's *Holy Roman Empire*, 1906 ed. p. 199 *n.*, says,
"Apostolic Majesty was the proper title of the King of Hungary. *The
Austrian Court has recently revived it.*" It would be as correct to say that the
Mikado has recently revived the imperial Chinese title of Son of Heaven.

ference. A lawgiver and organiser was wanted, not a
military leader as in the past, and his first act was to
destroy as far as possible the independent existence of
the tribes, and to fuse them into a nation by encouraging
the development of private ownership of land,[1] and by
appointing his own officials to the governorship of the
fortified places, and placing the foreign, non-Magyar, population directly under their control. The tribal divisions
were maintained for military purposes only, and the old
idea of the sovereignty of the people in general meeting
assembled was thrown into the shade, though the recollection of the tribal congregations of old never died, and
though the necessity of the people's assent to legislation
was always recognised.[2]

Hungarian writers have claimed that the institution of
the general meeting was at all times looked upon as
possessing an authority equal to that of the King, but as will
appear hereafter the assertion can hardly be justified. The
people divested itself of the greater portion of its sovereign
rights in favour of the monarch,—the personification of
national unity,—retaining only the guarantee afforded by
the elective nature of the monarchy, the principle that he
whom the popular will had raised to the throne could be
deposed by the same agency, and the fact that a nation
in arms could always get the better of a would-be tyrant
in the days which preceded the invention of gunpowder
and the introduction of the professional element in warfare.
The idea of the divine right of kings never existed at any
period of Hungarian history ; and if at any time the King
arrogated any right not specifically conferred by law, the
presumption was always, and, be it remembered, still is,
against the validity of the claim. Theoretically, the ownership of all land was vested in the King, who consequently

---

[1] *St. Stephen's Laws*, bk. ii. 3.

[2] Verböczy, *Jus Tripartitum*, ii. 3, cited by law xviii. of 1635. Kmety,
A Magyar Közjog Tankönyve, pp. xv. and 4, *n.*, 3rd ed., Budapest, 1905.

succeeded to the possession of all land escheated on conviction of treason, and to the estates of all persons dying
without male heirs.[1] Practically, he was the owner of all
lands not otherwise definitely appropriated, the power to
make grants of which was one of the chief causes of the
firm establishment of the royal power and of its subsequent
decadence. Theoretically he was the sole source of justice,
and practically the sole source of legislation. The general
meetings of the nation in fact continued, but it is evident
that they were summoned from time to time for judicial
purposes only, or for the purpose of publishing[2] the decrees
issued by the King on the petition,[3] or with the consent of
the royal council, which consisted of his own nominees,
and never had any effective control till the end of the
thirteenth century.[4] All officials were appointed by him,
and to him alone were they responsible. He was the
commander-in-chief, and could summon the nation to
arms; but his power was limited by the fact that the
obligation to serve was confined to home defence,[5] and to
service under the personal leadership of the King.[6] His
control was limited also as regards taxation; for the reason
that taxes could be imposed only on foreign immigrants and
on the remnants of the aboriginal inhabitants.

The rest of the population may be divided into three
main classes: the bishops and other chief ecclesiastics, who,
in the early days of Christianity, naturally had a preponderant influence in the King's council; the chief nobles
—the descendants of former heads of tribes and families—
from whom were selected the occupants of all official posts
not monopolised by the clergy; and the mass of the

---

[1] St. Stephen, ii. 26.

[2] Law I. of St. Ladislaus, 1092, was passed "*cum testimonio* totius cleri et
populi."—Preamble.

[3] St. Stephen's Laws, bk. ii. cl. 2. : "Consensimus petitioni totius senatus."
Cl. xxv., "decernimus nostrorum primatum conventu"; but i. 6 says "decrevi
mus nostra regali potentia."   [4] Law of 1298, cl. 23.

[5] Golden Bull, cl. 7.   [6] St. Stephen, ii. 43.

conquering race, all free and all noble, the lesser nobles or
"gentry" of a later date, theoretically on a footing of
absolute equality with the noblest, the richest, and the most
powerful. Naturally, as the result of the abolition of
collective ownership by the tribe, of the establishment of
private property, and of the exercise of the royal prerogative of making grants of land to useful adherents, some
became richer, some poorer, and a landed aristocracy arose ;
but, nominally, no Magyar, unless deprived of his rights
of nobility for treason to King or country, or for conviction
of certain specified offences against the law, was either
superior or inferior to his neighbour.[1] Every Magyar
freeman was liable to military service, under obligation to
attend the general meeting of the nation, and eligible for
any office of state. The Hungarian nobility was no privileged caste, but was synonymous and co-extensive with the
whole Magyar nation ; and it is essential to a comprehension
of subsequent history that this fact should not be forgotten.

In the counties[2] into which the country was divided
by St. Stephen for the organisation of home defence, the
royal power was represented by the governors[3] of the
fortified towns, henceforth no longer hereditary officials,
but nominated by the King, who naturally could not
afford to run the risk of leaving the country's strongholds in the hands of ambitious and disaffected nobles.
The military forces at the disposal of the governor were
formed by poor nobles,[4] who received land from the King
in return for service in arms, the right to possession
descending from father to son, but conferring no claim to
the freehold, and being dependent on continuity of service.
The rest of the lands in the immediate vicinity of the

---

[1] Verbőczy, *Jus Tripartitum*, i. 2, and law of 1351, cl. 11, "unâ et eâdem
libertate gratulentur."

[2] Apparently forty-five at this period, *Vienna Chronicle*, ch. xlv.

[3] Várispán, Comes Castri, Comes Parochiae or Provinciae. "Satrapa" in
the document recording the union of the Transylvanian nations in 1473.

[4] Kézai in Endlicher's *Monumenta*, p. 129.

town was held of the King by non-noble freemen, the
descendants of such of the original inhabitants of the
country as had been left in possession of their holdings,
and had, possibly because they offered no resistance to the
conquerors, avoided reduction to slavery.[1] These also
were liable to military service, and, in addition, paid over,
as a recognition of the *dominium naturale* of the King, half
the proceeds of the land, of which one-third went to the
governor and the remainder to the royal treasury.   The
great majority of this class eventually received rights of
nobility, and so became freeholders merged in the Magyar
nation and liable to military service on the same conditions
as the rest of the nobles.[2]   The remainder, with the
development of the fortress and surrounding land into a
town in the proper sense of the word, either sank in course
of time into the general body of non-free peasants, or
acquired burgess rights,[3] as did the artisan class—personally
free, but not land-owning, and the foreigners who settled
in the neighbourhood for the purpose of trade.   Thanks
to the example of St. Stephen, who manumitted most
of his slaves, slavery as an institution soon began to
disappear, though it continued to exist to some extent
to the end of the thirteenth century,[4] and the majority of
non-free peasants received allotments from their former
owners in return for fixed payments and services, the
difference between them and the free peasants consisting
in the fact that the former were *adscripti glebae*, while the
latter could migrate as they pleased.   From this class of
serfs sprang the great mass of the population, the *misera
contribuens plebs*, which bore part of the burden of military
service and nearly the whole of that of taxation, without
having any share in the political rights of the rest of

[1] Timon, *Magyar Alkotmány és Jogtörténet*, 3rd ed., Budapest, 1906, 129 *sqq.*
[2] Timon, *o.c.* p. 146.   Whole communes were occasionally ennobled in
return for exceptional services rendered to the State.
[3] Herczegh, *Magyar Jogtörténet*, Budapest, 1902, p. 70.
[4] Timon, *o.c.* p. 148.

the nation down to the abolition of class privileges in 1848.

The people must have been aware of its own inherent weakness as aliens in a strange land, surrounded by nations which considered it to be hardly human, and believed it to be guilty of cannibalistic proclivities, or the transition from socialistic republicanism to a monarchic *régime* would not have been effected so easily. But the influence of Christianity and the prestige which St. Stephen enjoyed as Defender of the Faith gave him an authority which he would never have possessed merely as the elected chief of a notoriously undisciplined race. Hence the anxiety manifested 'n his laws to guarantee the interests of the Church, which, in return for his fostering care, encouraged the monarchical idea, and propagated the legend of the King's miraculous powers. Of the laws as they have come down to us,[1] the first book is almost entirely concerned with Church matters, the position of the bishops, their judicial powers with respect to matrimonial and ecclesiastical offences, the observance of the Sabbath and decent behaviour during divine service, and, what was no doubt far more important to the clergy, who, it must be observed, were members of the nobility in virtue of their office, and as such were liable to military service, made the payment of tithes compulsory, and sanctioned the exaction of one-ninth instead of one-tenth of all produce in the case of fraudulent concealment.[2] The exceptional position of the clergy was still further strengthened by the enactment that no layman's evidence should be accepted against a priestly wrongdoer[3]—a tacit encouragement to misconduct which had its reward when the doctrines of the Reformation found their way into Hungary. The second book deals with offences against the person and property,

---

[1] Endlicher's *Monumenta*, p. 310 *sqq.*
[2] "Si quis decimam suam abscondit novem det," II. xviii.
[3] "Testimonium laici adversus clericum nemo recipiat," I. iv.

and the draconian severity of the penalties prescribed bears testimony to the condition of the country—disorderly, no doubt, but no worse than that which contemporary penal legislation proves to have existed in other parts of Europe. That there were other books is shown by frequent references in later laws to constitutional matters of which no trace remains in the existing series. The Golden Bull,[1] for example, and the law of Béla IV.[2] refer to the liberty granted by the sainted King, and Horváth[3] believes that the lost books defined the composition and functions of the King's council, and regulated the local government of the counties. Hartvic[4] says that after his coronation the King signed and published a decree in the nature of a "permanent treaty" between himself and his people, which looks like the prototype of the *diploma inaugurale* (or document signed by every king before his coronation) of a later date, and ordained that no one should be interfered with "*sine judicii examinatione*"—an apparent anticipation of the celebrated clause of the Golden Bull. Further, it is known that he ordained that he and his successors should periodically visit the county towns in company with the bishops and chief nobles for judicial purposes, and that, as he could not visit them all every year, each county should elect two judges for the trial of minor offences, from whom an appeal lay to the King's Bench. Presumably all these matters formed the subject of legislation at the general meetings, or Diets as they are usually styled, of which he is known to have held several at Székesfehérvár, attended not only by the people at large, but by the bishops, the chief officers of state, and the governors of the fortified towns.[5]

---

[1] Preamble.
[2] 1267.
[3] *Magyarország Történelme*, i. 128 *sqq.*   See also Kovachich, *Vestigia Comitiorum apud Hungaros*, Buda, 1790, i. 17 *sqq.*
[4] *Vita S. Stephani*, ch. x.
[5] Kovachich, *Vestigia Comitiorum*, i. 30 *sqq.*

More light is thrown on the composition of these popular assemblies by the preamble of the first series of the laws of St. Ladislaus,[1] which, though they deal with secular as well as religious matters, are stated to have been passed by the "Holy Synod under the presidency of his most Christian Majesty, with all bishops and abbots of the kingdom, and all *optimates* (members of the royal council and other great officers), and with the *testimonium* of the whole clergy and people."[2] The preamble to the second series shows the existence of a true legislative assembly acting without special reference to the King, in fact in his absence : "We, the whole body of the chief nobles (*optimates*) of the Pannonian kingdom, held a meeting on the Holy Hill in the time of the most pious King Ladislaus, and took counsel as to how it might be possible to prevent the intentions of evil men and advance the interests of the nation, and ordained as follows."[3] The third series begins simply with the words, "This they decreed and this they ordained," and the three books taken together show clearly that the days of independent royal decrees issued without reference to the wishes of the nation, constitutionally expressed, were over. On the other hand, they contain evidence of the confirmation of the power of the King as the paramount judicial authority, not only in lay but in ecclesiastical causes,[4] and of his control of the executive. The bishops and lords-lieutenant of the counties govern the country in his name, and he punishes and rewards them according to their deserts.

Ladislaus may claim to have strengthened, by the laws which bear his name, the foundations laid by St. Stephen

[1] Endlicher's *Monumenta*, p. 326 *sqq.*

[2] Kovachich, *o.c.* i. 60.

[3] *Ibid.*

[4] Ladislaus's charter, given to the monastery of Somogy, "omnium bonorum consensu (the nobles so described sometimes) regalis est prohibitio ne quis mortalium praeter ipsum regem super res ecclesiae judicare praesumat." See Marczali's *Enchiridion Fontium*, p. 100 *sqq.*

of the royal power, of the Church, and of the local government of the counties; to have improved the administration
of justice and enhanced the sanctity of private property.
That the Diet was not more frequently summoned is
probably due to the fact that the relations of society were
too little complicated to require much legislative regulation.
A few penal laws for the discouragement of disorder, and
a few regulations for the maintenance of the dignity of
the Church, its moral and material welfare, to purge it of
undesirables, and compel the reluctant to attend, and pay
for, its ministrations, sufficed for the needs of a country
the inhabitants of which had but recently abandoned the
nomad habits of their forefathers.[1]

Like all previous legislation the laws of King Coloman, 1100.
which, it should be noticed, are expressly stated to have
been enacted with the consent of the King and of the
entire nation, are chiefly concerned with the confirmation
and extension of ecclesiastical privileges.   Priests are to
be subject to the control of none but their bishops (§§ 5,
6, 65), to whom is also given judicial authority over
laymen in conjunction with a mixed tribunal of lords-
lieutenant and other lay officials, in a court to be held
twice a year for the benefit of those who, on account of
distance or want of means, are unable to apply for justice
directly to the King, and have reason to complain of the
action of the local authorities.   A strict system of
subordination of each rank of ecclesiastics to its immediate
superior in the hierarchy is established—the highest order

---

[1] Ecclesiastical legislation of the period deals, *inter alia*, with breaking the
Sabbath and talking in church ; penalty : prompt flogging in the porch and
compulsory head-shaving (St. Stephen, bk. i.).   Refusal to attend church,
refusal to pay tithes, bigamy of priests (*i.e.* remarriage, Szalay, *o.c.* i. 187),
bishops' refusal to abstain from unlawful cohabitation (St. Ladislaus, bk. i.).
" Ut ydiote (illiterates) presbiteri non ordinentur ; qui vero ordinati sunt discant
aut deponantur."   " Ut canonici in claustro et canonici in curia *literatorie*
loquantur."—*Decree of the Synod of Esztergom*, cl. 5, 6 ; Endlicher's *Monumenta*,
p. 351.   N.B.—The first mention of the official use of Latin in the law courts,
of which so much is heard later.

being responsible to the King alone, whose independence
of the Pope is guaranteed by insistence on the royal right
of investiture, by the exclusion of papal legates from the
kingdom unless their admission is expressly authorised by
the King, without whose knowledge and consent all communication with the papal see is absolutely forbidden.
That Hungary of the period was not looked upon with
a particularly favourable eye by foreign ecclesiastics may
be concluded from the unflattering account given by Otto,
Bishop of Freising,[1] who passed through the country on
his way to the Crusade, and lays claim to an omniscience
worthy of a tourist of a later period. "Their language,
manners, and customs are barbarous and brutal, so much
so that Fortune is to be blamed, or rather the tolerance
of the Almighty is to be marvelled at, for having handed
over such a delightful country to such monsters—I cannot
call them human beings. In one respect they imitate the
intelligence of the Greeks, namely, that they never
undertake any business of importance without long and
repeated discussion . . . . the nobles bring their own
chairs to the King's court, and there they meet and deal
with and discuss the affairs of State, and they do the
same in their own houses in the cold winter days. They
have such reverence for their King that they think it
unlawful, not only to annoy him by open contradiction, but
even to give vent to whispered abuse behind his back."

The period of obsequiousness described by the bishop
did not last long, if it ever, in fact, existed. The strong
monarchy founded by Stephen and buttressed by Ladislaus
soon began to show signs of decay, caused by the rapid
growth of a powerful landed aristocracy, both lay and
ecclesiastical, due to excessive grants of land, privileges,
and exemptions, made by weak kings to secure the
support of the influential. The grantees soon manifested
a tendency to emancipate themselves from the King's

[1] *Gesta Frederici Imperatoris*, i. ch. xxxi. *circa* 1150.

authority, to become great feudal lords, and to increase
their power and wealth at the expense of the lesser nobles.
Thus began the conflict which gave rise to the Golden
Bull, and runs through the whole of Hungarian history
down to the importation of the Habsburg dynasty. In
order to preserve the independence of the mass of the
nation and the authority of the Crown, it became necessary
to protect the King from himself, rather than to protect
the nation from royal encroachment on the popular
liberties. Andrew the Second was the first King of
Hungary to do what all others, with one exception, have
since done—to take a solemn oath on his coronation to 1205.
observe and respect the rights and privileges of the people.[1]
His own he could not maintain ; and thus was brought
about the alliance between King and people which finds
its expression in the Golden Bull,[2] the main object of
which was to preserve the authority of the Crown—the
chief defence of the people's rights against oligarchical
interference. Herein lies the difference between the
Golden Bull and Magna Charta, its elder by five years,
in which some have sought to find its source of inspiration.[3]
In the Hungary of the period no defence was necessary
against royal encroachment or attempted autocracy ; " in
such a state of society as that which existed all over
Europe during the Middle Ages very slight checks sufficed
to keep the sovereign in order. His means of corruption
and intimidation were very scanty. He had little money,
little patronage, no military establishment. His armies
resembled juries. They were drawn out of the mass of
the people ; they soon returned to it again, and the
character which was habitual prevailed over that which
was occasional. . . . Such a military force as this was a
far stronger restraint on the royal power than any legis-

[1] Herczegh, *Magyar Jogtörténet*, p. 59.
[2] So called from the *aurea bulla*, or gold seal, dependent from it.
[3] *E.g.* Szalay.

lative assembly. The army, now the most formidable instrument of executive power, was then the most formidable check on that power, . . . the legal check was secondary to that which the nation held in its own hands, . . . the guarantee is the opinion of a community of which every individual is a soldier. There were representative assemblies, but it was not necessary that those assemblies should meet very frequently, that they should interfere with the operations of the executive government, that they should watch with jealousy and resent with prompt indignation every violation of the laws which the sovereign might commit. They were so strong that they might safely be careless. He was so feeble that he might safely be suffered to encroach. If he ventured too far, chastisement and ruin were at hand. In fact the people generally suffered more from his weakness than from his authority. The tyranny of wealthy and powerful subjects was the characteristic evil of the times." [1]

The King's unfortunate marriage with Gertrude of Meran led to the importation of foreign favourites whose influence was intolerable in the eyes of the native noble. Bishop Berthold, the Queen's brother, a man of notoriously evil life, and other disreputable priests, showed a growing inclination to dispute the royal authority, to regard themselves as owing allegiance to none but the Pope, and to take advantage of the King's absence to make themselves masters of secular property. The office of the lords-lieutenant had again become hereditary, and, instead of suppressing the growing oligarchy, the 1219. King tried to purchase its support by perpetuating the results of usurpation, by issuing an edict which made all previous grants of lands and titles hereditary and irrevocable. The Diet had not been summoned for years. The more complete the independence, financial and military, of the great nobles, the less they cared for the constitu-

[1] Hallam's *Constitutional History*, i. 154 *sqq.*

tional rights of the nation. A number of *regna in regno* were formed. Local tyrants imposed their own taxes, issued their own debased coinage, exacted customs dues from foreign traders, and so paralysed the development of the country. Officials originally intended for the maintenance of the royal authority did most to undermine it. The King was so far stripped of the possessions which should have provided the funds necessary for national defence that he had to look for new sources of income. Fresh taxes were imposed; octroi duties were introduced; the price of salt, a royal monopoly, was raised; the currency was continually altered to the disadvantage of the holder;[1] and the collection of revenue was entrusted to Jews and other undesirables who made the position of the tax-payer intolerable. The King was even reduced to making excessive use of his " right of descent," *i.e.* of staying with nobles at their expense, a relic of old days when the Court had no fixed habitation, but moved about from place to place and judicial perambulations were a necessary institution. Signs of a daily intensified discontent became more and more manifest; local risings against petty tyrants proved the country to be on the eve of a general upheaval. Appealed to on a case of conscience, Pope Honorius advised the King that it was not only his right but his duty to revoke his unconstitutional edict at the expense of his oath, and to maintain the royal property and privileges intact.[2] Encouraged by the papal casuistry, the Archbishop of Esztergom, and other patriots, succeeded in stiffening the King's back, and inducing him to summon the Diet, and to issue the decree which later ages agreed in regarding as the fundamental guarantee of the liberties of the nation, though no such importance appears to have been

---

[1] Theodoric, *Life of St. Elisabeth*, quoted by Csuday, *Geschichte*, p. 235. Three new coins were issued in return for four of equal value withdrawn from circulation.

[2] Letter to the Bishop of Kalocsa, *Mag. Nem. Tört.* ii. 393, *n.*

attached to it by contemporary authorities. The later chronicles do no refer to it, neither is it mentioned by Bonfini ; and the fact is that it failed in its purpose, and practically was a dead letter till, three hundred years later, the *Jus Tripartitum* of Verbőczy gave it a posthumous celebrity.

It is an entire mistake to suppose, as many apparently do, that Hungary became a constitutional monarchy by virtue of the Golden Bull. The Bull was, in the first place, the charter of the liberties of the lesser nobles, that is to say, of the mass of the nation—a confirmation or re-affirmation, as clearly appears from the text, of existing rights and of the old established principle of the equality of all Magyar freemen. In the second place, it was intended not to circumscribe the royal power, but to strengthen and protect it against the effects of its own feebleness ; to restore its former prestige, and revive the authority which the encroachments of the oligarchy had diminished. The essential difference between this document and the Charter, which made King John exclaim, "By God's teeth, I will not grant them liberties which will make me a slave," is apparent ; but the points of resemblance are equally striking ; and if Hallam's words are true, that the Magna Charta is still the keystone of English liberty, that all that has since been obtained is little more than a confirmation or a commentary, and that if every subsequent law were to be swept away there would remain the bold features that distinguish a free from a despotic monarchy, a similar eulogium may be claimed for the Golden Bull. The document in question is a true charter, granted by the King without reference to the council, the prelates, or the nobles. It consists of a preamble, which explains the circumstances of its origin, and of thirty-one articles, of which the more important are set out below.[1]

---

[1] For the full text see Marczali, *Enchiridion Fontium,* p. 133 *sqq.*

Whereas the liberties of the nobles (*i.e.* all freemen) and others,[1] as established by St. Stephen, have been diminished in many respects by the power of certain of the Kings, sometimes for the satisfaction of their anger, sometimes in consequence of their lending ear to the false counsels of evil men, or of pursuers of private gain; and whereas the nobles have often urged and entreated Us and Our royal predecessors to take in hand the reform of the kingdom; now therefore, as in duty bound, desiring to satisfy their petition in all matters, more especially inasmuch as no slight bitterness has often arisen between us which should be avoided in order that the dignity of the Crown may be more effectually preserved; and whereas the desired object can be attained by none better than by the said nobles themselves; We hereby confirm unto them and to all other Our subjects the liberties granted by the Royal Saint, and at the same time, as regards other matters pertaining to the reform and welfare of the State, declare as follows :—

(i) That We bind Ourselves to hold a court[2] every year on the feast of St. Stephen at Székesfehérvár, unless prevented by some difficult matter or by sickness, and that if We Ourselves are unable to be present, Our Palatine shall be there without fail in Our stead to hear causes on Our behalf, and that all nobles who so desire may attend without let or hindrance.

(ii) It is Our will that neither Ourselves nor Our Successors shall seize any noble, nor destroy him out of favour to any powerful person, unless he shall first have been summoned and convicted according to law.[3]

(iii) That We will collect no tax and will exact no money payments,[4] and will not visit, uninvited, the estates,

---

[1] Foreigners, clause xix.

[2] "Solemnizare."

[3] Magna Charta, clause 39 : "No freeman shall be taken or imprisoned or disseised or outlawed or in any way destroyed . . . unless by the lawful judgment of his peers or by the law of the land."

[4] "Liberos denarios" · aid by non-noble freemen, in recognition of the *dominium naturale regis* and by foreigners *pro libertate.* (Timon, *c.* p. 240, and clause 80 of Coloman's Laws; Endlicher's *Monumenta*, p. 37: Clearly "without consent of the Diet" is implied in the case of non-clerical nobles. The tenants of the Church have, on the other hand, unconditional exemption. Clause 14, Magna Charta, evidently recognises the King's *right* to scutage and aids, but the assessment must be made by the general council.

houses, or villages of the nobles; and that from the Churches' folk we will collect no tax whatsoever.

(iv) If any noble shall die without male issue, his daughter shall obtain one-fourth of his possessions; of the rest he may dispose as he pleases. If death shall have prevented his making such disposition, his near kinsmen shall inherit; but if he shall have no heirs whatever, his property shall devolve on the King.[1]

(vii) If the King shall wish to lead an army outside the kingdom, the nobles are not bound to go with him save at his expense, and shall not be tried by court-martial (for refusing to go) on his return. But if a foreign army shall come against the kingdom, all are bound to go with him. But should We Ourselves go in person with an army outside the kingdom, all lords-lieutenant of counties, or others who receive money from Us, are bound to accompany Us.[2]

(viii) The Palatine may judge all our subjects without distinction, but he shall not determine the cause of any noble involving capital punishment or forfeiture of property without the King's cognisance, and he shall employ no substitutes save one judge in his own court.

(ix) If foreigners, be it understood men of good standing, shall come into the kingdom, no office shall be conferred on them without the consent of the council.

(xii) Neither the wives of those who die a natural death, nor of those condemned to death by legal sentence, nor of those who fall in battle,[3] or have died in any other way, shall be defrauded of their dowry.[4]

(xiv) If any lord-lieutenant shall not conduct himself in accordance with the dignity of his office, or shall despoil the people under his authority, he shall on conviction be publicly degraded and stripped of his office, and shall make restitution of that which he has extorted.

Clause xvi. forbids the granting of "whole counties" (*i.e.* hereditary lord-lieutenancies), or of any other offices

---

[1] *I.e.* no lord-lieutenant or other great noble has any feudal claim on the property of the nobles. The King alone is general heir.

[2] "Comitatus tenent vel pecuniam nostram," *i.e.* state officials.

[3] "Duello," single combat (Horváth), but query.

[4] Cf. Magna Charta, clause 7.

in perpetuity, in order to put an end to the attempted establishment of a feudal aristocracy. Clause xx. provides that tithes are to be paid in kind and not in money—a necessary provision at a time when the value of coins was continually changing, and a protection to the tithe-payer in view of the scarcity of metal currency. Clause xxiii. declares that new money shall not be issued at shorter intervals than twelve months. Clause xxviii. enacts that if any one has been legally condemned, no protection of powerful persons shall avail to protect him from the consequences ;[1] and clause xix. that strangers, of whatever nationality, are to be left in enjoyment of the privileges originally granted to them, and that Ishmaelites (Mohammedans) and Jews are not to be employed in the Treasury, or in the Mint, or in the collection of taxes, or in the control of the salt-monopoly.

And that these Our concessions and commands may stand and hold good at all times, during Our own life and the lives of Our Successors for ever, We have ordered the same to be committed to writing in seven similar documents, of which the first is to be sent to Our Lord the Pope for inscription in his registry ; the second is to be kept by the Knights of St. John ; the third by the Knights Templar ; the fourth by the King ; the fifth by the chapter of Esztergom ; the sixth by the chapter of Kalocza, and the seventh by the Palatine for the time being, to the end that having this document ever before his eyes, he may never deviate in any respect from the terms thereof, nor allow the King, or the nobles, or any other person, to transgress the same, so that they may rejoice in their liberty, and that the obedience due to the Crown may not be withheld. We also ordain that if We, or any of Our Successors, shall at any time contravene the terms of this statute, the bishops and the higher and lower nobles of Our realm, one and all, both present and future, shall by virtue thereof have the uncontrolled right in perpetuity of resistance both by word and deed without thereby incurring any charge of treason.[3]

[1] Magna Charta, 40 : "We will neither sell nor deny right or justice to any man nor defer the same."   [2] *Ibid.*, clause 41.

[3] The somewhat similar right of resistance conferred by cl. 61 of Magna

This charter, which, it will be observed, not only ratifies and confirms the ancient liberties of the kingdom, while providing for the maintenance of the King's authority —the best guarantee of the immemorial equality of all free Magyars against the attempted establishment of a feudal oligarchy—but guarantees the personal liberty of the subject against the possibility of arbitrary punishment or imprisonment, introduces the principle of responsibility for official action, and raises the Palatine to the position of intermediary between the Crown and the people, of guardian of the nation's rights, and of keeper of the King's conscience.

There is, perhaps, a tendency to read between the lines of early legislation, to discover in it a fuller meaning than its authors intended it to convey, and possibly some commentators have been inclined to exaggerate the importance both of the Great Charter and of the Golden Bull ; but, in any case, it is hardly too much to say that the latter enactment recognises, by implication if not expressly, the ancient popular right to regular legislative participation in the government of the country, and to the control of taxation and of the executive. It was intended to be, and was looked upon as a victory both for the Crown and for the lesser nobles, and as such it was expressly ratified and con-

Charta has given rise to the idea (entertained by Ladislaus Szalay among others, *o.c.* i. 294) that the Bull is derived from that document. A comparison of the two and of the circumstances which gave rise to them should suffice to refute the theory. Marczali, *Enchiridion Fontium*, p. 132, suggests that it was inspired by the laws of Aragon with which Hungary was connected by the marriage of King Emerich (Imre) with Constance, daughter of Alphonso II., but Beöthy (*Magyar Államiság Fejlődése Küzdelmei*, i. 44) points out that the charter of Aragon was considerably later in date. The " General Privilege of Aragon " is dated 1283, and the right of maintaining liberties by force of arms was granted by charter of Alphonso III. in 1287, which also provided that none should be proceeded against forcibly without previous judicial sentence, also for a yearly meeting of the Cortes. (Hallam, *Middle Ages*, ii. ch. iv.) But armed combinations, or " Hermandades," formed for the purpose of resisting arbitrary encroachment on constitutional rights apparently existed earlier.

firmed as a whole by the coronation oath of all Habsburg kings from Ferdinand to Leopold I. Temporarily, however, it failed to attain the desired result.   No more than nine years later King Andrew was obliged to issue a supplement[1] 1231. to the Bull, apparently on the advice of the Pope, to whom the clergy had complained that the great nobles were as oppressive as ever, that laymen interfered in ecclesiastical matters, and that Church property was taxed in spite of the promised immunity. The second clause of the Golden Bull is amplified by the enactment that henceforth not only no noble, but no person whatever can be imprisoned or destroyed without previous judicial process, thereby putting the guarantee of personal liberty on an equality with that provided by section 39 of Magna Charta, sections 30 and 31[2] of which find their Hungarian counterpart in clause 22 of the new law, which forbids the King to demand unpaid labour of the peasants for the purpose of building fortifications or for any other reason. The importation of foreign favourites and the development of foreign influence on affairs of state is further limited by an amendment of the eleventh section of the Golden Bull, which provides that no alien whatever shall have office or dignity conferred on him unless he be naturalised—a clause consistently neglected by later, Habsburg, kings of Hungary in spite of their confirmatory oath. The popular control of the executive is increased by section 11, which says that " if the Palatine shall mismanage the King's affairs and those of the kingdom, and we are prayed to appoint some more suitable person according to our pleasure, we will assent to the request." As regards all other matters, the law of 1231 confirms and closely follows the wording of that of

---

[1] For the text see Kovachich, *Vestigia Comitiorum*, i. 98 *sqq.*, and Marczali, *Enchiridion Fontium*, p. 134 *sqq.*

[2] " No sheriff or bailiff of ours, or any other, shall take horses or carts of any freeman for carriage, except with the consent of the said freeman.   Neither shall we, nor our bailiffs, take any man's timber for our castles, or other uses, save with the consent of the owner of the timber."

1222, save in so far as the interests of the Church are concerned—evident inspirer of this supplementary piece of legislation. The guarantee of observance is no longer the right of armed resistance, but excommunication by the Archbishop of Esztergom in the event of infringement. Ecclesiastical persons are exempted from the jurisdiction of the Palatine,[1] who is, at the same time, forbidden to hear matrimonial causes and others of an ecclesiastical nature (cl. 17), and a confirmatory document,[2] handed by the King to the Papal legate two years later, raises the exceptional position of the clergy to its highest point. Neither the King nor his judges are henceforth to interfere in matrimonial causes. Priests are to be subject to the judicial control of none but the ecclesiastical authorities except in matters concerning the title to land ; the amount of the royal contribution to the funds of the Church is fixed ; and the King renounces his right of episcopal investiture, thus depriving himself of one of the chief privileges of the *legatio apostolica* conferred on St. Stephen.

During the reign of Andrew's successor, Béla IV.,[3] the kingdom was torn and greatly weakened by the incursion of the Tartars. In the latter part of Béla's life his son Stephen rose against him ; in fact the country was practically divided between the king and his two sons, with the result that all three tried to obtain adherents by promises of favour and grants of land, which so increased the arrogance and attempted tyranny of the greater nobles that the lesser ones were obliged once more to bring pressure to bear on the King in order to force him to summon the Diet and to remedy their grievances. The 1267. resultant legislation provided for the return of lands usurped by great and tyrannical nobles, reaffirmed the privilege of all freemen of immunity from taxation, unless

[1] Altering clause 8 of the Golden Bull.
[2] *A Magyar Nemzet Története*, ii. 432.
[3] Albert.

imposed with their consent expressed in general meeting,[1] and emphasised the fact that there was no obligation to accompany the King on a war of foreign conquest, and that those who might voluntarily accompany him did so at his expense. "Likewise we have ordained that in every year one of us (*i.e.* the King and his two sons) shall go to Székesfehérvár, on the feast of the Sainted King, and that from every county[2] two or three nobles shall meet us there, in order that in their presence satisfaction may be given to all complainants for all injuries and wrongs inflicted no matter by whom"—a further recognition of the popular control of the executive, of the rights of the counties to take part in legislation,[3] and a second indication of a tentative elective system. The laws in question are expressed to be passed *habito baronum consilio et assensu* ; and it is impossible to say with certainty whether the phrase refers merely to the members of the council, or implies, as has been suggested, the recognition of an intermediate, not necessarily official, class between the King and the general body of the people ; but the presumption, based on the theoretical equality of all nobles, is in favour of the former interpretation, as is the preamble to the laws passed at the beginning of the reign 1291. of Andrew III. with the consent of the bishops and barons and " of all the nobles of the kingdom."

On his accession to the throne Andrew took the usual coronation oath[4] to be a faithful son of the Church, to do justice to all men, to keep the laws, to defend the

---

[1] That this is the correct interpretation of the clause is shown by the circumstance that the nobles had in fact recently paid taxes, as appears from the diploma of privileges granted to the nobles of Szepes, which says that they are to pay taxes only if imposed on *all* nobles.—*A Magyar Nemzet Története*, ii. 258.

[2] The number of counties had now been increased to seventy-two.—Magistri Rogerii *Carmen Miserabile*, § 10.

[3] Clearly the meeting was for legislative and not for judicial purposes, as otherwise the presence of the county representatives would be inexplicable at a time when there was an organised judicature but no jury system.

[4] *Magyar Nem. Tört.* ii. 576.

kingdom and its' territorial integrity, and to preserve the
rights of the people—thus guaranteeing "the most notable
and necessary liberties of the nation." [1]

1292.   The laws passed the following year at the Diet of
Székesfehérvár for the most part closely follow the wording of the Golden Bull, but there are notable additions.
No foreigner is to be appointed to any office or allowed
to have a seat in the council (cl. 3), and the right of the
nobles to influence the appointment to the chief offices of
State is definitely recognised by the ninth clause, which
provides that appointments shall be made to the offices of
Palatine, Treasurer, Vice-Chancellor, and Chief Justice, on
the advice of the nobles, "in accordance with the ancient
custom of the kingdom"—apparently of the pre-Stephanic
days, as there is no reference to any such custom in
recorded legislation.   All barons and nobles are to meet
in Diet once a year to deliberate on affairs of State, and to
inquire into the acts of the lords-lieutenant, "how
they have acted in their several counties and have preserved
the rights of the kingdom," and to punish or reward
them according to their deserts (cl. 25)—a considerable
advance in the direction of official responsibility to the
nation instead of to the King.   Further, the rights of the
counties and the principle of judicial responsibility are
extended by a provision to the effect that whenever the
Palatine holds a court in any county the Lord-Lieutenant
and four subordinate judges are to be present, and if any
injustice be done or attempted are to inform the King
(cl. 14).   The Lord-Lieutenant and four good men are
charged with the regulation and introduction of new
coinage in the counties (cl. 12), and the succeeding,
mutilated, section apparently prohibits local magnates
from making issues on their own account.   For the
further protection of the people from the oppression of

1 Constitutions of Pest, 1298, preamble and cl. 33 in Endlicher's *Monumenta*,
p. 630.

the great, it is provided (cl. 19) that all castles built to
the common injury (nests of robber barons and seats of
local autocrats) are to be destroyed ; and the laws of 1298
impose on the King and the Palatine the duty of seeing to
their demolition (cl. 9), and to the punishment, after
excommunication, of any great noble who compels freemen
to enter his service.

The Diet at which this law was passed was perhaps
the most important that had ever met in Hungary, as
here at all events we have an unmistakable, true legislative
assembly, which originated legislation without royal
interference, and subsequently, and for confirmation only,
submitted the results of its deliberations to the King, who
now takes his proper constitutional place, as the equal, as
regards legislative capacity, of the Diet, whereas hitherto
the initiative had rested solely with the Crown.[1] Not
only was the King himself absent from the Diet, but all
office-holders dependent on him, and hereditary magnates,
were, as the preamble states, expressly excluded. For the
purpose of checking the threatening growth of a feudal
oligarchy, the law allows the King to obtain armed
assistance from abroad if he is unable to put down
insurgent nobles with his own unaided forces (cl. 6), and
to prevent the establishment of a landed aristocracy it is
decreed that, in the event of any noble being forced by
pecuniary difficulties to sell his land, his brothers, or other
relations, shall have a right of pre-emption. Of far
greater importance is the twenty-third clause, which
contains the germ of the principle which, owing to the
importation of a foreign dynasty, did not attain its natural
development till a much later period, that no royal order
is valid without the counter-signature of a responsible
Minister. It is enacted that two bishops and two paid
nobles, elected representatives of the nation,[2] changing

---

[1] See Kmety, *A Magyar Közjog Tankönyve*, 3rd ed. p. xv. *sqq.*
[2] "Totidemque et *quasi omnes* nobiles."

every three months, shall be in constant attendance on the
King, whose acts as regards the conferment of dignities
and offices, "and other matters of greater importance,"
shall be void and of no effect without the consent
previously obtained of these temporary ministers *a latere*
—a notable addition to the guarantees of popular control
over legislature and executive, a parallel to which did not
exist in contemporary England.

1301.   On the death of Andrew III. the main line of the
house of Árpád became extinct, and the nation's unrestricted right of election to the vacant throne, which had
been limited by the compact of Etelköz, revived. Though
in fact the principle of hereditary succession had generally
obtained, the right of a son to succeed to his father had
never been actually recognised, and the people were at
all times entitled to select the most suitable member of
the Árpád family.   For example, Andrew I. was succeeded,
not by his son, but by his brother Béla (1061) ; and
Stephen II. was elected to the throne to the exclusion of
his predecessor's son (1114). Thenceforward the right
of primogeniture was recognised in fact, though in theory
the elective principle was maintained as rigorously as ever,[1]
and the taking of a satisfactory oath[2] to maintain the
rights and liberties of the people continued to be an
essential preliminary to coronation.[3]

[1] It was the same in England in Saxon times.   Stubbs, *Constitutional
History*, i. ch. vi.

[2] In any case from the time of Andrew II.   See the letter of Pope Gregory
IX. in Kovachich, *Vestigia Comitiorum*, p. 82, and probably earlier.   Timon,
Magyar Alkotmány és Jogtörténet, p. 105, n., quotes Fehér, *Codex Diplomaticus*,
ii. p. 508, showing that Ladislaus IV., 1279, in taking the oath to the
constitution was following an ancient precedent, "nec non omnia alia et
singula quae nostri progenitores in sua consueverunt coronatione jurare."

[3] "Though from the twelfth century the principle of hereditary succession
to the throne superseded in Aragon as well as Castile the original right of
choosing a sovereign within the royal family, it was still founded on one more
sacred and fundamental, that of compact.   No king of Aragon was entitled
to assume that name until he had taken a coronation oath to observe the laws
and liberties of the realm."   Alphonso III., 1285, being in France at the time

Pope Boniface VIII. wished to force the election of his vassal, Charles Robert of Anjou, who, through his mother, the daughter of King Stephen V., had Árpád blood in his veins, but the Magyars insisted on their unrestricted right of election, and fearing to compromise their independence by the acceptance of the papal nominee, chose Venceslas of Bohemia, and crowned him with the usual formalities. When, however, the new king 1305. succeeded, on the death of his father, to the crown of Bohemia, he resigned his right to the Hungarian throne, and Charles Robert ultimately succeeded to the vacant place. On November 27, 1308, a meeting of the bishops and great nobles, at which the mass of Magyar freemen was largely represented, was held at Pest. The papal Legate attended to urge the acceptance of Boniface's candidate, on the ground that as St. Stephen had accepted the crown from the hands of Sylvester, the latter's successor in the papacy had *ipso facto* the right to nominate the new king in default of male issue of the house of Árpád. The claim was resolutely and noisily contested [1] by the meeting, which, all the same, ended by unanimously electing Charles Robert, whom a section had chosen the previous year, stating at the same time that it had no objection to the confirmation [2] of the election by the Pope, but that that was a mere formality, and a totally different thing to the recognition of an obligation to accept the papal nominee. Charles therefore was duly elected [3] and took a

of his father's death, assumed the title, but the states protested and obtained an apology, at the same time acknowledging Alphonso's right to the throne, "so oddly were the hereditary and elective titles jumbled together."—Hallam, *Middle Ages,* ii. ch. iv.

[1] Horváth, *Magyarország Történelme,* ii. 21 ; Szalay, *Magyarország Története,* ii. 136.

[2] "The Popes of the Roman Church may confirm and crown the King of Hungary who springs from the royal family and shall have been unanimously elected by us," quoted by Timon, *Magyar Alkotmány és Jogtörténet,* p. 494, from document of 1308.

[3] "Diligenti collatione praehabitâ dominum nostrum Carolum *ac posteritatem ejus* prout regalis successio exigit in regem Hungariae ac naturalem

solemn oath[1] to maintain the privileges, not only of the
people, but of the Crown, the rights and possessions of
which he undertook " not to diminish or alienate (as had
been done by previous kings in favour of powerful nobles),
but rather to increase the same . . . to maintain the
nobles of the kingdom of Hungary in the exercise of
their approved and ancient rights ; to protect them from
the oppression of tyrants . . . to be satisfied with
legitimate wedlock . . . to do good and not harm to the
people committed by the divine Providence to my care ;
and to condemn or execute no one without fair and legal
trial."

The introduction of a foreign dynasty marks the
beginning of a new phase in the history of Hungary.
As would be expected, the importation of the Anjou
dynasty had a " western " influence. The badges and
trappings of European civilisation were introduced ; the
relations of noble and peasant received a feudal tinge ;
and that which had hitherto been regulated by custom
was now consecrated by law.   That the true feudal system
was never established on a firm basis was due to the
hostility of the very numerous lesser nobles, who resented
the formation of large domains and of a feudal hierarchy
which would increase the power of a few at the expense
of the great mass of the people, and to the considerable
political influence which the latter exercised at the Diets,
at which, in theory at all events, one noble was as good as

dominum perpetuum suscipimus."—Kovachich, *Vestigia Comitiorum*, p. 157.
I.e., the family of Charles Robert was placed in the position formerly occupied by
the house of Árpád.   The elective right was maintained, but the King had to
be chosen from the male members of the reigning house.   When the coronation of Charles Robert took place the Pope's Legate was not allowed to be
present for fear that the people should look on his presence as a proof of papal
interference.—Herczegh, *Magyar Jogtörténet*, p. 297, *n.*

[1] Kovachich, *Vestigia Comitiorum*, p. 170 *sqq.*   In the oath of Andrew II.,
the chief point is the maintenance of the rights of the Church ; here it is the
preservation of the rights of the whole body of nobles and of the Crown
against the oligarchy.

another. Vassalage to great nobles did in fact exist, but only to a limited extent,[1] and the recognition of the necessity of preventing its extension, in the interest both of the throne and of the lesser nobles, finds its expression in the establishment of the so-called "Doctrine of the Sacred Crown," and in a gradual development of the constitutional idea of the equality of King and people as legislative factors. The Crown, the outward and visible sign of the unity of the King and people, began to be looked upon as a person, as the true owner of the country,[2] and not as a mere symbol of kingship. Every Magyar freeman is a "member of the Sacred Crown" of which the King is but the first member, possessing no power but that conferred on him by the people, in conjunction with whom he forms the *totum corpus Sacrae regni Coronae*. Till the Sacred Crown has been placed on his head the King has no legislative and little other authority, and its imposition with the proper formalities is a condition precedent to the obligation of obedience.[3]

Charles Robert observed the terms of his oath so far as the privileges of the Crown were concerned, by compelling the return of fortified places and royal domains improperly obtained by grasping nobles; but he was too much occupied with the task of developing the military resources of his kingdom to trouble himself much with

[1] 1298, cl. 33, allows voluntary service to the great nobles as distinguished from the King: "Item statuimus quo nobiles servire valeant quibuscunque voluerint sua spontanea voluntate."

[2] "Radix omnium possessionum." The expression "sacred crown" first appears in the time of Béla IV.— Timon, *o.c.* p. 484, *n.* See especially Kmety, *A Magyar Közjog Tankönyve*, p. xv.

[3] Verbőczy, *Jus Tripartitum*, i. 4, by whom the doctrine was finally consecrated. "Nobiles . . . membra sacrae coronae esse censentur nulliusque praeter Principis legitime coronati subsunt potestati." This should be remembered in connection with the succession of Francis Joseph. Though Charles Robert was crowned three times with a new crown he was not considered to be *legitime coronatus* till on a fourth occasion the sacred diadem of St. Stephen was used.

constitutional questions. He did in fact summon the Diet on four occasions,[1] if not oftener, at the urgent instance of the bishops, but in 1338 we find the latter complaining to the Pope that the holding of the " general meetings of the Estates " is forbidden, and all approved and ancient customs and rights established by the royal saints, Stephen and Ladislaus, are neglected or suspended.[2] Presumably the chief grievance of the ecclesiastics lay in the fact that the alien King was the first to introduce a system of direct taxation by imposing a land tax[3] for military purposes on every peasant allotment, no matter whether it belonged to the Church or to a lay owner ;

1323. but as the tax was imposed with the consent of the Diet, thereby establishing a fresh precedent for the principle of popular control of taxation, the temporary inconvenience may be considered as more than counterbalanced by the permanent constitutional gain.[4] Save for the above-mentioned innovation, and for the establishment of an improved judicial system based on the French model which continued in use for several centuries,[5] no immediate and striking change was brought about by the introduction of a foreign dynasty, and by the inception of the period of Hungary's military glory, which reached its highest point during the

1342. reign of Louis the Great, Charles Robert's successor, when

1382. Poland, Volhynia, Podolia, Moldavia, Bessarabia, Wallachia, Bulgaria, and Servia were included in the limits of an empire which extended from Pomerania to the Black Sea.

The country paid somewhat heavily for its glory, for

[1] 1318, 1320, 1323, and 1322.
[2] Fehér, *Codex Diplomaticus*, viii. 4, 321, quoted by Herczegh, *Magyar Jogtörténet*, p. 331, *n.*
[3] See *infra*, p. 75.
[4] The necessity of application to the representatives of the nation for funds for military purposes was the origin of all the real power of the Diet, in fact, of all parliaments.
[5] Verböczy, *Jus Tripartitum*, ii. 6, " Usus processuum quem in causis incohandis prosequendis discutiendis et terminandis observamus."

it resulted in a period of legislative stagnation, broken only by an interval of retrogression which introduced a new page into the statute book, the evil consequences of which remained till 1848. The law of 1351, which it should be observed is passed "*de voluntate Genetricis Nostrae*," whose Árpád blood made her, in the popular eye, of equal importance with the King, recites and confirms, except in one detail, the Golden Bull, and restates the principle "that all and singular the nobles, both of Hungary proper and of the 'duchies' pertaining thereto, enjoy identical privileges." The most important point is contained in the preamble, which expressly alters the Golden Bull, in so far as the fourth clause of that charter declares that nobles dying without issue may grant in their lifetime, or bequeath on their death, their possessions to churches or to individuals, or may sell or otherwise alienate the same. Henceforward "they shall have absolutely no such power, but their possessions shall descend directly and as of right to their brothers and their issue, whose claim none shall be able to dispute." On failure of direct and collateral heirs, the land reverts to the Crown, the theoretical source of all individual ownership, the object being to strengthen the landed interest by the preventing the subdivision of properties and the establishment of large feudal estates, in order that it might be better enabled to answer the requirements of the new military system. Thus was established the so-called "principle of aviticity," [1] which, by preventing the alienation, and, consequently, the mortgaging of property, so long as any, no matter how distant, scion of the original owning family remained, offered an almost insuperable obstacle to the obtaining of credit, and to the material development of the country. Military exigencies were also answerable for the clause (6) which regulates the relations between landowner and serf. Henceforth the

---

[1] Ősiség, not abolished until 1848.

former is not only entitled but bound to exact the payment in kind of one-ninth of the produce of all holdings
in order to be able to carry out his military obligations.[1]
During the reign of Louis the provincial meetings
of nobles,[2] hitherto held at rare intervals and for
special purposes only, became gradually periodical,
and thus made up to some extent for the King's illegal
irregularity in the matter of summoning the national
Diet, due in all probability more to the pressing nature
of his military occupations than to any unconstitutional
inclinations.[3]

On the death of Louis, who left no son, his daughter
Maria was " crowned as King,"[4] after the usual formalities
of an election had been gone through.   Subsequently her
husband, Sigismund,[5] son of the Emperor Charles IV.,
1387. was also elected and crowned, but not until the Diet had
imposed, and he had accepted, conditions calculated to
guarantee the country against the dangers of possible
foreign interference.   He undertook, by his coronation
oath, not only to maintain all the rights of the nation, but
also to admit no foreigners to the Council of State, and
to confer bishoprics, which gave the right of admission to
that body, on none but Magyars.   Though further
1397. guarantees were exacted from him by the Diet of Temesvár,

[1] The fixing of the dues at one-ninth was probably no innovation, but
the legal confirmation of an existing custom.—Marczali, *Enchiridion*, p. 213.

[2] See *infra*, p. 95 *sqq.*

[3] Though there is no actual record of any Diet but that of 1351, it is
evident from references made at the Diet of 1397 to otherwise unrecorded
regulations that at least one other was held.—*A Magyar Nemzet Története*, iii.
348. See also Kovachich, *Vestigia Comitiorum*, p. 184 *sqq.*

[4] " Coronata in regem," Horváth, *Magyarország Történelme*, ii. 178, which
explains the famous cry "Moriamur pro Rege nostro Maria Terezia." Her
seal bore the inscription, "Sigillum Marie Dei gratia Regis Hungarie,"
Szalay, *Magyarország Története*, ii. 257, *n.*

[5] Sigismund admits in several documents that he was elected, and so did
not become King in virtue of his marriage with a descendant of Árpád. The
Doge of Venice writes to him of his "*regnum non jure haereditario sed electionis
scrutinio ad te delatum.*"—Szalay, *o.c.* ii. 271, *n.*

which was attended by four deputies from each county
and by delegates from the chief towns, now for the first
time invited to send their representatives,[1] Sigismund
surrounded himself with alien adventurers and favourites,
with the result that a conspiracy was formed to dethrone 1401.
him, and he was seized and imprisoned, for the country
never at any time entertained a doubt as to its right to
depose an unsatisfactory king whom the free-will of the
nation had raised to the throne. A section of the nobles
decided to exile him, and a council was formed for the
purpose of carrying on the government of the country
pending the making of a satisfactory arrangement as to
the succession. As, however, captivity seemed to be
having a sobering effect on the deposed King, and as the
nobles feared the result of competition for the vacant
throne, it was decided to reinstate him on his giving a
promise (not strictly observed) to expel all foreign parasites
and adventurers, and to refrain from taking vengeance on
the conspirators.[2] The chief object of his resentment was
the Pope, Boniface IX., who had taken the side of Ladislaus
of Naples, whom a faction had wished to elevate to the
temporarily unoccupied throne ; and it is probably fair to
assume that the legislation of 1404 was due more to
a wish to annoy Boniface than to a desire to protect
Hungary from papal interference. The Placetum Regium,[3]
issued "after consultation with all prelates, barons, and
nobles," declares that henceforth, "*sub poena capitis et
privationis beneficiorum*," no papal Bull shall be published
in Hungary without the express consent of the King ;
and that all attempts at outside ecclesiastical interference[4]

[1] Horváth, *o.c.* ii. 224, *n.*
[2] Kovachich, *Vestigia Comitiorum*, p. 194.
[3] Kovachich, *Vestigia Comitiorum*, p. 198 *sqq.* Cf. the English statute of
Praemunire, passed eleven years earlier, prohibiting, *inter alia*, bulls, excom-
munications, etc., touching the King or his realms.
[4] The Placetum was revived by Maria Therezia in 1768, and by Joseph II.
in 1781. It was last referred to in 1870 when papal infallibility was declared.

"by way of citations to Rome, inhibitions, rescripts,
executions, and processes," shall be void of effect—
the intention clearly being, not only to reassert the
King's right of investiture,[1] but to put an end to the
baneful influence of Rome on the tranquillity of the
country, an influence which was liable to be exercised
at any moment in support of any pretender to the
throne who would undertake to back the claim of papal
suzerainty.

1410.   The election of Sigismund to the imperial throne, and
his consequent long and frequent absence from Hungary,
gave rise to military disorganisation, to confusion at home
and disasters abroad in the wars with Venice and with the
Turks.   The immediate cause of disorder was a recrudescence of the tendency to establish local despotisms on
the part of certain nobles to whose action the restoration
of Sigismund had been due, a fact which made him a
puppet in their hands and reduced the royal authority
to a shadow.   As usual the lesser nobles sought the
antidote to threatened ruin in an attempt to strengthen
1435. the King, their natural ally.   The Diet was summoned,
and it was resolved to increase the counties' power of
self-government by allowing them to elect officials on

Bishop Jekelfalussy, who had published the Bull without previously obtaining
the royal consent, was summoned "ad audiendum verbum regium," and
publicly rebuked by the Prime Minister, Count Andrássy, in the King's name
in the presence of the whole cabinet.—Radó-Rothfeldt, *Die Ungarische Verfassung*, p. 13. Berlin, 1895.

   [1] See the letter written by Mathias Corvinus to Sixtus IV. in 1480
(*Enchiridion Fontium*, p. 275) on the subject of the "*jus electionis quae mihi
legitime competit.*"   "Your Holiness might have known, or, if ignorant thereof,
might have heard from others, of the nature and character of the Hungarians,
who, rather than allow appointments to benefices in this kingdom to be made
by the apostolic throne without election and presentation by their kings,
would prefer some other religion to the Catholic faith, and would join the
ranks of the infidels." As mentioned above, Coloman, in 1106, first gave up
the right of investiture. See his letter to Urban II., *Enchiridion Fontium*,
p. 115, but the royal assent to appointments to bishoprics was still required.
Herczegh, *Magyar Jogtörténet*, p. 116. Sigismund regained full command of
the "*jus supremi patronatus*" originally conferred on St. Stephen.

whom the duty was to be imposed of keeping the greater
nobles in order, of seeing to the proper collection of the
King's taxes, and to the regular provision of the necessary
military forces. The King admitted that it was his duty
to see to the defence of the frontier fortifications, and to
the protection of the country in general, so far as his
means allowed, and requested the Diet to put him in a
position to fulfil his obligations. It is noticeable that the
law which gave, *inter alia*, assent to this request was
declared to be passed " with the unanimous vote, advice,
deliberation, and consent of our prelates and barons, and
of nobles, representative of the whole *corpus* of the said
kingdom, and invested with full authority to represent the
absent," and thus confirmed not only the, hitherto tentative, representative principle, but the people's exclusive
control of taxation and its right to interfere in military
affairs.

The confusion of the hereditary and elective principles,
to which Hallam draws attention, is well exemplified by
the fact that when Sigismund died and left no son his
daughter Elisabeth and her husband Albert of Austria
were both, formally and simultaneously, elected : the 1439.
former, to emphasise the fact that the rights of a daughter
of the late King, and of a late Queen who had Árpád
blood in her veins, were recognised, and that she received
the crown not merely as the wife of the chosen sovereign;[1]
the latter, in order to prove that the mere fact of marriage
with a scion of the Árpád family conferred no claim to
the throne. As Albert was a foreigner, the Diet naturally
wished to exact exceptional guarantees, and made him take
a vow which was looked upon as a model for all future
coronation oaths. In addition to the usual undertaking
as to the confirmation and observance of existing laws

---

[1] Elisabeth admits that both she and her husband owed their throne to
election. See her letter to the Empress Frederick in Kovachich, *Vestigia
Comitiorum*, p. 473. " Als unser lieber Herr und gemahl Kunig Albrecht . . .
und Ich zu dem Reich Ungern erwelt und gekrönt ware."

forbidding, *inter alia*, the employment of foreigners as officers of State, and of foreign mercenaries, who might easily become a source of danger to the national liberties, he was made to swear that he would spend his whole time in Hungary, "after the manner of previous kings" (cl. 22); that he would not give away or otherwise alienate Crown property; and that, "in accordance with the requirements of ancient custom,"[1] appointments to the office of Palatine should be made only on the advice and with the consent of the prelates, barons, and nobles of the kingdom.[2] The reason for insistence on this recognition of the people's right to control the appointment of the chief officer of State is, of course, to be found in the fact that the King being an Austrian, and having been recently elected Emperor with the Diet's consent,[3] it was necessary that the Palatine should be some independent person and one not likely to be swayed by alien influence. For the same reason Albert was made to promise that the command of no camps or fortified places, and no possessions, honours, ecclesiastical offices, baronies, lord-lieutenancies, or other ecclesiastical or secular dignities, should be conferred on any foreigner. The Diet's control of monetary matters is established by the tenth clause, which provides that no change shall be made in the coinage without the consent of that body. As a further protection against foreign interference, it is enacted that in the matter of the marriage of the royal princesses the King must take the advice of the Diet, and not that of his relations in the Austrian Archduchy. The King admits (cl. 3) that it is his duty to provide for the defence of the kingdom at his own expense, binds himself not to call for the assistance of the nobles except in case

[1] The reference is to the law of Andrew III., 1291, cl. 9.

[2] "Pari voluntate eligat."

[3] He had been made to promise before election to the Hungarian throne that he would not accept the Imperial crown without the Diet's consent, "ne suo injussu imperium acceptaret."—Aeneas Sylvius, *History of Bohemia*, ch. lv.

of absolute necessity, and undertakes that, "as required by their ancient liberties," they shall under no circumstances be asked to serve beyond the limits of the kingdom. Further, he promises (cl. 14) to accept the advice of none but Magyars in matters concerning the defence of the kingdom. In return for his guarantees and undertakings the Diet promised to recognise the claims of his and Elisabeth's children to the throne of Hungary. The meeting of the Diet of 1439, at which these bargains were made, is important from the point of view of constitutional development, as the proposed laws were not, as had generally been the case in the past, laid before the assembly by the King in the form of ready-made propositions for discussion, acceptance, or rejection, but the Diet itself took the initiative, drew up the laws, and subsequently presented them for ratification, thereby asserting its right to initiate legislation, and placing itself, in this respect, on a footing of complete equality with the Crown.

Albert's reign was short, but long enough to give him the opportunity of neglecting his promise with regard to the appointment of the Palatine, and his undertaking to stay in Hungary and to provide for the defence of its frontiers. The result was that while he was absent fighting for the crown of Bohemia the Turks laid Transylvania waste, and carried away seventy thousand persons into captivity—a foretaste of what was to occur under later Habsburgs. His absence and his death produced a 1439. recrudescence of disorder, and of the attempts of powerful and ambitious barons to secure a preponderating influence at the expense of the legitimate authority of the whole body of nobles. Elisabeth, who was expecting her confinement, claimed the throne for herself and for the anticipated heir, and when Ladislaus was born the following year procured his coronation. But the nobles, aware of the danger liable to result from the long minority of a

useless infant, which might give a free hand to would-be
oligarchs, refused to be bound by the undertaking given
to his father, and elected Vladislav of Poland, who
accepted all the conditions they imposed, gave the necessary guarantees,[1] and undertook that Poland should help
to keep the Turks in order. The rejection of Ladislaus
amounted to a strong affirmation of the country's uncontrolled elective rights, more especially in view of the
fact that the nobles had agreed only a few years back to
recognise the claims of Elisabeth's and Albert's possible
issue, and to choose their King from among the descendants of the founder of the Anjou dynasty.[2] The identity
of Hungary's interests with those of Poland, and the
ancient principle that "election to the throne is dependent
on the will of the people, and that popular approval is the
sole source of the efficacy and virtue of the Crown,"[3] were
the chief reasons for the breach of the undertaking referred
to. Except as a matter of principle, the refusal to elect
the posthumous son of Albert was of no great importance,
1444. as after the death of Vladislav in battle against the Turks,
Ladislaus was in fact raised to the throne, in spite of the
opposition of two sections, one of which desired the
election of Philip of Burgundy,[4] and the other that of a
native Magyar noble.

The government, which, until the presumption of
Vladislav's death became a certainty, had been carried on
by "seven principal barons" or "captains,"[5] who soon
proved their inability to deal with disorderly nobles, was
1446. entrusted to John Hunyadi, voyvode of Transylvania, as
Regent during the King's minority. The limits of his

   [1] For the maintenance of constitutional liberty, and more especially for
the observance of the terms of the Golden Bull and the laws of 1298 and
1351, Kovachich, *Supplementa ad Vestigia Comitiorum*, i. 478, Buda, 1798.
   [2] *Suprà*, p. 47.
   [3] Kovachich, *Vestigia Comitiorum*, p. 239.
   [4] *A Magyar Nemzet Története*, iv. 68.
   [5] *Ibid.* pp. 65 and 72, *n.* The King's ecclesiastical authority was transferred to the Council of State.

authority were fixed by resolution of the Diet,[1] which
invested him with the same power as that hitherto exercised by the Crown (cl. 6), except in so far as it
restricted his power of making grants of land, and strictly
defined his relations with the Council of State and the
functions of that body. Hitherto the council had consisted of the King's nominees, summoned for consultation
as and when their nominator pleased. Henceforth the
Regent was to be allowed to select as many members as
he considered desirable, but there must in any case be
twelve permanent councillors—two, the Palatine and the
Chief Justice, *ex officio*, and ten elected by the Diet (cl. 7).
A further democratic guarantee was provided by the prohibition of indictment for treason without the knowledge
and approval of the Diet ; and in order to avoid the
possibility of rival claims and civil war in the event of the
King's decease, it was resolved that in case of dissension 1447.
representatives should be summoned from each county
to confer with the bishops and barons and a unanimous
vote obtained (cl. 30). In the course of Ladislaus's reign 1454.
the Diet successfully asserted its right to interference in
military affairs, by enacting that a committee should be
chosen from among its members for the purpose of fixing
the number of soldiers to be provided at the expense of
the Treasury, and of regulating the collection and employment of the royal revenues with a view to the punctual
payment of the troops. Further, it was resolved that the
counties should elect committees to decide questions of
exemption from service, and to see to the details of recruiting.[2]

Effect was given to clause 30 of the law of 1447 on 1458.
the death of Ladislaus, when Mathias Corvinus, one of
the Hunyadi family, was elected to the throne out of
gratitude and respect to the memory of the late Regent.

[1] See Kovachich, *Vestigia Comitierum*, p. 253 sqq.
[2] *A Magyar Nemzet Története*, iv. 130.

The nobles were largely influenced in their choice by the recollection of the disorder and disasters not infrequently consequent on the election of a foreign king, and it was this consideration which prevented the selection of Casimir of Poland or of the Emperor Frederick, both of whom considered they had claims—the one as brother-in-law and the other as uncle of the late King.[1] The first act of the Diet was to take steps to prevent the recurrence of an attempt made in the last reign to impose a tax without the consent of that body, to forbid such an infringement of its undoubted rights "under any pretext whatsoever—even in the most difficult circumstances.[2] The King, by his coronation oath, promised compliance with the law, and the fact that he was no foreigner, and frankly recognised the supreme authority of the representatives of the nation in the matter of taxation, led to their treating him at all times with exceptional liberality, though in the course of his reign protests were more than once raised in consequence of the frequency with which the Diet was summoned, and the regularity with which

1462. fresh taxation was asked for at each of its meetings.[3] General principles, the Diet's control of taxation, and its right to interfere in administrative questions,[4] having been established, the legislative assembly was able to turn its attention to matters of detail, with a view to the protection of the whole body of nobles against their traditional antagonists, the would-be oligarchs, and to purge the

---

[1] Csuday, *Ungarische Geschichte*, i. 441.

[2] Cl. 55, "Nullo unquam tempore . . . taxae . . . aut aliae executiones indebitae ex quacunque ardua ratione petantur vel imponantur."—Kovachich, *Vestigia Comitiorum*, p. 328.

[3] The law of 1471 says that the Diet is to meet every year in case of necessity, but that of the following year says that the frequent holding of the Diet is a burden, and that none is to be held for the next two years.

[4] "Ea quae ad publicam pertinent utilitatem . . . communi omnium consilio discutienda sunt et decidenda" (Letter of Mathias Corvinus). Kovachich, *o.c.* p. 364, styles this phrase, "illustre monumentum quo Cardinale illud Principium Juris nostri publici stabilitur."

law courts of the pernicious influence of aristocratic preponderance. By the Decretum Majus of 1486,[1] the object of which, according to the preamble, was to put an end to "enormities and unheard-of scandals" in legal procedure, the Palatine was deprived of his power as chief judicial authority of the kingdom, the criminal jurisdiction of the counties was enlarged, and it was ordained that a court, consisting of not less than two judges, should sit twice a year as long as might be necessary for the dispatch of business. The scandals referred to consisted in the fact that great nobles were in the habit of attending the courts [2] with an armed retinue for the purpose of intimidation (cl. 64), and that the delay in obtaining justice was so great, "especially in cases relating to the possession of land, that sometimes a cause could scarcely be disposed of in a man's lifetime" (cl. 4). In order to safeguard the principle of the equality of all men before the law, nobles are enjoined to leave their arms at their inn ; their ignoble retainers failing to divest themselves of their weapons are to be put in the pillory for two days and two nights without food ; the "immunity" enjoyed by many families, in virtue of which they were exempt from the control of the ordinary courts, and subject only to the King's personal jurisdiction, is abolished ; and all, with the single exception of hereditary lords-lieutenant, become subject to the authority of the local justices. It was presumably this law, which, as the preamble states, was passed on the motion, and

---

[1] Marczali, *Enchiridion Fontium*, p. 90 *sqq.*

[2] The so-called "Proclamatae congregationes," or perambulating courts hitherto held in the counties by the Palatine, are here referred to, generally identified, but wrongly, according to Szalay, *Magyarország Története*, iii. 289, *n*, with the "judicium generale" which the Palatine held, in case robbery and disorder was specially rife in certain districts, at which summary justice was done, executions were frequent, and heavy fines were imposed for the benefit of the treasury on whole districts, as well as on individuals, and was very unpopular, more especially for the reason that the holding of this extraordinary court was looked upon as an interference with the growing autonomy of the counties.

with the unanimous consent of the whole body of prelates, barons, and "elected nobles from each county representing the entire kingdom," which gave the reign of Mathias its reputation [1] as the golden age of even-handed justice.

The disciplined and orderly government established by the native king [2] was a great contrast to the general feebleness and disorder which marked the reigns of his foreign predecessors and of his immediate successors. His popularity was not destroyed even by his request for funds, repeated again and again in spite of the promise already mentioned.   The glory obtained by the capture of Vienna, and the fact that the king of Hungary became Archduke of Austria and King of Bohemia, and joined Moravia and Silesia to his dominions, justified his demands in the eyes of his subjects.   So many properties, communes, and even whole districts, had been exempted from the payment of the *lucrum camerae*, the fixed contribution of the peasants to the royal treasury, by the foolishness and weakness of his predecessors, that Mathias had to find 1465. a new source of income.   With the consent of the Diet he abolished the old impost and substituted an annual "treasury tax" of one-fifth of a gold florin on every town house and peasant homestead, including those of the Saxons and other, hitherto exempted, races—a tax which the Diet voluntarily quintupled in the following year, and

1 "Mathias is dead and justice has fled the earth" became a proverb. Clause 18, abolishing trial by combat, is interesting : "Whereas in trial by single combat frauds of various kinds may be committed, and it is rare that parties to the suit fight themselves, and usually hire fighters (*pugiles*), who at times are corrupted by gifts, favours, and promises, with the result that a suitor, though his cause be just, may lose the same owing to his being unaccustomed to fighting" . . .   Clause 69 ordains that "whereas lawyers are in the habit of undertaking for the sake of lucre the cases of many suitors at the same time, and conduct their defence *satis negligenter*, and care nothing if their principals are mulcted," in future no one is to be allowed to undertake more than fourteen cases in one term.

2 The Roumanians claim Mathias as of their race, but it was more likely he was of Slav origin.   In any case his family had been completely magyarised since many generations.

at its meeting in 1478 made payable for five successive years. As a compensation for this exceptional burden it was resolved that no military service should be asked from the nobles during that period unless the country were invaded by the Emperor, the Sultan, and other, specified, possible antagonists ; in which case it was agreed that all nobles without exception should take the field.[1]

Unfortunately for Hungary, Mathias left no legitimate heir, and the question of the succession to the throne was complicated by a provisional agreement which he had made at the beginning of his reign with the Emperor Frederick III. It was agreed that in the event of Mathias dying without heirs the crown should go to Frederick, or to such son as he should appoint ; or, if the throne should not become vacant before the Emperor's death, to his surviving son ; or, should he leave more than one, to such son as Hungary might select ; and the Diet of 1464, strange to say, had confirmed this infringement of its right of free election. However, on the death of 1490. Mathias, the Diet, which cannot be accused of exaggerated scrupulosity in matters which might be construed as constituting a breach of its privileges, did not hesitate to set aside the arrangement, on the ground that its authors had acted *ultra vires* and without consulting the wishes of the country, and to elect Vladislav of Bohemia, who had some particles of Árpád blood in his veins, being a son of Elisabeth, the daughter of Elisabeth and Albert. Maximilian, son of Frederick, consequently declared war on the new King in order to enforce his rights, such as they were, but peace was soon arranged on the terms that if Vladislav should leave no legitimate male issue, the crown should go to the house of Habsburg. Vladislav succeeded with difficulty, and amid loud protests from the lower

[1] The Diet made the imposition of the tax conditional on the acceptance by the king of the clause relating to military service. See the address cited in *A Magyar Nemzet Története*, iv. 267.

nobles, in obtaining the Diet's consent to the compact ; but the general attitude of the country was so evidently hostile to Austrian pretensions that Maximilian threatened to enforce his claims at once and without more ado.   The 1506. result was that a fresh agreement[1] was made, to the effect that in the event of the existing King having no male heir the crown shall go to such descendant of Maximilian as the nobles should select,[2] who should thereupon take the customary oath to maintain all the rights, privileges, liberties, and customs of the country.   It was at the same time arranged that Ferdinand, grandson of Maximilian, should marry Anna, daughter of Vladislav, in order that the, probable, future occupant of the throne should have some connection with the house of Árpád.   There can be little doubt that Hungary never had any intention of considering itself, and constitutionally could not be, bound by a compact which would curtail its elective rights, and was ratified chiefly for the reason that the Sacred Crown, the emblem of the people's liberties, was in Austrian hands, and that its return was one of the considerations specified in the contract.   The episode requires to be noted for the reason that at a later date Ferdinand asserted, and that German writers have supported his assertion, that the House of Habsburg succeeded to the throne of Hungary, not by election, but in virtue of the compact between Vladislav and Maximilian—a proposition which, as will be seen hereafter, unquestionable facts prove to be untenable.

The selection of Vladislav was an unhappy one for Hungary, for he was a feeble creature, deliberately chosen by the bishops and great nobles, not in the interests of the country, but as a tool for the prosecution of selfish ends and with a view to the preservation of their oligarchical privileges.   In addition to the usual coronation oath, Vladislav was made to sign a document or Diploma

---

[1] Marczali, *Enchiridion Fontium*, p. 328 *sqq.*
[2] " Quem eligendum duxerint."

Inaugurale,[1] nominally guaranteeing the rights and liberties of the nation at large, but in reality conceived with a view to the concentration of all power in the hands of the oligarchy. " Whereas the bishops, barons, and other nobles, and the whole body of the people, in exercise of the most ancient custom and privilege of electing their King, have cast their eyes on Us, and have elected Us their King and Lord and Prince in accordance with the terms and articles below written," Vladislav undertakes that he will maintain all and singular the ancient rights, privileges, immunities, liberties, and approved customs of the nation ; that he will not allow the Sacred Crown to be taken out of the kingdom under any pretext whatever ; that he will make no agreement with his Imperial Majesty Frederick V., or with Maximilian, King of Rome, " without the express free and voluntary consent" of the bishops and barons (cl. 7) ; that no foreigner shall be admitted to the Royal Council, all members of which, as well as all court officials, are to be Magyars ; and that he will ratify and confirm in writing all laws voted by the Diet before his coronation, "just as other kings our predecessors have always done in accordance with the approved and laudable custom of the kingdom" (cl. 18). Further, Vladislav admits the necessity of asking consent of the bishops and barons to the issue of new coinage, to the King's ecclesiastical nominations, to the alienation of the towns in Styria, Carinthia, and Carniola acquired by Mathias Corvinus, and, in the event of the redemption of such towns by Maximilian, to utilise the proceeds for the defence and for the general benefit of the kingdom in

---

[1] For the text see Marczali's *Enchiridion Fontium*, p. 307 *sqq.* This is usually considered to be the first occasion on which such a Diploma (a similar one to which was signed by all succeeding kings with one exception) was exacted, but Timon, *Magyar Alkotmány és Jogtörténet*, p. 105, *n.*, says that Andrew III. signed such a document, and the law of 1298, 41, refers to "libertates regnicolarum et ecclesiarum tempore coronationis suae in literis expressas" confirmed by him. See also cl. 18 of Vladislav's *Diploma*, *infra*.

accordance with the advice and wishes of the bishops and barons (cl. 5). The document is of importance not only for the reason that it strictly limits the royal authority in numerous particulars, but on account of its containing the first express recognition (cl. 7) of the Council's right to interfere in foreign affairs, hitherto regarded as belonging exclusively to the King's province. The continual reference, however, to bishops and barons, to the exclusion of the general body of nobles, proves a retrograde intention, and section 25 of the law of 1495, providing that the King and Council shall prepare Bills for presentation to the Diet, discloses a desire to deprive that body of its powers of initiative, rather than to facilitate and expedite legislation—the ostensible object of the measure. The attempted encroachment on the Diet's privileges was only temporarily successful, and three years later we see a return to the old practice.

Relations between the barons and lesser nobles soon became dangerously strained. The latter insisted on their right to a proper share in the executive, from which the former had excluded them by reorganising the King's Council, and by limiting membership to the Palatine, the Chief Justice, the Treasurer, the Chancellor, four barons, and four bishops. The last straw was provided by a resolution of the Council, to the effect that none but the peasants of those who had not the privilege of leading their retainers to war under their own flag should pay the increased war-tax—thus exempting the well-to-do at the expense of the poorer members of the community, and by the fact that the Council entrusted their own creatures with the collection of the tax [1] and failed to account for the proceeds. An attempt to impose taxation without the consent of the Diet, to jockey the opposition by unpunctuality, and by prolonging the meetings of that body to such an extent that the poorer members, unable

[1] Andrássy, *A Magyar Állam Fönmaradásának Okai*, i. 404.

to stand the expense of prolonged attendance, dispersed to
their homes, and thus enabled the great nobles to snatch a
vote with the semblance of legality, led to concerted action
on the part of the majority and to the passing of the law
of 1498.[1] It was thereby enacted that the Diet should
meet annually at the plain of Rákos for the ensuing four
years, and thereafter every third year ; that its business
must be finished within fifteen days, and that any one
failing to appear punctually on the first day should be
fined.[2] The sphere of action of the sixteen lesser nobles,
who had been appointed three years ago to take part in
the judicial functions of the Council, was enlarged by an
instruction of the Diet which ordered its representatives
" faithfully and under pledge of secrecy to take part in
all discussions relative to the common welfare " ; and thus
practically converted them into ordinary members of the
Council. Two years later the influence of the lesser nobility 1500.
on the executive was again increased. The Diet resolved
that the said representatives should be elected for a period
of three years ; that half their number should always be
in attendance (thus ensuring a perpetual majority in the
Council over the four barons or bishops who were bound
to be present), and declared it to be their duty (1507) to
report to the Diet any action of the Council which might
be contrary to law or dangerous to the liberties of the
country. But in spite of these constitutional safeguards,
the great nobles, with their money and their armed
retainers, still kept their access to the King's ear and their
general influence, and the Council still had less real power
than the actual executive officers, such as the Palatine, the
Treasurer, the Chief Justice, and others whose orders the
country was accustomed to obey.

By far the greatest and most permanent success
obtained by the Diet was the final establishment of its

---

[1] *Enchiridion Fontium*, p. 315 *sqq.*
[2] Barons and high ecclesiastics 800, others 400 florins.

control of taxation; and the celebrated law of 1504,[1] never repealed or amended, was often referred to in the first half of the nineteenth century as one of the strongest bulwarks of the Constitution. "If any county of its own motion and without the consent of the whole realm, that is to say of the general Diet of the kingdom, shall offer or grant to his Majesty any subsidy or contribution whatsoever under any pretext or in any form in contravention of the ancient liberties of the kingdom, the entire nobility of that county shall be deemed to be guilty of treason, perjury, dishonourable and disgraceful conduct, and *ipso facto* shall be removed and excluded from the society of the rest of the nobles."[2]   Thus, not only every tax not voted by the Diet is irregular and illegal, but even the making of voluntary contributions is penalised as liable to infringe the solidarity of the people, and to open the door to attempts at oppressive taxation and to the exercise of undue influence.

1505.   At the next meeting of the Diet a solemn protest was entered against the importation of foreign kings — Hungary's final kick as a completely separate State now so soon to be connected in perpetuity with the hereditary provinces of the Habsburgs, and so of historical, but not of practical interest, save in so far as it subsequently provided John Zápolya and his party with a justification for their fight against the introduction of an alien dynasty. "Whereas this kingdom has frequently been ruled by foreign kings and princes, and whereas it would be easy to prove, if necessary, that the kingdom never suffered greater injury, danger, and desolation, than at times when it was under the rule of foreigners, men of an alien tongue . . . in consequence whereof Rama, Servia, Galicia, Lodomeria, Bulgaria, and Dalmatia, and many fortified places, have been lost to the Crown, by reason

[1] In Marczali's *Enchiridion Fontium*, p. 317 *sqq.*
[2] Cf. 1 Richard III. ch. 2, forbidding the exaction of "benevolences."

whereof it is to be feared that, owing to the dilaceration
of the kingdom's extremities, hostile attacks may penetrate
into the interior . . . henceforth, whensoever the throne
shall become vacant, and there shall be no male heirs
entitled as of right and according to custom to succeed
thereto, no king shall be chosen from any foreign nation
or of foreign tongue, but a Magyar, and only a Magyar,
shall be elected by fair voting[1] and unanimous consent
on the plain of Rákos and nowhere else."[2]   Any one
daring to act in contravention of this resolution is to
be judged guilty of treason to the nation, to be
deprived of all privileges of nobility, and to be reduced to perpetual servitude.   In order to exclude
all possibility of foreign interference, the Diet of the
following year, as a condition precedent to its consent 1506.
to crown Louis, Vladislav's son, as " Junior King,"
according to not infrequent custom, made Vladislav
undertake[3] that in the event of his decease during Louis's
minority neither the Emperor Maximilian nor any
other foreigner should be appointed guardian—so strong,
apparently, was the presentiment and dislike of coming
foreign interference.

Of the remaining legislation of the reign only two
enactments need special notice.   The law of 1507 (5, 7-8)
declares that royal edicts unconfirmed by the Council of
State are void and of no effect, and that if any member
of that body shall, as such, offend against the "liberty,
common weal, and statutes of the kingdom," he shall be
looked upon as a traitor, brought before the Diet, and
punished according to his deserts,—thus putting the act
of proposing measures injurious to the interest of the mass

---

[1] *Parili voto*, one vote one value, in contradistinction to the more usual
principle, *Vota ponderantur non numerantur.*

[2] It was to this resolution that Napoleon I. referred in his manifesto of
1808, when he tried in vain to seduce the Hungarians from their allegiance to
the Habsburgs.

[3] See Kovachich, *Vestigia Comitiorum*, p. 455 *sqq.*

of the nobles on the same footing as actual illegal action, and establishing the principle of the responsibility of the executive to the representatives of the nation. The other measure to which reference must be made is the law of 1514, which deals with the position of the peasants. The law was passed under the fresh impression of the terrible Jacquerie associated with the name of Dozsa, the leader of the peasants, who are now deprived of the right of migration, their chief protection against exaction and oppression, and thus are reduced to complete and perpetual subjection to their landlords, whose customary claims to the forced labour and other services of their tenants now receive legal confirmation. It must not be forgotten that the peasantry comprised not only "Saxons, Germans, Bohemians, and Slavs who profess Christianity, Wallachians, Ruthenians, Servians, and Bulgarians who follow the errors of the Greeks, Philistines (Jazyges) and Cumanians (Polovtses)," [1] but Magyars also, who were in no respect in a better position than their alien fellows. They were not serfs in the true sense of the term, as they could not be sold away from the land or mortgaged. Their personal property was their own and could be disposed of by will ; they could marry as they pleased,[2] and, until 1514, could migrate from one landowner to another ; but the peasant had no right of perpetual occupation, and no claim to anything except to "the reward of his labour." [3] To the King he paid a land tax and extraordinary war taxes. To the clergy he paid tithes, and his lord claimed dues and services from him in accordance with the "urbarium" or contract existing between them. The dues were first fixed,

1514

---

[1] Verbóczy, *Jus Tripartitum*, iii. 25.

[2] This they could not do, neither could a peasant choose his own occupation before the middle of the 19th century in the Austrian possessions of the Habsburgs, who posed as the protectors of the peasants in Hungary.

[3] "Rusticus praeter laboris mercedem et praemium in terris domini sui quantum ad perpetuitatem nihil juris habet sed totius terrae proprietas ad dominum terrestrem spectat et pertinet."—Verbóczy, iii. 30.

as has been mentioned, by the law of Louis the Great [1] at one-ninth in kind of the product of the land, in addition to which the law of 1514 imposed on him the yearly payment of one florin in gold, and the provision for the lord's use of one chicken every month and two geese every year, while every ten houses in a village had to produce a fat pig at Christmas. Further, the lord was entitled to claim the unpaid labour of the peasant on fifty-two days in the year.[2] Before the passing of the law of Louis the Great, the landlord had jurisdiction only in civil matters, unless the *jus gladii* had been conferred on him by the King; but that law gave him jurisdiction in all criminal matters also, except in the case of crimes, including larceny and robbery,[3] which involved the death penalty. If the lord delayed or refused justice, he could be summoned before the lord-lieutenant, and the judicial officials of the county were bound by the law of 1405 (cl. 10) (which, however, seems to have remained more or less a dead letter) to hear and decide the case. The peasant could be transferred with his holding to another owner, and if he occupied land not held of some noble, he could dispose of half only by will, the rest going to his lord. Originally the right of migration was unrestricted, but the landlords did their best to curtail it. Laws were therefore passed in 1298 and 1405 reaffirming the right; but their operation was limited, if not nullified, by a subsequent enactment (1492), which required the tenant to obtain the consent of the landlord and to pay all his debts prior to removal. Even Mathias the Just could do little to ameliorate the peasant's lot, and the reactionary law of 1514 perpetuated a sore in the body politic which was more injurious to

[1] 1351, 6.

[2] That is to say, in the case of a peasant occupying a whole *sessio* or allotment. Such allotments varied in size in different parts of the country. In the case of a peasant who occupied a half or quarter *sessio* the dues and services were proportionately reduced.

[3] Timon, *o.c.* p. 574, *n.*

Hungary's interests, and more fatal to progress, than all the incursions of the Turks or the deadening influence of religious obscurantists.[1]

If on no other grounds, the reign of Vladislav was memorable for the reason that it saw the production of a codification of the customary and statute law of Hungary, which had hitherto justified its claim to be considered the land *par excellence* of custom. As Verbóczy says in the preface to his work,[1] "the laws of Hungary and the edicts of dead kings being confused, disconnected, and often contradictory, and so liable to give rise to intestine dissension, which is more injurious than foreign wars," it was advisable that, "neglecting mere ancient fables," a codification should be undertaken of the statute and customary law which actual experience had proved to be of actual force and validity, to which effect had been given from time immemorial in Diet and law courts. The author, who is described in the King's *Approbatio* as Protonotary of the High Court, was commissioned by the Diet of 1507 to draw up a document containing the fundamental laws of the kingdom. The result, the so-called *Jus Tripartitum*, was considered by a special committee of ten members, who reported in favour of its accuracy. In November 1514 the King gave it his *imprimatur*, and undertook to have a copy sent to every county for the guidance of its judicial authorities. Though this was never done, and though the *Jus Tripartitum* was never actually consecrated by law, yet, for more than three hundred years, it continued to be the chief if not the only document regulating the relations of King and people, of nobles and their peasants, of Hungary and the dependent States. In the dark days of Turkish domination the common use of Verbóczy's code was

---

[1] Báthory, one of the most powerful nobles of the day, is reported to have said that any one who complained of him to Mathias required two heads, as one would certainly be cut off before the complainant reached the palace.— Andrássy, *A Magyar Állam Fönmaradásának Okai*, i. 401.

[2] *Opus Tripartitum Juris Consuetudinarii Regni Hungariae.*

the chief tie which bound the *disjecta membra* of the Sacred
Crown together, and it is a remarkable document, which
requires to be studied carefully by any one who wishes to
obtain an insight into the circumstances of the age in which
it was written, when the monarchy had lost much of its
ancient authority and prestige, and the great body of
freemen had succeeded in asserting its claim to equality with
the greater nobles. The doctrine of the Sacred Crown,
and the conception of its wearer as the personification of
national unity, and as the delegate of the nation's rights,
had begun to give place to the idea of the actual
sovereignty of the whole body of Magyar freemen, of
whom the King was no more than the representative,
invested with the power of proposing and sanctioning
legislation, but not with that of forcing its acceptance
or directing its application—a life-president of a semi-
oligarchical state in which the mass of the peasants
had no influence whatever, and the trading population
of the towns little or none. From the point of view
of subsequent history the chief interest centres in
Verbóczy's enumeration of the royal privileges, and
Vladislav's solemn ratification of the Code is a sufficient
indication of the fact that no sign was discernible of
an attempt to give less unto Caesar than that to
which he was constitutionally entitled, and that the
Crown could claim no privileges other than those
specifically enumerated. The second part of the work
is specially devoted to the investigation of the problem
of the initiative in legislation : of the question whether
the King can himself make laws and statutes,[1] or whether

---

[1] The latter, apparently, are measures affecting the Constitution, if there is
any distinction. Herczegh suggests that the difference is that the King could
withdraw the former without the Diet's consent, but not the latter (*Magyar
Jogtörténet*, p. 330) ; but query, as section 5, dealing with the question of the
binding force of laws, says that both *constitutiones* and *decreta* bind the King ;
and section 3, that "*omnia,*" i.e. *leges, constitutiones, statuta et sanctiones*
mentioned therein "*specialiter Principis et non populi statuta nuncupantur* . . .

the consent of the people (the free *populus*, the members of the Sacred Crown distinguished by Verbóczy from the unprivileged *plebs*) is necessary to their validity. The answer is that "the King cannot of his own motion and uncontrolled power make laws, more especially laws which are prejudicial to divine and natural law, or derogate from the ancient liberty of the whole Hungarian nation, but can legislate only by summoning and interrogating the people as to whether it accepts his propositions or not. If the reply is in the affirmative, such propositions thereupon become law. "But the people itself, often by unanimous consent, decrees measures which it considers conducive to the public welfare, and hands the same in writing to the King, praying that laws may be passed in accordance with the same, and if the King accepts and approves the said measures, they obtain the force of law, and are, in fact, regarded as such." [1] The laws are declared to be binding, in the first place, on the King himself who promulgated them at the request of the people. The above is no doubt a correct presentment of the King's position as regards legislation, and the statement of the other rights of the Crown is equally precise. They comprise the right of granting the privileges of nobility, of succession to the property of nobles dying without heirs, of conferment of ecclesiastical benefices and titles, and there is no mention whatever of any other *jura reservata* which German writers have tried to read into the Hungarian constitution, such as the right of regulating all details of military organisation, of sole control of diplomatic negotiations, or of making treaties without

verum generali nomine constitutiones ipsae saepenumero regni decreta vocitantur." So clearly *decreta* are not merely by-laws of the executive or laws issued by the King without reference to the Diet. On the other hand, Verbóczy says, that the annexed States can make *leges*, or local regulations, but not *statuta*, or laws of general application for the whole kingdom.

[1] Part II. tit. iii.

reference to the Diet. We have already seen how Vladislav admitted the Diet's right to interfere with the making of agreements with foreign monarchs, and in so doing he was only following the example of his predecessor.[1] Louis's treaty with Poland in 1376 was expressed to be confirmed by the bishops and the " *barones regni Hungariae principaliores* " ;[2] that of Sigismund in 1369, as " *consilio barcnum nostrorum* " ;[3] and so long ago as the beginning of the twelfth century the Venetian ambassador was informed by the King (Coloman) that the proposed terms of peace would not be valid without the consent of the Council of State.[4] The personal rights and privileges of the nobles *vis-à-vis* the King are likewise defined by Verbőczy. " All bishops, priests, barons, and other magnates, nobles and patricians of this kingdom of Hungary, in virtue of nobility and of the possession of temporal goods, enjoy one and the same liberty, the same exemptions and immunities, nor has any one of the lords more nor any one of the nobles less thereof." [5] There can be no King unless he be elected by the nobles, and no rights of nobility can be conferred by other than the King. A noble so created *ipso facto* becomes a member of the Sacred Crown, is subject to the authority of none but the legally crowned King, and cannot be imprisoned unless he has previously been summoned and condemned by process of law. All nobles have complete freedom in the exercise of their

---

[1] 1462. Mathias writes, *re* his treaty with Frederick : " Certos tractatuum articulos attulit quibus respondere et eos firmare aut infirmare prout ab eo percepimus non est nostrum, cum non personam nostram ut dicunt sed totius regni universitatem concernant, imo nec adhuc in specie ostensi sunt et publicati, sed in hac proxima generali omnium regnicolarum nostrorum congregatione, ob hoc praecipue advocata, sunt publicandi."—*Epistolae Mathiae Corvini*, cited by Szalay, *Magyarország Története*, iii. 199, *n.*

[2] Szalay, *o.c.* ii. 241, *n.*

[3] *Ibid.* i. 228, *n.*

[4] Andrássy, *A Magyar Állam Fönmaraddsának Okai*, i. 127.

[5] Part I. tit. ii.

rights and in the use of their property, and are exempt from all servitudes, taxes, contributions, tribute, or other obligations save that of military service in defence of the country. Further, they have the right, conferred by the Golden Bull, of contradicting and resisting the King should he attempt to interfere with the rights and privileges of the nation, without thereby incurring a charge of treason—*sine nota alicujus infidelitatis.*

The greater part of the *Jus Tripartitum* is concerned with such questions as the difference between natural and civil law, between statutes and municipal regulations, with the conditions essential to the validity of an alleged custom, with the law of succession to property, and with the relations of the clergy to the civil law, and many other matters which have no immediate bearing on the subject matter of this book. It is enough if the reader remembers Verbóczy's statement as to the equality of all Hungarian freemen and his definition of the King's rights and privileges—a knowledge of which is essential to an appreciation of the terms of the contract on which Ferdinand of Habsburg received the crown of Hungary, and of the manner in which those conditions were observed by him and by his successors.

1516.   Louis II. was only ten years old when he succeeded to the throne; it was therefore decided that during his minority the affairs of state should be managed by a Council to consist of two bishops, six barons, and sixteen lesser nobles annually elected by the Diet, which thus secured an unquestioned control. The chief difficulties with which it was confronted were of a financial nature, the result, as usual, of the squandering by former kings of the revenues of the Crown and of the mortgaging of royal property. The Diet of 1518, with a view to the prevention of a recurrence of the financial scandals of the previous reign, decided that two members of the Council should be chosen as comptrollers of the royal expenditure;

that without their knowledge and consent the Treasurer should neither receive nor disburse any monies ; and that death should be the penalty for carelessness or dishonesty.[1] 1526. It was also made part of the Treasurer's duties to take steps for the defence of the fortified places on the frontiers, for the proper payment of officers and men, and for the provision of military necessities. Thus on the very eve of the era of national disintegration the Diet confirmed its control of the chief departments of State, and reaffirmed the principle of official responsibility to the representatives of the nation.[2] But these measures were insufficient to avert the fate (the result of a succession of incapable kings, of consequent internal disorder, and of the un-patriotic ambitions of a selfish aristocracy) which, but for the strong government and organising ability of John Hunyadi and Mathias Corvinus, would probably have overtaken the country at a considerably earlier period. Probably the chief cause of a national debility which invited disaster was the gulf fixed between the two sections of the population—the nobles, with their immunity from taxation and their monopoly of power, and the *misera contribuens plebs*, which could have little interest in the maintenance of the territorial integrity of the country, and in fact constituted a danger rather than a source of strength.[3] The Crown had lost its prestige, and the King was reduced to begging the Diet for money for his personal expenses. Faction, and corruption of morals, especially among the clergy, contributed to the general

[1] Kovachich, *Vestigia Comitiorum*, p. 446.

[2] The Rákos Diet of 1525 resolved that though bishops and barons take part in the Council as before, the control is to be in the hands of the elected members. "*Summa tamen auctoritas omnium rerum apud electas personas maneat.*" The Council had already ceased to be styled "Royal Council," and was known as the *Consilium Hungaricum.*—See Timon, *Magyar Alkotmdny és Jogtörténet*, p. 628, *n.*

[3] The Papal Nuncio wrote in 1526 to the Pope, that if the Sultan were to proclaim himself the protector of the peasants they would join him.—Andrássy, *A Magyar Állam Fönmaraddsdnok Okai*, i. 436.

decadence and disintegration which rendered the country an easy prey to its enemies. The King, twenty-eight of the chief barons, 500 nobles, seven bishops, and 22,000 men, were killed at the battle of Mohács; the Turks laid waste the country as far as Buda, the period of Hungary's separate existence came to an end, and therewith the possibility of expansion south and west, to the Balkans and to the sea, which in time would have converted Hungary into a great European power.

CHAPTER II

BEFORE we attempt the description of the disorder and territorial disintegration characteristic of the period which immediately followed the disaster of Mohács, some reference must be made to certain details of administration as well as to certain officials and races whose names will recur from time to time, some acquaintance with whose functions and position during the pre-Habsburg period is necessary to a proper comprehension of subsequent events.

It has been seen how the King gradually developed into a constitutional monarch with a right of veto, a divided authority as regards legislative initiative, a partial control of military and foreign affairs, and none whatever of direct taxation. The executive officials, by a similar process of development, gradually lost their character of court functionaries, appointed by and responsible to the King alone, and were converted into officers of State responsible to the Diet, and liable to execution for treasonable conduct [1]—an expansive term, and one which gave almost unlimited control over life and property to that body which was itself judge in all cases of treason.

The Palatine, Nádor,[2] or Comes Palatii, was originally, as the name indicates, no more than the chief court official ; but already in the time of St. Ladislaus[3] his

[1] Law of 1518.
[2] Properly Nádorispán, probably from the Slav, nadvor zsupan = Pala i Comes. German, Obergespan. *A Nádori és Országbírói Hivatal*, Frankl. (Fraknói). [3] Law iii. § 3 of 1092.

sphere of action had widened, and we find him representing the King in his character of chief judicial authority.
Under Coloman [1] he is not only the general representative
of the King in his absence, but accompanies him on his
judicial tours. In the reign of Béla III.[2] the Nádor goes
on judicial perambulations instead of the King, as "*judex
de latere regio missus*," to hold a *proclamata congregatio* in
each county; [3] and in the succeeding reign the nobles
recognise his authority, whereas, previously, he had no
jurisdiction over them unless they made voluntary submission.[4] Thirty years later he had acquired independent
judicial power not derived from his representation of the
King, and a new and distinct character as president of the
Diet in the King's absence and as custodian of one of the
copies of the Golden Bull, "in order that having the
document always before his eyes he may not deviate in
anything from the contents thereof, nor allow the King or
nobles or others to do so, that they may enjoy the liberty
which is theirs, and may therefore ever be faithful to Us
and Our Successors, and that the obedience due to the
Crown may not be withheld."[5] He thus became, in a
sense, the responsible guardian of the Constitution. By
the law of 1231 [6] the King undertook to remove unsatisfactory Palatines from office at the request of the nobles,
and from 1291 [7] he was bound to ask their advice before
making an appointment. The law of 1397, 14, enacts
that the Nádor may be called to account for misconduct
by the Diet and ejected with disgrace from an office, the
final development of which to the position it occupied
down to 1848 occurred in 1439,[8] when it was declared
that the Palatine should thenceforth be elected by the
nobles, not merely as intermediary between King and

---

[1] 1095-1115. [2] 1172-1196.
[3] Herczegh, *Magyar Jogtörténet*, p. 82.
[4] St. Ladislaus, Law iii. § 3, "qui spontanea voluntate iverint ad eum."
[5] Golden Bull, 1222, cl. 31. [6] *Ibid.* cl. 3.
[7] *Ibid.* cl. 9. [8] *Ibid.* cl. 2.

people, and representative of the constitutional principle, but as judge[1] between the two in questions of rights and obligations.   The law of 1485 further defines his duties : to summon the Diet on the throne becoming vacant, to cast the first vote at the election of the new King, and to act as guardian of the monarch during minority.   As such he may claim the same obedience as the King himself would be entitled to exact if of full age.   He is the Commander-in-Chief of the national forces and the "mediator between the King and his people."   He is responsible for the security of the kingdom and of the fitness of the fortified towns for purposes of national defence.   If the King is absent from the country, the Nádor is *ex officio locum tenens regius*, invested with all the royal powers save of pardon and of conferring privileges and titles.   If the monarch is of feeble intellect, or remiss in the execution of his duties, the Palatine can receive foreign ambassadors and negotiate with them.   This is evidently no innovation, but a legal confirmation of ancient practice, as from 1414 to 1419 the Palatine as "*vicarius*" governed the country during Sigismund's absence.[2]   By the law of 1525 (cl. 22) it was enacted that the office should be held for life.

The Chancellor's office developed in a similar manner. At first he was the Notarius who drew up and sealed documents on behalf of the King, and was not styled Chancellor till 1138.[3]   The clergy, being better educated than the rest of the nobles, for a long time monopolised the post, which for a considerable period was always held by the Archbishop of Esztergom.   Not till 1366 was a layman appointed.   The power of the Chancellor gradually increased, as it depended on him what matters were brought before the King, especially as regards the grant-

---

[1] "Judicium et justiciam facere potest et tenetur."
[2] He.zegh, *Magyar Jogtörténet*, p. 355, n.
[3] Timon, *Magyar Alkotmány és Jogtörténet*.

ing of pardons and the conferment of privileges, exemptions, and titles. He represented the Crown in judicial matters, and was custodian of the *liber regius*, the official record of State documents signed by the King. Next to the Palatine he was the most important member of the Council of State, and that he had become a public official instead of a mere court functionary in the course of the thirteenth century is shown by clause 9 of the decree of 1290, which requires the consent of the Diet to the appointment even of his deputy the Vice-Chancellor.

The Treasurer (Magister Tavernicorum or Fótárnok-mester) was no more than the manager of the King's private finances during the whole period of the Árpád dynasty, though clause 9 of 1291 required the advice of the Diet to be obtained, "according to ancient custom," before any candidate was appointed to the office. Under the Anjou dynasty he was promptly converted into a public official (Summus Thesaurarius or Fókincstartó), and had control of the tax voted from time to time by the Diet (*hadi adó*), the proceeds of which were utilisable only for military purposes. Numerous laws were passed for the purpose of controlling his actions :[1] *e.g.* 1496, 33, for auditing his accounts, which proving unsatisfactory, his arrest was ordered ;[2] 1518 and 1521, 33, providing for the election of two barons and two nobles to see to the collection and disposal of the military tax— the nearest approach to Dietal budget control. Strictly speaking there was no State Treasury or State financial system, only a Fiscus Regius or Camera Regia, which was supposed to bear all the expenses of State ; but the King's sources of income (*peculia Sacrae Coronae*) might not be alienated without the Diet's consent (1439, clause 18), and certain lands were specially intended to provide for the maintenance of the Court. Árpád and his descendants took a large slice of land for themselves (the *propria*

[1] Timon, *o.c.* p. 656.　　　　[2] Herczegh, *o.c.* p. 369, *n.*

haereditas mentioned in St. Steph.en's time), and all unoccupied lands belonged to the King, as did the domains or lands in the immediate neighbourhood of the fortified towns, lands forfeited for treason of their owners, and the property of nobles who left no heirs. Originally these were the chief, if not the only sources of revenue, but they were supplemented at an early period by the *regalia majora*, *i.e.* the salt monopoly, the customs duties, the right of coining, and the sole ownership of mines—inalienable and unmortgageable without the consent of the Diet. The collection and employment of the proceeds were also controlled by that body, which passed many laws dealing therewith (*e.g.* 1439, 11 ; 1464, 9 ; 1492, 30 ; 1514, 1). The right of coining was a source of considerable profit to the Crown,[1] which evidently was not over scrupulous as to the way in which it made use of its privilege. The Golden Bull shows that continual changes were made in the value of the coins. They were frequently called in and reissued at a discount, or were composed of metal not cf the standard value, as is proved by innumerable protests of the Diet.[2] Originally all highways were looked upcn as military roads, and as such were under the control of the King, who thus became entitled to make all merchants pay for using them.[3] Both exported and imported goods paid one-thirtieth of their value, and a duty was charged on all merchandise using highroads and internal waterways, as on goods exposed for sale at fairs and market-places.[4] The Diet determined what articles of import and export should be subject to

[1] Falsifiers of the coinage were punished as for high treason.

[2] Charles Robert left the mines of gold, silver, and copper in the possession of the surface-owners on terms of receiving two-thirds of the produce, but under Louis the Great the right of resuming possession was reserved to the Crown (1351, clause 13) on giving estates of equal value elsewhere.

[3] Herczegh, p. 124 *sqq.*, and Timon, *o.c.* p. 235.

[4] The *tricesima*, as it was called, was first imposed by King Sigismund. It was temporarily abolished by Mathias Corvinus, but was soon revived.

payment of duty and provided for the collection[1] of
the proceeds.

The first indication of a distinction between Crown and
national revenues is found in the law of 1444, clause 3 of
which provides that the proceeds of taxation are to be
applied to the payment of Court expenses and of the cost
of national defence, while other income may be utilised
according to the King's pleasure.[2]   Direct taxation was
first introduced by Coloman (1100), or in any case was
regularised by his law.   A *census regalis*, or *collecta regalis*,
was paid at that period by all freemen who were not nobles,
as a recognition of the King's *dominium naturale*, by tenants
of the King's land, and by foreigners *pro libertate* (cl. 80).
Hence the proceeds were known as *liberi denarii*, referred to
in the Golden Bull.[3]   The nobles at all times considered
the payment of taxes as beneath the dignity of free men,
and saw no difference between taxes paid to the King and
the rent paid by serfs to their lords.   Hence the numerous
laws from the Golden Bull onwards guaranteeing and
reaffirming the immunity from taxation enjoyed by all
nobles or freemen.   When the Crown had partially
pauperised itself by excessive grants of land and of wholesale immunity from taxation, it had to make extraordinary
levies on the non-noble freemen, at first only for the
purpose of building fortifications, or of portioning the
King's son on his marriage, but later for all purposes at
the King's discretion;[4] and immunities granted by the
Crown were held not to apply to extraordinary taxation of
this nature.   During the reign of the house of Árpád the
chief regular taxes were the hearth-tax (*fumarii*) payable
by every non-noble, free, householder, and the *terragium* or
land-tax.[5]   Besides these there were the so-called *munera*,
nominally free gifts payable by the towns on New-Year's

[1] Law of 1405, 17 ; 1439, 6 ; 1492, 27 ; 1498, 29 ; 1514.
[2] Herczegh, *o.c.* p. 416.   [3] Timon, *o.c.* p. 240.
[4] Herczegh, p. 126.   [5] Timon, *o.c.* p. 243.

day or on other festivals, and by lords-lieutenant, who were bound to entertain the King once a year, and to give him one or two hundred marks when he got up from dinner. In the middle of the eleventh century this custom annually produced ten thousand marks for the King's treasury,[1] which also received one-twentieth of the Church tithes.[2] The introduction of a regular system of taxation was necessitated by the establishment of a paid army under the Anjou dynasty, the basis of taxation being originally the *porta* (*i.e.*, the peasant homestead with a gateway large enough for a hay-cart to pass through) without reference to the number of persons living within it. This tax, which varied at different times from, roughly, one-seventh to one-third of a gold florin, was changed in the reign of Mathias Corvinus into a tax payable by all peasants except those of the clergy and of nobles possessing more than one *sessio* or peasant's allotment. Though this produced a large sum, it did not put an end to the necessity of occasional extraordinary taxation, to the extent even of a gold florin on every peasant household, and of the imposition of a poll-tax on the landless. Though from Albert's time no tax could be imposed without the consent of the Diet, Charles Robert, Sigismund, and Vladislav imposed such extraordinary taxes with varying success, without reference to that body, which invariably protested against the infringement of its privilege. The result was the law of 1453, absolutely prohibiting the collection of any extraordinary taxes whatever, an enactment which, as a matter of fact, did not prevent the Diet from subsequently voting special subsidies under exceptional circumstances. Thus, by degrees, were established the two principles : that of the Diet's complete control of direct taxation, and that of the nobles' absolute immunity therefrom. That the nobles

[1] Timon, *o.c.* p. 246.
[2] Granted by Pope Alexander IV. to Bela IV. in 1259. Herczegh, *o.c.* p. 127, *n.*

were not entirely altruistic in their resistance to the King's demands for money is obvious from the fact that the greater the exigencies of the public service the less the probability of the landlords obtaining their dues in full.

It must be remembered that the nobles had some justification for their rooted objection to pay taxes, and for the immunity which they maintained down to 1848. Every noble landowner,[1] no matter what the size of his property might be, was liable to be called out for military service at his own expense to resist foreign invasion,[2] and to pursue and take vengeance on the aggressor ;[3] and in a country like Hungary, "set in the midst—in the very jaws—of enemies, and requiring at all times to be defended by the sword,"[4] the obligation was no insignificant one. Apart from the *levée en masse* of the nobles the King had his own forces, and these he could utilise both at home and abroad. They consisted, in the first place, of the poor nobles (*várjobbágyok*), who held land of the King, and were under an obligation to perform military service in return therefor. These provided the mass of the army at the disposal of the Crown. Secondly, there were the forces which the chief officers of State were bound to provide in virtue of their official positions, viz. the Palatine, the Bán of Croatia, the Voyvode of Transylvania, the lords-lieutenant of counties, certain bishops, and others, to whom the King had made grants of land, the consideration for which was the performance of military service.[5] Thirdly, there were the soldiers whom the royal towns and privileged peoples like the Saxons were bound to provide. The non-noble free were under no obligation to serve, but eight, or sometimes ten, had

---

[1] In the case of brothers, joint owners, only one, the *utilior et acrior*, was bound to serve. Constitutions of Pest ; Endlicher's *Monumenta*, p. 635, cl. 19.

[2] Golden Bull, cl. 7.

[3] Law of 1231, cl. 16, "pro vindicta persequi."

[4] Verbőczy, i. 18.

[5] "Et quibus amplas concessimus possessiones," 1231, 15.

to club together to provide one soldier. If the king thought fit to employ mercenaries, he had to pay for them out of his own funds. With the Anjou dynasty the principle was introduced that while poor nobles were not bound to do more than give personal service, the great landowners must take a share in the defence of the country's interests proportionate to their means. Hence the law,[1] to which reference has already been made, fixing the peasant's dues at one-ninth of the produce of his land payable to the landlord, and one-tenth to the clergy, who, as nobles, were also liable to military service in defence of the country down to 1523, when they were allowed to find substitutes. For every hundred florins so received two mounted men had to be provided. The number of soldiers to be found under the new system in proportion to the number of peasants on an estate varied, from time to time, from three from every hundred to one from every twenty,[2] the so-called *militia portalis*. Nobles with no peasants originally had to give personal service only ; but from the middle of the fourteenth century three, four, ten, or twenty, according to the country's necessity and the decision of the Diet, had to find a mounted man between them,[3] as well as to serve themselves under the flag of the lord-lieutenant of their county. The forces so raised amounted to from 100,000 to 200,000 men at various times out of a population of between four and five millions, of whom seventy to eighty per cent were Magyars.[4] The local justices were entrusted with the task of registering all peasants liable to serve ;[5] and by a law of the reign of Ladislaus V., nobles failing to provide their proper contingent of soldiers according to the number of their

---

[1] 1351, 6.
[2] Timon, *o.c.* p. 744, *n.* The origin of the word *hussar*—húsz=20. "Gentes potissimum levis armaturae sive húszarones," 1486, cl. 31.
[3] Timon, *o.c.* p. 745, *n.*
[4] *Mátyás Király Birodalma.* Beksics, p. 39.
[5] Law of 1435.

tenants, had to pay sixteen florins for each mounted man whom they failed to supply, and ten for every foot-soldier. In case of non-payment within fifteen days, defaulters were to be kept under arrest until their obligations were fulfilled.[1] The number of men called out for service in every case depended on the decision of the Diet, as did the assessment of the military tax ; except, therefore, as regards the forces provided *ex officio* by the great officers of state and by the King, the control of the Diet was complete in military matters. Charles Robert, relying on the love of display of the Hungarians, introduced the so-called Banderial system, which allowed nobles who found one hundred or more soldiers [2] to bring them under their own flag instead of fighting under that of the lord-lieutenant of their county. The result was a competition among the nobles for the distinction of having brought the greatest number of retainers. The qualifying number was subsequently reduced, and from 1492 onwards the privilege was extended to all who brought not less than fifty armed men. For foreign expeditions the King could rely only on his own forces, and on the *banderia* of the officials already referred to,[3] each of whom provided not less than 500 mounted men.

The want of a permanent body of disciplined troops began to be felt. Consequently King Mathias organised a force of 14,000 infantry and 20,000 cavalry, known from their uniform as the Black Brigade,[4] the pay and cost of maintenance of which was voted from time to time, as required, by the Diet, which stipulated that the officers of the Brigade as well as those in charge of the fortified places on the frontiers should be exclusively

[1] *A Magyar Nemzet Története*, iv. 130.
[2] Timon, *o.c.* p. 746. Herczegh, p. 314, *n.*, says 500.
[3] The so-called Zászlós urak, or Bannerets.
[4] Herczegh, *o.c.* p. 414. Horn, *Le Compromis de 1868 entre la Hongrie et la Croatie*, says they were mostly Croatians.
[5] 1471, 6, and 1492, 8.

Magyar. The establishment of a permanent force led to the decay of the Banderial system, and as, after the death of Mathias, the Black Brigade became disorderly and fell to pieces, the country became unable to defend itself against the better organised and better armed Turkish troops. The result was the disaster of Mohács.[1]

As has been mentioned, the nobility never constituted an exclusive caste, for all free Magyar landowners nominally enjoyed precisely the same privileges. In practice, however, this was not entirely the case, wealth and official position being differentiating factors; and though, nominally, no difference of birth was recognised before 1608, there were certain families which possessed the hereditary right of admission to the Council[2] (membership of which otherwise depended on the holding of certain high offices), and others, the members of which were known, at all events as early as the reign of Béla IV.[3] as *barones naturales* or *barones solo nomine*. These latter

---

[1] The Turks had 300 guns at Mohács, the Hungarians only 80.—*Mátyás Király Birodalma.* Beksics, p. 21.

[2] Marczali, *A Magyar Nemzet Története,* ii. 639, cites a patent given to the Frangepán family by Béla IV., in return for a money subsidy required for the purpose of raising mercenaries, in virtue of which all its members became *primates*, and received in perpetuity the right to a seat in the King's Council, and to all the privileges, honours, and franchises attaching to the chief lords of the kingdom.   So it would appear that higher nobles were recognised *as a class* in 1263.   Further, Szalay, *Magyarország Története,* iii. 187, *n.,* says that down to the time of Sigismund "*Immunitas*" from the jurisdiction of the county authorities carried with it the title of baron.   For an example of "*Immunitas*" see Marczali, *Enchiridion Fontium,* p. 209 *sqq.* : a charter granted in 1330 to the Báthory family.   The family and all living on their land, including foreigners, are excluded from the jurisdiction of the Palatine and county authorities in perpetuity, and the peasants are exempt from payment of all State taxes and dues ; jurisdiction is given to the family in all civil and criminal cases, and power to inflict the penalty of death, mutilation, and branding, and to keep a gallows always standing for the discouragement of evil-doers.   These immunities, which also gave the right to build castles, gave rise to an oligarchy, to an attempt to bring the smaller landowners into a state of feudal dependence, and to the pauperisation of the Crown.   They produced a breach in the solidarity of the people, which was largely answerable for the disaster of Mohács.

[3] Beöthy, *o.c.* i. 332.

possessed the title, but not the office of the *veri barones regni*, the Palatine, Chief Justice, Bán of Croatia, Voyvode of Transylvania, and other officials, members of the Council of State enumerated by Verbóczy, in which recognised class of great nobles the bishops were included in virtue of their office. The title of Count (gróf) was held in the fifteenth century, if not earlier, by such nobles, *comites liberi et perpetui*, as exercised completely independent authority over whole districts.[1] Though the conferment in perpetuity of the right to exercise such authority was forbidden by the Golden Bull,[2] grants continued to be made in Croatia and Slavonia.[3] The creation of Counts without reference to landed possessions or special authority did not begin till after the introduction of the Habsburg dynasty, which, after 1608, created Counts of the Holy Roman Empire largely with a view to obtaining a majority in the Upper House. The same may be said of the Duces or Princes created by the House of Habsburg, who thus became possessed of a title confined under the Árpád dynasty to members of the reigning family.[4]

It will be remembered that all barons, that is to say officials dependent on the King and hereditary lords-lieutenant, were excluded from the Diet of 1298; but there is no evidence to show that this was the usual practice, and that their influence was permanently confined to the council chamber. In the first place, both custom and law not only allowed, but in early days, compelled

1 Timon, *o.c.* p. 534.   2 Cl. 16.
3 Herczegh, *o.c.* p. 316.
4 It was the custom from St. Stephen's time to confer the government of districts on sons or brothers of the King, with the right of coining, keeping troops, etc., and the heir to the throne was often crowned as "rex junior" in his father's lifetime. As such he had his own officials, chancellor, treasurer, etc., but held his position only *ex veluntate patris*. Emerich (Imre), son of Stephen, was apparently the first Duke, as governor of Slavonia. Béla, brother of Andrew I., governed a third of the kingdom.—Herczegh, *o.c.* pp. 64, 65.
The title of Prince was conferred for the first time on one not of royal blood, on the Voyvode of Wallachia, by Louis the Great.—Timon, *o.c.* p. 538.

the attendance of all nobles ;[1] in the second place, the
established principle that votes should be weighed and
not counted[2] makes it improbable that those who, owing
to their position and attainments, were best qualified to
form public opinion in such an unwieldy body as the Diet
of early days should have been habitually excluded from
its deliberations.   The fact of its unwieldiness soon led
to an attempt to alter its composition by the introduction
from time to time of the representative principle ; but the
fact that a recurrence to the old system frequently took
place shows either that the recollection of the old mass
meetings of the tribes died hard, or, what is more probable,
that the people had little confidence in the ability of their
representatives to resist the blandishments, or the attempts
at bribery or intimidation, of the powerful nobles[3] or of
the King.   The latter would, no doubt, find it easier to
get subsidies voted by a comparatively small body of
representatives than by the great mass of the impecunious,
and, consequently, would be the warmest partisan of the
representative system.   But there was another reason for
the introduction of that system.   It came to be regarded,
not as a deprivation of a right, but as an alleviation of a
burden.   The law of 1526 (cl. 16) says that "poor
nobles have become so exhausted by the frequency of
the meetings of the Diet that they have been compelled
to mortgage their property to meet the excessive expense,
and so have degenerated into a condition of perpetual
rusticity."   The great nobles dragged out the meetings

[1] "Omnes servientes (i.e. nobles) libere illic (Székesfehérvár) conveniant,"
1222, cl. 1, and 1290, cl. 25.

[2] Verbőczy says : "Verum si populus in duas divideretur partes, tunc
constitutio sanioris et potioris partis valet.   Sanior autem et potior pars illa
dicitur in qua dignitate et scientia fuerint praestantiores atque notabiliores,"
iii. 2.   The law of 1495, 25, ordains that each member of the Council is to
be asked his opinion ; but still the "Saniores" had it their own way, and
though continual disputes arose in consequence, the system continued till
after 1825.

[3] See Andrássy, A Magyar Állam Fönmaraddsdnak Okai, i. 392.

in order to tire out the opposition,[1] and non-attendance became a habit. It was resolved, therefore, that business must be begun on the fourth day after that fixed for the opening of the Diet, and concluded within fifteen days ; and that all who failed to attend should be heavily fined.

Fear of expense and distrust of their representatives alternately influenced the lesser nobles. It seems that in the twelfth century all attended every year. In 1267 it was enacted (cl. 8) that "two or three from each county" should appear. The law of 1290 (cl. 25) demands the attendance of all nobles ; and it is the same in 1318. In 1385 four representatives are summoned from each county. In 1486 an unspecified number of "elected nobles representing the whole kingdom" attended the Diet of Buda according to the decree of that year. Nine years later the entire body of nobles was summoned ; and we may take it that the right of all nobles to appear was never abolished till 1608, though after Mohács circumstances made its exercise an impossibility.[2] In early times the Diet, or *parlamentum publicum*,[3] as it was styled in 1288, was summoned annually ; but, apparently, it became the habit early in the fourteenth century to call it together at uncertain intervals when required, as it was then no longer summoned for judicial purposes. The law of 1498 decreed its convocation every year for the next four years, and then every three years ; that of 1563 requires an annual sitting to be held, but the rule was not observed. Ferdinand II., in his *diploma inaugurale*, undertook to summon the Diet at least every third year ;[4] and this continued to be, nominally, the rule till 1848.

[1] By 1492, 108, the Diet was bound to wait three days for the bishops and barons, and then could proceed without them.

[2] Apparently the whole body of the nobles was summoned for the last time, and under penalty for non-attendance, by Maximilian in 1572, for the coronation of his son.

[3] Also styled *Parlamentum generale, Concilium commune Regni, Conventus Regni generalis, Diaeta generalis.*—Beöthy, *o.c.* i. 48, and Kmety, *Közjog*, 248, *n.*

[4] Timon, *o.c.* p. 599. How long the Diet continued to be held in the

Till 1608 the Diet consisted of one chamber only, though the King's Council contained the germ of the Upper House of a later day. It is evident that in the time of the Árpád dynasty it was the usual practice for the King to consult the Council as to proposed legislation before the meeting of the Diet took place; and cl. 25 of the law of 1495 made it obligatory to do so.

In early days the Magyar population had little inclination for anything but country life, and the towns developed but slowly from the communes, in which strangers were encouraged to settle for purposes of trade by the grant of immunity from the payment of customs duties[1] and of the permission to hold fairs and markets under the supervision of the governor of the fortified town[2]—the political centre of every county. The urban population consisted chiefly of Germans and Jews, who did not speak Hungarian, and so lived a life apart and took no part or interest in the common affairs of state. Their very privileges were a cause of, and accentuated, their isolation, made them dependent on the King,[3] and hostile or indifferent to the constitutional rights of the rest of the people. As early as 1230 town councils existed, invested with judicial authority, and consisting of a judge

open air after the manner of the old tribal meetings is uncertain; anyway it was not so held after the introduction of the Anjou dynasty. It was not always held at the same place, but Székesfehérvár was the traditional place for the Coronation Diet. After Mohács, Pressburg (Pozsony) became the regular place of meeting, and continued to be so, apparently for the reason that it was close to Vienna, and gave the Habsburgs a greater degree of control than they would have had over a Diet meeting at more distant Buda. The oldest extant *litterae regales*, or letters of summons, are of 1318. They state that the Diet is summoned under pressure, under threat of excommunication, apparently the only means the nobles had of compelling an unwilling King to convoke them.—Herczegh, *o.c.* p. 338, *n.* Since Sigismund's time the *litterae regales* specified the chief subjects for the discussion of which the Diet was to meet.

[1] 1405, cl. 17. [2] Herczegh, *o.c.* p. 73.

[3] "Bona et peculia Sacrae Regni Coronae." "Die Magyaren errichteten in Ungarn den Staat, die Deutschen schufen die Städte."—Hunfalvy quoted by Schwicker, *Die Deutschen in Ungarn und Siebenbürgen*, Vienna, 1881, p. 87. See the chapter entitled "Die Deutschen und das Städtewesen in Ungarn."

(Major villae or villicus)[1] and ten or twelve jurors elected by all householders. From the decisions of this body an appeal lay to the King's treasurer. The actual government of a town was in the hands of an outer and an inner council : the former consisting of forty to one hundred members,[2] the latter of twelve to twenty-four senators elected for life, with whom lay the appointment of all executive officers. There were no definite class distinctions, but certain towns had an exclusively racial character, and in many places the result was the establishment of a narrow German oligarchy, which took advantage of its privilege of making by-laws and regulations to refuse to allow Magyars or members of other races to own property within the town limits, and so excluded them from participation in municipal government.[3] For a long time the towns were unrepresented at the Diet. The representatives of the larger ones were in fact summoned from time to time for special objects,[4] for the discussion of terms of peace or of financial questions, but the first occasion on which they undoubtedly took part in the general business of the Diet was in 1405. In that year eight[5] free towns sent their representatives, elected for the purpose, not by the mass of the citizens, but, as in later days also, by the town councils. This fact deprived

[1] Timon, c.c. p. 204, n. See also the charter given to Buda in 1276, cl. 3, in Endlicher's *Monumenta*, p. 543, and law of 1405, giving jurisdiction in case of all offences committed within the town limits.

[2] In Pest 124.—Herczegh, o.c. p. 386.

[3] The exclusive tendencies of the Germans made it necessary to take measures for the protection of other nationalities, and cl. 12 of the law of 1608 declared that at elections to municipal offices no regard must be had to nationality, and that Magyars and Slavs must be allowed to own property within the town limits. As this law received the assent of an Austrian king, it may be concluded that the scandal which gave rise to it must have been considerable. In most towns less than one hundred persons possessed the rights of citizenship. — Horváth, *Huszonöt év Magyarország Történelméböl*, i. 619. [4] *E.g.* in 1397 to the Diet at Temesvár.

[5] Called *liberae et Regiae civitates*, to distinguish them from the *liberae*. Verböczy enumerates eleven such, and early in the sixteenth century there were fifteen.—Timon, o.c. p. 563, n.

them of their representative character, and justified the general view that they were mere tools of foreign trade-guilds, anti-Magyar in spirit, and blind partisans of the King whenever the interests of the Crown and the nation happened to be opposed. Hence the continued opposition in the Diet to the extension of urban representation, of which more will be heard hereafter, and the fact that all the privileged towns together were regarded as forming only one *nobilis persona* entitled as such to the apparently derisory, but actually sufficient, privilege of one vote. More they could hardly expect so long as they were under the thumb of the Court, and were not only indifferent, but actually hostile to the desires of the nation whose favoured guests they were,[1] whose language they were unable to speak.[2] In return for their privileges they paid a land tax and a military tax to the Crown, and were under an obligation to find a certain number of soldiers, but only in the event of the King taking the field in person.

Before Mohács, Transylvania, "antiqvissimum Hungariae Regni membrum," as it was styled by the Diet of Pressburg of 1691, formed an integral part of Hungary, and consequently had no separate legislative body, but sent its representatives to the Diet in the same way as the counties of Hungary proper sent theirs. Being somewhat shut off from the rest of the country, it was, from St. Stephen's time, placed under a Voyvode, or permanent governor, who, in time, came to occupy much the same position as that held by the Palatine in Hungary. The population consisted of Magyars, Szeklers, and Saxons, spoken of as "the three nations of Transylvania," each having their own separate organisation down to 1437, when, owing to a rising of Wallachian and other peasants,

---

[1] Michael Horváth, *Magyarország Történelme*, vi. 25.

[2] The deputies of Pozsony, Buda, Kassa, and Székesfehérvár to the Diet of 1446 could not understand Hungarian, as shown by a letter of one of their number quoted by Knaus, *Az Országos Tanács és Országgyülések Története*, p. 41 and note 179. But Szalay, *o.c.* iii. 89, *n.*, doubts this.

they formed, for purposes of defence, a "fraternal union," which was developed in 1507 by the establishment of a common judiciary. A general meeting of all the nobles is first spoken of as having taken place in 1291, and from that time forward frequent mention is made of meetings of the *congregatio generalis trium partium* for judicial purposes as well as for the discussion of questions of local finance and military matters.[1]

The origin of the Szeklers (Latinised as Siculi)[2] is uncertain. Procopius[3] says that 3000 Huns entered Erdeleu[4] after their defeat, "calling themselves, not Hungarians, but Zekul," and that the Szeklers were the descendants of the Huns who stayed in Transylvania until the return of their congeners under Árpád. The anonymous scribe of King Béla speaks of them as "formerly Attila's folk," but Timon[5] shows that this could not have been the case, as their language proves that they could not have separated from the main stock until the Magyar tongue had attained its full development, which did not take place until a considerable time after the occupation of Pannonia had become an accomplished fact. Marczali[6] thinks they were members of a kindred tribe, neighbours of the Magyars in their old home, who are known to have settled in parts of Hungary and Bulgaria.[7] Pauler, on the contrary, believes that they were pure Magyars transplanted to Transylvania by St. Ladislaus in order to have a permanent defensive force on the frontier; but if this was their origin, it is

---

[1] Timon, *o.c.* p. 695 *sqq.*
[2] Probably originally Scythuli. The Epitome of Peter Ransanius in the *Chronica minora*, ed. Flórián, p. 153, says they were the descendants of Sicilians who fought under Attila, a mere invention to account for the name.
[3] *De Bello gothico*, iv. 18.
[4] The Hungarian for Transylvania is "Erdély."
[5] *O.c.* p. 75 ; so too Hunfalvy, *Magyarorszdg Ethnographidja*, 200.
[6] *A Magyar Nemzet Története*, ii. 170.
[7] The Bessenyők or Patzinakites of Constantine Porphyrogenitus.

strange that it should have been forgotten so soon. In support of the theory is the fact that the obligation of military service was universal with the Szeklers, who were, in consequence, exempt from taxation. They long maintained the old family and tribal organisation with its military basis,[1] the King's authority being represented by an Ispán, known as the Comes Siculcrum, and the seven districts and the seven free towns elected their own military and judicial officers. The seven captains and seven judges of the district, as well as the Comes, attended the Hungarian Diet. Similarly, the Magyar part of Transylvania was divided into seven counties, each under its Lord-Lieutenant and corresponding officials, as in Hungary proper. Every county and each of the four towns sent two representatives to the Hungarian Diet.

In early times the Hungarians not only did not oppress but actually gave exceptional privileges to the strangers within their gates who, later, ill requited the hospitality they had received. Of the so-called Saxons the earliest settlement came into existence in the reign of Géza II., about the year 1147, when floods in Flanders [2] drove out a considerable section of the population, which betook itself to Saxony in search of a new habitation, but finding that country a prey to famine, resumed its wanderings, accompanied by many Saxon families, and eventually reached the northern part of Hungary. There, in 1147, King Géza allowed them to settle in the district of Szepes (Zips), recently devastated by the incursion of the Kuns, and gave them special rights and immunities which were confirmed by subsequent kings. At first they did not form a separate political body, but by charter of 1271,[3] confirmed in 1312 by Charles Robert,

[1] Herczegh, o.c. p. 102, n. Hunfalvy, l.c., states that the name Szekler signifies frontier-guard.

[2] In the thirteenth century they were known as Flemings, not as Saxons Regestrum de Várad, 1231-1235.—Endlicher's Monumenta, p. 701.

[3] Endlicher's Monumenta, p. 522.

the twenty-four so-called towns were formed into a separate *provincia*, at the head of which was a *comes* or *judex* chosen by the inhabitants, who were thus withdrawn from the jurisdiction of the King's justices[1] and kept their own laws and customs. In return for their privileges they paid the King three hundred marks of fir e silver every year, and were bound to provide him with fifty lancers in time of war.

It seems that the Saxons of Transylvania mostly came from the neighbourhood of Cologne and Düsseldorf, whence they were driven by the oppression of feudal lords.[2] By the charter of Andrew II.[3] (1224) these " Theutonici Ultrasylvani " were recognised as a separate political organisation, were allowed to choose their own lay and ecclesiastical officials, and were subjected to the authority only of the King and of their own Ispán.[4] Their traders were allowed to import their merchandise free of duty into all parts of Hungary and to hold fairs and markets. Originally they elected their own burgher-masters and judges, but in or before Sigismund's reign these offices had become hereditary in certain families. An end was put to this, and the elective principle was restored, by Mathias Corvinus in 1477. Each town had its popular assembly, its inner council of twelve members, and its outer one of fifty to one hundred. The Transylvanian Saxons were bound to find 500 soldiers for home defence, provided the King took the field in person, and 100 for service abroad. They also paid 500 marks per annum to the royal treasury. Like their

[1] " Quia homines sunt simplices et in jure nobilium nequeunt versari."— Timon, *o.c.* p. 217, *n.*

[2] Keinzel, *Ueber die Herkunft der Siebenbürger Sachsen. A Magyar Nemzet Története,* ii. 412 *sqq.* See also *Enchiridion Fontium,* p. 145. Schwicker, *Die Deutschen in Ungarn und Siebenbürgen,* p. 80 *sqq.,* and especially Teutsch, *Geschichte der Siebenbürger Sachsen,* Hermannstadt, 1899, p. 8 *sqq.*

[3] Teutscn, *o.c.* p. 27.

[4] Appointed by the King—official title, Comes Cibiniensis, Count of Szeben.

fellow-countrymen elsewhere the Saxons would in all probability have lost their individuality, and have become merged in the Magyar nation, but for the special privileges which kept alive the spirit of racial distinction, the results of which were felt all through Hungarian history.

Slavonia formed part of Hungary from the earliest times, as is proved by reference to the treatise of Constantine Porphyrogenitus already referred to,[1] but was not converted to Christianity till the time of St. Ladislaus.[2] It enjoyed a certain measure of self-government, had its own Congregatio, which could pass by-laws of local application, paid only half the taxes paid in Hungary,[3] could elect its own Comes and bishops, and used its own laws and rules of judicial procedure. No Magyar or other foreigner could live or hold property in the privileged towns[4] without the express consent of the municipal authorities. The Congregatio[5] sent elected representatives to the Hungarian Diet.[6]

Croatia,[7] annexed in 1091 by St. Ladislaus, revolted

[1] De Administrando Imperio.

[2] This statement is not borne out entirely by the document which Timon (o.c. p. 224, n.) quotes in its support, "László qui terram slavonie" (i.e. the parts between the Száva and Dráva) "sive banatum ab errore ydolatrie ad Christianitatem convertem corone Hungarie subiugavit."

[3] Szalay, Magyarország Története, iii. 265, n.

[4] See the charter granted in 1108 to the town of Traun by King Coloman, in Marczali's Enchiridion Fontium, p. 126, regarded as the model for all such charters.

[5] Timon, o.c. p. 716 sqq.

[6] Law xxiii. of 1751. After Mohács Slavonia came under Turkish domination, and was not restored to the Sacred Crown till 1699—the peace of Karlócza. Since 1751 it was under the authority of the Bán of Croatia.

[7] See Timon, o.c. p. 716 sqq. ; and Herczegh, o.c. p. 226 sqq. Croatia of to-day is territorially distinct from the original country of that name. In the twelfth century Croatia was the name of the district lying between the Kulpa and the Verbász, and included the present Bosnia and parts of modern Dalmatia. Such was the independent kingdom of Zvonimir before it was united to Hungary. This original territory was subsequently occupied by the Turks, and the Christian population took refuge in the strictly Hungarian district lying between the Száva and Dráva. The rights enjoyed under

after his death, and was reconquered in 1105 by Coloman, who assumed the title of King of Croatia and Dalmatia, and placed both countries under a Dux or Bán invested with the functions of governor or chief justice. By the "Privilegium libertatum," granted a few years later, Coloman allowed the Croatians to keep their old laws, and to forbid the ownership of real property by Magyars, exempted the nobles from the payment of taxes to the royal treasury, and permitted migration to all who might consider themselves aggrieved by Hungarian rule. Except for the fact that they had no right of armed resistance to the King, the Croatians in most respects enjoyed rights similar to those possessed by Magyar nobles, as, apart from immunity from taxation, they were liable to military service outside the limits of Croatia only under the personal leadership of the King, and at his expense. Croatia had its own *diaeta generalis*, which could pass laws of local application only[1] and provided for the assessment and collection of the military tax and the enrolment of the military contingents required by Hungary. Dalmatia[2] received similar rights from Coloman, and, though in general under Hungarian law, had certain old privileges confirmed later by Charles Robert and Louis the Great. For instance, the Dalmatians elected the governors of the

Hungarian predominance were continued to those in the new, which gradually lost its essentially Magyar characteristics, though it continued to be subject to the spiritual lordship of the Magyar bishop of Kalocsa.

[1] Verböczy, *Jus Tripartitum*, iii. 2.

[2] Occupied by the Venetians early in the Anjou period, restored to Hungary in 1358, but again occupied by Venice in 1420. In 1432 the whole of Dalmatia came into the possession of Venice, which continually had to fight the Turks to maintain its rights. By the Peace of Campoformio Francis I. recovered Dalmatia as belonging to the Sacred Crown of Hungary, but kept it only till 1805, when it became a French possession. Recovered in 1815, it was incorporated in Austria, illegally, as Francis's claim to it was based solely on the fact that it belonged to Hungary. Fiume formed a "separatum Regni Hungariae coronae adnexum corpus," a detached but integral part of the Magyar kingdom, in accordance with the "Benignum Rescriptum" of Maria Theresa, 1779.

towns, the bishops, and the lower judicial authorities; and one-third of the customs duties was applied to local purposes, the remainder being paid into the Hungarian treasury. In Dalmatia the King did not claim the right of investiture or any judicial control of ecclesiastics. These three districts of Slavonia, Croatia, and Dalmatia, at first spoken of as *partes subjectae*,[1] and later, out of deference, it appears, to Croatian susceptibilities, as *partes adnexae*, never seriously claimed more than a certain degree of municipal independence, though the Croatians asserted, in their address to Ferdinand I., that they had joined themselves of their own free will to the Crown of Hungary, and in pursuance of their historical rights had voluntarily elected him to the throne. The value of such claim is indicated by the fact that though, possibly, some early kings of Hungary caused themselves to be crowned kings of Croatia,[2] Sigismund absolutely declined to do so, and from that time forward coronation with the Crown of St. Stephen was all that was required to give Kings of Hungary authority over the annexed or subject parts. Deputies sent by the provincial Congregatio had seats in the Hungarian Diet, and six towns and the district of Turopolya each sent representatives to that body, which passed many laws dealing with purely Croatian affairs, as the Corpus Juris Hungarici shows[3]—a suffi-

---

[1] Diploma of 1490 and Verbőczy, iii. 2, who distinctly states that Dalmatians, Croatians, and Slavonians, and any other people "*quae alterius subest dominio nulla potest condere statuta nisi cum consensu sui superioris.*" The laws of 1579, 1715, 2, and 1723, show that the usual phrase was "*Regnum Hungariae partesque eidem adnexae vel subjectae.*" Appeals from the local courts went before the High Court, the Királyi Curia of Hungary, both in Verbőczy's time and later in accordance with laws of 1723 and 1807. Beőthy, *A Magyar Államiság Fejlődése Küzdelmei*, ii. 271, cites a document of 1492, signed and sealed by the Bán and sixty-two chief nobles of Croatia, in which were the words "*coronae atque regno subjecti sumus.*" They are styled "*Subjectae*" in clause 8 of the Peace of Nagy-Várad, 1538, and in the preamble to the laws of 1608.

[2] Kmety, *A Magyar Közjog Tankönyve*, p. 148, says that Coloman was the only one to be crowned King of Croatia.

[3] *E.g.* 1351, xii., provides for the payment of the *lucrum camerae* by the

cient proof of the baselessness of Croatia's claim, advanced at a later date, to be considered an allied and not a sub-ordinate state.[1]   The key to later history is to be found in the fact that Croatia desired to be united to its congeners, Styria, Carinthia, and Carniola, and so to form a Slav state of greater importance than it could ever aspire to attain as a constituent part of the realms of the Sacred Crown.

The Wallachs or Roumanians claim to be descendants of Roman colonists, but there is not a vestige of evidence to show that any Roumanians lived in Transylvania at the time of its occupation by the Magyars.[2]   They were a

inhabitants of the district between the Dráva and Száva. 1471, vi., enacts that the fortifications on the Croatian frontier shall be entrusted to Magyars. The sixth decree of Sigismund shows that the form of the oath to be taken by all Croatian officials, from the Bán down to the lowest judicial authorities, was fixed by the Hungarian Diet.

[1] Horn, *Le Compromis de 1868 entre la Hongrie et la Croatie*, tries to show that Croatia was never a Hungarian province, but an allied state which had never been conquered. He admits, however, a "partial" conquest by St. Ladislaus, and that when Coloman advanced later with an army to enforce his claims, the Croatians accepted his terms rather than fight, which scarcely looks like voluntary alliance. His argument for the independence of Croatia, based on the fact that the Bán Imre issued instructions "auctoritate regia," pp. 41, 42, proves, if anything, precisely the contrary, as the Bán was son of the King of Hungary and ruling *ex voluntate patris*, who obviously had complete control of Croatia if he could delegate regal authority without reference to that country. It should also be observed that Báns were almost invariably Hungarians down to 1848, when the usual practice was departed from for an obvious reason. No conclusion can be drawn in favour of Croatia's independence from the fact that its deputies did not attend the Hungarian Diet from 1527 to 1593, as owing to the Turkish occupation everything was in an abnormal condition. Later they invariably attended, took part in the election of the Palatine, and demanded that their Bán should have a seat at the Diet, p. 80. In fact Croatia, as M. Horn admits, was proud of its connection with the Sacred Crown until it conceived ideas of expansion and of absorption of other Slav elements ; and indeed, until then, it never looked upon its privileges as other than municipal rights. Laws of 1439, 26, and 1492, 8, required the Bán to be a Hungarian, and the Croatians themselves demanded that it should be so, as they would not obey one of their own race.—Szögyény Marich László, *Emlékiratai*, p. 66. See also Auerbach, *Les races et les nationalités en Autriche-Hongrie*, Paris, 1898, pp. 315-316. For the argument based on Croatia's action *re* the Pragmatic Sanction, see below, p. 186, *n*.

[2] Paul Hunfalvy, *Die Rumänen und ihre Ansprüche*, Vienna, 1883, p. 39 *sqq.*, as to the evidence of names of rivers and places showing no vestige of a

race of nomad shepherds who gradually wandered into Hungary from the Balkan peninsula in the course of the twelfth century, bringing their Slav liturgy, an indication of their true origin, with them.[1] The theory of Roman origin, mentioned by Bonfini,[2] was seriously revived by Sinkai in 1807 on the authority of Eutropius,[3] who says that Trajan, after the conquest of Dacia, brought thither an immense number of people from all parts of the Roman world to till the land and occupy the towns, for the male population had been exhausted by the long war with Decebalus. But even if this statement is correct, it does not necessarily imply the total extermination of the

Romance population. See also De Bertha, *Magyars et Roumains devant l'histoire*, Paris, 1899, ch. vi., and Hunfalvy's *Magyarorszdg Ethnographidja*, pp. 479 *sqq.*, 499.

[1] Herczegh, *o.c.* p. 104. For the evidence of language see Hunfalvy, *o.c.* pt. ii. The Cyrillian characters were used down to the end of the eighteenth century, when Sinkai issued the first Roumanian grammar, 1780. Cihac's *Etymological Dictionary* shows that the Slav words in use vastly exceed those of Romance origin (*ibid.* 222). See also Auerbach, *Les races et les nationalités en Autriche-Hongrie*, Paris, 1898, p. 290 ; and Baloghy Ernö, *A Magyar Kultura és a Nemzetiségek*, Budapest, 1908, pp. 98, 106 *sqq.* ; also Beksics Gusztáv, *A Román Kérdés*, Budapest, 1895, p. 20 *sqq.* The Bible was not translated into the Rouman language till the time of George Rákóczy in the middle of the seventeenth century. Pič, *Zur Rumanisch-Ungarischen Streitfrage*, Leipzig, 1886, admits, p. 42, that the post-position of the definite article in Roumanian is a serious stumbling-block in the way of those who would assign a Roman origin to that language. Even the Roumanian name for Transylvania, "Ardeal," was clearly taken from the Hungarian Erdély, a proof that the Wallachians came on the scene after Transylvania had received the Magyar stamp. Pič can do no more by way of answer to the above fact than refer to the existence of a Rutulian town, Ardea, in Italy, *o.c.* p. 80.

[2] *Rerum Hungaricarum Decades*, 7th ed., Leipzig, 1771, p. 284. Of modern partisans of this theory see especially Pič, *Zur Rumanisch-Ungarischen Streitfrage*, Leipzig, 1886, ch. i. The letter of Pope Innocent III. in 1204 to the Hungarian King shows that he believed the Wallachs to be Bulgarians, but apparently he himself suggested to the Wallachians the theory of their Roman origin in the hope of weaning them from the Eastern Church.—See Hunfalvy, *Die Rumänen*, etc., p. 69. Niketas Choniates, writing at the end of the twelfth century, speaks of the Blacchi, " formerly called Mysians," as having previously been under the same rule as the Bulgarians. See also the reply of the Transylvanian Orders to the *Supplex Libellus Valachorum* in 1791. Jancsó Benedek, *Szabadsdgharczunk és a Dako-Román Törekvések*, Budapest, 1895, pp. 2, 3, 25 *sqq.*

[3] Book viii. 2-3.

Dacians;[1] and if the imported colonists were "*ex toto orbe Romano*," they were obviously anything rather than Roman. Mommsen, who clearly shows that the Dacians, so far from being exterminated, gave considerable trouble to later Roman emperors, says that the imported colonists were Dalmatians and inhabitants of Asia Minor.[2] Sinkai, in his anxiety to find a respectable origin for the Wallachs, quotes Eutropius when that writer apparently supports his theory, but not when his evidence is destructive. He therefore omits all reference to the passage[3] in which his author states that the Emperor Aurelian, "despairing of his ability to retain the province of Dacia, which Trajan had constituted beyond the Danube," withdrew the Romans therefrom in A.D. 270, abandoning it, according to Gibbon,[4] to the Goths and Vandals. Little is heard of them in early Hungarian history. The Blacchi[5] are mentioned some-

[1] See Hunfalvy, *o.c.* p. 12 *sqq.*, and, as to the evidence of inscriptions, p. 8, which prove the existence of a very strong Dacian element.

[2] *The Provinces of the Roman Empire*, bk. viii. ch. vi. Mommsen, in fact, says that Roman rule was never effective in the parts of Moldavia, Bessarabia, and Wallachia, which were "nominally" incorporated in the Roman Empire. "Even the language of the country maintained its ground." According to the same authority, the Dacians, Moesians, and Thracians all spoke the same language. The two legions posted on the left bank of the Danube were finally withdrawn in 260 A.D., and therewith disappeared the last vestiges of Roman control. The Roman coin and inscription of latest date are of 255 A.D.

[3] viii. 15.

[4] *Decline and Fall of the Roman Empire*, ii. 11 *sqq.* Gibbon is often cited in support of the Roman origin of the Wallachians, who, he wrongly says, "boasted in *every age* of their Roman descent," vol. ii. ch. xi., but in vol. vii. ch. lv., he says that they are of kindred origin with the Bulgarians, Servians, etc.

[5] Vlachs, from the German expression for Romanised races, Wälsch, see Hunfalvy, *o.c.* pp. 76 and 241-250. Verantius, a writer who lived at the court of John Zápolya, in the sixteenth century, mentions the Vlacchi, and says they had no freedom nor property, and lived a miserable life scattered about the mountains with their cattle.—See Kovachich, *Script. Minor.* ii. 106. Simon Kézai, *Gesta Hunnorum*, i. 5, mentions the Blacki as living mixed up with the Szeklers in early days, but evidently he and the other chroniclers who mention the Wallachs could account for their existence and for the servile position they occupied only by assuming that they were aborigines conquered by the Magyars. The anonymous scribe of King Béla refers to the existence of a

what contemptuously by the anonymous scribe of King
Béla, and a document of the reign of Andrew III. (1293)
refers to them as serfs of the King whose wanderings must
not be allowed to continue, apparently on account of their
predatory habits, by reason of which the edict of 1625
forbids them to ride or carry arms. The Diploma of
Leopold, 1691, which confirms the religious and civil
liberties of the other races of Transylvania, does not even
mention the Roumanians. On the other hand, the report
of Joseph to Maria Theresa, on his journey to Transylvania in 1768, refers to their "indescribable ignorance
and stupidity," and to their blind obedience to their priests,
and mentions the fact that not one in a thousand could
either read or write his own language. The troubles of a
later period are directly traceable to this servile obedience
to the priests, who desired an independent ecclesiastical
organisation of their own, and fomented the hatred engendered by subjection to Saxon as well as Magyar landlords. The Roumanians of Transylvania had no political
rights down to 1848, in which respect they were on precisely the same footing and had the same grievance as all
Magyar peasants.

St. Stephen abolished the old tribal divisions and
divided the country into counties[1] in order to facilitate
the collection of taxes, the establishment of a form of
military organisation, and the consolidation of the royal
power. At the head of each county was the Comes Castri
(Főispán or Lord-Lieutenant) appointed by the King—at

Wallachian Duke Gelou in Transylvania, but there is no other record of such
a person ; and Hunfalvy, *o.c.* p. 92 *sqq.*, shows that the Wallachian word
Kenez (Russian Kniaz, Prince or Duke) signified no more than the head of a
village or district.

[1] Probably forty-five at first (Timon, *o.c.* p. 188.) The oldest reference
is of the year 1150, in the *Gesta Frederici imperatoris* of Bishop Otto of
Freising, who says there were seventy or more, *Enchiridion Fontium*, p. 120.
See also the *Carmen miserabile Magistri Rogerii, circa* 1245, in Endlicher's
Monumenta, p. 262, and Petri R..nsani Epitome in *Chronica minora*, ed. Flórián,
p. 144.

first, probably, a purely military official, governor of the fortified town and commander-in-chief of the county forces,[1] who soon developed into the responsible head of all branches of local government. With the decline of the royal authority the autonomy of the counties rapidly increased, the purely military character of their organisation disappeared, and they became political units whose will was voiced by the Congregation or general meeting of the whole body of inhabitants,[2] originally convened only for judicial purposes [3] under the presidency of the Palatine, but as early as the middle of the thirteenth century, for the discussion and decision of all matters of local interest under the presidency of the lord-lieutenant.[4] In his character of "Comes naturalis" of every county, the King could appoint any local landowner to the lord-lieutenancy down to 1486,[5] when the law required the consent of the nobles to be obtained prior to the making of an appointment to that office. Though the sixteenth clause of the Golden Bull had forbidden the conferment of hereditary lord-lieutenancies, the dignity was, in fact, still hereditary at the beginning of the eighteenth century in no less than

[1] He appointed the hadnagy, or captain of the forces—the várnagy, the captain of the castle—and the centuriones, the lower officers.

[2] Till the introduction of the Anjou dynasty, nobles and non-nobles alike attended, but with the development of the feudal tendencies of the great nobles the peasants lost their right, though a letter of summons of the period of Louis the Great exists addressed "omnibus nobilibus et ignobilibus nec non alterius cujusvis status et conditionis hominibus."—Herczegh, o.c. p. 373, n.

[3] The Comes was the chief judicial authority of the county, but he had no authority over the nobles except in the matter of tithes and coinage (clause 5 of Golden Bull). There was also in early times a Judex Regis, at fiist independent, later under the control of the Comes, who, in his turn, was subject to that of the Palatine, and responsible at first to the King (sect. 14, Golden Bull), then to the Diet (1290, clause 25), for his general conduct. The "bilochi regales" referred to in Golden Bull, clause 5, were apparently judges sent specially for the trial of "furts et latrones," as assistants to the Comes.

[4] Herczegh, o.c. p. 92, n., cites a document of 1254, which shows that the congregation already then dealt with all matters "quae totam provinciam tangerent."

[5] Clause 60.

nineteen families, and was enjoyed *ex officio* by two arch-bishops and seven bishops.[1] The result was the converse of what might have been expected. The lords-lieutenant, both hereditary and nominated, being, in the majority of cases, great nobles who desired either a wider field for their activities or more satisfactory opportunities of spending their money than the county could afford them, developed in course of time a not unnatural tendency to absenteeism. Hence a gradual weakening of the King's hold on the organs of local government, and a corresponding accentuation of the democratic character of county organisation.

At first the Vicecomes was merely the nominee and representative of the Lord-Lieutenant;[2] but in 1548 the "Universitas nobilium,"[3] or whole body of freemen, asserted their right to elect whom they pleased, and thenceforward the Deputy-Lieutenant became the chief representative of the principle of local autonomy and the practical head of both the judiciary and the executive. In the absence of his superior he presided over the Congregatio, took a leading part in its deliberations, summoned meetings for the election of officials, and when the representative system was finally established, was usually chosen as one of the two deputies who represented the county at the national Diet. Next to the Vicecomes the four *judices nobilium* (szólgabirák) were the most important officers, and with him formed the *sedria* or County Court. They also owed their position, which they held for one year,[4] to election by the Congregatio; and refusal to accept office entailed the payment of a fine.

[1] Non-hereditary Főispáns held their appointments "durante beneplacito Regis," according to the usual form of patent.—Herczegh, *o.c.* p. 375, *n.*

[2] The text of the law of 1486, clause 60, makes it uncertain whether the King or the Lord-Lieutenant appointed the Vicecomes at that period

[3] The official title, "*nos universitas Praelatorum, Magnatum, et cunctorum nobilium.*"

[4] In the seventeenth century the tenure of his office was extended to three years.

Originally they exercised exclusively judicial functions ; but gradually the sphere of their activity came to include all details of administration, and they were entrusted with the duty of supervising the collection of taxes, the registration of all persons liable to military service, the maintenance of public order and of the means of communication. Their assistants, the Táblabirák, eight to twelve in number according to the size of the county,[1] were also elected officials.   They received no salary, and consequently met with the reward which is not unusually meted out to those who are patriotic enough to give their services to their country for nothing.   Though in later times it was the fashion in governmental Viennese circles to sneer at these Justices of the Peace, who performed their self-imposed duties neither better nor worse than their British counterparts, the office of Táblabiró was much sought after by the young and the energetic, and formed a stepping-stone to higher office and an excellent school for future legislators, in which nearly all the great politicians of the first half of the nineteenth century served their apprenticeship. At an earlier period the most desirable candidates were not always elected, as is evident from the law of 1486, which put an end to the practice of election by acclamation, conducive to the selection of unsuitable persons and to the perpetration of " levities, the result of fear, favour, and corruption," and entrusted the Lord-Lieutenant with the duty of preparing a list of candidates from among " the good, the worthy, and the well-to-do " (clause 9).

It would seem that at one period the counties showed some disinclination to put up with interference from the central government, and a disposition to claim for their local statutes a force and a validity equal to that possessed by the general laws ^ the realm.[2]   However, by

[1] According to the law of Math: ^ Corvinus, 1486.   Four according to
the law of 1444.

[2] See Verböczy, *Jus Tripa: :tum*, iii. 2.   In the nineteenth century the
Vienna Government objected, without effect, to the custom of some counties of

the beginning of the sixteenth century the limitations of the "*jus statuendi*" were clearly recognised, and the Congregations confined themselves to the making of rules of procedure and such by-laws of local application as did not run counter to the general statutes of the realm. In the matter of local taxation the Congregations had a free hand. From the year 1486 they were in the habit of imposing a tax to provide for the payment of the expenses of their elected representatives at the Diet, but this soon developed into a general power of taxation for all local purposes,[1] to which noble,[2] and peasant, and citizens of the free towns, alike contributed from 1537 to 1733, when land-owning nobles selfishly claimed the privilege of exemption on the strength of Verbőczy's dictum which limited the obligations of the nobility to military service. All matters of national as well as of local interest were discussed at the general meetings, and, if necessary, the results of the deliberations of the Congregatio, its requirements, and its objections, were communicated to the King, the Executive, and the Diet. On the last-mentioned body the counties exercised a direct and possibly, an excessive influence. It was customary for the King's letter of summons, directing the election of deputies, to set out the "propositions" or measures which the Crown intended to submit for consideration by the Diet. The Congregations debated these embryo Bills and gave binding instructions[3] to their representatives how to vote on each individual matter. The mandate could be withdrawn, modified, or supplemented, at any moment, and if any matter came before the Diet as to which the deputies had received no instructions, members were bound to refer to their constituents. Under

allowing the *honoratiores*, *i.e.* non-noble members of the liberal professions, to take part in and vote at the Congregations.

[1] Háziadó, *contributio do. sestica.*

[2] Except those personally summoned to the Diet by the King. Before 1537 only nobles paid.

[3] First mentioned in 1545. Beőthy, *o.c.* p. 352.

such circumstances there was no possibility of mistaking the opinion of the country, and, in fact, as will be seen hereafter, in the early years of the nineteenth century the fate of any Bill was practically known before the meeting of the Diet. But the system had grave disadvantages : there were practically fifty-two Diets instead of one, and the initiative and discretionary powers of the deputies were reduced to a minimum. Further, it became possible for an unscrupulous Government to obtain a momentary majority by inducing a few counties by corrupt means to disfranchise themselves temporarily by withdrawing the mandate given to their representatives. As a matter of fact the counties could rarely be reproached with a want of true patriotic interest in the affairs of the nation. Their chief power resided in the fact that it was not only their privilege, but their bounden duty to defend the Constitution and to refuse to obey illegal edicts.[1] The execution of all royal rescripts and ordinances of general application rested with the county authorities, to whom they were sent for publication, and if, after due consideration, the same were found to be not in accord with law and immemorial custom, the Congregation addressed a protest to the King, the Executive, or the Diet, and if the objectionable order was not withdrawn, could " respectfully disregard it." [2] The only remedy of the Crown was the dispatching of a commissioner to carry out the royal instructions by force, or the summoning of recalcitrant officials *ad audiendum verbum regium*, to be cajoled or browbeaten ; but if a county chose to continue its policy of passive resistance, to be steadfast in its refusal to elect officials, collect taxes, and provide recruits until its grievances were removed, it could effectually paralyse all attempts at unconstitutional action.

The pre-Habsburg period saw the gradual develop-

---

[1] 1444, cl. 3.

[2] This originated, no doubt, from the old right of armed resistance.

ment of the essential features of constitutional government,
of the idea of the personal liberty of the subject, of the
responsibility of the Executive to the nation, of the
representative principle, and of the equality of King and
people as legislative agents ; but in the state of debility to
which Hungary was reduced by internal faction and
external attacks, it is doubtful whether any constitutional
principles would have alone sufficed to defend the country
against the persistent attempts to germanise and absorb it,
of which it was the object in the ensuing period of its
history.   The fact that the Constitution was not cut and
dried and inelastic, but that it gradually took shape and
was formed by degrees, partly by crystallisation of customs,
partly by legislative enactments scattered over many years,
naturally gave rise to uncertainty which easily lent itself
to exploitation in the interests of absolutism.[1]   The
Hungarian Constitution was weak, inasmuch as it provided
no sufficient means of compelling a king to observe the
sworn guarantees he had given, or of punishing remissness
or intentional infringement.   The right of armed resistance to royal illegality and the threat of excommunication
—of a boycott in this world and of damnation in the next
—had been proved to be inefficient safeguards of popular
liberty.   A Constitution which members of a national
dynasty had successfully infringed had little chance of
avoiding violation at the hands of kings of an alien race,
whose watchwords were absolutism, Catholicism, centralisation, germanisation.   The Diet's right of financial control
was a powerful weapon, but, as will be seen hereafter, was,
alone, an insufficient means of defence.   Apart from the
inherent vitality of the Magyar race, it is, before all, to the
autonomous institutions of the counties, and to their
power of passive resistance, that Hungary owes the
maintenance of its individuality and its escape from

---

[1] "Der Absolutismus macht sich in den gewaltigen Lücken der Ungarischen Verfassung breit."—Tezner, *Der Oest. Kaisertitel*, etc., Vienna, 1899, p. 7.

absorption. It was the misfortune of Hungary that the
later kings of the pre-Habsburg period allowed themselves
to be dependent on the goodwill of the great nobles,
and feared a frank alliance with the mass of the people.
If the kings had boldly identified their interests with those
of the lesser nobles, they would have had a strong
kingdom, financially and militarily, instead of one rent
by faction and class-hatred. Hungary, set in the midst
of enemies, could not afford to make the mistakes which
England, secure in its insular position, could commit with
impunity. Internal dissension necessarily opened the door
to foreign interference, and after five centuries spent in
consolidating and extending itself, on constitutional development and foreign conquest, Hungary suddenly found
itself face to face with the task of maintaining its existence,
of escaping reduction to a mere geographical expression.

CHAPTER III

AFTER the battle of Mohács it at once became evident that little serious resistance could be offered to the Turk until a new king had been elected and time had been gained for the reorganisation of the scattered forces of the country. The first idea was to elect Sigismund, King of Poland, to the vacant throne, and he, in fact, sent envoys to negotiate on his behalf; but they arrived too late to have any chance of success, more especially as Hungary was disgusted with him on account of his failure to keep his promise, made some weeks before the great disaster, to send help against the Turks. The country was divided into two parties, of which by far the larger was in favour of the election of John Zápolya, Voyvode of Transylvania, a Magyar and a man of great wealth, who had long been looked upon as a possible candidate for the throne. It was mainly with a view to the exclusion of foreign pretenders and to his succession that the resolution formulated by Verbóczy had been adopted by the Diet at Rákos in 1505. The probability of promotion in the event of a vacancy occurring, was considered by some to have been the cause of Zápolya's absence from the fatal field of Mohács, a neglect of duty which his supporters tried to explain by suggesting that he had been kept away by the intrigues of a hostile faction in order that he might have no share in the anticipated glory.[1] In any case he was popular with the majority, and those who had escaped

the battle of Mohács

[1] Radó-Rothfeldt, *Die Ungarische Verfassung*, p. 26.

from the disaster at once began to gravitate towards him. For a time, at all events, there was practical unanimity in his favour. Soon, however, the opinion began to gain ground that the election of Ferdinand of Austria would result in the throwing of the might, not only of the hereditary provinces—a comparatively small matter—but of the whole of Germany into the scale against the Sultan, and special stress was laid upon this consideration by the Palatine, Stephen Báthory, and other personal enemies of Zápolya.

Ferdinand, grandson of the Emperor Maximilian and brother of Charles V., had married Anna, sister of Louis, the late King of Hungary and Bohemia, who in his turn had married Maria, Ferdinand's sister; but connexion by marriage with a former King could give no claim to an elective throne. The Archduke Ferdinand, born in Spain and living at Innsbruck, had hitherto concentrated his attention on Western-European politics and took no interest in Hungary, where he was entirely unknown. It was not he, but his sister Maria, who took the Habsburg cause in hand. A suggestion had been made that Zápolya should marry Maria, and so secure to Hungary the double advantage of a native King and of a connexion with Germany; but though the idea was favoured by the Pope Clement VII., and was well received in the country, the ex-Queen, partly out of loyalty to her brother [1] and partly, to judge from her subsequent reputation, for the reason that widowhood presented more attractions than the bonds of holy matrimony, would not hear of the scheme. A meeting of the Diet was called for November 5, and this fact and Maria's energy finally galvanised Ferdinand into life, who conceived the ingenious idea of sending Thomas Nádasdy to begin his electoral campaign by squaring the chief nobles and the influential clergy [2] by promises of money and by holding

---

[1] Michael Horváth, *Magyarország Történelme*, iii. 9.   [2] *Ibid.* pp. 3, 6.

out hopes of preferment to the seven vacancies which Mohács had fortunately created on the episcopal bench, and by promising observance of the rights and privileges of the people and the speedy ejection of the Turks.[1] Knowing nothing of the Hungarian Constitution, Ferdinand did not understand that election by the Diet was essential, and thought that, at the most, half a dozen or so influential electors could, as in Germany, dispose of the crown. In any case he had no idea of the necessity of calling the whole body of nobles together, and restricted his summons to selected representatives of the counties, who were to meet, not for the purpose of electing him, but for the formal recognition of his claim to the throne as brother-in-law of the late king. In the meanwhile, as he had neither men nor money with which to back his pretensions, his and Maria's chief wish was to gain time. He therefore began a correspondence with Zápolya, with a view to keeping him quiet while negotiations were begun, with the object of obtaining diplomatic backing in Western Europe on the strength of his alleged rights to the Sacred Crown and of the supposed interests of Christendom in the erection of a strong barrier against Turkish encroachment. In spite of the disturbed and desolate state of the country, a vast number of nobles attended the opening of the Diet, which took place at the traditional place of meeting, Székesfehérvár, on November 9. Though Ferdinand's envoy was present, and did all he could to obtain an adjournment of the meeting, the result was never in doubt, and John Zápolya was elected unanimously and by acclamation.[2] The only thing wanting to make the election and the ensuing coronation complete and legal in all respects was the fact that the Diet had not been summoned by the Palatine, but, Báthory being a personal enemy of Zápolya, by a document signed by thirty of the

[1] Michael Horváth, *Magyarország Történelme*, iii. p. 5.
[2] Fraknói, *Magyar Országgyűlési Emlékek*, i. 13-30.

principal barons and nobles, and that the first vote for the
new king was not cast, as it should have been, by the
Palatine. Zápolya, who was not a man of war, and was
not anxious to be King, appointed the famous Verbőczy
to the post of Chancellor, in the hope that the ingenuity
of the great legist, and the weight of his name, would
obviate the necessity of a recourse to arms for the
vindication of the claims of a native monarch to the
throne of St. Stephen.

Ferdinand, who had recently been elected King of
Bohemia, now thought it time to take a decided step, and
summoned a meeting at Pressburg, to which only those
on whose support he could rely were admitted. His
envoy, Christopher Rauber, solemnly promised in his
name that he would drive out the Turks,[1] and produced
a formal letter written by Ferdinand from Vienna in which
he undertook to indemnify his partisans against any loss
they might suffer in consequence of their support of his
pretensions, and promised that they should have the first
call on all temporal and ecclesiastical offices in the event
of his obtaining possession of the kingdom. In a document
of the same date (Nov. 30), which is important for the
reason that it refutes the claims which have been advanced
on behalf of the house of Habsburg to the throne of
Hungary by right of conquest, conferring a license to
disregard historic rights and constitutional guarantees,
Ferdinand undertook to maintain inviolate all the privileges
of the people and to govern in accordance with the
ancient laws of the country :—" We, Ferdinand, by the
grace of God King of Bohemia, Infante of Spain, Archduke
of Austria, etc. . . . promise the entire kingdom of
Hungary that We will preserve and maintain the Lords
Spiritual and Temporal, the nobility, the Free Towns, and
all the Estates of the Realm, in the enjoyment of all
liberties, laws, and decrees which they have enjoyed

---

[1] Beőthy, *A Magyar Államiság Fejlődése Küzdelmei*, p. 292.

from the time of former kings, even if We shall obtain the said kingdom by force of arms, in exactly the same manner as if We had been elected by unanimous vote. We will confer no bishopric, benefice, hereditament, or office on any alien, nor will We admit foreigners to the Council of the said kingdom. More especially will We observe the decree of his most exalted Majesty King Andrew, to the observance whereof the Kings of Hungary have been wont to take a solemn oath at their coronation. . . . And to the firm observance of all these presents We do hereby bind Ourselves and Our heirs." [1] This was good enough for Ferdinand's anti-nationalist and self-seeking partisans, but could not obviate the necessity of holding a formal meeting of the Diet, as foreign nations would recognise none but an elected King of Hungary. Therein lay the difficulty of the situation. as it was almost impossible to get together anything decently resembling a quorum. The meeting had to be postponed for the purpose of sending a whip round, and when it was ultimately held at Pressburg on December 17, the attendance was lamentably sparse, the representatives of the counties were conspicuous by their absence, and those who did attend were mostly Croatians, who subsequently transferred their allegiance to Zápolya, whose election the meeting declared void for nine reasons, chief among which was the fact that the Diet of Székesfehérvár had not been convened by the Palatine.[2] In this respect Ferdinand had the advantage of strict legality on his side, while, on the other hand,

---

[1] A similar promise was made to the meeting on Ferdinand's behalf five days later by Bishop Rauber. It is stronger in some respects. "Promittens quoque eisdem Statibus et Ordinibus quod omnia et singula regni hujus privilegia libertates, decreta, et consuetudines hactenus observatas de cetero non tantum conservare firmiterque tenere et adimplere, sed etiam illa eis majora amplioraque efficere velimus et intendamus. Nec eos vereri debere quod exteros suis adhibere consiliis aut alienis a natione Hungarica beneficia dignitatesque ecclesiasticas conferre velimus."—*Enchiridion Fontium*, p. 392. Michael Horváth, *o.c.* iii. 18.

[2] Szalay, *Magyarország Története*, iv. 31

Zápolya had been crowned with the Sacred Crown, the imposition of which was essential in the eyes of the majority to the validity of the coronation ceremonial. It was evident that arms alone could decide the questions at issue.

1527. On March 17 a meeting of the Diet was convened at Buda, as a counterblast to that held at Pressburg, and in order to show which of the rival claimants had the sympathy and the support of the nation at large. The meeting, which was attended by the representatives of fifty-three counties, and of Slavonia and Croatia, showed no hesitation in declaring for Zápolya, voted him one-tenth of all personal property, renewed its adherence to the principle enunciated by the resolution of Rákos, and declared those who should have any dealings with Ferdinand traitors to their country. To Ferdinand, who sent a protest asserting that he, not Zápolya, was the true King of Hungary, a reply was sent pointing out the fact that Hungary was not the fief, nor was its crown in the gift, of any man ; that the monarchy was an elective one, and that the best thing Ferdinand could do was to cease calling himself King and interfering in the affairs of the country, and to do his utmost, as a Christian, to help the cause of Christendom against the Turks.[1] Ferdinand thereupon concluded that he would have to fight, or, rather, to get some one to fight for him. As a preliminary, he tried to win over Zápolya's supporters by promises of money or promotion, more especially in Transylvania, the strong-hold of the national party, in which he could rely on the support of the Saxons, naturally in favour of a German king, and of the Jewish and German population of the towns, whose pocket interests led them to wish for the Austrian connection. Ferdinand, in pursuance of his policy of promising rather than fighting, sent seventy-nine letters to Maria, with instructions to date them from

[1] Michael Horváth, o.c. iii. 29.

Hungary, and distribute them to bishops, or would-be bishops, and to influential barons. The result of the manœuvre is unknown, but one thing is certain, namely, that the Hungarians began to show signs that they were tired of Zápolya's inactivity, and to waver in their allegiance to him.[1] Nearly a year had passed since Mohács, and nothing had been done either against the Turks or against the Austrian pretender, and many Protestants inclined towards Ferdinand in the mistaken belief that, as a German, he would favour the German reformed faith, which had already made considerable way in Hungary.

Without any expectation of success, and chiefly with a view to gaining time for the collection of men and money, Ferdinand offered Zápolya 300,000 florins for the crown of Hungary, and when the offer was indignantly refused, with the remark that no Habsburg "had any more right to the throne than a Babylonian or a negro," gave the order to his army to advance into Hungary. On September 26, Count Salm defeated Zápolya's forces, and captured all his artillery. The victory was welcome, as it enabled Ferdinand to convene something resembling a proper Diet, which hitherto he had been unable to do for the reason that, until it was clear which way the cat was likely to jump, comparatively few nobles were inclined to take any step which might jeopardise their necks. The coronation, which was carried out at the beginning of November with proper pomp and circumstance, gave Ferdinand a legal status, but no more solid gain, as more than half the country still refused to recognise the validity of his election. It is noticeable that the oath taken by Ferdinand before coronation differs in an important detail from the terms of the document of November 30, to which reference has been made, for he takes the oath for himself only, not for himself and his

[1] Some of those who had two sons sent one to Ferdinand and one to Zápolya.—Michael Horváth, *o.c.* iii. 41.

heirs, thus indicating the fact that his right to the throne was based solely on election, and that his successors would have no other claim than that which the people itself might give them. The oath is incorporated with the heading, "Ferdinandus in Regem Hungariae rite eligitur" in the *Corpus juris Hungarici*, and as the Corpus was published in 1822 with the special permission of Francis I., who was most jealous of his rights and prerogatives, and at a time when the censorship was exceptionally rigorous, mention of the fact of election would not have been allowed if there had been any basis for the Austrian contention that Ferdinand owed his crown not to election but to conquest, or to the compact made between his grandfather and Vladislav. By the oath, which may be regarded as embodying the terms of the contract between Ferdinand and Hungary, the new King binds himself "to maintain God's Church, the high ecclesiastics, the barons, the nobles, the free towns, and all the inhabitants of the kingdom, in the enjoyment of their exemptions, freedom, possessions, privileges, and ancient and approved customs ; to do justice to all and every one of them ; to observe the terms of the decree of his former Majesty, Andrew II. (the Golden Bull) ; not to alienate or diminish the territories of Hungary, or of any countries pertaining thereto by any title whatsoever, but to the best of his ability to increase and extend the same, and to do all that is legally possible for the common weal and for the honour and increase of the realm." To what extent the compact was observed will appear hereafter.

Neither Salm's victory nor Ferdinand's election did anything to quiet matters down. On the contrary, civil war was now in full swing, though there was no concerted plan on either side, and skirmishes between the two factions were of daily occurrence. It soon became evident that neither party was strong enough to demolish the other, and that the perpetuation of disorder and a permanent division of the country must be the result. Under the circumstances, Ferdinand broke with the traditions of his house and of Christendom, which forbade all dealings with the Turk, and influenced only by personal considerations and the fear that Zápolya might anticipate him, began bidding for the Sultan's support. Martinuzzi, or Friar George as he was generally known, Zápolya's chief supporter and adviser, began an agitation in Poland, resulting in the collection of a considerable armed force, which, however, was unable to stand against Ferdinand's superior numbers. Till now Zápolya had refused to listen to the suggestion that he should negotiate with the Sultan, believing that the Christian principles of Europe would back him in a new crusade ; but his defeats, and the failure of his hopes of foreign help, at last made him consent to approach Constantinople. The way had been already prepared, without his knowledge, by Venice, the most resolute enemy of the Habsburgs, which, fearing that the rival kings might come to terms, pointed out to the Sultan the fatal consequences which might result to Turkey if Hungary became a German dependence, and urged him to come to the assistance of Zápolya.[1] Negotiations with the Porte were begun on the basis of the recognition by the Sultan of Zápolya as an equal or allied monarch who, in return for assistance in the task of obtaining undisputed possession of the throne of Hungary, would make an annual present, a euphemism for tribute, to his ally. The proposal was accepted by the Sultan with a view to utilising Zápolya's claims as an excuse for the conquest of Hungary for his own benefit, and Austria's prospects looked blacker than at any previous period.

Ferdinand was not in Hungary to look after his own interests. Disgust was everywhere expressed at the brutality and misconduct of his German mercenaries ;[2] his warmest partisans began to waver when the news of

1528.

[1] *A Mag. Nem. Tört.* v. 62.   [2] Michael Horváth, *o.c.* iii. 47.

Zápolya's agreement with the Turks became public property, and Maria sent urgent messages entreating him to take the conduct of affairs into his own hands, and insisting that a prolonged absence from Hungary meant 1529. ruin to his prospects. By the beginning of January not a town in the south remained to Ferdinand, and on May 2, Zápolya issued a proclamation announcing his alliance with Suleiman and calling on all Hungarians to rally round him. With few men and no money Ferdinand could do nothing, even if he wished to do anything, for the defence of Buda, which the Turks, followed by Zápolya, entered early in September. Thence the Sultan advanced in person to Vienna and began the siege, but soon after abandoned it, though the defence could not have held out more than a few days longer, as soon as he heard that Ferdinand, whose capture was the main object of the expedition, was not in the town. In any case the result of the campaign was that not a vestige of authority was left to Ferdinand in Hungary ; for the army which he had collected ·in the hereditary provinces refused to advance as soon as it heard that Vienna was no longer in danger. Still, as Ferdinand had not been captured, or forced to admit defeat and withdraw his claims to the Sacred Crown, the Sultan's object had not been attained. The opinion now became general in Hungary that neither claimant would be able definitely to oust the other, and the desire for the end of a destructive, and apparently useless, civil war became more and more acute. Zápolya, established in Buda, was nearly at the end of his tether, for though the Diet voted subsidies he could not collect them, and so was almost penniless. Both rivals were ready and anxious for peace, but while Ferdinand was quite prepared to buy terms from the Sultan, Zápolya would not listen to the suggestion of a compromise with the Turks involving a surrender of part of Hungary to the Porte and the definite acceptance of

Suleiman's suzerainty.   Ferdinand was too fully occupied
in Germany with the task of procuring his election to the
imperial throne, in which he succeeded early in 1531, to
be able to show any activity elsewhere.   He therefore
confined himself to carrying on simultaneous negotiations
with Zápolya and with the Porte, which had announced
its intention of making a fresh attack on the Austrian
provinces.   With the former he arranged a truce for
three months on the basis of each party keeping what it
had got (a more accurate definition of spheres of influence
being an absolute impossibility at the moment), and thus
a provisional division of the kingdom resulted which
prepared the way for final dismemberment.

In the spring of the following year Ferdinand sent 1532.
envoys to Constantinople to offer an annual tribute of
100,000 florins in gold if he were given the opportunity
of obtaining the whole of Hungary, or of 50,000 if he
were allowed to remain in undisturbed occupation of the
fraction then actually in his possession.   He was even
prepared to relinquish all claim to Hungary, with the
exception of certain frontier districts the control of which
he considered essential to the safety of the hereditary provinces of Austria.   Finally, he expressed his readiness to
abandon even this modest claim if Zápolya would undertake the constitutional impossibility of nominating him as
his heir to the throne.   At first the Sultan's plenipotentiary
would listen to none of the suggestions of Ferdinand's
envoy, saying that there was room for only one person
at a time on the throne of Buda, and adding that it was
impossible to deal with a man who never kept his word,
whose ambassadors alternately threatened and begged for
peace.[1]   Eventually, however, he submitted the last of the
above-mentioned offers to Suleiman, whose reply took the
form of a promise to visit Ferdinand in his own country,
and to talk the matter over in Vienna.   The Sultan

[1] *A Mag. Nem. Tört.* v. 90.

did, in fact, penetrate into Austria and ravage Styria, but his visit had no great results, though Ferdinand, whose money difficulties were so well known that his Italian mercenaries refused to budge without money down, could oppose no effective resistance. In Hungary all political life was suspended ; whole districts were ravaged by Turk and Austrian alike, and rendered uninhabitable. The whole country was pining for peace and for the re-establishment of national unity. The nobles bitterly regretted the fact that two rival kings had been elected, and did not much care which of the two succeeded in making his claim effective provided the result was the withdrawal of the Turks on the one side, and of the far more hated German mercenaries on the other. The Diet, summoned at Buda by Stephen Báthory, Ferdinand's chief supporter, passed a resolution in this sense, and wrote saying, " If your Majesty cannot defend the kingdom, be kind enough to say so openly, and we will then discover some means of helping ourselves and of warding off the peril which threatens us." [1]   But

1532. Ferdinand, then at Augsburg, replied only with smooth words, and the Diet, at its next meeting, expressed its willingness to acknowledge whichever claimant first proved his ability to maintain the territorial integrity of the kingdom.

The poor result of his last expedition convinced Suleiman of his inability to evict the Austrians, completely and for ever, from Hungary. He therefore received, with a greater degree of politeness than he usually showed, a fresh embassy sent by Ferdinand to express his willingness to renounce all claim to the bird in the bush, provided he were allowed to retain what was actually in the hand. The Sultan agreed to the proposal on condition that the keys of Esztergom should be sent him as a sign of recognition of his

[1] *A Mag. Nem. Tört.* v. 97.

suzerainty, and Ferdinand submitted to the unprecedented humiliation. Both parties in Hungary were furious when it became known that a king, who had been elected solely with a view to the ejection of the Turks, and had solemnly sworn to maintain the integrity of the country, had recognised the overlordship of the infidel. They were still more enraged at the partition of the kingdom, and at the prospective loss of individuality as a nation and of the very name of Hungary.[1] Ferdinand did not care. He wanted leisure to turn his attention, as a good Catholic, to the extermination of the Protestants, and, for the moment at all events, was ready to abandon his hopes of obtaining an undivided throne. But his women would not agree to his sharing a crown, and spoiled the negotiations which otherwise would probably have ended in the abandonment of Hungary to Zápolya, and in the nomination of Ferdinand as his successor. Ferdinand, therefore, again collected an army, the biggest 1537. he had ever got together for use in Hungary, but only to incur a disastrous defeat at Gorján—after Mohács, perhaps the greatest blow Christendom ever suffered at the hands of the unbeliever. He began to realise the obvious fact that of himself he could do nothing, and that Martinuzzi was the only man capable of effecting any lasting results. Brother George, the tortuousness of whose ways earned him an unenviable reputation in certain quarters, was a statesman and a diplomatist who realised the fact that peace was his country's essential necessity, and desired above all the maintenance of Hungarian independence. He was quite ready to come to terms, but the archbishop, Ferdinand's emissary, acting on instructions, so haggled over details, that Zápolya's representatives

[1] Maria warned him against neglect of Hungarian interests, and told him Hungary might be easier to win than to keep. He replied that as soon as he had troops enough he would know how to deal with the Magyars. (Fessler, *Geschichte der Ungarn*, iii. 417.) His idea was to occupy the fortified places with hired troops to assure the subjection of the country to Austria.

dropped the discussion in disgust, and the matters in dispute were adjourned to a meeting to be held the 1538. following year at Várad, where peace was signed on the following terms :—maintenance of the *status quo* ; Ferdinand to succeed to an undivided throne on the death of Zápolya, even if the latter should have a legitimate heir ; if Ferdinand and Charles V. predeceased Zápolya, the crown to go to Zápolya and his heirs ; if he left no heir, Hungary's right of unrestricted election to revive. It was further agreed that should Zápolya have a son he should be confirmed in the possession of the family estates, and should receive a separate principality and a daughter of Ferdinand in marriage. In the meanwhile, Ferdinand gave up all claim to Transylvania, and Zápolya to Croatia and Slavonia. Result—a temporary peace and a worthless defensive alliance against the Sultan. Brother George induced Zápolya to consent to this sacrifice of the constitutional rights of Hungary and of his own claims, in the belief that the true interests of the country demanded it ; that if it had rest and time to recuperate it might be able to maintain its individual existence and eventually to eject the Turks. True, he admitted the claims of the House of Habsburg, but on conditions, and by the eighteenth clause of the compact Ferdinand undertook that " should the succession fall to Us, neither We ourselves nor Our son or heir shall take possession of the said kingdom, or of the provinces and parts subject thereto, before taking a solemn oath as King, in accordance with the custom of former kings of Hungary, to maintain and observe the liberties, decrees, laws, and customs thereof."

The sworn brotherhood did not last long. The country had imagined that Charles V. would now do his utmost to defend the family inheritance against the Turks, but the death of his wife, and anti-Catholic disturbances in Germany and the Netherlands, put all plans for the liberation of Hungary out of his head. It was necessary, therefore, to attempt to keep the Sultan in the dark as to the terms of the peace of Várad, for fear he should reply by invading the country, which, indeed, was incapable of effective resistance. Moreover, Zápolya had another reason for wishing to keep Suleiman in good humour, which had not been without influence on him at the time when preliminaries to peace with Ferdinand were under discussion. He had, in fact, matrimonial designs on Isabella, daughter of the King of Poland, who had no inclination to allow her to marry while matters in Hungary wore such a threatening aspect. The signing of the convention of Várad, and the apparent acquiescence of the Sultan, satisfied all parental scruples, and I .bella was married and crowned at Székesfehérvár early in the following year. Ferdinand must have been anxious about the 1539. possibility of the birth of an heir to Zápolya, and to this circumstance may probably be ascribed the fact that he insisted on the publication of the terms of the peace of Várad, knowing that it would bring the Sultan on to his ally's back ; and in fact the Turks promptly carried 10,000 Magyars into slavery at Constantinople. This necessitated further intrigues in order to checkmate Zápolya, whom Ferdinand believed to be now ready to recognise, definitely and unconditionally, the suzerainty of the Porte ; but Zápolya's days were numbered, and he died on July 11, 1540, only eleven days after the birth of his son, commending his country, his wife, and his child to the care of Brother George. In better times he would probably have n.ade a respectable king, but he was not strong enough to stand up against Turk and Austrian at the same time, and to reorganise the country after the disaster of Mohács. He saw, or rather Brother George made him see, that the only hope for Hungary was to improve the position of the peasants, reduced to the level of brute beasts by the law of 1514 ;[1]

[1] At his instigation the Diet of 1531 passed a law re-establishing the

and the last native king of Hungary was the first to
devote attention to the maintenance of the Hungarian
language,[1] seeing therein the best bond of national union,
and anticipating thereby the efforts of the patriots of the
early part of the nineteenth century. Though by the
peace of Várad the country was nominally divided into
two more or less equal parts, Zápolya's influence was out
of all proportion greater than that of Ferdinand, who, as
a Hispano-German, with no knowledge of Magyar customs
or laws, was always treading on the national toes, and put
no faith in his Hungarian followers. They in their turn
had no confidence in him, hated his German advisers and
sycophants, and looked with something like contempt on
a king who was useless in war and financially feeble. Even
the German population of the towns soon lost their illusions.
His mercenaries, instead of defending them against the
Turk, were no better than undisciplined looters.[2] With
the Church he was equally unpopular, for the reason that
he appointed foreigners to the most coveted ecclesiastical
offices in contravention of the law. His idea was to
govern Hungary from Vienna, and to visit it as rarely
as possible ; but in one matter, at all events, the Diet
had the whip-hand of him. It did not fail to remind
him that he was the elected king of a constitutional country
bound by law and his oath, and emphasised the reminder
by a refusal to abandon one particle of its control in the
matter of taxation. Hitherto the importation of the
Habsburgs had proved a disastrous failure. Whole
districts had been ravaged and depopulated by German
mercenaries, by the janissaries, and by the plague—also a
Turkish export. In one year 100,000 men, women, and

peasant's right of migration, but circumstances prevented it from becoming
effective. See Acsády, *A Magyar Jobbágyság Története*, 201 *sq.*

[1] Tinodi, whose poems passed from mouth to mouth, did much to keep
the Magyar spirit alive.

[2] "Who live on the tears (iacrimis vivunt) of the poor people," Law xvi.
of 1536.

children were carried captive into Turkey. Only in one respect were the rival kings agreed, namely, as to the necessity of keeping the country pure from the pernicious doctrines of Protestantism, and of extirpating a heresy which possessed the fatal attraction that it permitted matrimony to a clergy which had always been inclined to regard the vow of chastity as an unnecessary institution.

For a time it looked as if Ferdinand would now hold undisputed sway, but Isabella, Brother George, and Verbóczy had no intention of sacrificing Zápolya's son, John Sigismund, or what they considered to be the interests of the country. Two courses were open to them : either to secure the family estates and a suitable position for the boy at the price of recognising Ferdinand's claim to an undivided throne, or to throw the interests of Christendom overboard, make friends with the Turks, and, with their aid, secure the independence of as large a slice of Hungary as possible. Ferdinand had only himself to blame for the existing state of affairs. Elected for the purpose of expelling the Turks, he had proved himself unwilling or unable to satisfy even the most modest expectations of his supporters. Any hesitation which Brother George may have entertained as to which of the alternative courses he should follow were promptly dispelled by Ferdinand's attempt to make himself master of Buda by a trick. The Sultan was quite ready to accept the office of patron and protector of Zápolya's son. In the summer of 1541 he advanced with a large army and utterly defeated the Austrians who, under Roggendorf, were besieging Buda. The terror of Ferdinand and other princes lest the Turks should continue their victorious advance through Austria into Germany may be imagined ; but for the moment the Sultan had plenty to do in Hungary, which he knew the Austrians to be totally incapable of defending. Naturally, he took good care to reward himself properly for his efforts on behalf of Zápolya's son : in fact, there had never been any altruistic motive for his actions. He decided that Buda was no fit habitation for John Sigismund ; assigned him Transylvania as his place of residence, and entrusted him to the guardianship of Isabella and Brother George. Thus was the tripartite division of Hungary brought about. Practically the whole of Hungary proper was in the hands of the Sultan ; Transylvania became a separate principality under Turkish suzerainty ; and Ferdinand, with the title of King and no certainty as to the fixity of his tenure, occupied the western districts. The irony of fate willed it that Verbóczy, incarnation of legal wisdom, author of the book which the Magyar nobles looked upon as their Bible, should receive from the Sultan the appointment of Chief Justice of the Christian subjects of the Porte.

1541.   Brother George was now inclined to regret what he had done, and began to renew negotiations with Ferdinand at the request of the chief nobles, who entreated him to save the country from definitive dismemberment. But he could not make up his mind to be off with the Turks before he was on with Ferdinand. Probably he hoped that if he played one off against the other Hungary might eventually come by her own ; or that both Turkey and Austria might come to see the advantage of having an independent buffer-state between them. The result of the negotiations was the treaty of Gyalu, confirming and continuing that of Várad, with the addition of a clause, of the uselessness of which Ferdinand's previous record gave convincing proof, to the effect that the Austrians undertook to expel the Moslems. It was resolved that there should be a *levée en masse* of the Hungarians in the event of Ferdinand taking the field in person ; and an army of 60,000 men was collected, which, though Ferdinand had the good sense not to command it himself, met with complete failure in its attempt to recover Buda. General recrimination resulted ; Ferdinand, like other weak rulers and people before and since, consoled himself with the German equivalent of the classic phrase "*nous sommes trahis*," and threw the most influential of the Magyars into prison to encourage the rest. The result was the inception of a new period of distrust and hatred fatal to any possibility of effective action. The Magyars were utterly disgusted with the Austrians, whose predatory mercenaries gave the country no rest and proved quite incapable of ejecting the Turks.[1] The inclination to settle down quietly under the heathen yoke, which allowed, at all events, more religious liberty than Ferdinand's fanaticism could tolerate, became more and more pronounced. The Diet was lavish in the matter of subventions,[2] and Ferdinand in the making of promises. This, however, did not make him ashamed to buy peace from the Sultan for a year and a half at the 1543. price of 50,000 gold pieces, thereby still further estranging the Magyars,[3] who continued, in places, an unequal struggle on their own account, while Ferdinand devoted his energies to an unsuccessful attempt to extirpate Protestantism in Styria and the Tyrol. In the meanwhile Brother George continued his policy of keeping the Turks quiet while doing all in his power to help Ferdinand to extend his influence. "Until," wrote Brother George, "your Majesty's affairs take a turn for the better, I will keep the enemy out of the country by means of the artifices which I have hitherto employed," and there is no reason to doubt his sincerity, though it is clear that he was unwilling that Isabella should hand over Transylvania until he was satisfied that Ferdinand was both able and

---

[1] The law of 1546, 5, recognises the necessity of employing foreign help against the Turks, and authorises Ferdinand to maintain a permanent force of Hungarians and foreigners to be paid out of the proceeds of the military tax, the profits on coinage, and the customs duties. The nobles and clergy to maintain a certain number of soldiers proportionate to the size of their landed property. "Equites vel milites continui."—Timon, *o.c.* p. 761.

[2] Michael Horváth, *o.c.* iii. 165, 168 ; Szalay, *Mag. Tört.* iv. 240, 298.

[3] Michael Horváth, *o.c.* iii. 164.

willing to carry out the obligations imposed on him by the conventions of Várad and Gyalu.

1547.   The Porte, now fully occupied with affairs in Persia, consented to a peace for five years on terms which constituted a fresh and complete humiliation for Ferdinand, nominal King of Hungary. The Sultan, described in the document in which the terms of peace were embodied as Padishah of Buda, Transylvania, and the parts pertaining thereto, in consideration of the payment of a yearly tribute, consented to allow the King to remain in undisturbed possession of the parts then actually in his occupation, provided he undertook to abstain from interference elsewhere. Transylvania, and the district lying east of the Tisza, were left to John Sigismund, who, like Ferdinand, was to pay annual tribute in recognition of the suzerainty of the Sultan. The Magyar nobles, who had been kept in the dark as to the progress of the negotiations,[1] were greatly disgusted when the result became known ; but the country was utterly worn out by the events of the last twenty years, and had no alternative but to acquiesce in the disgraceful bargain, the effect of which was that Ferdinand was left in possession of thirty-five counties of upper Hungary, the Slavonian districts lying between the Száva and the Dráva, and the parts of Croatia adjacent to the sea.[2] Government was organised on a purely military basis, and a chain of fortified towns was established along the frontier as a defence against the Turks and as a haven of refuge for the country population when harried by irresponsible raiders. The rest of Hungary became an Ottoman pashalik in which no vestige of the old political life remained. Buda became a Turkish city, the cathedral was converted into a mosque, and the whole

---

[1] "Ea quae sunt in articulis praesentibus inclusis secretiora et quae non sunt necessaria ad publicandum teneatis apud vos secreta."—Ferdinand's instructions. The price of peace, 30,000 florins, was concealed from the Diet. —Michael Horváth, o.c. iii. 170.

[2] Law xix. 1548.

country was treated in precisely the same way as any Mussulman province.

In religious matters the new masters of the country interfered little, if at all, and looked on with an amused smile when Catholics and Protestants fought, and the latter reviled and destroyed the images which they had recently adored. Preferring convenience to dogma, some Magyars took refuge in Allah, and risked their souls for the sake of material advantages; but the fact that few, if any, became definitely denationalised, while many Slavs were permanently absorbed in Islam, gave fresh proof of the vitality of the Magyar nation. The rich nobles who had lands outside the limits of the Turkish pashalik retired thither; the poor ones were reduced to beggary. The peasants perforce remained where they were, and found their dues and their forced labour neither more nor less distasteful when exacted by alien masters than they had been when Hungary was under purely Christian government. In any case they were better off than the peasants of the outlying districts of Ferdinand's dominions, which enterprising Turkish raiders harried and laid waste at their pleasure. Their German King could not protect them, and at least a third of the district nominally under Habsburg sway was in reality subject to the Sultan. Transylvania was in a more enviable position, thanks to Brother George, who kept the Turks at arm's length, not by organised defence, but by ingenious diplomacy. Combining in one person the functions of Prime Minister and all other Ministers, he saved the country from the financial straits from which Ferdinand's dominions suffered, kept the nobles in order, bettered the position of the peasants, and at the same time met with little opposition, except from a section of the Saxons who had prejudices in favour of a German ruler.

Now that peace was temporarily secured, Ferdinand set about the task of establishing his rule in his fragmentary

Hungarian dominions on a firmer basis. He had every opportunity to do so, as the population was ready and crying for a ruler who would introduce order and give them rest. The nobles were becoming reconciled to the idea of Habsburg rule, but at the same time had no idea of abandoning their right to be governed in accordance with their ancient Constitution. Ferdinand had learned his lesson and now showed himself in another light. Personally he seemed to be friendly, and ready and anxious to listen to proposals ; but German Court officials, with no sympathy for Hungary and no comprehension or experience of constitutional government, formed an insuperable obstacle to the realisation of Magyar aspirations. Order was gradually restored, and powerful nobles who had taken advantage of the recent troublous times to make themselves uncontrolled tyrants of the lower classes, and considered license the first condition of liberty, were brought to book and made to disgorge their ill-gotten gains. Consequently, the lesser nobles, who, at the beginning of the reign, had been the most uncompromising opponents of the foreign king, began to look upon him with a more tolerant eye,[2] readily voted the necessary taxes, and gave voluntary subsidies in addition. At the same time they took care to stipulate that such action on their part should not be looked upon as a precedent for treating their legal immunity from taxation as lapsed.

The King, prompted by Brother George, recognised the necessity of doing something, if only out of a spirit of competition with the Turk, to lighten the lot of the peasants, and

[1] Maurice, Duke of Saxony, warned Ferdinand that he could never govern Hungary with foreigners, and advised him to hand it over to one of his sons, as Hungarians would obey none but a king who lived among them.—Horváth (Janos), A Közös Ügyek Előzményei és Fejlődése.

[2] Ferdinand said, "I am obliged to favour them, for if I didn't every man would become a Turk." The Magyars are said to have threatened to return to Asia en masse if their grievances were not remedied.—Istvánffy, Historia regni Hungariae, quoted by Beöthy, A Magyar Államiság Fejlődése Küzdelmei, i. 348.

to establish his popularity on a broader basis.   After much 1548. difficulty and delay, he induced the Diet to agree in principle to the abolition of the enactment forbidding the migration of the peasants ; but the nobles evaded the law in every possible way, and after ten years of legislation on the subject, it was still to all practical purposes a dead letter,[1] as in fact were the majority of the seventy-one laws passed in the session of 1548, which was chiefly remarkable for the fact that it was the first in which any attention was paid to the question of popular education.   Now that Charles V. had been completely successful in his anti-Protestant campaign in Austria, Ferdinand thought the time had come to imitate him in Hungary, and urged the Diet to take steps for the extirpation of heresy.[2]   That body, however, had the good sense to object to a régime of fire and sword, called upon the clergy to restore the Church to its former position by good example and by the inculcation of wholesome principles, and recommended that only " men of approved life " should be admitted to orders—showing thereby that, though the majority in the Diet was Catholic, it was fully alive to the fact that the spread of Protestantism was, in a large measure, due to the notoriously disreputable character of the parish priests.[3] From the point of view of Hungary's historic rights, the importation of the House of Habsburg was disastrous. True, the old court offices remained, but no Palatine, the proper intermediary between the King and the people, and the sworn defender of the country's rights, was appointed. True, the management of the national finances was nominally left in the hands of the Hungarian Treasury, and a separate Hungarian Chancery was established for the management of Hungarian affairs, but Treasury and

[1] Though the Diet had unanimously declared that " nothing had done greater injury to Hungary, formerly in a flourishing condition, than the oppression of the serfs, whose cry of suffering rose up to Heaven."—*Corpus Juris Hung.* i. 408, quoted by Szalay, *Mag. Tört.* iv. 253.

[2] Michael Hovráth, *o.c.* iii. 173.   [3] 1548, cl. 6.

Chancery were mere empty names, and their every act was dictated by Vienna. The opinion of the Hungarian Treasury was rarely asked, and if asked was neglected by the Viennese Ministry of Finance, in which all financial control was vested. Though the Hungarians had paid in blood for the inability of Ferdinand to defend his kingdom against the incursions of the Turks, they had no share in the management of military affairs, and none but Germans found places in the new War Council, the sphere of action of which included Hungary. A Privy Council was established in Vienna for the control of all important home affairs, and for the decision of all questions of foreign policy. Thus the Magyars were deprived of all voice in the three great departments of State—Finance,[1] Foreign Affairs, and Army—and the first definite step was taken in the direction of stripping Hungary of the most important elements of constitutional life. It is a question whether this high-handed action constituted a deliberate attempt to absorb Hungary in Austria ; but in any case it had the result of reducing the former country to a subordinate position from which it failed to emerge till three hundred years of ceaseless struggle had elapsed. The Magyars seem to have been unconscious, for a time, of the fact that they were letting their birthright slip from their fingers. Thirty years of internal discord and foreign oppression had so worn and wearied them that they had begun to forget the traditions of free Hungary. So soon, however, as they regained their strength they began the fight for the recovery of the ground that had been temporarily lost.

Naturally the Turks were not satisfied with the state of affairs in Transylvania, which they looked upon as temporary and as requiring modification in their interests so soon as a convenient opportunity should present itself. Ferdinand was equally discontented, and equally de-

[1] See Acsády, *Magyarország Pénzügyei I Ferdinand Uralkodása alatt*, Budapest, 1888, 35 *sqq.*

termined to alter what he regarded as an impossible position. It was Martinuzzi's business, now that a larger policy of national unity and independence was an impossibility, to hold the balance between the two rival parties. In 1549 he was ready strictly to carry out the terms of the compacts of Várad and Gyalu, so far as it was possible to do so in view of Ferdinand's inability to secure John Sigismund in the possession of his family estates. It was, therefore, agreed that the latter was to receive the title of Prince of Oppeln and Ratibor in Silesia, that Isabella should be given 100,000 florins, and that Ferdinand's rule should be acknowledged in Transylvania. As soon as Suleiman heard of the arrangement he gave instructions for the decapitation of Martinuzzi, but as usual Brother George succeeded in finding a satisfactory explanation, and in allaying the Sultan's suspicions of Ferdinand's intentions. The latter now made a serious attempt to put his new rights in force. His first step was to collect a large force of mercenaries, consisting of half the unattached blackguards of Europe, whom he placed under the command of Castaldo, an Italian, and of the appropriately-named Teufel. Between this particular devil and the deep sea of Islamism the Hungarians began to doubt whether the balance of discomfort was to be found on the side of the Turkish disease or of the Austrian remedy. Brother George, at last at the end of his tether, admitted to Isabella that he was no longer able to preserve her and her son from the tender mercies of both Sultan 1551. and Ferdinand, and induced her to abandon Transylvania to the latter, and to retire with her son into private life. Martinuzzi's task was now ended. He wrote to Ferdinand explaining the motives which had influenced his tortuous policy in the past, claiming credit for having restored Transylvania to the Sacred Crown, and asking to be relieved from the burden of office.[1] To this request

[1] See the facsimile letter in *A Mag. Nem. Tört.* v. 306.

Ferdinand refused his assent, as he could not spare sufficient troops to secure his position in Transylvania, and so could not dispense with the services of a past master in the art of deceiving the Turk. But Brother George's release was not long delayed, as Ferdinand, having conceived suspicions of the friar's single-mindedness, in order to avoid further complications, took the simple course of having him assassinated. He made no concealment of his complicity in the murder,[1] and openly declared that matters in general showed a decided improvement after the removal of the turbulent priest. But his boast was hardly justified by the facts, as the next ten years of more or less intermittent war with the Turks were more disastrous to Hungary than any preceding campaign. The terms of peace which, in 1562, brought an inglorious episode to a disgraceful end, left Transylvania still outside the pale of the Habsburg dominions, and provided for the payment to the Sultan of an annual tribute disguised under the name of a Christmas present.

Brother George was undoubtedly the greatest statesman and diplomatist Hungary had yet produced. It was not his fault that Ferdinand was negligent of the country's interests and incapable of defending them. He had to utilise the weapons with which nature had endowed him, and to call him deceitful and dishonest is but to compliment him, for the deceptions which he employed were never directed to selfish ends, and the arts of insincerity produced results which straightforward virtue could never have attained. For thirty years he played Suleiman against Ferdinand—a shifty Habsburg against an overbearing Turk—with the result that Transylvania retained a measure of independence, kept alive the Magyar spirit,

---

[1] Michael Horváth, o.c. iii. 201 sqq. Pope Julius III. held an inquiry into the circumstances of the assassination, and at the Emperor's urgent request acquitted Ferdinand of complicity, but this had no effect on public opinion.— Istvánffy, xvii. 310. Castaldo and his fellow-assassins, who, so far from denying the murder, claimed credit for it, were also acquitted.—Ibid. 314.

and handed on the torch of Hungarian tradition which otherwise would infallibly have been extinguished. It is eternally to Transylvania's credit that while the rest of Europe was bathed in blood by the quarrels of fanatics over questions of dogma, religious equality was proclaimed 1557. in that country. This, and the fact that in spite of the Habsburgs some vestiges at least of constitutional government remained in Hungary throughout the following period, during which absolutism was supreme on the Continent, was in a large measure due to the courage and ingenuity of Brother George.

On the death of Charles V., Ferdinand was elected to 1558. the imperial throne, and, consequently, paid less attention than ever to Hungarian affairs. His activity was confined to an attempt to deprive the country of its last means of defence against autocracy—of the right to fix the amount, and arrange for the collection, of taxes.[1] But here he had to contend against the passive resistance of the counties, now, as in the future, the one reliable bulwark of constitutional liberty. The Diet pointed out that the attempt to impose taxes without its consent was an unconstitutional act, and though Ferdinand argued that the welfare of the country, by which he meant that of the Austrian provinces, was of greater importance than constitutional forms, the Golden Bull, and other antiquated guarantees, which were all very well in their day but were out of place in an up-to-date monarchy, the resistance of the nobles was completely successful. In the matter of the maintenance of the elective character of the monarchy the results were not so satisfactory. Ferdinand felt that 1561. he was getting old, and, desirous of seeing the succession of his eldest son Maximilian assured, requested the nobles to crown him in his father's lifetime. The nobles replied

[1] Ferdinand wished the taxation to be fixed for a period of six years. Naturally the Diet objected, as it knew that it was only the necessity of obtaining votes for money and men that made Ferdinand convene it.—Szalay, *Mag. Tört.* iv. 318 ; Fraknói, *Magyar Országgyűlési Emlékek*, iv.

that election was a condition precedent to coronation, and some expressed the wish to elect the younger son, Ferdinand,[1] in the belief that he possessed greater military ability than his brother. The King was furious, and requested the Magyar to cease talking about the "superfluous and offensive" formality of election, and to crown Maximilian without more ado.[2] Temporarily, however, the nobles stood their ground, and it was not till two years later that, Ferdinand being seriously ill, Maximilian was crowned : the Diet contenting itself with a protest against the absence from the Letter of Summons of all reference to the necessity of election—a formality, perhaps, but at the same time an essential one if the continuity of the nation's rights was to be preserved.

Nine months later Ferdinand died. By electing him Hungary had made the worst possible bargain. The very fact of his being a Habsburg prevented any possibility of Hungary arriving at a reasonable *modus vivendi* with the Sultan, who, but for the fact of the identity of the King of Hungary and the head of the Holy Roman Empire, would have been quite ready to leave the Magyars in peace on acceptance of his suzerainty and on payment of a moderate tribute. The treaties which Ferdinand arranged with the Porte were made at the expense of Hungary, which the Turks continued to ravage while the hereditary provinces of Austria were left in comparative peace. From Mohács to the final ejection of the Mussulman, Vienna looked on Hungary as a buffer-state, specially intended by Providence to intercept the kicks to which Austria would otherwise have

---

[1] Salamon, *A Magyar Királyi Szék Betöltése*, p. 50. The idea was given up for the reason that it was imagined that the task of expelling the Turks would be taken in hand more seriously if King and Emperor were combined in one person.

[2] Ferdinand required the nobles to "recognise," not elect, Maximilian as King.—Michael Horváth, *o.c.* iii. 247. As a compromise, the word "nominatus" was used instead of "electus."—Szalay, *Mag. Tört.* iv. 326, *n.* ; Fraknói, *Magyar Országgyülési Emlékek*, iv. 371 *sqq.*

been exposed, and to pay at the same time for its privilege of vicarious suffering.   As Hungary alone could not, and Ferdinand and Charles V. would not if they could, effect the expulsion of the Turks, it would obviously have been more satisfactory to pay the Sultan and be left in peace than to pay the Habsburg and be harried and dismembered into the bargain.

CHAPTER IV

1564. THE Hungarians who had hoped for a Magyar King found that, in Maximilian, they had got a purely German one who did nothing to gain their goodwill, but subordinated their interests in every detail to those of the hereditary provinces, of which, but for its control of taxation, what remained of Hungary practically became a part. And yet it was the possession of the ancient crowns of Hungary and Bohemia, not that of the provinces of Upper and Lower Austria, Styria, Carinthia, and Carniola, which gave the Archdukes of · Austria their *locus standi* in Europe and ensured the election of Maximilian to the imperial crown. The new King was well acquainted with the doctrines of the Reformation, described Lutheranism as the true religion, and the opponents of Church reform as the servants of the devil ; [1] consequently, his succession to the throne seemed to promise a period of respite for the Protestants. But for this fact there was little to recommend him. He knew no Hungarian and little Latin, and so was obliged to address the nobles in the, to them, repulsive and unfamiliar German tongue. He regarded their notions of independence as mere impertinence, and took no pains to conceal the fact. Though the law of 1563 made it obligatory to convoke the Diet every year, unless circumstances (*i.e.* the Turks) made it impossible,. his idea was never to summon it except when he was in

---

[1] *A Mag. Nem. Tört.* v. 361.

want of money. The climax of unconstitutionalism was reached when he invented the plan of deliberately altering the text of laws after they had been finally approved by the representatives of the nation. The desultory war with the Turks continued with no more success than in Ferdinand's time, and ended in the now familiar way : 1568. *uti possidetis* and the payment of an annual tribute, or *munus honorarium* [1] as it was euphemistically called, to the Sultan. The peace of Drinápol nominally gave the country the blessings of peace for twenty-five years ; but in reality it was only a truce between King and Sultan, and the Turks still raided Hungary, and burned, and ravaged, and carried off slaves to Constantinople. Maximilian could do nothing but look on. He did, in fact, try to get German aid, but the Augsburg Diet of 1566 made it a condition precedent to the grant of assistance that Hungary should be fused in the Empire [2] and share its expenses and obligations, and nothing was done except to increase the nervousness of Hungary, to which the possibility of absorption in Germany was an ever-present nightmare. The complaints to which Ferdinand's unconstitutional proceedings had given rise were even better justified during the reign of his successor. The old grievances remained : the neglect of Hungary's interests, the abominable behaviour of the mercenaries, the failure to appoint to the chief offices of state, and the subordination of such functionaries as were in fact appointed to the corresponding officials in Vienna. With respect to the withdrawal or control of the mercenaries, [3] plenty of promises were made, but none were kept, while as regards the grievances of a constitutional nature, Maximilian made no secret of his intention that things should go on as they had in his father's time. In his view, military and financial matters were not even "affairs of common interest," but

[1] Szalay, *Mag. Tört.* iv. 354.   [2] Michael Horváth, *o.c.* iii. 265.
[3] As to their conduct, see *ibid.* pp. 275, 323.

were entirely outside the province of Hungarian influence; and the Magyars should be more than satisfied if a Hungarian or two found a place from time to time in the Council of War and in the Treasury. Of the one remaining constitutional safeguard he tried to deprive Hungary by a trick : by proposing that the counties which would undertake the expense of provisioning the troops quartered on them—thereby, so he suggested, obtaining the whip-hand of the disorderly mercenaries— should be relieved of an equivalent amount of taxation. But the Diet was not to be hoodwinked, and seeing that the object of the suggestion was to deprive it of its financial control, repudiated the proposal with an unparalleled outburst of protestation against the " hitherto unheard-of system 'of slavery, tyranny, and oppression introduced under his Majesty's *régime*," [1] and threatened to meet no more and to vote no more taxes till the country's grievances were remedied. The just complaints of the Diet, qualified as impudence by Maximilian, were, as usual, disregarded ; and want of combination, of leadership, and of the knowledge where and how to begin, reduced the nobles to practical impotence. They could do no more than continue the policy, which plays so large a part in Hungarian political history henceforward down to 1848, of making formal presentment of their grievances, of waiting and hoping. As regards the Turks, nothing shows the real feebleness of the Habsburgs at this period better than the fact than when the throne of Poland became vacant the Sultan's nominee, Stephen Báthory, was chosen, to the unspeakable disgust of Maximilian, who had spared no effort to secure election.

1576. The most characteristic event of the next reign, Rudolph's, was the attempt not only to fuse Hungary in Austria, but to force Catholicism on her at the point

---

[1] He used to bring some thousands of mercenaries to the Diet in order to overawe and coerce the members.—Beöthy, *o.c.* i. 309.

of the sword ; and it is, in a large measure, to the hold which Protestantism had obtained on the country that Hungary owed the success of her resistance to attempted incorporation. Rudolph's chief title to fame consists in the fact that he spent twelve million thalers on the purchase of pictures and statues — a sum which, if judiciously distributed among the unattached adventurers and impecunious princes of Europe, might have produced an army large enough to drive the Turks into the sea.[1] But Hungary's wishes had no influence on the new King, though, like his predecessors, he had sworn to maintain not only the Constitution, but the territorial integrity of his kingdom as well. He never summoned the Diet if he could possibly avoid doing so, and infuriated all strata of the population as much by subordinating the offices of state to the central bureaucracy of Vienna as by his indifference to the question of providing for the defence of the frontiers. The result was, that as the Hungarians had no hope of promotion in the Austrian service, and had no outlet for their energies at home, the disillusioned patriotism of the country transferred its allegiance to Stephen Báthory, in Transylvania, where Magyars found good and regular pay, and an opportunity of giving vent to their combative instincts. Rudolph was, apparently, both surprised and annoyed, and the gulf between him and his subjects widened perceptibly. The policy of concentrating all executive authority in Vienna was followed more consistently than ever, till the Diet brought the King up short by refusing to vote any taxes, with the result that he appointed Hungarians to various posts, and expressed his readiness to utilise their services in connection with all matters of common interest to Hungary and Austria, military as well as financial. But the Diet had lost all patience ; palliatives were of no use to a disease which required radical treatment ; Hungary

1580.

---

[1] *A Mag. Nem. Tört.* v. 431.

for the Hungarians was what it wanted, and exclusion of German influence and the restoration of constitutional government was, in its view, the only panacea.[1] Rudolph was "surprised," not to say pained, and nothing could ever induce him again to have any direct dealing with

1588. the Hungarians or with their ungrateful Diet. To a repetition of that body's demands for proper financial and military control, and for the re-establishment in its primitive form of the Hungarian Council, he replied by omitting to convene the representatives of the nation for a period of five years.

1593.   Matters began to assume a threatening aspect, and it was, on the whole, fortunate for Rudolph that war with Turkey broke out again and distracted the thoughts of the Magyars from the grievances which twenty-five years of peace had done nothing to mitigate. Transylvania, the last stronghold of Hungarian independence, now became the chief object of Rudolph's attention. His intrigues were ably seconded by the Jesuits, arch-enemies of liberty, traducers of the Magyars, and glorifiers of Austrian despotism, who had been recently introduced into the country, and had succeeded in getting Sigismund Báthory completely under their thumb. Tired of Turk and Habsburg alike, and sick to death of his wife, Christina, Sigismund came reluctantly to the conclusion that the only way to be quit of all three was to resign

1598. his throne in Rudolph's favour. General Basta, a man of proverbial brutality, now came upon the scene as the representative of the blessings of Habsburg rule, and treated Transylvania as a conquered country,[2] with the result that the inhabitants soon sighed for the

---

[1] Contarini, ambassador of Venice, wrote : " Odiano naturalmente la casa d' Austria perchè lor pare d' esser stati tenuti non solo soggetti ma sprezzati assai, avendoli essa sempre sottoposti al governo de Tedeschi loro naturali inimici."—Sayous, *Histoire générale des Hongrois,* ii. 125, n.

[2] " Pillia avec un soin méthodique dont le souvenir n'a jamais disparu." —Sayous, *l.c.* ; Michael Horváth, *o.c.* iii. 377-379 *sqq.*

days when they were so miserable under Turkish domination. The Protestants were, naturally, the chief victims of the unholy alliance of Basta and the Society of Jesus, and their churches were destroyed and their clergy were expelled. These were the halcyon days of the Catholic Church, and the officers of State were so many instruments of religious oppression. Of the bishops who occupied fourteen out of twenty places in the Council, perhaps the worst was Stephen Szuhai, Bishop of Eger. He told the King that it was quite unnecessary to summon the Diet, and that it was far simpler to order the counties to collect the taxes and, if they refused, to dragoon them into submission. It was Szuhai who conceived the idea of accusing wealthy nobles of treasonable dealings with the Turks, and of confiscating their property on the strength of trumped-up evidence. Millions flowed into the Treasury in this way, to the great satisfaction of Rudolph, who was ready to do anything for money.[1] What Basta did in Transylvania, Belgiojoso did in Upper Hungary. He openly declared his intention of feathering his nest at the expense of the Protestants : of extirpating heresy to the eternal profit of his Catholic soul, and for the temporary satisfaction of his disreputable appetites. Rudolph, who suffered at intervals from nervous collapse, was a mere puppet in the hands of the priestly organisers of the anti-Protestant campaign, who robbed, and confiscated, and tyrannised to their heart's content. What specially annoyed land-owners and peasants alike was the fact that as, owing to troublous times, the value of produce had greatly increased, the priests wriggled out of the bargains which they had made with respect to tithes. Lay farmers of tithes, who had, in many cases, paid cash down to the Church at a time when money was scarce and produce was cheap, lost both capital and income, and the peasants found themselves again face to face with the

[1] *A Mag. Nem. Tört.* v. 569 *sqq.*

tender mercies of ecclesiastics who had a short way of dealing with heretic unpunctuality in the matter of payment. Thus, the general discontent had an economic as well as a religious basis. The success of the Reformation in Hungary was largely due to the tendency to identify Catholicism with Austrian autocracy : to look upon the established Church as an instrument of oppression, the means of escape from which might perhaps be found in the adoption of a new religion. Hatred of the Jesuits was another important factor. They were looked upon as Habsburg spies, and detectives in priestly garb presented a particularly unattractive spectacle. They encouraged the King in the belief that Protestantism was the one obstacle to the success of his germanising efforts, and that Hungary could never be properly incorporated in Austria until heresy was extirpated. The influence of the higher members of the Catholic hierarchy was always anti-national, and, with few exceptions, the bishops were at all periods of Hungarian history ready to sacrifice the individuality and the Constitution of the nation, provided the hegemony of Catholic dogma could be thereby assured. Pázmány, for example, who turned from the Reformed to the Catholic Church, was reported to have said that he would rather the country were inhabited only by wolves and foxes than that heretics should be allowed to exist there.[1] When the Court of Vienna wanted an instrument of oppression it could always find an appropriate tool among the Catholic bishops ; no wonder, therefore, that the Catholic Church was looked upon, not as the provider of the means of salvation, but as a department of the hatred bureaucracy of Vienna. As in political, so in educational matters, the influence of the Jesuits was purely anti-Magyar. Their object was the discouragement of the idea of Hungary a nation ; their weapon, the substitution of dog-Latin for the national language, and

[1] Beöthy, o.c. i. 372.

the suppression of all reference to the past glories of the period of independence.

The Diet continued to present its usual list of complaints : of the absence of the King from the country ; of the disregard of laws he had sworn to observe ; of the exclusive employment of foreign advisers ; of the blackguardism of the German mercenaries, and of the sacrifice of Hungary's material interests to those of Austria. In 1597 the Diet raised for the first time the question of the economic grievances, of which much will be heard hereafter. It pointed out that Hungary was a country which depended for its welfare, and for its power to bear the burden of taxation, on its ability to find a market for the raw materials which Austria excluded by means of protective duties, while it flooded Hungary with its own surplus products. But to this, as to all other complaints, Rudolph turned a deaf ear. Not satisfied with his sins of omission, he attempted the deliberate fraud of falsifying the law, and inserted in the laws of 1604 the celebrated twenty-second clause, which forbade the Diet to occupy itself in future with the discussion of any matter connected with religion.[1] When the forgery was discovered, he attempted to justify himself on the ground of good intentions, and of the discretionary power vested in the wearer of the Sacred Crown, though he was, of course, quite aware that the Constitution, which he had sworn to maintain, gave him neither a license to forge nor any independent legislative authority. This was the last straw on the back already strained to breaking by the Bastas and Belgiojosos. Rudolph saw, without regret, that a crisis was at hand, for he had no doubt as to his ability to suppress any rising that might take place, and, in fact, was pleased with the prospect of a reasonable excuse for establishing Church and autocracy on a sounder basis.

The nation's necessities brought forth the requisite

---

[1] Károlyi, *A. xxii. Articulus.*

leader in the person of Stephen Bocskay, a fervent Calvinist, a diplomatist, and a soldier, whom a mass meeting held at Szerencs[1] acclaimed Prince of Hungary and Transylvania. Liberty of conscience for all was proclaimed, and all who should fail to rise in defence of their country were stigmatised as traitors. Having secured the benevolent neutrality of the Porte, Bocskay in a short time collected an army of such dimensions that Rudolph had reasonable justification for a fresh nervous breakdown. Though himself a Protestant of the strictest type, Bocskay did not trouble about the religious opinions of his followers. It was enough for him if a man was a patriot and ready to fight for his country. At first Basta obtained 1604. some success, but by the end of the following year all Transylvania and practically the whole of Upper Hungary were in Bocskay's hands, and his Haiduks were making incursions into Lower Austria, Moravia, and Silesia. It must be admitted that he took a leaf out of Basta's book, and destroyed and confiscated the property of the Catholic Church and of the Catholic nobles ; but considering the provocation received and the class from which the majority of his followers were derived, it would have been a matter for surprise if nothing in the nature of reprisals had taken place. For this was essentially a popular rising from which the chief nobles of Upper Hungary, and bastard Magyars, who cared more for their pockets than for the ancient liberties of the nation, held aloof. Bocskay, like his lieutenant, Stephen Illesházy, one of the victims of Szuhai's policy of extortion,[2] fought, not for his own hand, but against compulsory germanisation : to win back Hungary for the Hungarians, and to preserve the national language and individuality. Consequently, he was ready to make peace at any moment provided satisfactory

[1] At this meeting resolutions were drawn up in the Hungarian language for the first time since the country's conversion to Christianity.—*A Mag. Nem. Tört.* v. 603.

[2] Michael Horváth, *o.c.* iii. 381.

guarantees of political and religious liberty were forthcoming. It is possible that he might have driven the
Austrians clean out of Hungary, but the country wanted
rest, and there was always the danger that the attempts
of the Catholics to induce the Sultan to interfere might
be crowned with success : for an alliance of Cross and
Crescent was quite admissible in the eyes of the Church
in the sacred cause of tyranny and religious obscurantism.
Rome tried to stiffen Rudolph's back by promises of help,
as did the Venetians, whose interest it was to keep him
fully occupied in the South ; and the Jesuits threatened
him with excommunication if he made any concession to
the insurgents and to Protestantism. But his troops
were utterly demoralised, and his brother Mathias, sick of
his incompetence and mad outbursts of impotent rage,
pressed him to make peace.

Bocskay embodied the terms on which he was willing 1605.
to suspend hostilities in fifteen articles, which demanded,
inter alia, religious liberty for Calvinists and Lutherans ;
the abolition of the forged twenty-second clause of the law
of 1604 ; the exclusion of the bishops from political office,
and, generally, from interference in Hungarian affairs ;
the expulsion of the Jesuits ; the appointment of a Palatine [1]
with complete authority to represent the King during his
absence from Hungary ; the confiding of the management of Hungarian military and financial affairs [2] to
Hungarians ; the exclusion of German advisers ; the
exclusive employment of Magyar officers and Magyar
troops within the limits of Hungary ; and a general
amnesty to put an end to accusations of treason and the
consequent extortion. The news that a large Turkish 1606.
army was advancing finally induced Rudolph, after months

[1] None had been appointed for forty-six years in spite of continual protests
of the Diet.

[2] For the financial position at the end of the sixteenth and the beginning
of the seventeenth centuries see Acsády, *A Magyar Adózás Története, 1598-
1604-ben*, Budapest, 1906, pp. 49 *sqq.* 59 *sqq.*

of haggling, to give way on the main points, and to sign
the convention known as the Peace of Vienna, in which,
as a final wriggle, he inserted the clause "without prejudice
to the Catholic faith," in order to qualify the obligations
imposed on him and to have a weapon for future use.
Five months later the peace of Zsitvatorok arranged
matters with the threatening Turk, for the first time on
a basis not altogether disgraceful to Christian Austria, as
no annual tribute was exacted, though 200,000 florins were
in fact paid as the price of a twenty years' peace which
confirmed the Habsburgs in possession of, roughly, one-
quarter of the Hungary of seventy years ago.[1]   The
peace is remarkable for another reason ; for the fact that
the terms were submitted to the Diet for consideration
and were embodied in a special law ; and thus the
principle of the ratification of foreign treaties by the
representatives of the nation as essential to their validity
received fresh confirmation.   Bocskay had not fought in
vain.   Protestantism, which hitherto, like Judaism, had
been a nominally tolerated, but not a recognised religion,
now received legal sanction ; and, thanks to him, Magyars
were Magyars still, when Austrian poison ended his career
only a few months after the achievement of his object.[2]
The death of Bocskay would, no doubt, have had the
result of encouraging Rudolph to violate the compact
recently made, but, fortunately, his family was tired of the
sick man, who at times "bellowed like a bull or roared like
1607. a lion," and failed even in his attempts to commit suicide,
and a bloodless palace revolution put his brother Mathias
in possession of the throne of a fragmentary Hungary.

In pursuance of the terms of the peace of Vienna,[3] the
1608. Diet was summoned, and proceeded to add a fresh chapter
to the constitutional history of Hungary, and new clauses

[1] Szalay, *Mag. Tört.* iv. 460.   [2] Michael Horváth, *o.c.* iii. 429.
[3] It has been termed the first *Ausgleich*, or "Compromise," between Austria
and Hungary.

to the fundamental laws which no Habsburg ever frankly obeyed or openly impugned. The elective nature of the monarchy[1] received fresh confirmation, though Mathias struggled hard to get himself "recognised" instead of elected ; and the historic rights and privileges of the nation were again formally guaranteed in writing before the coronation took place. Clause 22 of 1604 was abrogated, " the same having been added to the Statute Book *extra Diaetam*, and without the consent of the people."[2] Religious freedom was assured to the Protestants, and places of worship confiscated by either party during the late disturbances were to be returned to their true owners. It was provided that the Palatine should be elected at the next meeting of the Diet, and that in the event of the King being unable to live permanently in Hungary, or being obliged to be absent for a long period, the Palatine, in accordance with the full powers to be granted to him by his Majesty in that behalf, should, as ancient custom demanded, have as complete authority to govern and administer the country with the help of the Hungarian Council as the King himself would possess were he not absent.[3] It was further provided that the King should submit the names of two Catholics and two Protestants as candidates for the office in question, from among whom

---

[1] Clearly recognised by non-official Austria, the Protestants of which begged the Hungarians not to elect Mathias unless he guaranteed religious liberty to them also.—Michael Horváth, *o.c.* iii. 458, 462.

[2] Clause 1 of the Terms of Peace.

[3] Clause 18 of the law of 1608, ratified by Mathias before coronation and as a condition precedent to election. This clause is of special importance, as a similar one in the laws of 1848 was said by the enemies of Hungary to be a revolutionary innovation, justifying the taking of extreme measures. Clause 3 of the terms of peace says : " Statutum et constitutum est quod sua Serenitas (the Palatine) secundum plenipotentiam sibi per suam Majestatem non ita pridem concessam in negotiis regni Hungariae per Palatinum et Consiliarios Hungaricos, non secus ac si sua C. R. que Majestas personaliter praesens adesset, audiendi, proponendi, judicandi, concludendi, agendi et disponendi in omnibus iis quae ad conservandum regnum Hungariae ejusdemque regnicolarum quietem et utilitatem videbuntur esse necessaria, plenariam potestatem et facultatem habeat."

the Diet should elect one; and that in the event of the Palatine's decease the King should be bound to summon a special meeting of the Diet within one year for the election of a successor (clause 3). Clause 4 requires the Sacred Crown, the symbol of national independence, to be brought back to Hungary and left there in the custody of elected Magyar laymen. Clause 5 provides that the Treasurer must henceforth be a Magyar and a layman, and that no foreigners are to be allowed to meddle with any branch of the national revenues, the management of which is to be entirely independent of the Austrian treasury. Hungary proper, as well as the parts thereto annexed — Dalmatia, Croatia, and Slavonia — are to be governed by Magyars only; appointments are to be made without regard to religious belief; and his Majesty is to take care that no foreigners are ever allowed to interfere in any governmental department (clause 10). German and other foreign mercenaries are to be withdrawn from the country as soon as possible (clause 12). The King is to undertake to maintain the "privileges, liberties, customs, and immunities" of the people in "undiminished sanctity;" and all decrees which may be in contradiction with the ancient laws of the kingdom are to be amended and put in order by a special commission, and, as amended, are to be adopted by the Diet and ratified by the King. Further, the clause of the Golden Bull and of its amending Act, which prohibits the punishment of any person without legal citation and conviction, receives fresh confirmation (clause 16); and the Jesuits, the fount and origin of half the discord and disasters which rent the kingdom, are forbidden to own real property in Hungary. Thus the conflict between Magyar patriotism and Austrian autocracy apparently resulted in the complete victory of the former. The Protestants are no longer to be harried and oppressed at the discretion of the Jesuits. Hungary is to cease to be a milch cow to be drained and debilitated by foreign adventurers and parasites of the Habsburgs. It is no longer to be a mere province of Austria, privileged to intercept the blows of the Turks, and to pay for the privilege in blood and taxes. The contract between Hungary and the Habsburgs, which each successive King had done his best to tear to shreds, was again patched up —to be violated again so soon as convenient occasion offered. The legislation of the year 1608 is memorable also for the fact that the indiscriminate right of all nobles to appear at and take part in the deliberations of the Diet was abolished, and the representative system was definitively introduced. Further, the Diet was divided into two Chambers. What we may call the Upper House henceforward consisted of the magnates and hereditary barons, the bishops, and certain other high ecclesiastical functionaries; the Lower House, of the deputies from the counties, from certain chapters and free towns, and of the representatives of absent barons. Thus for the first time the existence was recognised of an aristocracy separate and distinct from the common aristocracy of the whole body of freemen.[1]

After the Peace of Vienna the Protestants tried to secure the results of their victory, and the Catholics to win back by fair means or foul what they had lost. The resulting conflict fills the history of the next thirty-seven years. The law providing for the re-establishment of Hungarian control of Hungarian finances remained

---

[1] The barons and magnates included the Comes of Pressburg, the guardians of the Sacred Crown, the governor of Fiume (later), hereditary and appointed lords-lieutenant, hereditary counts and barons, and other High Court and judicial officials (Kmety, *Közjog*, p. 85, *n.*). In the Lower House the judges of the High Court had seats, but took no part in the debates and had no vote. The number of the county representatives was not fixed till 1681, when the Lower House complained that only two were summoned from each county. The Upper House did not agree that there was reason to increase the number, which thus was tacitly fixed in perpetuity, down to 1848, at two. The number of the free towns entitled to be represented was fixed at eight, in accordance with the decree of King Vladislav, but apparently others sent deputies also.

L

practically a dead letter, and Vienna continued as before to turn a deaf ear to the protests of the Diet. Mathias, who never had the least intention of giving effect to the laws of 1608, tried his hand at Rudolph's old trick of altering the text of laws after they had received their final form at the hands of that body, which eventually had to pass a law (1618) to emphasise the fact that the King had no right whatever to omit anything from, or interpolate anything in, the Bills submitted to him for confirmation —that he possessed indeed the right of veto, but not the privilege of forgery. It is noticeable that the Magyars did not fight for their own hand only, but did their best to improve the position of the Protestants in the hereditary provinces. Mathias, however, pointed out to them that Austria was Austria and not Hungary, and politely requested them to mind their own business. And in fact they were soon fully occupied with their own affairs, for as soon as Mathias was elected Emperor at Frankfurt, he felt himself strong enough to begin a systematic anti-reformation campaign against the "dog's creed," as he styled it, and the Jesuits again raised their heads in Hungary, and opened schools just as if there never had been such a thing as the Peace of Vienna or the laws of 1608. Of course it would be absurd to suppose that the Protestants were nothing but injured innocents, passive victims who turned both cheeks in turn to the smiter and confined themselves to making verbal protests. As in England, so in Hungary, as regards readiness to give their opponents the opportunity of earning the martyr's crown, there was little to choose between Catholics and Protestants. It was merely a question of opportunity ; and as the former were members of the established Church, and Vienna identified Protestantism with Hungarian nationalism and hostility to benevolent despotism, it is obvious that the votaries of reformation got comparatively little chance of indulging their propensity to persecute their opponents. Bishop Khlesl summed up the official Catholic view in the phrase, "Between Christ and Belial there can be nothing in common," *i.e.* that the King could at any moment take away with his left what his right hand had been forced to concede, and that no moral obligation could originate in a treaty made with heretics. Protestantism was therefore at a permanent discount.

Transylvania, the refuge and stronghold of Magyar nationality, cared even more for freedom of conscience than for political independence, and the schemes of Gabriel Bethlen were directed to the recovery of the former rather than of the latter.[1] Personal aggrandisement was not his ultimate object when he took the side of Bohemia in the war with Austria, which ended so disastrously for the former at the battle of White 1620. Mountain and led to the conversion of the hitherto existing trialism into the dualism of to-day. His notion was to secure the independence of Protestant Hungary, increased by the addition of the hereditary provinces in Austria (in which Protestantism had taken root as strongly as anywhere), which had already cried to the Magyars to come over and help them. He had hoped, in alliance with Bohemia and with the Protestant German princes, to obtain a Protestant majority at the Diet of Frankfurt, and so to put an end for ever to the great enemy of Calvinistic and Lutheran humanity—the domination of a Catholic emperor. The ease with which Ferdinand II. destroyed the historic independence of Bohemia, established the predominance of an intolerant Catholic minority, substituted German for Czech as the official language, and foisted a German bureaucracy on the conquered country, encouraged the Habsburgs in the work of reducing Hungary to the position of a province or a

---

[1] See the manifesto issued by him on the eve of insurrection.—Szalay, *Mag. Tört.* iv. 518, *n.*

colony of Austria.   It was in the Turks that Gabriel
Bethlen saw the chief defence of Hungary against
germanisation.   He did not want the Turks any more
than he wanted the Habsburgs, but a long residence
among the former had taught him that from many points
of view, more especially as regards respect for the given
word, the former were vastly superior to the latter.   It
was his object that the Hungarians should be masters in
their own house, and in order to attain it he never hesitated
to utilise a heathen against a Christian despot.

During the whole of Ferdinand's reign the complaints
of Jesuit influence and of evasions of the laws of 1608 [1]
continued without interruption.   The underground rumb-
lings were unintermittent, but nothing took place in the
nature of an earthquake beyond an advance into Upper
Hungary by George Rákóczy of Transylvania, who,
guaranteed by treaty the financial support of France and
Sweden, thought the time had come to effect the final
liberation of his country from political and religious
oppression.   Unfortunately, the Magyars were temporarily
divided by the spirit of religious intolerance.   The Protestant members were at one moment on the point of
seceding in a body from the Diet ; and throughout this
period national politics were completely swamped by
religious dissensions, as is shown by the terms of the
1645. Peace of Lincz concluded between Rákóczy and Ferdinand
III., and incorporated in the Statute Book by the Diet
of 1646.[2]   Except for clauses 9 and 65, which provide
for a general amnesty and forbid the sending of Magyar
troops out of Hungary, the convention is concerned solely
with guarantees of the free exercise of religion and of
the free use of chapels, bells, and churchyards ; with the

---

[1] In the Diploma Inaugurale he undertook to observe them "*in omnibus
suis punctis, clausulis, et articulis, firmiter et sancte, per aliosque omnes inviolabiliter observari faciet.*" It is set out in Marczali's *Enchiridion Fontium*,
p. 514 *sqq.*
[2] *Enchiridion Fontium*, pp. 522-542.

prohibition of interference by landlords in the religious
affairs of their peasants; and with the distribution of
honours and offices without regard to religious opinions.

Hitherto, as we have seen, Transylvania and its princes
had done much to preserve the existence and the liberties
of Hungary, but now it spent its force in useless internal
and external wars under George Rákóczy II. The result was that there was no one to interfere with the process
of grinding Hungary to pieces between the Turkish
and the Austrian millstones. The country was never
more exposed to the horrors of Turkish irruptions than
during the early part of tne reign of Leopold I. (1657-
1705), while he and his Jesuit advisers were occupied with
the task of extirpating heresy and destroying the last
vestiges of political liberty.[1]   In the Diploma Inaugurale,[2]
and by his coronation oath, Leopold undertook to observe
and maintain the laws and liberties of Hungary; to
summon the Diet at least once every three years; to
employ exclusively Magyar counsellors in Magyar affairs,
and Magyar soldiers and officers in Hungary; not to
remove the Sacred Crown; and above all to obey the
laws of 1608—the guarantee of religious freedom. But
the ink of the Diploma was scarcely dry when he began
to follow his father's footsteps, to renew the campaign of
which the ultimate object was the abolition of all constitutional guarantees and the establishment of an unlimited
despotism. In order that he might have a free hand, and
that the Porte should have no excuse for interference, he
did not even remonstrate when the Turks annually raided
Hungary and killed and carried off the inhabitants to
the number, according to a contemporary estimate, of
10,000 every year. Though the great majority of the
population was Protestant, the lords-lieutenant and other

---

[1] For details see Alfred Michiel, *Histoire secrète du Gouvernement autrichien*,
p. 126 *sqq.* Unreliable.
[2] Confirmed and incorporated in the Statute Book by the Diet of 1659.

officials were mostly Catholics, who used their influence in an anti-Protestant, anti-national direction,[1] by forcing the counties to send Catholic representatives to the Diet, thus strengthening the forces of intolerance and multiplying the instruments of autocracy. The peasants, for the most part, clung to Protestantism, for the services of the reformed Church were conducted in Hungarian, instead of in Latin which no one understood[2]; but nine-tenths of the great landowners were Catholic, and as intolerant as the Jesuits, who, within a year of the coronation of the new King, already felt themselves strong enough to begin a campaign of compulsory conversion and the extirpation of the recalcitrant. Stankovics, the Jesuit, clearly expressed the true aim of official Austria in his prayer : " God grant that we may soon see the day, the glorious and blessed day, when the whole of Hungary will speak but one language and will be united in the ancient faith." So the real object was not to ensure the salvation of mankind by turning all hearts to the Virgin, but to extirpate the national language and therewith the feeling of Magyar nationality. Nicholas Zrinyi in vain urged the King to put an end to the three great evils—mercenaries, Turkish raids, and religious persecution ; but the King listened to none but Montecuccoli, and replied that if the Diet would drop the religious question, something might be done against the Turks. As a matter of fact, the Turks were a far lesser evil than the German mercenaries,[3] as the former looked upon

[1] Catholic landlords considered themselves justified in compelling their peasants to attend Catholic services, and to hand over Protestant churches on their estates to the Catholics, even where the majority of the population was Protestant.—Michael Horváth, o.c. iv. 26. The principle on which they acted was expressed by the phrase, "cujus regio, ejus religio."

[2] The Jesuits of Munkács, seeing that the peasants took no interest in services which they could not understand, tried them with mass in their own language, and with success, until the Pope in 1661 forbade the substitution of Hungarian or any other language for Latin.

[3] See Law iii. of 1596 as to robberies, murders, arson, and sacrilege " which no words can describe."

Hungary as on their future inheritance, and consequently set a certain limit to their destructive instincts, while the latter, who generally engaged themselves for a single campaign only, considered war as a commercial undertaking. Whether they killed Turks or Magyars they did not care; in fact, understanding neither, they hardly distinguished between the two. Money, not glory, was their object, and if, as was generally the case, they did not receive the wages promised by their Austrian paymasters, they indemnified themselves at the expense of the peaceful inhabitants, and what they could not turn into cash they ruthlessly destroyed.[1] The general discontent must have eventually ended in a national revolt against Austrian rule; but once again the Turks acted as a lightning conductor for Austria, and all the energies of Hungary were directed against them until the complete defeat of the Sultan's troops at St. Gothard led to the Peace of Vasvár, when Austria again sacrificed Hungary's interests, in spite of the oceans of blood the Magyars had shed in defence of their country. Not only were the Hungarians not consulted as to the terms of peace;[2] not only was no part of their country recovered as the result of a successful campaign, but four additional counties were handed over to the Turks. The Magyars came to the natural conclusion that the Court of Vienna had no intention of freeing them from the Turkish yoke, and that they had therefore no alternative but to make the best terms they could with the Porte in order to save themselves from the destruction as a nation which Vienna thought could easily be brought about, now that religious differences made concerted action an impossibility, and as the country had lost its only possible leader by the death of Nicholas Zrinyi.

1663.

1664.

---

[1] "Rather *Allah* than *wer da*," *i.e.* than the "who goes there" of the Germans, was a popular phrase of this period.
[2] Szalay, *Mag. Tört.* v. 98.

Zrinyi's brother, Peter, Nádasdy, and Frangepán, after futile negotiations with Louis XIV., who, though anxious that troubles at home should prevent Austria from interfering abroad, was not, for the moment, disposed to help the Hungarians, did in fact raise part of the country in revolt. After a few small successes they were induced to lay down their arms by a promise that Hungary's grievances should be remedied, and a general amnesty granted to all who had taken part in the rising. The value of Habsburg promises was, as usual, too highly 1671. estimated, and the three counts, Zrinyi, Nádasdy, and Frangepán were executed after a mock trial before an Austrian tribunal.[1] A reign of terror followed; executions were a daily occurrence; over 2000 nobles were thrown into prison, and the foreign mercenaries were given a free hand to murder, burn, and impale in the name of Christ and Mary.[2] "Poor Nádasdy! May he rest in peace. I have had two masses said for the repose of his soul." Having thus salved his conscience, Leopold informed the Protestants that owing to insurrection their religious liberty was forfeited, and proceeded to the wholesale confiscation of schools and churches. Public opinion made Leopold personally responsible for the massacres which followed, but it is probable that he was in reality a more or less blind instrument in the hands of Lobkowitz,[3] the moving spirit in the anti-Protestant, anti-Hungarian campaign,[4] who was ably seconded by Bishop Kollonics

[1] Wagner, *Hist. Leop.* i. 249; *Histoire des Révolutions de Hongrie*, 1739, i. 237 *sqq.*; Szalay, *Mag. Tört.* v. 134 *sqq.*

[2] A gold piece was given to any mercenary who killed an ex-insurgent, and six months' pay for killing an officer.

[3] Lobkowitz said to Gremonville, ambassador of Louis XIV.: "The Emperor is not like your King, who sees everything, and himself gives the lead in all matters. He is like a statue which we put in the position which suits us best."

[4] Michael Horváth, *o.c.* iv. 90 *sqq.*; Wagner, *Hist. Leop.* i. 265. Wagner was himself a Jesuit, but lets the truth come out in spite of his violent anti-Magyar prejudices.

when any dirty work was to be done.   To complete their victory, and to erase the last vestiges of Hungarian liberty, an attack on the organisation of the counties was begun.   Owing to the devastated condition of the county the collection of the ordinary taxes was an impossibility. Orders were therefore given that each county should 1672. maintain its oppressors, the German mercenaries who were quartered upon it, and that failure to do so should entail "the most terrible consequences."   Every family was to be taxed according to its *presumed* normal consumption of meat, beer, wine, and brandy (it was even proposed to tax every pair of shoes), and this at a time when half the land was out of cultivation and the depredations of the mercenaries made the obtaining of supplies from a distance an impossibility.[1]   How and where the people were to get the articles of food scheduled as the basis of taxation the Viennese Court neither knew nor cared. That peasants starved was a matter of no importance provided the taxes were paid.   The noble landowners who should have helped and protected them were refugees, if Protestants, and occupied in currying favour with Vienna, if Catholics ; and so the soldier tax-collector had a free hand.

According to the Swedish ambassador, Puffendorf, Leopold took an oath in 1670 that if, by the grace of God, he succeeded in putting down Zrinyi's insurrection, Hungary should become a true *Regnum Marianum*, and every Protestant should be expelled from the Virgin's territory.   When Puffendorf remonstrated with him on the subject of religious persecutions and Turkish raids, he replied that it was no great misfortune if the Sultan pocketed a bit or two of Hungary, and that, personally, he would rather lose the whole than endure the presence of any heretic.[2]   But, for the moment, even Leopold had

[1] *A Mag. Nem. Tört.* vii. 300.
[2] *Ibid.* vii. 301.

qualms of conscience on the subject of the oath he had
taken at his coronation to maintain the liberties and the
Constitution of Hungary, and turned to Kollonics, an
authority on matters of conscience, who appointed a
committee consisting of four Jesuits and three monks to
decide the moral question involved. The committee
unanimously decided that Hungary had forfeited a'l
historical and natural rights, and that the King was under
no obligation to treat its inhabitants as human beings.
Thus with a clear conscience, knowing for certain that his
actions smelled sweet in the nostrils of the Almighty, for
the committee told him so, Leopold proceeded with his
work of extirpating heresy and pulverising his sacred
engagements. A mild protest was raised by Bishop
Szelepcsényi against the abolition of the shadow of
constitutional government which remained, but his action
was evidently due to fear of losing his place and emoluments as viceroy, and on being guaranteed the continuance
of his salary he reconsidered the matter and withdrew his
opposition. On March 11, 1673, Leopold published the
decree which he imagined was to reduce Hungary for
ever to the position of a hereditary province of the
Habsburgs. All constitutional forms were abolished, and
Ampringen, a licentious and self-seeking soldier, was
appointed governor-general, with a council consisting of
Szelepcsényi and Kollonics, the typical representatives of
religious intolerance, and ten others to aid him in the task
of germanising the country and of " taking care of the
interests of the Roman Catholic Church." [1] But the
scheme was still-born. Dissensions among the German
officials condemned it to failure from the start, and
absolute anarchy reigned in the land, to the satisfaction of
none but mercenaries, who were thus left undisturbed in
their orgy of brutality and depredation. [2]

[1] Instructions, Szalay, *Mag. Tört.* v. 155, *n.*
[2] If the peasants complained they were robbed of their last farthing and

Kollonics' boast that he would make Hungary first a slave, then a beggar, and then Catholic,[1] lacked justification only as regards the last item. Wherever the population could manage to keep in touch with its clergy it still adhered to its religion. Kollonics, therefore, directed his persecution mainly against the clergy, in the hope that when the last of its members had been killed, imprisoned, or driven out of the country, such Protestants as still wished to be married, or to christen their children, or to be buried, in accordance with some kind of Christian formality, must perforce be converted to Catholicism. The result, to judge from the number of shepherdless sheep who returned to the true fold, was eminently satisfactory. Of the conversions which took place in the course of the succeeding three years, 6000 are ascribed to Bishop Szelepcsényi and 7000 to Bishop Bársony ; while the Jesuits, who are more exact in their figures, are credited with having won 15,219 souls for Christ in the single year 1673.[2] A *judicium delegatum extraordinarium*, 1674. or special tribunal, for the wholesale trial of Protestant clergy, was established at Pressburg, which summoned 336 pastors and schoolmasters before it, and expeditiously condemned those who were foolish enough to obey the summons, or did not die in prison, to death—the sentence being subsequently commuted by the tender-hearted Kollonics to hard labour in the galleys at Trieste and Naples.[3] The general disgust of Europe led to remonstrance on the part of certain German princes and of Sweden and Holland.[4] A temporary halt was called ; but the feeling of hatred engendered throughout Hungary

received corporal punishment into the bargain.—Michael Horváth, *o.c.* iv. 99. Even the Austrian Court was shocked by the "godless excesses" of the German mercenaries, and in 1696 ordered the military authorities to take steps for their prevention, lest the wrath of Heaven should be incurred.—Wagner, *Hist. Leop.* ii. 313.

[1] Szalay, *Mag. Tört.* vi. 30.   [2] *A Mag. Nem. Tört.* vii. 328.
[3] Michael Horváth, *o.c.* iv. 97.   [4] Wagner, *Hist. Leop.* i. 325.

was too deep to be allayed by trifling concessions, and
the national aspirations found a new leader in the person
1676. of Imre Thököly, whom the Turks, as well as Louis
XIV., then at war with Leopold, helped with men and
money.

His object was much the same as that of other national
champions, his predecessors: religious liberty, the
restoration of confiscated property, the recognition
of his claim to the title of Prince of Transylvania,
and constitutional government for Hungary.[1] At first
he obtained only minor successes, in Moravia and elsewhere, but by the beginning of 1683 nearly the whole
of Upper Hungary was in his hands. The Court of
Vienna soon became aware of its inability to put down
the insurrection, but at the same time was disinclined to
make substantial concessions. The failure of the new
system of government and the retirement of Ampringen,
its moving spirit, made Leopold see that something must
be done to quiet popular discontent for fear lest the
revolt, which at first showed signs of taking a slow and
1681. indecisive course, might end in a general conflagration.
The Diet was summoned, and its first demand, the
election of a Palatine, was conceded. More than this
Kollonics had no intention of allowing Leopold to grant ;
and the Protestants[2] could do no more than bring
forward series after series of complaints : that churches
were turned into stables or used for profane purposes ;
that schools were closed, and that submission to extortion
was a condition precedent to permission to bury their
dead.[3] Eventually, more out of weariness than for any
other reason, and, possibly, influenced by the wish to get
his second wife Elenora Magdalene crowned quietly,
Leopold gave way to some extent, reconfirmed the terms

---

[1] Wagner, *Hist. Leop.* i. 558.

[2] Being in a minority. They were forty-two to sixty-six Catholics—
Szalay, *Mag. Tört.* v. 197.

[3] Marczali, *Enchiridion Fontium*, p. 544.

of the peace of Vienna,[1] which had nominally guaranteed religious liberty to all, gave permission to the ejected 1681. Protestant clergy to return to their parishes, annulled the forcible conversions of the past years, and specified certain districts in which schools and churches might be built.[2] This, of course, contented no one; neither the Catholics who objected to any interference with, or diminution of the right to persecute their religious opponents which they had hitherto enjoyed, nor the Protestants, who would be satisfied with nothing short of absolute religious equality with the Catholics. The outrageous system of taxation introduced in 1672 was withdrawn, and arrears of taxes, it being impossible to collect them in the impoverished state of the country, were remitted. The office of Governor-General was abolished; a general amnesty was proclaimed; the withdrawal of German soldiers was promised; and the subordination of the Hungarian Treasury to the corresponding institution in Vienna nominally ceased. But Kollonics remained president of the Treasury, in spite of the law forbidding the holding of that post by an ecclesiastic, and Esterházy, the new Palatine, made little or no attempt to restore the old authority of his office. In fact, the laws of 1681 were merely a sop thrown to public opinion, and an attempt to throw dust in the eyes of the Protestant Powers of Europe.

The instant Thököly's defeat at Pressburg caused his 1683. retirement, and John Sobieski's victory over the Turks under Kara Mustapha raised the siege of Vienna, Leopold began to regret the concessions of 1681. Careless of what might happen to Hungary, he secretly offered terms

---

[1] Clause 25 of the law of 1681: "*Liberum Religionis exercitium a parte nonnullorum interturbatum,*" is the unexaggerated description of the horrors of the past years.

[2] Clause 26. It was at the same time enacted that Hungary should have its own diplomatic representative at the Porte, who was to be on a footing of equality with the Austrian envoy.

of peace to the defeated Vizier in order to save himself the trouble and expense of pursuing his advantage. But the offer was refused, and the Pope and the Venetians, believing that the time had at length come to drive the Turks out of Europe, compelled the Austrians to continue the war.[1] Otherwise, for all Leopold cared, Hungary might have waited till doomsday for its liberation from the Turkish yoke. Now that Thököly was temporarily out of the way, the King conceived fresh conscientious scruples about keeping a promise made to Protestants ; and fearing to compromise his soul's salvation, cast about to find some new method of extirpating heresy, and, incidentally, of incorporating Hungary in his hereditary dominions. His advisers pressed upon him the view that the complete reconquest of the parts occupied by the Turks, which now seemed probable, justified him in regarding Hungary as a country conquered for his own benefit and not for that of its inhabitants. Hungary, so Kollonics said, owing to the long duration of the Turkish occupation, had lost its Magyar character,[2] and Austria could deal with it as she pleased. Two committees, in which, naturally, no Hungarian found a place,[3] were appointed to consider the question of the proposed incorporation in the hereditary provinces, and that of the introduction of a permanent system of taxation without
1686. representation The recapture of Buda by Charles of Lorraine after a century and a half of Turkish occupation, and the complete defeat of Kara Mustapha at Mohács, the scene of the great disaster of 1526, temporarily put an end to disturbances in Hungary. Thököly, to whom the Vizier attributed his misfortunes, was thrown into prison

---

[1] Beöthy, o.c. i. 422.

[2] The fact that this was not true, though the greater part of Hungary had been occupied by the Turks for a century and a half, is one of the most remarkable facts in Hungarian history, and should have satisfied the Habsburgs as to the futility of attempting to germanise the Magyars.

[3] Beöthy, o.c. i. 503.

at Belgrade, and with the exception of Munkács, where the
heroic Ilona Zrinyi, his wife, still held out, the whole
country was in the hands of the imperial troops. But the
lies of Caraffa led Leopold to believe that a fresh insurrection, of a far more dangerous character than any of its
predecessors, was pending ; a new extraordinary tribunal
was established at Eperjes, and the butchery of innocent
but inconvenient persons which followed recalled the worst
days of the Spanish Inquisition, and acquired for Caraffa[1]
a permanent reputation for brutality rivalled only by that
of Basta and Belgiojoso in the past, and of the butcher
Haynau at a later date. A recrudescence of persecution
followed all over Hungary, especially in the reconquered
parts, where, under the heathen rule of the Turks, the Protestants had exercised their religion in comparative peace.

The fear of torture rather than that of death had 1687.
reduced Hungary in the course of twelve months to such
a state that Leopold thought the time to be ripe for the
realisation of the scheme cherished by the Habsburgs for
the last 150 years, namely, the abolition of Hungary's
elective rights, and the establishment of hereditary
monarchy. The disgust generated in Europe by the
butchery of Eperjes made it advisable to give the
semblance of legality to the execution of the scheme,
instead of abolishing Hungary's rights merely with the
stroke of a pen and incorporating it once for all in the
hereditary dominions. The Diet was therefore convoked,[2]

[1] Of Neapolitan origin. He owed his rapid advancement to the Jesuits, to
whom his fanaticism and cruelty recommended him.—Michael Horváth, o.c. iv.
183. Arneth, a non-Magyar authority, in his life of Field-Marshal Starhemberg,
quoted by Szalay (*Mag. Tört.* v. 352, *n.*) says, "Sehr ist zu bedauern, dass der
Glanz der erfochtenen Siege durch die Grausamkeit befleckt wurde, mit welcher
der unmenschliche Antonio Caraffa zu Eperies gegen die angeblichen Theil-
nehmer einer *kaum wirklich bestandenen Verschwörung* verfuhr."

[2] Kollonics expressed surprise at the sparse attendance of the representatives
of the counties, and at the youth of those who were in fact present. He himself supplied the answer to the enigma : "Of course, if all the older men have
been decapitated, you can send only young ones."—"A Történelmi Tár,"
cited in *A Mag. Nem. Tört.* vii. 465.

and the King announced that though he would be justified
in treating Hungary as a conquered country to be dealt
with as he pleased, he was disposed, of his mercy, to
re-establish the Constitution under three conditions :[1]
Firstly, that the inaugural diploma should henceforth
take the form of that signed by Ferdinand I. Secondly,
that the hereditary right of the male line of the house of
Habsburg to the throne of Hungary should be acknowledged in perpetuity. Thirdly, that the clause of
the Golden Bull giving the right of armed resistance to
unconstitutional acts of the monarch should be abolished.
It is perhaps surprising that the last condition had not
long ago been insisted upon, as though, in reality, it gave
no protection to insurgents if the King got the better
of them, it yet gave a sort of legal sanction to in-
surgence, and justified to some extent the expectation of immunity in case of failure. Only one
speaker,[2] the Chief Justice, Count Draskovsics, was bold
enough to urge the retention of the clause and the
maintenance of the elective nature of the monarchy.
All the conditions were accepted with little, and that
chiefly formal, opposition.[3] And thus, after 687 years,
Hungary ceased to have an elective monarchy ; and
as, in fact, it had ceased from the time of Ferdinand I.

---

[1] " Posset equidem eadem sacratissima Caesarea Majestas Regno huic . . .
omni jure leges dare nec non vi armorum recenter acquisita jure belli sibi
suisque augustis haeredibus separatim attribuere placitisque et convenientibus
legibus gubernare." October 31, 1687. The King's "propositions" at the
opening of the Diet.

[2] Marczali, *Enchiridion Fontium*, p. 677 ; Wagner, *Hist. Leop.* ii. 30.
He died suddenly a day or two later, and was popularly supposed to have
been poisoned on account of his independence.—Katona, *Historia Critica*,
xxxv. 441.

[3] Even the extension of the right of hereditary succession to the Spanish
branch of the Habsburgs which became extinct in 1700. In the event of the
extinction of all male descendants of both branches "the ancient and approved
custom and prerogative of the Estates and Orders in the matter of the election
and coronation of their kings" revives —Cl. 2, 1687. This is of importance
in connection with the Pragmatic Sanction.

to be elective, except on paper, the country lost little by the concession.[1]

The real pinch was in the first condition, for the diploma of Ferdinand I. contained no guarantees of religious freedom, as in 1526 the right of freedom of conscience was not questioned, and the idea, now rooted in the Habsburg mind, that religious unity was essential to, and would necessarily lead to, political unity, had not been conceived. The Protestants protested in vain. The Catholic majority had its way, and, satisfied with the triumph of dogmatic intolerance, gave way almost unasked on other points of far greater importance than the question of an hereditary crown.[2] The form of diploma, as finally settled, contained no reference to the obligation of convening the Diet at least once in every three years ; to the exclusion of foreign interference in Hungarian affairs, which a dozen laws and previous diplomas had guaranteed ; to the election and sphere of influence of the Palatine ; to the employment of Hungarian officers in Hungarian regiments ; or to the obligation of withdrawing foreign mercenaries from the country. In accordance with the terms of the new law—the work of an intolerant Catholic majority which in no sense represented the opinion of an intimidated country—Leopold's son, Joseph, was crowned in his father's lifetime [3] first hereditary King of Hungary,[4] in grateful remembrance of the benefits conferred by the

---

[1] Clause 2 provides that in future the states and orders of Hungary, *and the parts thereto annexed*, will have none other for their King than the legitimate descendants of the King in accordance with the law of primogeniture. Thus the King of Hungary becomes *ipso facto* King of Croatia, which M. Horn would have us believe was an independent, allied, kingdom.

[2] At this Diet the representatives of over a hundred non-Hungarian families were foisted on the Upper Chamber with a view to creating an entirely anti-national aristocracy as had been done with success in Bohemia after the battle of White Mountain.—Beöthy, *o.c.* p. 504.

[3] *Rex junior*, as in the reigns of Andrew II. and Béla IV.

[4] But the coronation, the diploma, and the oath still remained conditions precedent to investiture with royal power.

ejection of the Turks from Buda,[1] which, if successive Habsburgs had attempted to perform their most elementary duty to the nation which had voluntarily elected them to the throne, could undoubtedly have been effected a century earlier.

The Catholics were not yet satisfied with their work. To the complaints of the Protestants as to the disregard of old laws and of solemn guarantees of religious freedom, they retorted by quoting other ancient enactments enjoining the burning of heretics.[2] Laws were passed in the same session providing for the re-establishment of the Jesuits (sec. 20), and " with a view to the maintenance of concord and public tranquillity," it was ordained that none but Catholics should be allowed to own property in Croatia, Slavonia, or Dalmatia (cl. 23).

Having converted Hungary into a hereditary dependency of Austria, Leopold now thought it worth while
1689. seriously to set about the task of expelling the Turks. All Europe was at war, and Louis XIV. had his hands too full to render much assistance to the Sultan, while Austria could rely on the help of Poland, Venice, and the German Princes. It seemed at last as if nothing could prevent a victorious march to Constantinople and the incorporation of the Balkan provinces in the realm of the Habsburgs; but at the critical moment the death of Pope Innocent XI., who gave millions to the Christian cause out of gratitude for Austria's exemplary treatment of the heretics, deprived Leopold of his most important supporter. Thököly, freed from imprisonment at Belgrade, had again started, more or less successfully, on the war-path; but by the end of 1690 Louis of Bavaria had made Transylvania too hot to hold him. Though he

1 With the aid of men and money contributed by all Catholic countries.
2 E.g. 1525, iv. "Lutherani etiam omnes de regno extirpentur, et ubique reperti fuerint per ecclesiasticas, verum etiam per saeculares, personas libere capiantur et comburantur."

returned again the following year, and destroyed half of the imperial army, and in spite of the fact that the child Michael Apaffy II. was nominally recognised as Prince of Transylvania, that country was practically reduced, by the end of 1698, to the position of one of the hereditary provinces of Austria. The appearance on the scene of Eugene of Savoy (the importation of capable foreigners was always a necessity for Austria down to the days of Metternich and Beust), led to the final overthrow of the Turks and their expulsion from all parts of Hungary with the exception of the Banate of Temes. Leopold was, however, too much occupied with the task of securing his succession to the throne of Spain to follow up his victory and to carry out ambitious plans in the Balkan peninsula. Peace was therefore made at Karlo- 1699. vicz and signed by Leopold as Emperor only, which showed his opinion of the effect of the laws of 1687, and that he now considered it unnecessary to ask Hungary's opinion as to the terms of peace, though the law of 1681 bound him to do so. The Palatine, Eszterházy, made no attempt to render effective such rights as were left to Hungary, and for the rest of his reign Leopold did not think it necessary to go through the form of convening the Diet. Every department of State was germanised. The parts beyond the Dráva recently occupied by the Turks were not rejoined to Hungary, and Croatia and Slavonia were governed directly from Vienna. Kollonics was all-powerful, and under him Hungary was reduced to a position similar to that which it occupied during the Bach *régime* of a later period. The counties nominally retained their independent organisation, but in reality were mere tax-collecting agencies. Kollonics was not yet satisfied, and suggested to Leopold the advisability of introducing foreign settlers, especially Austrians, " in order that the kingdom, or at least a large part of it, may be gradually germanised, and that the Magyar blood, accustomed to revolutions and disturbances, may be diluted by the admixture of a German element."[1] His whole policy was, in fact, directed to this one end : to the ejection of the Magyars from Hungary. In pursuance of this scheme new German communes were established in many parts of the country. Buda received an almost entirely German population, as did Esztergom, Várad, Eger, Fejérvár, in fact, all the chief towns recovered from the Turks ; and the Saxons of Transylvania had such privileges conferred on them as their Magyar co-religionaries could never hope to receive.

To this period belongs the introduction of the Servians, 70,000 to 80,000 of whom under their patriarch Arsenius Csernovics took refuge in Hungary. Already in 1495 Servians who had fled from the Turks enjoyed certain privileges,[2] such as exemption from the payment of tithes ; but hitherto their religion,[3] like that of the Jews, had been tolerated but not recognised. Circumstances had now changed, and Leopold "in order that on the very threshold of our kingdom they may appreciate 1691. the mildness and benignity of our rule and government," secures them in the free exercise of their religion ; allows them to choose their own archbishop, and to build churches and monasteries wherever they please. Further, the patent confirms their exemption from the payment of tithes, and subjects them to no control but that of their own elected magistrates.[4] This then is the origin of that considerable factor in modern politics—the Servian population of Hungary, established by Leopold with the deliberate intention of introducing a permanent foreign

[1] "Einrichtungswerk des Königreichs Ungarn," cited in *A Mag. Nem. Tört.* vii. 512.

[2] Law of 1495, 45. They, originally, did not intend to take up their residence permanently in Hungary.

[3] Greek Church.

[4] The patent is given at length in Marczali's *Enchiridion Fontium*, p. 597 *sqq.*

element hostile to the idea of Magyar nationality.[1]   "He builded better than he knew."   To make room for them Magyars were unceremoniously kicked out of their holdings—the intention being to get the land out of Hungarian hands, and so to destroy the influence of the land-owning "gentry," the backbone of county organisation.   To give a semblance of legality to the evictions, the so-called Neo-acquistica Commissio was appointed, for the purpose of investigating all titles to land in the re-captured districts, and all landowners were called upon to justify their occupation within six months.   Naturally, after the country had been occupied by the Turks for the better part of two centuries, and had been for years the battlefield of Moslem, German, and Magyar, the production of documentary evidence of title was difficult, if not impossible ;[2] hence, many hundred square miles of land fell into the hands of the Austrian Government and were promptly sold to Germans and other foreigners. Prince Eugene, Caprara, and others who had deserved well of Leopold, were not forgotten, and the grant of enormous estates recompensed them at Hungary's expense for their services to the autocracy.

The reconquered districts offered a fine field for re-ligious intolerance, being for the most part occupied by Protestants whose religion the Turks had looked upon as contemptible rather than blameworthy.   The Government's first step was the issue of an order that, henceforth, none but Catholics should be eligible for office in the counties ; but as this to some extent failed to effect the desired results, owing to the numerical insufficiency of Catholic candidates, recourse was had to the old and tried expedient of driving out the clergy and confiscating their churches and schools.   The next move in the campaign was directed against intellectual freedom, and a rigorous

[1] See Baloghy Ernő, *A Magyar Kultura és a Nemzetiségek*, Budapest, 1908, p. 139 *sqq.*   [2] Michael Horváth, *o.c.* iv. 261.

censorship was established under the control of a Jesuit, authorised to suppress any book he might consider pernicious, and to destroy the press that had printed it. Foreign Governments protested against the new crusade, not only on humanitarian grounds, but also for the reason that such proceedings must eventually lead to a fresh revolt. The Viennese Government was ready with a satisfactory explanation. It replied that not 5 per cent of the population of the reconquered districts belonged to the Reformed Church, and that exceptional treatment could not be expected for a numerically trifling body of dissenters. It was not the fault of Kollonics and of his policy of extermination that the statement as to the relative numbers of Protestants and Catholics was a lie.

Taxation was now to give the finishing touch to the ruin which other forms of persecution had been unable to complete to the satisfaction of the camarilla. In the seven years from 1683 to 1690 Hungary was made to pay 30,000,000 florins in taxes, or more than it had paid in a whole century to the Turks. In 1699 the whole of Austria and Hungary paid 10,800,000 florins, of which the latter had to pay 4,500,000, while the hereditary provinces, which were much richer, and had been left comparatively uninjured by late wars, escaped with the payment of little more than 6,000,000. The basis of taxation was fixed without convening the Diet and without consulting any Hungarian as to the taxable capacity of his country.[1] Further, it being the deliberate policy of the War Council

[1] In 1684 an attempt was made to impose a tax of 5,000,000 florins on Hungary in addition to its own expenses for home defence, while Lower Austria, which had never been ravaged to anything like the same extent, was exempted for two years from the quartering of troops. In 1685, though worn and exhausted by the war, Hungary was made to bear 70 per cent of the cost of maintaining the army—Austria 30 per cent. In 1686 Hungary bore 51¼ per cent, and in addition had to feed and find forage for the troops which, as they could not get their pay from Vienna, took it out of Hungary.—Horváth, *A Közös Ügyek*, p. 38 *sqq.*; Acsády in *A Magyar Nemzet Története*, vii. 522; Michael Horváth, *o.c.* iv. 248.

in Vienna to quarter as many troops as possible outside Austria in order to save the hereditary provinces the expense of their maintenance, Hungary had to find quarters, rations, and fodder for 12,000 horses and for 44,000 men, who were chiefly occupied in the collection of taxes, and were not particular as to what kind of torture they employed in order to compel payment. In 1702 recourse was had to a new method of oppression, and the pressgang was introduced with instructions to collect 20,000 men for use in the war with France from among peasants " having no visible means of subsistence "— in other words, from among those whom Austrian tyranny had reduced to the verge of starvation.[1]

In Transylvania the position of affairs was no better than in Hungary proper, in spite of the Diploma Leopoldinum[2] of 1690 (granted at a time when Thököly, and the fear of foreign interference, forced the hands of the Vienna Government), which guaranteed the religious liberties of the recognised sects, fixed the maximum of taxation, and provided for the convocation of the Diet at fixed intervals, and for the exclusive employment of Transylvanian officials in the management of Transylvanian affairs. Young Apaffy was driven to resign his title of 1701. Prince of Transylvania, and to retire abroad in order that there might be no obstacle to the process of compulsory germanisation which Kollonics proceeded to inaugurate with a complete disregard of the recent Diploma. The taxes were increased far beyond the legal maximum, and the German collectors repeated the brutalities which had made them an object of detestation in the rest of Hungary. Many of the inhabitants fled to escape torture ; others took their daughters to the Turks and sold them in order to obtain the money necessary to satisfy the extortions of Vienna. In Transylvania as well as elsewhere the *régime*

[1] Beöthy, o.c. i. 518 ; A Mag. Nem. Tört. vii. 526.
[2] In Marczali's Enchiridion Fontium, p. 577 :77.

of Kollonics had brought about such a state of affairs that an eruption of the volcano was bound to ensue. That it did not come earlier was due to the denationalisation of the majority of the great nobles—the natural leaders of the people, who from motives of self-interest remained blind to the sufferings of their compatriots, and thought only of currying favour with the Court of Vienna. The results of absenteeism soon became apparent. The peasants who had hitherto respected, even if they disliked, their landlords, lost all touch with them, and a Jacquerie on a large scale, winked at by the camarilla, whose policy it suited that the landowners should be exterminated, was the natural result. The homeless and the persecuted, the victims of Vienna and of the Society of Jesus, took to the highway for their livelihood, and the bands of robbers who infested the country assumed such proportions that an organised campaign had to be undertaken for their suppression. These forces of discontent were ready to the hand of any leader who could impress their imagination sufficiently to induce them to drop fighting for revenge or profit and to start a war of liberation.[1] The leader was found in the person of Francis Rákóczy, grandson of a former Prince of Transylvania, and of Count Zrinyi, one of the three Counts who had been executed in 1671 in spite of the promised 1703. amnesty. The opportunity was afforded by the outbreak of the war of the Spanish Succession.

Rákóczy had been confided in his childhood to the care of the Jesuits with a view to distracting his mind from earthly ambitions ; but the priesthood possessed no attractions for him, and he obtained leave to travel. Unjustly suspected of complicity in the insurrection of the peasants in Transylvania and thrown into prison, he proceeded, on his escape, to justify Vienna's suspicions of

[1] According to Beöthy the last straw was the introduction of the press-gang already referred to.—o.c. p. 518.

his reliability. At the start he had but 50 horse and 200 foot, but his name was sufficient to cause peasants and refugees to flock to his camp, and by the end of the year he had 70,000 men and a miscellaneous collection of arms. At first a strong feeling of hostility existed between the peasants and the nobles.[1] In its early stages the rising was distinctly one of the lower orders ; but as the movement proceeded it lost, to some extent, its class character, and ended by becoming a national insurrection in which noble and peasant, Catholic and Protestant, alike took part. To Rákóczy's army, though badly armed and suffering from a deficiency of officers, Austria, now deeply engaged abroad, could offer but little resistance. Leopold was in his dotage—more worried about the future of his sinful soul than about that of Hungary; and the spring of 1704 saw Hungarian scouts at the gates of Vienna. In a manifesto[2] addressed " to all Christian princes and states," an eloquent vindication of the sacred right of insurrection against tyranny, and an unanswerable indictment of the House of Habsburg, which had sworn times innumerable to maintain the liberties of Hungary, but had deliberately reduced its people to slavery, Rákóczy calls God, His saints and angels, and all the civilised world, to witness that he took up arms, not for purpose of private gain or ambition, but in order to liberate his country from the yoke of a perjured and tyrannical dynasty.[3] England and Holland,

[1] Rákóczy mentions in his memoirs the difficulty of getting peasant and noble to work together harmoniously. He says that nine-tenths of his followers were Calvinists.—Szalay, *Mag. Tört.* vi. 149. *Mémoires du Prince François Rákóczy*, in vol. ii. of *Histoire des Révolutions de Hongrie.* The Hague, 1739. *Principis Rákóczii Confessiones.* Ed. of Hungarian Academy of Sciences, 1876.

[2] Dated June 7th, 1703, but Szalay has shown, *Mag. Tört.* vi. 140, *n.*, that it was not issued till the next year. For the text of the manifesto see Marczali's *Enchiridion Fontium*, p. 601 : " Ad perpetuam rei memoriam.. Recrudescunt inclytae gentis Hungarae vulnera," etc.

[3] Rákóczy has been accused of ambition, and of playing for his own hand, but it is improbable that ambitious motives would have led him to begin such

which recognised the importance of the movement, saw with concern the enforced division of Austria's forces required on western battlefields, and Stepney, the British envoy at Vienna, was instructed to urge the King to make terms with the insurgents.[1]   The camarilla, however, was obstinate, and the news of Heister's success against Rákóczy, and of Prince Eugene's and Marlborough's victory over the French and Bavarians at Hochstädt, made it less inclined towards a compromise than ever. 1705. The following year, in spite of a severe defeat at the hands of Heister at Nagy-Szombat, the insurgents devastated the hereditary provinces, and this fact, and the death of Leopold, who, desirous of making his peace in time with the Almighty by coming to terms with those whom he had so deeply wronged, urged his successor to settle with Rákóczy[2] on the basis of the recognition of Hungary's historic rights, led to the inception of negotiations.

On succeeding to the throne Joseph issued a manifesto disclaiming responsibility for past errors,[3] and announcing his intention of ruling in accordance with the terms of his coronation oath, and of doing all that was in his power to do to remedy the existing discontent.   Popular opinion attributed to him an abstract fondness for justice and a desire for reform to which he could not in reality lay claim.   He soon became bored with the business of state, and dropped the Jesuits and the Ministers for the more congenial society of ladies who possessed the physical attractions in which his German wife was deficient.   So the Government, left to its own devices, required little

an unequal contest with such inadequate forces. He was no soldier of fortune, but the owner of 2,000,000 acres, and a Prince of the Holy Roman Empire, whose wife and child were in the hands of the Habsburgs.—Beöthy, o.c. p. 524.

[1] Szalay, Mag. Tört. vi. 147. See Stepney's letter to Rákóczy, Histoire des Révolutions, etc., i. 241 sqq.

[2] Hist. des Révolutions de Hongrie, ii. 330.

[3] According to Beöthy, o.c. p. 535, he had negotiated with Rákóczy behind his father's back.

encouragement from Prince Eugene, the chief partisan
of the fire and sword method, to induce it to abandon
negotiation and to resume the fight. It soon became
evident that Rákóczy with his irregulars [1] could not long
continue the unequal contest with the trained soldiers of
Vienna which the hope of European intervention alone
induced him to maintain. The futility of his expectations
was proved before long by the offer of Peter the Great to
put the Russian army at Joseph's disposal, and by the
fact becoming evident that Louis XIV. cared for the
cause of Hungary only so far as it served to create a
diversion in Austria's rear,[2] and that no effective support
could be expected from him. Rákóczy, therefore, opened
negotiations on the basis of the restoration of the constitutional liberties of the country, and of the recognition of
the newly-acquired hereditary rights of the Habsburgs.
But his offer of peace met with no response, and but for
the efforts of Sunderland, sent by England to Vienna with
instructions to insist on a reconciliation, the fight would
have gone on to the bitter end. The pressure exercised
by England and Holland was so far successful that Joseph 1706.
notified the Powers of his willingness to recognise the
constitutional rights of Hungary;[3] but he changed his
mind when the news came of Prince Eugene's victory
over the French at Turin, which left Austria's hands free
to deal with the insurgents.

Rákóczy's last move was the convocation of a meeting
of nobles at Ónod, who solemnly passed a resolution,[4] in

---

[1] He had twenty-five French officers with him, excellent so far as technical
matters were concerned, such as artillery and fortification, but they wanted to
turn Magyar irregulars into troops of the line, and make them adopt a
manner of fighting which was foreign to their habits and nature.—Beöthy,
o.c. p. 556.

[2] He for a time subsidised the insurgents to the extent of 50,000 livres per
mensem.—Fiedler, *Aktenstücke zur Geschichte, F. Rákóczy*, p. 195. Vienna,
1855.

[3] Credentials of the Dutch envoy cited by Szalay, *Mag. Tört.* vi. 313, *n.*

[4] *Enchiridion Fontium*, p. 613 *sqq.* When reproached for issuing his

their own name and in that of their descendants, to the effect that they renounced for ever all allegiance to the perjured Habsburgs. But this was only a paper thunder-bolt, and as a kind of counterblast thereto, and in order to give proof in the eyes of Europe of his tolerant spirit and of his devotion to the Constitution, Joseph was induced to summon a meeting of the Diet at Pressburg. His refusal, however, to make any concession in the direction of religious liberty, and the appearance of the plague and of the insurgents, dissolved the Diet before any result had been attained. In the meanwhile Heister had inaugurated a fresh campaign, which began with a notice to all wives and children of the insurgents to leave their homes within 1708. fourteen days, and ended with the battle of Trencsén—the final blow, as it turned out, to the hopes of Rákóczy, though he made superhuman efforts to raise a new army. Again England interfered and sent Lord Peterborough to Vienna to insist on peace being made ; and 1711 saw the end of the long struggle, Joseph having removed all remaining obstacles to peace by dying in the early part of the year.

Rákóczy, who had retired to Poland in order to negotiate with the Tsar with a view to inducing him to intervene on behalf of the insurgents,[1] made a last attempt to prevent the success of the negotiations, which Alexander Károlyi had carried on during his absence, by making an appeal to Hungary to hold out to the last, and protesting against a peace which would "lead to the everlasting slavery and entombment of the once glorious Magyar race." But all were longing for rest, and the insurgent nobles of

manifesto on the ground that it was likely to bring about reprisals, Rákóczy replied that if the people won, the manifesto could do no harm ; and that if they lost, declaration of independence or no, the Habsburgs would massacre them.—Beöthy, *o.c.* p. 486. According to Michael Horváth, *o.c.* iv. 415, Louis XIV. insisted on a renunciation of allegiance to the Habsburgs as a condition precedent to the giving of further assistance.

[1] Fiedler, *Aktenstücke*, p. 197.

Hungary and Transylvania, convened by Károlyi in the church of Szatmár, accepted the terms which he had negotiated on their behalf. Rákóczy was to be allowed to keep his estates and live where he pleased, in Hungary or Poland, provided he took the oath of allegiance to the King within three weeks. A general amnesty was to be proclaimed; widows and orphans of insurgents were to receive back the property of their husbands or fathers, and foreign soldiers, who had taken part in the rising, were to return unmolested to their own countries. Provision was made for the revival of the old guarantees of religious freedom, and the King was to promise " to maintain and hold sacred and inviolate the rights, liberties, and immunities of the kingdom of Hungary and Transylvania." [1] Though the results of the struggle were not so great as those secured by Bocskay and by the Peace of Vienna, in any case they justify Acsády's statement, that they realised the most important point in the national programme. Hungary was Hungary still. Rákóczy, still irreconcilable, retired to Paris, and thence to Turkey, where he ended his days. But his country never forgot him, and popular pressure recently induced the present head of the House of Habsburg to give a tardy consent to the return of his harmless bones to his native land.

[1] Clause ix.

CHAPTER V

1711. THE violent phase of the anti-reformation campaign ended with the Peace of Szatmár. The bankruptcy of the Caraffa-Kollonics system was evident. If Thököly and Rákóczy failed to compel a complete restoration of Hungary's rights, they had, at any rate, given convincing proof of the fact that violence and oppression could never reduce the country to a position of permanent subordination to the hereditary provinces. It seemed as if Charles, the new King, had been long enough absent from Austria to be unaffected by the influence of the Viennese camarilla with its fixed idea as to the necessity of extirpating Protestantism by violent means as the first step towards the compulsory germanisation and absorption of Hungary. "I will strive with the whole force of my soul, in order that my beloved Hungary, which has been tossed and disturbed by so many storms and troubles, may enjoy certain peace, and may be comforted after the heavy blows it has suffered." This, Charles's first manifesto, showed that the lesson of successive insurrections had not been entirely lost, and that there was no intention, for the moment at all events, of attempting a recurrence to the policy of intimidation. But much more than smooth words was necessary to restore to Hungary even a semblance of its former position. The districts recaptured from the Turks required to be reincorporated in the kingdom, and freed from the control of the military and financial authorities of Vienna. The

reduction of taxation was an absolute necessity, and something definite required to be done for the improvement
of the material condition of the people, which could never
thrive while German soldiers, ill-paid or unpaid, lived on
the country. Further, the inalienable right of the Diet
to decide all questions of taxation must obtain fresh and
unequivocal recognition. The aspirations of the nobles
soared no higher than this. They had no idea of the
necessity of far-reaching reform, of abandoning the exclusive privileges of the nobility, and of establishing the
State on a broader basis. The great nobles had, to a
considerable extent, been tarred with the Viennese brush,
and were out of touch with the great mass of the people ;
but the "gentry" who attended the meetings of the Diet
were really representative of popular opinion, and that
opinion was overwhelmingly conservative, and, before all,
hostile to the introduction of any kind of innovation
which might bring with it the infringement of the nobles'
privilege of immunity from taxation. The Diploma
Inaugurale,[1] the first to be signed since the monarchy had
lost its elective character, and therefore regarded as exceptionally important, gave satisfactory guarantees ; but
as, hitherto, every Habsburg had systematically violated
his oath, too much importance could easily be attached,
in forecasting probabilities, to the paper promises of the
new King. Like his predecessors, Charles undertook,
"firmly and sacredly," to preserve and maintain, and to
see that all others of whatever rank or position did the
same, "all the liberties, immunities, privileges, statutes,
common rights, laws, and customs," conceded and confirmed by previous kings ; and more especially the Golden
Bull, with the exception of the clause permitting armed
resistance ; to keep the Sacred Crown in Hungary, and to
reincorporate all the districts recovered from the Turks.

---

[1] Incorporated together with the coronation oath in Law i. of 1715.—
Marczali, *Enchiridion Fontium*, p. 687 *sqq.*

The crown now being hereditary, the King bound all possible successors to swear before coronation to observe the terms of this diploma, and guaranteed the revival of the ancient elective character of the monarchy in the event of his leaving no male heir—a matter of great importance to Hungary, in view of the fact that at the moment Charles had no son, and seemed unlikely to have any. Further, the law of 1715, in which the diploma and the coronation oath are incorporated, formally reaffirmed Hungary's right to be governed solely in accordance with its own existing laws and those which might thereafter be passed by the Diet. The maintenance of historic rights and constitutional liberties seemed, therefore, to be sufficiently guaranteed, though in reality, as subsequent events proved, Charles had no more intention than any of his predecessors of allowing inconvenient promises to interfere with the introduction of innovations or with the establishment of dynastic continuity.

The King's experience in Spain had taught him that war was no longer what it used to be; that it had become more scientific, and required a better organisation than that provided by the Banderia of the nobles or the *levée en masse* in time of necessity. He therefore induced the 1715. Diet to consent to the establishment of a standing army,[1] and to vote the taxes necessary for its maintenance.[2] This new institution was, naturally, unpopular with the taxpayers, who not only had to find the money for the soldiers' pay, but—a still greater burden to an agricultural population which had by no means recovered from the

[1] 1715, Art. 8, "regulata militia tum ex nativis tum externis constans."
[2] Though the principle of a standing army was adopted, Hungary did not bind itself to find either a fixed number of men or a fixed sum of money for their maintenance. Both were to be fixed from time to time as occasion required. The nobles, in consenting to the innovation, were apparently influenced by the consideration that the establishment of a permanent native force would relieve the country from the extortions and brutalities of the German mercenaries.

effects of the late wars and disturbances—was obliged
to provide quarters, rations, and forage for 15,000 men,
who, if they did not get what they wanted by asking, took it by force. So the new army was no more
loved than the imperial troops, which were still quartered
on the country, not for fear of a Turkish invasion, the
alleged reason, but in order to prevent the possibility of
a fresh Hungarian rising—now as ever the bugbear of
the Viennese bureaucracy. The nobles as well as the
peasants soon discovered that they had cause for complaint. Though in one respect the authority of the Diet
was undisputed, for neither men nor money could be
raised unless voted "*diaetaliter*," they found that the
control of the force which they had brought into existence was vested in the Austrian Council of War, and
that reiterated demands for the establishment of a Hungarian War Office to deal with the new Hungarian troops
were persistently disregarded. Apart from the risk involved in the institution of a permanent army controlled
by the Viennese bureaucracy, the nobles had another
reason for feeling nervous as to the outcome of the new
experiment. Their immunity from taxation had hitherto
been justified by the obligation to perform military service,
and though the law of 1715 expressly maintained the right
of the King to call upon all classes to serve in case of
necessity, the establishment of a standing army practically
nullified the obligation and destroyed the justification for
exemption.

As regards religious questions, the position of affairs
was far from being satisfactory to the Protestants.
Charles's long stay in Spain had saturated him with the
spirit of dogmatic intolerance, and his whole reign consisted
of a series of acts of injustice and partiality though not of
open persecution. His idea was to root out heresy without
scandal to Europe, and he considered that the object in
view could best be attained by subjecting the Protestants

to petty annoyances, by refusing to allow churches to be built in certain districts, and by restricting the rights of citizenship and membership of trading guilds to Catholics. Scandal was not entirely avoided, and Frederick William of Prussia, actuated either by charitable motives or by the idea that Hungary might produce some useful recruits for his corps of grenadiers, instructed his Ambassador in Vienna [1] to do what ne could to help the Protestants, and to promise an asylum in Prussia for such as cared for the *flebile migrandi beneficium*. Possibly Prussian mediation had some effect, but it is probable that the desire to obtain Protestant support in the matter of the succession to the throne was the real cause of the adoption of milder methods, and of the issue of an order forbidding the sequestration of churches, the ejection, on religious grounds, of Protestant tenants by Catholic landlords,[2] and the separation of parties to mixed marriages (1722-23). Catholic annoyance at these concessions found its expression in the application of a sort of tyrannical Test Act. It was decided to exclude Protestants from the exercise of legislative functions and from the holding of all offices by insistence on the taking of an oath containing a reference to the Virgin and saints, refusal to take which rendered the recalcitrant liable to fine and imprisonment. Passions became so inflamed, and the relations between Catholics and Protestants were strained to such a degree, that Charles finally had to interfere and annul the sentences passed on the non-jurors. Section 30 of the law of 1715 declared that the King confirmed the laws of 1681 and 1687 (which, as has been seen, nominally put the two religions on a footing of equality) "for the present"; Calvinists

---

[1] See his letter to Canngiesser.—*A Magyar Nemzet Története*, vol. viii. p. 124, *n.*

[2] Landlords entertained the opinion that he who paid the piper was entitled to call the tune; that they were justified in compelling their tenants to conform to the religion of their lord, and in refusing to allow churches built on their lands to be used by members of a heterodox sect. "Cujus regio, ejus religio."

and Lutherans were therefore sitting on a volcano which was liable to eruption at any moment. A committee was appointed in 1721 to decide all matters of dispute; but the demands of the Catholic clergy were of such an outrageous nature that the King could not accept them, and was compelled to reserve the decision of debated questions. The result of his deliberations was embodied in the so-called Carolina Resolutio, published ten years later.[1] The Protestants as a body are thereby deprived of their right of appeal to the King in case of illegal oppression; so, while the principle of toleration is nominally maintained by the Resolutio, they are in reality stripped of their only defence against persecution (ci. 9). Apostates, especially those who, having originally been Lutherans or Calvinists, have joined the Catholic Church and have subsequently apostatised, are to be severely punished (*gravi arbitraria poena*) by the civil magistrates (cl. 5). Protestants are obliged to observe the festivals of the Catholic Church and to take part in the usual processions (cl. 8). The oath to the Virgin and saints is to be taken by all judges, advocates, and officials, but witnesses are to be allowed to take the ordinary oath to the Father, Son, and Holy Ghost, " in order that the course of justice may not be delayed " (cl. 9). Mixed marriages may be celebrated only by Catholic priests (cl. 7), who of course threw every possible obstacle in the way of their celebration, and exacted a promise that all children resulting from the marriage should be brought up in the Catholic religion. The rights of the landlords to interfere in the religious affairs of their peasants are maintained, but in case of any alteration in the established practice approval of their actions must be obtained from the King as Defender of the Faith (cl. 4). The result of the edict in question was that the peasant had no legal protection in the exercise of his religion, and that his right to pray, to marry,

[1] 1731, Marczali, *Enchiridion Fontium*, p. 706 *sqq.*

to christen his children, and be buried, according to the rites of his own Church, was made absolutely dependent on the arbitrary discretion of landlord and King, *i.e.* on the discretion of the landlord if he was a Catholic. Thus it is clear that the sole object of that which was euphemistically described as a " benign " concession to Lutherans and Calvinists, was the maintenance of the outward forms of legality and the extirpation of Protestantism by indirect means and petty persecution.[1]

It was evident from the first that Charles had little or no intention of keeping his promises and of respecting the constitutional rights of Hungary. It might be supposed that a full and frank observance of the terms of the Diploma and of the coronation oath would deprive the King of all influence on governmental matters, and of all rights save that of veto ; but in reality this was far from being the case. In the first place, article vii. of the law of 1715 made the King himself judge in all cases of *lèse majesté* and treason, and persons accused of those offences could be imprisoned before trial, and so deprived of the protection enjoyed for the last five hundred years in virtue of clause 2 of the Golden Bull and of clause 4 of the Act of 1231—the excuse for the innovation being the alleged necessity of avoiding " the most dangerous consequences arising from the formality of citation " before a Court of first instance. In the second place, apart from his position as head of the Church, which involved the right of appointment to all ecclesiastical offices and the complete control of all ecclesiastical educational establishments, the

---

[1] *A Magyar Nemzet Története*, vol. viii. p. 147, gives several instances of the way in which Protestants were dealt with : *e.g.* a drunken Protestant cut off the nose of a crucified Christ which a boy was carving. Condemned to death. Sentence commuted by the King to three years' hard labour. A Lutheran peasant was visited on his death-bed by a Catholic priest. The dying man by accident or design let the sacred wafer fall from his mouth. After death his body was dug up and burnt, and the ashes were scattered. His wife and daughter were obliged to swear that they had not induced the committal of the offence, and *then* were fined fifty florins. Sentence confirmed by the King.

King appointed every official of state (with the exception of the Palatine and the guardians of the Sacred Crown) down to the humblest clerk—a privilege which gave him immense influence, more especially on the Upper House, the members of which were to a large extent holders of official positions, and on fortune, place, and title hunters, who naturally had their eye on the King, the sole fountain of honour and distributor of emoluments. Moreover, the frequency and duration of the sittings of the Diet depended almost entirely on the royal will, as well as, to a large extent, the choice of subjects for discussion. Further, the employment of the proceeds of taxation and of other sources of revenue was a matter solely for the determination of the King, who also decided all questions relating to the imposition of import and export duties, and to the raising of loans, without reference to the Diet. Every Hungarian matter, even the resolutions of the Diet, had to run the gauntlet of the Viennese bureaucracy before they reached the King. The want of independence, in spite of oft-repeated guarantees, was especially noticeable in military and money matters. The Financial Board, established in 1715, controlled the entire finances of Hungary as well as of the hereditary provinces; consequently, the supposed financial independence of the Hungarian Treasury, guaranteed though it was by innumerable laws, became more of a myth than ever, as every act of that institution was reported to and controlled by the Viennese Board, of which it thus became a mere subordinate branch-office. Only one Hungarian found a place on the Financial Board, and the "reporter" for Hungarian matters was a German. The Council of War did not contain a single Magyar member. Practically, the Palatine was the only surviving representative of the old *régime*, and even his influence had been greatly reduced in spite of legislation specially directed to its preservation. In military matters the control of the Palatine, who in former times had been the commander-in-chief of the national forces, had entirely disappeared. He was no longer the direct intermediary between the nation and the Crown, his functions, as such, being performed by the Hungarian Chancery sitting in Vienna. His Council was no longer the chief authority in executive matters, and he was reduced to the position of a mere representative of the King in his quality of president of the new Council of Lieutenancy and of the highest Court of Justice. Nicholas Pálffy, who held the office from 1714 to 1731, was an old man and a tool of the Viennese bureaucracy, and when he died no successor was appointed—a direct contravention of the law. The government of the country was carried on by the King through the medium of the Hungarian Chancery, which consisted of the Chancellor, the Vice-Chancellor, and twelve councillors, whose functions comprised the "nullification of everything which might conduce in any way to the curtailment of the royal power and dignity, and, on the other hand, the preservation in their integrity of the royal rights, privileges, and prerogatives, the execution of the King's commands, and the maintenance of the system and laws of the country." Nominally it was its duty to maintain the constitutional rights of Hungary, but in reality it did little more than transmit the royal instructions to the corresponding officials in Pressburg, and submit the resolutions of the Diet for confirmation by the King. As the worldly prospects of the members of the Chancery depended on their ability to keep on good terms with the King and the Viennese authorities, they would have been more than human if they had thought of nothing but the maintenance of the Constitution. True, they were asked their opinion on all matters which concerned Hungary, but it depended entirely on the King's discretion whether effect was given to their advice or not. Though the laws of 1569 and 1715 affirmed their complete independence of all other

authorities, their position was in reality one of complete
subordination and empty magnificence.

The chief organ of government was the Council of
Lieutenancy established by the law of 1723, articles 97,
101, and 102 of which define the sphere of its activity.
Though it was expressly declared to be independent of all
other governmental departments, and to have the right of
communicating directly with the King without interference
on the part of the Viennese bureaucracy, the fact that its
twenty-three members were appointed and paid by the
King, and not by the country, was not conducive to independence.   The Council had no originating or executive
power ; its duty was to "cause the resolutions of the Diet
to be carried out by those whose business it was to see
to their execution," and to receive the reports and presentments of the county authorities.   Like the Chancery,
it could make recommendations which the King accepted
or disregarded as he chose ; consequently, its actions were
condemned to sterility from the start.   Though it was
divided into five sections dealing respectively with ecclesiastical, educational, military, economic, and general matters, as a large proportion of its members were Catholic
ecclesiastics it is not surprising to hear that "its only
serious business was the oppression of the Protestants."[1]

The position of affairs was no more satisfactory in
Transylvania than in Hungary proper, though the rights
and liberties of that country had been specially confirmed
by the Peace of Szatmár.   The only matter of importance
discussed at the annual meeting of the Diet was the
amount of taxation to be voted ; and practically all power
was vested in the Transylvanian Chancery in Vienna—
like its Hungarian counterpart a mere organ for the trans-
mission of royal orders.   Though the three recognised
religions were nominally on a footing of equality, the
Catholic, being that of Vienna and of the King, naturally

[1] *A Mag. Ncm. Tört.* viii. 73.

got the upper hand. In 1699 the Catholics, in contravention of the Diploma Leopoldinum, obtained an order from Vienna to the effect that of candidates for government appointments at least one must be a Catholic, and that at least half of the members of town councils and trade guilds must also be of that religion. Consequently, Transylvania, which had been the first country in Europe to adopt the principle of religious equality, lost its special characteristic, and the influence of the Romish clergy and of the King gave a religious tinge to all questions, and did much to diminish the spirit of loyalty to the dynasty which had never been conspicuous for its intensity.

In Hungary proper the smooth words used by Charles on his accession had not failed of their effect, and the loyalty shown by the Magyars to an alien dynasty at this and at all subsequent periods can only excite the amazement of those who have some knowledge of the history of Hungary since 1526. The words were not followed by deeds tending to alleviate the existing distress. For centuries the normal condition of the country had been one of war. Four times within a few years the population of Debreczen had been dispersed to all quarters of the kingdom.[1] The country was full of robbers; discipline of all kinds was hopelessly relaxed, and landlords were not only unable to collect their dues, but were exposed to the reprisals of any tenants who considered that they had old scores to pay for religious or other reasons. Peasants left their holdings and migrated to the lands vacated by the Turks in southern Hungary, where the Ten Commandments were temporarily in abeyance and there were no landlords. The want of labour was severely felt in the deserted districts, and the land went out of cultivation. The Treasury soon felt the result of the departure of the taxpayers. In 1715 the Government decided to re-enact the old laws forbidding the migration

[1] *A Mag. Nem. Tört.* viii. 98.

of peasants without the express consent of the landlords ; and in 1718 impressed on the latter the necessity of treating their tenants well and of assisting them financially till a succession of good harvests had put them on their feet again.[1]

Neither materially nor from the point of view of the restoration of its constitutional rights can Hungary be said to have received the promised "comfort." How little Charles intended to be bound by his obligations is best shown by the fact that within a few months of signing the Diploma Inaugurale, which provided for the revival of Hungary's elective right in the event of the extinction of the male line of the Habsburgs, he began to take steps to abolish that right, so far as possible, for ever. In 1703 his father, Leopold, had made a so-called Hausgesetz—Pactum Mutuae Successionis—confirmed by will in 1705, by which it was provided that the testator should be succeeded by Joseph and his sons, whom failing, by Charles and his sons ; and that should the latter have no male issue, the succession should go first to Joseph's daughters and then to those of Charles. From the moment of his succession Charles had no intention of being bound by any such arrangement, and at once began to take steps to secure the succession, in default of male heirs, of his own daughters (should he have any), to the exclusion of Joseph's daughters (Maria Josepha and Maria Amalia), who obviously had superior rights to any which any possible female issue of Charles might claim. In any case it was to the interest of all that the question of the succession should be arranged before the death of Charles with a view to the prevention f internal dissension and foreign interference, and his subjects were not slow to recognise the fact. As early as March 1712 the Croatian

---

[1] The Vienna Government always claimed credit for humanitarian motives for its interference between landlord and tenant, but a study of the cases in which it interposed makes it clear that interference was invariably prompted by motives of financial self-interest.

Diet busied itself with the matter, no doubt on receipt of a hint from Vienna, and with a view to emphasising its loyalty at Hungary's expense, and requested the royal confirmation of a resolution to the effect that Croatia accepted as its ruler whatever person might succeed to the possession of the hereditary provinces of Austria.[1] As is shown by the terms of his reply to the resolution, Charles himself clearly recognised the fact that as Croatia formed part of the dominions of the Sacred Crown of Hungary, the resolution was *ultra vires* and of no possible effect ; but all the same it gave him a useful start, and a lever for use with the other constituent peoples among whom the Magyars were the only important, and doubtful, factors. A certain degree of nervousness is shown by Charles in broaching the subject with Hungary. In July of the same year a meeting of Hungarian nobles was convened to consider the possibility or advisability of submitting the question of female succession to the Diet. The result was, to some extent, encouraging ; but the meeting expressed the opinion that certain conditions must be observed, and concessions made, before the Diet

---

[1] Salamon, *A Magyar Királyi Szék Betöltése*, p. 36 : Croatia at a later date, and its historians (*e.g.* Horn, *o.c.*), refer to this resolution as a proof of its independence of Hungary ; but Croatian representatives to the number of ten were present at the meeting of the Hungarian Diet which accepted the principle of the Pragmatic Sanction on behalf of Hungary and the parts annexed without protest from the Croatian deputies. Further, the Croatian Diet of 1740 refers to the terms of the law passed at Pressburg in 1723 as the governing enactment, and to its own resolution of 1712 only as a proof of ready loyalty ; and Maria Theresa, in her rescript to the said Diet, refers only to the Hungarian law of 1723. Salamon, *o.c.* p. 225. In his reply to the Croatian Diet of 1712 Charles mentions the fact that in the event of his having no son the crown of Hungary "and of the parts annexed" will go to the person whom the Hungarian Diet may elect, *i.e.* that coronation with the Sacred Crown *ipso facto* makes the wearer King of Croatia, etc. (see Csuday, *o.c.* p. 224). Further, the operation of Law i. of 1715, providing for the revival of Hungary's elective rights, is extended to the "*partes adnexae,*" and the Croatian representatives raised no objection, which they obviously would have done if they thought that the resolution of March 1712 had any constitutional significance. See Kónyi Manó, *Deák Ferencz Beszédei*, 2nd edition, Budapest, 1903, ii. 601 *sqq.*

would consent to abandon its elective rights which now seemed likely to revive in the near future. The question of the contribution of the hereditary provinces to the maintenance of the army, kept in Hungary just as much for the defence of Austria as for that of Hungary itself, must first be settled. Hungary's right to a separate and independent government must be recognised. In the event of Charles's successor being a minor, the Palatine must be entrusted with the regency, and not some Austrian Minister. The future Queen must marry a Catholic, and her husband must be crowned in Hungary. Generally, the historic rights of the kingdom must be properly guaranteed and confirmed. Charles was not at all pleased with the bargaining spirit shown by the nobles, and affected to look upon the whole business as a mere matter for private family arrangement, and as giving no occasion for any negotiation with Hungary, though of course he was perfectly well aware that no Hausgesetz had any validity in that kingdom.

On April 19, 1713, the document known as the Pragmatic Sanction[1] was produced at a meeting of the Privy Council in Vienna. It recited the Pactum Mutuae Successionis of September 12, 1703, and provided that in default of male heirs the hereditary provinces, regarded as one and indivisible, should descend in the first instance to Charles's daughter, should he have one, and then, in default of male heirs of such daughter, who would succeed, in accordance with the law of primogeniture, to the daughters of Joseph, and lastly to those of Leopold. This arrangement was accepted without demur by the members of the

---

[1] Kmety, *Magyar Közjog*, p. 172, *n.*, says that the term Pragmatic Sanction was that applied by German princes to documents regulating the succession to their principalities. Hubner, *Reales Staats-Lexicon*, cited by Marczali in *A Magyar Nemzet Története*, vol. viii. p. 198, *n.*, says " Pragmaticae Sanctiones sunt Edicta oder Rescripta generalia von wichtigen Sachen, welche zur Erhaltung der allgemeinen Wohlfahrt so wohl in Polizysachen gehören und von der höchsten Rathscollegiis aufgesetzet werden."

Council, but neither they nor Charles attempted to conceal the fact that, though the hereditary provinces had neither right nor power to object, Hungary was under no obligation whatever to give effect to a mere family compact, more especially in view of the Diploma Inaugurale of 1712, which expressly recognised the revival of the right of election in the event of Charles having no male heir. A considerable amount of discussion therefore followed as to the advisability of convening the Diet, and as to the possibility of inducing it to consent to the abandonment of its elective rights. Eventually, fear of Magyar opposition, and the fact that all hope of male issue had not yet been abandoned, led to a decision to postpone for a time the taking of any decisive step. A son was in fact born in April 1716, but he died the same year, and it was not till September 1718 that the birth of Maria Theresa provided the desired heir. In order to get rid of the superior claims of Joseph's daughters, Charles married Maria Josepha to the Elector of Saxony, who later became King of Poland, and Maria Amalia to the Elector of Bavaria, and made both of them, before betrothal, renounce all claim to the Habsburg succession.

The ground being thus cleared, it was now time to obtain the formal recognition of Maria Theresa as Charles's heir by the various provinces of Austria. Beginning with the line of least resistance, the consent of Upper and Lower Austria was secured without difficulty; and in fact the Tyrol was the only province to show any serious inclination to object. In the case of Hungary no such obsequiousness could be anticipated. The Palatine was commissioned to win over the chief nobles; the Archbishop to square the ecclesiastics; and the Chief Justice to deal with the "gentry," from whom the greatest amount of opposition was expected. The arguments of Charles's agents were supplemented with lavish promises of titles, money, and promotion. The same procedure was adopted in Transylvania, though in reality there was no reason for so doing, as, constitutionally, that country formed an integral part of the domains of the Sacred Crown of Hungary, and possessed no separate elective rights.

The Palatine addressed himself first of all to Francis Szluha, an old insurgent under Rákóczy, and a man of great influence, and asked him what the price of the Diet's consent would be. Szluha returned evasive answers: pointed out the possibility of Charles having a son, the impossibility of forecasting the action of the Diet in view of the number of the unremedied grievances of which it had cause to complain, such as the failure of the King to reincorporate in Hungary the districts recovered from the Turks, the burden of taxation, the neglect of Magyars in the matter of official appointments, and the exclusive employment of Austrians. He drew attention to the fact that the Diet had, in 1687, accepted the hereditary principle as regards the male line on the distinct understanding that Hungary would be better treated, and that its rights would be respected, with the result that it had been worse treated than ever. But in spite of these objections and of the fact that the general opinion of the country showed itself to be distinctly hostile to the proposal, the leading men, both in the Upper and in the Lower House, including the recalcitrant Szluha himself, were so easily won over that there is justification for the belief that in reality there never was any doubt as to Hungary's acceptance of the principle of female succession, and that the only question was what guarantees could be obtained in return for the abandonment of a constitutional right. The Diet met at Pressburg on June 30, and 1722. though the King's summons[1] contained no reference to the question of female succession, no doubt every member

[1] Kovachich, *Supplementum ad Vestigia Comitiorum*, iii. 432.

was aware of the reason for its convocation.   Szluha
opened the discussion with an ingenious speech[1] on the
subject of the necessity of peace and quiet, which could be
guaranteed only by a settlement of the question of the
succession to the throne.   He pointed out that discord
and a separation of Hungary from Austria would only
have the effect of reopening the door to the Turks, and
ended with an appeal to sentiment—to the notorious
loyalty of the Magyars, another proof of which would
win the admiration and applause of the whole world.   The
proposal was accepted almost without discussion, and it is
fair to doubt whether the success of the Viennese Court
should be ascribed entirely to Szluha's oratorical powers.
The distribution of rewards in money and money's worth
which followed gives colour to the supposition that other
agencies were at work besides eloquence and assurances
that the acceptance of the principle of female succession in no sense involved a diminution of Hungary's
independence.[2]

By the laws of 1723, which gave effect to the resolution of the Diet in favour of accepting the principle of
hereditary succession in the female line, the King " first
and before all, and without any previous humble petition
of his faithful States and Orders in that behalf, promises
to maintain all the said States and Orders of his hereditary
Kingdom of Hungary, and of the Parts, Kingdoms, and
Provinces thereto annexed, in all diplomatic[3] and other
rights, liberties, privileges, immunities, customs, prerogatives, and laws hitherto granted, established, and
enacted, and to be enacted "[4] by the present and future

---

[1] Salamon, *A Màgyar Kiràlyi Szék Betöltése*, p. 149 *sqq.*

[2] Szluha was made a baron and received 20,000 florins; Stephen Nagy,
24,000 ; and many others lesser sums.—Beöthy, *o.c.* p. 713.

[3] *I.e.* referred to in the Diploma Inaugurale of 1712.

[4] Recognising the fact that no change is made as regards the immemorial
equality of Diet and King as legislative factors and of the former's powers of
initiative.

Diets (Art. 1). In its turn the Diet "proclaimed by free and unanimous vote" its acceptance (failing male issue) of the principle of female succession to the throne of Hungary and of the Parts, Kingdoms, and Provinces pertaining to the Sacred Crown. The order of succession is to be the same as that established in the hereditary provinces, which are at the same time declared to be inseparable [1] (subsec. 3). Hence it follows that whatever male or female descendant of the specified members of the House of Habsburg becomes entitled, according to the law of primogeniture, to the possession of the hereditary provinces, he or she, necessarily and *ipso facto*, becomes entitled to the Crown of Hungary and of the Parts, Kingdoms, and Provinces inseparably thereto annexed (subsec. 4). Should Charles have no male issue, the succession devolves, first on his daughter and her legitimate Catholic descendants; then on Joseph's daughters and their issue; lastly, on the offspring of Leopold's daughter in accordance with the law of primogeniture, and in conformity with the new Act of Settlement obtaining in the indivisible and inseparable hereditary provinces of Austria, which, together with Hungary and the Parts, Kingdoms, and Provinces thereto annexed, form the hereditary possessions of the House of Habsburg (sections 5, 6. 7). All succeeding kings or queens, as the case may be, are to guarantee and confirm, on the occasion of their coronation, the liberties and prerogatives of Hungary as confirmed by Charles's Diploma Inaugurale and by the laws of 1687 and 1715 (subsecs. 9 and 10), and will maintain the same inviolate (Art. 3, sec. 1). The King not only confirms and promises to maintain inviolate all the rights, liberties, privileges, immunities, prerogatives, laws, and approved customs of Hungary, but will cause

---

[1] *I.e.* the Austrian provinces are not to be partitioned among the members of the House of Habsburg, as had been done in times past, but are to form an indivisible whole just as Hungary and the parts thereto annexed—Transylvania, Croatia, etc.—are an indivisible whole.

the same to be observed by all his subjects of whatever rank or condition (Art. 3, sec. 2). The eleventh section of the second article makes the express reservation that on the extinction of the descendants of Charles, Joseph, and Leopold, "the ancient, approved, and accepted custom and prerogative of the States and Orders in the matter of the election and coronation of their King shall revive."

These laws formed a new contract between Hungary and the House of Habsburg,[1] and were regarded and accepted as such by both parties. They form the basis of their relations down to the present day in spite of the *coups de canif*, not to say the tearing to tatters, to which they have been subjected by successive kings, and of repeated attempts to read into them a meaning which they cannot possibly bear. They in no sense form a contract between Hungary and Austria. They in no sense bring them into closer contact than had hitherto existed. Though the elective nature of the Hungarian monarchy had been recognised by Ferdinand I: and by every one of his successors, Hungary had, as a matter of fact, invariably exercised its right of election in favour of the person entitled by right of heredity, or by virtue of a family compact,[2] to the possession of the hereditary provinces of Austria. Apart from the question of female succession, from the point of view of Hungary's relations with

---

[1] Not, it must be observed, between Hungary and the hereditary provinces (as Tezner declares it to be, *Die Wandlungen der österreichisch-ungarischen Reichsidee*, p. 66 sq.). The laws of 1723 do not differ, as regards their essential character, from any other laws passed by the Diet and sanctioned by the King, and strictly maintain their validity only until abrogated by a similar law similarly sanctioned, "*legibus in futurum diaetaliter constituendis*," as Law iii. of 1715 puts it.

[2] As in the case of Mathias II. Deák points out that, but for the Pragmatic Sanction, when Charles died in 1740, Hungary would probably not have elected Maria Theresa, but would have put an end to the Habsburg connection, as both the French Court and Frederick the Great were anxious to weaken Austria, which could best be done by severing its union with Hungary.— Kónyi, *Deák Ferencz Beszédei*, iii. 41.

Austria, the laws of 1723 amount to no more than to an affirmation of the indivisibility of the hereditary provinces on the one hand, and of the indivisibility of Hungary and its dependencies on the other, and of the indissolubility of the union of Austria and Hungary, which exists for defensive purposes only, and is a necessary consequence of the identity of the monarch of the two countries. Should the identity of the Austrian monarch and the King of Hungary cease, the union between Austria and Hungary *ipso facto* comes to an end, and Hungary is again free to elect its king. Thus, the union between the two countries is a purely personal one, depending on the existence of an individual qualified to combine in his person two distinct characters, and in no sense amounts to unification. On the contrary, Hungary's distinctive and independent position *vis à vis* Austria, and its historic rights, privileges, and laws, receive fresh and express recognition and confirmation. That is the *quid pro quo*. The recognition of its complete independence is the consideration for the, possibly temporary, abandonment, or rather suspension, of its constitutional elective right so long as legitimate Catholic issue of certain specified persons shall exist. If any contract has any definite meaning the import of this particular compact is clear, namely, that the full and frank observance by members of the House of Habsburg of their obligation to observe and respect the laws and Constitution of Hungary in all their details is a condition precedent to their right to the Sacred Crown. Their obligation is not merely moral, it is contractual. If it were otherwise the Diet would merely have passed a law accepting the principle of hereditary female succession without reference to the Diploma Inaugurale and the laws of 1687 and 1715 in particular, and all other the kingdom's rights, laws, and prerogatives in general.[1] No

---

[1] The consequences of combining the main point of the Pragmatic

O

new rights and privileges were conferred on Hungary by the Pragmatic Sanction, or by the laws of 1723. The latter, the only enactments connected with the question of the succession of which Hungary has official cognisance, the details of which, in fact, differ from those of the .Pragmatic Sanction,[1] are, apart from the above-mentioned question and that of the duality of the monarchy, or the personal union of the two countries involving the obligation of mutual defence,[2] merely a reaffirmation of rights,

Sanction in the same law with a reaffirmation of Hungary's independence was pointed out to the King by a member of the Council before he confirmed the law ("Reflexiones in Articulis," quoted by *A Mag. Nemzet Tört.*, viii. p. 222). Springer, however, does not hesitate to say that since 1526 Hungary was "a province of the Habsburgs just like every other crown-land."— *Grundlagen und Entwicklungsziele der österreichisch-ungarischen Monarchie*, Vienna, 1906, pp. 8, 18, 19. Tezner states that the reaffirmation of constitutional rights which Hungary was careful to obtain, applied only to the nobles' immunity from taxation (*Der österreichische Kaisertitel*, etc., Vienna, 1899, pp. 36 and 45, *n*.). He says the same of Law x. of 1790-91, *o.c.* p. 36, the heading of which " De independentia Regni Hungariae partiumque eidem annexarum " would alone almost prove the erroneousness of his view apart from the phraseology of the law itself : "Hungaria est regnum liberum et relate ad totam regiminis formam . . . independens."—See *infra*, p. 232.

[1] It is noticeable that the law of 1723 does not mention the Pragmatic Sanction in order to avoid any appearance of dependence on Austria or recognition of the validity, as regards Hungary, of a document which, in fact, affected the Austrian provinces only. The Law of 1715, iii., which says "nec status et Ordines Regni eadem Sacra Regia majestas secus regi aut dirigi vult quam observatis propriis ipsius Regni Hungariae hactenus factis vel in futurum Diaetaliter constituendis legibus," being subsequent in date to the Pragmatic Sanction, is complete proof that the law of 1723 was entirely independent of the Pragmatic Sanction, which differs from it, in the first place, owing to the fact that its promulgation was an act of an uncontrolled autocrat, while the law of 1723 was the act of the elected representatives of a nation confirmed by a constitutional king. Secondly, the Pragmatic Sanction gives the right of succession to all female members of the House of Habsburg, "alle abstammenden Erben des Geschlechts," while the law of 1723 confines the right to the descendants of three specified persons. This fact alone suffices to disprove Lustkandl's statement that the law of 1723 was a mere registration by the Diet of the terms of the Pragmatic Sanction (*Das ungarisch-österreichische Staatsrecht*, 1863, p. 226 *sqq.*). Further, there is the fact that while Hungary's right of election revives in a certain event no such right is reserved to the hereditary provinces.—See Deák's, *Adalék a Magyar Közjoghoz*, Pest, 1865, p. 56 *sqq.*

[2] As obviously the King of Hungary must defend the Archduke of

privileges, and customs which had existed for centuries, which every King in turn had sworn to observe and respect, and a declaration of the indivisibility of the realms of the Sacred Crown—Hungary, Transylvania, Croatia, Dalmatia, and Slavonia. The Habsburgs gained by the contract, as now that their hereditary right to the throne of Hungary was acknowledged, their realms for the first time presented to Europe the appearance of a strong, united monarchy—a matter of considerable importance, and a compensation for the loss of prestige involved by the fact that a female Habsburg obviously could not become a Holy Roman Emperor, and that, consequently, only the possession of the crown of Hungary could assure her status *vis à vis* other royal houses.

Austria, and *vice versa*, though the law does not in fact refer to the obligation of defence. No obligation is imposed on Hungary of joining Austria in a war of conquest not necessary for the preservation of the territorial integrity of the realms of the King and Archduke. Charles's proposal bears this out : " Ut adversus omnem externam vim et quosvis etiam motus internos salutare inveniatur statuaturque remedium, eaeque necessariae diaetaliter fiant dispositiones ut per vicinam et amicam cum reliquis Regnis et provinciis nostris haereditariis divinitus nobis et Augustae Domui nostrae subjectis cointelligentiam et unionem publica quies, pax constans et inperturbata, ac in quemvis casum optata Regno tranquillitas in aevum perduratura stabiliatur." No doubt, as Bidermann says (*Geschichte der Österreichischen Gesammt-Staats-Idee*, Innsbruck, 1889, ii. p. 51), Charles's object was the " gezetzliche Begründung einer Vereinigung" but the Diet accepted " das Mittel, liessen aber den eigentlichen Zweck damit unerfüllt." Count Virmont declared Charles's object to be " a fusion of and an indivisible ' Aneinanderhängen' of all provinces and hereditary kingdoms, with the object of *mutual and reciprocal defence*" (*ibid.* p. 56). Certainly " cointelligentia" is not the word which would be chosen to indicate the existence of the *real* union which Lustkandl and his disciples see in the law of 1723. Deák cites the fact that during the minority of the King of Hungary the Palatine is his guardian according to Law ii. 1485, confirmed by i. 1681, v. 1715, and *after* the Pragmatic Sanction by ix. 1749 and v. 1790, whereas in Austria the guardianship devolves on the Emperor's nearest paternal relation (Kónyi, *Deák Ferencz Beszédei*, iii. 41). Further, Austria being a member of the German Empire, and later of the German Confederation, was obliged to take part in a defensive war with the other members, but Hungary not being a member was under no such obligation—an inconceivable position if a real union of Austria and Hungary existed.

Save for the final conversion of the monarchy from an elective to an hereditary one, and for the definitive establishment of the principle of duality, the reign of Charles is memorable only on account of the victory of Prince Eugene at Petervárad, the capture of Temesvár, and the final ejection of the Turks from Hungary, one result of which was the completion of the organisation of the military frontier begun some twenty years earlier. The defence of the frontiers was entrusted to Slav refugees, Servians, Roumanians, and Germans, who in return for military service enjoyed exemption from taxation. They were commanded by Austrian officers who were responsible for their acts only to the King and to his Council in Vienna, and so were entirely withdrawn from Hungarian control, though the land they occupied strictly formed part of Hungary, and should have been reincorporated therein in accordance with the King's solemn undertaking to maintain the territorial integrity of the kingdom.[1] The existence of an organised foreign military force directly dependent on Vienna was naturally regarded as a standing menace to Hungarian independence, more especially as all danger of Turkish invasion, the only excuse for the maintenance of a special military organisation, had finally disappeared.[2]

1740.

Maria Theresa gave the same constitutional guarantees before coronation as her father had given, and throughout her reign of forty years made few direct attacks on the rights and liberties of Hungary. The process of germanisation took a new and more subtle form, and violent anticonstitutionalism was replaced by an attempt to kill the spirit of nationality by kindness. The Queen was

---

[1] The coronation oath, "Fines regni nostri Hungariae et quae ad illud quccumque jure aut titulo pertinent non abalienabimus nec minuemus sed quoad poterimus augebimus et extendemus."

[2] The abolition of the force and the reincorporation of the frontier districts was continually demanded by the Diet henceforward down to 1848, but in vain.

animated by a sincere desire for the welfare of the country, but, at the same time, entertained the ineradicable conviction that that welfare consisted only in assimilation to, or fusion with the hereditary provinces of Austria. She relied to a considerable extent, and with success, on the effect of her personal appearance, and of the idea of having a woman for their King, on the chivalrous and susceptible Magyars. She early recognised the fact that the Hungarians, if properly treated, formed the one solid and reliable support of her throne ; and the readiness with which they responded to her demands for men and money more than answered to her expectations during the hard times of the war of the Austrian Succession, when no one in Europe believed that the monarchy could maintain the form in which Charles had left it, and paper plans for its partition, and speculations as to its future, were as rife as they are to-day. In view of the simultaneous attacks by Prussia, France, Bavaria, and Spain, it certainly looked as if the gloomy prognostications of complete dismemberment would be justified ; and the fact that, after eight years of fighting, Maria Theresa was able to conclude peace with honour, and with no greater loss than that of Silesia and of a few districts in Italy, while, on the other hand, the Pragmatic Sanction obtained complete recognition, was due in a great measure to the freedom with which Hungary spent its blood and treasure in a cause which was, at the most, only partially its own, and on behalf of a dynasty which had no claim whatever on its gratitude. Conscious of its own importance as the chief constituent element of the monarchy, more especially now that the connection with the Holy Roman Empire had temporarily ceased, Hungary was more able and more disposed than hitherto to take a firm stand in defence of its Constitution ; and the enthusiasm evoked by the young Queen on her coronation was insufficient to make the Diet forget its

unremedied grievances, or to omit to insist upon its
undoubted rights. It is a mistake to suppose that the
oft-quoted and lauded words, "*moriamur pro rege nostro
Maria Therezia*,"[1] showed that at the moment of their
utterance, and till then, Hungary was all loyalty and
devotion to its Queen. As a matter of fact, throughout the year which elapsed between her accession and
September 21, 1741, the date on which those words were
uttered, there had been a considerable amount of acrimonious discussion, friction, and bargaining. There was
the natural fear that in the probable event of Francis
of Lorraine, Maria Theresa's husband, obtaining the
imperial crown, Hungary might lose its position as the
most important factor in the monarchy, and again be
looked upon by Vienna as a mere appanage of the House
of Habsburg. It was desired to limit Francis's right of
interference in Hungarian affairs as much as possible, and
in order to emphasise the fact that Maria Theresa was
the only recognised King of Hungary, and that Francis
was only her consort, the Lower House refused to allow
him to be crowned simultaneously with his wife. The
instant the coronation was over the Diet gave bitter
expression to its grievances, and to its hatred of foreign
interference ; so, while giving every credit to the Magyars
for the enthusiastic generosity of their promises, and still
more for the manner in which they redeemed them,[2] we
must not forget that the old insurrectionary spirit was
only dormant—sleeping, moreover, with one eye open.
The fact that it did not wake to active life was due

[1] The phrase really used was, "*vitam et sanguinem pro domina et rege,
corona et patria nostra*," or "*vitam et sanguinem consecramus*."
[2] The *bona fides* of the cry "Vitam et sanguinem" is shown by the fact
that, before the end of the year 1741, Hungary had 80,000 men-in-arms,
exclusive of the frontier garrisons.—Beöthy, *o.c.* p. 724. In 1751 the Diet
increased the military tax, amounting to 2,500,000, by 700,000 florins, and
then was abused by the Queen for its stinginess. Further, during the Seven
Years' War the Counties voluntarily found 52,000 more men.—Csuday, *o.c.*
ii. 250.

chiefly to Maria Theresa's personal charm, and to the tact of Pálffy, the newly-elected Palatine.

In the dangerous position in which the Queen found herself, the Diet had little difficulty in exacting a declaration that both within and without the limits of the kingdom Hungarians should have the exclusive control of Hungarian affairs, and a recognition of the complete independence of the Hungarian Treasury, Chancery, and Council of Lieutenancy, and of the obligation to fill all official posts, whether secular or ecclesiastical, by the appointment of suitable Magyars. The indivisibility of Hungary and Transylvania obtained fresh recognition, and special grievances, such as the prolonged existence of the Neo-acquistica Commissio,[1] and the right claimed by the Crown, and several times exercised, of imposing taxation behind the Diet's back by virtue of the eighth section of the Act of 1715,[2] on the pretence that war was imminent, were remedied by law. In all these questions the Diet must have our entire sympathy, as it did no more than reassert its undoubted rights ; but its action in the matter of taxation served only to prove once more the selfishness of the governing class, which affected to believe that the abolition of its privilege of exemption from taxation would entail the ruin of the country and the extinction of its independence. The nobles forced the Queen to consent to a fresh legal affirmation of their exemption and privileges, as defined by their champion, Verbóczy, two hundred and thirty years ago, and to a declaration that the payment of taxes was a personal obligation of the peasant in occupation of land,

[1] *Supra*, p. 165.

[2] It provided that "in the extraordinary case of an unexpected hostile irruption" not admitting the ordinary method of procedure, the Palatine, Primate, members of the High Court of Justice, and as many barons, prelates, and representatives of the counties and free towns as can be got together, shall be summoned to deliberate and decide as to the amount of the financial contribution to be made by Hungary, if they consider one to be necessary, and not for any other purpose.

and not a charge on the land itself: for if it were the latter, any noble who came to hold land hitherto occupied by a tax-paying peasant would *ipso facto* become liable to, taxation, and the exemption of the nobility would become a thing of the past.

After this exhibition of egotism the Diet had no opportunity of showing its fighting powers for eight years, as the war gave the Queen a tolerable excuse for omitting to convene it; but when it met again in 1751 the old grievances were ventilated anew: the burden of excessive taxation, the oppression, extortions, and general misconduct of the soldiery, and the unfairness of the Austrian customs regulations, framed with the deliberate intention of excluding Hungarian corn and cattle. The Queen would give no promise of doing anything to lighten the burdens which were crushing the country,[1] and the disgust generated by her refusal was intensified by her demand that representation and voting rights should be given to certain new privileged towns, the inhabitants of which, almost exclusively German, would naturally use their votes in the interest of their benefactress, and so would increase the control of the Court on a body which was already far too subject to its influence. The Diet refused its consent to Maria Theresa's demand, also to the request that Hungary should make a fixed contribution to provide for the interest on a proposed State loan of ten million florins—a refusal which found its justification in the fact that Hungary had never received the slightest benefit from any loan raised by Austria for public purposes. The attempted taxation of ecclesiastical property, a side attack on the cherished exemption of the nobles, was also successfully resisted, and the only result of the manœuvre was that it drove the Catholic priests, who had hitherto been on the side of the Court, into the arms of its Protestant opponents,—a

---

[1] Though she admitted in her rescript of February 16, 1754, that the existing tariff system was unfair.

consummation which no amount of legislation on religious questions could have effected. So things went on much as before ; the country had still no idea of the necessity of any real reform ; defence of class-privileges was still the main object of the Diet, whose sessions in 1751 and 1764 were, except for some patchwork, parish-pump legislation, practically barren of results.

That the Diet should have adopted a defensive, almost hostile, attitude is not surprising. Maria Theresa had no notion of the meaning of constitutional government. She openly stated her view that " when a royal rescript is under discussion in the Diet, the States and Orders have not to consider the question of the advisability of what is demanded of them, but only the method in which the royal requirements are to be met." [1]   Her idea, and that of her Minister, Kaunitz, was that everything should be done mechanically, by word of command, according to Prussian pattern ; and not content with the importation of foreign notions, the Queen imported foreign officials to carry them out, though the law bound her to consult none but Hungarian advisers in all matters affecting Hungary.[2] From her point of view two matters imperatively required settlement : the provision of a sufficient army, and, its consequence, the adoption of a proper system of taxation. On neither of these questions could Maria Theresa expect anything but hostility from Hungary.[3]   The first necessity, therefore, was to get rid of Magyar statesmen, who, though personally loyal to the throne, were patriots according to their lights — defenders of the Constitution first and courtiers afterwards, and to

---

[1] Arneth, *Maria Theresa*, quoted by Beöthy, *o.c.* p. 601.

[2] 1741, xi. " Tam intra quam extra regna."

[3] Maria Theresa originated the policy of germanising the army. Only German words of command and Austrian flags were allowed to be used. The spirit of Magyar nationality was to be suppressed or discouraged, and driven into the background as much as possible, and the army subjected in all details to the control of the Vienna Hofkriegsrath.

substitute creatures of the Court, tools of a would-be-autocracy. Count Paul Festetics, who throughout the sittings of the Diet had supported the Queen's policy through thick and thin, was entrusted with the task of elaborating a scheme of reform of the relations of landlord and tenant. Since 1715 the lot of the latter had become harder than ever; for now that the liability of the nobles to military service had ceased in fact, though not in theory, the peasants not only had to provide the recruits for the standing army, but also had to bear the whole burden of the taxation necessary for its maintenance. So between the demands of the landlord and those of the state the country population was in an unenviable position. The more the landlord took the less remained for the Treasury; and this is the sole explanation of Viennese interference in the Hungarian peasant question. Humanitarian motives were entirely absent: the desire for the punctual payment of taxes was ever present; consequently, Vienna has no more claim to our respect than the nobles have who clung with such tenacity to the principle that the poor must be taxed in order that the rich may go free. When, during the session of 1764, Maria Theresa made a demand for increase of taxation, the question of lightening the peasants' burden was raised; but the Diet would not even consider it, and the remarks of a liberal-minded ecclesiastic were drowned in laughter.[1] The result of the Diet's obstinacy was that in 1765 the Queen, on her own initiative, issued an order regulating the relations of landlord and tenant, the main result of which was that the current scale of dues and payments was thenceforth regarded as the maximum to which the landlord was entitled, and that any attempted increase justified the aggrieved party in appealing to the Queen.[2] Thus, the peasant was, for the first time, brought directly in contact

---

[1] Marczali, *Enchiridion Fontium*, p. 797.
[2] See Acsády, *A Magyar Jobbágység Története*, 362 *sqq*.

with the Crown. The peasants were again allowed to migrate, and their obligations were made proportionate to the size of their holdings. In return for every allotment [1] of, roughly, twenty-three to forty acres of arable land according to the district in which it lay, and ten to eleven of pasturage, the peasant was obliged to do fifty-two days' work per annum with a cart or plough, or one hundred and four without one, in addition to a certain amount of wood-cutting, cartage, and beating for game. One-tenth of all produce belonged to the Church, and one-ninth to the landlord, to whom an annual poll tax of one florin was also payable. In the case of a lawsuit between the landlord and tenant the Manorial Court was still the court of first instance, but an appeal lay to the County Court, in which the county lawyer was bound to undertake the peasant's case. These slight improvements of the peasant's position, which still gave him little or no protection from the arbitrary exercise of the landlord's authority, the principle of governmental interference between landlord and tenant, and the legal recognition of an authority superior to that of his lord, convinced the nobles that the country was going to the dogs, and the peasants that complete emancipation was intended. The inability of the peasant to understand any form of liberty which did not entail the immediate abolition of landlordism, and the conviction that the good intentions of the Queen were concealed and thwarted by a malevolent aristocracy, led to a refusal to do forced labour, and to the outbreak of an epidemic of disorder which had to be forcibly suppressed, and incidentally strengthened the position of the nobles *vis à vis* the Queen, who had not the slightest desire to bring about a social revolution. No further legislation was attempted with a view to the improvement of the peasants' lot. The new system was

[1] A *sessio*, or allotment, could be divided into two, four, or eight parts, and the dues and services apportioned.

simply disregarded in many districts, and did not receive general application till ten years had passed.

One great benefit was conferred on Hungary by Maria Theresa.[1] By charter of 1779, Fiume and the surrounding district were incorporated in Hungary; and thus was realised the long-cherished desire of the Magyars to have their own outlet to the sea—a convenience which was rendered all the more necessary by the burden imposed by the unfairness of the Austrian customs regulations and by the excessive dues imposed on Hungarian produce in transit. The result of having its own port was that Hungary again became a wheat-producing and wheat-exporting country, whereas for a long time past its trade had been almost entirely confined to the export of cattle, which had to pay a heavy duty at the Austrian frontier. Corn also was heavily penalised except during war time, when the duty-free export of the wheat required by Austria for its troops was kindly allowed. The loss of Silesia, the chief manufacturing district, made it a matter of vital importance to Austria to foster its remaining industries. The desired object could best be attained by rendering Hungarian and foreign competition impossible by means of tariff barriers, and by compelling Hungary to draw exclusively on the hereditary provinces for all its requirements.[2] The duty on Hungarian manufactures exported to Austria was raised in 1774 from, roughly, eleven to twenty per cent,[3] and a heavy duty was also imposed on all raw products which Austria itself was capable of producing.[4] The export of Hungarian cattle

[1] In addition to the reincorporation of the parts beyond the Máros, the last district to remain in Turkish hands.

[2] Michael Horváth, o.c. v. 240 sqq. The commercial relations of Hungary with Austria and the outside world were under the exclusive control of the Viennese Commerzien-Rath, established in 1746, which numbered no Hungarian among its members. Thirty to sixty per cent duties were imposed on all foreign goods imported into Hungary which Austria was capable of producing.   [3] Mag. Nemzet Tört. vol. viii. p. 321.

[4] The export to foreign countries of Hungarian raw materials which

to Carinthia was prohibited, and, climax of absurdity and undue preference, no Hungarian wine was allowed transit through Austria to foreign countries unless the exporter shipped at the same time an equal quantity of Austrian wine. In order to make the competition of Hungarian cloth factories an impossibility, those in Austria were provided with capital by the State at three per cent interest, and the free importation of skilled foreign workers was allowed. Every branch of Hungarian trade was at a very low ebb by reason, in a great measure, of the obstacles thrown in the way of the export of its surplus products, and owing to the fact that Hungary was surrounded by countries which produced the same kinds of raw material as it provided. Consequently, the complaint of Austria that the Magyars did not bear a proper share of the expense of the monarchy was not well founded, for Hungary's taxable capacity was vastly inferior to that of its neighbour, and was at the same time unduly depressed by the stepmotherly treatment to which Hungarian trade interests were subjected. It was Maria Theresa's opinion [1] that as the richer classes in Hungary enjoyed an immunity from the taxation to which those in Austria were liable, it was only fair that the latter country should be commercially favoured at the expense of the former. The result was that Hungary was treated as if it were a colony which existed only for the purpose of exploitation by the mother-country, and its export trade sank to an almost hopeless level.

By nature as well as by education the Queen was as

Austria required was either prohibited or rendered impossible by the imposition of such high export duties that the producer had no alternative but to sell to Austrian consumers at a price far below that obtainable elsewhere.

[1] Influenced by Adam Kollár's book (1764), attacking the principle of the nobles' immunity and advocating an equitable system of direct taxation for all classes. The outcry against the book was so strong that Maria Theresa had to order its withdrawal from circulation (Michael Horváth, o.c. v. 211). She forgot that owing to the unfair tariff system Hungary indirectly paid a large proportion of the taxation which was nominally paid by Austria.

intolerant in religious matters as any of her predecessors. Though her struggle with Protestant Prussia was not calculated to make her look with a favouring eye either on Lutherans or on Calvinists, the genius of statesmanship with which nature had endowed her occasionally proved stronger than the spirit of religious fanaticism. The difficult circumstances which surrounded her at the beginning of her reign compelled recognition of the magnitude of the risk which acts of intolerance would surely entail. Nevertheless, the inward struggle between the statesman and the fanatic continued uninterruptedly, and it was at all times uncertain which of the contestants would gain the upper hand. At first she expressed her intention of following her father's example, and refused to receive Protestant deputations; but when the French and Bavarian armies were only a few miles distant from Vienna she changed her mind as to the advisability of exhibiting an intolerant spirit, only to change it again so soon as the threatening danger had passed. Thenceforward she openly identified herself with the party of persecution. The question of the oath to the Virgin and saints, as a condition precedent to eligibility for office of any kind, was still as burning as ever, and on Christmas Eve 1742, as a message of peace and goodwill to all men, she issued a rescript announcing her inflexible resolution to maintain the objectionable ordinance. Only when the impossibility of finding a sufficiency of Catholic candidates for office in certain districts became evident did she change her mind, and then only to the extent of admitting Protestant candidature in case of absolute necessity. The minor authorities naturally took their cue from the Court, and the confiscation of schools and churches was almost as common an event in Maria Theresa's reign as in any previous period.[1] Special permission had to be

---

[1] As many as two hundred were confiscated during this reign, *A Mag. Nemzet Tört.* viii. 331.

obtained to build school or church, and the unauthorised inception of the work of construction entailed severe punishment. The Protestant clergy were fined if they failed to notify from the pulpit the approach of Catholic festivals, and licence to work on a saint's day had to be obtained from a Catholic priest. Apostacy from the Romish faith was severely punished : both converter and proselyte were fined and imprisoned if of the better class, and a long term of penal servitude was the penalty imposed on poorer offenders. It was only when the Queen wanted the co-operation of the Protestants for the execution of her plans of reform that some concessions were made. Pope Benedict XV., fearing reprisals on the part of Frederick of Prussia if Maria Theresa's system of persecution was carried too far, advised her to be more tolerant ; but the recognition by his successor, Clement XIV., of her right to the title of Apostolic King was intended, and served, as a direct incitement to oppression. By refusing to allow any form of higher education to be given in Protestant schools she thought to compel the more intelligent to attend the Catholic establishments ; but her manœuvres were attended with little success, except in the case of nobles ambitious of distinction or office, to which apostacy was the easiest and most certain road.

Notwithstanding the above facts, it must be admitted that Maria Theresa was animated by a genuine desire to raise the general level of instruction. Hitherto the education of the people had been almost entirely in the hands of the Jesuits and of the monks, and the Queen's intelligent advisers were not slow to perceive that little could be done until the exclusive control of religious obscurantists was abolished.[1] The suppression of the

[1] The laws of 1715-74 and 1723-70 reserved to the Crown the control of all schools, and the latter indicated the Council of Lieutenancy as the educational authority. It confined its activity to the restriction as far as possible of non-Catholic establishments.—Marczali, *Enchiridion Fontium*, p. 717. The German language was made a compulsory subject in all seminaries, and a

Society of Jesus by Clement XIV. was by no means
1773. approved by Maria Theresa, but it was the best thing
that ever happened for the cause of education in Hungary,
as the property of the Jesuits was utilised for instructional
purposes, and all classes profited without distinction of
creed. The control of all educational establishments
from university to village school was placed in the hands
of the Council of Lieutenancy ; the country was divided
into eight educational departments, and the programme
of every school was arranged according to the language
and level of intelligence of each district. The Ratio
1777. Educationis[1] provided for the establishment of schools
of three grades : National schools for those who intend
to be agriculturists, artisans, or "fathers of families " ;
grammar schools for future National School teachers, and
for those intended for business or for the army ; and
Academies "*severioris literaturae,*" in which " *disciplinae
sublimiores,*" philosophy, jurisprudence, theology, and
medicine "*a viris lectissimis explanantur.*" Further, the
High School of Nagyszombat, formerly in Jesuit hands,
was transferred to Buda and converted into a university—
"*emporium quoddam artium ingenuarum et scientiarum ubi
licebit audire viros celeberrimos.*" The Protestants, who
could not forget the recent persecutions, naturally looked
upon the whole scheme with distrust, and thought they
saw the old wolf under a new disguise ; but their
suspicions were not justified, for the Ratio Educationis constituted a serious attempt to promote the
educational welfare of the whole nation, not only of a
single religious sect, and the subsequent renaissance of
Hungary, and the consequent maintenance of its individuality, was largely due to Maria Theresa's zeal in the
cause of learning.

knowledge of it was essential to all candidates for public, civil, military, or
ecclesiastical employment.
   [1] See Marczali's *Enchiridion Fontium*, 718 *sqq.*

"I am a good Hungarian," wrote the Queen in 1778,
"and my heart is full of gratitude towards that people."
She proved the fact by leaving the Constitution under a
glass case; "it fared like old shields and coats of mail . . .
the ancient panoply was thrown aside to rot in lumber-
rooms or be exhibited as part of an idle pageant."[1] The
office of Palatine was for a long period left unfilled,[2] and
the Diet was summoned only three times in the course of
forty years. But perhaps the severest blow she inflicted
on the cause of Magyar nationality was the encouragement
she offered to the great nobles to settle in Vienna and
to enter the Government service.[3] This, and matrimony
with Austrian ladies, widened the gulf already existing
between the aristocracy and the "gentry." The former
became denationalised, forgot its native language, and
looked with contempt on its own country which supplied
the absentees with the means of living a life of idle
magnificence in Vienna, where they spent the money which
would have been better employed in the country of its
origin. Hungary found some compensation in the fact of
the consequent development of the class of lesser nobles,
of the "gentry," for whom country business provided the
school in which they acquired the experience of public
affairs which a later generation employed to such good
purpose in the Diet and elsewhere for the preservation of
constitutional privileges and of Magyar nationality and
characteristics. Neither the insidious favours of Maria
Theresa nor her religious intolerance succeeded in undermining the patriotism and *esprit de corps* of the Lower
House. However much its members might quarrel
amongst themselves on questions of dogma, as soon as
their constitutional rights, or, it must be added, pocket
interests, were attacked, their solidarity was unbreakable.

[1] Hallam, *Constitutional History*, i. 157.
[2] For fifteen years from 1765.
[3] Michael Horváth, *o.c.* v. 179-94.

Attempts to interfere with their control of taxation were doomed to failure from the first, and attacks on the impregnable rock of county organisation were so evidently useless that they were not even attempted. The younger generation might, perhaps, have been seduced from its allegiance to the national party if a military career had been open to it; but promotion to the higher grades was reserved almost exclusively for Germans, and the fact that a knowledge of the German language was essential for admission to the commissioned ranks, deprived the Queen of the services of many Magyars in whom the hatred of that tongue was ineradicable. Such national literature as there was was in Latin; but dog-Latin was an inefficient medium for the conveyance of modern political and scientific notions, so the Magyars were confronted with the alternative of either learning German or of developing and improving their own language. The first to point out the necessity of polishing and enriching the mother tongue was an evangelistic clergyman,[1] who reproached his countrymen with the neglect of their own language in favour of Latin, which the early kings had introduced of necessity, as in their day it was the only medium of communication between different countries.[2] But his voice was that of one crying in the wilderness, and Hungary still had to wait a few generations for anything to be done in the desired direction owing to the conservatism of the Magyar, who regarded the use of Latin as the chief means of differentiating the Noble from the peasant.

---

[1] John Ribiny, *Oratio de cultura linguae Hungaricae*, 1751.

[2] When St. Stephen introduced Christianity he imported Polish, German, and Italian priests to help him in the work of conversion, who did not lose sight of their own interests. They induced him to believe that now Hungary was a member of the happy Christian family he would do well to adopt the language of the Church in order that they might obtain for themselves the lion's share of political influence. This was the origin of the use of Latin as the language of Government.—Kossuth, *Schriften aus der Emigration*, ii. 159.

CHAPTER VI

Joseph II. had already been Emperor of Germany for 1780. fifteen years when he succeeded to the throne of his mother, who had carefully brought him up on the system which "magyarised the princes in order the better to germanise the Magyars." As usual, the exaggerated piety of the mother was the cause of free-thinking in the son. Joseph took Frederick the Great for his model, and resolved to be a crowned philosopher and a benevolent autocrat. In old days birth had been the matter of supreme importance; later, membership of the Catholic Church had been the passport to preferment; henceforth education and ability, and a knowledge of the German language, were to be the only qualifications for admission to the ranks of officialdom. Respect for tradition, and the idea that an institution must be good because it is old, became a thing of the past. Religion must be encouraged for the sake of the weaker spirits and in so far as its ministers can be utilised as promoters of the new policy. The pedantic exactitude of Frederick, the great martinet, was to be applied to all branches of the Government service. The Procrustean system of cutting down what was too long and stretching what was too short was to be introduced; and in order to reduce all as near as possible to the same standard the privileges of the Nobles were to be curtailed, and the peasants and lower classes were to be raised. The unification and simplification of government was Joseph's ideal, which naturally brought

him into conflict with Hungarian conservatism.   He
hoped in vain that a general development of material
prosperity, improvements in local government, in the
administration of justice, and in the means of communication, as well as the promise of a career for conspicuous
talent, would atone in Magyar eyes for interference with
the prerogatives of birth.   He made the mistake of
supposing that his philosophy could overcome the
prejudices of pocket patriotism, which saw in the
attempt to abolish class distinctions the spectre of
taxation for all—the bugbear of the privileged and the
true aim of Joseph's reforms.

One of the earliest acts of the philosopher was to burn
22,000,000 florins' worth of notes and bonds, which his
father had put by against a rainy day, on the ground
that it was a scandal for a king to hold the promissory
notes of his subjects—a harmless piece of theatricalism,
and on a par with the action of a banker who would
destroy his own note issue and claim to be actuated by
altruistic motives.   He refused to be crowned King of
Hungary, as he would have been obliged to take the
coronation oath to maintain the Constitution, rights, and
privileges which he was absolutely determined to abolish.
In a spirit of toleration, hitherto unknown in a Habsburg,
the outcome of a philosophic contempt of dogma, he
protested against the traditional policy of persecution ;
and though he would have liked to secure uniformity in
religion as well as in the clothes of its professional adepts,
limited his interference to the establishment of his position
as head of a Church in the tenets of which he did not
believe.   The connection with Rome must be weakened,
and the Pope's power of interference must be curtailed.
Sigismund, Vladislav I., and Maria Theresa had already
established the principle that no papal Bull could be issued
in the country without the Placetum Regium ; but Joseph
went a step further in announcing that not only every

Bull, but every letter, order, and instruction from Rome must obtain the royal sanction and approval before publication ; and that the Bulls "Unigenitus"[1] and "In Cena Domini"[2] must be expunged.   Thus, not only matters of church government, but of dogma also, were subjected to Joseph's control.   The relations and communications of the monastic orders with their titular heads were regularised, pilgrimages to Rome were forbidden, and bishops were no longer to swear allegiance to the Pope on the occasion of their consecration.   Pope Pius VI. became anxious, and went to Vienna in order to reason with the royal innovator, a step unheard of for the last three hundred years, and one in which the free-thinkers saw a revenge for Canossa.   Though the Pope was treated with great respect, he obtained little satisfaction, as during his visit Joseph not only took the precaution of avoiding an interview, but ordered an inventory to be taken as a preliminary to the confiscation of the property of all religious orders which preferred a life of ease and contemplation to the work of ministering to the wants of the poor and the ignorant.   At the same time he appointed a commission to inquire into the whole matter of ecclesiastical property, with a view to the establishment of State control, to the more equal distribution of its revenues, and to subjecting it to taxation.   The result was a storm of protest.   The bishops protested more loudly than any, but the laymen also objected, as ecclesiastics, in virtue of their possession of real property, enjoyed the privileges of nobility, and the nobles saw in the proposal to tax church revenues the thin edge of a wedge intended to be driven into their own most cherished prerogative.   The privilege of ignorance was also attacked by the establishment of

---

[1] Against the Jansenists (1713) and Quesnel's *Moral Reflections on the New Testament*, confirmed 1725.

[2] A wholesale excommunication of all heretics.—See Marczali, *Magyarország Története II. Jozsef Korában*, Budapest, 1885, ii. 73 *sqq.*

State-controlled seminaries for intending priests; for
Joseph saw in the withdrawal from the influence of the
bishop of juvenile ecclesiastics—henceforth to be regarded
as State officials and as the mouthpiece of the central
Government—the best means of combating superstition
and of eradicating the spirit of intolerance.[1]   Some of
the details of his system of interference were comic rather
than beneficial ; for instance, his directions with respect
to sermons.   Women were to be exhorted from the
pulpit to abandon the pernicious habits of wearing stays
and defrauding the customs house ; and the use of candles
on the altar was prohibited, not for any ritualistic reason,
but for fear of fire.

1781.   Soon after his accession the uncrowned King issued
an edict proclaiming the complete political equality of
Protestants and Catholics, and this was followed a few
months later by the Tolerantiae Edictum,[2] which marked
a great advance, not only as regards the previous position,
but in comparison with that obtaining in the England of
the period, not to mention other European countries.
" His Majesty being persuaded of the injurious effects of
all coercion which does violence to the human conscience,
and believing that the greatest benefits to religion and to
the State emanate from that genuine spirit of tolerance
which is agreeable to the principles of Christian charity,"
proceeds to break with the tradition of the Habsburgs,
which made it incumbent upon them to preserve Hungary's
character as a Regnum Marianum with the aid, if need be,
of the stake, the wheel, and the sword.   (Sect. 1) The
free, private exercise of their religion is to be allowed
everywhere to Lutherans, Calvinists, and members of the
Greek Church.   (Sect. 2) Wherever there are more than
one hundred non-Catholic families they can build their
own church (which, however, must have no tower or

---

[1] Marczali, Mag. Tört. II. Jozsef Kordban, ii. 173 sqq.
[2] Enchiridion Fontium, 709 sqq.

bells) and may keep their own priest.   (Sect. 3) Non-Catholics may hold any dignity, position, and property, both in Hungary and the parts thereto annexed.   The sole qualifications for office are henceforth to be merit, capacity, and a Christian life.   (Sect 4) No oath is allowed to be exacted the terms of which contravene the religious principle of Calvinists or Lutherans ; and Protestants are no longer to be compelled to take part in Catholic ceremonies.   (Sect. 5) The seventh section abolishes the rule that all children of mixed marriages are to be brought up in the Catholic faith.   Henceforth, if the father is a Catholic, all the children are to be Catholic ; if he is a Protestant, the males follow the father's, the females the mother's religion.[1]   All this was of great importance to Hungary, where, hitherto, a large section, if not the greater part of the population, had recently been excluded from participation in political life, and even from membership of Trade Guilds ;[2] but it must not be supposed that an end was put to all religious strife by a stroke of Joseph's pen.   The Catholic bishops struggled hard to keep open the gulf which divided their country into two hostile camps[3]—an unpatriotic action in justification of which they referred to the sacred right of oppression conferred by old legislation, a reference which only disgusted Joseph

[1] Sects. 1 and 2 still restrict the public worship of Protestants to certain specified places.   Sect. 16 declares that no one shall be fined or suffer corporal punishment for a religious cause.   Sect. 10 allows Protestant priests to attend their co-religionaries *even* to the place of execution.   The details of the Edict of Toleration supply a sufficient answer to Austrian apologists who try to minimise the amount of persecution to which the Protestants had hitherto been subjected.

[2] Sect. 5 Edictum Tolerantiae.

[3] The reservation as to children of mixed marriages, whereby alone the superiority of the Catholic Church was maintained, gave them the desired weapon.   They did all they could to throw obstacles in the way of mixed marriages, and continued to exact, as the price of consent, a promise that all children should be brought up in the Catholic faith.   Their power in this respect was not destroyed till 1843-44.   They were specially annoyed by the recognition of the contractual aspect of marriage and the consequent admission of the possibility of divorce.

the more with them and it, and made him more resolved than ever to persevere in his abolitionary campaign. The Jews were not forgotten. Hitherto they had been tolerated but not recognised, and had to pay a special tax to justify their claim to existence. Henceforward they were allowed to attend Christian schools and to hire land and carry on trades, whereas up to now the majority had earned a miserable livelihood as travelling pedlars. Joseph wished to abolish the distinction existing between them and the rest of the population, and tried to compel them to shave their beards and abandon the use of distinctive clothes; but the Jews protested, and so the matter dropped, to the relief of the Christians who objected to the abolition of the outward signs of racial difference, almost as much as they objected to Jewish emancipation for fear of the competition of Semitic intelligence.[1]

The removal to Vienna, in spite of a howl of protest, of the Sacred Crown (which the Magyars looked upon as the symbol of their national independence) without more ado than if it were the most ordinary piece of personal property,[2] was an indication of Joseph's contempt for the law when it stood in the way of the execution of his plans, and a proof of his intentions with regard to Hungary. They amounted to nothing less than the recasting of the whole of its social, religious, and governmental institutions. With a view to the simplification of government the Treasury was united with the Council of Lieutenancy; the Transylvanian and Hungarian Chanceries were amalgamated; and the seat of government was, as reason demanded, transferred from Pressburg to the more central Buda. Joseph refused to recognise any distinction between constitutional Hungary and the hereditary provinces of Austria where his autocratic rights were undisputed.

1782.

---

[1] Marczali, *Mag. Tört. II. József Korában*, ii. 271 *sqq.*

[2] "*Bonum mobile*" was the phrase Joseph contemptuously applied to it.— *Ibid.* ii. Appendix xxii.

Henceforth all feet were to be squeezed into the same shoe.   Linguistic uniformity was essential to complete 1784. centralisation.   Joseph therefore issued an order[1] to the effect that henceforth German was to be the official language of Hungary, and was to be used in all Chancerial documents at the expiration of six months from the date of the order.   Within three years German was to be exclusively used in the law courts, and ignorance of that language was to entail exclusion from all public employment.   Hence, special attention was to be given to it in gymnasium and seminary, and a knowledge of it was made a condition precedent to employment in the humblest educaticnal capacity in the primary schools.   Further, German was to be the exclusive medium of instruction in the University.   Joseph was mistaken in his estimate of the extent to which German was known in Hungary, and it is easy to imagine the horror of grey-headed officials at the prospect of having to learn a new and repulsive language at their time of life on pain of loss of employment. For Joseph made no secret of his intentions.   " If any one does not conform with my desires, the door is open and he can walk out, whether he be a member of the Chancery or the humblest clerk in the county organisation." He was perfectly indifferent as to what people learned provided they learned it in the German language, and to the fact that what may be admirable as a means of education is purely detestable as an end.   The measure, which was intended as a direct blow to the spirit of nationality, had precisely the contrary effect to that which was expected.[2]

[1] Instructions to the Council of Lieutenancy, May 6, 1784 : " Alle Provinzen der Monarchie sollen nur ein Ganzes ausmachen, in allen die Kräfte des Volkes auf ein gemeinsames Ziel, Österreichs Macht, gerichtet sein."

[2] Joseph justified his action on the ground that the use of a dead language proved that the national language was deficient, and that a country should not be governed and judged in a language which the majority of the population does not understand—a good reason for the abolition of Latin but not for the introduction of German in its place.   See Joseph's edict of April 26, 1784.— Marczali, Mag. Tört. II. József Korában, ii. 385.

It made the Magyars, perhaps for the first time, recognise the importance of language as a preservative of distinctive nationality, and realise the fact that the recognition of the superiority of German as the language of all branches of Government must sooner or later be equivalent to an admission of the right claimed by Austria to the position of predominant partner, of the superiority of the German race, and of the necessity of ultimate fusion therewith. The revival and development of the Hungarian language dates from this period, and the contemporary works of Kazinczy, Báróczy, Bacsanyi, Bessenyei, and Révai are a lasting proof of the progress made within the limits of a single generation.

After making an inventory of ecclesiastical property with a view to its taxation, Joseph proceeded to deal in the same way with that of private owners. A census of the population [1] was begun, and a system of registration of land and house property was instituted with a view to the formation of an estimate of the taxable capacity of the country and of the number of available recruits. A swarm of foreign surveyors descended on the counties, as hateful to the landowners who had to contribute to their maintenance as to the peasants who had to give them unpaid assistance ; but owing to the incompetence of the surveyors and the hostility of the population the work was never finished, and the only result was the increase of Joseph's unpopularity.[2]

The organisation of the counties, the real stronghold of national independence, was the next object of attack. The first step was to get rid of opposition in high places, and to appoint to the most important office in the country

[1] According to Pauler, *o.c.* p. 130, the population was 8,000,000 in 1785. Count Albert Apponyi, in his pamphlet on *The Juridical Relations of Austria and Hungary,* p. 8 *n.*, says that out of the 7,500,000 inhabitants of Hungary, 340,000 enjoyed the rights of nobility as compared with 122,000 in France out of a population of 26,000,000.

[2] Michael Horváth, *o.c.* v. 397.

Count Christopher Niczky, who was obviously qualified for the post by the fact that he possessed the confidence of none of his fellow-countrymen. Owing to the suspension of the meetings of the Diet, which Joseph never once convened in the whole course of his reign, the counties formed so many uncontrolled *regna in regno*, a fact which was not conducive to the attainment of Joseph's ideal—uniformity of government. The counties must therefore be abolished, and the country must be divided into ten districts, each under a royal nominee, a paid commissioner, or Kreishauptmann, whose sphere of authority was to include all matters relating to taxation, to trade questions, to the registration of land and population, to the relations of landlord and tenant, to the means of communication, to the appointment and dismissal of officials, and to the control and distribution of the soldiery. Not only was every vestige of the old popular elective organisation destroyed at one stroke, but the personal liberty of the subject was at the mercy of the Kreishauptmann, who could arrest any one in the Emperor's name, and could apply direct to him for instructions without regard to the Council of Lieutenancy in which the control of the country was nominally vested. No doubt Joseph was animated by the best motives. With a view to the development of trade he sketched out a whole network of roads, prescribed the regulation of the waterways, and laid special stress in his instructions to the commissioners on the necessity of religious tolerance, of the abolition of the *corvée*, and on the undesirability of encouraging the migration of the country population to the great towns. The fact is that Joseph was born before his time, and that the country was not ready even for the proposed improvements in its material condition, in his advocacy of which the Emperor to some extent anticipated the great reformer of half a century later—Count Stephen Széchenyi. He wished to plant ready-made, full-grown trees, and was too impatient to cast a seed and leave it to germinate. The only real result of his hasty reforms was the production of a conviction in the minds of the peasants that he intended, and in fact had ordered, their complete emancipation, and that his good intentions and instructions were thwarted and disregarded by a malevolent officialdom, in which they discerned not the protectors of the poor, whom Joseph had wished them to see, but the agents of their natural enemies, the landlords, and of a new and more subtle form of oppression. Consequently, the Jacqueries which followed in certain districts were, in a way, a tribute of gratitude to the imperial liberator whose remissness in suppressing the disturbances gave some colour to the belief that he was not an entirely reluctant spectator of the process of landlord-baiting.[1] The good intentions above referred to were expressed in the order of August 22, 1785, whereby the term serf (*jobbágy*, *Leibeigen*) was abolished, and the peasants' right of migration received fresh confirmation. Henceforth the peasant can marry without consent, and is not controlled in his choice of trade or profession. He can freely dispose of his personal property, cannot be deprived of his tenant right except by legal process, and in case of oppression can claim the assistance of the official lawyer of the district.[2] All these reforms, beneficial in themselves, were acts of benevolent tyranny realised in total disregard of the laws of the country, and over the head of the sole legal legislative authority. The idea of conferring proprietary rights on the peasants apparently never entered Joseph's mind, but as the body which paid the

[1] Like Stepanovitch, the most heartless and successful of the anarchistic agitators of Russia, Hóra and Kloska, the authors of the Jacqueries here referred to, produced documents written in letters of gold, purporting to contain Joseph's authorisation to the peasants to exterminate the landlords.— Michael Horváth, v. 351, 357; Marczali, *Mag. Tört. II. József Korában*, ii. 526. See also Jancsó Benedek, *A Román Nemzetiségi Törekvések Története*. Budapest, 1899, 110 *sqq.*, 114, 123.

[2] Acsády, *A Magyar Jobbágyság Története*, 379 *sqq.*

taxes and provided the recruits for the army, they were entitled to protection from gross acts of tyranny; and every fresh immunity conferred on them drove another nail into the coffin of the nobles' exemption from taxation, the desire for the abolition of which was the motive for all Joseph's reforms of the relations between landlord and tenant. However great our sympathy may be for the desire of the nobles to maintain their independence and legislative rights, we must admit that they cut a poor figure when they could produce no better justification for the maintenance of a barbaric system and of inequitable privileges than Verbóczy's two and a half centuries' old dicta, and tacitly insisted on the theory that their national individuality could be preserved only by the perpetuation of injustice and class distinction.

If Joseph's reforms had been prompted only by notions of abstract justice, and not by considerations of expediency, he would not have maintained the one-sided system of protection which reduced Hungary to a position of complete economic dependence on Austria,[1] the price of escape from which was complete fusion with the hereditary provinces, and that no patriot was prepared to pay. The desire for uniformity and for the abolition of class and national distinctions was at the bottom of the Emperor's economic policy [2] as well as of his reform of

[1] In 1785, Joseph wrote to the Chancellor, Pálffy, admitting that Hungary was exploited as a colony, but saying that he would do nothing to remedy its position unless it would undertake to pay more taxes (Beöthy, o.c. vol. i. p. 728). It must not be forgotten that the nobles made large voluntary contributions in money, first in 1439, and in men; much less that Hungary had no control whatever of expenditure, and that all proceeds of taxation went to Austria, which never spent a penny on the material or moral welfare of the country from which it annually drew a sum of money out of all proportion greater than that which it provided itself, having regard to the relative taxable capacity of the two countries.

[2] The "Isolirungs-System," as he himself styled the system of out-and-out protection of Austrian trade interests maintained at Hungary's expense. On the economic relations of Austria and Hungary during this and the preceding period, see Michael Horváth's Az Ipar és Kereskedelem Története Magyarországban a három utolsó századadszad alatt.

the judicature and of the criminal law. The jurisdiction of the landlord over his tenant was taken away, and thirty-eight local courts of first instance were established. These were subject to the control of the supreme judicial body, the Court of Seven Judges, whose duty it was, *inter alia*, to select and submit to Joseph the names of candidates for judicial appointments. Henceforward, nobles and peasants were to be tried by the same tribunals, and both classes were to be liable to the infliction of the same penalties—no doubt a great and admirable reform as far as it went, but the punishments prescribed for various offences showed little advance from the humanitarian point of view, and the absence of any idea of the desirability of reforming the criminal, rather than of merely taking vengeance on the offender, is shown by the enormous length of the sentences prescribed for comparatively trifling misdeeds. And here again, the tendentious character of the reform is shown by the number of offences enumerated by the new code which entail the loss of the rights of nobility, and the consequent enlargement of the tax-paying classes.

1788. Joseph paid for the unpopularity of his reforms and innovations as soon as foreign complications arose, and where Maria Theresa found help and enthusiasm, met only with indifference and open hostility when men and money were wanted for the Turkish war, success in which might encourage the Emperor in the prosecution of his centralising policy, whereas a fiasco might afford the opportunity of recovering at least some measure of independence. The distress caused by the slow progress of the war, and the news of the outbreak of the French Revolution, made the probability of a general upheaval of the country greater than ever ; more especially when Joseph gave orders that the troops should be employed to collect, by force if necessary, the arrears of taxes which the pauperised population was quite unable to pay. But the spirit of hostility found its expression, not in any outburst of violence, but in a passive resistance to the demands of the Government, and in a deliberate development of the spirit of nationalism, the outward and visible signs of which were the revival of the national costume, and the universal use of the national language. With the outbreak of the revolution in Belgium came the beginning of the end, and the general collapse of the edifice which Joseph had so laboriously reared. Fearing that he would find another and more formidable Belgium in Hungary, he began the process of climbing down the ladder, and was unable to stop until he had arrived at the bottom. First he issued a decree suspending the work of the survey-commission, followed by the rescript of December 18, 1789 (which it is to be observed is written in Hungarian as well as in German), promising to convene the Diet as soon as the war should be over. Last of all came a death-bed recantation—the withdrawal of the objectionable ordinances, and the destruction at one stroke of the whole work of his reign, excepting only the Edictum Tolerantiae.

We have of Our clemency decided to restore the public administration and the judicial system, as from the first day of May next, to the position it occupied in the year 1780 on the decease of Her Most Serene Majesty the widowed Empress and Apostolic Queen Our Mother . . . and now that We are convinced that you prefer the old form of government, and in it alone seek and find your happiness, We make no delay in deferring to your wishes ; and as Our sole desire is for the prosperity of the nations entrusted to Our charge . . . to all the counties of the kingdom, royal free towns and districts, their former legal authority is restored, both as regards matters to be dealt with in general or other meetings and as regards the election of officials. The rest of the ordinances issued by Our authority, which may seem to be contrary to the usual interpretation of the laws, We hereby declare to be suspended, void, and of no effect . . . whereby you will receive an irrefragable proof, and one valid for all times to come, of Our determination to maintain in undiminished force the rights of the Estates in the matter of legislative authority, which, by virtue of the fundamental laws of the Kingdom is equally divided between the King and the various Estates of the Realm, and to transmit the Constitution inviolate to Our descendants in the same form as that in which we ourselves received it from Our predecessors, in the hope that you will assist the country which implores your assistance by supplying provisions for the troops now mobilised for its security, and by voting of recruits to the extent which you may consider necessary for the carrying out of the campaign during the current year.

Strange irony of fate that the bitterest enemy of the Magyar language should be the first of the Habsburgs to submit to the obligation of addressing his subjects in that idiom, and that the great innovator should be compelled to subscribe to a document containing the plainest possible recognition of the constitutional rights of the Diet as regards legislative initiative, control of taxation, and the fixing of the military contingent. The last clause of the rescript gives complete proof of the success of the policy of passive resistance, and of the impossibility of coercing a country which Maria Theresa found it easy to lead by appealing to its generosity. Whatever one's opinion may be of the wisdom of Joseph's attempted innovations, it is impossible to be blind to the many merits of the would-be reformer, or to withhold one's sympathy from the individual. He chose for his epitaph the words : "Here lies a monarch whose intentions were good, who failed in all his enterprises." [1] A more courtly, but equally just inscription records the fact that "*Saluti publicae vixit, non diu, sed totus.*" [2]

[1] Michael Horváth, *o.c.* v. 440.   [2] *A Mag. Nem. Tört.* viii. 464.

CHAPTER VII

THE return of the Sacred Crown to Buda was the signal 1790. for an outburst of joy on the part of the Hungarians, who saw therein the outward and visible sign of their victory, the re-establishment of their Constitution, and the recognition of their historic rights. But their recent experiences were not calculated to make them entirely contented with the prospect of returning to the position of affairs which had existed at the death of Maria Theresa. It was evident that a stronger safeguard was required than that provided by the Pragmatic Sanction[1] against attempts to annihilate the nation's individuality. The law of 1723 was intended to form, and had been looked upon by all as constituting, a contract between the Habsburgs and Magyars; and the deliberate pulverisation of that contract by one of the parties thereto, in the opinion of many, justified the other party as treating the whole compact as null and void, and in returning to the *status quo ante*. It was pointed out that Joseph had succeeded to the throne solely by virtue of that agreement, which had guaranteed the liberties and the Constitution of the Hungarian nation, and that by his disregard of his contractual obligations "the thread of succession had been broken";[2] whence it followed that the people had recovered its ancient elective rights. This

[1] The term Pragmatic Sanction is used for convenience, though, as has been pointed out, it is not that document but the laws of 1723 which contain the terms of the contract between Hungary and the Habsburgs.

[2] "*Filum sanctionalis successionis regiae interruptum.*"—Marczali, *Az. 1790-91-diki Országgyűlés*, Budapest, 1907, i. 15.

opinion, and the general unrest, was encouraged and fomented by Prussia, which saw with concern the successes of Loudon in Turkey, and was quite alive to the advantage either of securing active assistance in the event of war with Austria, or, at all events, of paralysing the right arm of the Habsburgs by encouraging the Magyars to sulk in their tents. When war seemed unavoidable the Hungarian leaders kept in close touch with Jacoby, the Prussian envoy, and were anxious that no terms of peace should be arranged between Prussia and Austria which did not provide some kind of guarantee of the maintenance of the liberties and independence of Hungary, and new and more certain protection for class privileges. Few, however, went so far as to wish for the deposition of the perjured dynasty, or as to be disposed to shed their blood "*pour le roi de Prusse.*"

The Counties addressed themselves with pleasure to the task of destroying the relics of "Josephism." Compulsory German instruction was promptly abolished, and the opportunity was taken for the first time of extending the teaching of the Hungarian language among the non-Magyar population. It is perhaps not to be wondered at that the reaction manifested itself in places in a somewhat exaggerated form. In some Counties the books of the foreign land-surveyors were solemnly burnt. German, *i.e.* non-Hungarian, clothes were either voluntarily laid aside or stripped from the backs of the wearers. A cry was raised for a return to ancient Hungarian manners and customs, to the simple life of "Scythian" ancestors, and for the re-establishment of the ancient relations of landlord and serf.[1] Of all Joseph's innovations the principle of religious toleration alone escaped attack; for the people was convinced of the necessity of putting an end to the disputes which had so long divided the nation into two camps, the hostility of which had lent itself

[1] Marczali, *Az. 1790-91-diki Orszdggyülés*, i. 42 *sqq.*

so easily to exploitation in the interest of alien domination.[1] The immediate convocation of the Diet was demanded, and it was resolved that a failure to convene it within a month should be followed by the suspension of the collection of taxes. The catchwords of the French Revolution, " sovereignty of the people " and the rest, came into fashion, and the establishment of a national army, and the recognition of the nation's right to be heard on the question of making war and peace, was insistently demanded. Both the illegality of interference with old class privileges, and the modern ideas of liberty and equality, provided a basis for an attack on the Habsburg connection. The continuance of the war with Turkey, and the position of Austria *vis à vis* the Anglo–Prussian–Dutch convention, made it essential for Vienna to come to terms with Hungary, which saw the opportunity not only of obtaining security for the maintenance of its historic rights, but of limiting the privileges of the Crown and of establishing a national army which should make a repetition of the brutalities of foreign mercenaries an impossibility. The sudden abolition of Joseph's reforms produced a recrudescence of unrest among the peasants, who discerned nothing but humanitarian motives in the innovations of the past reign. The " Peasants' Decree," issued in certain districts, showed the spirit which animated the Hóras and Dozsas to be still alive, and gave fresh expression to the ineradicable idea that nothing but the malevolence of officials prevented the realisation of the desires of the Liberator-King for the complete emancipation of the oppressed. The proclamation in question threatens extermination of the landlords if they venture to depart a hair's-breadth from the terms of Joseph's edict, as well as of any blackleg peasants who dare to pay

---

[1] " Qu'on ne craigne pas la révolution dans un pays où il y a six partis puissants qui se détestent, le clergé, catholique, grec et protestant, les magnats, gentilshommes et paysans?"—Le Prince de Ligne to Kaunitz.—Marczali, *o.c.* i. 54.

the rent, or perform the services hitherto incident to the tenure of land. The p•tition addressed to Leopold II., Joseph's successor, shows hardly any sign of the influence of the French Revolution, and no idea of demanding any form of political rights or anything more than the abolition of the most crying forms of injustice. The requirements of the peasants are limited to the redemption of the feudal dues, the fair division of the *corvée* between the different seasons,[1] the employment of non-nobles in inferior official positions,[2] freedom from corporal punishment without previous legal condemnation, and a lightening of the burden of taxation. Luckily for the nobles, Leopold was either too busily occupied with external complications, or was too conscientious, to raise a peasant Frankenstein and to utilise the forces of discontent for selfish purposes. Without his interference the nobles were brought to reason by the threat of peasant risings, and consented to the passing of certain measures, based, not on Joseph's decree, for that would have been equivalent to the recognition of the legality of extra-Dietal interference in the internal affairs of the kingdom, but on the laws passed in Sigismund's, Ferdinand's, and Maximilian's reigns, which had abolished the principle of perpetual servitude. The right of free migration, subject to the satisfaction of the peasant's legal obligations to his landlord, was re-established,[3] and the tenant's right to fair compensation for unexhausted improvements was recognised. On the other hand the manorial courts were revived, and the *régime* of the stick continued.

It was fortunate for Hungary that one royal innovator

---

[1] Hitherto the landlord could compel the tenant to do the prescribed forced labour all at once at any period of the year, thus making it impossible for the peasant to prepare his own land for the season's crops.

[2] *E.g.* in the postal service.

[3] Migration was allowed only at the festival of St. Gregory, *i.e.* before the spring labour begins, and for fear lest whole districts might be depopulated to the detriment of the Government in the matter of taxation (1790-91 Art. 35). This law was the last passed with a view to bettering the position of the peasant till a new era of reform began with the Diet of 1832.

was not succeeded by another of the same type. Leopold had already had twenty-five years' experience of the work of government at Florence, where he had earned the respect and admiration, not only of his own subjects, but of all who had come in contact with him.[1] But Tuscany was not Hungary, and presumably he recognised the fact that the benevolent despotism, based on a well-organised secret police, which had sufficed in the former would, in the present condition of public opinion (the result of the French Revolution), and in view of the threatening nature of the general European outlook, infallibly lead to a national upheaval in the latter. This, rather than any philosophic attachment to the abstract idea of Liberty and Constitutionalism, dictated the letter in which he informed Hungary of his accession to the throne and of his intention to maintain the freedom, laws, and Constitution of the country, and to summon the Diet without delay. The lesson afforded by the deathbed recognition by his predecessor of Magyar tenacity of purpose and by the victory of passive resistance made him indisposed to submit to the influence of reactionary bureaucrats who saw in the collapse of "Josephism" the prospective loss of remunerative occupations. The justifiable suspicion with which the Diet at first looked upon Joseph's brother was evidenced by the insistence of the Lower House on the taking of an oath by all its members to the effect that no one would accept any honour, decoration, or present, without the knowledge and consent of the Diet ;[2] and by the contest which raged over the question as to the form which the Diploma Inaugurale should take. By the demand for separate diplomatic representation in the peace negotiations with Turkey, and for a separate Hungarian army using only Hungarian words of command, officered exclusively by Magyars and subject only to the control of a Hungarian

[1] Doran, *Men and Manners at the Court of Florence.*
[2] Marczali, *o.c.* i. 163.

War Office, a definite attempt was made to give proper expression to the principle of the personal nature of the union between Hungary and the hereditary provinces deducible from the terms of the Laws of 1723. To the former of the two demands the King yielded; and it is probable that had his relations with Prussia continued much longer to be strained almost to the breaking-point he would have been forced to a complete surrender. Though at the discussion of the terms of the Convention of Reichenbach the Prussians threw over the Hungarians, whose attitude had paved the way for Prussia's diplomatic success, the fact that Leopold felt his position to be insecure is shown by the letter which he addressed to some of the leaders of Hungarian opinion on July 20. "Animated by attachment to the Constitution of the kingdom as interpreted by the Pragmatic Sanction, His Majesty neither desires to infringe the accepted terms of that enactment, nor will he permit the same to be violated by others. His Majesty is not averse to the adoption by the Diet of suitable measures directed to the preservation of the said Constitution in accordance with the dignity of the Crown and the welfare of the country, but at the same time cannot allow that His Majesty's right of succession, based on a fundamental law of the State, the Pragmatic Sanction, should be called in question. . . . The King is prepared to exercise his executive authority in accordance with the laws, but cannot agree to any alteration which is contrary to the spirit of the Constitution of the kingdom." For a moment Leopold entertained the idea of inducing Magyar officers, by promises of reward and advancement, to issue a counterblast to the demands of the Diet, in the name of the Hungarian forces, in the form of a *pronunciamento* protesting their loyalty to the dynasty, and announcing their refusal to be separated in any manner from their Austrian brothers in arms; but a more effective, if less reputable, means was adopted of showing the Diet that it could not have things all its own way, and of proving the essential weakness of a body which was only partially representative of the inhabitants of the country, viz. a deliberate incitement to racial dissension. The Servian population was encouraged in the assertion of its demands for territorial separation which found violent expression at a so-called Illyrian congress [1] attended by many Austrians, and among others by the governor of Petervárad, who compelled, by threats of imprisonment, the partisans of unity to sign a petition for national dismemberment. Leopold clearly had no intention of giving effect to the separatistic tendencies of the Servians, but thought to utilise them for the purpose of frightening the Diet, which he vainly tried to terrify by an attempt to procure the indictment, on a charge of high treason, of those who had negotiated with Jacoby for Prussian support.[2] Another useful bugbear was the suggestion of the imminence of a peasant-war with which the officious Press threatened recalcitrant nobles; and, in fact, the attitude assumed in some districts by the lower orders did induce the Diet to adopt a less uncompromising attitude than that which the instructions of certain counties would have justified it in assuming. Thus, it was to a combination of circumstances that the acceptance, after a deal of haggling, of a Diploma Inaugurale, containing practically the same terms as those signed by Charles III. and Maria Theresa, was due. The liberties, immunities, and privileges of the kingdom received fresh confirmation, and the revival of its elective rights in the event of the extinction of the issue of the three persons specified by the Pragmatic Sanction was guaranteed. Further, the acceptance of the terms of this Diploma, and the taking of an oath recognising its validity, was made a condition precedent to the right of Leopold's successors to occupy the throne.

[1] Michael Horváth, o.c. vi. 48 sq.
[2] Schwicker, Politische Geschichte der Serben in Ungarn, Budapest, 1880, p. 363 sqq.

Though the Hungarians had to renounce their desires for complete military and diplomatic independence, the meeting of the Diet of 1790 is in any case memorable for the fact that to it is due the strongest expression of the constitutional rights and independence of the country that had ever been put in black and white. The laws then passed suffice, alone, as a justification, if any is required, of the attitude adopted by subsequent generations towards the encroachment of successive monarchs. A new and solemn recognition was obtained from the King of the independence of Hungary and of the parts thereto annexed, and a clear definition of the position occupied by the two parties to the Pragmatic Sanction. The personal nature of the union existing between Austria and Hungary is underlined and emphasised, and the equality of King and Diet as legislative factors is definitely reaffirmed. No change is imported into the relations existing between the two countries, but a clear restatement is made of principles which every Habsburg king, with the exception of Joseph II., had sworn to observe, and had consistently infringed.[1] The most important clause of the law passed by the Diet of 1790–1791 is Article 10, which reads as follows :—

[1] Tezner, the most violent modern critic of Hungary's Constitution, asserts in order to get over the obvious meaning of the laws of 1790, that the affirmation of Hungarian freedom and independence is no more than a reaffirmation of the rights and privileges of the nobles as regards exemption from taxation, a "Privilegien Assecuranz," as he styles it. — *Der Oesterreichische Kaisertitel*, pp. 36, 91. An acquaintance with the details of the law in question, a comparison of Article 1 of 1723 and of Joseph's rescript of January 28, 1790, and the fact that Law x. makes no reference to the nobles, only to the "Jura et libertates *Regni*," and the words of the heading of that law, "*De independentia Regni Hungariae Partiumque eidem annexarum*," should suffice to refute the assertion. Though no special mention is made of foreign affairs and of a separate national army, Idenczy, a renegade Hungarian, a supporter of Joseph's *régime* and an avowed enemy of the Constitution, wrote a book drawing attention to the effect of the wording of Article 10, "a free Kingdom and independent as regards the whole legal form of government," and logically deducing therefrom, as others have since done, the complete independence of the armed forces of Hungary from the military authorities of Vienna, complete financial independence, and the right to separate diplomatic representation.—*A Mag. Nem. Tört.* viii. 523.

"Hungary, together with the parts thereto annexed, is a free Kingdom, and independent as regards the whole legal form of government, in which term is comprised each and every governmental department; that is to say, it is dependent on no other Kingdom or people, but is possessed of its own separate existence and Constitution,[1] and consequently must be ruled and governed by its hereditary King, crowned according to law, namely, by His Most Sacred Majesty and his successors, Kings of Hungary, in accordance with its own laws and customs and not after the manner of other provinces, as is prescribed by Articles 3 of 1713,[2] and 8 and 11 of 1741."[3]

Article 3 provides that in future kings must be crowned without fail within six months of the death of their immediate predecessors, and that until the ceremony of coronation has taken place the royal right of conferring titles and privileges is suspended.

Article 12 declares that His Majesty voluntarily recognises the fundamental principle that the power of passing, abrogating, and interpreting laws is exercisable jointly by the King and the States and Orders of the realm in Diet assembled and not otherwise, and that His Majesty will himself maintain the said legislative rights of the States in full force and inviolate, just as they existed in the time of his predecessors, and will so transmit them to his successors; "assuring the States and Orders of the Realm that the Kingdom and the parts thereof annexed shall never be governed by Edicts or so-called Patents which in any case can never be accepted in any governmental departments."[4]   Further, the King under-

---

[1] "Propriam habens consistentiam et constitutionem."

[2] "Nec Status et Ordines Regni eadem Sacra Regia Majestas secus regi aut dirigi vult quam observatis propriis ipsius Regni Ungariae hactenus factis vel in futurum Diaetaliter constituendis legibus."

[3] Guaranteeing the nobles' exemption from taxation (8) and providing that Hungarian affairs shall be managed by Hungarians exclusively.

[4] "Judiciis." This does not mean law courts, but is equivalent to "dicasteriis" as used in Article 10, the technical word for governmental departments.

takes that he will not interfere in judicial matters or in the execution of sentences, and that the executive power shall be exercised in strict accordance with the laws. A meeting of the Diet is to be convened every third year or oftener if necessary in the public interest (Art. 13). The Council of Lieutenancy, as the supreme executive organ, is declared to be independent of all other official departments (Art. 14). His Majesty assures the States and Orders that no foreign language shall be used in any governmental business of any nature whatsoever (Art. 16). Officials are not only to take an oath of allegiance to the King, but are also to swear to observe the laws (Art. 18). No subsidies in money or kind, and no recruits, shall be asked for by the King, even in the form of free gifts or under any other pretext whatsoever, *extra Diaetam*, except in the case provided for by Article 22 of 1741 ;[1] and the amount of taxation required for the maintenance of the standing army must be fixed only by the Diet, and only for the period intervening between two meetings thereof. The taxes payable by Croatia and Slavonia are also to be fixed by the Hungarian Diet (Art. 59).

In one respect the Diet suffered a slight defeat. It was especially anxious to establish its control of the price of salt—a royal monopoly and one of the chief sources of income, the raising of which to an excessive figure inflicted considerable hardship on the lower classes. Article 20 enacts that the price shall not be raised without the consent of the Diet, but the result of the popular victory was nullified by the insertion of the phrase, " except in case of urgency," which had already done good service in cases where the King wished to perpetrate an illegality. As regards ecclesiastical matters also, the legislation of 1790 was not entirely satisfactory, though some progress was in fact made in the direction of establishing the

[1] In the case of sudden invasion making it impossible to summon the Diet.

principle óf religious equality.   The Catholic bishops
thought it their duty to put matters back, as far as it was
possible to do so, to the position in which they were left
by Maria Theresa, in order to revenge themselves for the
inequality of treatment to which Catholics were subjected
in Protestant States, and on the principle that liberty of
conscience must necessarily be fatal to the interests of
Catholicism.   For a moment Leopold was disposed to
maintain the Catholic Church in its privileged position,
in order to punish the Protestant section which had
indulged in a flirtation with Prussia prior to the meeting
of the Congress of Reichenbach.   Fortunately, however,
the great majority of the lay Catholics were animated by
a reasonable spirit, which induced them to prefer national
unity to the interests of the party of dogmatic intolerance.
The King, therefore, withdrew his opposition, and
Article 26 was passed, as it declares "in spite of the
opposition of the spiritual lords and of a certain section
of the lay Catholics."   The Article in question is based on
the Tolerantiae Edictum of Joseph II., the operation of
which is now extended by the grant of equal rights to
members of the Greek Church (Art. 27).   Henceforth
the Protestants may have the church towers and bells
which the above-mentioned edict had denied them ; the
distinction between public and private religious exercises
is abolished, and Lutherans and Calvinists may build as
many churches as they please, provided that they can
satisfy the members of a mixed commission that there is
money enough available to provide for the maintenance of
a new place of worship in the district in which they
propose it should be erected.   In one respect the law is
of a retrograde character.   Clause 3 of the Tolerantiae
Edictum allowed non-Catholics to hold property and
office in Croatia, thereby abolishing the restrictions
imposed by the law of 1687, which had confined that
privilege to Catholics.   These restrictions were revived

by the law of 1790-91. But for this fact, and but for the maintenance of the advantage enjoyed by the Catholic Church in the matter of the religious education of the issue of mixed marriages, and for the restriction to Catholic priests of the right of celebrating such marriages, the members of all recognised religions were put on practically the same footing.[1] In any case the Catholic Church renounced the political supremacy it had so long enjoyed with the connivance of the Habsburgs, whose aim it had been to effect the uniformity of their dominions in religious matters with a view to ultimate uniformity in all branches of government.

The equalisation of Protestant and Catholic was important also from the point of view of the reincorporation of Transylvania in Hungary. Hitherto, as the Protestants were far more happily situated in the former country where the Catholic religion had never occupied the dominating position it had held in the latter, they naturally had contemplated with a certain degree of apprehension the possibility of a reunion which might entail the loss of religious freedom. Now that their fears as to the possible consequences of reincorporation were allayed, the desire revived for a reunion which would strengthen them in their resistance to autocratic encroachment on their liberties and privileges. Kaunitz, the chief exponent of the advantages to be derived from the dismemberment of Hungary, had no difficulty in convincing Leopold of the dangers which would be entailed by the realisation of the wishes of the Hungarian population of Transylvania, and encouraged the opposition of the Saxons, who never lost an opportunity of currying favour with the Court, and of emphasising their loyalty at the expense of the Magyars. The fact that the question of the position of the Transylvanian Roumanians was raised (for the first time) at the

---

[1] Catholics may freely convert Protestants, but the latter are strictly forbidden to seduce a Catholic from his faith.

Transylvanian Diet of 1790 gave further proof of the necessity of reincorporation. The numbers, as well as the want of education, of the Roumanians, made them, then as now, a source of danger to the Magyar principle to which the reunion of the severed member of the Sacred Crown would bring an accession of strength. It is not surprising, therefore, that successive Habsburgs showed themselves to be indisposed to give effect to the Magyars' desire for reunion, and remained true to the motto " *divide ut imperes*."

At the beginning of the reign both the King and the nobles had played a game of bluff, for the purposes of which one party utilised the bugbear of Jacqueries and Servian separatism, the other the spectre of revolution and of Prussian interference. When both agreed to put a stop to their flirtation with each other's antagonists, a period of mutual confidence followed, based on a far more solid foundation than that afforded by the temporary enthusiasm which Maria Theresa and Hungary had entertained for each other. The return of the Sacred Crown, the coronanation, and Leopold's promise to confirm the appointment of whomsoever the Diet might select for the office of Palatine, won the confidence of the nation. In order to show its willingness to consign Joseph and his innovations to oblivion, and to begin a new era of affectionate loyalty, the Diet elected Leopold's son, the Archduke Alexander, to the vacant post. A reasonable compromise settled all disputes. The towns which the Magyars looked upon as the strongholds of Austrian imperialism, the foreign population of which might become the instrument of an anti-national policy, were encouraged by the success of the French *bourgeoisie* to demand better representation at the Diet. As on previous occasions, the elected representatives of the nation protested against the undue exercise of the right of the Crown to increase the number of royal free towns, and Leopold agreed to consult the Diet on each occasion before exercising his privilege. Possibly it was a mistake on the part of the Magyars to resist the establishment of a *tiers état*, which, as subsequent history shows, once received within the pale of the Constitution, would have been as active as the nobility itself in its hostility to unconstitutional interference ; but Josephism and the French Revolution had engendered a feeling of nervousness, and the nobles feared to open a door for the admission of German influence, the exclusion of which they had only recently effected. The creation of a separate Servian Chancery, which the Diet naturally looked upon as an indication of an intention to dismember Hungary and to treat a comparatively recent importation as an independent people, was more or less satisfactorily explained by the King's assurance that it indicated no separatistic intention ; that it was solely due to consideration of administrative convenience ; and that the sphere of influence of the new department would be strictly confined to ecclesiastical matters. The establishment of the Servian Chancery was in fact a mere temporary move in the game of bluff, the necessity for which soon ceased to exist, as indeed, did the Chancery itself.

By Article 16 of the law of 1790 a first step was made in the direction of official recognition of the Hungarian language, and Article 7 of the law of 1792 marks a further advance. The study of the national language is thereby elevated to the position of an ordinary subject of instruction within the limits of Hungary proper, and to that of a *studium extraordinarium* in the "annexed parts." Non-Magyar students in academies and university are dispensed from the necessity of learning the language provided they have no intention of gaining a livelihood in Hungary. A knowledge of Hungarian is ultimately to be essential for admission to the public service, and in the meanwhile public offices are to be gradually filled as vacancies occur by the appointment of candidates acquainted with that

language. Thus the principle that non-Magyars earning
their living in Hungary may reasonably be expected to learn
the national idiom obtains recognition for the first time.

It is remarkable that the Diet did not take the
opportunity presented by Leopold's conciliatory disposition
of passing, or of attempting to pass, in spite of the
opposition of the Viennese bureaucracy which it would
have infallibly encountered, some measure of reform of
the fiscal relations of the two countries. Frequent
reference was, indeed, made to the scandal of the one-sided
Austrian protective system as one of the causes, if not the
chief cause, of the poverty of the country, and the question
of the customs barrier erected between the two halves of
the monarchy and the expediency of doing something for
the encouragement of trade was referred to a committee ;
but there the matter ended. Presumably, the shock inflicted
on Hungary by Josephism had produced a temporary
paralysis of the progressive instinct, and the energy of the
Diet was exhausted by its efforts to "entrench" the
constitutional position, and to put an end to the hatred
engendered by the conflict of rival religions. In any case,
the country had little reason to be dissatisfied with the
results attained in the short time which had elapsed since
the death of Joseph. It is a question whether the fact
that the duration of his successor's reign was limited to
two years was in reality a misfortune for Hungary, and
whether Leopold would have succeeded in maintaining
the spirit of confidence engendered by his early acts in the
minds of his Magyar subjects, but for which, when the
storm and stress of the Napoleonic period began, Austria
would have found itself in a far weaker position than that
which it actually occupied.

CHAPTER VIII

1792. FRANCIS was a sickly, petty creature, whom his father would gladly have excluded from the succession, had it been possible to do so, but for the fact that his second son, Charles, was no better fitted than the legal heir to occupy the throne.[1] The new King, half educated, virtuous, obstinate, and impatient of contradiction, prided himself before all on his pedantic attachment to the minutiae of government,[2] and was easily flattered by his ministers into the belief that he was a heaven-born genius who carried the whole weight of government on his own shoulders. In reality, he was a puppet in the hands of Colloredo and Thugut, in spite of the fact that he distrusted them to such an extent that he employed the secret police to watch their every action. So long as the detective force succeeded in making him believe that no detail of the public or private life of his subjects could escape the royal omniscience,[3] and provided that a sufficient number of new State documents were submitted for his signature, and that the old ones were properly docketed and pigeonholed, no suspicion of his own futility ever crossed his mind.

[1] For Joseph's opinion of his son see Anton Springer, *Geschichte Oesterreichs seit dem Wiener Frieden*, Leipzig, 1863, i. 109.

[2] He continually said that he would have made a good head clerk in a government office.—Hartig, *Genesis der Revolution in Oesterreich*. "D'esprit étroit et mesquin il prenait la signature des pièces pour l'exercice du pouvoir et l'ingérence dans tous les détails des affaires pour la marque de l'autorité."—Eisenmann, *Le Compromis Austro-Hongrois*, p. 53.

[3] Anton Springer, *o.c.* i. 118.

The French Revolution not only shook thrones but also shattered preconceived notions as to the divine origin of class distinction ; it is therefore not surprising that when Francis came forth in the face of Europe as the champion of the monarchical idea, and, incidentally, of the privileges of the nobility, he had the almost solid support of the governing classes of Hungary. The nobles expressed themselves as ready to shed the last drop of their blood in the cause of the security and dignity of His Majesty, and Francis in his turn declared his anxiety to do all in his power to promote the welfare of his beloved Hungarians, and to encourage their national aspirations.[1] He badly wanted their backing in his combat with the democratic hydra, " the spirit of the age," " the malady of the time," in which, at a later date, Metternich saw the root of all evil.[2] He bid for it boldly by promising to find places for Magyars in the Council of State and in the holy of holies of the military hierarchy, as well as by gratifying the landlords by still further strengthening their juridic control of the peasants—the protection of whom was ever, according to Austrian apologists, the pride and pleasure of the House of Habsburg. The objectionable Servian Chancery was at once abolished, and the Diet showed its gratitude by receiving the Metropolitan and bishops of the Greek Church into its body. There was a considerable party which embraced the doctrines of liberty and equality, but the fear of the spectre of revolution threw all questions of social reform into the background, and would-be

[1] "Mit der Offenherzigkeit, welche auf der Reinheit meiner Absichten und meinem Selbstbewusstsein beruht, erkläre ich vertraulich, dass auch die grossmüthige Nation es nie bereuen wird, mir vertraut zu haben. . . . Euer Liebden werden den Mitbürgern nach der Heimkehr sagen, dass ich der eifrigste Hüter der Verfassung sein werde . . . meinen Willen stets das Gesetz, mein Herz nur Aufrichtigkeit und das Vertrauen des Volkes leiten wird."— Speech to the Hungarian deputation sent to invite him to Hungary to be crowned. Csuday, ii. 300.

[2] *Memoirs,* iv. 249, 255 and *passim.*

reformers had to possess their souls in patience while the unnatural alliance between Hungarian constitutionalism and Austrian autocracy, based on an inquisitorial detective system, held the field.

It is, unfortunately, impossible to blink the fact that the enthusiasm of the governing classes for constitutional government was, in the early part of Francis's reign, to a great extent the outcome of anxiety to maintain the privileges of the minority at the expense of the great mass of the people.[1] Consequently, but little inclination was manifested to open the door to new ideas, or to protest when the introduction of a strict censorship barred and bolted it. The mere suggestion of a connexion between Jacobinism and Protestantism was considered to provide a sufficient justification for a recrudescence of religious intolerance ; and the general nervousness was shown by the treatment meted out to Martinovics and his associates 1795. who were hanged, or imprisoned for years, for complicity in a plot which never existed. True, one of the conspirators had translated the Marseillaise, and Martinovics himself had produced a revolutionary catechism [2]— a

[1] When in 1807 Paul Nagy, the most radical of contemporary politicians, urged on the Diet the necessity of taking steps to lighten the burden of the lower classes, he was shouted down by the Diet and told "not to play the fool."—Michael Horváth, o.c. vi. 255.

[2] Divided into four parts : (1) What is man? What is wisdom, and what should be done to combat superstition and ignorance ? (2) What is Society and Citizenship ? Of the sovereignty of the people, and of the duties of Citizenship. (3) Of servitude. No difference between the serfs and beasts of burden. (4) The right of resistance to governmental violence, to put an end to slavery, and open the door to freedom. Kings are men of like passions with ourselves and may be deposed if they make improper use of their power (this hardly goes further than the clause of the Golden Bull). Of the evil caused by the power of priests and nobles—ignorance and fanaticism the result. Hungary enclosed in a Chinese wall by the exclusion of books. The people's rights must be restored, or it will take them for itself. These platitudes were described in the indictment as "*scripta jam in se ipso crimen laesae majestatis involventia.*"—De Gerando, *Der öffentliche Geist in Ungarn*, Leipzig, 1848, pp. 36, 46. Michael Horváth, o.c. vi. 142. The incriminated documents were not circulated but kept locked up by the seventy-five "conspirators." Even those who took no part in the discussions of the society, but were aware of its

declaration, of the rights of man which justified resistance to the monarch, in fact, the abolition of royalty as an institution; but it contained nothing but general principles, no reference to Austria or Hungary in particular, and there is no evidence to show that its author, or any one of his associates, contemplated the creation either of a revolutionary movement directed against the Habsburgs, or of a peasant insurrection, the nightmare of the privileged classes. But Thugut[1] had no difficulty in persuading Francis that he had had a narrow escape, and convinced him of the necessity of keeping the country free from contamination by foreign revolutionary notions, and of discouraging pernicious originality in all its forms. And so the spirit of reaction triumphed, and the advent of Napoleon found King and nobles united to an extent that would have seemed impossible to previous generations, that alone explains the fact that after the defeats and humiliations which preceded the Peace of Pressburg[2] the House of Habsburg was able to come up smiling for the next round.

By a reference to the traditional liberality of Hungary, 1796. evidenced by its chivalrous treatment of his respected ancestress, Maria Theresa, Francis obtained without any difficulty a vote for 50,000 men, 10,000 horses, and an enormous quantity of supplies. Francis's younger brother, the Archduke Joseph, was elected Palatine, and after this

---

existence, were condemned. Seven of the accused were hanged. For the history of this "conspiracy" see especially Fraknói Vilmos, *Martinovics és Társainak Összeesküvese*, 2nd ed.; for the catechism, *o.c.* p. 427 *sqq.*, Budapest, 1884.

[1] Thugut, originally Thunichtgut, son of a carpenter. Maria Theresa discerned his abilities. He obtained Bukovina for Austria, in order to connect Transylvania with Galicia, on the ground that it formerly belonged to Hungary, in which, however, it was never incorporated. He was credited, not without justification, with having invented the Martinovics conspiracy to terrify public opinion.—Beöthy, *o.c.* p. 652. Michael Horváth, *o.c.* vi. 126. He succeeded to the place left vacant by the death of Kaunitz in 1794.

[2] Austria lost the Venetian provinces, Tyrol and Vorarlberg, roughly 3,000,000 of its population, and its access to Italy and Germany.

affirmation of the solidarity of King and people the Diet was dissolved—a blank session so far as legislation was 1797. concerned. When the Peace of Campo Formio was signed the following year, Hungary had already lost 100,000 men and 30,000,000 florins, but that did not damp its ardour, and in 1802 the Diet voted the increase of the Hungarian contingent to 64,000 men, and the provision of 12,000 more in the event of a renewal of hostilities. In 1809, the *levée en masse* was decreed ; the summons was responded to with the utmost enthusiasm, and one can only marvel at the loyalty evinced throughout the whole Napoleonic period to a dynasty which had already proved its ability to astonish the world by its ingratitude to a nation which had saved Austria in 1741 when birds of prey were preparing to tear it to pieces. For twenty-two years Hungary fought almost without interruption in order to maintain Austria's position in Germany and Italy, as a rule under incompetent generals,[1] and with little encouragement in the way of promotion for Magyar officers, except when Vienna saw signs of slackening in the national enthusiasm for the Habsburg cause.

1804. For a moment Hungarian suspicions were aroused when, after Napoleon had announced his assumption of the Imperial title, Francis followed suit by taking that of Emperor of Austria, which might in some measure be regarded as implying, if not the fusion of the two countries, at all events the subordination of Hungary to the hereditary provinces. It was not the first time that the House of Habsburg had considered the advisability of adopting a title which should symbolise its hereditary rights to the Crown of Hungary, as well as to the heterogeneous congeries of duchies, principalities, and countships comprised in its Austrian dominions. The

1 Who, with two exceptions, did not know the Hungarian language, and openly expressed their dislike of, and contempt for, the Magyars.—Michael Horváth, *o.c.* vi. 298.

style of Emperor of Pannonia had been suggested in the
time of Joseph II., and even before that period slipshod
diplomatic documents and careless speakers referred, not
infrequently, to a non-existent "Austrian Empire," under
which misnomer Hungary was supposed to be included.
To speak of the head of the House of Habsburg as "the
Emperor" was perfectly correct, as there was in fact only
one Emperor, namely, that of the Holy Roman Empire,
for the title of Emperor, qualified by the addition of
the words, "of all the Russias," was merely adopted for
convenience in dealing with West European Courts, and
had no meaning except as a sort of translation of
the proper appellation, "Tsar."[1]   The shaky and
precarious position of his German throne, the practical
collapse of which led to his abandonment of the Holy
Roman title two years later, made it advisable that
Francis should invent some phrase which should prevent
his being reduced to calling himself by his proper
appellation of King of Hungary and Bohemia and Archduke of Austria.   It is doubtful whether the assumption
of the new title was intended as a step in the direction
of the amalgamation of Hungary with the hereditary
provinces ; but the Magyars naturally viewed the move
with apprehension, though in all probability it was only
the outcome of an idea that it is more distinguished to be
styled "Emperor" than to be one of a crowd of mere
Kings.   In any case, Francis found it necessary to allay
Hungarian suspicion by issuing a rescript in which he
declared that "that which We have done for the glory of
Our monarchy has no effect on the individuality, laws,
or constitution of Our beloved Hungary and of the
parts thereto annexed," though, but for the fact that
the principle of the indivisibility of the hereditary provinces of the Habsburgs received fresh confirmation,

[1] See Freeman's introduction to the translation of Léger's *History of
Austria-Hungary*.

Hungary was in no way affected by the conversion of the Archduke of Austria into an Emperor.[1]

1805.   Some reward was clearly due to Hungary in return for the enthusiastic loyalty of which it continued to give proof, and at the next meeting of the Diet Francis agreed to make further concessions in the direction of establishing the official position of the Hungarian language.[2] Henceforward the Diet is to communicate with the King in Hungarian and Latin (columnaliter), and only in Hungarian with the Chancery and the Council of Lieutenancy. Hungarian may be used in the County Courts, and the King undertakes to give full effect to the seventh article of the law of 1792 already referred to.[3] But at this point the concessions with respect to the language question came to a full stop, and, though the Diet of 1807 made further attempts to obtain complete official recognition for the national language, Francis

---

[1] "Salvis semper juribus, legibus et Constitutione Regni Hungariae." It is absurd to lay stress, as Tezner (Der Österreichische Kaisertitel, Vienna, 1899) does, on the fact that the Diet used the expressions "tota monarchia" and "monarchia Austriaca," and to argue therefrom that Hungary recognised the fact of its inclusion in a uniform Austrian Empire, as the words are "utilitas Regni Hungariae partiumque adnexarum et totius monarchiae," which show that a distinction is drawn ; otherwise the words "tota monarchia" would suffice alone, and a separate reference to Hungary would be superfluous. Further, we f.nd the phrase "tota monarchia et Regnum Hungariae," 1805 (see infra, p. 301, re the title of Ferdinand, 5th of Hungary and 1st of Austria). Friedjung's offhand statement that Hungary was, and recognised the fact that it was, "ein Theil Österreichs" requires no refutation.—Österreich von 1848 bis 1860, Stuttgart, 1908, I. vi.

[2] 1805, Art. 4. The importance of language as a preservative of national individuality was now fully recognised, thanks to Révay, Kazinczy, and others, for whom see Riedl's Hungarian Literature, London, 1906. Paul Nagy pointed out, for the first time in 1807, that the language was of greater importance than the Constitution, as the latter might be won back, but language and nationality never, if once lost.—Beöthy, o.c. p. 884 ; Tezner, Der Österreichische Kaisertitel, etc., Vienna, 1899, says that Hungary's objection to the official use of the German language was "nur ein Agitationsmittel, durch welches das eigentliches Ziel desselben die Abwehr der Vernichtung der ständischen Steuerprivilegien verdeckt wurde," p. 39, a statement which he does not attempt to support by evidence.

[3] Supra, p. 238.

successfully took refuge in a policy of procrastination, 1807. and the members dispersed with nothing to their credit save an undertaking on the part of the King that he would never do anything to curtail the right of free speech, and with further sacrifices of men and money on the debit side. It was resolved that the nobles, merchants, and tradesmen, should contribute one-sixth of their income, and one per cent of the value of all personal property;[1] and as if to prove that the words, first used at this meeting of the Diet, "we are the representatives not only of the Nobility but are the protectors of the entire population," were no meaningless phrase, the peasants were exempted from the imposition of this exceptional burden.   Neither King nor country was satisfied with the results of the session of 1807; the latter, on account of the magnitude of the sacrifices demanded of it and of the ill-concealed disinclination of the Crown to do anything to promote the national welfare by encouraging the trade purposely sacrificed to Austrian interests; the former, because he realised the fact that temporary votes of men and money could not suffice to maintain his position in Europe in view of the growing intimacy of France and Russia, and that nothing would answer his purpose short of putting the military organisation of the country on a permanent basis and thereby depriving the Diet of its most cherished rights—the control of taxation and the voting of the annual contingent.

When the Diet met again Francis had little reason 1808. to complain. With a few flattering words he obtained more than he could ever have got by appeals to reason. Not only did he obtain a vote of 20,000 men, but he was invested with authority, hitherto unparalleled, to proclaim the *levée en masse* without reference to the Diet in the event of a renewal of the war at any time during the next three years. He thus was enabled

---

[1] Michael Horváth, o.c. vi. 244.

to exhibit in the eyes of Europe the spectacle of the solidarity of King and people, and a proof of the readiness of the Magyars to make any sacrifice when the dynasty was in danger.[1] Napoleon did not sufficiently appreciate the intensity of Hungarian loyalty when he issued the celebrated proclamation[2] from Schönbrunn.

1809.   It is the Emperor of Austria, not the King of Hungary, who has declared war against me. By your Constitution he had no right to do so without your consent. . . . Hungarians, the moment has come to recover your independence. I offer you peace, the integrity of your territory, your liberty, and your Constitution. . . . I want nothing from you : only to see you free and independent. Your union with Austria has been your misfortune. Your blood has flowed for her on distant fields, and your dearest interests have been continually sacrificed to those of the hereditary States. You formed the fairest portion of the monarchy and yet were reduced to the position of a subject province, and made the sport of passions to which you were strangers. You have your national customs and a national language. You boast of an ancient and illustrious origin. Regain, therefore, your national existence. Have a King of your own choice who reigns for you only, who resides in your midst, who is surrounded only by you and your soldiers. Hungarians, this is what Europe, which has its eyes on you, what I also ask of you : a lasting peace, commercial relations, and an assured independence. That is the prize that awaits you if you are worthy of your ancestors and of yourselves. You will not refuse these liberal and generous offers. You will not squander your blood in the cause of feeble Princes, ever dominated by corrupt ministers who are in the pay of England, that enemy of the Continent, which has founded its prosperity on monopoly and on our divisions. Meet, therefore, in your national Diet on the plain of Rákos, as your ancestors did, and let me know the result of your deliberations.

---

[1] "*Cordi meo carissimi Hungari! Fecistis ea quae charactere vestro avito digna sunt. Videbit tota Europa Regem vestrum vobiscum ita unum sentire, ut nec mihi nec vobis carius esse possit quam antiquam constitutionem nostram usque ultimam guttam sanguinis defendere velle. Juncti fuimus, juncti sumus, juncti semper manebimus donec mors nos separabit.*" —*Diarium Comit.* 35, 376.

[2] Facsimile in *A Mag. Nem. Tört.* viii. 582.

To this 'document, which, with consummate ingenuity, touches every sore spot in the body politic and appeals both to passion and to sentiment, Hungary replied by making still further sacrifices[1] on behalf of the dynasty which it was invited to throw overboard, and at Aspern and Wagram justified the confidence which the imperial family[2] manifested by taking refuge in Hungary when the enemy, who would have seduced the Magyars from their allegiance, was at the gates of Vienna.   Hungary's reward for its devotion to a losing cause was the loss of Fiume and of the western parts of Croatia, and (as soon as the King thought his position to be sufficiently well assured by the marriage of Napoleon to Marie Louise) by the initiation of a new phase of reaction and repression.

The Archduke Joseph tried to press upon Francis the necessity of establishing the monarchy on a firmer basis, either by means of the extension of representative institutions to all the subject provinces, or by a complete restoration of the constitutional system of Hungary, and by a transference (suggested by Gentz in 1805)[3] of the centre of gravity to Buda : for the possession

---

[1] Hungary's contribution this year amounted to 40,000,000 florins.—Horváth, *Közös Ügyek*, p. 39. Beöthy, *o.c.* ii. 247 *n.*, says 28,000,000 and 50,000 men.   The *levée en masse* took place four times during the Napoleonic period —1797, 1800, 1805, 1809.   In 1796 Hungary gave 50,000 recruits, 6,100,000 bushels of wheat and oats, 10,000 horses, and 20,000 head of cattle.   In 1802 the contingent was 64,000 men.   In 1807 additional 12,000 recruits were voted, and in 1808 a further 20,000.—*Ibid.* i. 725.   And yet Austria complained that Hungary had done nothing and demanded that it should take the responsibility for a large part of Austria's public debt, not a penny of which had been spent in Hungary or for Hungary's benefit.

[2] 1805.   The Archduke Joseph, the Palatine, wrote on November 23 to Francis, "Let Your Majesty rely on the Hungarian people which will never desert its King."—Horváth, *o.c.* p. 113.   Francis said in a brave moment that he would not make peace with the French even after five defeats, and that if he had to retreat to Temesvár he would win the sixth battle there (Beöthy, *o.c.* i. 669), showing that he knew what the possession of Hungary meant to its dynasty, its resources, its sticking power, and its patriotism.

[3] *Correspondence*, iv 244.   Not only Gentz, the German political writer in the Austrian service, but Talleyrand also considered that the seat of government should be transferred from Vienna to Buda, which was less liable to attack

of the crown of St. Stephen seemed likely to be the one thing capable of preserving for the Emperor of Austria his importance in the eyes of Europe. Francis curtly replied that "the Hungarian Constitution must be remodelled and brought into harmony with the system obtaining in the other hereditary possessions." For the moment he thought of nothing but of restoring some semblance of order to the financial system of the monarchy. In the position of affairs which obtained in the rest of Europe the placing of an external loan was an impossibility. Notes were in circulation to the amount of 1,060,000,000 florins, which, in the absence of a sufficient corresponding metallic reserve, were accepted only at an enormous discount.[1] Hungary in vain protested against the adoption of this system of printing-press finance, as to which it had not been consulted, which, if not actually contrary to Hungarian law in any case was not sanctioned by it. The new Austrian Finance Minister, Wallis, reduced the value of the note issue by a stroke of the 1811. pen to 212,000,000, i.e. to one-fifth of its face value, and an illegal patent[2] was the first notification Hungary received of the accomplished fact. Further, the value of the 80,000,000 florins' worth of copper money in circulation was reduced by four-fifths in order, apparently, to complete the ruin of the tax-paying peasant, already reduced to the verge of starvation by the sacrifices

and was the natural centre of the Dual Monarchy.—Beöthy, o.c. p. 638. Bismarck wrote to Baron Schleinitz, March 13, 1861 : "If I had to be Emperor of Austria I should at once transfer myself to Pest, put on a hussar uniform and speak Hungarian. I should incorporate everything in Hungary which I could squeeze into it. I should tell the Magyar Diet that the first duty of an Austrian Emperor is to be a Hungarian King."—Beksics, *Mátyás Király Birodalma*, p. 122.

[1] At about one-tenth of their nominal value.—Michael Horváth, o.c. vi. 314. The ratio of paper to silver fell as low as one to twelve.—See also Anton Springer, o.c. i. 168 *sqq.*

[2] Rescript of May 8, 1811. The law of 1790-91 (Art. 12) declared such patents to be illegal, as the Diet did not fail to point out.

entailed by the war. The counties protested, but merely received a peremptory order to carry out the terms of the Patent within seven days, and a rescript from Francis rebuking their "insolence" and threatening "the most stringent measures." The ringleaders of resistance were summoned to Vienna "*ad audiendum verbum regium*," *i.e.* in order to be frightened into submission or corrupted by promises ; but the King, nevertheless, had to give way to the demands of the nation to the extent of summoning the Diet.

It met on August 25, and was at once confronted with a demand for an increase by 12,000,000 florins of the taxes raised for military purposes, and for a guarantee of 100,000,000 of the total, depreciated, paper issue of 212,000,000 florins ; *i.e.* of practically the same amount as that allotted to the King's Austrian dominions, which were far more prosperous and enjoyed the benefit of a gerry-mandered customs system at Hungary's expense. And this in face of a four-fifths depreciation of the cash in circulation.[1] In 1814, in spite of the Government's under-taking to issue no more paper money,[2] a further emission of 480,000,000 was made, which fell to one-third of its nominal value. The next step was the redemption of the depreciated notes by the exchange of 100 new paper florins for 250 of the previous issue. Had Francis shown any inclination to satisfy the wishes of the Diet in the matter of the language question, it is possible that he would have met with little opposition from that body. But he returned a point-blank refusal to all its requests, and ought not to have been surprised when it paid him in his own coin and refused to undertake any part of the burden of extra taxation which he would have imposed on the country. Twelve years of despotic government

[1] The value of the notes issued in 1811 fell 45 per cent in twelve months.— Michael Horváth, *o.c.* vi. 389.

[2] Patent of February 20, 1811.

was the result, and only in the political life of the counties
did any vestige remain of the Constitution likened by
Metternich[1] to "a precious jewel which ought to be kept
like a relic"—locked up, apparently, in a safe, to be
exhibited from time to time to prove to a careless Europe
the good faith with which the Habsburgs observed their
obligations.

Francis had no difficulty in forgetting what he had
said on the occasion of his accession to the Throne : that
Hungary would have no cause to regret its confidence in
the excellence of his intentions, and that he would be the
most ardent defender of the Constitution and of the laws.
A story is related to the effect that when Baron Stift, the
King's doctor, who was treating him for a persistent
cough, observed that there was no cause for anxiety as
His Majesty had an excellent constitution, Francis exclaimed, "Never let me hear that word again. Say, if
you like, that I have a *dauerhafte Natur*, but don't speak
of constitutions, for there is no such thing as a good one,
and never will be."[2] Whether the story is a true one or
not, from 1813 to 1825 the Constitution of Hungary
was practically non-existent. Metternich described the
Holy Alliance between Russia, Austria, and Prussia as
having come into existence "not for the destruction of
popular rights or for the promotion of absolutism or
tyranny, but as the outcome of the piety of the Tsar, and
for the adaptation to politics of the principles of Christianity." As far as Hungary was concerned these Christian
principles found their expression in an unexampled obscurantism, and in a total disregard of the contractual obliga-
1814. tions of the reigning monarch. The Council of State
was re-established in Vienna, and the Hungarian Chancery
and Council of Lieutenancy were reduced to the position
of mere instruments for the execution of its instructions.

[1] *Memoirs*, iv. 256.
[2] *A Mag. Nem. Tört.* ix. p. 10 ; Michael Horváth, *oc.* vi. 372.

The censorship of the Press reached a point of development hitherto unattained. The importation of foreign
periodicals "of a dangerous tendency" was strictly forbidden ; [1] and as the order was held to apply not only to
political but to purely literary productions as well, it
amounted to a total prohibition of all foreign literature.[2]
Some of the counties protested, but the Catholic ecclesiastics were on the side of the obscurantists. Their Synod
petitioned the King to instruct the censors to extend their
activity to the booksellers' shops, with a view to the
withdrawal of all "pernicious literature"—a comprehensive phrase as interpreted by religious and political reactionaries—and even induced him to prohibit the employment
of Protestant teachers in Catholic schools and private
families except as language and dancing-masters.

Though Francis had declared in his rescript addressed
to the Diet in 1807 that the independence of the Hungarian
Treasury should be strictly maintained, that institution
was not consulted on the subject of the new financial
measures adopted in 1816, nor was Hungary represented
on the commission appointed in August of the same year,
under the presidency of Metternich.[3] The result of the
deliberations of that body was embodied in the Patent of
October 29—the work of Stadion, the new Minister of
Finance. The Patent provided for the issue of five per
cent one hundred florin obligations, redeemable in specie
only, in exchange for notes of like nominal value and for
a like amount of short term bonds issued earlier in the
year. As if this depreciation did not inflict a sufficiently
serious loss on the holders, in 1820 outstanding paper
was redeemed at two-fifths of its face value,[4] and Stadion's
plan was so far successful that by 1827 the paper money

[1] Order of January 1, 1821.
[2] Michael Horváth, o.c. vi. 383 sq. Every possible obstacle was thrown
in the way of students wishing to visit foreign universities.
[3] Memoirs, iii. 15. See especially Anton Springer, o.c. i. 307-315.
[4] A Mag. Nem. Tört, ix. 45.

in circulation had been reduced from 1,060,000,000 to 99,000,000 florins.   It was no doubt good business for a Government to pay a penny for a shillingsworth of cash received or of services rendered, but the result to the individual was disastrous.[1]   The protests raised by Hungary on the promulgation of the Patent of 1811 was met by a royal assurance that the measure was of a temporary nature and would remain in force only until the meeting of the Diet ; but as the King in defiance of the law did not summon that body for the next thirteen years it was but cold comfort.   If the buying power of the depreciated paper and copper money had remained the same, it is conceivable that the peasant, who lived from hand to mouth, would not have been severely affected ; but this, of course, was not the case in a country which had to import most of its requirements, and, as will be seen hereafter, the Austrian Government would not accept its own paper in payment of taxes.

It might have been supposed that the Government would have made some concession to the poorer classes in return for the sacrifices entailed by the recent financial juggles.   Far from it.   The price of salt, a royal monopoly, which, as the King had admitted in his rescript of 1802,[2] could not be increased without the consent of the Diet,[3] was raised in 1811, 1815, and in 1816, without reference to the representatives of the nation.   A further rise of two florins the centner followed two years later, and the price had to be paid in silver then standing, owing to Stadion's measures, at a premium of 250 per cent.   If the Austrian Government had encouraged and facilitated the export of Hungarian products, something

---

[1] According to Michael Horváth, *o.c.* vi. 392, the result of the Government's financial measures was that in sixteen years the value of 100 florins paper fell as low as eight florins silver.

[2] September 23, and again December 14, 1807.

[3] Law xx. 1790, *nisi extreme urgentes circumstantiae aliud exigerent,* i.e. in case of war making it impossible to summon the Diet.

might have been said in its favour; but the duty imposed on Hungarian corn and cattle exported to Austria, and the octroi dues, made it impossible to compete with Bavaria and Turkey, while the duty imposed on Austrian wines exported to Hungary was comparatively trifling. Tobacco being a State monopoly in Austria the duty on the Hungarian product was raised, first from one and a half kreuzers to twenty, and then to twenty florins payable in silver.[1] Articles imported from abroad into Hungary and then into Austria paid duty twice over, while Austria could buy goods abroad, and after paying a single duty could export them, without further payment, to Hungary. So after forced depreciation of the currency had sheared the Magyars to the skin, the gerrymandered tariff system proceeded to remove the scalp also.

In the enforced absence of the Diet no one could make effectual protest against the system of organised spoliation of which Hungary was the victim. While war was in progress or in prospect the King was too busy to be bothered with a Diet, and when peace was assured he had no time to spare. Plenty of time, however, was available for the making of an insidious attack on the organisation of the counties—the last refuge of the constitutional principle. For some time past the Government had appointed to the office of lord-lieutenant only such denationalised Magyars as could be relied upon to raise no obstacles to the realisation of bureaucratic ideals; and in some counties meetings for the election of officials had not been summoned for ten or fifteen years.[2] Vienna had learnt by experience that a frontal attack on local autonomy was doomed to failure, and could only result in causing all classes to combine in defence of their interests. A new scheme must be devised, and a new weapon discovered

---

[1] Umrisse einer möglichen Reform in Ungarn, i. 17.
[2] Michael Horváth, Huszonöt év Magyarország történetéböl, i. 25 (cited henceforth as Horváth, Huszonöt év).

wherewith to break down resistance to intended centralisation.   No better instrument could be found than the
impecunious "noble," whose membership of the privileged
class made him, as regards voting power, the equal of the
richest and the most intelligent.   The "nobles in sandals"[1]
who might, and did, occupy any position from that of
postman to that of pig-tender, had hitherto taken but
little part in the political life of the counties.   Want of
time and money had prevented attendance at the meetings,
and the Government was not slow to recognise the fact
that here was an element which could be utilised to obtain
the complete exclusion from office of the educated classes,
and to ensure the election of pliant creatures who would
reduce the autonomy of the counties to a mere sham.
Free food and free drinks brought the impecunious in
their thousands to the polling-places, and the return of
the official candidate was rarely in doubt.   In order that
there might be no mistake, under the pretext of safeguarding the sacred rights of the people, an order was
issued from Vienna which abolished the old system of
election by acclamation and substituted therefor individual
voting, thereby assuring the preponderance of a corrupt
and frequently intoxicated majority.   The success of the
autocratic wolf in the sheepskin coat of the sandalled
nobility was especially precious to the Government at a
moment when the Freemasons of Spain and the Carbonari
of Italy were keeping Metternich fully employed.   With
Naples and Piedmont in a ferment the time was not yet
ripe for undisguised autocracy, and Francis thought it
necessary to repeat his assurances of love for Hungary
and of attachment to its Constitution.   "Hitherto, by the
grace of God, I have preserved your country from every
danger, and will take steps to avert all possible harm
in the future; for my happiness consists in that of my

[1] Later known as "five-florin Magnates."—Michael Horváth, Huszonöt
év, i. 580.

faithful people, the task of governing whom has been imposed on me by Divine Providence. Now, once more, peril is threatening the world. The whole universe is playing the fool (*stultizat*), and with ulterior motives is demanding a Constitution. You are blessed in having a Constitution inherited from your ancestors, which I wish you to love as I love it. I have preserved it hitherto, and it is my intention to hand it down unimpaired to my successors in the hope that you will not desert me in the hour of danger. The danger is not yet here, but should it ever come I count upon your assistance." [1]   Apart from the terminological inexactitude of the first sentence of this remarkable appeal, it may be pointed out that the monarch's affection for the Constitution had been shown in the past only by his failure to summon the Diet for the last eight years, and was to be manifested in the future by a refusal to convene the representatives of the nation for the succeeding period of five years.[2]   The Magyars' characteristic affection for the dynasty seemingly enabled them to swallow any inaccuracy provided it was clothed in the Magyar language, but a further attack on the depleted pockets of the tax-payer was more than they could stand. For the suppression of the commotions in Italy, the War Office and Stadion decided that Hungary must produce 28,000 recruits,[3] and that the taxes, fixed by the Diet at its meeting eight years ago at 5,200,000 florins, and payable in paper money, must thenceforth be paid in silver. The result was that the ratio of paper to silver then being as one is to two and a half, the contribution of Hungary

---

[1] Horváth, *Huszonöt év*, i. 28.

[2] Law xiii. of 1791 required the Diet to be convened every three years or oftener.

[3] In order to maintain a semblance of legality, but at the same time to avoid the necessity of summoning the Diet, which alone could grant recruits, the Government called for the balance (28,420) of the 90,000 recruits demanded by Francis in 1813 and 1815, but not actually called out owing to the declaration of peace in the latter year. The contingent not having been voted by the Diet it was *ab initio* illegal.

was raised to 13,000,000 florins without the consent of
Diet, the only legal taxing authority. As a matter of
fact there was not sufficient silver in circulation for it to
be possible to pay the amount demanded in that metal,[1]
but this was a detail to which Vienna was entirely indifferent, and Pharaoh's demand for bricks without straw
seems moderate in comparison with that of Stadion. In
1815 the Government had demanded and obtained taxes
and recruits behind the back of the Diet; but at that
time Napoleon was again at large, and there was the
excuse of imminent danger. In 1821 there was no such
justification for illegality, still less for the Government's
refusal to accept its own paper which it had arbitrarily
depreciated for its own ends. Neither the protests of the
counties nor the fact that a large percentage of previous
taxes was in arrear and uncollectable, and that the consumption of salt had dropped to an unprecedented level
—a certain proof of the destitution of peasant tax-payers—
could turn the Government from its purpose. The easy
1822. success of Metternich in Italy, and the knowledge that he
had the Holy Alliance at his back, prevented Francis from
paying attention to the warnings of the Palatine. Some
of the fifty-two counties paid the tax and found the
recruits; others, more numerous, only did so after the
receipt of threatening rescripts, while the remainder stood
firm for a long time. Eight refused to collect the taxes,
ten to provide recruits; and it was only by means of
moral terrorism or actual violence that the Government
was able to break down their resistance. Of the passive
resisters some were chained and imprisoned,[2] others were
arrested on a charge of treason, or on a trumped up
accusation of being in secret communication with Italian
insurgents; while those who resigned their offices,[3] rather

[1] Horváth, *Huszonöt év*, i. 116.

[2] At Komárom and elsewhere.—Horváth, *Huszonöt év*, i. 108.

[3] As in Bars County, where the whole official body resigned and so temporarily paralysed the illegal action of the commissioners sent to break down the

than be a party to illegality,[1] and refused to hold the necessary meetings, were surrounded by soldiers, driven to the meeting-place, and kept there till they gave way. As for the recruits, the press-gang looked after them, with the result that the forests were peopled with "poor fellows," the usual euphemism for highway robbers, and that agriculture came to a standstill for want of hands.[2]

In spite of the saying to the contrary, everything cannot be done with bayonets, and the King's advisers at last recognised the fact that violent coercion, though temporarily successful, must be beaten in the long run by resolute passive resistance. It was to the determined attitude adopted by a few counties in the face of tyranny and violence that the restoration of a semblance of constitutional government, after thirteen years of despotism, was ultimately due. The choice lay between the uncompromising utilisation of armed force for the final destruction of the Constitution and the convocation of the Diet which the counties had continually entreated Francis to summon in accordance with the law,[3] "not owing to passion or anarchical suggestion, but from motives of fidelity to him on whom we must look as upon the true Father of our Country. The mainspring of our action is the desire to protect the Throne and our ancient Constitution, and in our fidelity to both nothing shall shake us."[4]   The King was finally induced to accept the

resistance of the counties, by fair means or foul, by force or by bribing the impecunious "nobles," and so obtaining a majority at the county meetings over the intelligent opposition.

[1] Francis saw a revolutionary spirit where there was only conservatism anxious to maintain constitutional rights, and wished to indict the officials of Bars, but the attorney-general (Causarum Regalium Director) informed him that there was no law under which they could be indicted, and that the only result of prosecution would be to show up the illegality of the Government's action in the whole matter of taxes and recruits.—Marczali, *A Legujabb Kor Története*, p. 297, Budapest, 1892.

[2] Michael Horváth, *o.c.* vi. 246.

[3] xiii. of 1790-91.

[4] Address of Somogy County.—Marczali, *A Legujabb Kor Története*, p. 299.

second alternative and to adopt a comparatively constitutional attitude;[1] and though the Diet was summoned ostensibly only for the purpose of crowning Queen Carolina Augusta, and though Francis made no secret of the fact that he had no intention of complying with his legal obligation to summon the elected representatives of the nation at fixed intervals, the opportunity of airing grievances and of re-establishing the Constitution in accordance with the spirit of Law x. of 1790 was greeted with the utmost enthusiasm. With the opening of the Diet at Pressburg on September 11, 1825, began a new era of political development which ended with the capitulation of Világos twenty-four years later.

[1] Metternich claims the credit.—*Memoirs*, vol. v., letter to Gentz, Sept. 28, 1825.

CHAPTER IX

METTERNICH's success abroad blinded Europe to the inherent rottenness of the new-fangled Empire, and made it forget that Austria, as a united nation, was a diplomatic fiction, and consisted in reality only of a narrow bureaucracy, a disorganised army, an empty treasury, an all-powerful secret police, and a degenerate dynasty. For the last alone could any enthusiasm be expected from the monarchy's sole constituent race which was not a mere fragment of some greater political entity, and a time was bound to come when the policy of passive resistance to Viennese encroachment must give place to another ; when the Magyars would no longer be contented with " fencing round " their Constitution, but would see the necessity of advancing in the direction indicated by the liberal ideas of England and France. The weakness of the political situation lay in the fact that owing to a series of unconstitutional monarchs all energies had been directed to the maintenance of historic rights and not to the passing of progressive legislation. The change from mere defence to active progress is the characteristic feature of the period which was inaugurated by the convocation of the Diet of 1825.

The blackest darkness preceded the dawn. We are told that it is a mistake to suppose that Metternich had unlimited power over Francis, that while he ruled Europe he never ruled Austria or Hungary, and that

in matters of internal government he was purposely kept
at arm's length.[1] Be that as it may, it was certainly
Metternich who persuaded the King of the necessity of
preventing Hungary from coming in contact with the
notions of the outside world, in order to perform "the
task which Austria had undertaken of forming a dam
against the extension of the movement in favour of the
principle of the sovereignty of the people which was
spreading west of her."[2] The essence of the so-called
Metternich system was "zealous opposition to every
concession which would weaken the power of the monarch
either at home or abroad. It was a gigantic task to take
the field against the spirit of the age. No one Government could succeed in it alone. So long as the two
great Powers, Austria and Prussia, followed the same path
hand-in-hand, the supreme power could maintain an
undiminished control ; but as soon as the King of Prussia
decided to share his authority, though only in certain
matters, with the estates of the realm, it at once became
evident that the collapse of the autocratic principle
must soon follow in both countries. . . . The out-and-
out negation of the principle of a division of power, a
principle which the King of Prussia had half recognised,
became the task of Austria alone in Germany and
Western Europe."[3] For the execution of that task, so
far as Hungary was concerned, Metternich found willing
helpers in clerical obscurantists, and useful instruments
in the spies of Count Szedlniczky, Chief of the Secret
Police since 1817. The spy-system, first applied in
Austria, was extended to Hungary, where, before long, no
official could keep his place unless he was in Szedlniczky's
good books. The secret police took no notice of

[1] *Genesis der Revolution in Österreich,* 3rd ed., 1851, p. 15 (by Count
Hartig, the Austrian Minister).   Metternich said of himself : "J'ai gouverné
l'Europe quelquefois, l'Autriche jamais." See also Stiles, *Chargé d'Affaires* of
the United States in Vienna, *Austria in 1848-49,* London, 1852, i. 61.

[2] Hartig, *o.c.* p. 12.   [3] *Ibid. o.c.* p. 7.

Hungarian authorities, but took their instructions solely from Vienna. The introduction of foreign newspapers was forbidden ; passports could be obtained only with the greatest difficulty ; and only strong backstairs influence could obtain leave for Protestants, desiring to become professors, to visit foreign universities.   Innumerable protests from counties and individuals were addressed to the King, claiming that the behaviour of Hungary during the late wars justified it in looking for something better than suspicion, and warning the Government of the consequences of its policy.[1]   In spite of oppression, and partly in consequence of it, the party of progress and patriotism increased in strength.   Excessive severity was the cause of the censorship's failure ; the best foreign works were smuggled into the country, and forbidden fruit is proverbially attractive.   The process of literary revival which began at the end of the reign of Joseph II. had never entirely ceased.   The national literature was the begetter rather than the result of a national ideal, and the revival of letters was the chief cause of the gradual substitution of ideas of patriotism allied with progress for the narrow conception of that sentiment which had hitherto existed.   Hungary was still suffering from " insularity."   While the great nobles, austrianised by Maria Theresa, looked upon the Magyar language as a gipsy jargon, and, fearing the doctrines of liberalism and the loss of class privileges, stood shoulder to shoulder with the partisans of autocracy, the majority of the lesser nobles or gentry were inclined to be stagnant or retrograde ; to believe that what Magyar country gentlemen did not do could not be worth doing ; to be satisfied with the vegetable existence described in Eötvös's novel, The Village Notary, or to indulge in a swaggering prodigality exemplified by the Magyar Nabob of Maurus Jókai.   It was therefore essential to win back the great absentee

[1] Horváth, Huszonöt év, i. 78.

nobles to Hungary, to develop a less narrow form of patriotism, and to enforce recognition of the possibility of progress and of the substitution of a positive for a negative programme. There was plenty of scope for the energy of reformers. The peasants were practically in the same position as that which they occupied before the importation of the Habsburgs. The right of migration had again been conferred on them in 1790, and the school system established by Maria Theresa had done something for their intellectual improvement ; but though many landowners did all they could to improve the condition of their peasants the *régime* of the stick continued, and the great mass of the population, both Magyar and foreign, had no political rights, and consequently were not interested in the maintenance of Magyar nationality.

The gentry, who produced most of their own require- ments, were tolerably well off, but the depreciation of the currency made it difficult for them to maintain their standard of living, as nearly all articles of luxury required to be imported. Want of capital made the introduction of agricultural improvements an impossibility, and the raising of loans was hampered by the antiquated and exaggerated system of entail. The want of proper means of communication, of good roads, and of the regulation of the waterways, and the consequent difficulty of disposing of raw products, were severely felt, while the Austrian tariff system deliberately stifled Hungary's modest attempts to emerge from the position of a purely agri- cultural country. The Catholic clergy, who enjoyed the rights of nobility in virtue of their office, turned their eyes to the Government—the dispenser of preferment—and generally cared more for their prospects of promotion than for the constitutional rights of their country. With the increase of the wealth and importance of the towns, the, largely foreign, urban population had become dis- contented with the limitation of its political privileges, and hostile to the Magyar nobles, who, seeing in the organs of municipal government nothing but an alien oligarchy and a tool of Austrian autocracy, were justified in objecting to an increase of the influence of a permanently reactionary element. As it was, the Government's control of the Diet was excessive. The *Personalis Praesentiae Regiae locum tenens*, or president of the Lower House, was not elected by the members but was appointed by the King; and the High Court of Justice[1] provided the clerks and other officials, who consistently used their influence in favour of the Crown. Resolutions of the House were drawn up by an official of the High Court, and were handed to the Magnates by a deputation drawn from all classes of members; and the refusal of the Upper House to transmit such resolutions to the King, without even taking the trouble of considering them, nipped many salutary measures in the bud. An exchange of messages repeated ten times or more between the two Houses was no unusual occurrence; and if the two Houses finally managed to agree on a principle,[2] endless opportunities of quibbling and obstruction were afforded by the process of settling the form of the measure (*concertatio*) to be submitted for the royal sanction.[3] Delay is fatal to enthusiasm; members got bored with a subject owing to the procrastinating tactics of the Government, or changed their minds from conviction, or for the reason that the offer of place or title made it worth while for them to do so. The Upper House,[4] in which high officials and

---

[1] The judges had seats in the Lower House, but did not speak or vote.

[2] The holding of a *sessio mixta* of the two Houses was an extremely rare occurrence. Law xxvi. of 1790-91 *re* the Protestant religion was passed in such a session.—Beöthy, *o.c.* i..797. *Re* the exchange of messages, see Eötvös, *Reform*, 11.

[3] Horváth, *Huszonöt év*, i. 165, says that the Government, in drawing up the text of laws, always tried to make it as obscure as possible in order to be able to give its own interpretation to inconvenient enactments. Horváth was a member of the Hungarian Ministry in 1849.

[4] In 1844 there were 165 members, de Gerando, *Über den öffentlichen Geist in Ungarn*, p. 63. About thirty-four were ecclesiastics.

ecclesiastics were present in overwhelming numbers, was the stronghold of the Court party, and its unlimited powers of obstruction could reduce the progressives to almost permanent impotence.   At the elections of 1825 a considerable number of Magnates caused themselves to be elected members of the Lower House [1] in order to avoid condemnation to comparative inactivity in an assembly which was generally regarded as hostile to the interests of the nation.

The instructions given in 1825 by the various counties to their members agreed in demanding that steps should be taken to prevent a recurrence of the illegalities which the Government had recently perpetrated, and to "fence round" the Constitution ; but they contained little or no indication of a desire for far-reaching reforms except as regards the customs tariff.   For the most part they were limited to a demand for the establishment of an institution for the training of Hungarian officers (the Ludoviceum), and its corollary, the exclusive employment of Magyar officers in Magyar regiments ; for the recognition of Hungarian as the official language instead of Latin ; for the convocation of the Diet every three years ; and for the establishment of a Hungarian bank with power to issue notes.[2]   The moderation of these demands seems to have astonished Metternich, to judge from the letters he wrote a few days after the opening of the Diet.   "A good spirit prevails, but a great deal of inexperience is evident.   The fatherly attitude adopted by the Emperor in his speech has taken the Estates by surprise, and, as is usual in such cases, has inspired them with great enthusiasm. . . . . Certainly a democracy does not exist here.   The struggle goes on

---

[1] In which the Court party consisted only of the ecclesiastics, the urban representatives, and the members of the High Court.   Most of those who had distinguished themselves in the counties by activity in resisting the recent illegalities were elected.

[2] Horváth, *Huszonöt év*, i. 149 *sq*.

between the pure Royalists and the friends of the Constitution."[1] The speech in question contained the usual platitudes; as usual with the Habsburgs, the King posed as the champion of the Constitution which he had deliberately set at naught. "I ask nothing from you but zeal in taking measures for the increase of your own happiness . . . . . . and that the Constitution of the Kingdom may be fenced round and strengthened, and so be handed down to my descendants for the benefit of the Magyars, whom I regard as my beloved sons." The enthusiasm with which this expression of constitutional sentiments was received was somewhat damped by the King's reply to the first Address received from the Diet, in which that body complained that in direct contravention of Law x. of 1790-91 the country had been governed by royal edicts, in the same way as the hereditary provinces of Austria were governed; and that taxes and recruits had been collected by force. The Address declared that the principle that the convocation of the Diet depended on external circumstances and not on the Law was indefensible, and demanded that the representatives of the nation should be summoned every t ee years and that all officials should swear fidelity not nly to the Throne but to the Constitution as well, and ould be prosecuted if they violated their oath. The reply rebuked the Diet for wasting time; recorded the fact that His Majesty "noted with regret that many matters were again warmed up which had better have been forgotten," and justified the failure to summon the Diet for thirteen years on the ground of want of time and of suitable opportunities. The dissatisfaction evoked by this rescript induced the Palatine to press for a more satisfactory pronouncement. In a second rescript the King protested that nothing could be further removed from his intentions than an attempt to interfere with

---

[1] *Memoirs*, September 26, 1825, vol. v.

the Diet's control of taxation and recruiting, and
that the apparent misconception of his motives
"pained his paternal heart." He further pointed to
the fact that a law already existed providing for the
summoning of the Diet every three years (as though
that superfluous observation were of itself a sufficient
answer to a complaint that the legislative assembly
had not, in fact, been summoned since 1812), and
expressed his willingness to convene it at even shorter
intervals if necessary.

The receipt of this assurance, which was regarded as
a proof of the King's intention to turn over a new leaf,
encouraged the progressive party to begin the work of
reform. Law viii. of 1741 had affirmed the principle
that the payment of taxes was a personal obligation of the
peasants in occupation of allotments, and not a charge
on the land itself, which, consequently, if occupied by
a noble was exempt from taxation. A resolution was
now carried, condemning the inequitable system, and the
thin end of the wedge was driven into the principle of the
nobles' immunity from taxation, the abolition of which,
even to the limited extent now proposed, would materially
lighten the burden borne by the peasants, as the number
of nobles in occupation of land was large, and the
consequent increase in the ranks of the taxable would
be considerable. The Hungarian language next claimed
attention. It was pointed out that it was nothing less
than a scandal that the study of the national idiom should
be regarded as of less importance than that of a dead
language, that Catholic priests should think that a
knowledge of any tongue but that of their own ritual
was superfluous, and that the German and other foreigners
who made their money out of the Magyar population
should refuse to learn the language of their adopted
country. Paul Nagy suggested that the prime necessity
was the establishment of a Hungarian academy, whose

members should devote themselves to the task of polishing and developing the language and of encouraging its use ; "but all this is vain talk," he exclaimed, "while those who could do most in this direction hang back. The chief necessity is money, money, money." His words did not fall on deaf ears. Count Stephen Széchenyi, a member of the Upper House, promptly offered a year's income, some sixty thousand florins ; many others followed his example ; subscriptions poured in ; a committee was appointed to carry out the scheme outlined by Nagy, and a new era in the history of the Hungarian language began.

At first quite a sensation was caused in the Upper House when Széchenyi addressed it in Hungarian, but soon others followed suit, and in a short time the importance of the national idiom as the best preservative of Magyar nationality was generally recognised. The proposal that Hungarian should thenceforth be the official parliamentary language met with some opposition on the part of Croatian representatives and of some Hungarians of Upper Hungary, where Austrian influence was strongest, and it was evident that the Court was anxious to do all it safely could do to prevent the realisation of Magyar aspirations. The King's reply to the request of the Diet that laws should thenceforth be published in Hungarian as well as in Latin, a request that had already been formulated in 1811 but without success, was evasive and unsatisfactory, and afforded further proof in Hungarian eyes of the hostility to the idea of Magyar nationality of a King who saw no objection to issuing proclamations in Hungarian at the time of the French war, when the enthusiastic loyalty of his Hungarian subjects was a matter of vital importance, but would make no concession when he felt his position to be secure. In reality there should have been no question of gracious concessions ; in this, as in other matters, the Diet asked nothing but that to which it was entitled, and the

Palatine admitted to Széchenyi that he knew of no law which prohibited a Hungarian from using his native language. But the Court thought otherwise, or affected to do so, and, except for the foundation of the Academy, the session of 1825 marked no advance in the direction of establishing Hungarian as the official language. And, indeed, the general legislative gains of the Diet were infinitesimal. Academic resolutions, and fresh paper guarantees of constitutional rights, could hardly be looked upon as a result commensurate with the energy and enthusiasm manifested by the progressive party.[1] " His Majesty, being entirely convinced that his own and the Kingdom's welfare is based solely on the punctual observance of the law, and that if any part of His Majesty's rights or of those of the Estates be lost, the entire legal edifice established by centuries of use would collapse, has graciously thought fit to declare that it is his chief care to defend and maintain the Constitution, and to cause others to maintain the same, more especially Laws i., x., xii., and xix. of 1790 "[2] (Law iii.). " His Majesty assures the Estates that in the matter of recruits and taxation he recognises the binding force of the laws of 1715-18 and 1790-91, and that he will not cause any change to be made in the nature or amount of taxation without the consent of the Diet" (Law iv.). " As custom and the experience of centuries proves that the holding of the Diet is the chief promoter of the welfare of the Kingdom, and a beneficent remedy and preventive of grievances, His Majesty assures the Estates and Orders that he will not fail to give effect to Law xiii. of 1790, relating to the

[1] In the 1825 Diet, questions were for the first time decided by direct voting. Hitherto the Personalis, after hearing the chief speakers, declared the motion carried or rejected on the principle that " *vota non numerantur sed ponderantur.*" As he was a nominee of the Government the result of such a principle may be imagined.

[2] Recognising the independence of the Kingdom and the division of legislative power between King and Diet, *supra*, p. 232 *sqq.*

Diet "[1] (Law v.).   The expression of constitutional sentiments contained in the new laws must have been too
familiar to excite much enthusiasm, as in the past such
declarations were generally the precursors of a fresh period
of autocratic illegality.   At the same time it was not
discouraging. Though the session came to an end, the
political activity of the members did not cease.   Numerous
committees laboured unceasingly at the work of laying
the foundations of constitutional reform, and of preparing
the materials intended to be utilised at the coming meeting
of the representatives of the nation, now, perhaps for the
first time, imbued with the idea that their duties were not
confined to maintenance of the constitutional *status quo*,
or to the promotion of local rather than of national
interests.

The fear of complications with Russia made it necessary
that the Court should be on good terms with the Magyars,
for a disturbed and discontented Hungary would make
the re-establishment of the army on a proper basis, and
effective interference abroad, an impossibility.   Since 1815
the Hungarian forces had greatly decreased in numbers,
and comparatively few volunteers came forward to fill the
vacancies.   Owing to the accepted principle, "once a
soldier always a soldier," many of the rank and file had
passed the serviceable age, and the establishment was
several thousand short of the proper complement.[2]   The
Magyars entertained a rooted objection to military service
in peace time and the Government did nothing to overcome their antipathy.   The Hungarian regiments were
full of Austrian officers, promoted over the heads of
qualified natives, and the fact that it was the settled policy
of the Government to keep down the number of Magyar
officers was proved by its refusal to sanction the establishment of the Ludoviceum projected as long ago as 1808.

---

[1] Providing for its convocation every three years.
[2] Marczali, *A Legujabb Kor Története*, 312.

Further, the use of the military to enforce the illegal
collection of taxes made the army unpopular, and caused
it to be looked upon as the blind instrument of an alien
and hostile Government. The committee appointed to
consider the whole question wished, now that in the days
of scientific soldiering the *levée en masse* was out of date,
that every noble should serve for a period as a private
soldier as a condition precedent to eligibility for public
office, an innovation which would soon have provided a
national army controlled by the national representatives ;
but this was the last kind of force which the Government
wished to bring into existence.

In 1830 Metternich again urged the necessity of convening the Diet. It was as well that he did so, as before
the session began the July revolution had taken place in
France, as well as revolutions in Germany, Italy, and the
Netherlands. The proclamation which summoned the
Diet referred to the proposed coronation of Ferdinand,
the heir to the throne, in accordance with ancient precedent,
and to the necessity of voting recruits to fill the vacancies
in the Hungarian regiments, "the model of bravery,"
and promised a satisfactory reply to the statement of
grievances presented during the past session, and a
reference to a special commission of the question of re-
annexation to the mother-country of the parts which had
been torn from it and never returned, in spite of unceasing
protests. Fortunately, the Hungarian chancellor, Adam
Reviczky, possessed the confidence not only of his
countrymen but also of the King, whom he convinced of
the legality of the position adopted by the Opposition, and
of the impossibility of silencing the party of reform, which
wanted no violent innovations—only that the King should
put himself at the head of the movement and be the first
gentleman of Hungary.[1]   Thanks to Reviczky, the secret
police of Vienna, hitherto the chief source from which

[1] Marczali, *A Legujabb Kor Története,* 317.

Francis drew his information about Hungarian men and matters, temporarily ceased its baleful interference, and the relations between King and people assumed a more satisfactory aspect.

The question of the military contingent was the first matter for discussion. The House demanded an explanation of the Government's reason for requiring recruits, and though the Personalis objected to the demand on the ground that it constituted an interference with diplomatic affairs outside the purview of the Diet, the majority insisted, the Court gave way, and the President of the War Council was deputed to give the necessary explanations. The recruits were thereupon voted, the House declaring in its resolution that it did not wish to fall short of the standard of patriotism and fidelity to the dynasty set by its predecessors in the time of Maria Theresa, and that in the case of unwarrantable attack on the country, it was prepared to make the utmost exertions to provide for its defence.[1] This episode was important, not only from the military standpoint, and for the reason that it showed Europe that Hungary, as hitherto, identified its interests with those of Austria in face of the possibility of foreign complications, but still more so from the constitutional point of view, as it established the Diet's right to receive information as to the facts which necessitated an appeal for recruits on the part of the Government, and amounted to a recognition of Hungary's right to make its voice heard on questions of foreign policy. The required contingent was not voted without a considerable amount of acrimonious discussion. The fact that corporal's rank could not be attained without a knowledge of German, and the dislike of Austrian officers and Austrian uniforms were emphasised as the chief causes of the unpopularity of the service. It was pointed out that often ten, or even fifteen, foreign officers were to be found in the higher

[1] Marczali, *A Legujabb Kor Története*, 317.

ranks of a single Hungarian regiment, and that no
Magyar, however competent, could expect promotion to
a higher post than that of captain.[1]   The Lower House
threatened to refuse the vote unless reference were made
in the resolution to these grievances, and the reactionaries
had to give way.   The text, as finally settled, stated that
the recruits were voted " on the Diet being informed as
to the position of foreign affairs and of the Hungarian
forces, as a special grant in view of exceptional circumstances, which must not be regarded as constituting a
precedent for future use."   " Inasmuch as the prompt,
reward of professional merit would spur the military to
exert themselves in their profession, His Majesty has been
pleased to assure the Estates that he will carefully bear in
mind the provisions of Law ix. of 1792 and i. of 1807,
and will appoint born Magyars to the command of
Hungarian and frontier regiments, and to the rank of
General and to the Staff."   As usual, the royal promises
were made only to be broken, but the fact that the King
accepted the conditions of service insisted upon by the
Diet, and so reaffirmed that body's right to decide questions affecting the " internal organisation " of the army,
gave permanent importance to the law of 1830.[2]

In the same year the language question received further
consideration, and the desire of the Government to get
the military contingent voted made it more disposed to
be accommodating than it had hitherto been.   Even in
Croatia there was little disposition to resent the placing
of the Hungarian language on a footing of equality with

[1] Horváth, *Huszonöt év*, i. 239-40.   Paul Nagy named a Hungarian
regiment in which only twenty-two officers out of fifty were Hungarians.—
Marczali, *A Legujabb Kor Története*, 318.

[2] The immediate grant of 28,000 recruits was voted, and of a further
20,000 in the event of Austria being invaded before October of the following
year.   The period of service was fixed at ten years.   Recruits on proof of
unavoidable necessity for their presence at home must be allowed to return.
The number of recruits to be provided by each district is to be determined by
the Diet, which even fixes the minimum height for eligibility for service, etc.

Latin, until such time as the use of Hungarian should become universal among the Croatians. Several Croatian members spoke in favour of the extended use of that language, none against it ; and at a meeting held at Agram the Croatian electors gave instructions to their deputies to the Diet, which deserve to be recorded as an answer to the charge brought against Hungary of attempting the forcible magyarisation of other races. " The Estates and Orders, recognising the necessity of spreading the knowledge of the Magyar Language in these Kingdoms (Croatia, Slavonia, Dalmatia) *in order that a closer bond may bind them to the Magyar Kingdom*, request their Deputies to use their endeavours in order that the Hungarian language may by law be made a regular subject of instruction." [1] The language question was, in fact, made the subject of legislation, and the King sanctioned a measure which provided (Law viii.) that the Council of Lieutenancy should reply in Hungarian to all communications addressed to it in that language, and issue its instructions in the same idiom ; that the Court of Appeal should use the Hungarian language when considering Hungarian cases ; that local courts should do likewise except where Hungarian was not in general use (*e.g.* Croatia), in which case their deliberations might be conducted either in Latin or in Hungarian ; that in future no one should be eligible to public office who was ignorant of the latter language, or, after 1834, be admitted advocate. Further, it was enacted that all military officials in Hungary, including those of the frontier establishment, should be bound to take cognisance of all communications addressed to them in Hungarian. All this marked a considerable advance in the desired direction, though the patriotic party in the Lower House failed to realise one of its chief desires, namely, that Hungarian should be made the language of command in Hungarian regiments, experience having

[1] Marczali, *A Legujabb Kor Története*, p. 323.

shown that the difficulty of obtaining recruits was largely due to the use of German, and to the employment of Austrian officers and non-commissioned officers to the exclusion of qualified Magyars.[1]

In all directions indications were to be found of a revival of a spirit of nationality and of a desire for reform. It might be said that the same manifestations were visible, though in a lesser degree, in the early years of the previous reign, but in truth, at that period, the desire of the nobles to obtain fresh confirmation of their privileges was the mainspring of action, and the prospect of the spread of the liberal notions of Western Europe excited almost as much fear in the mind of the upper classes of Hungary as in that of the Austrian Government. The constitutional guarantees then obtained did not put a stop to the traditional germanising policy of which Joseph II. had been the chief exponent, or to the attempts to surround Hungary with a Chinese wall, which should prevent the possibility of contact with the ideas of the outside world. The vast majority of the educated population still failed to realise how backward the country was both materially and politically, as compared with its western neighbours ; and what guarantee was there that the country would not again relapse into a slumber of apathy and self-satisfaction—hypnotised by momentary success in obtaining fresh paper guarantees of the maintenance of its ancient Constitution ? The spirit of retrospective patriotism had indeed been aroused by the literary revival to which reference has already been made ; but the credit of having turned men's eyes to the future, of having created a desire for progress and compelled the recognition of its necessity, was due almost entirely to the genius of an individual. From the moment when Count Stephen Széchenyi made his offer of a year's income, as a first contribution towards the cost of establishing a Hungarian

[1] Horváth, *Huszonöt év*, i. 233.

Academy, he became a marked man. Born in 1791, son of Count Francis, the founder of the National Museum, who died "despairing as a Magyar," Stephen Széchenyi entered the army, but finding therein no field for his energies, no prospect of obtaining the advancement habitually denied to capable Magyars in the Austrian service, left it in 1826 to travel in France and England, where his eyes were opened to the possibility of material and political progress unknown to Hungary. He conceived the idea of regenerating his country, and thenceforward devoted his whole energies to the task of preparing himself for what he conceived to be his mission. At first, while still under the numbing influence of the years passed in the Austrian service, he appears to have considered that Hungary must find salvation in the general welfare, and as a subordinate factor, of the Austrian monarchy; that the ideal of a practically independent Hungarian monarchy, of a Magyar Holland, without its commercial prosperity, was antediluvian and unrealisable. His conviction that Hungary was neither desirous nor capable of regaining its national independence was modified to some extent at a later date, but it was the guiding principle of his whole career that material regeneration must precede constitutional reform, and that the first duty of a patriot was to force this view on public opinion. His first effort in the desired direction was the publication of a book on *Horses*, in which he showed how antiquated the notions were which prevailed in Hungary on the subject of horse-breeding, and pointed out how much more profitable it would be to adopt modern methods of improving the breed, as in England. With a view to encouraging such improvement, the first horse-races were held under his auspices at Pest, and in order to facilitate intercourse and contribute to the formation of public opinion, he founded the National Casino, the establishment of which was followed by the formation of similar clubs in many of the chief towns of

Hungary—a potent factor in the development of the political education of the upper classes.

In 1829 his first great book appeared—*Credit*.[1] Every intelligent person read it and quarrelled over it, agreed with its tenets or burnt it as unpatriotic, and Széchenyi's reputation as the apostle of national regeneration became firmly established. The book begins by addressing a rebuke to those who see patriotism in mere opposition to Austria, " and salvation in vain insistence on a catalogue of unredressed grievances. Let us not seek the cause of our backward condition solely in the Government. Let us not stay motionless in our old state of stagnation merely because the Government has not removed every obstacle to our well-being. Instead of everlasting complaints, sterile recriminations, and idle demands, let us set ourselves to work ; and if everywhere the road does not lie clear before us, let us at least try to develop ourselves mentally and morally, and increase our material well-being, where and when, and in what manner it is possible to do so." The causes of Hungary's poverty are enumerated in turn ; its antiquated agricultural methods ; the absence of the requisite capital ; and before all the want of *credit*, due to the feudal relations of landlord and peasant. The landowner is tied hand and foot by the antediluvian system whereby, in accordance with the law of 1351, land is entailed down to the most distant member of a family[2] on the death of whom the ownership reverts to the Crown, without the regard to claims of creditors,[3] the result of which is that no one can lend money on land owing to the impossibility of realising his security. The peasant has no interest in the country beyond the " reward of his labour," as Verbóczy put it over three hundred years ago, and the forced labour of serfs notoriously

---

[1] " Hitel," *Gróf Széchenyi István Munkái*, vol. i. Budapest, 1904.

[2] Ösiség, jus aviticitatis. According to Horváth, *Huszonöt év*, i. 420, there was hardly a family in the country which was not engaged in a lawsuit as to the title to property.   [3] Fiscalitas.

produces only a third of the result obtained by hired hands or peasant ownership. Trade is practically non-existent, owing, partly, to want of proper means of communication and to the idea that road-making consists in heaping mud on mud, in consequence of which it is more troublesome to go to Vienna than to Philadelphia. The inconsiderable home market is made still smaller by the absenteeism of the great landlords, while export is hampered by duties, by continual governmental interference, and by guilds and monopolies which operate in restraint of trade. The establishment of a national bank to provide the money for improvements and for the encouragement of enterprise is one of the chief national requisites ; but before all the whole nation must be welded into one, and to this, and to the maintenance of nationality, the development and modernisation of the national language is a condition precedent. Progress is visible in all directions, except in Hungary, where people still are satisfied with the contemplation of a glorious past, believe that " *extra Hungariam non est vita* " and see no necessity for educational development and a wider horizon. " They are wrong who say Hungary was. I love to believe that Hungary will be."

The book, which jumps from one subject to another in bewildering fashion, appeals rather to the imagination than to the intelligence. It speaks much of the essential necessity of credit, but gives little practical indication of the way in which the desired object is to be attained. It is full of Bentham and Adam Smith, and the charge of Anglomania brought against it by its chief but ineffective critic, Count Joseph Dessewffy, was undoubtedly justified. Széchenyi replied to his opponents in a second volume, *Light*,[1] in which he develops the thesis enunciated in *Credit*, convinced those whom his first effort had left doubting, and drove not one nail, but many, into the

[1] "Világ," *Gróf Széchenyi István Munkái*, vol. ii. p. 39 *sq*.

coffin of the feudal relations of landlord and peasant. But the benefits he conferred upon his country did not end there. Had there been no Széchenyi, Hungary would have long remained in the old state of somnolence and stagnation, and would have waited for years for a first tentative effort to be made in the direction of economic development.

His next book, *Stadium*, written in 1831, forbidden by the censorship, and printed abroad two years later, is less emotional and more constructive than his previous works. In it he formulates a distinct programme in twelve sections, the most important points of which are the abolition of exaggerated entail ; the commutation of the Crown's reversionary right for the payment by each successive owner or purchaser of one per cent of the value of the estate ; the extension of the right to own land to all members of the community ; the equality of all before the law ; contribution to the cost of parliamentary and local government by all classes, not only by the non-nobles as hitherto ; and the abolition of monopolies and trade guilds. Further, he demands that the Council of Lieutenancy shall be the only intermediary between the King and the nation, which would thus be free to work out its own political salvation, freed from the numbing influence of Austrian bureaucracy, and that in Hungary no law, order, or judgment which is not couched in the Hungarian language shall have any force or validity. Széchenyi was convinced that if once the land were freed, if all classes could become landed proprietors, complete emancipation would follow, and that the nation would consist of ten million freemen, which, politically, had hitherto consisted of eight hundred thousand privileged persons. The race, he said, must die if nine millions continued to be excluded from the possession of rights which should belong to the nation as a whole. Freedom for all is essential to material prosperity ; "the steamship cannot endure the smell of feudalism," and for every shilling the nobles give up they will receive back eighteenpence in another form. Let them have the courage to cast their bread on the waters, and they will soon find it again.[1]

Széchenyi was anxious to proceed hand in hand with the Government, not in spite of it, and this wish influenced his whole career. Therein lay his mistake. He failed to see the uselessness of expecting any good from the Vienna of Metternich, which looked on Hungary merely as a colony to be exploited in the interests of Austria, and as the possessor of a Constitution which required not reform but abolition.[2] It must be remembered that the last word in all matters rested with the Crown, and that the King of Hungary was never a match for the Emperor of Austria. Every matter, though purely Hungarian, had to run the gauntlet of the Council of State in Vienna, and of the Conference of Ministers. The Hungarian Chancery, the Palatine, and the Treasury, did little more than register and give effect to the decisions of Vienna. There was no question of the power being in the hands of the majority in the Diet ; the majority was always in

[1] The influence of *Hitel* and *Stadium* is clearly visible in the anonymous work, *Umrisse einer möglichen Reform in Ungarn*, said to have been written by Count George Andrássy, which appeared in 1833 and insists on the necessity of improving means of communication in order to attract the foreigner, of regulating the waterways, of encouraging improvements by means of proper patent laws, etc.—Part i. It complains of Austria's habit (which is still in favour in the twentieth century) of deliberately traducing the Magyars in order to alienate from them the sympathies of other nations, but makes the admission that "here there is no question of a nation, only of the interests of a few Magnates whose chains the nation has to endure."—Part ii. 17 *n*.

[2] "Die Regierung . . . so wenig eine reformirte Verfassung wie die Altbestehende liebte, und die Todtenruhe der deutschen Erbländer gern auch auf Ungarn übertragen hätte. Darum kann man aber auch den ungarischen Reichstag nicht tadeln, dass er den Widerstand bis auf das Äusserste trieb, und sich freiwillig nicht beugen liess. Er hatte nicht zu wählen zwischen der bestehenden, theilweise veralteten Constitution und einer neuen vernunftgemässen Verfassung, sondern zwischen der Herrschaft des Gesetzes und der Regierung durch Cabinetsbefehle."—Anton Springer, *o.c.* i. 198.

opposition, not in office, hence the essence and foundation of parliamentary government were wanting. The opposition, since 1825, was the originating, creative force, while the Government was the drag on the wheel, and relied for the successful prosecution of its policy of inertia on the traditional hostility of the greater and lesser nobles, and of Protestant and Catholic, which was now fast disappearing. Party organisation and discipline of the English type were unknown. Every fresh question was liable to weaken or destroy such slight cohesion as existed, and it was only the influence of individuals which served to maintain some semblance of unity of action, which the changing and contradictory nature of the "instructions" of the constituencies, the mutual distrust caused by the acceptance of office by some of the most important members of the reform party, and the attempts of the Government to sow discord among its opponents,[1] did much to diminish. The Magnates were hypnotised by Court influence and prestige, and the party of progress in the Upper House was in a hopeless minority. The place-hunters and the bishops cast their votes in favour of reaction with machine-like regularity, the former for obvious reasons, the latter because they were aware that the curtailment of the privileges of the nobles would lead to the diminution of their influence, both as ecclesiastics and as the largest landowners in the country.[2] The steady opposition of the Government party to the proposals of the Lower House gradually wore out the patience of the elected representatives, who, not unnaturally, ended in many cases by losing the enthusiasm for reform with which they had begun the session. The

[1] Louis Wirkner, author of the memoirs frequently cited below, an agent of the Vienna Government, did much to undermine mutual confidence.

[2] In old days their tenure of land was to a large extent subject to the performance of military duties, the maintenance of fortresses, and the supply of troops. These obligations had long ceased, but the bishops retained their estates.

proceedings of the Diet tended to degenerate into a haggling-match in which the *vis inertiae* of Magnates and retrograde ecclesiastics was bound in the long run to defeat the efforts of the representatives of public opinion.

As a matter of fact, it was not always possible to know what was the trend of public opinion at any given moment on any particular subject. The Press at this period possessed but little weight, and the counties were always liable to alter the instructions given to their deputies. It was not unusual for a member to speak in favour of a motion and yet be obliged to vote against it, in consequence of the receipt of a fresh mandate from his constituents. The binding force of these instructions naturally lessened the authority and originating power of the Diet, tended to prevent the development of the true form of parliamentary government, and made it impossible to predict with certainty the fate of any measure, however great the enthusiasm which greeted its introduction. Of enthusiasm there was, in fact, plenty since 1825; the catchwords of reform were in every one's mouth; many travelled in order to inform themselves as to the economic and political progress of foreign nations, more especially of England and France, and a feeling of shame was caused by the idea that Hungary did not stand in the same rank as other European nations. Hence the seed cast by Széchenyi did not fall on barren ground. Since the July revolution even Metternich was inclined to the belief that the best preventive of similar outbreaks was the encouragement of ideas of moderate reform; and the violence of the peasant disturbances brought about in 1831 by the cholera, and by the belief that the medicine provided at the expense of the Government was intentionally poisoned, confirmed his newborn opinion that only increased educational facilities and the improvement of the material position of the country population could prevent the recurrence of the outrages to which the landlords were subjected. . The great nobles shared Metternich's views, and the idea of the necessity of some measure of reform which should better the condition of their tenants, but at the same time should not undermine their own privileges, gradually took shape in their minds. Few, however, were far-sighted enough to realise the fact that half-measures would not suffice to stop the rising flood of discontent ; that the tide which had swept over France and Germany could not be stopped at the Hungarian frontier, or that the greater the receptivity of Hungary for foreign ideas, the greater its ability and determination would be to maintain its national individuality and to work out its salvation on its own lines.

1832.   When the time came for the reassembling of the Diet, though the majority of the counties, which ascribed the poverty of the country to the gerrymandered customs system, put commercial and tariff reform in the forefront of their programme, Reviczky wished to obtain prestige for the Government · by giving the impression that it was itself at the head of the reform movement, and to begin with the line of least resistance — the reform of the relations between landowner and peasant, and of judicial procedure. The King's speech, therefore, referred specially to these two questions, but as the Government gave no indication of the length to which it was prepared to go in its concession to the ideas of the progressive party, there is justification for doubting its good faith, and for believing that its anxiety to begin with the discussion of urbarial relations was due to the belief that that subject of all others was calculated to bring about a split in the ranks of the Opposition, and that the raising of awkward questions and the warming up of old grievances would be thereby avoided.   On the one hand were politicians of the type of Paul Nagy, who said that it was useless to "fence round" the Constitution so long as it protected the interests only of a privileged class, and the millions of non-nobles were left outside the pale ;[1] on the other were those, found even among the members of the Lower House, who raised their voices in opposition to the policy of concession to the peasants on the ground that it would destroy the independence of the country : as if, as Deák said,[2] everlasting servitude, the landlord's judicial powers, and the *régime* of the stick formed the only foundation of the Hungarian Constitution The Catholic bishops were also against emancipation, "trembling lest that rock should split on which Peter's Church is built '''; [3] but the great majority of elected members were on the side of the angels ; with them there was no question of fighting for profit or privilege, but for permission for self-sacrifice in the interests of an oppressed class. The Government was always glad to lighten the burden of the peasants at the expense of the landowners, and to pose as the protector of the poor, but it had no intention of giving them real freedom, or of doing anything in the direction of emancipation which might tend to democratise the country. As before, it tried to undermine the Opposition in the Diet and in the counties by bribery and corruption, and in several constituencies succeeded in bringing about a modification of the liberal "instructions" which had been issued to the deputies.[4] But the session was by no means barren of results so far as the peasant question was concerned. The small vexatious dues, the payment of which had not been interfered with by the ordinances of Maria Theresa,[5] were abolished ; the *corvée* was reduced and regularised in such a way as to prevent the exaction of the landlord's rights from making it impossible for the peasant

---

[1] Marczali, *Enchiridion Fontium*, p. 798.

[2] Horváth, *Huszonöt év*, i. 398.   [3] Horváth, *Huszonöt év*, i. 399.

[4] Kölcsey, the noted poet, and one of the boldest champions of the peasants' cause, retired from the representation of his constituency, as, owing to the machinations of the Government, the liberal instructions given him on election were withdrawn.   [5] *Supra*, p. 202 *sq.*

to give proper attention to his own land at seasons when such attention was most wanted.[1]   The right of free migration, subject to the satisfaction of all debts whether of a public or private nature, and without the necessity of obtaining the landlord's consent, was conferred on the peasant[2]— after all but a small boon, for the peasant could only migrate to the land of another proprietor ; he could not yet become a free man and have property of his own.

The spirit which animated the King and his advisers was clearly shown when the Bill which embodied these and other moderate concessions was submitted for the royal assent.   After a delay of nine months, a reply was received, refusing consent to the most important provisions of the Bill, such as the permission thereby granted to commute all dues in perpetuity for a money payment, though such redemption had been allowed in Austria since 1772, without fatal democratic consequences.   The King was perpetually under the impression caused by the French Revolution, and dead against emancipation, fearing that " it would bring into existence a new and hitherto unrecognised class, and that trouble might easily arise owing to a change of this nature.[3]   He even refused his consent to the abolition of the landlord's jurisdiction ; but Deák and his followers did not abandon hope.   Though the permanent commutation of dues did not receive legislative sanction, it was admitted in principle, as it was enacted that landlord and tenant might enter into contracts for the redemption of such dues by payment of a fixed annual sum, and some of the more liberal nobles at once took advantage of the permission.   Further, a step was

---

[1] Law viii. 1836.   [2] Law iv. 1836.

[3] See his conversation with Wirkner, the Government agent, *Élményeim*, 2nd ed. p. 71, which disposes of the oft-repeated legend that it was to the Crown that the peasants always had to look for their salvation.   It must be admitted that the reforms of Maria Theresa and Joseph II. were introduced in spite of the nobles, who thought that the country must necessarily go to the dogs if their privileges were interfered with, but those reforms were due to economic, rather than humanitarian motives.

taken in the direction of peasant proprietorship by granting permission to the peasants to enclose for private or common use part of the land over which they and their landlords had joint rights of pasturage. During the same session a measure (Law viii. of 1741), which declared the payment of taxes to be a personal obligation of the peasant, not an incident of real property, was repealed, and of course in this case the royal assent was not refused, as the result of the law was a considerable increase in the number of tax-payers. As a large number of nobles now, for the first time, became liable to taxation, it was obvious that they would never rest until the rest of the privileged classes were in the same boat with themselves, and so the propagandists of emancipation would find fresh partisans in the ranks of the self-interested. The Government, therefore, did not enforce the new tax, but winked at its evasion in order to obtain the support of the now taxable "sandalled nobility," which, consequently, became a willing instrument in the hands of the retrograde. A further, though inconsiderable, breach in the privileges of the nobles, and a further advance in the direction of making the liability to taxation common to all, was effected by the passing of a resolution that all classes should pay toll at the suspension bridge which it was now proposed to erect between Buda and Pest in accordance with the cherished scheme of Széchenyi. Many nobles still regarded the obligation to pay taxes, no matter in what form, as a badge of servitude, and nothing illustrates the mental attitude of the ultra-conservative better than the fact that Chief Justice Cziráky [1] would never cross the chain bridge for the reason that he considered that the payment of toll was contrary to the principle of the nobles' immunity from taxation. But such fossils were fortunately rare, and the Diet, admitting the inequitableness of the existing system, in accordance with which the

---

[1] The author of the *Conspectus Juris Publici*.

unrepresented, non-noble, tax-payers bore the whole cost of its meetings, shifted the burden on to the shoulders of the privileged classes.   The same course should in fairness have been adopted with respect to the expenses of local government, which were borne entirely by the class which derived least benefit from that institution.   The *Pesti Hirlap*, the most influential of the newspapers, started an agitation in favour of a change of system, and some of the Conservatives, whose spokesman was Count Emil Dessewffy, gave it their support, but a " No tax " cry was got up in the counties, and the question did not come up for discussion by the Diet.   Many nobles, however, thenceforth voluntarily bore their share of the expenses in question, and the change which was gradually taking place in public opinion was indicated by the fact that numerous counties took advantage of their statutory rights to admit non-noble members of the intelligent classes to take part in the deliberations of the local assemblies.

The general disgust caused in the ranks of the Liberal party by its inability to overcome the resistance of the Upper House [1] and of the Government to necessary reforms, made many consider the advisability of retirement from the unequal struggle as a protest against the absurdity of the existing system, and Deák had considerable difficulty in convincing them of the futility of a policy of boycotting the Diet, which could only have the effect of facilitating the task of the partisans of reaction.   One of the greatest difficulties with which the Liberals had to contend, and one of the chief causes of discouragement, was to be found in the absence of proper means of informing public opinion.   The Austrian and Hungarian

[1] The feeling entertained against that body first became really acute at the Diet of 1832-36, on account of the obstructive exercise of its powers of stopping legislation.   " Mending or ending " was demanded, not on account of objections to the hereditary principle, but because it was felt that the Upper House was merely the tool of Vienna.

newspapers 'gave accounts of the proceedings of the French and English Parliaments, but none of those of the Hungarian Diet. The official journal of that body gave the most meagre summary of its transactions ; no members' names were mentioned, and no reference was made to the extra-Dietal meetings at which the real business of the Lower House was transacted.[1]   Consequently, the constituencies and the country at large had but scanty means of informing themselves of the march of events and of the shifting currents of parliamentary opinion beyond that afforded by the presence at the meetings of the Diet of a considerable body of youthful politicians sent by the counties to serve a kind of political apprenticeship in the gallery of the House.[2]   In 1825 the "instructions" of many counties referred to the need of having a proper official journal of the proceedings of the Diet, and that body expressed its desire for such an organ, which should confine itself to recording the speeches of members without comment, and should be subject to the censorship only of a committee of the House itself ; but when the required permission was demanded, the Government returned no answer, and the matter dropped, only to be raised again, and dropped again in 1832, when the President of the

[1] Most resolutions were taken in "district meetings" (Kerületi ülések) or committees held outside the House, in which the Government was not represented, and so exerted no influence. Originally the deputies of the two Tisza and two Danube districts sat separately, but at this period they all sat together, so forming a sort of committee of the whole House, excluding the members of the High Court.—Kmety, Közjog, 268, n. The result was that discussion in the Lower House was often reduced to a minimum, and the most important motions were declared carried on a cry of " Agreed " without more ado.

[2] In 1825 fifteen to twenty were sent by each county.—Horváth, Huszonöt év, i. 298. In 1836 their number totalled 1200 or more.—Wirkner, Élményeim, p. 91. Filled with liberal notions and at the same time with devotion to the historic rights of the country, they exercised a considerable, and possibly undesirable, influence on the proceedings of the Diet. Reactionary speeches were greeted with demonstrations of disapproval, and the Government was justified in objecting to the existence of a noisy and disorderly chorus.

Lower House declared, amid protests from the deputies, that the right of censorship was the inalienable prerogative of the Crown. Louis Kossuth, who made his first political appearance at the Diet of 1832, stepped into the breach and began the issue of his lithographic reports of the proceedings of the Diet,[1] which, subscribed for by the county clubs, at once greatly increased public interest, subjected the members to the control of public opinion, and encouraged a healthy ambition. For a time the publication continued its bi-weekly appearance, but as soon as the Government got wind of Kossuth's enterprise it confiscated the lithographic press, and the policy of obscurantism again triumphed.

The Government was well served by its agents. Ferstl, an ex-officer, was head of the secret police, and "under his orders were those persons who were entrusted with the duty of observing the acts of the more conspicuous public men, and those whose function it was to give their opinion on the political questions of the moment," as Wirkner euphemistically styles the spies of Vienna.[2] Further, there were "at the head post-office two entirely trustworthy persons in charge of the so-called Black Cabinet. These opened the letters of those individuals whose views and intentions it was desired to know."[3] As a matter of fact, there was no legal justification for police interference in Press matters. The Palatine issued a *pronunciamento* to the effect that no political or literary periodical could be issued without express permission from the King, but no law restricting such publication existed. A statute of 1790 (xv.) spoke of the freedom of the Press, which was thereafter to be regulated according to law, but there was no legislative justification for the existence of a

---

[1] *Országgyűlési Tudósítások.*   [2] *Élményeim,* p. 67.

[3] *Élményeim,* p. 68. Ferstl was instructed by Metternich to give immediate information of any important fact to Wirkner, who none the less resented the imputation of being a spy in the pay of Vienna.

preliminary censure such as that exercised by the police-bureau, against the severity of which the counties protested in vain. After the close of the Diet, Kossuth continued his work by distributing manuscript accounts of the proceedings of the county meetings, and no amount of prohibitive orders and illegal tampering with the post could entirely prevent the circulation of his reports. The Government, therefore, took the absolutely illegal step of sending soldiers to arrest him, seized his writings and correspondence, and caused him, after a long period of strict preliminary confinement, to be condemned by a servile tribunal first to three, and then to four years' imprisonment.

It was the deliberate policy of Vienna to stifle free discussion. There was hardly a county in which some chief speaker was not prosecuted and imprisoned. In 1834 a society was formed among the youths attending the Diet on the lines of the *Société des Droits de l'Homme* for the discussion of political questions. No doubt the juvenile debaters entertained notions of too advanced a character for the Viennese stomach, but they confined themselves entirely to theory, and there was no possibility of danger to the Government. True, they organised a torchlight procession in honour of one of the victims of the muzzling policy, but that did not justify the arrest of the chief members, and the condemnation, by a mockery of justice,[1] of one of the leaders of the society [2] to ten years' confinement in a fortress. The counties protested, but in vain,[3] and public opinion became violently inflamed when it was realised that the liberty of the individual was at the mercy of judges, who, from motives

---

[1] Witnesses were not confronted with the accused, who were not brought into court, but examined separately in their cells, and were not allowed to choose their own defenders.—Pulszky Ferencz, *Életem és Korom*, 2nd ed., i. 101. Pulszky was himself a member of the society.

[2] Lovassy.

[3] Neither the King nor the Chancellor would receive deputations.—Marczali, *A Legujabb Kor Története,* p. 392.

of self-interest, were ready to obey the instructions of Vienna, no matter how illegal they might be. A more notable victim was Széchenyi's friend, Baron Wesselényi, who had made himself objectionable to the Government by his activity in connexion with the question of the reunion of Transylvania, his native land, to the mother country. With him and Kossuth out of the way it was hoped that the task of stifling free speech might be more easily accomplished.

From the time when Transylvania was first occupied by the Magyars it was spoken of as the "*partes Transylvanae*," and sent its representatives to the Hungarian Diet. After Mohács and the consequent division of the realms of the Sacred Crown, from the year 1540, Transylvania had its own Diet, and the King, and the representatives · of the Magyar, Szekler, and Saxon populations, exercised joint legislative authority. After the first ejection of the Turks, neither the Viennese Government,[1] nor the Diet of Transylvania,[2] attempted to deny Hungary's 'right to demand the reincorporation of the severed parts, but for a long time the Transylvanians had no wish for reunion, chiefly for the reason that during the period of religious intolerance and despotism they feared the loss of their special privileges, and that the equality of the four recognised religions would become a thing of the past.' Now, since 1825, a strong feeling existed among the Magyars of Transylvania in favour of reunion, which, as they believed, constituted their sole defence against Austrian interference. The only serious

[1] As shown by Law viii. of 1791.

[2] Clause 6 of the law of 1791 passed by the Transylvanian Diet : "Tam sua Majestas sacratissima quam secuturi ejusdem ex augustissima domo austriaca successores qua legitimi reges Hungariae Transylvaniam tanquam ad sacram regni Hungariae coronam pertinentem eodem cum Hungaria imperii et successionis jure tenebunt." Which refutes Brote's statement, that only a federal tie existed between Hungary and Transylvania, and that the latter was always independent.—*Die rumänische Frage in Siebenbürgen und Ungarn*, p. 11.

opposition came from the Saxons.[1]   The organisation of
the Diet differed in certain respects from that of its
Hungarian prototype.   It consisted of one Chamber only,
in which the representative members were far out-
numbered by the official element, consisting of the members
of the High Court, the lords - lieutenant of the Magyar
counties, and the chief officials of the Szekler and
Saxon districts.   The Diet had the right to appoint
the members of the Transylvanian Chancery in Vienna,
the Chancellor and Governor, the judges of the High
Court, and the lords-lieutenant ; but since 1809, the
King, in contravention of the law, had failed to convene
the Diet, and the Austrian Government appointed its own
subservient nominees to all vacant posts, without reference
to the wishes of the country.   Only one official remained
who had been appointed in accordance with constitutional
usage, and a further grievance was to be found in the
fact that the Government had no regard to the relative
numbers of the members of the various Churches, but
chose its nominees almost exclusively from the ranks of
the Catholics, in spite of the fact that by far the greater
part of the Magyar population, and the vast majority of
the chief nobles, belonged to the Reformed Church.   The
average of education was considerably lower in Transylvania than in Hungary proper, and there were few of
sufficient energy and independence to make a firm stand
against the unconstitutional interference of the Government, whose intention it was gradually to prepare the way
for the final absorption of Transylvania in the hereditary
provinces, by omitting to convene the representatives of

---

[1] There were twice as many Magyars as Szeklers, and four times as many
Magyars as Saxons.   The Roumanians, by far the biggest element of the
population, were not represented, though many of Roumanian origin were
among the elected representatives and specially summoned nobles.—Horváth,
Huszonöt év, i. 427.   There was no limit to the power of the King to
summon the last-mentioned (regalisták) ; it was easy therefore to swamp the
Opposition.

the people. Baron Nicholas Wesselényi was the chief promoter, if not the creator, of the desire for reunion with Hungary. He first came into prominence in 1818, when the Government attempted to regulate the question of the relations between landlord and peasant without reference to the wishes of the people constitutionally expressed through its elected representatives. He travelled all over the country, urging the inhabitants to resistance to the illegal actions of Vienna, and exciting the enthusiasm of the youth for the Hungarian language and nation. As in 1790 so in 1825, one of the chief questions raised by the Diet at Pressburg was the question of reunion, if not with Transylvania as a whole, at all events with certain districts in which the Magyar feeling was strongest ; and Wesselényi was the life and soul of the movement in favour of reincorporation. Thenceforward he devoted himself almost entirely to the cause. He attended innumerable county meetings, which he induced to pass resolutions petitioning the King to remedy their grievances, and, pending the convocation of the Diet, to initiate a policy of passive resistance in order to paralyse the unconstitutional action of the Government. In May 1832 the King gave some indication of an intention to summon the Diet, but vague promises were no longer capable of satisfying the people. In the following year the Bán of Croatia, sent as Royal Commissioner with full powers to Transylvania, became convinced of the fact that a recurrence to constitutional government alone could restore tranquillity to the country, and succeeded in satisfying the King of the unwisdom of the policy hitherto adopted. The Diet was, therefore, summoned in 1834, and an opportunity was at length obtained of ventilating long-standing grievances.[1] No practical results were obtained ;

---

[1] Some of the chief causes of complaint were, apart from those arising out of the deliberate violation of the Constitution, the favouring of Catholics at the expense of Protestants, the prohibition of foreign travel, and the op-

but that very fact served to strengthen the conviction entertained by the Protestant-Magyar population that the only hope of political salvation lay in reunion with the mother country. The King's reply to an Address voted by the Diet took no notice of the grievances therein enumerated, and his intentions were shown by the fact that he passed over the two candidates for the presidential chair who had received the greatest number of votes, and appointed a person on whose subservience to the wishes of the Government more reliance could be placed. The printing of the journal of the Diet was prohibited, and when Wesselényi distributed lithographed accounts of its proceedings his press was confiscated. The Diet entered a formal protest, and the King replied thereto with a rescript severely rebuking the members for having dared to stand up for their constitutional rights, dissolving the Diet, and enjoining obedience to the edicts which he proposed to issue.

In Hungary proper, Wesselényi and Kölcsey did not allow the question of reunion to drop, though it was now more obvious than ever that the Government would not consent to the reincorporation of the severed province for fear that the spirit of Magyar nationality and the power of resistance to the policy of centralisation would be thereby strengthened. Wesselényi's activity naturally marked him out for destruction. The Government wished to get him out of the way at any price, and in May 1834 caused him to be indicted on a charge of disturbing the public order, the accusation being based on a distorted interpretation of words he had used in a speech made at Szatmár at the end of the previous year. He accused the Government of having for centuries sucked the blood of the peasants while it posed as their protector, and warned his country that Austrian interference with the Jacqueries, which would

pression of the Szeklers by the soldiery, which exacted provisions at half the market price, and generally misconducted itself.

ensue, would be withheld till the houses of the nobles were reduced to a mass of smoking ruins, and then—" Woe to our national independence ! " [1] He was accused of *lèse majesté* immediately the words were spoken, but refuted the charge, and the matter was allowed to drop by the meeting, which had power to punish him if it considered that he had made use of improper language. Six months later the Government seized the opportunity of suppressing an active and capable opponent, and Wesselényi, after long delay, was sentenced to three years' imprisonment.[2] The question was raised in the Hungarian Diet whether a prosecution would lie for words spoken in a country where no law existed curtailing the right of free speech ; and, secondly, whether an attack on the Government could be treated as an attack on the King, and so justify indictment for "infidelity," or minor treason ; but the Upper House twelve times rejected the petition which the elected representatives wished to be addressed to the King on the subject, so the presentment never reached its destination, and the only result was that the feeling of resentment against the obstructive tactics of the Magnates became more inflamed than ever, and the conviction more rooted that the Government would shrink from the adoption of no means, however illegal, of suppressing the opponents of unconstitutional action.

To belong to the Opposition, or to call one's self a Liberal, meant the loss of all possibility of advancement, involved a liability to persecution at the hands of spies, and made it almost impossible to obtain permission for

---

[1] De Gerando, *Über den öffentlichen Geist in Ungarn*, p. 190 *sqq.* ; Marczali, *A Legujabb Kor Története*, p. 390 ; Kónyi, *Deák Ferencz Beszédei*, i. 162 *sqq.*

[2] The influence of Deák, who applied direct to the King, saved Wesselényi from imprisonment, and he was allowed to retire to Gräfenberg for the benefit of his shattered health. But the Government's object was attained. " The Government succeeded in obtaining a conviction."—Wirkner's expression, *Élményeim*, p. 99.

foreign travel. Nothing shows the spirit which animated the partisans of the Government better than their action in resisting the substitution of a living for a dead language in official documents. They urged that it was inadvisable to proceed too quickly ; but as the language question had been raised, without satisfactory result, on every possible occasion during the past forty-three years, no one could be accused of undue precipitancy. The subject was again mooted during the session 1832-36, and again it engendered a feeling of passionate hostility between the parties, comparable only to that evoked by the question of the emancipation of the peasants. The deputies demanded that the messages of the Upper to the Lower House should be couched in the Hungarian language, as well as petitions and addresses to the King, and that the Hungarian text of the laws should thenceforth be regarded as the official version. To this latter demand the Magnates refused their consent, and the King insisted that the Latin text should continue to be considered the only authentic one. " A dead language means a dead people," protested one of the deputies who had already suffered for his outspokenness at the hands of the Government.[1] " From our graves we cry to the King to open our tombs and to let us arise to a life of freedom ; but instead of lifting the cover, our rulers only drive a few more nails into our coffin, and condemn the living to everlasting death." [2] Deák, who during this session of the Diet finally established his influence, not so much by means of his speeches as by his moderation and common sense, and by the absolute straightness and unselfishness which were his striking characteristics, expressed himself in a similar strain. " No one was born with a ready-made knowledge of Latin. The action of the Government is comparable

---

[1] John Balogh, who had been indicted for openly expressing approval of the speech for which Wesselényi was condemned.

[2] Marczali, *A Legujabb Kor Története*, p. 380.

to that of the tyrant who inscribed the laws on the top of a high tower in such small characters that no one could read them with the naked eye and yet punished those who transgressed them." [1]   Finally, the King gave way on the intervention of the Palatine, and a further advance was made towards the abolition of the compulsory use of a dead language, partisans of which desired its maintenance solely for the reason that it served as an obstacle to the development of the spirit of Magyar nationality.   Henceforth, when any doubt arose as to the interpretation of laws, the Hungarian version was to be regarded as the authentic one.   High Court actions were allowed to be conducted and judgment delivered in Hungarian, and registers of births and marriages were to be kept in that language ; but, that other nationalities might have no cause of complaint, only in places where divine service was celebrated in Hungarian.   Further, the King undertook to take steps for the provision of facilities for the acquirement of a knowledge of the Magyar tongue in Roumanian seminaries. [2]

It is no exaggeration to say that the Government considered all progress in Hungary to be contrary to Austrian interests, and this is especially true as regards economic [3] and educational matters.   Széchenyi realised this fact, and consequently took a comparatively inconspicuous part in general politics, for fear that he might excite insuperable hostility to his pet plans, such as the regulation of the Danube, the removal of the obstacles to navigation known as the Iron Gates, and the development of the port of Fiume, the natural channel for Hungarian exports, with which heavy freights, and want of accommoda-

---

[1] Marczali, *A Legujabb Kor Története*, p. 381.   According to Kossuth and Deák only fifteen to twenty thousand persons understood Latin.

[2] Law iii. of 1836.

[3] *E.g.* a prohibitive duty was imposed on the import of Hungarian beet sugar into Austria, while the Austrian article was imported into Hungary duty free.

tion for shipping, seriously interfered.   Educational as
well as material progress was consistently opposed.   As
Hungary showed signs of a coming development in the
arts of manufacture, of ceasing to be a purely agricultural
country, the Diet in 1836 urged the establishment of
technical schools in the chief towns, and of a polytechnic
in Pest, in order to remedy the want of practical mechanical
and commercial knowledge, the chief obstacle to be overcome ; but the Government, which wished to keep the
control of all educational matters in its own hands,
opposed the introduction of a Bill dealing with the subject.
"His Majesty," said a royal rescript, "will take the
establishment of such institutions into consideration ;
consequently, legislation is superfluous,"[1] and the disgust
of the Diet may be imagined in view of the fact that no
money for the furtherance of the scheme, or help in any
form, had been asked of the Crown.   The same obstructive
tactics were adopted with respect to the Ludoviceum.   At
the beginning of the century, during the Napoleonic wars,
the Diet had agitated in favour of the employment of
Hungarian officers in Hungarian regiments, though, as
a matter of fact, there was an insufficiency of qualified
persons, to remedy which it was proposed, in 1808, that a
sum should be privately raised for the establishment of a
military academy.   Eight hundred and ninety-five thousand
florins were subscribed, and a college was built with accommodation for two hundred students, but the Government
would not give permission for it to be opened, on the
ground that its statutes required revision, but in reality
because it objected to the request that the language of
instruction should be partly Hungarian.[2]   Thus, every
action of the Government proved its desire to do all in its

[1] Horváth, *Huszonöt év*, i. 474. Not till 1846 was permission given for the
establishment of a commercial school bearing the name of the Archduke
Joseph, which later developed into a polytechnic.

[2] The building remained unoccupied till 1848, when it was opened. After
the war it was shut again till 1872.

power to retard the development of the country and to crush its aspirations.

Francis died on March 2, 1835. His last actions, his refusal to allow the adoption of the desired reform permitting commutation of feudal dues for a money payment, and the dissolution of the Transylvanian Diet, had destroyed the last vestiges of the popularity which he had gained by his consent to the convocation of the Hungarian Diet in 1825. The establishment of the secret police and the development of the censorship had been the characteristic events of the last years of his life. He desired to keep his subjects free from the infection of the liberal ideas of Western Europe ; believed that prevention was easy, but that cure was difficult, and persecuted ideas on principle, in the hope that the march of civilisation could be arrested at the Hungarian frontier. The futility of his efforts was proved by the fact that the closing period of his reign was rendered illustrious by the rise of the three greatest sons of Hungary—Széchenyi, the prophet of material progress ; Kossuth, the political idealist ; and Deák, the personification of strict legality and of the invincible tenacity of the Magyar race.

CHAPTER X

I⊤ was notorious that Ferdinand, the new King, was of 1835.
less than mediocre ability.   His father had not failed
to realise the fact, and knowing the feebleness of his
character impressed on him the necessity of allowing
himself to be guided by Metternich, who, with Kolowrat and the Archdukes Louis and Francis Charles,
Ferdinand's younger brother and presumptive heir, henceforth formed a camarilla which held all strings and made
the puppet King dance to its liking.   The tendency of
Ferdinand's advisers was at once shown by their action as
regards the royal title—seemingly unimportant, but not
so in reality.   To style the new King, Ferdinand the
First, as they attempted to do in official documents,
instead of Ferdinand the Fifth, his proper designation,
would have been equivalent to an interruption of the
continuity of succession of Hungarian kings, would have
implied, to a certain extent, at all events, the incorporation of Hungary in Austria, and would undoubtedly have
been used as an argument to prove the voluntary relin-
quishment of national independence.[1]   The next slap in

[1] The Diet declared, August 19, 1835, that the title of Ferdinand the First
"Austriae Imperator quo sua Majestas utitur," can derogate in nothing from
the rights and independence of Hungary guaranteed by Law x. of 1790-91.
The result of the protest was that Ferdinand used the style of "First of Austria
and Fifth of Hungary of that name."   Springer's statement (*Grundlagen und
Entwicklungsziele des Oesterreich-Ungarischen Monarchie*, Vienna, 1906, p. 23),
that "Ungarn gestattete ohne Wiederrede das der Kaisertitel auch auf Ungarn
radizirt werde, dass der König von Ungarn unter dem Kaiser von Oesterreich

the face which Hungary received was the appointment of a new Chancellor in the place of Kevicsky, who had always exercised a moderating influence on Francis, and consequently was hated by the more retrograde of the great nobles. Count Fidél Pálffy received the vacant place, a denationalised opportunist, ignorant of his country's language,[1] whose only wish was to earn the favour of Vienna and to maintain the privileges of the aristocracy. To appoint to the most important official position a man who knew no word of Hungarian, the nephew and nominee of Kolowrat, the chief protector of the Pan-Slav agitators now coming into prominence, was a deliberate insult to the Diet which the Government looked upon as an unmitigated evil, the influence of which should be curtailed by fair means or foul, and more especially by limiting the freedom of speech and of the Press, as is proved by the treatment meted out to Kossuth and Wesselényi. The new Chancellor opposed every form of progress ; obstacles were thrown in the way even of the construction of the new bridge at Budapest on the ground that it was too important a matter to be left to private enterprise, and of the improvement of the Danube for purposes of navigation, for the reason that it would open the door not only to foreign trade competition, but to the importation of foreign ideas as well. No one's correspondence was safe from interference at the hands of the police, and every possible means was adopted to prevent concerted action on the part of the various counties.[2] A great change had recently come over the latter, for whereas formerly only the meetings held for

völkerrechtlich verschwinde, dass es ein Land neben den vielen anderen Ländern des Kaiserreiches sei," is clearly untrue. — See Kónyi, *Deák Ferencz Beszédei*, i. 157.

[1] Szögyény-Marich László, *Emlékiratai*, p. 9.

[2] The "instructions" of the counties given to their deputies before the Diet of 1825 insisted on the inviolability of their correspondence, without which unity of action was impossible.—Horváth, *Huszonöt év*, i. 157. Then as later the motto of the Government was "*divide ut imperes.*"

the election of officials were well attended, the newly
aroused interest in the political questions of the day,
and the repressive action of the] Government, caused
hundreds to come where hitherto tens had congregated.
Disorder and violence were not uncommon when the
main questions which divided opinion were being discussed. Neither side can be acquitted of the charge of
bribery and corruption. The partisans of the Government, being drawn from the richest classes, were the first
to adopt illicit means of gaining the day, and the
Liberals had to follow suit, on pain of being left out in
the cold, though quite aware of the demoralising effect
of their action. The excitement caused by the persecution of ideas and the prosecution of individuals reached
such a pitch that the Viennese camarilla became nervous
and recognised the advisability of providing a safety
valve for popular passions by summoning the Diet, the
convocation of which was moreover demanded by the
necessity of getting the military contingent voted in
view of the threatening nature of the European outlook.
Pálffy had to go, for even his partisans in the ranks of
the retrograde Magnates were not prepared to see their
country sacrificed to Austria, and reduced to the position
of a dependent province, and Count Antony Majláth, a
highly-educated and broad-minded man, was appointed in
his stead.

The chief result of the reactionary policy recently 1839-
pursued by the Government was the complete victory of 1840.
the Opposition at the polls, and a noticeable change in
the ideas of the Upper House, where few, with the
exception of the bishops, were now disposed to offer an
uncompromising resistance to Liberal innovations, or saw
salvation only in the retention of old forms and antiquated privileges. Széchenyi's example was contagious,
and many who had been satisfied with the *rôle* of spectator, now wished to play a part in the affairs of the

country. Among the Conservatives the most distinguished were Count Aurelius Dessewffy,[1] a politician of distinguished ability, Baron Samuel Jósika, Count George Apponyi and Baron Nicholas Vay, men of exceptional education and breadth of view, who formed the " party of deliberate progress "[2] which supported the Government, but not in the former servile manner, and desired to avoid conflict with the Crown and with Austria's interests in order to lessen opposition to the promotion of the material welfare of their country. Count Louis Batthyány was the leader of the Liberals in the Upper House. He accepted Széchenyi's ideas on the subject of economic reform and material progress, but cared more than his teacher for the maintenance of the national Constitution, and was not inclined to barter liberal ideas and independence for financial prosperity, in which respect he resembled his predecessor in the leadership, Baron Nicholas Wesselényi, driven into retirement by ill-health and persecution. Among his followers were to be found such distinguished persons as Baron Joseph Eötvös, not less celebrated as a politician than as a writer ; Count Ladislaus Teleki, a debater who was always ready to enforce his arguments with the aid of the duelling sword, and many other nobles, whose presence in the ranks of the Liberal party went far towards realising the wish long ago expressed by Széchenyi, that the aristocracy should take its place at the head of the reform movement instead of being dragged at its tail. Their programme comprised the emancipation of the peasants ; an equal distribution of the burden of taxation ; the grant of political rights on the basis of a property-qualification irrespective of class or religion ; the provision of extended educational facilities, and the abolition of the customs barrier between Hungary and Austria, and of

---

[1] Son of Count Joseph Dessewffy, the chief critic of Széchenyi's *Hitel*.

[2] The *Fontolva Haladó* Party, as it styled itself.

the Aviticitas and Fiscalitas[1] which, as Széchenyi had
shown, constituted the chief obstacles to the economic
regeneration of the country.

The opening of the session was marked by an episode
which augured ill for the prospects of peaceful progress.
The county of Pest was deprived of the services of one
of its members, Count Gideon Ráday, whom the Government had prosecuted on a charge of *lèse-majesté*, on account
of a too free expression of opinion on the subject of the
Government's sins of omission and commission, and
forbade to take his seat for the reason that the case was
still pending—an outrage on the principle of parliamentary
independence, as the unchecked exercise of such autocratic interference would have enabled the Government
to arrange the constitution of the House as it pleased,
to disfranchise any county which had elected Liberal
representatives, and, in fact, to disqualify the whole
Opposition by the simple process of indictment.[2] The
Lower House refused to proceed to business till its
grievance was remedied, and the Government was in a
quandary, as the withdrawal of the prohibition would
have amounted to the abandonment of its cherished
principle that the Crown and its Ministers were invested
with equal sanctity as regards immunity from criticism,
and would have been equivalent to an admission of the
illegality of its proceedings in the case of Count Ráday.
The Magnates refused to endorse the remonstrance which
the Lower House addressed to the King, but as the
Deputies stuck to their guns and refused to begin work
(though Ráday was ultimately allowed to take his seat),
until they received satisfactory guarantees for the maintenance of their parliamentary privileges, the Upper House
had to give way and the address was forwarded to the
Crown. In reply thereto the King sent a rescript on
March 24, 1840, promising that the right of free speech

---

[1] *Supra*, pp. 41, 278.   [2] Kónyi, *Deák Ferencz Beszédei*, i. 318 *sqq.*

should not be restricted, and that a full amnesty should be granted to Wesselényi, Lovassy, and others who had been prosecuted for political reasons since the last session of the Diet, if that body would consent to begin without more ado the discussion of the Government's request for recruits. Eventually Deák and his party accepted the King's offer, and the contingent was voted, the Law[1] in which the grant was embodied stipulating that the recruits should serve only in Hungarian regiments, and thereby further affirming the Diet's right of interference in matters affecting the internal organisation of the army.

The twelve points of the programme which bore the name of the county of Szatmár, the basis of whose instructions to its deputies it formed, may be taken as typical of the demands of the Liberal party at this period: —(1) the abolition of the existing system of entail; (2) land registration and the establishment of a land mortgage bank; (3) compulsory redemption of feudal dues and of peasants' allotments; (4) abolition of guilds and monopolies operating in restraint of trade; (5) eligibility to office and the right to own land to be extended to all without restriction; (6) the revival and extension of the law of the reign of King Mathias relating to the taxation of nobles and the higher clergy;[2] (7) popular education; (8) freedom of the Press; (9) emancipation of the urban population and the reform of municipal government; (10) revision of the civil and criminal law and the introduction of trial by jury; (11) the separation of executive and judical functions in the counties; (12) popular representation at the Diet. Of this list, which might have passed as the programme of the Liberal party in almost any contemporary European country, the last

---

[1] 1840, Law ii.

[2] LXIV. of 1486, providing for the payment by the clergy and nobles of the expenses of the " *nuntii electi* "—a dead letter.

point was clearly the most important.   The county organisation was all very well as a bulwark of the Constitution, as a barrier against autocratic encroachment, but its very strength was its weak point.   The conflict of local interests was always liable to be fatal to the possibility of united action, and it was evident that the salvation of the country, its political independence and its economic development, could be guaranteed only by a strong central Parliament elected on a basis which admitted within the pale of the Constitution the majority of those who had been hitherto excluded.   The idea that that majority could continue indefinitely to be taxed to provide for the expenses of local and parliamentary government without being represented at the councils of the nation was soon to be exploded.   The principle of universal liability to taxation had been championed to good purpose by Kossuth, who pointed out that complete exemption therefrom was in civilised countries a privilege enjoyed by beggars alone; but it was still opposed by some who, though they called themselves Liberals, put their pocket interests before those of the nation at large.   The Government was influenced by conflicting considerations ; for while, on the one hand, it had always recognised the advantage of increasing the number of tax-payers, on the other hand it was opposed to anything which would tend to strengthen the feeling of national unity.

One of the chief obstacles to that unity and the chief battle-ground of the antagonism which had hitherto existed between Catholics and Protestants, was provided by the question of mixed marriages.   Originally, no restrictions on such unions existed, and the question was first raised by the bigotry of Maria Theresa in the interests of the domination of the Catholic Church.   In accordance with the edict of Joseph II., if the husband were Catholic, all his children were brought up in the father's religion ; if he were a member of the Reformed Church, his boys were brought up as Protestants, while the girls followed the mother. The same principle, though distinctly unfair to the Protestants, was adopted by Law xxvi. of 1791, which, at the same time, enacted that no obstacle was to be thrown in the way of the celebration of mixed marriages. In spite of the last-mentioned provision, the Catholic priests tried to compel Protestants desiring to marry Catholics to sign a document giving an undertaking that all children of the marriage should be brought up in the Catholic religion,[1] and refused to perform the ceremony until such guarantee were given. A further injustice inflicted on the Protestants consisted in the fact that any one desiring to leave the Catholic Church was unable to do so without first submitting to religious instruction by a priest, in order that the eloquence and erudition of the latter might have a chance of bringing the wandering sheep back to the fold. The instruction was not allowed to be taken in homœopathic doses from various priests, so the ingenious ecclesiastics hit upon the plan of interrupting their lectures before the full six weeks' course was ended, and of compelling the would-be pervert to betake himself to a fresh instructor. This manœuvre might be continued indefinitely, with the result that it might take years to complete the process of transference from one religion to another.[2] The whole question of mixed marriages was raised at the end of the Diet in 1830, but nothing was done. In 1833, the Lower House appointed a committee which proceeded to draft a Bill remedying the above-mentioned grievances, and providing that thenceforth Protestants might own land in Croatia, visit foreign universities, and that Protestant members of trade guilds should not be penalised for refusal to observe Catholic festivals and holidays. To their credit the Catholic members [3] of the Lower House

---

[1] The so-called " *Reversalis.*" The Catholic priests justified themselves by reference to an illegal Royal Order of 1792.

[2] Horváth, *Huszonöt év,* i. 312.

[3] Deák, who first attracted special attention by his speech on this question,

rose one after the other to support the Bill, which was consequently carried; but the bishops strongly opposed the first reading, and it was sent down again unread in spite of the efforts of Széchenyi and Eötvös, himself a Catholic, in its support. Seven times the Bill was sent up to the Magnates, only to be rejected, to the great satisfaction of the bishops, two of whom issued pastoral letters instructing the clergy to prevent the celebration of mixed marriages by all means in their power, and to refuse the Church's blessing to such unions, unless the Protestant bridegroom gave the "*reversalis*" undertaking, in spite of the law of 1791, which made it obligatory on Catholic priests to officiate unconditionally. Finally, after an eighth exchange of messages with the Magnates, the Lower House dropped the Bill, which had found its most ardent supporters among the Catholic members, rather than that it should be passed in a mangled form. But the excitement increased rather than waned, owing to the ill-advised action of the bishops in sending one of their number to Rome to obtain the instructions of the Pope, who, though he decided that mixed marriages without "*reversalis*" must be looked upon as "*illicita sed valida*," approved the action of the bishops, and gave them written encouragement in their resistance to the law. As no papal communication could be published in Hungary without the *Placetum Regium*, furious protests were raised in the counties, and the general election, which took place in 1843, was largely influenced by this episode, which did much to eliminate the previously preponderating influence of the Catholic clergy. The development of a spirit of freethinking was

was one of them. The Palatine was in favour of the Bill, having himself married a Protestant. The Croatians, both lay and ecclesiastic, were, next to the bishops, the most violent opponents of the Bill, for the reason that it would abolish Law xxvi. of 1791, and so remove the restrictions imposed on Protestants (not, be it observed, on Jews or members of the Greek Church) which forbade them to own land in Croatia. So the opposition had an economic as well as a religious side. Hungary and Croatia came into collision for the first time over this question.

one of the characteristic phenomena of the period, and the Catholic Church, feeling that its influence was slipping away, tried in vain to retain it by entering into an unholy alliance with the party of reaction—nominally "for the defence of throne and altar,"[1] but in reality because it feared the loss of political power and the secularisation of its enormous possessions.

Only in the matter of the language question was any notable success obtained by the Liberal party in the Diet of 1839-40. Law vi. of that session enacted, *inter alia*, that Addresses to the King, the official communications of the county authorities[2] with the Government offices, and the circulars of the Council of Lieutenancy, should be couched exclusively in the Hungarian language. Henceforth the possession of a knowledge of Hungarian was to be a condition precedent to appointment to all ecclesiastical offices, and the King undertook to see to the extension of the knowledge of that idiom in the frontier districts, and to its employment by the Magyar regimental authorities in their communications with Hungarian official bodies. Further, after the expiration of three years from the close of the session, all registers of births, marriages, and deaths were to be kept in the Hungarian language.[3]

As regards the reform of the criminal law, one of the chief necessities of the period, the Liberal party failed to realise its desires. The conviction now obtained that the existing law was of too Draconian a character, though, as recently as 1825, the "instructions" of one county required that the King should be petitioned in favour of greater

---

[1] The motto of its organ, the *Nemzeti Ujság*, which never possessed much influence, and had still less when the control was taken over by the reactionary Count John Majláth.

[2] Határaibani Köztörvényhatóságok, *i.e.* Hungarian authorities only, *intra fines regni*, so Croatia had no ground of complaint.

[3] Wirkner, in his letter to Metternich, admits that not one-tenth of the nobles understood Latin.—*Élményeim*, p. 136. The Government feared that the universal use of a language understood by all would be fatal to its policy of reaction and obscurantism.

frequency in the application of capital punishment, on the ground that the long confinement of prisoners was a cause of excessive expense.[1] The Diet appointed a committee to consider the question of reform, which included in its members many of the best known and most enlightened deputies, among others Deák, Pulszky, Eötvös, George Apponyi, and Aurelius Dessewffy; and a commission was sent abroad to study the various prison systems. The Bill, for the most part the work of Deák, which was intended to give effect to the recommendations of the committee, provided for the introduction of trial by jury and the abolition of the death penalty; it is needless to say, therefore, that it was thrown out by the Upper House.

The results attained by the efforts of the Liberal party since 1825 were far from being commensurate with the energy expended, and it became more and more evident that the struggle between the old ideals of Austrian despotism and Hungarian constitutionalism must soon take a decisive turn one way or the other. Hungary recognised the need of democratic reform, of abolishing the hard and fast line which divided the population into two classes, the privileged and the unprivileged,[2] and was no longer content to limit its exertions to the prevention of the more flagrant violations of its historic rights. Austria, on the other hand, saw that its only chance of keeping its preponderance lay in the maintenance of the *status quo* as regards the question of the emancipation of the peasants and of its economic relations with Hungary. The antagonism which existed between the two countries was brought to a head, but was not in any sense caused, by recent events in Western Europe. It was the conflict of ideals—liberalism on the one side, autocracy on the

1843-
1844.

---

[1] Marczali, *A Legujabb Kor Története*, p. 360.

[2] As long ago as 1807 Paul Nagy had urged the necessity of extending the benefits of the Constitution to all Hungarians "in order that in the moment of danger the entire people may stand together in its defence."—Wirkner, *Élményeim*, p. 25.

312 THE POLITICAL EVOLUTION

other, which rendered a peaceful solution an impossibility. The wall with which Metternich had sought to surround Hungary had failed to stop the spread of modern notions.

In 1841, Kossuth, whose term of imprisonment had recently terminated, became the editor of the *Pesti Hirlap*, and dealt in its columns with every subject of public interest from the national point of view. Landerer, the publisher, was an agent of the secret police, hence the fact that the Government raised no objection to the inception of the new journalistic enterprise,[1] which it certainly would not have permitted if it had had an idea of the magnitude of the influence which Kossuth would exert on public opinion. Széchenyi was mistaken in supposing that economic progress must necessarily precede constitutional reform. Kossuth's view was sounder, namely, that only the development of a middle class, by means of an extension of the franchise, could bring about a lasting change for the better in economic conditions. He saw that the future of the country depended on the "Gentry," not on the Nobles, whom he plainly told that reforms would be effected "through them and with them if they were willing, without them and in spite of them if necessary." Dessewffy, who wrote in the *Világ*, the organ of the "Party of Deliberate Progress," was Kossuth's only possible antagonist in the journalistic world. He feared the possibility of an orgy of tyrannical Liberalism as much as the recrudescence of Austrian autocracy, and therefore was in favour of the establishment of a strong, but limited and responsible, central government, which should control the excessive power of the counties. Unfortunately, he died in 1842, at the age of thirty-six, and there was no one to take his place. Széchenyi lost no opportunity of attacking Kossuth and of accusing him of setting poor against rich, class against class, and, more especially, of stirring up hatred against the

[1] Szögyény, *Emlékiratai*, p. 19.

Upper House; but his efforts were ineffective, possibly for the reason that he created the opinion that the main-spring of his action was a petty jealousy which prevented him from supporting any scheme which he himself had not initiated.[1] He published a pamphlet[2] with the special object of pressing home the attack, in which he admitted that he did not doubt the purity of Kossuth's motives, and agreed for the most part with his views. He reproached his rival with addressing himself to the heart and not to the head of his readers, and tried to impress on him the futility of progress without regard to the means employed and the goal in view. According to Széchenyi, Kossuth, in his thirst for popularity, mistook the applause of the crowd for public opinion, and demanded unlimited publicity for his own views while he encouraged the mob to shout his opponents down. Between himself and Kossuth, Széchenyi considered the same difference to exist as there is beween peaceful reform and revolution. But the nation was tired of waiting in vain for reform to come from above, and though the pamphlet in question had to some extent a moderating influence on the tone of the *Pesti Hirlap*, its chief result was the destruction of the remains of Széchenyi's popularity and the splitting of the reformers into two parties—the moderates and the Kossuthites. Kossuth, whose paper was not so much the organ of public opinion as the creator of it, made a polite but crushing reply, suggesting that his adversary renounced his own opinions so soon as he heard them enunciated by another, and the victory was never for a moment in doubt, more especially as Dessewffy and Eötvös threw their weight into the balance on Kossuth's side. Thenceforth Széchenyi's influence was supreme only in economic matters, and even in this department the rivalry of Kossuth was soon to make itself felt.

---

[1] Pulszky, *Életem és Korom*, i. 158.
[2] *A Kelet Népe*, Gróf Széchenyi István Munkái, vol. ii., Budapest, 1905.

The King's Speech, on the occasion of the opening of the Diet gave unusual satisfaction, on account of the number and the nature of the legislative proposals which it contained.[1] It appeared as if the Government at last recognised the necessity of constitutional and economic reform. Even Kossuth was inclined to believe in the good intentions of Vienna; but the cloven hoof was soon shown by the inspired refusal of the Upper House to allow the publication of an official, uncensored report of the proceedings of the Diet. The reform of the municipal franchise, and the extension of urban representation at the Diet, were favoured by the progressive party, not only as the first step in the direction of a thorough alteration of the existing basis of parliamentary representation, but as being likely to bring a considerable accession of strength to the Liberals. A Bill was therefore introduced providing that both municipal officials and deputies to the Diet should be elected by manhood suffrage, and that sixteen seats should be allotted to the towns. The Magnates insisted on a high property qualification for the franchise and on the adoption of a system of indirect voting, which would have excluded the great mass of the urban population from participation, and would merely have had the effect of giving the Government sixteen more votes in the Lower House, whose "saturation with dependent elements, whose servility would in the course of five or six years suffice to destroy not only that chamber itself, but liberty and the Constitution as well."[2] So after fruitless negotiation the Bill was dropped, and the disingenuousness of the Government's legislative proposals became patent to all. True, the Upper House allowed an Act to pass making non-nobles eligible for all

[1] Establishment of land mortgage bank, improvement of means of communication, regulation of the Danube, urban representation at the Diet, etc.—Horváth, *Huszonöt év*, ii. 190.

[2] Széchenyi, quoted by Horváth, *Huszonöt év*, ii. 233.

offices,[1] but small thanks were due to them for the concession ; for what could be more useless than to give peasants, who, as non-nobles, could not vote at elections, the right to be themselves elected ?   In other respects the Act in question conferred a considerable boon on the lower classes.   Law vii. 9 of 1840 had admitted in principle the peasant's right to redeem all feudal dues, and to divide his holding by will among his children, and now that of 1844 conferred the right on all non-nobles, belonging to any recognised religion, to own real property.   The change which had taken place in public opinion since 1834 is noticeable.   Notions which had horrified people at that date met with almost universal acceptance ten years later.   The laws of 1840 and 1844 were, in fact, generally regarded merely as an instalment, and the movement in favour of complete emancipation of the peasants continued unabated.

Hungarian had now completely ousted Latin as the language of debate, though there was still some opposition on the part of the representatives of the "annexed" or "subject parts," encouraged by the Government and by the partisans of reaction.   The Croatian deputies to the Diet of 1843-44 all belonged to the so-called Illyrian party, to which reference will hereafter be made, and had been elected by a snap vote in the absence of the Hungarian electors, who were tricked into the belief that the election had been postponed.   When these deputies began to address the Diet in Latin, they were met with cries of "Speak Hungarian!" and shouted down, chiefly for the reason that the trick to which they owed their election was known, and on account of the recognised fact that they were the representatives of a disloyal faction, and not of the public opinion of Croatia.   The King, who was quite ready to wink at the existence of a Pan-Slav agitation, if he could utilise its promoters to the detriment

---

[1] 1844, Law v., without regard to religious distinctions.

of Hungary, took no notice of the protests of the Hungarian party in Croatia against the illegalities which had marked the recent elections, but sent a rescript to the Diet ordering it.to allow the Croatian deputies to address it in Latin.   The House denied the right of the Crown to interfere, persisted in its refusal to listen to Latin speeches, and resolved to ignore them in the official journal of proceedings.   Finally, an end was put to the dispute by the receipt of the royal assent to an Act,[1] which provided that the Hungarian language was to be used to the complete exclusion of Latin in all royal communications with the Diet, as well as in the drawing up of laws, and in the Crown's confirmatory rescripts.   Thenceforth Hungarian was to be the sole language of debate, but a period of grace was granted to non-Magyar deputies, permitting them to continue the use of Latin for the space of six years.   The use of Hungarian was made obligatory in all documents issued by the Chancery and by the Council of Lieutenancy, as well as in all the law courts of Hungary.   In future the Magyar language was to be taught in the secondary schools of the "annexed parts" as an ordinary subject, and was to be the medium of instruction in all schools in Hungary proper.   The authorities in the said "parts" were bound to accept official documents couched in the Hungarian idiom, but might continue to use Latin in their correspondence with Hungarian officials.   Thus, after a struggle which had continued almost without interruption since 1790, the Magyar language was raised to the position to which it was entitled as that of the dominant nation, or of the "predominant partner," if that familiar phrase is less offensive to racial susceptibilities.[2]

[1] Law ii. of 1844.

[2] Under what may, for convenience, be called the feudal system only birth could give rights ; so long as the Catholic Church was supreme membership of that Church was essential to their full enjoyment.   With the approach of the abolition of the former and of the dethronement of the latter the language

If the Croatians had wished to address the Diet in their own language something might have been urged in their favour, but nothing but the wish to annoy could have prompted a sudden recurrence to the use of Latin, voluntarily abandoned for years past in favour of Hungarian, which the Croatian deputies spoke without difficulty. As a matter of fact, 'they had no wish whatever to preserve the use of Latin, as they knew there was no feeling in its favour in their own country, where it was understood by only a trifling minority, but they wanted a weapon of offence, and could find it only in the Latin language, as there was no tongue in existence which could be described as the national language of the Slavs of Hungary, unless it were Servian, and to the exaltation of that jargon to an exclusive position no Croatian would have agreed. In Slavonia only 12,000 out of 145,000 spoke Croatian, and in Croatia 280,000 out of 570,000 spoke Servian,[1] and as the Palatine, the Archduke Joseph, wrote to Metternich, there was no question of any *national* feeling of hostility to Hungary on the part of the subordinate races. "The use of Latin has declined, as in the rest of Europe, and the people see no objection to the official use of the Magyar language, provided that they are not

question acquired a new and greater importance, as the majority of those who would now receive political rights for the first time were of non-Magyar origin.

[1] Horváth, *Huszonöt év*, ii. 214. Fényes's and other statistics, quoted by De Gerando, *Über den öffentlichen Geist in Ungarn*, p. 262, give the population of Hungary in 1842 as 13,784,170 ; of which 4,870,000 Magyars, 1,262,000 Germans, 2,311,000 Roumans, 4,273,860 Slavs. De Gerando, *o.c.* p. 237, states that all races where in contact with the Magyars spoke Hungarian, while Slováks, Croats, Ruthenians, and others spoke Hungarian to each other, as it was the only language they could all understand. In their intercourse with each other Hungarian was used as pidgin-English is used in the Treaty Ports by Chinese from different provinces. Count Albert Apponyi, in his pamphlet already referred to, *The Juridical Nature, etc.*, says that in 1848 the nobles numbered 675,000 out of a population, according to him, of nearly 12,000,000. To the numbers of the privileged must be added over 16,000 clergy, members of enfranchised liberal professions (*the honoratiores*), and the burgesses of the free towns, p 8 *n*.

interfered with in the use of their own dialects in private.
All peoples and races inhabiting the Kingdom, without
exception, entertain this view, and in recent times the
younger section of the population evinces a lively desire
to acquire the Magyar language, even in places where it
is not generally spoken."[1]   Better evidence of the artificial nature of the agitation could not be asked than that
provided by this letter of a member of the House of
Habsburg.   The fact was that the Croatian deputies
found that the triumph of Hungarian Liberalism meant
the triumph of the principle of religious equality, and that
the right of owning land in Croatia could then be no
longer denied to the Protestants.   There was no question
of fighting for the maintenance of national rights.   It
was only the fact of the enjoyment of the benefits of the
Hungarian Constitution by Croatia as a constituent part
of the Hungarian kingdom that saved the Croatians from
Austrian despotism — as they were to discover to their
cost at a later period, when they allowed themselves to be
used as the catspaw of autocracy.

Since the Habsburgs abandoned the old Hungarian
tradition with respect to the Balkan Peninsula, turned
their eyes from the road which led towards Constantinople,
and kept them fixed on Frankfurt, the central point of
the German Confederation, the Slav races had begun to
develop a tendency to look to Russia for their future.
The Tsars naturally regarded with complacency a movement[2] which, even if it did not end in permanently increasing
their realms or their influence in Western Europe, would in
any case provide them with a useful weapon to hold over
the head of Austrian Emperors, the population of whose
patchwork dominions was more than half Slav.   The
possibility of the arrogation by Russia of a sort of
"sacerdotal supremacy" over the Slavs of Hungary was

1 Horváth, Huszonöt év, ii. 281. See also Beöthy, o.c. ii. 279.
2 Bidermann, Russische Umtriebe in Ungarn, Innsbruck, 1867, p. 18 sq.

not lost sight of by the author of the apocryphal Will of Peter the Great,[1] but according to Kossuth,[2] the idea of Pan-Slavism as the union of all Slav races under Russian protection with a view to the formation of the largest political organisation the world had ever seen, was first suggested by Prince Adam Czartoryszki in 1815, as affording some consolation to the Poles for the dismemberment of their country. The idea was accepted with enthusiasm by the Tsar Alexander, and only the wedge, to use Palacky's phrase, driven into the Slav body by the Magyars,[3] seemed to make the ultimate realisation of the dream an impossibility. Hence the hatred of the Pan-Slavs for Hungary. In any case there would seem to be evidence enough to show that the affection evinced by successive Tsars for the Slavs of Hungary was not purely unselfish, and was due to some other reason than a laudable desire for the spiritual welfare of their co-religionaries.[4] At the time of the cholera epidemic in 1831, Russian agents were busy stirring up the peasants, and the Russo-Turkish war afforded a favourable opportunity of encouraging the idea of the identity of interests of all Slavs, and of fomenting hatred of the inconvenient Magyars.[5] Austria, hypnotised for the moment by its fears of the nearer danger, the establishment of a united and democratic Hungary, lost sight of the possible ultimate consequences of Russian interference, and encouraged the mutinous tendencies of the Slavs in the hope of thereby checking the progress of Magyar Liberalism. Kolowrat, Austrian Minister and chief of the pro-Slavs, saw no inconsistency in encouraging the national desire of

---

[1] Bidermann, *Russische Umtriebe in Ungarn*, n. 98.

[2] *Schriften aus der Emigration*, ii. 168.

[3] See *supra*, p. 3.

[4] Horváth, *Huszonöt év*, i. 510, cites instructions given to Admiral Tsitsakoff in 1812 emphasising the necessity of stirring up the Slav races in Bosnia, Servia, Croatia, and Dalmatia, of promising them freedom and the establishment of a great Slav state.

[5] Marczali, *A Legujabb Kor Története*, p. 417 *sq.*, and Bidermann, *o.c.*

the Czechs as regards the maintenance of their language, and in thwarting at the same time similar aspirations on the part of the Magyars.[1] In the reign of Joseph II. the Croatians were anxious for the maintenance of Hungarian independence, and protested against centralisation and germanisation as energetically as any Magyar. When, after the Peace of Schönbrunn, the parts lying beyond the Száva were given up to Napoleon, Croatians apparently resented the dismemberment of their country less than the prospect of absorption by Austria. The short period spent under the French flag gave a great impetus to trade and to education, and greatly increased the Croatians' idea of their own importance, and to some extent is responsible for the development of separatistic tendencies.[2]

At first the Pan-Slav movement was purely literary, but a new turn was given to it by the raising in the Diet of 1830 of the question of the exclusion of Protestants from the ownership of land. The fear of the removal of Protestant disabilities contributed to the production of a form of pseudo-patriotism among the Catholics of Croatia, and to the creation of a feeling of hostility to the Magyars, which, but for its economic origin, would soon have disappeared. The poet of the movement was John

[1] Count Leo Thun came forward as the champion of the Slováks, alleged to be oppressed by the Magyars. See his controversy with Pulszky, who effectively answered him.—*Die Stellung der Slovaken in Ungarn*, Prague, 1843. No doubt Hungary did its best to establish the use of Hungarian among the uneducated Slováks by making a knowledge of that language essential to employment in church and school. The priests hated the Calvinists of Hungary as much as they hated the Catholics of Austria, and then, as to-day, exploited the ignorance of the common people, and created a hostility to Hungary which otherwise would not have existed. Thun's idea was that timely concessions to the Austrian Slavs would prevent their looking to Russia for their future.

[2] Beöthy, *o.c.* ii. 279, says that after the collapse of Napoleon's Illyria, the parts of Croatia which had been incorporated therein petitioned Francis for re-union with Hungary, and declared that they wished to live and die under the aegis of the Hungarian Constitution. But the pocket interests of the Catholics caused this pro-Magyar enthusiasm to be short-lived.

Kollár, an evangelistic preacher, who in 1827 wrote a kind of Divine Comedy entitled *Slawy Dcera* (Glory's Daughter) in which he drew a glowing picture of the future of Russia—fated to extend from the Arctic Seas to Constantinople—and vilified the Magyars and all alleged oppressors of the Slavs.[1] A more redoubtable protagonist was Louis Gáj, to whose machinations such bitterness as was felt in Croatia with regard to the language question was almost entirely due. In 1835 he founded an anti-Magyar newspaper, the *Illyrian National Gazette*, in which, knowing that the Croatians alone were no match for the Magyars, either in numbers or intelligence, he urged the necessity of a union of the southern Slavs, and of its necessary corollary, Croatian hegemony, under the protection of Russia, the tender mother of all Slavs, the predestined ruler of the world.[2] Russia's treatment of the Poles should have made Gáj's Croatian readers hesitate as to the advisability of sacrificing their local autonomy and the certain benefits enjoyed under the Hungarian Constitution; but the prospect of a reconstituted and glorified Illyria apparently obscured their judgment as to the respective merits of King Stork and King Log. The difficulty presented by the absence of a medium of communication between all southern Slavs was more or less got over by the adoption of the Ragusan dialect, which, under Italian influence, had developed into something resembling a modern language, which could not be said of the Croatian and Servian dialects to which it was allied.[3]

[1] Árpád, Charlemagne, and others guilty of interfering with the prospects of Slav expansion, are accommodated with special places in his Inferno, where they drink the filthy water of dungheaps while devils dance on their stomachs. In 1837 Kollár wrote a pamphlet on the relationship of the different Slav dialects, the moral of which was that no matter how many Slav branches there may be, they possess a common Fatherland in Russia. His first work was published in 1832, entitled, *Shall we become Magyars?*

[2] He was generally reputed to be in the pay of Russia.—Horváth, *Huszonöt év*, i. 523. Pulszky, who was particularly well informed on the subject, also says that Gáj's press was run with Russian money.—*Életem és Korom*, i. 101.

[3] Pulszky, *ibid.* i. 137.

In spite of unlimited abuse of the Magyars, the Illyrian movement made but little headway, though the Viennese Government, which had censored and suppressed to the best of its powers the attempted development of a periodical literature in Hungary proper, threw no obstacles in its way, and winked at the treasonable propaganda of Gáj and his followers.[1]   If any one had a reason for complaint it was not the Croatians (with whose limited autonomy, enjoyed for centuries, no Hungarian had attempted to interfere), but the Magyars of Croatia, as the scandals which had marked the elections of representatives to the Diet of 1844 were repeated the following year, and the nobles who were not members of the Illyrian party were deprived of their votes.   The Bán produced a royal rescript which stated that the right of voting at the provincial Diet belonged only to those summoned by writ of the Bán and personally present, and as that official had taken care to summon only the high Catholic clergy and members of the Illyrian party, the Croatians who were loyal to Hungary, and the Magyars of Croatia, were stripped of the rights which immemorial custom had given to every noble.[2]

Now for the first time the notion was propagated that fractional nationalities, settled in a country which had indisputably belonged to the Hungarian kingdom for nearly a thousand years, were entitled to form *regna in regno* and renounce allegiance to the paramount nation, but for whose protection they would long ago have been absorbed in Austria, if, indeed, Austria had itself escaped the dismemberment with which it was threatened in the days of Maria Theresa.   The words used by the Palatine, who was also an Austrian archduke, in the Upper House

---

[1] Francis sent Gáj a diamond ring, and an Order to Count Draskovitch, his chief supporter.—Horváth, *Huszonöt Év*, i. 531.   Metternich, on the other hand, disapproved of the encouragement given to the Pan-Slavs.

[2] Pulszky, *o.c.* i. 213.

of the Diet on June 28, 1843, with respect to the Illyrian movement should not be forgotten, for they are no less to the point to-day than they were sixty-five years ago : *" When every fraction of the Hungarian people lays claim to a separate individuality, the general welfare of the country is threatened.·   I belong to those who think that every inhabitant of Hungary, whatever his language may be, while he enjoys the rights, the privileges, and the benefits of the Magyar Constitution, should consider himself a Magyar.* Here there is no Illyrian nation ; there is only one nation, the Hungarian.   I repeat that the welfare of the country has hitherto been derived from the unity of the constituent nationalities."   Baron Rauch, a Croatian magnate, followed in the same strain, and attacked Gáj and his followers for their attempt to impregnate the youth and the clergy with ridiculous notions, and for " assuring them that in the near future the Russians will dictate laws in Pressburg, and will grant a constitution to all nationalities which join them." [1]   The agitation was in fact fictitious, and at this period had but little effect on the masses, whose free use of Slav dialects in church [2] and daily life was in no way threatened.   But the view entertained by the Palatine was not that of the Viennese Government.   " It is certain that Metternich's Government gladly availed itself of the opportunity of drawing to itself the non-Magyar-speaking races, more especially the Croatians, by the grant of secret support, or at least by the promise of it, and so prevented the disappearance of the evident antagonism between them and the Magyars. . . . It is undeniable that the Government's plans were put into practice with great skill, with the result that very few among those whom the Government intended should play an active part in the strife of parties saw through its designs and

[1] De Gerando, *Über den öffentlichen Geist in Ungarn*, p. 325.
[2] Except where the great majority of the population were Magyars, and wished for the use of their own language in Protestant churches.

realised the fact that, while nominally fighting the battle of the nationalities, they were in reality only catspaws utilised for the attainment of ends which had nothing in common with their racial aspirations."[1]   The truth of this statement is proved by the fact that the publication of Gáj's disloyal and anti-Magyar paper was allowed, while that of Kossuth's account of the proceedings of the Diet was forbidden ; and the answer to the charge brought against the Magyars of oppressing the Slavs by attempting to suppress the use of their dialects, is to be found in the fact that no steps were taken in Hungary to interfere with the dissemination of Pan-Slav extravagancies.   The result of Viennese encouragement was that Croatia began to have pretensions to be looked upon as an allied country, not as a constituent part of the Hungarian kingdom, to demand union with Dalmatia, and to object to any interference in Croatian affairs[2] while maintaining its influence on Magyar politics by means of its representatives at the Hungarian Diet.   If racial suicide is to be commended, and the Magyars are to be blamed for acting in self-defence and for attempting to utilise school and church for the maintenance of their existence as a nation, well and good ; but if the instinct of self-preservation is not wholly vile, the feeling of resentment aroused by the connivance of the Viennese Government at the separatistic propaganda of the so-called Illyrian party was amply justified. Wesselényi, the earliest Hungarian prophet of federation,[3] saw in the disabilities of the peasants the chief justification

[1] *Ost und West*, the pro-Slav Viennese publication, March 1862.—Horváth, *Huszonöt év*, i. 530.   [2] Kónyi, *Deák Ferencz Beszédei*, i. 397.

[3] In 1843 Wesselényi published his *Szózat* or appeal, in which he pointed out that Austria should prevent the nationalities from turning their eyes to Russia by developing the spirit of freedom and contentedness.   He suggests a form of federation and the formation of five groups :` (1) The German provinces, including Carinthia and Carniola, whose scattered Slavs should have the same privileges as the Saxons of Transylvania ; (2) Bohemia and Moravia ; (3) Galicia ; (4) Lombardo-Venetia and the Italians of Dalmatia ; (5) Hungary and the parts annexed.—See Horváth, *Huszonöt év*, ii. 126 *sq.*

for the fear aroused by the spectre of Pan-Slavism. In his view a strong Hungary was essential to Europe as a defence against the spread of Russian obscurantism, and the right of citizenship should be conferred on all who could read and write Hungarian. Above all things, all semblance of an attempt to deprive the constituent nationalities of their languages should be avoided, lest Croat, Slovák, and Servian should be driven into the arms of Russia, or become willing instruments in the hands of the reactionary Government of Vienna.

That the object of that Government still was the retardation of the moral and material progress of Hungary, was clearly shown by the attitude which it adopted towards the movement in favour of the emancipation of the peasants, and with regard to the commercial relations of Austria and Hungary. The basis of those relations was formed by the principle that it was Hungary's business to supply Austria with raw material, and Austria's exclusive privilege to provide Hungary with the manufactured article. Consequently, any attempt of the latter to develop its incipient manufactures was looked on with disfavour by the former, for fear that the Hungarians might ultimately become commercially self-sufficing. Though, since 1825, the Diet continually complained of the fact that the customs tariff was all in Austria's favour, and was intentionally fatal to the possibility of Hungarian commercial development, the Austrian Government turned a deaf ear to all remonstrances and denied the right of Hungary to have a voice in the matter. So long as that country was purely agricultural its only wish was for the removal of the customs barrier erected in Austria's interest between the two countries ; but when the fact was realised that the want of local manufactures was one of the chief causes of the nation's poverty, ideas changed, and the maintenance of that barrier was desired in order to prevent the swamping of nascent industries by Austrian

exports, but with modifications which would put an end
to the existent one-sided arrangement. Three, four, and
even ten times as much duty had to be paid on goods
exported from Hungary to Austria as on those sent from
Austria to Hungary. A heavy transit duty was imposed
on exports from Hungary to foreign countries passing
through Austria, which, consequently, constituted the only
market for Hungarian products, and thus could practically
fix its own price. As between the two countries, the
balance of exports over imports was enormously in favour
of Austria, four-sevenths of whose products went to
Hungary in 1841. Money flowed out of Hungary.
Seventeen million florins were paid to Austrian manufacturers in one year for cotton goods alone, which could
perfectly easily have been produced locally.[1]

In 1844 the Diet sent an Address to the King, asking
for commercial reciprocity, for statistics of imports and
exports, for information as to the working of the existing
tariff system, and on other matters affecting the commercial relations of the two countries. The Government,
in order to burke inquiry, delayed the despatch of its
reply till only three days remained before the dissolution
of the Diet. The reply stated that "the fact that more
had not hitherto been done for the advancement of
Hungary's commercial interests must be ascribed to the
difficulties presented by attendant circumstances, but that
the Government has the matter at heart, and will take
steps with a view to the promotion of the material welfare
of the Kingdom." The wished-for statistics were not
sent, and the vague nature of the long-delayed answer
gave fresh proof of the Government's intention of doing
nothing to remedy the grievances which had been the
subject of incessant complaint for nearly a century. The
excuse usually put forward in justification of the maintenance of the unfair tariff system was that Hungarian

[1] Horváth, *Huszonöt év*, ii. 246-47.

landowners paid no taxes, and, consequently, so it was
alleged, were at a great advantage as regards the cost cf
production of raw materials as compared with Austrian
producers, and that the tariff system to some extent
redressed the resultant inequality.   A second excuse was
found in the fact that the tobacco traffic was a State
monopoly in the hereditary provinces, but not in Hungary,
and as that monopoly was the chief source of Austrian
revenue, a protective duty to exclude Hungarian tobacco
was an absolute necessity until the Diet consented to the
extension of the monopoly to Hungary, in which case
Austria would be compensated for the abolition of the
customs barrier.   The first-mentioned excuse would
promptly have disappeared if the Government had used
its influence in favour of the principle of universal taxation, one of the chief desires of the Liberal party, instead
of retarding its adoption for fear of its necessary consequence—a stronger and more democratic Hungary.
The tobacco question the Government approached in a
characteristic manner.   It established its factories in
various parts of Hungary, and proceeded to undersell the
Hungarian producers at a loss to itself, under the pretence
of benefiting the poor consumer, but in reality in the confident belief that a few years of "dumping" would ruin
the local manufacturer, and that thenceforward Austria
would obtain the desired monopoly without having to
make any concessions as regards the tariff question.   The
execution of this plan was facilitated by the fact that the
better class of leaf for mixing purposes had to be imported
by Hungary from abroad ; consequently, by raising the
duty on that article the ruin of the Hungarian manufacturer could be assured.   As usual, Austria was using
loaded dice, and it was evident that Hungary must play
its own game without reference to the susceptibilities or
the convenience of its antagonist.[1]

[1] Széchenyi's schemes for the improvement of the breed of horses,

Stephen Bezerédj voiced the common discontent and suggested the remedy when he exclaimed in the Lower House: "Some time or other we must awake from our lethargy and set up on our own doorsteps that which we are not allowed to erect on our frontiers. If we do not wish to groan eternally under the commercial yoke of the foreigner, let us combine to form a protective union."[1] The idea was greeted with enthusiasm, as affording a means of escape from the economic tyranny of Austria, and October 1844 saw the establishment of the Protective Association, the members of which, drawn from all classes of society, bound themselves, for a period, to the exclusive use of home-made products. The object of the association was not merely to boycott goods "made in Austria," but to prevent the migration of skilled labour, which found insufficient opportunity at home, to promote trade in general, and to encourage the establishment of manufactories of those articles which could just as well be produced in Hungary as across the frontier.[2] Here, it seemed, was an idea

agriculture, etc., did not run counter to Austria's interests, and consequently were not altogether discouraged, but those of his proposals which would tend to make Hungary commercially self-sufficing were opposed. For instance, the proposed land mortgage bank had to be dropped, as the Government insisted on keeping the control in its own hands instead of appointing officials from a list of candidates submitted by the Diet. The Government clearly wished what was intended to be a benefit to the country to be degraded into an instrument of bureaucratic interference and corruption.—Horváth, *Huszonöt év*, ii. 266 *sqq.* The same fate befell another of Széchenyi's proposals (first made in the *Jelenkor* or "Present Time," and developed into a pamphlet, *Az Adó és Két Garas,* "The Tax and Two Kreuzers"), suggesting that each noble should pay two kreuzers every year for every acre and a half he owned. The resultant six and a quarter million florins per annum would enable a loan of a hundred millions to be raised for public purposes. The Lower House accepted the idea of a public fund of this nature, and offered 10,340,000 florins, to be spread over the next three years to form an interest and sinking fund for railway loans, etc.; but the Government's supporters in the Upper House would only agree to 1,000,000 per annum for that period—too small a sum to be of any practical use. So the idea was abandoned.

[1] Marczali, *A Legujabb Kor Története,* 556.
[2] Kónyi, *Deák Ferencz Beszédei,* ii. 64 *sqq.*

that would unite all parties without distinction, but the natural hostility of the Government prevented the Conservatives from co-operating, and membership soon became a party question. Széchenyi opposed the establishment of the Association on the ground that it would do Austria so much harm that it must infallibly provoke a fatal retaliation, but neither his prognostications nor the opposition of the reactionary party could stop the ball which Bezerédj had started rolling. Within three weeks the Association numbered 60,000 members, and 146 branches were quickly established in various parts of the country.[1] The leaders of society set the example of wearing dresses made exclusively of Hungarian materials, and all who claimed to be patriots were bound to follow suit. An exhibition of local products was held, and factories were started. Some succeeded, others failed; but in any case the foundation was laid of future commercial development. In the first year of its existence the Association reduced the proceeds of the sale of imported cigars by 3,000,000 florins, to the great disgust of the Viennese Treasury,[2] and Metternich suggested to the Palatine the advisability of taking steps to suppress the dangerous innovation; but the Archduke pointed out that the Association was a private society, in no sense illegal,[3] and of course the Government could no more compel the members to use Austrian products than the British Government could compel the English to eat German sausages. Austrian manufacturers began to find themselves squeezed out of the market which they had hitherto monopolised, and resorted, but without success, to the modern trick of marking their goods "Made in Hungary."[4] The inspired Austrian Press started a campaign of calumny, which finds its counterpart in modern times, and alleged that the

---

[1] Horváth, *Huszonöt év*, ii. 364.

[2] Horváth, *Huszonöt év*, ii. 369.   [3] Beöthy, *o.c.* ii. 342.

[4] De Gerando, *Über den öffentlichen Geist in Ungarn*, p. 443 *n*.

formation of the Association proved that Hungary wished
to sever all connection with Austria. Magyars of all
shades of opinion protested against the insinuation, and
the only result of the Press campaign was still further
to incense public opinion against rich absentees who
spent in Vienna the money which they drew from
Hungary. Count George Apponyi, the leader of the
"Party of Deliberate Progress," who had been recently
appointed Vice-Chancellor, saw that the only way in
which the Government could combat a dangerous movement was to take the wind out of the Association's sails
by parading a conciliatory spirit, and by abolishing the
most crying abuses of the one-sided tariff system. But
it had always been the principle of the Viennese Government to give way only an inch at a time, with the result
that in the long run it had to concede an ell, where the
concession of half a yard in the first instance would have
brought peace with honour. It consented to a reduction
of the duty on certain articles, but in many instances the
new tariff maintained the same proportionate difference in
Austria's favour,[1] and in all cases unfairly penalised the
incipient trade of Hungary.

It was evident that no serious concession could be
expected. The Government was, in fact, more disposed
to abolish the customs barrier, as that would be a step
in the direction of the absorption of Hungary, than to
modify it to Austria's loss ; and abolition was out of
the range of practical politics unless compensation were
obtained by the establishment of a monopoly of the tobacco
traffic, which the "dumping" policy was intended to bring
about. It affected to believe that Hungary had no right
to be heard on the tariff question, but could cite no law

[1] See the instances given by Horváth, *Huszonöt év*, ii. 382-83. In the
case of raw silk, for instance, which Austria worked up and exported,
and consequently wanted cheap, the duty was 4 florins 10 kreuzers per
centner, while the duty on the same material imported into Hungary was
100 florins.

in support of its view. The Pragmatic Sanction provided no justification, and Law x. of 1790 clearly recognised the mastery of Hungary in its own house, subject to the constitutional authority of its King, who must know how to dissociate himself at times from the Austrian Emperor. Hungary was to be, as far as the Government could make it so by the imposition of an import duty which was almost prohibitive of foreign competition, a private market to be flooded at Austria's will with inferior Austrian productions. Baron Sinai, the first financial authority of the period, in the course of conversation, which Wirkner[1] records, gives the view of the hard-headed Austrian business man of the economic relations of the two countries. "It is a question whether Austria would gain anything if Hungary were to attain a high state of civilisation. People believe that Hungary contributes nothing to the common expenses. Far from it. Hungary is a little West Indies for Austria. Every handful of grain, every product of Hungary pays a high duty at the Austrian frontier, and, on the other hand, Hungary takes the very worst manufactured articles from Austria, and thereby increases the tax-paying capacity of the latter. What money is left in their country the Magyar cavaliers bring to Vienna and spend it there."

Here, at least, we have an unprejudiced foreign opinion on the financial aspect of the question, a strong confirmation of the Hungarian view on the subject of the organised exploitation, not to say spoliation, of which Hungary had been the victim since the days of Maria Theresa. Some Hungarians saw the sole chance of escape from an impossible position in the inclusion of Hungary and Austria in the German customs-union[2]—influenced by the fact that in case of a good harvest in both countries the former had no market, in existing conditions, for its surplus products; but the suggestion received but little support.

[1] Élményeim, p. 121.   [2] Horváth, Huszonöt év, ii. 157.

Seeing that the Zollverein brought closer political union between the parties to it in its train, the great majority of the Magyars came to look upon the customs barrier erected between Hungary and Austria as an obstacle to possible ultimate incorporation in the hereditary provinces, and realised that to consent to its abolition might be equivalent to political suicide. It was realised that the establishment of a customs-union between Hungary and Austria, and the maintenance of a protective system *vis-à-vis* the rest of the world, must eventually make the commercial monopoly enjoyed by Austria in Hungary still more complete, and postpone, perhaps for ever, the realisation of Hungary's desire for economic independence. This was the view maintained by Kossuth, who rightly refused to be satisfied with sops thrown from time to time by Austria in the hope of effecting a temporary pacification, but took his stand on the Constitution and declared that Hungary required no concessions, only its strict legal rights — freedom to work out its own economic salvation on its own lines. He laid special stress on the necessity of obtaining direct connexion with the outside world, on building a railway to Fiume, Hungary's port, in order to avoid the necessity of transit through Austria to Trieste. In 1840, the export of goods *via* Fiume had increased threefold in comparison with the figures of the preceding six years, and yet the Government, which spent millions on the development of Trieste, and a considerable sum on that of Venice, would not spend a penny on the provision of proper shipping accommodation at Fiume. Forty-seven counties instructed their representatives to support the scheme, in order that the traffic originating in the basin of the Danube might obtain a direct outlet to the Adriatic—the key to foreign markets. The Lower House was ready to guarantee four per cent interest on the cost of construction, and to push the scheme with all its power, but when the

Magnates passed an amendment to the effect that the Government should be requested to build the line, the scheme was shelved.[1]   The meaning of Governmental control was too well known—endless obstruction, delay, and discouragement, for fear that Trieste would suffer from the competition of a Hungarian port, and that Hungary's dependence on the Austrian market might ultimately cease.[2]

Not only in economic matters, but in the general field of politics as well, the results attained by the Diet of 1843-44 were far from being in proportion to the amount of energy expended.   A notable success had been obtained as regards the recognition of Hungarian as the official language of the kingdom of Hungary, an advance had been made in the direction of religious equality,[3] and one of the disabilities of the non-nobles had been removed by making them eligible to public office.   Henceforth the peasant might own land; but this concession could be of no great value except as a matter of principle, until the existing system of entail (ósiség) was abolished.   Abolition was, however, sure to follow, now that the first steps had been taken in the direction of non-noble ownership; and electoral rights could not long be withheld now that eligibility to office was no longer confined to the privileged classes.   But it must not be supposed that progress was to be measured only by the number of laws added to the statute-book.   As Horváth points out, in the abnormal position of affairs, the result of Hungary's " mixed marriage " with Austria, and of the absence of an effective

[1] Kossuth did not abandon hope. He visited Trieste in 1845, and the result was his article in the Heti-ap, January 27, 1846, "Tengerre Magyar!" (Seawards, Magyar!).

[2] Horváth, Huszonöt év, ii. 166, 247 sq.

[3] Law iii. of 1844. At mixed marriages the ceremony may be performed by Protestant clergy. Any Catholic wishing to become a Protestant can do so by making a declaration in the presence of a priest and two witnesses. If the priest refuses to grant a certificate of conversion, the witnesses can do so. As regards the first point the Act is retrospective also.

uncensored Press, one of the chief functions of the Diet was to create public opinion, not merely to give effect to it ; and judged from this point of view, the Liberal party had not laboured in vain, but had laid a solid foundation which could not long remain without a superstructure.[1]

[1] *Huszonöt év*, ii. 259.

CHAPTER XI

THE Government was not slow to realise the fact that the popularity and strength of the Opposition had greatly increased now that the country's eyes had been opened to the possibility of commercial development and of freedom from economic dependence on Austria. With a view to the recovery of its waning prestige, the Government decided that, henceforth, it would itself be the initiator of reforms and not wait to have them forced on it by the Liberals. It hoped to dish the Opposition : to beat the reformers at their own game, and to compel them to follow the governmental lead on pain of losing their popularity. Count George Apponyi, the leader of the " Party of Deliberate Progress," was entrusted with the management of Hungarian affairs, and commissioned to inaugurate the new policy, for the success of which two things were essential. In the first place, the abnormal, unparliamentary, position of the Government must be altered ; at all costs the perpetual majority of the Opposition must be destroyed. In the second place, a leaf must be taken from the book of Joseph II., and the power of the counties to paralyse unconstitutional action must be abolished. In Hungary there was a divergence of opinion as to the merits of the county organisation. Some looked upon it as an incomparable institution, the product of an almost supernatural wisdom, while others considered it to be the chief obstacle to

progress.   Ladislaus Szalay,[1] the editor of the *Hirlap*
since Kossuth's resignation in July 1844,[2] and Eötvös
and Csengery, the chief contributors,[3] were among the
latter.   They objected to the existence of fifty-two *regna
in regno*, to the compulsory nature of their "instructions"
to deputies, and to their power of bringing the whole
governmental machine to a standstill by a simple refusal
to obey orders.[4]   They wished the influence of the
counties to be limited to local affairs, and the executive
power to be transferred to the hands of a strong central
government operating on true parliamentary lines.   In
their opinion the patriot should not content himself with
opposition to the Government, but should strive that the
Government may be so organised that there may be as
little cause as possible to oppose it.[5]   But the larger party
took the view that if the power of resistance of the
counties were weakened or abolished, the Government
would find the task of destroying the Constitution comparatively easy, and that it was a mistake on the part of
Eötvös to cast ridicule on the county organisation,[6] and

[1] The celebrated historian.

[2] He failed to get permission from the Government to start a new paper.
It is evident from Wirkner's account that Metternich tried to get hold of
Kossuth, though he declared that he hated bribery, despised the man who
allows himself to be corrupted, and would never ask anything of Kossuth that
could hurt his moral feelings.   At the same time he asked him "to name the
compensation for his time and trouble which would best answer to his wishes
from the material point of view."—Pulszky, *Életem és Korom*, i. 173 ; Wirkner,
Elményeim, 123 *sq*.   "Utilise him or hang him," was Széchenyi's advice to the
Archduke Louis.

[3] Beksics' *A Magyar Doctrinairek*, 1882.

[4] For the powers of the counties, see Cziráky, *Conspectus Juris Publici*,
Bk. I. ch. v.

[5] Eötvös's articles were reprinted in *Die Reform in Ungarn*, Leipzig, 1846,
reprinted in Hungarian, Pest, 1868.   He takes as his starting-point the impossibility of the continued existence of a privileged minority with all the
power and no obligations ; the fatal results of the non-severance of executive
and judicial functions ; and the necessity of abolishing the oligarchy and
opening wide the gates of citizenship.

[6] In *A Falu Jegyzöje*, 1845 (The Village Notary).   See Grünwald Béla,
A régi Magyarország, Budapest, 1888, pp. 436-451.

to weaken its hold on the popular affection unless and until a proper system of representative government, and a national and responsible Ministry, were brought into being. The justice of this opinion was soon to be proved.

In 1844 the idea occurred to Kolowrat to appoint a commission to consider the whole question of the county organisation with the object of converting the lords-lieutenant into active instruments of governmental control. In many counties the lord-lieutenancy was a hereditary office, or was vested in the chief ecclesiastical authority, and absenteeism was the rule rather than the exception. It was decided that this state of affairs must end, and immediately after the dissolution of the Diet a rescript was sent to the Palatine giving instructions that henceforth the lord-lieutenant must reside in the county, preside at all meetings of the local Diet, audit the finances, see to the collection of taxes, and generally become the central controlling figure of the official body. In return for the increased demands on his activity his pay was to be trebled, and he was to be assisted by a " well disposed " secretary, in other words, by a creature of his paymaster the Government. If the existing lords-lieutenant refused to accept these conditions, which amounted to a recurrence to pure Josephism, they were to be allowed to keep their titles, and the Government would appoint administrators in their place. These latter, together with the lords-lieutenant, would be responsible for the good government of the counties and would be liable to severe punishment if guilty of remissness or of connivance with the Opposition. " Apart from their strict official duties," said the rescript, " it is incumbent on the heads of the county organisations that they should take steps to obtain a majority loyal to the Government and to the Constitution, that they should report on every meeting and on the nature of its delibera-tions, and should inspect the minutes of the same. With regard to the appointment of officials they are to put themselves in communication with the Government and to carry out its instructions with every means at their disposal." Thus, the constitutional guarantees afforded by the county organisations were to be destroyed; a bureaucracy directly dependent on the Government was to take the place of elected representatives; and a subservient majority was to be scraped together by fair means or foul. Eötvös declared that the administrators could only succeed by means of bribery, and subsequent events justified the statement. The new *régime* was initiated on February 26, 1845, in spite of the objections of the Palatine, the Archduke Joseph, to the curtailment of the counties' elective rights. Thirty-two Administrators were appointed, who proceeded to justify the confidence reposed in them by their Viennese paymasters by packing meetings, holding them without due notice, using soldiers to eject the Opposition at the point of the bayonet,[1] bribing on a large scale,[2] and drawing up the "instructions" to deputies in accordance with the requirements of the Government, or modifying them after the session had begun.[3] In Croatia the Bán imitated the Administrators and jockeyed the Opponents of the "Illyrian" tools of Vienna out of their votes.[4] All over the country the prospects of the Liberals looked so black that Széchenyi asked Apponyi to be careful not to annihilate the Opposition lest Vienna

---

[1] Bihar County.—Horváth, *Huszonöt év*, ii. 327 *sq.* De Gerando, *Über den öffentlichen Geist in Ungarn*, p. 232.

[2] Hont County, where in January 1845 the Administrator distributed 17,000 florins, and in Miskolcz, where the agents of the Government openly bought votes in the streets.—De Gerando, *l.c.* No doubt the Opposition also used bribery and corruption. Wirkner (a tainted source) says that candidates would entertain their supporters by hundreds and that many families were in consequence reduced to beggary (*Élményeim*, p. 185), a state of affairs to be paralleled only by county elections in England in the same century. See also Kónyi, *Deák Ferencz Beszédei*, ii. 89 *sq.*

[3] Beöthy, *o.c.* ii. 379.

[4] A deputation was sent to Vienna to complain of the illegality of the Bán's action, but was not received.

should have matters all its own way.[1] In October 1846,
Apponyi was appointed Chancellor, a proof of the
confidence of the Government in the success of the new
régime, and in its ability to overwhelm the Liberal Party.
But the Opposition was not dead; on the contrary,
though the general hatred of governmental interference
in the counties and the fear of possible reduction to
impotence made it more radical, more Kossuthian, mistrust
of Vienna led to a rapprochement between it and the more
advanced of the Conservatives; and the idea that the
institution of a responsible ministry and a wide extension
of the franchise alone could guarantee the maintenance of
Hungarian independence met with far more general
acceptance than hitherto.[2]

Count Antony Széchen at a meeting held on 12th
November 1846, formulated the programme of the Conservatives, who were now to form an organised party,
declaring their belief in the loyalty of the expressed
intentions of the Government,[3] which now announced its
determination to adopt a policy of active reform, and
promising consistent support, so long as due regard was
had to the moral and material interests of the country,

---

[1] Marczali, *A Legujabb Kor Története*, p. 578. Unfortunately Széchenyi
had been induced by Apponyi to accept the appointment of chairman of a
commission appointed to consider improvements in the means of communication, which created the impression that he approved Apponyi's policy.

[2] For the "Stimmung" of Hungary at this period see Anton Springer, *o.c.*
ii. 90. "Eine ähnliche mächtige Bewegung, wie man sie nach dem Tode
Kaiser Josephs und dann wieder kurz vor dem Reichstage 1825 bemerkt hatte,
durchzitterte das Land von einer Grenze zur andern, die Politik verdrängte
abermals alle anderen Interessen, die öffentlichen Angelegenheiten liessen jede
andere Sorge zurücktreten, dem Vaterlande unmittelbar zu dienen, mitzurüsten
für den Streit, mitzukämpfen die Schlacht, hielt sich jedes Individuum im
Gewissen verpflichtet."

[3] The Government's concessions on the language question were referred to
as a proof of its goodwill. The fact that it had taken fifty years of incessant
struggle to extort such "concessions" was forgotten, as were the connivance of
the Government with the Illyrian separationists, the censorship. the illegal
arrest of members, the administrators, and the tariff system. For the
programme, see Horváth, *Huszonöt év*, ii. 438-45.

The programme condemned the tactics of the Opposition, whose principle, so it alleged, consisted in doing everything against the Government and nothing with it, and declared the readiness of the Conservatives for reform under the aegis of Vienna. Apponyi's plan of campaign, submitted for the acceptance of the Viennese Cabinet in January 1847, suggested that, in place of the sketchy legislative propositions usually contained in the King's Speech, the Government should come forward with cut and dried Bills, and should no longer leave the initiative to the Diet. The idea was that this innovation was an approximation to a true parliamentary system as exemplified by England, but the essential fact was lost sight of that in England the power is in the hands of the majority, whereas in Hungary the Government had hitherto been in a perpetual minority—a circumstance which made all analogy between the two countries illusory. But this was a matter of no consequence to Apponyi, who wished that reform should come in a moderate form from above rather than in a more radical guise from below. His proposals,[1] therefore, touched all questions which chiefly agitated the public mind, but at the same time took care to safeguard the interests of Vienna. The immunity of the nobles from taxation was to be abolished, and the tobacco monopoly was to be introduced, the Diet's consent to which was to be purchased by the provision of improved means of communication. The question of urban representation and of the organisation of the royal free towns was to be dealt with—naturally not in a way that would diminish the Government's hold on the Diet, from which the representatives of absent Magnates were henceforth to be excluded. The system of entail and the Crown's rights of succession were to be "regulated" but not abolished. An end was to be put to the disorderly proceedings of the occupants of the gallery, and the "misuse of the right of

[1] Hartig, *Genesis der Revolution*, Appendix I.

free speech " at the provincial Diets was to be restrained.
The penal code and the prison system were to receive
attention, and the regulation of non-commercial associa-
tions, "the abolition of which by the Government might
be justifiable but impolitic," was to be taken in hand.
Finally, the redemption of feudal dues was to be
facilitated, "in order to impregnate the country population
with a spirit of confidence and with a feeling of attachment
to the Government." [1]

It was evident that only half-measures were intended,
and that the semblance rather than the reality of reform
was the object in view. The origin of this programme
is to be found in an extraordinary letter,[2] dated May 9,
1844, and addressed to the Palatine by Metternich, whose
ideas on the subject of Hungary had hitherto been limited
to the view that the essence of good government consisted
in steady opposition to the wishes of the majority.
Between platitude and misrepresentation some particles of
truth manage to ooze out. " Those States which remain
stationary are necessarily retrogressive ; those which
advance in a wrong direction march to destruction. For
States to thrive it is essential that they should advance in
accordance with principles, and in a direction which is in
conformity with the requirements of the age. Hungary
has remained at a standstill for the reason that it was for
a long period under the Turkish yoke, and, consequently,
was subjected to foreign political influence, was involved
in civil strife, and for more than a century had no strong

---

[1] The reality of the desire of the Government to improve the peasants' lot
may fairly be questioned. In 1846, a Leipzig bookseller, Otto Wigand,
published a pamphlet on the urbarial question dealing with the *corvée* and
other feudal relics, and demanding their abolition in the name of humanity.
It contained no word of attack on the King and his Ministers, but attacked
the privileges of the Nobles. Result, that the Government decreed that *all*
books published by Wigand should be confiscated in future.—De Gerando,
Über den öffentlichen Geist in Ungarn, p. 245.

[2] Set out in Wirkner's *Élményeim*, 151 *sq.* Horváth's version differs somewhat.—*Huszonöt év*, ii. 274 *sq.*

government.   The country was tired during the reign
of Maria Theresa, the beginning of which was occupied
in a struggle to maintain the throne, and wanted
scarcely anything but internal peace.   From this slumber-
ous state it was aroused by Joseph II.   The period of its
revival was marked by the Diet of 1790-91, which had more
or less the character of a constituent assembly. . . .
The long reign of His late Majesty did nothing for Hungary.
The fault did not lie in the ideas of the Monarch,
but was due to the dearth of men capable of answering
the requirements of the situation.   The unfortunate
state of affairs which obtained was the result not
of want of will on the part of the governmental
authorities but of failure to understand the necessities of
the situation ; *for two conflicting principles stood face to face,
those of Hungarian constitutionalism and German despotism.*
. . . The Diet of 1825 marks the beginning of a new era
in Hungarian history, not only because it began with a
declaration on the part of the King that he had irrevocably
entered on the path of constitutionalism, but also for the
reason that the democratic elements of Western Europe
began to exercise an influence on the confused position of
Hungarian affairs. . . . Public life in Hungary is paralysed
. . . this is the plain unvarnished truth . . . it is paralysed
for the reason that *the Government has lost its moral force*
. . . because the power is in fact in the hands of fifty-two
counties, which fact is, of itself, enough to make the
general welfare of the country a mere *pium desiderium* ;
for the reason that the democratic principle is in direct
contradiction with the whole body of circumstances existing
in Hungary, beginning with those affecting the ownership
of land, and finally, because there is no possibility of
obtaining a majority for the Government in the Lower
House.   A State with constitutional representative institutions cannot survive but must come to an end if the
Government cannot command a majority."   That majority

was to be obtained by fair means or foul in order to maintain the hold of " German despotism " on Hungary, of a Government which had " lost its moral force." As if Vienna had not sufficient influence already. It controlled the army, completely controlled the revenues, could force its bank-notes on the country in exchange for cash and then depreciate the paper currency at will, education was entirely in its hands, the censorship controlled the thoughts of the people, and the one-sided tariff system emptied their purses. A creature majority in the Lower House must now be concocted in order to accomplish Hungary's final destruction.[1]

The pronouncement of the practical identification of the desires of the Conservative party with those of Vienna, and the activity displayed in attempting to secure a majority for reaction masquerading under the cloak of progress, provoked the Opposition to issue a counter-manifesto,[2] the work of Deák, which did much to bridge the gulf fixed between the doctrinaire Liberalism of Eötvös, moderate Conservatism, and the Radicalism of Kossuth and his followers. Stress was laid on the necessity of adherence to principles and not to leaders, and of keeping a close watch on the Government, whose action in connexion with the Croatian illegalities and with the appointment of the administrators showed that the organisation of the Counties no longer afforded a sufficient guarantee of the maintenance of the Constitution, which could be preserved only by the establishment of a central and responsible Government.

[1] " It is obvious that if the system were suffered to take root a kind of Austrian bureaucracy would by degrees be engrafted on the Hungarian institution. . . . The ultimate result of the system would probably be the conversion of Hungary into an Austrian province and the Diet into a mere registrative Board, or, at most, an Administrative Council similar to the Landstände of the hereditary provinces."—Mr. Blackwell (British diplomatic representative at Pressburg) to Lord Ponsonby, January 28, 1848. *Correspondence Relative to the Affairs of Hungary presented to both Houses of Parliament*, 1850.

[2] For the text see Kónyi, *Deák Ferencz Beszédei*, ii. 163-69.

For the preservation of national individuality, religious equality, freedom of the Press, reunion with Transylvania, and equality of all before the law were declared to be essential. Before all, the privilege of the franchise and the burden of taxation must be enjoyed and borne by noble and non-noble without distinction, and the landlords must be compensated for the loss entailed by the compulsory abolition of the urbarial system which could now be delayed no longer. The Opposition would forget neither the responsibilities towards Austria deducible from the Pragmatic Sanction, nor the fact of the independence of Hungary reaffirmed by Law x. of 1790-91. The Opposition justly complained that the Government now presented itself to the country in the guise of a parliamentary party, but at the same time insisted on the provision, by fair means or foul, of an unconditionally submissive majority instead of asking for independent support on the strength of a meritorious programme. How much could be expected from the Government in the way of fair treatment had recently been shown by its action in the matter of the primary schools, the exclusive control of which had been handed over to the Catholic bishops, whose sectarian zeal augured ill for the Protestants. The Opposition wished religious and secular instruction to be kept distinct, that each denomination should receive its spiritual training at the hands of its own clergy, and that the control of elementary schools should be given to the communes, subject to the supervision of the county executive, which could not legally be deprived of its general supervisory authority.

Though plenty of inflammable material had accumulated, no one save Széchenyi appears to have believed in the possibility of an explosion. Apponyi and Metternich considered the Opposition to be a nuisance but not a danger, and Wirkner led the Government to believe that an obsequious majority could be obtained by the expenditure of a few hundred thousand florins.[1] Széchenyi, who now feared the development to its logical conclusion of the progressive tendency which he had been the first to stimulate, issued a passionate appeal[2] to his countrymen— a last effort to restrain their advance along the path which he feared would lead to revolution. Hungary, he said, was unfair to Vienna—looked for evil motives where none existed, and lost sight of, or took a perverted view of, the consequences necessarily arising from the "mixed marriage" with Austria. He still believed in the incompatibility of material progress with radical reform, and, though in favour of the emancipation of the peasants, and of the equal distribution of the burden of taxation, feared that a hasty and simultaneous realisation of both these *desiderata* would divide the country into two hostile camps instead of fusing all classes to their common advantage. He admitted the genuineness of Kossuth's motives, but declared that the road to hell is paved with good intentions, that Kossuth was "full of phantasy and self-confidence," fancied himself to be the Messiah of a new political era, and would be responsible for all the evil that might ensue if he did not retire from the leadership of the Opposition. The pamphlet, which invited the people to work in harmony with, and not in opposition to, the Government, and was intended to assist Apponyi in his task of concocting a majority, failed to attain its object. The general opinion regarded the appeal as an outburst of personal animosity against Kossuth, who neither read nor replied to the attack of "the greatest of the Magyars," as he had himself styled his adversary. No *modus vivendi* was possible between the two, and in the absence of Deák from the fighting line[3] there was no one to dispute

---

[1] Pulszky, *Életem és Korom*, i. 248.

[2] *Politikai Programmtöredékek*, Gróf Széchenyi István munkái, Bp. 1905, vol. ii.

[3] In his constituency, Zala, the principle of the contribution of the nobles to the costs of local government was rejected, owing in a large measure to

Kossuth's claim to the leadership of the Opposition, for which his debating powers and his hold on the popular imagination obviously qualified him.

Both in Austria and in Hungary there was a general feeling of unrest—a conviction that a change was impending, that with the disappearance from the scene of Metternich and Marshal Radetzky, the main supports of the existing *régime*, both nearly eighty years old, the position of the Habsburg monarchy *vis-à-vis* the rest of Europe in general, and Germany and Italy in particular, could not fail to be sensibly modified. In these circumstances the Government was impressed with the necessity of doing something to allay the growing discontent of Hungary, of avoiding internal complications, the presentment of the spectacle of a house divided against itself, and the consequent destruction of its credit in the European money-market. Metternich and Apponyi talked glibly of the introduction of reforms which should increase the material prosperity of Hungary, but the shaky condition of Austrian finances was a matter of common knowledge. In view of the known inability of the Government to raise money for works of public utility,[1] the opinion gained ground that the *bona fides* of the promise of material reform was more than doubtful, and that the real object in view was the postponement of the discussion of Hungary's grievances and of the remodelling of the Constitution on democratic lines for which the country was now ripe. The suspicion was justifiably entertained that the chief aim of Austria was to throw the burden of part of its public debt on Hungary, and that in the event of all classes consenting to bear their share of taxation the

wholesale bribery, and Deák had made the acceptance of the principle a condition precedent to his acceptance of election.—Beöthy, *o.c.* ii. 253 ; Kónyi, *Deák Ferencz Beszédei*, ii.

[1] For example, Kübeck, the Finance Minister, pressed by Széchenyi for a loan of only a million florins for the regulation of the Tisza, avowed his inability to find the money.

proceeds would be utilised to bolster up the Austrian financial system rather than for the benefit of the Hungarian tax-payer. Now that the principle of the equal distribution of the burden of taxation had come within the range of practical politics, it was more than ever necessary that the nation's finances should be directed by a responsible Minister invested with control, not only of the sources of revenue, but also of its application. A refusal to bear that burden was to be found in the "instructions" of only three or four counties, and the practical unanimity with which ideas were accepted which, but a few years ago, were to be found in the programmes of only the most radical constituencies, proved that the intelligent section of the community was in practical agreement on questions of principle, though a considerable divergence of opinion still existed as to the method in which the desired reforms should be effectuated. The instructions of the metropolitan county of Pest demanded the recognition of Hungary's right to make its voice heard on questions of foreign policy; the revision of the tariff system; the introduction of a new criminal code and of trial by jury; the annual convocation of the Diet at Pest, the natural centre of national life; a wide extension of the franchise; reunion with Transylvania; the emancipation of the Jews, and the abolition of the nobles' exemption from taxation.[1] To not one of these demands, which

---

[1] Stephen Bezerédj, who had already set an example of being the first to make a contract with his tenants for the redemption of feudal dues, voluntarily paid his share of the cost of local government in his county. Over two hundred nobles did the same in Deák's old constituency, Zala, and sixty followed suit in Csongrád.—Horváth, *Huszonöt év*, ii. 362 ; Kónyi, *Deák Ferencz Beszédei*. Széchenyi objected to this as premature, and for fear that it would excite the opposition of the larger landowners. For the same reason he opposed Kossuth's scheme of land purchase. Kossuth saw the necessity of the complete emancipation of the peasants and of indemnifying the landlords, and believed that if the nobles' exemption from taxation were abolished there would be no difficulty in providing interest and sinking-fund on a loan of sufficient magnitude for the purpose. Wesselényi's idea was that the peasants should

may be taken as fairly representative of the desires of the nation, was the Government likely to yield without a struggle.

During the last session of the Diet, the Opposition had always been sure of a majority of ten to twenty-five votes on any important question, but owing to the action of the Administrators, and to the system of bribery and corruption now rampant in many constituencies, it was evident that it would be impossible to prophesy with certainty the fate of any motion in the Lower House. The Opposition, therefore, felt that it would be fighting with its back to the wall, and that it must strain every effort to prevent the country from being hypnotised by the hope of material progress under the aegis of Austria, for the reason that the loss of the present opportunity of converting the semblance of independence into a reality meant the postponement to an indefinite period of the realisation of their hopes. Széchenyi and the Conservatives were still inclined to mumble spells over a disease that needed the knife, and but for Kossuth the most burning questions of constitutional reform might have waited for years for a satisfactory solution. The Government moved heaven and earth to prevent the election of Kossuth, and Széchenyi gave up his seat in the Upper Chamber in order to oppose him in the Lower House, seeing, as he thought, the opportunity of forming a united party of his own by the exclusion of both Conservative and Radical extremists, and so of destroying the preponderating influence of his great antagonist, the continuance of which would, in his opinion, infallibly lead the country to destruction. Everything pointed to the probability of a stormy session, a probability increased by the recent death of the Palatine, the Archduke Joseph, who, throughout his fifty years' tenure of office, had never forgotten

relinquish part of their holdings to their landlords, and should hold the balance in fee simple, free of all dues.

the fact that, though he was the representative of the authority of the Crown, he was, at the same time, the representative of the principle of Hungarian independence.   His experience and his popularity had enabled him to exercise a moderating influence on the acrimony of party politics which unfortunately showed signs of reaching its acutest stage at the very moment of his inopportune disappearance from the scene.

Ferdinand opened the Diet in person, in November 1847, and for the first time since the early years of the sixteenth century the representatives of the nation heard their King address them in their own language.   The programme outlined by the Speech from the Throne comprised, *inter alia*, proposals for legislation on the subjects of the reform of municipal government, and of urban representation at the Diet ;   recommended the abolition of the *corvée*, and suggested that steps should be taken with a view to the regulation of the commercial relations of Hungary and Austria, in a manner conformable to the interests of both countries—in his Majesty's opinion best to be served by the abolition of the customs barrier.   The Speech was well received, not only for the reason that it was couched in the Hungarian language, but because the proposals it contained, and the manner in which they were expressed, were thought to indicate the abandonment of the old ideals of germanisation and centralisation, and to amount to a recognition of Hungary's legally indisputable right to manage its own affairs without the intervention of the Viennese bureaucracy.   Paul Somssics, the leader of the Conservative party, moved an address thanking the King for his Speech, and for the proposals it contained, which " so happily correspond with the most ardent desires of the people," and proposed that instead of the usual discussion and presentment of the country's grievances, of the list of the Government's sins of omission and commission, all matters connected with the infringement of the country's constitutional rights should be referred to a special commission. Such an attempt to burke public inquiry and discussion was not to pass unchallenged. Kossuth declared that the great wish of the Diet was not to remedy grievances after their infliction but to prevent their occurrence. He attacked the whole system of government as deliberately intended to deprive Hungary of the independence which the law of 1790, confirmed by successive kings, had unreservedly acknowledged, and pointed out, " as a member of His Majesty's most faithful Opposition who allows no one to surpass him in loyalty to the Throne," but distinguishes the King from the King's Government, that it was not the first time that legislative propositions of an encouraging nature had been laid before the Diet with little or no result save that of shelving the discussion of the nation's grievances, and of postponing the adoption of remedial measures. He enumerated in turn the chief grounds of complaint, laying especial stress on the Government's continued neglect of the Diet's demand for the re-incorporation in Hungary of certain districts of Transylvania,[1] and on the illegality

---

[1] The Transylvanian Diet of 1837 did not accept Wesselényi's ideas on the subject of reunion, as the landlords feared that emancipation of the peasants would follow as well as abolition of the nobles' exemption from taxation. Wesselényi also had to contend against the opposition of the official class which feared the loss of remunerative occupation under the Austrian Government, also of the Saxons who were desirous of incorporation in a Greater Germany under Austrian hegemony. The numerical preponderance, on the other hand, of the Roumanians convinced the Magyar population that the emancipation of the peasants would be fatal to their interests unless the protection which would be afforded by reunion with the mother-country were previously obtained. In 1847 the Diet of Transylvania, reactionary in other respects, was prepared to enter into negotiations for reunion. Certain districts and counties had been ceded to the princes of Transylvania by various treaties between 1583 and 1645. In 1687 Transylvania again came into the possession of the Sacred Crown, and the said districts and counties were declared, by a law of 1693, to be integral parts of the Kingdom of Hungary. In 1731 King Charles improperly caused three counties and one district to be incorporated in Transylvania in spite of the protest of the Council of Lieutenancy. The Diet of 1741 also protested and passed an Act, which received the royal assent, providing for their re-incorporation ; but the Act remained a dead

of the recent appointment of Administrators; insisted
that the Address should specifically allude to each unremedied grievance, and, as a guarantee against repetition
of unconstitutional action, should demand the annual convocation of the Diet at Pest.. The Address, as moved by
Kossuth, was carried by a narrow majority (the representatives of twenty-six counties voting for the motion,
and of twenty-two against it), but was rejected by the
Upper House, which adopted the view that the Address
should be limited to an expression of thanks to His
Majesty, and should contain no reference to grievances,
or that, if the Lower House insisted on alluding to them,
it should do so only in general terms. Rather than
submit to the emasculation of the Address, Kossuth proposed that it should be dropped altogether, and after a
long and stormy debate his motion was carried. For the
first time in history no reply was sent to the Speech from
the Throne.

The new Palatine, the Archduke Stephen, elected by
the Diet out of gratitude for the services of his father,
threw all his influence into the scale in favour of Széchenyi,
whom he considered to be the only person capable of acting as a counterpoise to Kossuth and of inducing the Diet
to abandon its insistence on the removal of its constitutional grievances. Signs of the formation of a "cave"
in the Opposition were not wanting. Kossuth wished to
be as omnipotent in the Diet as he had been in the
journalistic world, loved popularity, and wished to mono-
polise the applause of the country. The result was that a
section of his party, the inferior talents, was inclined to

letter in spite of the remonstrances of the Diets of 1751 and 1764, and of a
fresh Law (xi. of 1792). Representations were again and again repeated, and
a third Act was passed in 1836 (xxi.) and received the royal assent. Still,
nothing was done, and the Diet again renewed its request, but in vain. The
explanation of the Government's barefaced illegalities is to be found in the
fact that it feared that the re-incorporation of Transylvania would strengthen
Hungary.

revolt, and so caused the Palatine to believe that a conciliatory pronouncement on the part of the King with
respect to the appointment of the Administrators would
go far towards destroying the supremacy of Kossuth, and
bridging the gulf fixed between the Government and the
Progressives.   He therefore induced the King to issue a
rescript to the effect that the appointment of Administrators was intended only as a temporary measure, that no
more would be nominated " except in exceptional circumstances, and that there never had been any intention of
interfering with the rights of the counties."   The " misunderstanding," to quote the words of the rescript, " was
all the more painful to His Majesty's paternal heart, as
from the very first moment of his reign he had given so
many proofs of his unconquerable determination to maintain inviolate the ancient Constitution, and its firm foundation—the organisation of the counties, and to observe the
laws of the country, more especially the fundamental
statute of 1790."   But the rescript satisfied neither the
Conservatives, who ·discerned in it an unwelcome indication of weakness on the part of the Government, nor the
Progressives, who looked upon it as amounting to a mere
empty promise, made only to be broken, like similar
undertakings which successive kings had given when
desirous that the Diet should drop the discussion of its
grievances and be humbugged into a temporary belief
in the Crown's attachment to constitutional principles.
An Address of thanks to the King for his gracious
rescript, and the rejection of Kossuth's counter-pro-
position demanding the prompt dismissal of the Administrators and the reinstatement of the Lord-Lieutenant was
carried, thanks to the Croatian vote and to the fact that
several members disobeyed the instructions of their constituencies which insisted on the abolition of the Government's illegal innovation.   The result was received with
howls of disapproval from the youthful occupants of the

gallery; disorder spread to the floor of the Chamber, and the House adjourned without any declaration from the Chair as to the fate of either the motion or the amendment.

The Government would have liked to dissolve the Diet without delay, but in view of the inflamed state of public opinion in Hungary, and of the uncertainty of the general European outlook, feared to take any step which might conceivably fan into flame the smouldering discontent. Consciousness of its own inherent weakness led it to overestimate the amount of explosive energy with which Hungary was charged. On February 25, at a conference of the Opposition, the question was debated whether the time had not come for the presentation of an Address to the King requesting the grant of a Constitution to the hereditary provinces, Kossuth being firmly convinced that one of the chief sources of Hungary's troubles was to be found in the fact that his country was united in a " mixed marriage " with another, which had no experience, and consequently no idea of the meaning of constitutional parliamentary government, and therefore not only was unable to understand, but viewed with actual hostility, Hungary's manifestation of attachment to its historic rights. Kossuth and his followers were outvoted —a proof positive of the fact that at that date the Opposition, in spite of its ardent desire for reform, was determined to proceed with caution and had no idea of committing itself to a revolutionary policy the outcome of which it would be impossible to foresee. Kossuth alone seems to have been convinced that the hour had come for Hungary to put an end to an intolerable situation, and to establish its independence of a Government " by whose unconstitutional acts the legislative, the executive, and the judicial powers of the State have been utterly degraded. If such acts," he cried, " can be endured any longer, and at a moment when despotism trembles before the renascent spirit of liberty, and nations benumbed and decrepit show signs of their pristine vitality, then indeed shall I despair of my country."[1]   But not even Kossuth contemplated the possibility of a recourse to active revolutionary methods.   No doubt he was determined that the near future should see the end of Austrian interference in Hungary's internal affairs, and the establishment of a responsible Ministry at Pest, but he relied for the attainment of his object on constitutional weapons and on the rottenness of the foundations of Austrian autocracy, which required no more than the rumble of a distant earthquake to bring the whole structure clattering about Metternich's ears.

[1] Speech on the question of the reincorporation of part of Transylvania, January 14.

END OF VOL. I

Printed by R. & R. CLARK, LIMITED, *Edinburgh.*

The Political Evolution

of the

Hungarian Nation

The

Political Evolution

of the

Hungarian Nation

BY

THE HON. C. M. KNATCHBULL-HUGESSEN,

IN TWO VOLUMES
VOL. II

LONDON
THE NATIONAL REVIEW OFFICE
23 RYDER STREET, ST. JAMES'S
1908

The Political Evolution of the Hungarian Nation

CHAPTER XII

On February 29 tidings reached Vienna of the out- 1848.
break of the Revolution in Paris and of the flight of
Louis Philippe. The first result of the news was a run
on the banks and a scramble for silver, due, of course, to
the probability of a fall in value of paper money, but
ascribed by Metternich to the machinations of Hungarian
Radicals anxious to ruin the credit of the Austrian Government.[1] The panic spread from Vienna to Pest and other
chief towns, and on March 3 Cornelius Balogh addressed
the Diet on the general monetary position, calling on
the Government to abandon the policy of reticence which
caused the public to take a more gloomy view of the
financial outlook than possibly was justified by the facts,
and demanding the publication of an official statement,
which alone could allay the public anxiety as to the
proportion borne by cash in reserve to the note issue.[2]
Kossuth, who had long been of the opinion that parlia-

---

[1] "In Folge absichtlicher Discreditirung."—Hartig, *Genesis der Revolution*,
121. There is not a shadow of evidence to justify the suggestion, which,
apart from the improbability of note-holders deliberately depreciating the
value of their own property, is refuted by the fact that the news of the Paris
Revolution did not reach Pressburg till March 1.

[2] According to Horváth, *Huszonöt év*, ii. 569, there were only 20,000,000
florins in cash against over 200,000,000 in paper.

mentary government, and the appointment of a responsible Ministry, was the only possible cure for the unsatisfactory state of affairs existing in Hungary, was quick to seize the opportunity presented by the confusion which the echo of a foreign revolution had sufficed to produce in Vienna. Taking Balogh's motion as his text, he declared that the panic afforded incontrovertible proof of the necessity of establishing a separate Hungarian Ministry of Finance, which alone could save Hungary from the disastrous consequences of the chronic financial muddle in which Austria was involved. The whole existing system of Government was, in fact, bankrupt, and the annoyance naturally felt by its architects at the prospect of its collapse must not be allowed to interfere with the interests of the people. "The men of a past generation to-day or to-morrow descend into their graves, but the people is everlasting, and a glorious future awaits both the nation and the throne which derives its strength from the freedom of its subjects. Loyalty, and enthusiasm for the dynasty, can exist only in the hearts of free men whose interests are indissolubly bound up with those of the ruling family ; for a bureaucracy no such sentiments can be entertained." The French, he continued, had won back their liberties, of the return of which they did not dream three months ago, while Hungary went on labouring at its futile, Sisyphean, task. He concluded by moving an Address to the Throne, conceived from the dynastic point of view, which, he thanked God, was identical with that of the interests of his country. The Address recites the efforts made by the Diet in the direction of reform, and points out that the chief cause of present trouble is to be found in the fact that a retrospective view of history proves that the Government has never been in harmony with the idea of Hungarian independence as guaranteed by law ; and that, consequently, for the last three centuries, all efforts had to be directed to the maintenance of the Constitution instead of to its development in accordance with the spirit of modern times. The maintenance of the existing system would involve, so the Address declared, the Throne and the Monarchy, to which Hungary is attached by the grateful bonds of the Pragmatic Sanction, in consequences of which the final issue cannot be foreseen. The country's Constitutional life needed development in the direction of a truly representative system, and its intellectual interests required the fostering hand of freedom. The defensive system wanted radical reorganisation and to be brought into conformity with the national character and with the interests of the Throne, and of the different classes of society. The question of the responsible administration of the Hungarian revenue and finances could no longer be postponed. With respect to various matters the conflicting interests of Hungary and of the hereditary provinces required equitable adjustment, for the effectuation of which the Diet, while careful to defend the nation's interests and independence, was ready to lend a helping hand.

We are, however, convinced that the laws which require enactment in order to give expression to our constitutional rights, and to promote the moral and material welfare of the nation, can be endowed with effective vitality only when an independent national Government, exempt from foreign interference and called into existence as the constitutional expression of the will of the majority, has been entrusted with their execution. We therefore regard the conversion of the existing departmental system of government into a responsible Hungarian Ministry as the indispensable condition and essential guarantee of all reform. This is our conception of the duties of our calling, and it is our fixed and earnest design to bring these matters to a satisfactory conclusion in harmony with your Majesty's desires during the current session. This is what our country and the unenfranchised millions expect of us. This is what we are prompted to ask by the instinct of loyalty and fidelity, which binds us with indissoluble ties to the reigning House, for we are convinced that it is only thus that tranquillity, peace, and mutual confidence can be established on so firm a foundation that no unforeseen storms will be able to shake it, and that concord and contentment can alone produce an enthusiastic and harmonious spirit on which your Majesty and the reigning House can, in all circumstances, confidently rely. . . . It is impossible for us to view without apprehension those symptoms of disorder which are only too apparent in many parts of that monarchy to which we are united in virtue of the Pragmatic Sanction. The unforeseen complications produced by recent events which have taken place abroad will necessarily multiply those symptoms and increase their intensity. . . . We are thoroughly convinced that your Majesty will find the most effective antidote to possible untoward contingencies, the best means of uniting the dominions of the Crown in a friendly understanding, and the firmest support of your Majesty's Throne and dynasty, in surrounding that Throne with those constitutional institutions which are imperatively demanded by the requirements of the age. . . . Therefore, in a spirit of unshakable loyalty and steadfast confidence, we entreat your Majesty to be graciously pleased to send to the Diet with full powers to give effect to the royal will, while at the same time acting in accordance with the existing laws, individuals, corresponding in number with the various governmental departments, who, as members of the highest executive institution, the Council of Lieutenancy, enjoy your Majesty's gracious confidence, and will, under the guarantee of personal responsibility, be entrusted with the execution of the Laws hereafter to be enacted. It would be the duty of such individuals to take direct part in the proceedings of the Diet, to inform that body of your Majesty's gracious intentions, to furnish the necessary explanations and statements on behalf of the Government, more especially as regards financial affairs, and to afford effective assistance in bringing matters under discussion to a successful conclusion in order that the contemplated salutary legislation may be as soon as possible submitted for your Majesty's gracious sanction. Thus, whatever unexpected turn present affairs may take, peace and tranquil confidence will be established in our country and will form a foundation for the development of those moral and material capabilities in which, as in our unshakable loyalty to your Majesty, the Throne will find its firmest support no matter what the uncertain future may have in store.

The Address, which was adopted unanimously by the Lower House,[1] was the outcome of a conviction that there was no essential divergence between the interests of Hungary and those of the hereditary provinces, but that lasting confidence could be secured only by the establishment of constitutional parliamentary government, not only in Hungary but in Austria as well. It was believed that the fellow-feeling which one constitutionally governed country might be expected to entertain towards another would tend to dissipate the cloud of misunderstanding, emanating from the dingy pigeon-holes of the Viennese bureaucracy, which had so long obscured the relations of Hungary and Austria. The maintenance of Hungary's historic rights, and their logical development, could not be assured so long as an antediluvian autocracy and the baneful influence of bureaucratic tradition existed on the other side of the Leitha. Hungary had no quarrel with the people of the hereditary provinces, and no desire to sever its connexion therewith. So far from indicating an inclination to belittle the binding force of the ties which bound it to the Austrian dominions of the Habsburgs, it expressly recognised the existence of affairs of common interest, and desired that they should be settled in a manner satisfactory to both parties, in the confident belief that two constitutionally governed countries could easily arrive at a fair solution of questions which, if unsolved, or solved in the old, one-sided, manner, would make the attainment of lasting content an impossibility.

The old order was clearly doomed. Széchenyi, possibly unconsciously influenced by a feeling of personal hostility to Kossuth, was inclined to discern the approach of anarchy in the destruction of class privilege and in other items of the democratic programme, and believed himself to be the only man capable of arresting the

1 "Unanimiter die Dummheit angenommen" was Széchenyi's comment.— Pulszky, *Életem és Korom*, i. 279.

advance of Hungary on the path of Kossuth's tracing. He proposed that the King should send him as Royal Commissioner to Pressburg, where his credit and importance in the eyes of the people were not yet exhausted, with full powers to negotiate with the Lower House [1] with a view to emasculating the resolution which Kossuth had formulated, which, in Széchenyi's and Apponyi's opinion, was bound to lead to trouble. As an alternative, the dissolution of the Diet was suggested, and effect would no doubt have been given to the proposal, approved by Széchenyi, Metternich, and the Archduke Louis, but for the timely arrival in Vienna of the Palatine, who knew what effect such hasty action would have on public opinion in Hungary, already excited to a dangerous degree by the delay of the Upper House in meeting to discuss the Address to the Throne, the presentation of which to the King, Metternich was determined to prevent. It is possible that his obstructive tactics would have succeeded but for the occurrence of events in Vienna and Prague which turned the attention of the Government in another direction.

The Viennese Diet had long ago lost such little power of initiative and independent action as it had ever possessed, and since the early days of Francis's reign had been completely under the thumb of the bureaucracy. But modern Liberal ideas had penetrated even to Vienna. The February Revolution in Paris, the inflammable condition of the atmosphere in all parts of Europe, and the rotten state of the national finances, brought the general discontent to a head and confirmed the belief that the existing system must soon collapse.[2] The students, who,

---

[1] Szögyény, *Emlékiratai*, p. 50.

[2] Hübner, *Ein Jahr meines Lebens*. " The Bureaucracy absorbed everything. It was as if one part of the human body usurped the functions of all the rest, and that cannot occur with impunity. Thus, the Bureaucracy suffered from a kind of progressive decay. During the last reign it was reduced to complete impotence. It was so to speak mummified, suffered from senile marasmus, and was on the point of extinction when the events of 1848 gave it the death-blow, February 1849."

on the Continent, exert an influence on public opinion which is incomprehensible to Englishmen, were saturated with the spirit of insubordination, and the Juridisch-politischer Leseverein, of which Alexander Bach, the future reactionary Minister, was the presiding genius, was far from being the innocent association which its name would indicate it to be. Bach is said by Hartig to have been in close touch with members of the Pressburg Diet, but whether that statement is true or false, it is certain that Kossuth's speech of March 3[1] caused a great sensation in Vienna and was greeted by the Liberals with enthusiasm as indicating the only direction in which Austria could find political salvation.[1] A monster petition was presented to the Diet protesting loyalty to the dynasty and at the same time demanding the publication of an official pronouncement on the financial position ; the convocation at fixed intervals of a legislative assembly representative of all the constituent nationalities and invested with complete authority as regards the imposition of taxation and the audit of expenditure ; the emancipation of the Press ; publicity in judicial proceedings ; the establishment of a modern form of municipal government, and proper representation of the trading, agricultural, and intelligent classes. On March 11 the students of the University and of the Polytechnic resolved to present a petition on their own account to the Emperor demanding freedom for the Press, the improvement of educational facilities, and religious equality. Two days later, escorted by a crowd of sympathisers, they marched to the meeting-place of the

---

[1] Szögyény, Emlékiratai, p. 53. Hartig, Genesis der Revolution, p. 113, says that Kossuth was all along in communication with Bach, but Kossuth absolutely denied the truth of the statement.—See his letter to Marczali, A Legujabb Kor Története, p. 608, n. 2, also Anton Springer, o.c. ii. 178, n., re the Genesis: "Diese Schrift, welcher in Deutschland ein ungebührliches Gewicht als Geschichtsquelle verliehen wird, ist nur dort von historischem Werthe, wodurch die (der Feder eines Mitarbeiters entstammende ?) gallige Polemik die Bekenntnisse des Grafen Hartig hindurchschimmern und die Zustände im Regierungslager geschildert werden."

Diet, then in session, whose members accepted the task of presenting the petition handed to them by the students and proceeded direct to the Palace where the Council of State was sitting. The fact that the members of the Diet identified themselves with the students gave an unmistakably revolutionary aspect to an incident to which otherwise comparatively little importance would have been attached. Metternich alone was in favour of the adoption of violent measures ; the other members of the Council feared to add fuel to the threatening flames, and a reply was sent to the demonstrators to the effect that arrangements should be made for a special deputation to lay the petition before the Emperor, who would " soon take steps necessary to the welfare of his beloved people as a whole," in other words, would wriggle and shuffle to the last possible moment.[1]

Smooth words and procrastinating tactics could no longer avail. Small but bloody affrays took place in various parts of the town between the populace and the soldiery, who occupied the chief strategic points, and the leaders of the forces of discontent decided to force the resignation of Metternich and the grant of a Constitution. From hour to hour·the situation assumed a more threatening aspect, and the action of the Archduke Louis, who ordered the troops to fire on the people, produced precisely the contrary effect to that which was expected. The Government thought that a spoonful of water would suffice to extinguish a conflagration which threatened to destroy the whole fabric of autocracy, and announced that a new Press law would be immediately prepared. The inability of such a trifling concession to still the storm was at once apparent ; a suitable Jonah must be found, and Metternich was thrown overboard. The Archduke

---

[1] For the Viennese revolution see, besides Hartig's *Genesis*, Helfert, *Geschichte der österreichischen Revolution*, Freiburg im Breisgau, 1907. Also Reschauer, " Das Jahr 1848," *Geschichte der wiener Revolution*, Vienna, 1872. For a general view of the events of 1848 there is nothing to equal Professor Marczali's *A Legujabb Kor Története*, quoted *passim*.

Louis told the Chancellor that only his resignation could appease the popular fury, and Metternich retired, disclaiming all responsibility for the blood which had been shed, and expressing the hope that his own fall would not entail that of the monarchy, the burden of which he had so long borne on his aged shoulders.[1] His resignation only temporarily cleared the air ; signs of a probable recrudescence of disorder in a more violent form were visible on all sides ; doubts were justifiably entertained as to the reliability of the troops and of their readiness to obey an order to fire, and on March 14, at a conference of the members of the Government, at which the Emperor was present, it was resolved to yield to the wishes of the people. On the following day it was announced that the Emperor would " summon the representatives of the constituent peoples round the Throne and avail himself of their advice in legislative and administrative questions."[2] This vague promise of the grant of a Constitution produced a temporary lull in the popular excitement. As the essence of a constitutional State consists in the fact of the existence of a responsible Government, the heads of the various governmental departments were hastily converted into Ministers, and, in spite of the obviously intentional omission of the word " Constitution " from the manifesto of March, comparatively little doubt as to the genuineness of the imperial intentions found public expression.

The desire for political reforms was not confined to the Kaiserstadt. Bohemia, where the recollection of ancient independence still lived, and the hatred of the germanising interference of the Viennese bureaucracy had increased rather than diminished of late years,[3] could

---

[1] Princess Metternich's *Diary*, vii. 542. Hübner, *Ein Jahr meines Lebens*, March 1. Anton Springer, *o.c.* ii. 191. Helfert, *o.c.* 252 *sq.* Reschauer, *o.c.* i. 306 *sqq.* [2] Hartig, *Genesis der Revolution*, 154.

[3] Hartig, p. 81, speaks of the Bohemians' wish to preserve their national language as Czechomania, and of the "cheek," "Frechheit," of the Czechs towards the Emperor, who had inherited " unbeschränkte Macht " over them in consequence of the victory of White Mountain ; but where the relations of

not be expected to remain a passive spectator of the
struggle for liberty of which the greater part of Europe
was the battle-ground. A mass-meeting was held at
Prague on March 11, at which Bohemia's demands were
formulated amid general enthusiasm. Czechs must in
the first place be put on a footing of absolute equality
with the Germans ; and Bohemia, Silesia, and Moravia
must have their own Diet, which should meet alternately
at Prague and Brünn. The principle of ministerial
responsibility must be accepted, the censorship must be
abolished, and the obligation to perform military service
must be made universal. Other requirements comprised
the compulsory redemption of feudal dues and services,
and a declaration of the legal equality of all recognised
religions. A petition was drawn up embodying the
nation's demands, and it was resolved that it should be
laid before the Throne by a special deputation which
comprised several of the best known magnates and literary
men of the country.

The disturbances of which Vienna and Prague were
the scene, to which the above slight reference has been
made only for the purpose of drawing attention to the
fact that the desire for the abolition of bureaucratic
government was not confined to the Magyars, naturally
did not fail to exert some influence on the course of
events in Hungary, where since March 3 matters had,
more or less, come to a standstill, owing to the failure

Croat and Magyar are in question it is quite another matter. The Croatians'
language and other rights are sacred in Hartig's view, and Croatian pretensions
are worthy of all encouragement, though the position of Hungary *vis-à-vis*
Croatia, which had formed part of the dominions of the Sacred Crown for
eight hundred years, was, morally, far stronger than that of the Habsburgs,
whose rights over Bohemia had been gained by conquest a little more than
two hundred years ago. The influence of the Hungarian example on affairs
in Bohemia is unquestionable. The Czech Orders wrote to the Diet of
Pressburg, "All the peoples of Austria are following with redoubled attention
the course of events in Hungary, for they well know that their fate, their
future, depend on what is taking place there."—Horváth (John), *A Közös
Ügyek Előzményei és Fejlődése*, Bp. 1902, p. 143.

of the Magnates to hold a meeting for the purpose of discussing the Address, voted on Kossuth's motion in the Lower House. The absence of the Palatine and other chief officials excited a considerable amount of angry comment, but no serious breach of the peace occurred,[1] and, in fact, the spectacle of order and self-restraint exhibited by the Hungarians of all classes during this period of feverish tension is in marked contrast to the scenes of violence and bloodshed which characterised the proceedings of the students, the proletariat, and the Liberals of Vienna. In Hungary the feeling of loyalty was universal.[2] The dangerous position of the dynasty[3] caused Széchenyi to express the opinion that the time was come, or would shortly arrive, for the Magyars to prove once again their fidelity to the Throne with another cry of "*moriamur pro rege nostro*," and his words were received with enthusiasm.[4] A petition was prepared emphasising the identity of the interests of the Hungarian

---

[1] Mr. Blackwell, the British representative at Pressburg, writing to Lord Ponsonby, the Ambassador in Vienna, reports (March 15), "Pressburg is as quiet as the greatest lover of order could wish it to be."—*Correspondence Relative to the Affairs of Hungary.*

[2] As to Kossuth's attitude, see the evidence of Somssics, a political opponent. "Ich weiss es, dass Kossuth noch im Februar 1848, sich mit Berathungen befasste, welche entschieden beweisen, dass er damals noch keine Revolution wünschte, oder wenigstens an eine solche nicht glaubte. *Ich fande ihn stets monarchisch, ja dynastisch, gesinnt.*"—*Das Legitime Recht Ungarns und seines Königs*, Vienna, 1850, p. 18.

[3] The Empress asked Metternich if the abdication of the Emperor were necessary.—Marczali, *A Legujabb Kor Történéte*, p. 609.

[4] Wirkner, *Élményeim*, p. 199. "It is a characteristic trait of the pro-dynastic feeling general in Hungary, that in those troublous times (March 13), only one person was found to jump on a table and raise his voice in favour of a republic, and he had scarcely spoken the word when he was instantly knocked down, and the infuriated mob nearly tore the unfortunate man to pieces."—*Ibid.* p. 203. On the 14th, Wirkner, who, it will be remembered, was the agent of the Austrian Government in Pressburg, was notified by the Archduke Louis, that in case of necessity the Court would take refuge in Hungary. Wirkner replied that "ungrateful Vienna being in a state of actual revolution, the moment had come for Hungary once more to give proof of its centuries-old fidelity and magnanimity towards its King."—*Ibid.* pp. 204, 205.

people with those of the wearer of the Sacred Crown, and
begging the King to take refuge in the midst of his
faithful Magyars should Vienna, as seemed probable,
continue its riotous behaviour. The petition was never
sent, but the fact that its despatch was seriously contemplated is indicative of the spirit of loyalty which
animated the Hungarians at a time when revolutionary
excesses were taking place but a short distance beyond
the borders of their country. In Pest, it is true, the
youth, under the influence of Joseph Irinyi, a member of
the Diet, the poet Petőfi, and Jókai,[1] the novelist,
dissatisfied with the pace at which things were moving,
determined to give the country a lead, but maturer
politicians agreed in counselling abstention from all
semblance of revolutionary illegality.

The Upper House met on the 14th of March, and
the Archduke Stephen gave expression to the general
feeling when he proposed that the Address as voted by
the Lower House should be accepted without amendment.
The motion was carried unanimously, and the Archduke
thereon added the words, " I assure the House that I shall
consider it my duty to join hands with the Orders in the
task of promoting the Constitutional development of the
Country " : a statement which was received with general
applause. A deputation was chosen for the purpose of
presenting the Address to the King, and it left the same
day for Vienna. Among its members were to be found
the bearers of the most distinguished names in Hungary—
Prince Paul Eszterházy, Counts George Károlyi, Louis
Batthyány, Ladislaus Teleki, Julius Andrássy, Stephen
Széchenyi, Kossuth, and many others. Old dislikes were
forgotten. Széchenyi said, " We must support Batthyány
and Kossuth; hatred, ambition, and antipathy must be
silenced," and silenced they were.

---

[1] See his novel, *A Tengerszemü Hölgy* (translated into English under the
title, *Eyes like the Sea*).

The departure of the deputation and the march of events in Vienna made it impossible to restrain the juvenile enthusiasts of Pest, and on the 15th, Petőfi recited his poem, the "Magyar Marseillaise" (Talpra Magyar) [1] from the steps of the Town Hall, and the twelve points of a manifesto, drawn up two days previously by Irinyi, were read aloud and accepted with all possible demonstration of enthusiasm.

What does the Magyar people demand? (1) We demand the freedom of the Press and the abolition of the Censorship. (2) A responsible Ministry in Budapest. (3) A yearly meeting of the Diet in Pest. (4) Equal civil and religious rights for all (5) A national army of defence. (6) An equal distribution of the burden of taxation. (7) The abolition of feudal relations. (8) Trial by jury, and popular representation on the basis of equality. (9) A national bank. (10) That the troops shall take the oath of allegiance to the Constitution. That Hungarian soldiers shall not be taken out of the country. That foreign troops shall be removed. (11) Freedom for political prisoners. (12) Union with Transylvania. Finally—Equality, Liberty, and Fraternity.

This manifesto, it will be observed, contains nothing which can be stigmatised by the epithet revolutionary, and in no respect, save possibly as regards the soldiers' oath of allegiance, goes one whit beyond the limits set by Constitution to the aspirations of the nation, but in fact finds a justification for every item in existing laws. Volunteers invaded Landerer's printing-house and struck off copies, for distribution to the waiting crowds, of the first uncensored document ever printed in Hungary. Of

[1] It begins thus :—

> Magyars up ! your country calls you !
> Break the chain which now enthralls you,
> Free men be, or slaves for ever,
> Choose ye, Magyars, now or never,
> For by the Magyars' God above
> We truly swear,
> We truly swear the tyrant's yoke
> No more to bear.

—From Loew's *Hungarian Poetry*, Riedl's *Hungarian Literature*.

excitement there was plenty, of disorder practically none. A committee of twelve was appointed for the purpose of ensuring the maintenance of public order, whose proclamation issued the following day. ended with the words, " Our watchword is—long live the King ! Constitutional reform, liberty, equality, peace, and order ! " Other towns followed suit and appointed similar committees, and even the preponderating German section of their population greeted with genuine or feigned rejoicing the dawn of a new era.

In the meantime the deputation from the Diet had arrived at Vienna, where it was received with extraordinary enthusiasm. Kossuth, by reason more especially of the reference he had made in his speech of the 3rd to the necessity of the grant of a Constitution to Austria, was the popular idol. The horses were taken out of his carriage and he was dragged in triumph to his hotel. Széchenyi, who found it hard to conceal his jealousy of his rival, states in his *Diary* [1] that if Kossuth had spoken the word the people would have stormed the palace and utterly destroyed it. Kossuth's own statement of a later date that at that moment he " held the fate of the dynasty in the hollow of his hand " was strictly accurate. The Court was thoroughly frightened, and the same evening Ferdinand issued a statement to the effect that he had already done everything that was necessary for the re-organisation of the country on a constitutional basis, which promptly calmed the popular excitement. The wish to resist the demands of Vienna and of Hungary was ever present, but the requisite energy was wanting, and for the moment the chief anxiety of the irresolute Court was to " save its face "—to avoid the appearance of demoralisation. Kossuth had an interview with the Archduke Francis Charles, who said : " His Majesty

[1] See also Mészáros Lázár (the Minister of War in the first Hungarian Cabinet) *Élettörténete*, i. 41, and Pulszky, *Életem és Korom*, i. 285.

recognises the justice of your demands and would willingly
consent to them if only Vienna were quiet, so that it
might not appear that he does justice to his true
Hungarian nation not of his own free will, not in
accordance with the promptings of his paternal heart, but
under the pressure of revolution." Kossuth replied :
" If your Imperial Highness will give me your word of
honour that you will do what equity and justice bind you
to do for my country, I will make things quiet for the
House of Austria in Vienna." " And the House of
Austria will be everlastingly grateful to you for your
action," answered the Archduke, who thereupon gave
his word of honour and shook Kossuth's hand.[1] That
this was all part of a pre-arranged comedy there is only
too much reason to believe. At the conference of the
King and his Ministers held on the night of the 16th,
subsequent to Kossuth's interview with the Archduke
Francis Charles, the latter said that as heir-presumptive
to the Throne he refused to give his consent to the
demands of the Hungarians, and Szögyény,[2] who was
present at the meeting, says distinctly that there was no
intention of giving way but that want of energy and
determination finally compelled surrender. Pillersdorf,
the Austrian Minister of the Interior, who, at a subsequent
meeting, declared that he considered the demands of the
Hungarian Diet moderate enough and only hoped that
those of the Austrian representatives, shortly to be called
together, would be no greater, no doubt voiced the
general feeling of the Court party when he advised the
King to give way and to trust to subsequent events to
give him the opportunity of withdrawing or modifying
his concessions.[3] " Everything might be recovered in
a roundabout way," is Wirkner's phrase,[4] and that is
the key to the action of the camarilla on the night of

[1] Kossuth, *Schriften aus der Emigration*, ii. 207.   [2] *Emlékiratai*, p. 59.
[3] Szögyény, *Emlékiratai*, p. 74.   [4] *Élményeim*, p. 211.

March 16, and during the immediately succeeding period. The Palatine, the Archduke Stephen, alone played a straightforward game. He knew his duty towards Hungary and was anxious to do it ; and if, as he himself said, the double dealing of the Court subsequently made his position untenable,[1] he at least had the satisfaction of knowing that he fulfilled his obligations to the best of his mediocre abilities.[2]

Early on the morning of the 17th the battle was over. Ferdinand gave way, the Archduke Stephen was appointed Viceroy with full powers of representing the King in his absence from Hungary, and consent was given to the establishment of a responsible Ministry in Pest under the presidency of Count Louis Batthyány, the leader of the Opposition in the Upper House. The answer of the King to the Diet's Address is characterised by all the fulsomeness with which the manifestoes of previous members of the House of Habsburg, temporarily driven into a corner, have made us familiar :—

"Enlightened as to the desires of my faithful Magyars by the humble Address which I have received from you in the name of the Hungarian Orders, I hasten to declare, in accordance with the promptings of my paternal heart, that I will take pleasure in directing my thoughts to the fulfilment of all those requests which are now essential to the happiness and constitutional development of the country. I therefore notify your Highness that in your character of Palatine, chosen by the unanimous desire of the Orders and confirmed as such by me, you are invested, as my Viceroy, with full powers within the meaning of the law to govern in my absence the Kingdom of Hungary, and the parts thereto annexed, in the path of the law and the Constitution, maintaining the unity of the Crown and the connexion with the

[1] Anders, *Stephen Viktor Erzherzog von Oesterreich,* p. 290.
[2] "It will be your fault if we lose Hungary," said the Archduke Louis at the meeting of March 16 (Szögyény, *o.c.* p. 59). A suspicion was quite unjustifiably entertained that Stephen hoped to become King of an independent Hungary.

Empire in its integrity. I am disposed to accede to the desire of my faithful Estates and Orders for the appointment in accordance with the laws of the country of an independent and responsible Ministry, and give you at the same time authority to propose for appointment suitable persons from among those whom you have mentioned to me, also to take steps in order that suitable legislative proposals may be made by the Estates and Orders with a view to defining in an expedient manner the sphere of influence of such individuals, having regard to the close connexion, rightly considered to be of such importance, existing by virtue of the Pragmatic Sanction, between the Kingdom of Hungary and my hereditary dominions which are equally entitled to my paternal care. Such proposals, together with the other suggested laws referred to in the Address, should be laid before me by the Estates and Orders for my decision without delay. Make known the contents of these lines, my answer to the petition which has been presented to me through your Imperial Highness, to the Estates and Orders, and inform them my reply is prompted by my paternal desire for the happiness of my beloved Hungary, which I have at all times promoted as a father should.[1]

The contents of this rescript were regarded as entirely satisfactory and roused no suspicions of the existence of any *arrière pensée*. The Hungarian Commission, believing that a new era had dawned for the two countries, issued a manifesto to the people of Vienna before its departure from the capital :—

The bankruptcy of the godless principle of *divide et impera* which sowed the dragon's teeth of discord between us is now recognised. That tie which henceforth binds us all to the beloved reigning House of our country is no chain of servitude but the golden bonds of freedom, the maintenance of which can be assured only so long as each and all stand together. The desires of us Magyars have been satisfied ; for the future, a Magyar Government supported by free institutions will control our destiny, and the royal promise assures you that you also will henceforth enjoy similar blessings. Brothers, we shall be united in liberty, strong in our mutual understanding, powerful in our alliance, which fellow-feeling, genuine confidence, and fidelity to the reigning

---

[1] Horváth, *Huszonöt év*, ii. 609.

House have cemented. . . . . Once again we exclaim, as a final farewell and as a final expression of our thanks, long live the reigning House, long live the Austrian people, freedom, fraternity, and the community of interests which unites us all ! [1]

Thus, the realisation of Hungary's wishes, and the, apparently final, recognition of the principle of duality, of the personal nature of the union existing between the two countries in virtue of the Pragmatic Sanction and of the laws of 1790-91, was not regarded as in any way involving the severance of the bonds which united Hungary to Austria, or the abolition of the essential obligation of mutual defence. On the contrary, it amounted in the general view to a reaffirmation of the connexion from which neither party wished to escape, and as a final regularisation, in accordance with the law and the Constitution, of relations the true meaning of which had been wilfully distorted and obscured by centuries of autocratic encroachment.

On March 23 the names of the members of the first Hungarian Cabinet were published. The Prime Minister, Batthyány, recognised from the outset the difficulties which would result from the inclusion in the Ministry of a person of Kossuth's overwhelming personality, but at the same time was aware of the impossibility of excluding the chief author of the country's new-found independence. Kossuth himself wished for the post of Minister of the Interior, but the Palatine would not hear of it, as that would have put the control of the coming elections into Kossuth's hands.[2] It was thought that he would have less opportunity of exercising an overweening influence as Minister of Finance, and he eventually agreed to accept office in that character. Colonel Mészáros, actually serving in Italy, became Minister of War ; Széchenyi, Minister of Communications and Public Works ; Klauzál,

---

[1] Beöthy, o.c. iii. 54.
[2] Szögyény, Emlékiratai, p. 72.

of Commerce and Agriculture.   Deák accepted a portfolio
as Minister of Justice, Eötvös as head of the Department
of Public Instruction and Religious Worship, while
Szemere went to the Home Office.   The Prime Minister
took no portofolio.   Prince Paul Eszterházy, the greatest
landowner in Hungary, who had recently been Ambassador
in London, became Minister in attendance on the King,
charged with the task of supervising his country's relations
with Austria.   His duty was to personify the connexion
of Hungary with the King-Emperor, and to consult with
the Austrian Minister of Foreign Affairs on all external
matters of common interest to the two countries.   As to
what was to happen in the event of disagreement nothing
was decided ; it was one of those problems the decision of
which was left to the future, which mutual goodwill and
good faith would certainly not have found to be insoluble.

All shades of Liberal opinion were represented in this
Ministry-of-all-the-talents, which any country at any period
might have been proud to possess.   The Conservatives,
who had failed to keep pace with the times, were not
represented, but their spokesman Szécsen accepted the
situation on their behalf, and declared that though they
did not abandon their principles they bowed to the will
of the majority.   "Bolder, more daring, spirits, with
whom the Powers above seem to be in close alliance, have,
in the space of a few days, placed the future of our country
on a basis to which we ant-like workers could never have
raised it, or, perhaps, could have placed it only after the
lapse of generations." [1]   Thus Széchenyi ; but his optimism
was apparent rather than real, and his nature and his
experience made him view the future with misgiving.
Eötvös and Deák both thought that matters had moved
too quickly, "mais à un homme ivre on ne peut pas
parler raison, et la Diète en ce moment est ivre." [2]

[1] *Pesti Hirlap*, April 8, quoted by Marczali, *A Legujabb Kor Története*,
p. 614.   [2] Szögyény, *o.c.* 64.

Hungary certainly was intoxicated, if drunkenness consists in plunging into work with feverish enthusiasm; but if we compare the legislation of the next three weeks with that of the past thirty years, we can only come to the conclusion that Hungary drunk was greatly superior to Hungary sober. The temporary responsible Ministry under the presidency of Kolowrat, appointed in Austria on March 21, compares badly with that of its Hungarian counterpart. "On baptisa Ministres les présidents des Chambres, Offices, et Conseils, et tout fut dit. Ce fut une nouvelle gerontocracie."[1] No members of the victorious party of reform found a place. A Liberal Ministry could have worked hand in hand with Hungary and would have recognised the fact that its only chance of maintaining its existence lay in co-operation with a similar body in Hungary; but nothing could be expected from the old firm masquerading under a new trade-name.

Difficulties were not slow to arise. The Viennese bureaucracy, seeing in the establishment of separate Hungarian Ministries of War and Finance the final loss of its influence and a death-blow to centralisation—its ideal and the object of its labours—wished to keep its hold on those two departments of State, and thus, to some extent at all events, to nullify the results of Hungary's victory.[2] An imperial rescript brought by the Palatine to the Diet on March 29 showed how little the camarilla intended that the King should keep the word so solemnly pledged a few days ago. The rescript requires that the proceeds of taxation in Hungary should be sent to Vienna, as in the past, to pay for the expenses of the Court and to

[1] Eisenmann, *Le compromis Austro-Hongrois*, p. 78.

[2] It is perhaps unnecessary to remind the reader that the Pragmatic Sanction deprives Hungary of no single attribute of independence, except of that of choosing its own King in the event of the extinction of the male line of the Habsburgs, and that Law x. of 1790-91, so far from justifying any restriction of Hungary's sovereign rights, expressly declares that country's independence of the various departments of the Viennese bureaucracy.—See vol. i. pp. 191 *sqq.*, 232 *sqq.*

provide for the general necessities of the Empire; that the Diet should be limited to the discussion of questions relating to direct taxation, of which it had had complete control for centuries past, and that all matters connected with trade and the customs tariff should be treated in agreement with the Austrian authorities. As regards the Ministry of War, it was stated that His Majesty " clings to the principle of intimate connexion which derives from the Pragmatic Sanction,[1] and to his rights with respect to the employment of the armed forces in accordance with the law and to the nomination of officers." The maintenance of the Hungarian Chancery in Vienna was also demanded, the result of which would be that the independent Ministry would be reduced, as Kossuth pointed out, to the position occupied by the old Council of Lieutenancy, which existed merely for the purpose of executing the orders transmitted to it by the bureaucrats of Vienna. The Prime Minister drew the attention of the Palatine to the fact that the terms of the rescript were not in accord with the justifiable expectation or legal rights of the country, and requested him to use his influence with the King to induce him to give effect to his promise with respect to the appointment of a responsible Ministry. The Archduke replied, " The present serious and important moment will decide the fate of Hungary. . . . I give my solemn word that I will not only transmit to His Majesty the remarks which the Ministry may make to me but will see that effect is given to them, and will, if necessary, make the retention of our offices dependent on the success of my efforts." The Diet thereon unanimously passed a resolution to the effect that any attempt to render vain the sacred word of the King would be looked upon as an audacious move on the part of a discredited bureaucracy,

[1] The Pragmatic Sanction has nothing to do with the armed forces of Hungary, except that the obligation of mutual defence is a necessary consequence of the identity of King and Emperor.

and that any tampering with the royal promise must necessarily have the effect of diminishing belief in the King's good faith. The people's wrath was unbounded when the terms of the rescript became known, but no actual disturbance occurred, though here and there the cry was raised of "Down with the German Government!" The Palatine, no doubt, was a broken reed, but a law had already been passed providing for the establishment of a national defensive force, and a nation in arms would have stood behind the Ministry if any overt attempt had been made to coerce the Diet and to curtail the effect of the concessions obtained. Knowledge of this fact, and the arrival of the news of unexpected complications in northern Italy, brought Vienna to its senses and compelled the camarilla to postpone its attempts at reaction to a more convenient season. A second royal rescript, dated March 31, shows that the King felt himself constrained to abandon the unconstitutional attitude recently adopted. "While I recognise," said His Majesty, "the fact that the organisation of home defence and the vote for military requirements belong to the sphere of action of the legislature, and that the disposition of the regular forces and their employment are within the competence of the Viceroy's Government acting through the responsible Ministry, on my part I confidently expect from the attachment of my faithful Estates and Orders to my House and to the connexion, consecrated by the Pragmatic Sanction, with my Empire that they will readily see that the question of the employment of the Hungarian army beyond the limits of the Kingdom, as well as that of the appointment to military offices, can depend only on my royal decision, and that the counter-signature in such matters must consequently be entrusted to the Minister in attendance on my person."

It is important that the date of the last-mentioned rescript (March 31) should not be forgotten. As will be seen hereafter, ten days before the issue of that document, which, if black is black and white is white, gave the clearest possible proof of the King's intention to abide loyally by the terms of the promise contained in his communication to the Archduke Stephen of March 17, and to accept the full logical consequences of the concessions he had thereby agreed to make, the Viennese camarilla had already formulated its plans for the destruction of the newly-recognised independence of Hungary at the cost, if need be, of civil war. The Magyars, unaware of the underhand machinations of the Court party, now looked forward with confidence to the future. The country greeted the second rescript with orderly enthusiasm, recognising the truth of Wesselényi's saying, that anarchy is the bridge over which expelled absolutism returns. From all parts of the country expressions of thanks and loyalty reached the Throne. " Let His Majesty," said Kossuth, " come as soon as possible into the midst of his faithful Magyars and convince himself that our fidelity is no empty word, but that the Magyar can be manly, firm, and sincere, not only in winning liberty for himself but also in loyalty to his King."[1] The country's confidence in its future and in its monarch was confirmed, and seemed to be justified, by the fact that on April 10 Ferdinand came to Pressburg in order to be present at the ceremony of the dissolution of the Diet, and was accompanied by the Heir-apparent, the Archduke Francis Charles, and by his son, Francis Joseph, whose presence was looked upon as indicating the frank acceptance and final consecration of the new order of things, both by the actual occupant of the Throne and by his two immediate heirs. " I have come with joy into your midst," said the King, " for I find my dear Magyar people to be still the same as I have always found it to be. . . . It is a joy to me to see my

---

[1] On April 2 the Diet gave proof of the loyalty of its intentions by voting 3,000,000 florins for Court expenses.

faithful Orders round me. . . . From the bottom of my heart I wish happiness to my loyal Magyars, for it is in their happiness that I find my own. Therefore, that which they require for the attainment thereof I herewith grant and confirm by my royal word to you, my dear cousin (the Palatine), and through you to the whole nation, in whose fidelity I find my greatest joy and comfort."[1] Francis Charles, speaking in his own name and that of Francis Joseph (the present King), said, "In my opinion, all that this noble-minded people can desire for its glory and prosperity is to be found to the full in those laws at the ratification of which I consider it a special privilege to have been present."[2] The King may perhaps be acquitted of intentional duplicity on the ground that his intellectual feebleness made him the unconscious instrument of the tortuous policy of the camarilla, but no such excuse can be alleged for Francis Charles.

[1] Horváth, *Huszonöt év*, ii. 705-707.   [2] *Ibid.* ii. 706.

CHAPTER XIII

IT would not have been surprising if the laws passed between March 20 and the date of the dissolution, which transformed the old oligarchical Hungary into a modern constitutional State, had shown signs of hurried workmanship, but it would be hard to put a finger on any indication of precipitancy or of political immaturity in the legislation of 1848. Though framed at a moment of great anxiety and excitement, it needed only slight alterations to fit it to form the basis of the compromise[1] which, twenty years later, the wisdom of Deák and his contemporaries was able to effect without infringing the principle of historical continuity.[2] The laws of 1848 were, in fact, not the hasty product of three weeks of feverish activity, but were the result of twenty-three years of continuous struggle, and of a gradual educational process for which three great men were chiefly responsible—Széchenyi, Deák, and Kossuth. To Kossuth is due the lion's share of the credit of having raised the debates of the Diet to a higher level, and of having induced the abandonment of the old circular rut—the perpetual insistence on local interests and grievances, and on the necessity of maintaining the integrity of the Constitution, not on that of reforming it. The fact that the nobles were induced to denude themselves of their oligarchic privileges, and deplete their

---

[1] Tezner, *Die Wandlungen der österreichisch-ungarischen Reichsidee*, p. 10.

[2] *Ibid.*

pockets in the interests of the nation at large, is the best evidence of Kossuth's influence on the imagination of his countrymen.   No doubt the Viennese bureaucracy would, eventually, have bought the support of the lower orders for its centralising designs by abolishing class privileges, but the process of sweeping those privileges away would have infallibly swept away the Constitution also.   Kossuth was quick to grasp the opportunity afforded by the disturbed condition of Europe in general, and of Vienna in particular, to recast the whole political fabric, and, at the same time, to obtain recognition of constitutional rights which, if dormant, had always existed, and of their necessary corollaries.   Possibly, but for Kossuth, no baptism of fire and blood would have followed the rebirth of the Magyar nation ; certainly, but for him, the Hungary of to-day would not exist.

Law iii. provides for the establishment of an independent, responsible Hungarian Ministry at Budapest. The person of the King is declared to be sacred and inviolable (sect. 1).   In his absence the Archduke Stephen, as Palatine and Viceroy, is invested with all executive powers, exercisable, in accordance with the law and the Constitution, through the responsible Ministry ; and no ordinances, commands, decisions, or nominations made or issued by the King or his Viceroy, as the case may be, are valid unless countersigned by a member of the Ministry (sect. 3).   It was subsequently suggested by the reactionaries of Vienna that this devolution of authority to the Palatine was a revolutionary innovation; but a reference to the law of 1485, which defines the duties of that official, provides a precedent and shows that there was nothing unconstitutional or legally objectionable in the new clause. That law provided that in the absence of the King from Hungary the Palatine should be *ex officio locum tenens regius*, invested with all powers exercisable by the Crown, except those of pardon and of the conferment of privileges and titles, and that if the King should be weak-minded or remiss in the performance of his duties, the Palatine should have authority to receive foreign ambassadors and give them an answer : in other words, should have complete power to represent the Crown both in home and foreign affairs. Ferdinand was notoriously weak-minded. To call him remiss would be to flatter him. For years past it had been a favourite trick to take no notice of the Addresses of the Diet, or to wait so long before sending a reply thereto that no time was left to discuss the terms of the rescript before the dissolution took place. Such a state of affairs obviously could not be tolerated in a country which was henceforth to have a proper system of parliamentary government. The power could no longer be left to the Crown of reducing the Diet to a condition of farcical futility by means of a deliberate policy of procrastination. That the suggestion of revolutionary illegality was an afterthought of the camarilla is shown by the terms of the manifesto issued by the King to the Croatians on June 10.[1] " At the last Hungarian Diet, in accordance with the request made to Us by our faithful Estates, We, of our own free royal will graciously ratified a law in accordance with which Our beloved Cousin, his Imperial Highness the Archduke Stephen, Palatine of Hungary, has been appointed Our Viceroy, with full powers as such to exercise the executive authority through our Hungarian Ministry at the same time appointed, which said Ministry unites in itself all functions hitherto attributed to the Court Chancery, the Council of Lieutenancy, the Treasury, and the Council of War."[2]

[1] See also Law iii. of 1562, which was never objected to as revolutionary. " As his Imperial and Royal Majesty cannot reside in Hungary, it is ordained that his Imperial Highness (the Archduke Mathias) in accordance with the full authority granted him by His Majesty in that behalf, shall have *plenary powers* to act and ordain through the Palatine and the Hungarian Councillors in matters concerning the Kingdom of Hungary."

[2] Hartig, *Genesis der Revolution*, Appendix XV. p. 363.

Every member of the Ministry is to be responsible for his official acts of whatever nature (sect. 4). In all civil, ecclesiastical, financial and military affairs, and all matters connected with home-defence His Majesty will henceforth exercise his executive authority only through the responsible Ministry (sect. 6). By the 7th and 8th clauses the right is reserved to the King of nominating the military and higher ecclesiastical officials, as well as that of employing the Hungarian army beyond the limits of the Kingdom, but these rights can only be exercised with the consent of the responsible Minister in attendance on the person of His Majesty, signified by his counter-signature. Thus, the Hungarian army cannot be withdrawn from the country unless its withdrawal is sanctioned by the Ministry, which, of course, would obtain the authorisation of the Diet, before giving its consent. In the absence of the King the Palatine nominates the Minister-President, his nomination being subject to the royal approval (sect. 11). The Minister-President submits the names of the other members of the Cabinet to His Majesty for confirmation (sect. 12). The Minister *a latere* is to represent the country "in all matters which interest Hungary in common with the Hereditary Provinces" [1] (sect. 13). A Council of State is to be established at Budapest under the presidency of the King, or, in his absence, of the Viceroy or Prime Minister, which will include in its members the high officials of the former Chancery, and the chief members of the Treasury and of the Council of Lieutenancy (sects. 19, 22, 24).[2] Ministers can sit or speak in

---

[1] This phrase was subsequently construed as implying a recognition by Hungary of a closer tie uniting it to Austria than that of personal union—the result of the identity of King and Emperor. But the Pragmatic Sanction is in 1848, as twenty years later, alone recognised as the basis of the relations of the two countries ; consequently, matters of common interest are those, and those only, which flow from the obligation of mutual defence, which necessarily involves the adoption of a common, or, more correctly, an identical foreign policy for purposes of defence, but not for purposes of aggression.

[2] With respect to official appointments, due regard is to be had to sect. 58

both Houses, and can be called upon by both to appear
and give explanations personally or in writing (sects. 28,
29, 30). Ministers are not necessarily members of either
House, but can vote only if they are members (sect. 31).
The Ministers are responsible " for all acts or ordinances
which are injurious to the independence of the country,
to the constitutional guarantees, to the existing legal ordinances, to the liberty of the subject, or to the sanctity of
property, which they may do or issue in their ministerial
capacity, as well as for the embezzlement or illegal use
of moneys committed to their charge," [1] and for failure
to carry out the law or to maintain public order or
security, in so far as the executive powers entrusted to
them suffice to secure their maintenance (sect. 32). The
impeachment of Ministers may be voted by an absolute
majority of the members of the Lower House (sect.
33). Ministers are to render an annual account of
their dealings with the national revenues, and present
their estimates for the ensuing year to the Lower House
(sect. 37).

Law iv. provides that Parliament shall sit annually in
Budapest, and that Bills presented for the royal assent
shall be confirmed before the end of the session. The
mandate of the members is to be for three years ; the
King, however, has the right to prorogue or dissolve
Parliament at any time, but a new one must meet within
three months of the dissolution, and neither prorogation
nor dissolution may take place until the Budget for the
past year and the estimates for the ensuing period have
been passed. The King nominates the President of the
Upper House, while the Lower House elects its own
Speaker, and other officers, by ballot. The qualification

of the law of 1791, which provides that natives of the *partes adnexae* are to be
employed in proper proportion (sect. 23.)

[1] An almost exact translation of Sect. 4, Art. 1-5 of the French Constitution
of 1791. The influence of that Constitution is visible in many sections of the
laws of 1848.

for election as member of Parliament is the same as that
for the enjoyment of the franchise, except that the candidate must have attained the age of twenty-four and be
able to speak the Hungarian language.

Law v., which is stated to be a temporary measure,
provides for the introduction of popular representation.
All male citizens, whether native or naturalised, of
Hungary and of the parts annexed, are qualified for the
franchise irrespective of their religion, provided they have
attained the age of twenty years, are not under parental or
other guardianship, or in service, have not been convicted
of fraud, murder, theft, and other specified crimes, and
possess urban real property to the value of three hundred
florins, or property in the country equal in value to one
quarter of a *sessio*, *i.e.*, an allotment varying in extent in
different districts, but on the average approximately equal
to eight to twelve acres.   The franchise is also conferred
upon traders and manufacturers who possess their own
shops or factories, and on artisans who have their own
workshops and regularly employ at least one assistant.   It
is also given to those who do not come within the above
category, but are possessed of a fixed income of one hundred florins derived from land or investments, and to all
professors, surgeons, doctors, lawyers, apothecaries, clergy-
men, schoolmasters, and other members of the professional
classes, as well as to existing burgesses of the free towns,
without regard to their incomes or professions.   All who
have hitherto enjoyed the right to vote at elections of
members of the Diet, but do not possess any of the above
mentioned qualifications are temporarily [1] left in possession
of the franchise, it being the object of the present Diet to
widen the basis of representation, not to curtail existing
rights.   There are to be in all four hundred and forty-six
deputies, that is to say, three hundred and seventy-seven

---

[1] The Radicals objected to this on the ground that it was an obvious
infringement of the principle of equality.

for Hungary and the parts annexed, including eighteen for Croatia, and eight for the frontier districts, hitherto entirely unrepresented, and sixty-nine for Transylvania, if and when the re-union is effected : the question of reincorporation being left to the decision of the Transylvanian Diet, Hungary undertaking to maintain all the special rights, privileges, and distinctive laws of the Transylvanians, which are not in actual conflict with the principle of complete unity with the mother country (Law vii.).

Law viii. abolishes the nobles' immunity from taxation. Henceforth all inhabitants of Hungary and the annexed parts are to bear their fair share of the common burden on the basis of a system of assessment to be hereafter elaborated. Law ix. abolishes for ever the *corvée* and all feudal dues in money or kind, as well as the manorial jurisdiction of the landowners. The legislature places the latter, as regards indemnification for their loss, "under the protecting shield of the national honour" ; their rights are to be valued, and compensation is to be paid by the State on a five per cent basis (Law xii. 3). Law xiii. records the fact that the clergy voluntarily renounced their claim to tithes without asking for compensation. Lay impropriators are to receive compensation, and the needs of the poorer clergy are to be cared for by the State.

Law xiv. provides for the establishment of a Credit Bank, with a view to enabling landed proprietors to tide over the difficulties consequent on the abolition of feudal dues ; and Law xv. abolishes in principle the old system of entail (ósiség). Pending the elaboration of a law on the subject, all suits arising from that system are temporarily suspended.

Laws xvi. and xvii. place the management of county affairs in the hands of committees, until the next meeting of Parliament, the continuance of the autonomous rights of the counties in their existing form being clearly incompatible with the reformed Constitution, and with the executive powers now vested in the responsible Ministry.[1]

Law xviii. puts an end to the existence, never recognised by the Hungarian legislature, of the preliminary censorship, introduces the institution of trial by jury, and is specially strict as regards journalistic attacks on the King, on the Constitution, and on the connexion of Hungary with Austria arising out of the Pragmatic Sanction. A political daily newspaper is to deposit 10,000 florins caution-money, other papers a less sum. This law, which evinces a distinctly non-liberal spirit, and caused great dissatisfaction, was only a temporary measure, and perhaps finds its justification in the fact that a certain degree of severity was necessary during the period of transition from bureaucratic to parliamentary government.

Law xx. places all recognised religions, viz. the Catholic, Greek, Calvinist, Lutheran, and, henceforth, the Unitarian religion, on a footing of absolute equality. The clergy of all such religions is to be provided for by the State, and all schools are to be thrown open to all denominations.

Law xxi. restores their ancient rights to the national flag[2] and coat-of-arms, and the annexed parts may use their own colours and arms alongside those of Hungary.

[1] Széchenyi and the more Conservative politicians wished to maintain the old organisation, which they regarded as the focus of national life and the stronghold of the influence of the nobles. Kossuth also was inclined to preserve it, as he still considered it to be the chief defence of the Constitution, but not in its present oligarchic form. He wished to place it on a democratic basis. Deák and Eötvös were decidedly in favour of its abolition, on the ground of its incompatibility with parliamentary government.—See the latter's *Reform, passim.*

[2] It seems to be doubtful what these ancient rights were. In old days the Magyars apparently fought under a red flag. In the time of Andrew II. official documents were fastened together with a red, white, and green ribbon, and tradition says that those colours were adopted for the national flag by

Law xxii. refers to the organisation of the National Guard, in which all persons between the ages of twenty and fifty years, who are not in service and own urban real property to the value of 200 florins, or half a *sessio* in the country, or have a regular annual income of 100 florins, are liable to serve. Officers up to the rank of captain are to be elected by the force itself, all above that rank are to be appointed by the Commander-in-chief (in Hungary the Palatine, in Croatia the Bán), on the recommendation of the Minister of War. The members of the force are to take the oath of fidelity to the King and to the Constitution.

Laws xxiii. to xxvii. deal with the question of the reform of municipal government, pending legislation on the subject by the reformed Diet. Temporarily, the qualification for the enjoyment of the municipal franchise is practically the same as that for the right to vote at elections of members of the Diet.

The legislation of 1848 has been styled revolutionary, and its authors have been accused of attempting to destroy every link of the chain which bound Hungary to Austria, but the accusation is ill-founded, for apart from the fact that Law x. of 1790–91 declared the complete independence of Hungary as regards all branches of government, the germ and the justification of the new order of things are, as will be seen, to be found in innumerable laws sanctioned and confirmed by successive

Louis the Great.—Kmety, *A Magyar Közjog*, p. 514. Each Baron with banderial rights had his own flag, and the counties had theirs, but Law xi. of 1596 says "*suae Majestatis vexillo pareant et subsint*," which shows that the royal flag alone had "centrale Bedeutung" according to Tezner (*Wandlungen*, etc., p. 35), but there is no evidence as to whether that flag was the personal standard of the King, or the three coloured national flag of Hungary. Later, the regimental colours bore either a picture of the Virgin or something to show the origin of the regiment, and had no political meaning. In 1754 an order of the War Council prescribed the use of the double eagle, and since the adoption of the imperial title the use of the imperial eagle was intended to symbolise the non-existent political unity of all the realms of the Habsburgs.— *Ibid.* pp. 37, 38.

kings.[1] No new limitation was placed on the constitutional power of the Crown which was not the reasonable
consequence of a correct interpretation of the Pragmatic
Sanction; and it is only in matters of internal organisation,
in the abolition of the last traces of feudalism, and in the
substitution of a system of representative government for
the old oligarchical *régime*, that a distinct break with the
past is to be found. Even Hartig[2] admits that "the
movement in Hungary proceeded on legal, and not on
revolutionary lines," in other words, that no attempt was
made to deprive the Crown of rights based on statute
law or sanctioned by immemorial custom. "The nation
gained nothing new by means of the laws of 1848; His
Majesty gave it no share in those privileges which he
legally enjoyed; but those laws assured it, with the consent of course of the Crown, the enjoyment of those
rights which it had hitherto legally possessed, but had, in
fact, been exercised by the King in disregard of the
law."[3] Teszner[4] and others who would deny the very
existence of a Hungarian Constitution before 1848, see
an argument in support of their views in the fact that the
jura reservata of the Crown are not defined by statute;
but the very fact of the absence of hard and fast legal
definition is evidence of their restricted character, for the
King, being the delegate of the nation, which divested
itself of a portion of the sovereignty in favour of the
Crown, can by no process acquire rights which have not

---

[1] Even the principle of ministerial responsibility is not new. It will be
remembered that Law vii. of 1507 provides that if any member of the Royal
Council does anything contrary to the laws or injurious to the interests and
liberties of the country, the other members are bound to bring the matter
before the Diet, at its next meeting, which will punish the offender according
to his deserts.

[2] *Genesis der Revolution*, p. 278.

[3] Coloman Tisza, 1866, cited by Horváth (John), *A Közös Ügyek Elözé-
ményei és Fejlödése*, p. 56.

[4] *Die Wandlungen der österreichisch-ungarischen Reichsidee*, Vienna, 1905,
and *Der österreichische Kaisertitel*, etc., 1899.

been specifically delegated to him.[1] Time does not run against Acts of Parliament : it neither destroys nor diminishes their binding force, and in a constitutional country no length of illegal use can confer prescriptive rights as against the sole valid source of royal authority. However great the influence exercised by the Austrian Government on the internal affairs of Hungary since the disaster of Mohács had been, the success of a policy of encroachment on the constitutional liberties of the country cannot be taken to imply the abandonment in perpetuity of national privileges, or justify complaint when the coincidence of a period of political revival in Hungary with one of revolutionary disorder in the hereditary provinces enabled the Magyars to assert their right of re-entry into the possession of their birthright.

It cannot be denied that Vienna, since the importation of the Habsburgs, had exercised an influence on the internal affairs of the Magyars at times so preponderating that Hungarian independence practically existed only in the ink and paper of the Corpus Juris. On the other hand, only a perversion of historical facts can give a semblance of support to the assertion of Lustkandl,[2] the originator and the chief source of modern criticism of Hungary's historic rights, that the Constitution was a myth ; that before as well as after the Pragmatic Sanction Hungary was in reality incorporated in the realms of the Habsburgs, and that the Magyars acquiesced in such incorporation. What Bidermann[3] calls the Gesammt-Staats-Idee was conceived immediately after the battle of Mohács, and, though its manifestations and the relations of the Habsburgs to Hungary vary from time to time,

[1] Verbőczy.
[2] Das ungarisch-österreichische Staatsrecht, Vienna, 1863, as a reply to which Deák wrote his Adalék a Magyar Közjoghoz, Pest, 1865 (cited as Deák, Adalék).
[3] Geschichte der österreichischen Gesammt-Staats-Idee, Innsbruck, vol. i. 1867; ·vol. ii. 1889.

the desire to destroy everything that differentiated that country from the hereditary provinces, and to bring about its final incorporation in a uniform Austrian monarchy was ever present. The early period of Habsburg domination was one long anti-reformational campaign, in which the principles of absolutism in Church and State were opposed to those of religious freedom and constitutional government. The godless doctrines of Luther and Calvin were to be extirpated, and at the same time the liberties of Hungary were to be destroyed in the interests of uniformity, the ideal of the Habsburgs, in whose opinion heresy and rebellion were practically synonymous.[1] Later, when the attention of the Habsburgs was concentrated on the German Confederation, and all considerations were subordinated to the maintenance of Austrian hegemony therein, the presentment of the appearance of a united Austrian monarchy, all parts of which gave unquestioned obedience to Vienna, was a matter of vital importance. It was the same at the period during which the whole policy of Austria was influenced by the desire to maintain that country's domination in Italy, the heel of Achilles, the existence of which contributed more than anything else to Hungary's temporarily successful assertion of its rights in 1848. The Habsburgs considered Hungary's incomprehensible insistence on historic rights a nuisance, and an obstacle to the realisation of their ambitions. They were bored with a "nation of hussars and lawyers," as

[1] The idea of Austria's duties to Rome and reactionary principles, is well illustrated by a pastoral letter of the Bishop of Trient, issued in 1866, cited by Springer, *Grundlagen und Entwickelungsziele der österreichisch-ungarischen Monarchie*, 1906 :—"Austria is the most useless State in the world, unless as the champion of Catholicism and in the name of the Roman Curia it secures Middle Europe for the Papacy against the Protestant North and the revolutionary, unbelieving West. Its vassaldom to Rome must be the corner-stone of its policy, both internal and external ; Austria must maintain its position in Germany and Italy as Rome's policeman, and as the embodiment of the reactionary principle. The Concordat is the only Constitution Austria wants." The Concordat of 1855 showed that the Austrian Government realised the fact that without the backing of Rome reaction must fail.

Bismarck called the Magyars [1]—fighters and hair-splitters, who should, in their opinion, have been proud to sink their individuality in a common Austrian fatherland. But this was precisely what Hungary never had any intention of doing, though Lustkandl and his followers will not admit the fact. They tell us that since 1526 Hungary was a monarchically governed province of the Habsburgs on precisely the same footing as the hereditary dominions; [2] that it was under a completely centralised government down to 1848; [3] that the Hungarian Constitution amounted to no more than immunity from taxation for a privileged class; [4] that the Diet had no legislative power, such being vested solely in the King, [5] whose exclusive authority extended to all departments without exception. [6] Further, we are informed not only that a real and not a mere personal union was the result of the Pragmatic Sanction, but that such a real union existed before the law of 1723, [7] and was finally consecrated by the assumption of the imperial title in 1804, and that Hungary acquiesced without protest in the process of incorporation in the new-fangled Empire. That successive Habsburgs tried to bring about such an incorporation is an unques-

[1] *Reflections and Reminiscences*, ii. 252.

[2] Springer, *Grundlagen*, p. 8, following Lustkandl. *Das ungarisch-österreichische Staatsrecht*, p. 307. "Die österreichischen Länder mindestens seit der Pragmatischen Sanction eine einheitliche Gesammt-Monarchie gebildet haben, wovon Ungarn auch ein spezieller Theil war."

[3] Tezner, *Die Wandlungen*, etc., p. 2.

[4] Tezner, *Kaisertitel*, p. 45, following Lustkandl, *o.c.* 171.

[5] But see vol. i. p. 233, Law xii. of 1790-91, " *De legislativae et executivae Potestatis Exercitio*," which declares that the power of "passing, abrogating, and interpreting" laws is jointly exercisable by King and Diet, and not otherwise as his Majesty admits, "voluntarily and of his own accord." See also iii. 1715. " *Nec Status et Ordines Regni eadem Sacra Regia Majestas secus regi aut dirigi vult quam observatis propriis ipsius Regni Hungariae hactenus factis vel in futurum Diaetaliter constituendis legibus.*"

[6] Springer, *Grundlagen*, p. 13. According to this author the Pragmatic Sanction and the laws of 1790 resulted only in the "Stärkung des Absolutismus und die Befestigung der alten Privilegien des Adels," p. 15.

[7] Tezner, *Kaisertitel*, p. 106 *sqq.*

tionable fact, but the extent to which they succeeded in
their efforts is another matter.

The reader is acquainted with the terms of the
Pragmatic Sanction and of the laws of 1790-91,[1] but is,
perhaps, not equally conversant with other details of
legislation and executive practice on which Lustkandl
and his successors base their arguments. To begin with
financial matters. Bidermann, following Lustkandl,
adduces the fact that in 1562 a royal order was issued
providing for the introduction of the Austrian currency
system into Hungary as a particularly instructive indication of that country's recognition of its financial subordination to Vienna,[2] but omits all reference to legislative
enactments of the same reign and subsequent periods,[3]
which prove that in matters affecting the currency the
Magyars did not submit to Austrian dictation.[4] Bider-

[1] See vol. i. pp. 190 *sqq.*, 230 *sqq.*

[2] *Gesammt-Staats-Idee*, p. 15. "Ein besonders Hervorleuchtender, den
deutschen Hintergrund illustrirender Fall."

[3] *E.g.* 1547, xxiv., re-establishing the coinage on the previously existing
basis. 1548, li., as to relative value at which Bohemian money is to be
accepted. 1741, xxxii., as to acceptance of the Moravian Gröschl.—See
Deák's *Adalék Magyar Közjoghox*, p. 97 *sqq.*, also p. 131, where twenty-one
other Hungarian laws regulating the coinage are cited. See also the laws
cited by Horváth (John), *A Közös Ügyek*, p. 41 *sqq.*

[4] In 1752 Maria Theresa established a bank of issue in Austria, the notes
of which were accepted in Hungary though the Diet was not consulted on
the subject. In 1811, that body passed a resolution to the effect that "the
King has no power either by reason of his royal prerogative or otherwise to
issue notes or bring them into circulation in Hungary . . . without the
permission of the Diet (Horváth (John), *Közös Ügyek*, p. 91), and raised the
question of the advisability of establishing a separate Hungarian bank.
Austrian notes, however, continued to be circulated in Hungary, and in fact
formed the chief medium of exchange, but the proceedings of the Diet of
1825 show that the members never accepted the Austrian view that the
decision in such matters formed one of the *jura reservata* of the Crown.
When Francis in 1811 wished to force Hungary to undertake the liability for
100,000,000 florins out of the 211,000,000 of the Austrian public debt, if a real
union had existed, and if the King's power had been as illimited as Lustkandl
and his school suggest, he certainly would not have accepted, as he had to do, a
refusal. Maria Theresa submitted to a similar rebuff in 1763, and both in 1806
and 1809 the Diet obtained a recognition of the principle that no such burden as
Francis wished the country to undertake could be imposed without its consent.

mann finds further confirmation of his view in the fact
that during the reign of Ferdinand I. the Hungarian
Regalia or Crown perquisites, if the phrase may be used,
were under the management of an Austrian official,[1] but
eleven laws from 1492 to 1825 prove the Diet's control
of the mines,[2] four laws forbid the King to mortgage
or alienate Crown property,[3] a similar number deal with
saltpetre and gunpowder, which were also *Regalia*,[4] and
eight with salt, another Royal monopoly.[5] As regards
the trade relations of the two countries, it has been seen
that ever since the reign of Maria Theresa the monarch
arrogated to himself the right of unlimited control, but
he had no constitutional justification for so doing, as is
shown by the existence of legislation on the subject of the
customs duties emanating from the Diet and confirmed
by the Crown. Law xxiv. of 1622 enacts that the proceeds of all duties collected in Hungary or in the parts
annexed shall no longer be sent to the Austrian Treasury,
but shall be forwarded to the corresponding Hungarian
institution at Pressburg. That of 1659 (lix.) deals with
the question of the admission of Hungarian wines into
Austria, and that of 1662 (xlii.) provides that the King,
pro conservanda bona vicinitate mutuaque amicitia, shall
consult the Estates and Orders of the hereditary provinces
on the subject, which proves that in this case, at all events
the King of Hungary dissociated himself from the Archduke of Austria, and that he realised that in the latter
character he was not entitled to claim exclusive control of
the fiscal relations of the two countries.[6] Law xci. of

---

[1] *Gesammt-Staats-Idee*, p. 20. [2] *Adalék*, p. 130 *sq.*

[3] 1514, i., ii. ; 1608, xxii. ; 1609, liv. ; 1622, xlvi. [4] *Adalék*, p. 133.

[5] *Ibid.* p. 132. Law xx. of 1790 declares that the price is not to be raised
by the King without the consent of the Diet, except under exceptional
circumstances, which are not defined. No doubt it means in time of war,
but the phrase in any case does not justify the view that the Diet's control
was *nil*, or, at all events, illusory.

[6] *Ibid.* p. 105. Other laws bearing on the subject are 1490, xxiv.,
specifying the places at which duties are to be levied ; 1514, i., forbidding the

1715, referring to Law x. of 1655, provides for the appointment of a commission to inquire into the whole question of the customs " *in excessis et defectus diligenter inquirere . . . investigare, corrigere, addenda addere, tollendaque tollere*,[1] which alone suffices to refute Lustkandl's statement to the effect that the Austrian monarch had exclusive authority in such matters. Moreover, the continued existence of a customs barrier between Hungary and Austria is of itself an indication of the fact that the two countries continued to be regarded as two juridically separate and distinct units. That the Hungarian Treasury was, in general, dominated by that of Vienna to such an extent that the former was reduced to the position of a mere branch office of the latter is indisputable ; but it is equally clear that the domination in question formed at all periods one of the chief grievances of the Diet, and was always resented as unconstitutional. To take but two of the many enactments dealing with the subject— Law v. of 1608 provides for the election of treasurers, who are to be entirely independent of " foreign nations," *i.e.* of the hereditary provinces ;[2] and Law xiv. of 1741

King to alienate or mortgage the customs ; 1523, xlvi., and 1715, xc., declaring that duties are to be levied only at specified places. Seven laws between 1498 and 1681 abolish the duties on certain articles, *ibid.* p. 141 ; and five, in addition to those passed before Mohács, fix the tariff or grant exemption to various articles. [1] *Adalék*, p. 108.

[2] Deák cites five more Acts passed between 1608 and 1681 dealing with the same subject.—*Adalék*, p. 109. Ferdinand I., two years after Mohács, ordered all revenues to be sent to Vienna. In 1583 the Diet declared (Law i.) that no more taxes should be voted till the liberties of the country were restored, but the result of its resolution was *nil*, and the Treasury was deprived of its last vestiges of independence by Leopold I. In 1809 Baron Knesebeck, the Prussian statesman, wrote of Hungary, " Kein Schanzgräber, keine Metze Korn kann hier ohne Zustimmung der Stände ausgeschrieben werden " (Horváth (John), *Közös Ügyek*, p. 93), but in spite of that fact Hungary's financial control was, however great *de jure*, *de facto* extremely small. According to Eötvös (*Reform*, p. 8) in 1846 the *net* revenues amounted to 23,000,000 florins, of which 4,500,000 went to cover the expenses of local government. Of the remaining 18,500,000 only 4,500,000 florins were produced by the tax voted by the Diet for military purposes. Over the balance of 14,000,000, none of which was spent in Hungary, the Diet had practically no control.

was passed with the intention " *ut Camera Regia Hungarica in activitate, vigore legum patriarum, eidem competente plene et omnino conservetur.*" In theory, therefore, the independence of the Hungarian Treasury was fully maintained, but in reality it was almost non-existent, notwithstanding the continued protests of the Diet. In this constant insistence on grievances and in the *renovatio* or re-enactment of laws [1] in practically the same form over and over again, Tezner sees the reduction of the functions of the Diet to a mere "Petitions-Gravaminal-Postulatsthätigkeit" (a word of such monumental proportions that translation is impossible), "such as we find in all continental, monarchic States with a limited representative system, at the period of their transition to absolutism"; [2] but the mere fact of such re-enactment, which in every case received the royal assent, proves that the King of the period, no matter to what extent he had been guilty of encroachment on the rights of the Kingdom, fully admitted the existence of such rights, though he violated them to the best of his ability. Nothing but legislation such as that of 1848 could suffice to prevent the repetition of such encroachment on the part of monarchs whose chief desire it was to efface the distinction which existed between the King of Hungary and the Archduke of Austria. [3]

---

[1] *E.g.* as to removal of foreign troops five laws in a century—1536-1638—and five between 1550 and 1791 as to the obligation of the King to reside in Hungary. "Das gibt dann zusammen die Verfassung des *inclyti Regni Hungariae,*" exclaims Tezner, who before committing himself to the statement that the initiative power in matters of legislation was vested solely in the King, should have referred to the episode of the extra-Dietal insertion of Law xxii. of 1604 (see vol. i. pp. 139, 143), and to Verbőczy, *Jus Tripartitum,* Part ii. 3, 4. The King had of course a power of veto, which to some extent reduces the Parliaments of all constitutionally governed countries to a "Postulats-Petitions-Thätigkeit." In England the petitional form of laws continued till about 1470. As Stubbs pointed out, the importance of the petitional form lay in the fact that it gave Parliament the initiative. All the criticisms of Tezner and Springer would apply equally well to the British Parliament, any way to the middle of the seventeenth century, *i.e.* royal delay, evasions, etc. See Rudolf Springer, *Die Krise des Dualismus,* Vienna, 1904, 13 *sq.*; Stubbs, *Constitutional History,* II. xvii., III. xx.   [2] *Kaisertitel,* p. 18.

[3] Springer says that the Habsburgs rightly never looked upon themselves

The establishment of the War Council in Vienna in
1556 undoubtedly inflicted a severe blow to the principle
of Hungarian independence, but the statement of Lustkandl that the Diet neither then, nor at any time since
the beginning of St. Stephen's reign, exercised any control
over military matters, requires modification.   In the first
place, in the days of the old banderial system, and before
its establishment, the King could not call upon the national
forces to serve beyond the limits of the kingdom.   In
the second place, a whole series of laws exists to prove
that the control of the Diet was complete as regards the
number of men to be found by the counties and landowners, the period of service, the quartering of the
contingents, and the amount of the military tax.[1]   The
command of the Hungarian forces when brought into
existence by the Diet was vested first in the Palatine, later
in the King, but if the Diet had refused to vote recruits
from time to time, the King had no constitutional means
of compelling the grant of subsidies in men or money,
and after a time would have found his privilege reduced
to the command of a non-existent force.   But indeed,
the Diet, considering the fact that Hungary was not

as the mere successors of the Árpád and Jagellon dynasties, and that Hungary,
dismembered by the Turks and restored by the Habsburgs, should be looked
upon as the creation of the latter (*Grundlagen*, p. 11).   "Der gegenwartige,
abgerundete, befestigte, geeinigte Staat ist *ein Geschenk des Kaisers*, d.h. *Österreichs und seiner Völker*," *ibid.* p. 12.   It would be far more true to say that
but for Hungary, Austria would have ceased to exist in the time of Maria
Theresa, and that constitutional government was a present made by Deák to
Austria.   Besides, the ejection of the Turks was the work of Catholic Europe,
not of Austria alone.

[1] See Deák's *Adalék*, etc., p. 134 *sqq.*, where he cites twenty-three such
laws.   Perhaps the strongest is xix. of 1790, which declares individuals and
counties to be guilty of treason to the country if they offer the King subsidies
in men or money without the Diet's consent, which the King specially confirmed in Law iii. of 1825.   Law ii. of 1592, *re* defence of frontiers, provides
for the appointment of commissioners to consult with the envoys "*vicinorum
regnorum et provinciarum*," which has been used to show the existence of a
real and not a personal union.   It of course shows precisely the contrary, as
does the action of the Diet in 1792, which refused to vote recruits until
informed of the reasons for which they were required.

directly interested in the wars waged by the House of
Habsburg for dynastic purposes, was extremely lavish
both of blood and treasure, and never attempted to
exercise any separate control over the Hungarian forces,
which were practically merged in those of the hereditary
provinces, thereby justifying the erroneous view commonly
entertained by foreign countries, whose experience of
Hungary was mostly confined to the battlefield, of the
nature of the bond which united the Habsburg dominions.
The control of the Hungarian forces exercised by the
Consilium Aulicum Bellicum of Vienna was complete, and
the Diet did not, even in 1790, when it obtained the
most thorough recognition of the national independence,
aspire to the establishment of a separate military organisation for Hungary, but contented itself *temporarily*[1] with
the demand that places should be found for two Hungarians in the War Council.   The Magyar contingent,
except in Laws xxiv. of 1764 and i. of 1802, which speak
of the " Hungarian army," was nearly always referred to
as " the Hungarian legions " or regiments;[2] and the fact
that the law just referred to, which fixes the numbers of
the " Hungarian army " at 64,000 men, makes no reference to artillery, only to cavalry and infantry, shows that
no idea was then entertained of establishing a complete
military organisation separate from that of the hereditary
provinces, though no recognised *jus reservatum* of the
Crown would be infringed by its establishment.   No
argument in favour of the existence of a real union can be
fairly drawn from the fact that the defensive organisation

---

[1] " Animadvertentes Hungaricam militiam separato a reliquarum ditionum
copiis jure *pro hodiernis rerum conjunctis* vix aut ne vix quidem regi posse."—
Horváth (John), *Közös Ügyek*, p. 83. · At the same time the Diet demanded
that Hungarian regiments should be commanded only by Magyar officers.
Evidently the Diet considered that according to the Constitution it was
entitled to establish a separate military organisation, but that the middle of
the Napoleonic era was not a suitable moment for insistence on strict constitutional rights.

[2] In 1725 they are referred to as " *militia nostra nationalis Hungarica.*"

of the Hungarian frontiers was directed from Vienna
during the existence of the Turkish peril, for the defence
of the borderland was of vital importance to Austria,[1]
which had more than once seen the armies of the Sultan
at the gates of the capital ; and the fact that one country
guarantees the territorial integrity of another does not
betoken the existence of any form of union between the
two.   Till 1848, the control exercised by Austria over
the Hungarian forces was indisputably complete, but it is
equally indisputable that the Diet never abandoned its
right to interfere in questions affecting the internal organisation of the troops, such as the preferential employment
of Magyars in the higher ranks and on the staff,[2] the
standard of height, the exclusive employment of officers
and non-commissioned officers acquainted with the Hungarian language,[3] the period of service and the liability of
the Jews thereto,[4] and the non-transference of Magyars
to non-Hungarian regiments.[5]   The Diet of 1825-27 for
the first time raised the question of the use of Magyar
words of command instead of the German words in use
since Law viii. of 1715 admitted the insufficiency of the
old banderial system[6] and allowed the establishment of a

---

[1] " *Quandoquidem salus et permansio non modo afflictae hujus patriae, tanquam
clypei et antemuralis, sed aliorum quoque vicinorum Regnorum et Provinciarum
ex bona et secura confiniorum provisione dependeat.*"—Leopold I. in his Coronation Diploma.

[2] 1792, ix.   [3] 1807, i.

[4] 1830, vii. Law lix. of 1715, contemporary, it should be observed, with
the first establishment of a standing army, recognises the Diet's right of interference in military affairs.   It appoints a commission "*pro systematis elucubra-
tione in militaribus economicis rebus,*" and the King undertakes to appoint
commissioners on his part to confer with those chosen by the Diet to which
the result of the conference is to be submitted at its next meeting for revision.

[5] 1840, ii.

[6] The use of German was, according to Bidermann, intended "to produce
a complete feeling of brotherhood among all the nations of the Habsburg
monarchy" (*Gesammt-Staats-Idee*, vol. ii. p. 78).   "Doch das Gefühl der
Zuzammenhörigkeit . . . zu einem klaren thatkräftigen Bewusstsein ist ihm
nicht gelungen": a view which is not in accord with that entertained by
Tezner and Springer on the subject of Hungary's recognition of, and acquies-

standing army, consisting of foreign as well as of native soldiers. Nothing was in fact done to give effect to the wishes of the Diet in this respect, but no law or *jus reservatum* existed to make insistence on the realisation of its desires constitutionally inadmissible. Five laws[1] make the consent of Hungary a condition precedent to the exercise of the Crown's right of declaring war—a sufficient proof of the limited nature of the royal authority as compared with that wielded by the Archduke of Austria. The laws of 1848 made no change in the constitutional position as regards the military obligations of Hungary deducible from the terms of the Pragmatic Sanction, to which Kossuth and the Prime Minister[2] assigned the only reasonable meaning, viz. that it was Hungary's bounden duty to defend the territorial integrity of the Austrian Empire if it was attacked, but that there was no obligation to take part in a war of conquest, or to interfere in the internal affairs of the hereditary provinces. The common army, if and so far as it can be said to have had a constitutional existence by virtue of the obligation of mutual defence, was not destroyed by the legislation of 1848,[3] which did no more than provide for a Ministry of Home Defence, and required the consent of the Hungarian Government to the employment of the national forces beyond the limits of the Kingdom : that is to say, for purposes not strictly connected with the maintenance of the territorial integrity of Austria.

cence in, the unification with Austria. It is true that in 1655 the Diet demanded the admission of Hungarians to the Viennese War Council. This does not, however, prove abandonment of Hungarian rights ; it only shows that the Diet wished to assure its influence on the course of negotiations with the Turks, in accordance with Laws i. of 1536, ii. of 1622, and many others which forbade the King to make war or peace without its consent.

[1] 1608, ii. ; 1613, v. ; 1618, ii. ; 1622, ii. ; 1659, i. "*Ne Rex sine praescitu et consensu Regni ullum vel bellum moveat, vel militem extraneum introducat.*"

[2] In the debate on the rescript of March 31.

[3] Count Julius Andrássy, August 1, 1868.

As regards relations with foreign powers and diplomatic action, the influence of the King was always supreme, though his claim to exclusive control was not unquestioned. The Diet did not cease to insist on its right of making its voice heard when peace negotiations were in progress ; but, as in other departments, so in that of foreign affairs, Hungary failed to secure all the attributes of distinctive existence, and, both before and after the Pragmatic Sanction, the protestations of the Diet and its attempts to assert its strict rights were almost invariably ineffective. Though numerous laws declared that Hungary must be separately represented when terms of peace with the Turks were under discussion,[1] only on two occasions [2] do we find Hungarian commissioners acting on terms of equality with the diplomatic representatives of the hereditary provinces. As a general rule, Hungary was neither consulted nor represented, and this explains the fact, to which Lustkandl refers in proof of his statement that a *real* union bound all parts of the Habsburg dominions together, that in 1741 the Diet requested the Queen to find places for Magyars in the so-called Ministry of State to which all questions of foreign policy were referred.[3] Leopold II. assured the Diet in his Coronation

[1] *E.g.* 1536, i. ; 1546, iv. ; 1622, ii. ; 1659, i. ; 1681, iv.—See Kónyi, *Deák Ferencz Beszédei*, i. 14.

[2] At the Peace of Zsitvatorok, 1606, and that of Sistova. Hungary was not consulted *re* the terms of the Peace of Vasvár, 1664 ; or of Karlowitz, 1699 ; or of Passarowitz, 1718 ; or of Belgrade, 1739 ; nor was it represented at the Congress of Vienna, 1815.—Horváth (John), *Közös Ügyek*, 66 *sq*. Both in 1830 and 1840 the Diet would not vote the military contingent until it received explanations from Vienna as to the general European outlook, and the necessity of recruits, to emphasise its right to information on questions of foreign policy.

[3] Springer says that Hungary gave up its rights of independence in return for representation in the higher governmental departments of Vienna (*Grundlagen*, p. 18) which he styles "common" to both countries ; and Tezner (*Kaisertitel*) says that the Diet, at the beginning of the eighteenth century, made no objection to the fusion of Hungary with the hereditary provinces, and that that fusion was practically complete and accepted as such ; but he tries to prove too much. For instance, he refers to the demand of the Hungarian magnates

Diploma that he would respect the country's right to be consulted in all matters which affected its interests, but

made in 1712 that Hungary "*in perpetuum conjungeretur*" with the hereditary provinces, and that its representatives should be admitted "*ad suae majestatis consilia et intima quoque conferentialia*" as a proof of Hungary's acquiescence in the process of absorption. In reality, this particular request was the outcome of Hungary's wish for the abolition of obstacles to free trade with Austria, and not of a desire for incorporation. He sees a similar proof of acquiescence in the request addressed by the Diet to Maria Theresa in 1741, that she will consult the Primate, Palatine, Bán, and her faithful Hungarians on matters concerning "*tranquillitatem et salutem adeoque ipsam universorum regnorum et Provinciarum summam,*" and requests her in matters "*directe et praecise Regnum hoc respicientia negotia intimum Hungaricum consilium adhibere.*" The use of the phrase "regnorum et provinciarum *summam*" shows that a distinction is drawn between affairs of common interest arising out of the Pragmatic Sanction and the "*directe et praecise Hungariam respicientia negotia.*" In the case of the former the Diet wishes due weight to be given to its views ; as to the latter, it wishes to exclude foreign interference. That this is the correct interpretation is shown by the Queen's reply, in which she says that she will be guided by her Hungarian advisers in Hungarian affairs, which shall be dealt with "*legibus Regni stabilita modalitate,*" but that "*cum magis ardua occurrerint pertractanda negotia*" she will summon the Palatine, Primate "*et Regni dominos.*" The "more difficult matters" distinguished from the "*res et negotia Hungarica*" can only be affairs of common interest under the Pragmatic Sanction, *i.e.* mutual defence (the War of Succession was just beginning) and diplomatic questions arising therefrom. Law xi. of the same year, which embodies the result of the negotiations with Maria Theresa, also bears out this interpretation, Her Majesty "*clementer resolvit quod nimirum res et negotia Regni tam intra quam extra Regnum per Hungaros tractabit tractarique faciet.*" See also Law xvi. of 1790, which provides that Hungarians are to be admitted "*in ipsum Status ministerium*" and the "*cancellaria Status intima,*" "*ut tam interna quam externa illa quidem per Hungaros, haec vero cum influxu Hungarorum pertractentur,*" *i.e.* Hungarian affairs are to be managed only by Hungarians, and in foreign affairs Hungary's right of interference is to be recognised. Lustkandl says that before 1723 there was a real union—a confederation of all the realms of the Habsburgs—and cites the terms of the Peace of Vienna, 1606, to prove the statement. But they prove just the contrary, as they provide for the maintenance of "neighbourly relations and mutual love," as if "ancient pacts and treaties" had never been violated "*et ultro citroque commercium Christianorum.*" Further, both parties, Hungary and the Czechs, agree to unite forces against the Turks if a satisfactory peace cannot be arrived at. Such undertakings could not have been necessary if a real union existed (*Adalék*, p. 48 *sq.*). Almost the same words are used by Law xxvi. of 1622, "*De pace cum Ditionibus Regno Hungariae adjacentibus stabilienda et vicinitatis juribus invicem colendis.*" In 1641 delegates were summoned from Hungary and the hereditary provinces to discuss matters connected with preparations for war against the Turks, and the Diet was summoned to choose representatives. The things went on as before, and "neither military history nor the language of diplomacy recognised the existence of a King of Hungary or of a Hungarian army."[1] The laws of 1848 clearly did not contemplate the establishment of a separate Ministry of Foreign Affairs for Hungary. Deák is precise on this point. The first draft of sect. 13 of Law iii. provided that the Minister in attendance on the King should represent the Kingdom in all those *foreign* affairs which jointly interest Hungary and the hereditary provinces, but an amendment was carried omitting the word in italics,[2] and the nature of the "matters which interest the Kingdom in common with the hereditary provinces" is left undefined, and only a reference to the Pragmatic Sanction can supply the needed definition.

No one attempted to deny the existence of affairs of common interest. It will be remembered that the manifesto, the work of Deák, issued in 1847, declared the willingness of the Opposition to work hand-in-hand with Austria in such matters, and its inability to forget either the duties deriving from the Pragmatic Sanction, or the guarantees of independence contained in Law x. of

Palatine, thinking that the proposed joint action would excite the suspicions of the Diet, was careful to point out in his letter of summons that the conference was summoned only for the purpose of taking measures for common defence, and did not commit Hungary to joint action in any other matters. "*Super praedeclarato dumtaxat praecise negotio solo, aliud enim ibidem publice tractari minime patiemur.*"—Kovachich, *Supplementum ad Vestigia Comitiorum,* iii. 367. It is, therefore, misleading to adduce such cases of joint action in proof of Hungary's abandonment of its independence.

[1] Teznei, *Wandlungen,* etc., p. 5. See Lord Palmerston's reply to Pulszky, the Hungarian envoy in London, December 13, 1848 : "The British Government has no knowledge of Hungary *except as one of the component parts of the Austrian Empire* !"—*Correspondence Relating to the Affairs of Hungary, 1847-49,* p. 107. A deliberate misstatement or an unfortunate misconception of the relation existing between the two countries.

[2] Horváth (John), *Közös Ügyek,* p. 153. It must be remembered that in 1848 Austria was a member of the German Confederation, and consequently that Austrian and Hungarian interests were not identical. Hungary could therefore reasonably demand separate diplomatic representation.

1790-91. On November 12 of the same year, Kossuth, speaking from his place in the Diet, said: "I maintain that any one who strives to disseminate the opinion that our country's lawful interests are necessarily in conflict with those of Austria is doing a bad service to the reigning House. I flatly deny the existence of such a conflict, and repeat with absolute conviction the words used by the Diet in 1844, to the effect that the complete development of constitutional life in Hungary is perfectly compatible with the Austrian connexion." During the debate on the subject of the rescript of March 31 the same speaker said that it was undeniable that Hungary had duties to perform towards Austria resulting from the Pragmatic Sanction; and it was indubitably the intention of the new Government to send a commission to Vienna to discuss the nature and the means of fulfilling such obligations.[1] According to Deák, Hungary would have been quite ready in 1848, as well as on the morrow of its greatest military successes the following year, to come to an arrangement on the lines of the Compromise of 1867. "Common affairs," said Deák,[2] "did not now first come into existence . . . if so much Magyar blood had not drenched every battlefield of Europe, the Austrian State would not now exist. If German, Czech, and Moravian had not fought side by side with us right down to Belgrade, perhaps Hungary would to-day be a fragmentary province of Turkey." The laws of 1848 were intended to form the foundation of a permanent superstructure, the details of which required time and much consideration for their elaboration; but the camarilla in Vienna had no intention of laboriously untying the Gordian knot, which it believed could be cut without difficulty. History, as usual, repeated itself. Ever since 1526, the Habsburgs, from time to time, under the pressure of military or financial needs, renounced their policy of

---

[1] Beöthy, o.c. ii. 574.   [2] March 28, 1867.

encroachment on the liberties of Hungary, but as soon as their temporary necessities were satisfied, withdrew the concessions they had been forced to make, or tried to misinterpret their obvious meaning. From time to time Hungary had bowed to the force of circumstances, and temporarily submitted to the curtailment of its constitutional rights. But those rights were destructible only by legislative process, the result of an express agreement between two equal parties, King and Diet, and no such agreement is to be found in the pages of the Corpus Juris Hungarici. The laws of 1848 should have put an end to the long period of autocratic interference, and have assured to Hungary the position as an independent nation to which it was legally entitled but did not in reality occupy since 1526. It would be as idle to deny the fact that the Magyars had lost the chief attributes of independence as to assert with Lustkandl and his imitators that they acquiesced in the principle of incorporation in the hereditary provinces. The whole political history of Hungary from Mohács to 1848 is characterised by an incessant alternation of infringement and revindication, attempted or successful, of constitutional rights which Hungary enjoyed *de jure*, but *de facto* had partially lost. As regards their binding force, you cannot differentiate between one fundamental law and another, nor can you adhere to the advantageous clauses of a contract and reject the inconvenient obligations. The consideration for the acceptance by Hungary of the terms of the Pragmatic Sanction was the guarantee of national independence, subsequently interpreted and confirmed by Law x. of 1790, which declared that "Hungaria est Regnum liberum, et relate ad *totam regiminis formam* independens."

CHAPTER XIV

THE prospect of a new era of civil and religious equality was greeted with general satisfaction. Even the Servians expressed their gratitude for favours to come, and published declarations in their newspapers announcing that thenceforth they would "regard themselves as Hungarian citizens, ready, in consequence of the bonds of loyalty to the Throne, of filial love for the common fatherland, and of unshakable gratitude to the Magyar nation, to live and die for the Magyars."[1] At Temesvár, Servians, Roumanians, and Magyars, Catholic and Lutheran clergy, gave expression to their enthusiasm by singing the Te Deum in the market-place, and the purely Servian population of the frontier districts sent a petition to the Diet begging for complete incorporation in Hungary, and for the immediate abolition of Austrian military control. Since the recognition of the Greek Church all real reason for hostility to Hungary had disappeared, but the idea of Servian nationality still existed, and the Illyrian movement had raised visions of possible membership of a great Slav kingdom, and had created a feeling of discontent, which, though temporarily dormant, was always liable to be waked into life by the intrigues of the anti-Magyar agitators.

The Roumanians, next to the Magyars the most numerous race, though in an actual majority in Transyl-

[1] Horváth, *Huszonöt év*, ii. 674.

51

vania,[1] had never enjoyed any political rights, and were thoroughly discontented with the position which they occupied of complete subjection to their Magyar and German landlords, which the selfishness of the ruling classes had hitherto done nothing to alleviate, and of religious subordination to the Servian hierarchy. The events of March 15 caused a considerable amount of excitement among them, and they hailed with delight the prospect of the abolition of racial and feudal distinctions, which the reunion of Transylvania to Hungary would necessarily have entailed so soon as the March laws received the royal assent. The Transylvanian Diet met on May 30 at Kolozsvár, the streets of which were filled with crowds clamouring for " re-union at any price." Wesselényi proposed the motion which should put an end to the separation from the mother-country which had lasted for three hundred years, and it was carried unanimously. Even the Saxon deputies raised no dissentient voice after Augustus Roth, one of the most influential of their number, had expressed his adherence to the principle of re-union.[2]

At a meeting held at Kolozsvár on March 28 the necessity of having a State language for the sake of administrative unity was admitted, and the Roumanians asked only for permission to use their own idiom in matters of local government and in church and school, but not in the law courts,[3] where Hungarian was to be the official language. The *bona fides* of the Magyars' intentions toward the nationalities is shown by the Bill

[1] 1,050,000 as against 800,000 Magyars and Szeklers and 200,000 Saxons. —Horváth, *Magyarország Függetlenségi Harczának Története*, Geneva, 1865, i. p. 40 *n.* (cited henceforward *Mag. függ. harcz.*). Kossuth (*Schriften aus der Emigration*, ii. 154) puts the numbers of the Saxons at 250,000.

[2] Brote (*Die rumänische Frage in Siebenbürgen und Ungarn*, Berlin, 1895, says that reunion was voted "unter dem Terrorismus der aus Pest verstärkten Massen," but does not offer any evidence in support of a deliberately misleading statement. See Jancsó Benedek, *A Román Nemzetiségi Törekvések Története*, II. 436-447, 468-481, for Roumanian opposition. For the Saxons, *ibid.* 487, 517.

[3] See De Bertha, *Magyars et Roumains devant l'histoire*, p. 390.

introduced by Eötvös, the Minister of Education, which, while maintaining State educational control, provided that the language of instruction should be that of the majority in each district, so that no one could fairly complain that undue preference was given to the language of the predominant race. But Transylvania was destined still to suffer from the effects of its "seven deadly sins"—its three nationalities and four religions. Though the laws of 1848 would have satisfied all legitimate aspirations, it soon became evident that unscrupulous agitators would find ample scope for their intrigues among the uneducated Roumanians, whom, unfit for liberty and yet impatient of control, centuries of subjection had imbued with hatred of their privileged neighbours.[1] Opposition to reunion with Hungary first came from the Saxons, who feared to lose the dominating political position and the economic preponderance they had hitherto enjoyed. Though their representatives had raised no objection to the passing of the Act of Union, a few days later the Austrian flag was hoisted in many parts of the Saxon districts as a protest against absorption, and the report was disseminated among the ignorant Roumanians that the Magyars intended to cast off their King and found a republic, the yoke of which would be far heavier than that which the subordinate races had hitherto borne.

Though the Roumanians of Hungary proper sent

[1] It must not be forgotten that nationality conferred no rights. It was only nobility that did so. Roumanian, Croatian, and Saxon nobles had Magyar serfs who paid the usual feudal dues in money and labour to their alien lords. Of eleven princely families only four were Magyar. The members of thirty-five non-Magyar families had the title of Count, and of ninety-three baronial families thirty-nine were non-Magyar. Two hundred and fifty thousand Saxons enjoyed political rights, from the enjoyment of which thirteen-fourteenths of the Magyar nation were excluded.—Kossuth, *Schriften aus der Emigration*, ii. pp. 150, 154. Under the laws of 1848 the members of the Slav races of Hungary would have enjoyed a constitutional freedom denied to them elsewhere. According to Fényes (*Magyarország Statisztikája*, i. 118), twenty-one thousand Roumanians enjoyed the rights of nobility, *i.e.* two per cent : a small number perhaps, but considering the low level of education among the Roumanians, possibly a fair proportion.

greetings to their brothers across the border, and exhorted them to embrace the advantages which reunion would bring, the separatist movement soon attained formidable proportions.   On May 14 a meeting was held under the presidency of Bishop Siaguna, who at first had posed as a pro-Magyar and partisan of reunion, and a petition was sent to the King requesting a declaration to the effect that the Roumanians were entitled to complete equality in Church and State with other races, and demanding the abolition of feudal dues and tithes without compensation to landlord or tithe owner ; freedom of speech and of the Press ; trial by jury ; the equal distribution of the burden of taxation ; the abolition of the vexatious customs restrictions, and the establishment of elementary and secondary schools at the State's expense. Further, the petition demanded that the decision of the question of reunion should be held 'over until the Roumanians had been recognised as constituting a fourth nation, and as such were represented at the Diet.[1]

If any proof is required of the factitious nature of the anti-Magyar agitation fomented by Siaguna, it is to be found in the terms of this petition, the demands of which were purely superfluous now that provision had been made for the union of all races in one common nation, and that religious and political equality was guaranteed to all. The meeting was composed only of Roumanians who lived under Saxon domination, which is sufficiently indicative of the origin of the agitation.   Those who lived in the Magyar districts of Transylvania were strongly in favour of reunion, and as a counterblast to the above-mentioned petition sent a statement of their

---

[1] The Act of Union received the royal assent on June 11.   The King's reply to the Roumanian petitioners is instructive : "I rejoice to be able to assure you that by the law which gives the same rights and liberties to all the people of Transylvania without distinction of language, race, or religion, the greater part of your desires has been satisfied, consequently your future happiness depends solely on the execution of that law."

wishes to Pressburg expressing "loyalty to the Magyar King, thanks to the spirited champions of liberty, affection to their Magyar brothers, and their attachment to, and sincere confidence in, the first independent Hungarian Ministry." [1] Bishop Alexander Sulucz wrote to Wesselényi on May 22 : " Evil-minded persons are trying to root the dangerous belief in the hearts of the people that the Magyars wish to break away from His Majesty and the House of Austria . . . a thousand devils are trying by this hellish device to cast suspicion on the Magyar nation ; " [2] and Wesselényi, appreciating the situation, wished the feudal burdens to be removed immediately in order to create a feeling of confidence in the good intentions of the Ministry, and to send an influential person, Count Széchenyi for choice, to explain the meaning of reunion ; [3] but before anything could be done, bloody riots occurred in Transylvania, and all possibility of harmonious action was at an end.

Events took much the same course in Croatia. For a brief moment all party wrangles ceased. The twelve points of Pest, and, more especially, the prospective abolition of the relics of feudalism, created the most lively enthusiasm, and cheers greeted every mention of the names of Kossuth and Batthyány, to the disgust of Gáj and his Illyrian party, whose intrigues soon succeeded in changing the tune. An improvised committee summoned a national assembly at Agram on March 25 for the purpose of formulating a programme and sending an address to the King. Not a single Magyar or Servian member of the party in favour of closer union with Hungary was present ; but Baron Kulmer, Kolowrat's emissary, attended the meeting—a sufficient indication of the fact that the camarilla in Vienna was fully alive to the possibility of utilising the separatistic tendencies

[1] Horváth, Mag. függ. harcz. i. 61.
[2] Marczali, A Legujabb Kor Története, p. 632.
[3] Jancsó Benedek, Szabadságharczunk és a Dako-Román Törekvések, 89 sq.

of the various nationalities for its own ends, and was determined that no time should be lost in giving effect to the decision adopted at a meeting held at the house of the Archduke Frederick Charles on March 21. On that date, which, it will be observed, was only four days later than that of the King's formal acceptance of the demands of the Magyars for the appointment of a responsible Ministry, the question of the ultimate consequences of the promised concession to Hungary was debated, and the means of taking away with one hand what the other had given were discussed.[1] Baron Samuel Jósika, the Transylvanian Chancellor, spoke as follows :—
" The Monarchy is shaken to its foundations. Revolutionary movements have taken place in many parts. Croatia and Transylvania are still quiet. It is essential that they should not be disturbed and that our efforts should be directed to the utilisation and proper direction of those elements which are faithful to the Government. Those elements are the Szeklers and the frontier guards of Croatia. I can answer for the former ; for the latter we require a suitable and determined leader of their own race, who is capable of exploiting their devotion, their military organisation, and their injured racial feelings, in the interests of the Throne." [2] He proceeded to propose the appointment to the office of Bán of Baron Jellacsics, who had been recommended to him by Baron Kulmer, Kolowrat's emissary to Croatia, who was hand in glove with Gáj, the champion of Illyrian nationalism, " whose attachment to the reigning House was a mere cloak for dangerous designs." [3] All that was known of Jellacsics was that he was a colonel, a man of energy and decision, and deep in debt—just the person, in Gáj's opinion, to carry out the anti-Magyar designs of the Illyrian party.

[1] The account of this meeting is taken from the memoirs of Szögyény, who was present.—Szögyény Marich László, *Emlékiratai*, p. 65 *sq.*
[2] Szögyény, *o.c.* p. 66   [3] *Ibid.*

The Archduke Stephen protested against the appointment, and Szögyény pointed out the illegality of a nomination disapproved by the Palatine and made behind the back of the responsible Prime Minister, and emphasised the undesirability of exciting the suspicions of the Magyars by underhand proceedings. But the Archduke Louis persuaded the Palatine that the appointment of Jeilacsics was specially desired by His Majesty; opposition was withdrawn, and Szögyény was instructed to delay official notification of the appointment as long as possible.[1] Why? Because it was wished to create the impression that the illegal appointment of Jellacsics was due, not to any secret machinations of the Court party, but to the irresistible demand of the oppressed and enthusiastically loyal nationalities of Croatia.[2]

The meeting held at Agram on March 25, four days after the appointment of Jellacsics had been decided upon, adopted an Address[3] to the King, drawn up by Gáj, lemanding the confirmation of Jellacsics in the office of Bán for which the unanimous wish of the people had designated him; the summoning of a Diet representative of the three united kingdoms of Croatia, Dalmatia, and Slavonia, and of the military frontiers; complete separation from Hungary, of which Croatia had been a dependence for eight hundred years; the appointment of a responsible Ministry; the official use of the national language; yearly meetings of the Diet to be summoned in turn at Agram, Essegg, Zara, and Fiume; and the establishment of a national bank. Henceforth, the United Kingdoms

---

[1] Szögyény, o.c. p. 68. The appointment was gazetted on March 28, the day on which the unsatisfactory rescript (supra, p. 20), was issued, and three days before the rescript of March 31, which apparently withdrew all opposition to the Magyar demands. The double dealing of the Camarilla is plain.

[2] "So griff der Hof unter dem Einflusse der ungarischen Adelsparte zu dem Auskunftsmittel, die Slaven gegen den magyarischen Radikalismus zur Hilfe aufzurufen."—Friedjung, Österreich von 1848, etc., i. 45.

[3] Hartig, Genesis der Revolution, p. 195 sq.

were to have their own national army, which was to swear
allegiance to the new Constitution and to the Crown, and
was to be commanded by native officers using only the
national language.[1]   In future no foreigners were to be
appointed to ecclesiastical or other offices, and the clergy
were to be released from the obligation of celibacy.[2]   On
April 2 the Address was presented by a deputation led by
Gáj to the King, who replied that he was disposed to
take the demands therein formulated into consideration,
and to maintain the municipal privileges[3] of Croatia, but
that he was obliged to draw the deputation's attention to

[1] What the national language of the three United Kingdoms would have
been is questionable. It will be remembered that a few years earlier the
Croatians complained of what Hartig calls the "verfassungsmässige lateinische
Sprache" (*Genesis*, p. 73), though he would have hunted in vain in the pages
of the Corpus Juris for a law which made the official use of Latin compulsory.
He says that the demands of the Croatians amount to the "isolation" of
Croatia, and that they do not fall short of the stereotyped wishes of the other
races striving for freedom (p. 196) ; and on the next page describes Jellacsics
as "fighting at the head of the troops of his nation for the *unity of the
Monarchy*." Croatia, as subsequent history shows, was humbugged into the
belief that it was fighting for national Slav aims, while in fact it was being
utilised for the promotion of the anti-Magyar designs of the camarilla of
Vienna. Hungary could never understand how there could be any hostility to
reforms which did not attempt to oust any living language, but only abolished
a dead one, and did not attempt to force the use of Hungarian for magyarising
purposes on the subordinate nationalities. The necessity of a State language
had been proved by the fact that Latin had been used as such for centuries, and
Hungarian was the only tongue fitted to take its place. If the Magyars had
attempted to magyarise the subject races, they could easily have done so in the
course of a thousand years. That they did not do so was an unfortunate
mistake.

[2] Szögyény, *o.c.* p. 70.

[3] It will be remembered that non-Catholics could not own land in Croatia,
and that real property was subject to only half the burden of taxation borne by
land in Hungary. The origin of this remission was to be found in the fact
that in old days Croatia was specially liable to Turkish attack. The liability
to attack had long ceased, but the privilege was maintained, and the Croatians
feared to lose it. In 1843 Kossuth said at the general meeting of the nobles of
Pest County that if the Croatians were dissatisfied with their connexion with
Hungary they should go in peace, and his suggestion was incorporated in the
instructions given to the deputies of the county. The Croatian deputies
protested and entreated "*per amorem Dei*" that the idea of separation should
be dropped.—Kossuth, *Schriften aus der Emigration*, ii. 177.

their immemorial connexion with Hungary and to the necessity of respecting and maintaining the same. This ambiguous reply could have but two meanings—either that the feeble-witted monarch was still actuated by *bona fide* scruples, entertained conscientious objections to the breach of his promises to Hungary, and was kept in ignorance of the machinations of the camarilla ; or, that the Court party was anxious to lull the suspicions of the Magyars until such time as affairs in Italy had assumed a more reassuring aspect and Jellacsics had perfected his preparations for an open attack on Hungary in the interests of autocracy. The forces at the disposal of the new Bán consisted of the malcontents of the Illyrian party, the reactionaries who feared the loss of the profits to be derived from the maintenance of the feudal system, the Catholics who dreaded the increase of Protestant influence in Croatia, and the ignorant masses who had no idea that their nationalistic aspirations were to be exploited in the interests of Austrian domination, of which racial hatred, religious bigotry, and pocket patriotism were the blind instruments.

Mayerhofer, the Austrian consul at Belgrade, was untiring in his efforts to stir up hatred against the Magyars and promised the establishment of a separate Voyvodina such as that to which the Servians had aspired in the reign of Leopold II. Bishop Rajasics, the recognised head of the Serbs, whose apparent enthusiasm for the Magyar cause had led him a few days earlier to stick a cockade of Hungarian colours in his hat and to accompany the deputation sent by the Pressburg Diet to Vienna on March 14, was in close communication with both Mayerhofer and Gáj, who exhorted the Slav races to show their affection for the dynasty by shaking off the yoke of the "Asiatic tyrants." The underhand character of the agitation is shown by the fact that the petition presented by a Servian deputation to the Hungarian Diet on April 8 heartily accepts the principle of the predominance of the Magyar race and the Magyar language [1] in all matters of Church and State, but requests that the Serb dialect may continue to be used in private and local affairs. Not a word referred to the desire for territorial separation. The deputation warmly thanked the Diet for its fatherly care for Servian interests, and expressed its desire to live and die for Hungary and its Constitution ; but at a subsequent private interview with Kossuth, George Stratimirovics, a member of the deputation, raised the question of separation, and threatened that if the Servians' wish for independence was not acceded to they would "apply elsewhere." "In that case," replied Kossuth, "the sword must decide between us"—an unfortunate remark, which, as Horváth says, "poured oil on the glowing embers of passion."[2] The smouldering fires of discontent burst into flame, and within a few days in all Servian districts, armed mobs were attacking both Magyar and German landowners with impartial fury—an improvised prelude to the serious business of the anti-Magyar campaign, for which their leaders and the wire-pullers of Vienna had resolved to utilise the forces of race hatred and barbarism.

Nothing is more striking than the contrast exhibited by the political wisdom and constructive energy of the Hungarian Ministry and the disorderly *naïveté* of Austrian Liberalism. In Vienna the new Press laws and the unaccustomed freedom of public meeting opened the door to revolutionary licence. Violent speeches were made attacking the Emperor and the monarchical institution. A strong feeling was evinced in favour of union with Germany, and the German colours were everywhere to be

---

[1] At the beginning of the session of 1847, the Croatian deputies officially declared that though, in accordance with Law ii. of 1844, they were entitled to continue to speak Latin in the Diet, they would speak Hungarian "*in order to show the love and affection existing between Hungary and Croatia and to draw tighter the constitutional bonds which united the two countries.*"

[2] *Mag. függ. harcz.* i. 136 *sq.*

seen instead of the familiar black and yellow of the Habsburgs.[1] No one knew to whom he should look for orders, whether to the Ministry, to the Reichsrath, to the Archduke John, or to Frankfurt. No one knew whether Austria was to continue to be an independent monarchy, or was to become a subordinate part of the German confederation. Of the Ministry appointed on March 17, five members quickly retired, including Ficquelmont, the Minister for Foreign Affairs, a creature of Metternich, and especially odious to the Progressives and the students. Pillersdorf, the only moderately liberal Minister, was convinced that the sole way to avoid a recrudescence of violent disorder was to bring the promised Constitution into being as quickly as possible. The Emperor had undertaken, on March 15, to convene a constituent assembly, which should discuss the popular requirements, and decide as to the form which the new representative Government should take ; but the Ministers persuaded the Court party that a less dangerous course would be to produce a cut-and-dried Constitution, and to inform the people that it could have that or none. The Constitution, which Hartig[2] describes as " the bastard child of Viennese Radicalism and of ministerial vanity," by no means answered to the expectation of the reformers. The constitution of the Upper House, which carefully provided against all possibility of the infiltration of a Liberal element, aroused general indignation, which found its expression in " Katzenmusik " and less harmless demonstrations. The students and the National Guards forced their way into the Palace and the Council Chamber, and on May 16, an Imperial Proclamation announced the

---

[1] Hartig, *Genesis der Revolution*, pp. 184, 185. A resolution was passed by the Germans of Vienna and communicated to the Emperor that "only a firm and intimate union of interests with the common German fatherland can win back the old and oft-proved confidence."—*Ibid.* p. 184 ; see Stiles (an eye-witness of the revolution in Vienna), *o.c.* i. 119.

[2] *Genesis der Revolution*, p. 217.

withdrawal of the still-born Constitution and the convocation of a single constituent assembly.   It was evident that
the Emperor was sitting on a volcano which might fail to
respect his sacred person.   It was resolved that he should
retire to the cooler atmosphere of the Tyrol.   Just before
the issue of the proclamation His Majesty took an evening
drive to Schönbrunn, and only when he arrived there told
the coachman to drive on to Innsbruck, and sent a
message to the Minister of War informing him that the
Kaiser " had decided to make a journey to the Tyrolese
mountains for the benefit of his health." [1]

The Emperor's flight marks the beginning of the
counter-revolution.   The absence of the Court was disadvantageous to the pocket interests of the shopkeeping
class, and signs of a revulsion of feeling in favour of the
old order of things encouraged the trembling Ministry
to order the troops to disband the Academic Legion.   The
result was that the people believed that their leaders had
been bought by the reactionary camarilla which had
determined to deprive them of their promised liberties
by force of arms, and that Prince Windischgrätz was
advancing on Vienna at the head of a large army.[2]
Barricades were hastily erected, the Ministry was paralysed by terror ; a committee chosen from among the
students, the National Guards, and the general body of
citizens constituted the sole recognised authority, and
" the Kaiserstadt groaned under an ochlocracy, a parallel
to which is scarcely to be found in history." [3]

Prague also became the scene of violence and disorder.
At this epoch of general ferment, Bohemia apparently
had only two courses open to it : either to lend an ear to
the blandishments of Frankfurt, which summoned Czech
representatives to its councils with a view to the incorporation of Bohemia in the German confederation, or to

---

[1] *Genesis der Revolution*, p. 244.   Anton Springer, *o.c.* ii. 313.
[2] Hartig, *Genesis der Revolution*, p. 246.   [3] *Ibid.* p. 181.

stake its future on the promised Constitution, which was
to cement the union of all the constituent peoples of the
Austrian monarchy.   Its choice fell on a third alternative :
the maintenance of its Slav individuality and the relaxation
to the utmost of the bonds which united it with the
hereditary provinces.   On May 31 the National Committee summoned a meeting at Prague of all the Slavs
inhabiting the kingdom, with a view to the adoption of
measures which should safeguard Bohemia's interests.
With the consent, improperly given, of the Governor,
Count Leo Thun, who seems to have been actuated by
the desire to exclude as far as possible the influence of
the Viennese Ministry,[1] a provisional Government was
appointed, which included in its members Palacky, the
historian (the author of the much-quoted saying as to the
necessity of inventing an Austria if one did not exist
already), and the draft of a Constitution was drawn up,
which practically reduced the connexion with the Austrian
monarchy to a personal union, the result of the identity
of the Bohemian King and the Austrian Emperor.   The
prospect was not pleasing to the non-Slav inhabitants of
Prague.   Czech and German clubs came into violent contact, and Prince Windischgrätz, the military commander,
called out the troops to put an end to brawling.   On
June 12, a section of a Slav organisation attempted to give
expression to its dislike of the Prince's methods by
treating him to a cats' concert outside his head-quarters, in
spite of the protests of the sentries.   A shot was fired by
some unknown person from a neighbouring house, and
Princess Windischgrätz, who was standing at a window at
her husband's side, fell dead.   After two days of street
fighting, in which the Germans helped the troops, order,
à la Warsaw, again reigned in Prague.   The effect of
Windischgrätz's " methods of barbarism " was not
confined to Bohemia.   A useful hint was given to the

[1] Hartig, *Genesis der Revolution*, p. 255.

camarilla as to the means to be adopted, and the man to be employed, for the execution of its reactionary policy.

In the meanwhile Hungary was proceeding with the huge task of reorganising the Government in all its branches. The position of the new Ministry was not altogether enviable. Not one of its members had had any experience of the routine work of governmental departments. Perhaps it was well that it should be so. The fact that the old officials, who were used to their ruts and disinclined to leave them, had to be retained, prevented the adoption of ill-considered measures and a surrender to the wishes of certain sections of the people, which thought that the appointment of a national Government meant the immediate cure of all ills and the building of a new Rome in a day.[1] With the exception of a certain amount of Jew-baiting, due to the usual economic causes, no serious breaches of the peace took place.[2] The nobles accepted the new position of affairs with hardly a murmur. In a few cases, the peasants, temporarily intoxicated with the new wine of liberty, demanded with threats the immediate division of the nobles' land ; but such local disorders as occurred were not of a sufficiently serious character to require the intervention of the military. Except for a few juvenile doctrinaires, no one thought for a moment of the possibility of definite separation from Austria, and of breaking with the dynasty. The maintenance of the personal union and of the Pragmatic Sanction was looked upon as a sacred obligation, and the fact of the King and of his two immediate successors in title having been present at the recent dissolution of the Diet was considered to amount to the final consecration of the new order.

If any proof is wanted of the pacific intentions of the Magyars, it is to be found in the financial and military situation of the country. When Kossuth became Minister

[1] Pulszky, *Életem és Korom*, i. 314.
[2] Eötvös, *Die Garantien der Macht und Einheit Österreichs*, Leipzig, 1859.

of Finance the Treasury contained only 480,000 florins, while the estimated expenditure for the remaining six months of the year amounted to 28,000,000, and the receipts to 10,000,000.[1] Military affairs were in a still more unsatisfactory position, as the Austrian Government would not allow Mészáros to return from Italy to take charge of the Ministry of Home Defence to which he had been appointed. Nearly all Hungarian troops were absent from the country, and no reliance, in case of troubles arising with the Croatians, could be placed on the Austrian regiments quartered in Hungary, more especially on the higher officers, who, owing to the traditions under which they had been trained, and to fear of the diminution of Austria's military strength, resented the prospect of a dual control. The Ministers, especially Batthyány, were determined to keep on strictly constitutional ground, and the Throne did not begin to tremble until the conviction was forced on the country that the Croatian rebellion was receiving secret encouragement and active support from the Court of Vienna.[2] Rebellion is the correct expression, for Croatia had for centuries past formed a subordinate part of the realms of the Sacred Crown, pronounced to

---

[1] The deficit was to be supplied partly by imposing a temporary tax on spirits, partly by the proceeds of taxation of the hitherto exempted classes. The estimate of expenditure for the coming year was 62,000,000 florins. Kossuth emphasised the necessity of establishing a national bank, not only for State purposes, but to assist private enterprise. He appealed to the patriotism of the well-to-do to find the bullion required as a reserve against the note issue, rendered necessary by the one-sided tariff system which had drained the country of cash. Every one contributed what he could in cash and silver-plate, and an issue of 12,000,000 florins' worth of one- and two-florin notes was made possible to answer pressing requirements.—Beőthy, o.c. iii. 239 sq.

[2] Wessenberg wrote on July 12, 1849 : " Die Politik Batthyány's resümierte sich ungefähr in den Worten : 'Ungarn ist der österreichischen Monarchie koordiniert, aber nicht subordiniert.' So äusserte sich auch der ausgezeichnete Rechtsgelehrte Deák, der mich mit Batthyány gesuchte. Bei alledem sah man beiden an, dass sie die Unmöglichkeit des gegenwärtigen neuen Zustandes der Gesamtmonarchie anerkannten und in ihnen der Wunsch rege war, ihre Stellung in ein freundschaftliches Verhältnis zur Kaiserlichen Regierung zu bringen."

be for ever inseparable by the Pragmatic Sanction, the
benefits of which the Habsburgs could not claim to enjoy
unless they fulfilled the corresponding obligations.

In spite of the existence of an independent Hungarian
Ministry confirmed by the King, the Government of
Vienna was determined at all costs to retain an undivided
control of financial, military, and foreign affairs.   It
pretended that it had not been officially apprised of any
change involving the removal of such matters from its
sphere of influence.   The Minister of War instructed
commanding officers in Hungary to take instructions only
from Vienna, and the Minister of Finance gave orders that
the produce of the Hungarian mines should, as hitherto,
be forwarded to the Austrian Treasury.[1]   A royal rescript
of April 7 raised the question of Hungary's acceptance of
liability for part of Austria's public debt, contracted
without the sanction of the Diet, solely for the benefit of
the Habsburgs, and of their hereditary provinces.   The
rescript[2] in question did not, in fact, suggest that Hungary
was under any obligation to assume the proposed responsibility for the annual payment of 10,000,000, florins, one-
fourth of Austria's liability in respect of interest, but based
the claim solely on the "high-minded disposition of the
Magyars."   The fact remains, however, that Austria's
creditors looked on Hungary as forming part of their
security, which would be considerably impaired by the
latter country's refusal to give the required guarantee.
Consequently, in spite of the disordered state of its finances,
due to the period of transition from one form of Government to another, the view that Hungary made a tactical
mistake in neglecting considerations of expediency, and
refusing to budge from the strictly constitutional position,
is possibly justified.   The Palatine entreated the Viennese
Government not to insist on its demand at the present

---

[1] Horváth, *Mag. függ. harcz.* i. 97.
[2] Horváth (John), *Közös Ügyek*, 147.

juncture, and pointed out that in any case the question at issue was not one for the offhand decision of the Austrian Ministry, but should stand over for discussion by the two Parliaments. That of Hungary would in all probability have ultimately consented to undertake the suggested liability, if it had been convinced of the straightness and sincerity of Austrian intentions, but that it could not be since the appointment of Jellacsics ; and even Deák, the personification of equity and moderation, was unable, in existing circumstances, to counsel the acceptance of an unnecessary obligation.

The military question was the most difficult of all, as the revolutionary attitude of the Liberals of Vienna, and the position of affairs in northern Italy, made it' essential that the King should not be hampered as regards the disposal of the military forces of his dominions. The war in Italy was very unpopular in Hungary, which agreed with the predominating Austrian view, from which the Viennese Ministry was not averse,[1] that Lombardy should be handed over to Charles Albert, and that the new Italian State so to be formed should compensate the Habsburgs for the loss of a province by taking over the liability for a proportionate 'part of the Austrian national debt. As Lombardy formed a part of the Habsburg dominions, the integrity of which Hungary was bound by the Pragmatic Sanction to maintain, there can be no doubt that participation in the Italian war was strictly incumbent on the Magyars, but at the same time the fact that all their troops were liable to be required at any moment to defend their frontiers against the attacks of Croatians inspired by Vienna morally absolved them from their obligation. The belief was gaining ground that, if once the war in Italy were brought to a successful end, Radetzky and his army would be sent to Hungary, to deprive the Magyars, by force, of their constitutional

[1] Marczali, *A Legujabb Kor Története*, p. 644.

rights, and that it would be madness to denude the country of troops[1] when only the uncertainty of the issue of the Italian campaign, and the want of men and money, prevented the camarilla from throwing off the mask and openly making common cause with Jellacsics and his blind instruments of autocracy.[2]

Batthyány and his fellow-ministers were quite aware of the dangers which threatened their country, and were anxious to emphasise as much as possible the identity of its interests with those of its King. The belief was entertained .hat in view of the revolutionary ferment in Vienna, the King could be safe only in Hungary, and that the security of his Austrian throne could be guaranteed only by reliance on the Magyars, and by a frank recognition of the true meaning of the Pragmatic Sanction and of the binding force of his recent undertakings, more especially now that the extremists of Vienna were clamouring for absorption in a greater Germany. When the riotous behaviour of the capital drove the King to undertake his excursion to Innsbruck, a petition was sent to him entreating him to take refuge in the midst of his faithful Magyars. An undecided answer was returned, so the Palatine, Széchenyi, and Eötvös proceeded to Innsbruck and obtained a promise that the King would transfer himself and his family to Budapest so soon as Parliament voted the

[1] At this time there were only 18,000 troops in Hungary, mostly German and Czech, but though the country was without its natural defenders, the Austrian Government demanded that 40,000 recruits should be raised and sent to Italy.—Pulszky, *Életem és Korom*, i. 311.

[2] At a meeting held on March 25 in Vienna, attended by the Archdukes Louis and Charles, Windischgrätz, Ficquelmont, Kolowrat, Hartig (the author of *Genesis der Revolution*), Josika, and Szögyény, at which the concessions made to Hungary and a message of the Archduke Stephen proposing the sending of troops to Pest to repress disorder were discussed, Louis asked Ficquelmont if he had a sufficient military force at his command, and a representative of the Treasury if he had sufficient money. "A decided no was the answer to both questions."—Szögyény, *Emlékiratai*, p. 66. This was four days after the illegal appointment of Jellacsics, so it is obvious why the men and money were wanted.

desired forty thousand recruits for the purposes of the war in Italy. · In order that Hungary's fear of denuding itself of all means of defence might be allayed, an undertaking was given that a stop should be put to croatian and Servian excesses, and that the treasonable activity of Jellacsics should be effectively discouraged.   Whether the King was sincerely disposed to accept Hungary's invitation, and to shake off the influence of the camarilla, or whether he too only wished to gain time and obtain the desired recruits is uncertain, but in any case Jellacsics continued to refuse to have any communication with the Hungarian Government, or with the Palatine, the official representative of the Crown.   On April 22 he pronounced the final disruption of the ties which bound Croatia, Dalmatia, Slavonia, and Fiume to Hungary, appointed members of the Illyrian party to all official posts, and stirred up the rougher elements of the population to persecute the local Magyars, whose countrymen, so the Croatian clergy declared from the pulpit, intended to rob the Slavs of their property, religion, and language, to kill their children and to violate their wives.[1]   The youth of Hungary urged the Government to take energetic measures for the suppression of Jellacsics and his myrmidons, and no doubt the Ministry would have been justified in hanging him as a traitor, but unfortunately it had not the necessary means at its disposal of restoring order and of suppressing the propagandists of treason.   Moreover, Batthyány, knowing that the Bán had the reactionary camarilla at his back, feared to do anything that would involve a departure from the position of strict legality hitherto maintained, so contented himself with going to Vienna in company with the Palatine, to protest against Croatian misfeasance.   The result of his remonstrance was the issue of royal instructions to Jellacsics to submit himself in all matters pertaining to his office to the

[1] Horváth, *Mag. függ. harcz.* i. 168.

responsible Hungarian Ministry, and a statement of the King's "unshakable determination to maintain the unity of the dominions of the Sacred Crown." Further, permission was given to the Archduke Stephen to send a Royal Commissioner to Croatia with instructions to impeach Jellacsics on a charge of high treason. The Bán was, therefore, between the devil and the deep sea, and had to choose between unconditional submission to the Pest Ministry, which might entail unpleasant consequences, and open rebellion. Knowing that he could rely on the support of the camarilla, whose agent he was, he chose the latter alternative, got up a riot at Agram, pronounced the emancipation of the peasants, and issued a proclamation to the effect that whosoever should ascribe the passing of the liberation laws to the Magyar nobility, or describe the Croatians as Hungarian citizens, should suffer exemplary punishment.[1]

Preparations for an attack on Hungary were made with all possible expedition, on the ground that the King was no longer a free agent, and that it was the duty of the Slav population to free him from the undue influence of the Magyars. Hrabovsky, the royal commissioner sent to impeach the Bán, did nothing, and his inactivity, equivalent to connivance with treason, would seem to confirm Horváth's statement[2] that Jellacsics produced justification for his actions in the shape of letters from the Archduke Francis Charles and the Archduchess Sophia, which ordered him to take no notice of any instructions which might emanate from the King, but to proceed with his preparations for an active campaign. In the meanwhile,

[1] Horváth, *Mag. függ. harcz.* i. 164. Pejakovics, *Aktenstücke zur Geschichte des kroatisch-slavonischen Landtages,* 1848. Vienna, 1861.

[2] *Mag. függ. harcz.* i. 179. "That the imperial family encouraged the insurrections against Hungary was generally believed; and Jellacsics himself wrote to this effect in a letter, dated the 4th of June and addressed to the frontier regiments stationed in Italy."—Stiles, *o.c.* ii. 64 *n.* See also Anton Springer, *o.c.* ii. 435 *n.*, and Friedjung, *o.c.* i. 70.

the Hungarian Government was doing everything possible to satisfy legitimate aspirations. Arrangements were made for the establishment of a separate Croatian governmental department, official positions were left unfilled with a view to the appointment of Croatian candidates [1] and the right of the Croatians to use their own language in all matters of local government received fresh confirmation. Jellacsics, summoned by the King to Innsbruck to give explanations of his conduct,[2] took no notice of the summons. Batthyány, aware of the fact that but for the promised support of influential personages in Vienna, Jellacsics would not dare to disobey a royal command, saw that the time had come to put an end to an ambiguous position, and threatened to resign his office unless he were given a free hand in Croatia. His resignation would have produced such an uproar in Hungary, and might have had such a serious effect on the war in Italy, recruits for which were urgently needed, that the camarilla was obliged to give way to some extent, and the feeble King was allowed to issue a rescript,[3] commanding the Bán, for the second time, on pain of impeachment as a traitor, to take his orders from the Hungarian Ministry.

We have been mistaken in you Croatians and Slavonians, who have shared the fortunes of Hungary under the same Crown for eight hundred years, and *have to thank your union with that country for the constitutional liberty which you alone among the Slavs have enjoyed for centuries. We have been mistaken in you who have always had an equal share of Hungary's rights and privileges . . . to whom the last Diet of the Kingdom of Hungary and of the adjoining countries granted, in accordance with Our royal will, full participation in all the blessings of constitutional freedom, and equality of rights.* The legislative body of the Hungarian Kingdom has abolished the urbarial dues in your countries just as in Hungary,

---

[1] See the document presented by the Cabinet to the Archduke John, July 4.—*Mag. függ. harcz.* i. 278 *sq.*

[2] Hartig, *Genesis der Revolution*, Appendix xv. 1.

[3] *Ibid.* Appendix xv. 2, June 10.

and the serfs among you have been relieved of all burdens, and converted into free landowners. . . . As in Hungary, so in your own countries, the benefits of constitutional representative government have been extended to the people, in consequence whereof, not only the nobility, but all members of the community, including the frontier regiments, take part, through their elected representatives, in the general legislative assembly, as well as in your municipal gatherings, your direct participation in which enables you to promote your national welfare. Hitherto the nobility has borne but a small portion of the public burdens. The law has now provided for the equal distribution of such burdens among all, without distinction of class, and thereby a heavy load has been removed from your shoulders. Attempts have been made by means of the dissemination of malevolent and lying reports to inspire you with anxiety with respect to your nationality and your municipal rights. They are in no way threatened ; on the contrary, they are extended, and strengthened, and made secure against all attacks ; for the use of your mother tongue, in place of the Latin language which you have hitherto been accustomed to use, is assured to you by law for ever, not only in church and school, but in your public meetings as well. Calumniators have tried to induce you to believe that the Magyars suppress your language, or wish to hinder its development. *We, Ourselves, assure you that these suggestions are absolutely false,* and that your efforts to improve your mother tongue and extend its use in place of that of the dead Latin language receive due recognition. The legislature will support you in your efforts in this direction, and will provide for the proper maintenance of the priests, to whom are entrusted the care of your souls and the religious instruction of your children. During eight hundred years you have been united to the Magyars, and *during the whole of that period the legislation has always behaved with due regard for your nationality.* How can you therefore believe that that same legislation now adopts a hostile attitude towards your mother tongue, which it has consistently protected during eight centuries. . . . We have sworn by the living God that we will not only Ourselves preserve the integrity of the Hungarian Crown, and maintain the Constitution and laws, but will make others do the same. . . . Hear and obey the gracious word of your King, whose royal power will at all times protect your nationality and your rights, but who is determined to maintain with all his might the dignity of his Hungarian crown and of the law, no matter from what quarter attack may come.

Truth will out, sometimes, even in a Habsburg proclamation. Either the description given in the above rescript by Ferdinand and his advisers of the relations which subsisted between the Magyars and the Slav nationalities for the past 800 years is a correct one, in which case the statements of Gáj, Jellacsics, and others were baseless calumnies, and their subsequent actions and those of their Habsburg supporters were totally unjustifiable, to use no stronger expression ; or that description was deliberately false and misleading, and was issued for the purpose of throwing dust in the eyes of the Budapest Cabinet, and of gaining time for the completion of plans for the destruction of Hungary's independence and territorial integrity, which every Habsburg King (with one exception) had sworn to maintain.[1]

Jellacsics at last obeyed Ferdinand's command and went to Innsbruck ; but the fact that he behaved not as a person who had been branded as a traitor by his King, and had come to explain and excuse his mutinous conduct, but as a Slav plenipotentiary commissioned to negotiate with the Hungarian Ministry on equal terms, shows that the royal summons and the Bán's compliance were merely an episode in the comedy which considerations of expediency

[1] "Upon this document the Hungarians laid great stress, and vainly supposed that such a blow inflicted by the Emperor upon the very 'head and front' of that rebellious movement must subdue all opposition, and that peace and order would soon be restored to the country. But they were imposed upon by the treachery of the Court ; there was no sincerity in the act, and as subsequent events fully established, the manifesto was a mere blind for their deception. Had the Imperial Court considered him in the light in which it denounced him, Jellacsics would have been in the presence of his God instead of that of his Emperor, or, even if regarded as less criminal than originally charged, he would at least have been condemned to the castle of Olmütz or Spielberg, rather than called to the imperial palace ; while, on his own part, the Bán would never have ventured to disobey with such audacity, had he not been sustained secretly by the approbation and connivance of the Court."— Stiles, *o.c.* ii. 64.

required to be prolonged for a still uncertain period : that is to say, until affairs in Italy had taken a decided turn for the better. He stated that his actions had all been in accordance with the spirit of Sect. 2 of Law iii. of 1848, which refers to the unity of the Crown and the maintenance of the connexion with the Empire ; and that if such unity and connexion were maintained he was quite willing to come to terms with the Hungarian Government, provided Croatia were guaranteed against the continuance of a system of oppression, which, as we have seen, the King's manifesto declared to be non-existent. The falsity of the Bán's statement is proved by the terms of the petition which he presented on behalf of the Croatians. " The Croatian people cannot recognise the existing Hungarian Government. His Majesty is therefore requested to annul all its dispositions relative to Croatia, Dalmatia, and Slavonia, and to give those countries a separate and independent Government under the presidency of the Bán." The petition further demanded that the control of all military, financial, and commercial matters should be vested in the Austrian authorities, and that the official language should be Slav [1] —presumably that dialect which Gáj had selected for the use of the " Illyrian nation " as being most closely allied to the Servian and Croatian languages. The real object of Jellacsics, and the fact that his devotion to the cause of the Slav nationalities was fictitious—assumed merely for the purpose of concealing the fact that he was the agent and mouthpiece of the camarilla, were disclosed by the ungarded statement [2] made by the Bán to Batthyány, to the effect that the two essential points of his programme were the centralisation of military and financial control

---

[1] This shows the fictitious nature of the agitation of a few years back in favour of the retention of Latin.

[2] Recorded by Pulszky, who was present at the interview, *Életem és Korom*, i. 330 *sq.*

and the assumption by Hungary of part of the burden of Austria's public debt.   At the same interview the Bán enlarged upon the necessity of sending more soldiers to Italy, and expressed his willingness to abandon the position he had assumed with regard to the Servian question if the Hungarian Parliament would vote the desired recruits. In other words, the Servians should be left to shift for themselves if Hungary would consent to abandon the chief attributes of independence.

Jellacsics, reinstated in his office, and sure of his position now that the tide had begun to show signs of turning in Italy in Austria's favour, returned in triumph to Agram to be acclaimed dictator by his dupes, and to perfect his preparations for an attack on Hungary in the interests of despotism, which he knew would make short work of Slav aspirations if Lombards and Magyars could first be reduced to submission.   The prospects of selfish ambition had undergone a change.   Hitherto Jellacsics had posed as the champion of Serbo-Croatian separatistic ideals, which, if the threatened fusion of the hereditary provinces with the German Confederation took place, he might possibly have exploited for his own benefit ; but now that order had been restored in Prague, and Radetzky's Italian campaign seemed likely to be crowned with success, he was quick to realise the fact that the unification rather than the disruption of the realms of the Habsburgs would best serve his personal interests. Baron Kulmer, the Bán's confidant and mouthpiece, was appointed Minister without portfolio, and five days later his colleagues in the Austrian Cabinet wrote to the Hungarian Ministry urging it to come to terms with Jellacsics at any price, and stating that if it failed to do so they would be compelled to "renounce neutrality towards Hungary." [1]   In its reply the Hungarian Ministry drew attention to the fact that "renunciation

[1] Horváth, *Mag. függ. harcz.* i. 274.

of neutrality can have no meaning unless the Viennese Cabinet renounces obedience to the Austrian Emperor, who is at the same time King of Hungary, for otherwise, as the two crowns are united on one and the same head, and as the Austrian Emperor cannot make war on himself, his Ministry cannot renounce neutrality towards the Magyar King." Hungary would have been amply justified in regarding such a proclamation of the Court's solidarity with the rebellious subjects of the Sacred Crown as a declaration of war, and as a final disruption of the bonds of the Pragmatic Sanction, but Batthyány and his colleagues were determined that the camarilla should thereafter have no excuse for alleging that the Magyar had made no attempt to arrive at a peaceful settlement of debatable questions, and wrote to the Archduke John[1] that they had not only done nothing to justify the hostility of the southern Slavs, but had actually guaranteed them the enjoyment of liberties *which were unknown to the constituent races of Austria*. The Cabinet requested the Archduke to go to Agram to reprove the seditious and to explain to the misinformed the nature and effect of the new laws, and expressed its readiness to accede to all reasonable demands which the elected representatives of the Slav nationalities should present to the Hungarian Parliament, provided that they did not involve the disruption of the Hungarian monarchy; for no one was prepared to buy peace at the expense of territorial integrity. "The Magyar nation will be just and equitable both in peace and war, but cowardly it will never be." No reply was received to this document, and it became more and more evident that nothing short of a disaster to the Austrian arms in Italy would induce the camarilla[2] to abandon its intention of forcing Hungary to surrender the gains of the past three months.

[1] July 4. For this document see Horváth, *Mag. függ. harcz.* i. 278-84.
[2] Wessenberg, the Austrian Minister, said that there were two Govern-

The new Parliament met on July 5. The elections, which passed off quietly, showed the nation to be strongly in favour of the March laws. Members of the old Opposition were re-elected in nearly every case. Few Conservatives, and only forty representatives of the Radical section, which considered that the Government was not sufficiently advanced, sufficiently "national" in its views, secured seats. No idea of breaking away from Austria, or of weakening the connexion resulting from the Pragmatic Sanction, occurred to any one. All parts of the kingdom, with the exception of Croatia, sent their representatives. The places of the old retrograde Conservative magnates were, for the most part, occupied by younger and more progressive men, who were not averse to the idea of reforming the Upper House, a proposal to give effect to which was introduced early in the session. Indications of a split in the Cabinet were not wanting. Batthyány and his followers were anxious to avoid civil war at any price, and were agreed as to the necessity of voting the recruits required for the Italian campaign, while Kossuth and Szemere were unwilling to consent to the proposed grant so long as the Austrian Government

nents in Austria : "The public one of which he was a member and the secret one or so-called Camarilla."—Beöthy, *o.c.* ii. 573. Of this latter the Archduchess Sophia was the moving spirit. She was in close communication with Bach, who was either deliberately betraying his old friends the Liberals, or was trying to run with the hare and hunt with the hounds.—Helfert, *Die Thronbesteigung des Kaisers Franz Josef*, p. 70, *n.* The Hungarian deputation which went to see Ferdinand in September, wrote : "The Magyar nation does not doubt the existence of a conspiracy in the neighbourhood of your Majesty, which is gambling with the new liberties of the people and with the throne which your Majesty has inherited, the object of whose reactionary efforts is its own miserable, personal, profit." In the Holy of Holies of the camarilla were, besides the Archduchess Sophia, the Empress and Windischgrätz, all of whom possessed a spirit of determination in which the Archducal members were for the most part lacking. The outer camarilla consisted of Lobkowitz, the Emperor's A.D.C., and Count Grünne, that of Francis Joseph, and Bombelles, the Master of Ceremonies.—Beöthy, *o.c.* ii. 193, 205. As to the influence of the Archduchess Sophia and of the camarilla, see also Friedjung, *Österreich von 1848 bis 1860*, i. 67-9, 105-109, 110, 111.

refused to lay its cards on the table and to play a straight game. Kossuth, who at one time believed that Austria was fated soon to disappear in a united Germany, and that Hungary would stand alone, was now convinced of the impossibility of avoiding a struggle for the maintenance of his country's independence. The strength of his position lay in the fact that the other Ministers feared his resignation, which would have made the continued existence of the Cabinet an impossibility. On July 1, Kossuth's *Journal*, embued with the same spirit as that which had animated the *Pesti Hirlap* of earlier days, began to appear, and formed, rather than reflected, public opinion. In Parliament, though many of his colleagues were disposed to resent the dominating influence he exerted both in and outside the House, which they felt to be incompatible with the maintenance of peace with Austria, Kossuth was practically the uncontrolled mouthpiece of the Government, and Batthyány was hardly more than its figurehead.[1] Such opposition as was, in fact, from time to time raised to Kossuth's proposals was apparently due rather to a desire for oratorical distinction than to a belief in its inherent utility.[2]

Ferdinand was requested to attend the opening of Parliament, but the Palatine replied on his behalf, " that His Majesty's serious illness prevented him from giving effect to his paternal intention of opening and presiding over the councils of the representatives of the Hungarian nation." The King's Speech stated that :

His Majesty, desiring to promote the happiness of his Kingdom, followed the promptings of his own heart, when, during the last session of the Diet, he ratified, at the request of his faithful Magyars, those laws which the public welfare and the spirit of the times demanded. To his deep regret, the

---

[1] See Beksics, *Kemény Zsigmond A Forradalom s a Kiegyezés*, Budapest, 1883, p. 56 *sq.* ; and Horváth, *Mag. függ. harcz.* i. 287 *sq.*

[2] Marczali, *A Legujabb Kor Története*, p. 655, and *note*.

King has been apprised of the fact that in the southern districts of the Kingdom and in the annexed parts, evil-intentioned agitators have stirred up His Majesty's subjects of diverse languages and religions with lying and alarming reports, and with a calumnious statement to the effect that the said laws did not owe their origin to His Majesty's free will, and that they, the said agitators, have refused to obey the same, with His Majesty's knowledge and in the interests of his House. His Majesty therefore solemnly declares his irrevocable resolution to defend the unity of the Crown and the integrity of the Kingdom against all attack whether from within or from without, and to maintain the laws which he has sanctioned.

Nothing could have been more satisfactory than this speech if it had in any way represented Ferdinand's real views and intentions. It refers with regret to the fact that the war in Italy was not yet over, but says no word on the subject of the desired recruits, a reference to which would have resulted in Kossuth's retirement and the disintegration of the Cabinet. It was unfortunate that Hungary refused to fulfil its strict obligations in this matter, for there can be no doubt that the opinion of Batthyány, Eötvös, and Deák was the correct one: namely, that though it was no part of the country's duty to join Austria in a war of aggression, Lombardy was an integral part of the King's dominions, and, therefore, Hungary could not refuse to take part in its defence without incurring the reproach of having neglected the obligations imposed by the Pragmatic Sanction. The Minutes of the Ministerial Council [1] declared that the absence from the King's Speech of reference to the sending of troops to Italy "should in no wise be taken to indicate the existence of a desire on the part of the Government to throw doubt on Hungary's obligation, deriving from the Pragmatic Sanction and from the terms of the second section of Law iii. of 1848, to defend His Majesty against foreign attack," and emphasised the fact

---

[1] Horváth, *Mag. függ. harcz.* i. 297 *sq.*

that so soon as the territorial integrity of Hungary, and of the annexed parts, should be fully assured, all the military forces which should not be required for the maintenance of internal order and security should be placed at His Majesty's disposal. The Ministry was, in fact, confronted with a dilemma from which there was no escape; either the country must refuse to fulfil its obligations to its King, and so lend colour to the view that its intentions were revolutionary and disloyal, or, it must be denuded of troops and left exposed to the attacks of Jellacsics, whose hostile designs were known to, and encouraged by, the Government of Austria.   Kossuth's insistence on the choice of the former alternative was dictated by the conviction, which subsequent events proved to be well-founded, that so soon as the war in Italy should be finished, the whole forces of the Empire would be utilised for the destruction of Hungary's liberties, and if unconstitutional action is ever justifiable, it was so when the very existence of a nation was at stake.[1]

On July 11, in answer to a question on the subject of Servian disorder, Kossuth described the dangers which threatened the country. On the one side was Jellacsics with his mutinous Serbs and Croatians ; on the other, the Viennese Ministry, whose intrigues threatened to destroy the results of the constitutional struggle for independence. In the Lower Danubian provinces a Russian army was drawn up ready to cross the Pruth, and in reply to an official question as to its intentions, stated that it would take no warlike measures until it discerned signs of hostility to itself within the Hungarian borders. The chief difficulty was presented, he said, by the fact that Vienna refused to relinquish its financial and military control, and that he who has one hand in the pocket of a

---

[1] Even Helfert (*Die Thronbesteigung des Kaisers Franz Josef*, p. 74) admits that the Viennese Cabinet had no intention of solving the Gordian knot, but was determined to cut it.

nation and in the other holds its armed forces can do what he pleases. The Viennese Government supplied the Bán of Croatia with the sinews of war, and threatened to "renounce neutrality," in other words, that the Emperor of Austria would make war on the King of Hungary. No support was to be expected from abroad. "Poland relied on the sympathy of France, and that sympathy in fact existed, but Poland is no more. A nation which has no vital force cannot live ; that which is kept alive by the support of others, and not by its own inherent vitality, has no future before it." He concluded by demanding a vote of 200,000 men and 42,000,000 florins for the defence of the national liberty and independence, and before he could finish his sentence Paul Nyáry, the leader of the Opposition, rose with uplifted hand, in the attitude of one who takes a solemn oath, and cried : " We grant them." The whole House rose and repeated his words. "You have stood up as one man," were the concluding words of Kossuth's speech, "and I bow before the greatness of the nation. I will only add that if as much energy is shown in the execution of your promise as you have manifested in the making of it, not even the gates of Hell shall prevail against Hungary."

The enthusiasm of a nation, which a century earlier had manifested by its cry of " *Moriamur pro rege nostro* " its readiness to shed its blood in the thankless task of saving a dynasty which had little or no claim on its gratitude, was now to be enlisted in another cause. But no word of Kossuth's speech indicated the existence of hostility towards the reigning House. On the contrary, the speaker laid stress on the loyalty of the nation to its King, and on the identity of the interests of Austria and Hungary. The Address in reply to the King's Speech states that the Hungarian Parliament will be glad, so soon as peace and order have been re-established in Hungary, and a return to normal conditions has been assured, to

lend a helping hand to His Majesty, with a view to the
conclusion of such terms of peace as will be in accordance
with the dignity of the Throne, the principles of constitutional freedom, and the legitimate desires of the Italian
people."[1]   In his public pronouncements Kossuth was
still as pro-dynastic as ever, but his knowledge of the
shifty and tortuous policy which the camarilla had pursued
ever since the meeting of March 21 must have long ago
convinced him that the Court was determined to recover
by force the ground which circumstances had obliged it to
yield.   In any case, his demand that the organisation of
the national forces should be taken in hand, and his refusal
to allow more troops to be sent to Italy were amply
justified by the state of affairs which had existed in the
south since the early days of July, when the Serbs attacked
the Magyar population with fire and sword.   Though the
former were defeated on July 11 at Versecs, and again a
few days later at Futak, the majority of the engagements
had an indecisive result or ended unfavourably to the
Magyar cause.   The imperial Generals and higher officers
made no attempt to pursue an advantage when gained ;
attacks were not pressed home, and the opinion gained
ground among the disheartened troops that their leaders
were acting under orders from Vienna which forbade the
adoption of energetic measures.[2]   The repeated failure of
half-hearted attacks at Szent Tamás and elsewhere convinced the Government that reliance could be placed only
on Magyar troops commanded by Magyar officers, and
encouraged Jellacsics and Latour, the Austrian Minister
of War, in the belief that Hungary would prove to be
incapable of resistance when the time arrived to give open
effect to their secret desires.

---

[1] Horváth, *Mag. függ. harcz.* i. 326.

[2] "Selbst als Latour schon im Einverständnisse mit Jellacsics stand, wurde
die Maske zunächst nicht abgeworfen : und so wurde durch dieses Gaukelspiel
in die Armee Unsicherheit und Verwirrung getragen."—Friedjung, *o.c.* i. 76.

When the Reichsrath met on July 10, Vienna was no longer in a state of revolutionary ferment, and the desire for union with Germany had subsided. The Slavs were in a majority, and the Galician members consisted entirely of Polish and Ruthene peasants, whose ignorance lent itself to exploitation in the interests of autocracy. With the exception of Alexander Bach, ex-Radical opportunist, the members of the Ministry got together by Doblhoff were colourless nonentities. The victory of Radetzky at Somma Campagna showed that Lombardy was not lost, and that Austria still had an effective army.[1] It was therefore considered safe for the Emperor to return to Vienna, and for the Government to adopt a more decided attitude towards Hungary. The Cabinet of Budapest was soon made aware of the change which Radetzky's successes had effected, for Jellacsics again demanded not only territorial separation for Serbs and Croats, in spite of the King's repeated assurances and oaths " to the living God " that he would maintain the unity of the realms of the Sacred Crown, but that all military and financial affairs of Hungary should again be controlled by Austria : in other words, that the independent Hungarian Ministry should be deprived of its most important functions, and that the country should be reduced to the subordinate position from which it had so recently escaped. Batthyány went to Vienna to see Doblhoff, and to get, if possible, a straight answer to a straight question. " Does the Austrian Ministry, in the present disturbed state of affairs, intend to defend the rights of the Crown in the Hungarian

[1] According to Beöthy (o.c. iii. 5) the poet Grillparzer's much quoted lines, written a few months earlier, to the effect that Austria existed only in Radetzky's army, require modification, as that army was made up of Magyars, Czechs, Roumanians, Tyrolese, and other nationalities. Austrian patriots were conspicuous by their absence from an army of races which had no natural cohesion, which did not understand each other's languages and had no feeling of common patriotism. Possibly the officers agreed in their contempt for quill-drivers and politicians.—See also Radetzky's letter on this subject. Hübner, Ein Jahr meines Lebens, Oct. 28.

Kingdom having regard to the terms of the Pragmatic Sanction ? " The reply was of such a disingenuous nature as to leave no doubt as to the real intentions of Vienna. " As far as the Ministry is acquainted with the demands of the Croatians, the latter have no intention whatever of severing their connexion with the Magyar Crown. They also refer to the Pragmatic Sanction, and the question is which party's interpretation is the more correct. The decision of that problem would require a thorough investigation of the constitutional relations of Hungary and Croatia, which the Ministry's position does not permit it to undertake. Consequently, no decided pronouncement can be made in favour of either party. As, however, the Ministry hopes that a peaceful solution of the present difficulties will be arrived at, it will refrain from taking any step which might jeopardise the existence of the whole monarchy." [1] The Viennese Cabinet was perfectly well acquainted with the fact that Jellacsics had been branded as a traitor by the King's manifesto of June 10, and nothing had happened in the interval to alter his status. It knew very well that the Croatians, so far from caring about the true meaning of the Pragmatic Sanction, which had pronounced the inseparability of the realms of the Sacred Crown, aspired to territorial separation and desired to substitute a purely personal union for the real one which had existed between Hungary and the annexed, or subject, parts for more than eight hundred years. It was evident, therefore, that separatistic aspirations were to be temporarily encouraged with a view to the ultimate triumph of centralisation and uniformity—as regards Hungary the main objects of Habsburg policy ever since the disaster of Mohács.

By rescript dated August 14, the King withdrew the powers of representation conferred on the Palatine, and stated that thenceforward he intended to take the reins

[1] Horváth, Mag. függ. harcz. i. 331, 332.

into his own hands, which, legally, he had no power to do unless he resided in Hungary, and that he had no intention of doing. The real meaning of the rescript was that the question of the ratification of the laws of July 11, which granted men and money for national defence, would be left to the decision of the wirepullers of Vienna; and those who had resolved to destroy Hungary obviously had no intention of allowing effect to be given to measures which might eventually have the effect of checkmating their private designs. "Reaction has now come out into the open," wrote Batthyány, "and no longer conceals its plans and intentions. Hungary is indicated as the first victim. . . . at the most we have three weeks before us."[1] But he still hoped that it might be possible to avoid a conflict, and for the sake of peace was ready to counsel the sacrifice of Hungary's military and financial independence and the acceptance of the burden of part of Austria's public debt. Above all, he desired the avoidance of any semblance of illegality on Hungary's part, and that, if war must come, the responsibility should rest with Austria. Kossuth was no less anxious to avoid hostilities, but he believed that his country would prove to be strong enough to defend its rights, and was unwilling to buy peace on terms which would have been acceptable to Batthyány. In his opinion negotiation was useless, and nothing but complete surrender, or such a manifestation of strength as would make Austria realise the risk involved by an appeal to arms, could avoid bloodshed. On August 28 Batthyány and Deák went to Vienna in order to obtain the royal assent to the Bills passed by Parliament on July 11, providing men and money for the defence of the country, and to make a further attempt at negotiation with a view to the avoidance of hostilities; but they were informed that the King was too ill to see any one—in other words, that the camarilla was resolved that no

[1] Letter to Szalay, August 18. Horvath, *Mag. függ. harcz.* i. 346.

compromise should be accepted.[1] Three days later a
royal rescript was issued, which ordered the members of
the Hungarian Ministry to come to Vienna to discuss
matters with Jellacsics, who now demanded the cessation
of Hungary's military preparations, while he actively
continued his own, with the assistance of Latour, the
Austrian Minister of War. On the same date, August 31,
the Viennese Government issued a note[2] explaining its
views on the subject of the March laws, which it
declared to be incompatible with the Pragmatic Sanction
and destructive of the unity of the monarchy. It maintained that the powers conferred on the Archduke Stephen
were illegal, as involving the separation of Hungary from
Austria, and that Ferdinand, now that Austria was
possessed of a Constitution, had no power to sanction
laws which involved an alteration of the relations which
had hitherto existed between the two countries. The
authors of this note forgot the elementary fact that the
Pragmatic Sanction was brought into existence at a time
when Austria, being under a despotic Government, had no
voice, as a nation, in any arrangement made between the
two equal legislative factors, the King of Hungary and
the Hungarian Diet, and that, consequently, in the case
of the Pragmatic Sanction, there could be no such privity
of contract between Austria and Hungary as would give
the former the right to interfere in any modification of an
agreement made in 1723 between the Austrian autocrat
and the Magyar nation. But this fact, and the impossibility of finding any argument in the Pragmatic Sanction
or in Law x. of 1790-91 in proof of the existence of a
real union between Austria and Hungary as distinguished
from a personal union resulting from the identity of King

[1] According to Helfert, *Die Thronbesteigung des Kaisers Franz Josef,* this
was the Empress's doing.
[2] Text in Helfert's *Revision des ung.-öst. Ausgleichs,* i. 157. Horváth gives
only a summary.

and Emperor,[1] were of less importance than the necessity
of justifying in the eyes of Europe the subsequent actions
of the camarilla.   Though it was impossible to refer to
any law in support of its thesis, the note suggested that
Hungary's claim to act independently in the matter of
customs tariffs and the national finances was unconstitutional, and that a refusal to bear part of the burden of
Austria's public debt, and the action of Parliament in
voting men and money for purposes of national defence,
indicated an intention to sever all connexion with the
Austrian Empire.   The document ended with a demand
for the suspension of all measures taken by the Hungarian
Government since the beginning of March—in other
words, for the renunciation by Hungary of its right of
self-government, of which it had so recently obtained the
recognition.   "We will bargain with Hell if necessary,"
said Kossuth, "even with Jellacsics on a purely Croatian
basis, but with reaction, which would mutilate our independence, never, a thousand times never.[2]   Though the
note of the Austrian Government was a summons to
surrender rather than an invitation to negotiate, Kossuth
proceeded to give further proof of his pro-dynastic feeling
by proposing that Ferdinand should come to Budapest to
co-operate in the task of adjusting all differences, for
Vienna, he said, was under the influence of Frankfurt,
and only in Buda was the King's sovereignty complete.
"But if that is impossible, let His Majesty give us, without
in any way diminishing his sovereign rights, a younger

---

[1] "Die Pragmatische Sanktion war einfach eine Erbfolge-Ordnung . . .,
von einer Realunion . . . sagte sie nichts, im gegentheile garantirte sie Ungarn
die politische Selbständigkeit. . . . Aus den Reichstagsverhandlungen 1790
und zwar aus den Ansprüchen der Regierung selbst überzeugt man sich
am besten, dass die sog. pragmatische Sanktion ein bilaterale Vertrag war und
weit entfernt die Verfassungsrechte Ungarns zu schmälern gerade den festen
Rechtsboden für die Forderung politischer Selbständigkeit und unabhängiger
Administration gab."—Anton Springer, o.c. ii. 500, and note.

[2] Marczali, A Legujabb Kor Története, p. 661.

King [1] in the person of His Imperial Highness the Archduke Francis Joseph . . . thus will the future of the House of Austria be assured.".

Kossuth was mistaken as to the strength of the Austrian movement in favour of fusion with Germany, in which country Russia and Slavism were looked upon as constituting the greatest danger to Western Europe, and a strong Hungary was regarded as the best guarantee of peaceful development.[2] Two months earlier the eyes of Vienna were fixed on Frankfurt, but the victory of Custozza [3] had given a fresh turn to public opinion, and the easy success of Windischgrätz in Bohemia and the fiasco of Szent Tamás led the Court to believe that Hungary could be suppressed as easily as the rioters of Prague.[4] The complete success of the party of reaction and the determination of the camarilla to hesitate no longer as to the employment of the Slavs for the destruction of the Magyars, are shown by Ferdinand's letter to Jellacsics of September 4 :—

Dear Baron Jellacsics—The indubitable proofs which you have repeatedly given since your appointment as Bán of Croatia of your fidelity and attachment to my dynasty and to the whole monarchy, and the readiness you have shown to give effect to my orders issued in connexion with the negotiations with my Hungarian Ministry which have been taking place, have convinced me that you never entertained any disloyal or disobedient intentions with respect to my commands, nor intended to bring about the dissolution of those bonds which for

---

[1] The "*rex junior*" of ancient days.

[2] See the despatch to Szalay, the representative of the Hungarian Government at the Frankfurt Diet, July 19, with respect to a proposed defensive alliance of Hungary and the German Confederation.—Horváth, *Mag. függ. harcz.* i. 343, 345. Pillersdorf knew and approved the instructions given to Szalay. See Anton Springer, *o.c.* ii. 497.

[3] July 25.

[4] "What is the Magyar people and what are the Magyar nobles ? Rebels who ought to be extirpated or made harmless for ever."—Schwarzenberg to Wirkner, *Élményeim,* p. 235.

centuries united the parts annexed to Hungary to my Hungarian Crown.

On the same day as that on which this letter was dispatched, Jellacsics, to whom Radetzky had sent twenty-one battalions of infantry, seized Fiume, the port of Hungary, and occupied the Slavonian districts.

After fruitless attempts on the part of Batthyány and his colleagues to obtain the royal assent to the Bills passed on July 11, Kossuth proposed to Parliament that a deputation should be sent to Vienna to ascertain the King's will, which the proved loyalty of the nation, now strained to the breaking point, entitled it to know; to draw his Majesty's attention to the massacre of his Magyar subjects by Serbs and Croats, and to request that the Magyar troops, now no longer required in Italy, might be sent home for the defence of their native land. In the memorial[2] presented to the King in pursuance of Kossuth's proposal, loyalty makes a last effort to maintain the distinction which had hitherto been consistently drawn between the King and his malevolent advisers.

We come before your Majesty in the name of the united Kingdom of Hungary and Transylvania, whose immemorial and unshakable loyalty to the reigning House entitles them to ask their King to support them in their efforts to maintain the integrity of the country's rights. . . . Hungary is no dominion which has been won by the sword, but a free country, whose constitutional liberty and independence have been sealed and confirmed by your Majesty's coronation oath. The laws which were consecrated by your Majesty's royal assent on April 11 fulfilled the heartfelt desires which the nation had long entertained; and the nation, tranquillised and loyal as of old, borrowed fresh strength from liberty, and stood ready to defend your Majesty's throne

---

[1] The Hungarian Ministry was not informed of the sending of this letter, but read it in the newspapers two days later. Pulszky at once asked Wessenberg, the Austrian Prime Minister, for explanations. He replied: "I can give you none. I know nothing about it. It was done behind my back."—*Életem és Korom*, i. 339; *i.e.* it was dictated by the camarilla.

[2] Pulszky, *Életem és Korom*, i. 339.

against the dangers which threatened it from various quarters. Parts of Hungary are now in a state of rebellion, the ringleaders of which continually and openly declare that their seditious campaign against the freedom and independence of Hungary, which your Majesty has repeatedly confirmed and the laws have established, has been undertaken in the interests of the reigning House and in your Majesty's name. . . . The mainspring of that sedition, which, in lower Hungary, has reduced peaceful villages to ashes, has killed and tortured innocent women and children with a cruelty which surpasses that of barbarous races,[1] threatens Hungary with invasion from Croatia, and has occupied the Hungarian port of Fiume and the Slavonian districts without a shadow of justification, is none other than that reactionary policy which aims at annihilating Hungary's constitutional independence and the freedom of the people, and at tearing up the laws which your Majesty's predecessors of glorious memory, and your Majesty's own coronation oath have consecrated and confirmed. . . . We pray your Majesty to order all military forces now in Hungary, on pain of your Majesty's displeasure, punctually and bravely to perform their duty of maintaining the laws, and defending the Kingdom against the attacks of the seditious, no matter whose name or standard they may usurp. The Magyar nation is resolutely determined to solve, during the present session of Parliament, on the basis of liberty, equality, and fraternity, and of constitutional rights common to all, the racial questions and problems of internal government now pending between it and the Croatian people. Croatia is at the present moment subject to a military tyranny. Consequently, its citizens are prevented from making their legitimate requirements known to the legislative authority of Hungary. We therefore pray your Majesty to take effective measures for the liberation of the Croatian people from the yoke of the aforesaid tyranny, in order that it may give free expression to its desires, and for the immediate surrender of Fiume and of the Slavonian districts which the forces of sedition

---

[1] No doubt the Magyars took a bloody revenge for the "cannibalistic brutalities" of which the peaceful population was made the victim, but Anton Springer rightly remarks that "eines muss übrigens ausdrücklich bemerkt werden, dass über die von den Ungarn verübten Greuelthaten nur die slavischen Parteiblätter berichten, dagegen über die Unmenschlichkeit der serbischen Freischaaren zuerst und am lautesten die österreichischen Feldherrn Beschwerde führen."—o.c. ii. 484, n. See also Friedjung, o.c. ii. 208.

have seized. The Magyar nation does not doubt the existence of a reactionary party, which has no object save the promotion of its own selfish interests, and that your Majesty will not only remove its members from the neighbourhood of your Majesty's person, but will also mete out punishment to those who deserve it. . . . The present moment is of such importance to the life of the nation that procrastination will have a most disastrous effect on the faithful subjects of your Majesty, who is humbly entreated to grant our prayer, and, more especially, to deign to appear in Hungary without delay, for it is certain that unless our request is complied with, confidence will be shaken to such an extent that the Hungarian Ministry will be paralysed in its efforts to make effective use of those instruments with which the law provides it, and will be unable to answer for the maintenance of order and of internal peace. The avoidance of incalculable dangers depends on the swift decision of your Majesty, whom we entreat to throw his weight into the scale for the salvation of our country, which will give the support of its unshakable fidelity to your Majesty's throne.

The petition was presented on September 9 by a deputation to which admission was refused until all reference to the feeling of uncertainty and want of confidence existing in Hungary had been expunged. While it was being read Ferdinand nervously "fidgeted in his chair. He seemed to be in a state of fear, and could hardly read the reply contained in a document which he held in his trembling hands."[1] The reply was as follows :—

I deeply regret that owing to the weak state of my health I am unable to comply with the wish expressed by the deputation that I should visit my kingdom.[2] I will consider the legislative proposals which have been laid before me, and if I should have cause to make any comments thereon my observations must not be interpreted as indicating a desire on my part to set aside or

---

[1] Pulszky, who was present on the occasion of the presentation of the petition.—*Életem és Korom*, i. 342.

[2] "It will be a strong act indeed if the ruling party at Vienna refuse to permit the King of Hungary to visit his kingdom."—Despatch No. 38, the British Ambassador to Lord Palmerston (*Correspondence*, etc.).

infringe existing laws.[1] I repeat that it is my fixed resolve to preserve the laws, territorial integrity, and rights of my Hungarian Kingdom, to the maintenance of which I have pledged my royal word. Of the other matters on which you have touched, some have already been settled in accordance with the wishes of the nation, and as regards the others I will at the earliest possible moment declare my will by the intermediary of the Ministry.

In any other mouth this reply would have been equivalent to an undertaking to suppress sedition and to give full effect to the laws which Ferdinand and his predecessors had sanctioned, but the whole history of Hungary for the last four hundred years had been one long commentary on the value of Habsburg promises, and the members of the deputation withdrew in silence, feeling that through them the nation had taken final leave of its King.[2]

On the day preceding the reception of the deputation, Eszterházy, the Hungarian Minister in attendance on the King, foreseeing the inevitable consequences of the triumph of the reactionary party, resigned his office. Széchenyi had already disappeared from the scene. The strain of the last few weeks was more than his over-wrought nervous system could endure, and an attack of temporary insanity compelled his retirement to an asylum just at the moment when the moderating influence of "the greatest of the Magyars" might have been of supreme value to his country. Batthyány, now as ever, strove to keep within the bounds of strict legality. He considered that Hungary's desire to keep on good terms with Vienna could best be indicated by the resignation of the Cabinet, and by the exclusion of Kossuth from the reconstructed Ministry. On September 11 the Palatine announced the resignation of Batthyány and of his colleagues, and added that he himself would carry on

[1] The "existing laws" must necessarily include those which received the royal assent on April 11.

[2] Pulszky, *Életem és Korom*, i. 342.

the government of the country until a new Ministry had been appointed. The announcement was received with dissatisfaction, and the view prevailed that if all the Ministers resigned no new Government would be appointed.[1] Outside the House a universal cry arose for Kossuth, who thereon yielded to popular pressure, withdrew his resignation, and announced that he would retain his portfolio until a new Ministry should be formed. He pointed out that the feeble state of the King's health and the deleterious influence of the party of reaction made it indispensable that decided measures should be taken without delay for the protection of the country and of the true interests of the Throne. He proposed that provision should be made for immediate necessities, financial and military, by the issue of five-florin notes on the security of the whole national revenue, and that pending the sanction of the July laws volunteers should be enrolled, and officers and men of the regular army should be allowed to leave their regiments for the purpose of enlisting in the new auxiliary force. Just as Jellacsics had declared that the Magyars had taken advantage of the weak state of Ferdinand's health to extort concessions which otherwise would never have been granted, the Magyars in their turn invoked that illness as an excuse for the King's apparent hostility to a loyal nation, the result of the underhand machinations of the camarilla which exploited his feebleness and vacillation for the furtherance of selfish interests. And so the strange spectacle was presented of Serbo-Croatians on the one side and Magyars on the other preparing to cut each other's throats in the name of one and the same King, and, nominally, in defence of the rights of the Throne against separatistic encroachment. Hungary still did its utmost to maintain a cherished fiction—the abstract con-

---

[1] Szemere, *Politische Charakterskizzen aus dem ungarischen Freiheitskriege*, Hamburg, 1853, iii. 111.

ception of a constitutional King distinguishable from the
imperial instrument of a reactionary oligarchy.

On September ¯12 the ·Palatine again entrusted
Batthyány with the formation of a Ministry, which included Eötvös and Mészáros alone of the members of
the previous Cabinet ; but as the new Ministry could not
become an actuality until the new appointments had been
confirmed, and as the news that Jellacsics had invaded
Hungary with 36,000 men had finally removed all doubts
as to the intentions of Vienna, the demand for the adoption of a more resolute policy than that which the reconstruction of the Cabinet seemed to promise became almost
irresistible.   Many young Liberals came from Vienna to
Pest to express their sympathy with the Magyar cause
and to place their swords at the disposal of the country.
This encouraged Kossuth in the belief that the spirit of
Liberalism was stronger in Austria than it really was, and
that Hungary would find an effective ally in the hatred
of absolutism which might be expected to exist in a
land which had recently given proof of its revolutionary tendencies.   He therefore proposed that a fresh
deputation should be sent to Vienna, not to the King
this time, but to the Reichsrath, which, presumably,
would see in the maintenance of Hungarian independence the surest guarantee of the prolongation of its
own existence.   "It is expedient," said Kossuth, "that
we should speak as one people to another, who have affairs
of common interest and a common enemy . . . let us
arrange matters in a friendly fashion as one free nation
with another."   As Deák put it: "The deputation should
explain that on all those matters in which our interests
come in contact with those of the domains of the Austrian
Empire Hungary is heartily desirous of coming to an
arrangement on the basis of constitutionalism, justice, and
equity." [1]   Possibly it was a mistake to depart from the

<hr />

[1] Horváth (John), *A Közös Ügyek*, etc., p. 158.

logical basis of Hungary's position—its complete severance, except for the obligation of mutual defence, from the hereditary provinces, resulting from the laws of 1723 and 1790—but at all events fresh proof was given of the baselessness of the suggestion that Hungary was animated by a revolutionary desire to break the last link which bound it to Austria, and of its willingness to recognise the necessity of arriving at a more complete definition of its relations with the Empire than was to be found in the March laws or in previous legislation. On September 19 the deputation asked for admission to the Reichsrath, in order to present a memorial which laid stress on Hungary's desire to preserve the ties which united the two countries, to both of which the maintenance of constitutional govern-ment was essential, and expressed the intention of the Hungarian Parliament of regarding any encroachment on the political institutions of Austria as an attack on its own privileges, and its confident hope of meeting with reciprocal treatment at the hands of the Austrian Reichsrath.[1] But the deputation knocked in vain, though the German Liberals spoke strongly in favour of its admission. The Slav majority refused its consent, and reaction triumphed, as it could now allege with some show of justification that Austria was solid in its approval of the Government's attitude towards Hungary. "You Slavs," said Lohner, one of the Viennese deputies, "claim that you are serving the Empire, . . . but if Hungary fails it will be too late to restrain the victorious soldiery, and history will din into your ears the fact that you allowed a sister-race to be butchered, and a common slavery with it will be your fate." Another member of the Reichsrath asked the question : "Whether the Government is of opinion that the constitutional King approves of the war now in progress between his subjects, and whether the Ministry

---

[1] Horváth, *Mag. függ. harcz.* i. 493 *sq.* ; and enclosure in Despatch 58, Ponsonby to Palmerston (*Correspondence*, etc.).

approves of the supply of arms, money, and soldiers to the Croatians for the suppression of the Magyars?"[1] but the peasant deputies of Galicia were impervious to argument, and the Government had already made up its mind. "The Cabinet came to the tardy but sincere conclusion that the policy hitherto pursued with regard to Hungary would lead to destruction, and that the concessions wrung from the Crown were incompatible with the interests of the Monarchy. So far the Ministry was right; but did it take into consideration the inevitable result of a pronouncement in this sense? Latour undoubtedly, Bach hardly, did so. The others? No. But however that may be, they certainly provoked the Hungarian revolution."[2] If Latour and the camarilla acted deliberately, with a knowledge of the necessary result, Hungary did not do so. There the fight began in the name of the monarchical principle, and in defence of the unity of the realms of the Sacred Crown against rebellious Serbs and Croatians, whose separatistic desires were exploited by Vienna for the purpose of wiping out the March laws, which could legally be abrogated only by the joint legislative action of King and Parliament. In Hungary there was nothing in the nature of a revolution so long as Ferdinand remained on the throne. Till it became clear that his successor had determined to destroy the Constitution, which all his predecessors, save one, had sworn to maintain, and Austria openly joined hands with the rebels, the fight never lost its pro-dynastic and purely defensive character. At the same time, it is evident that Kossuth, at all events, entertained no illusions as to the intentions of the Court.

"What will be the issue of this business?" he asked.—"That the bravery or the cowardice of the people will decide. I rely on

---

[1] Horváth, *Mag. függ. harcz.* i. 493.

[2] Hübner, *Ein Jahr meines Lebens*, 1848-49, p. 211, "Jetzt greift das Ministerium nach ihm ; (Jellacsics) er soll in Ungarn Ordnung machen."

the instinct of self-preservation, and believe that the Magyar nation will not allow itself to be cut down like a coward, nor submit to wear the chains of slavery. One thing I know for certain, that the spirit of pious loyalty to the Crown has been undermined in the breasts of its most faithful subjects by the terrible events of the last two months, to an extent to which it never could have been shaken in the course of long years, by the greatest enemy of the Monarchy." [1] " The invasion of Hungary by Jellacsics will bring freedom in its train. . . . The further he advances the more certain it is that not a single man will see the waters of the Száva again. . . . There are only two things for the Magyars to do. One is to rise in their thousands to destroy the invaders of their country's soil ; the other is to remember ! If they do not do both, then are the Magyars such a cowardly despicable race that their name will be synonymous in the pages of history with shame and ignominy ; then are the Magyars a God-accursed people . . . which will wander homeless on the face of the earth, begging in vain for a crust of bread, and receiving in place thereof a blow in the face from the alien race which has made it a wandering beggar in its own land, like the homeless dog which any blackguard can knock on the head without reproach. In vain will the Magyar turn to religion for consolation ; it will give him none. God, whose creative work he will have degraded by his cowardice, will not forgive him his sins either in this world or in the next. The maid to whom he lifts his eyes will drive him like some mangy beast, with her broom, from the threshold. His wife will spit in his face with repulsion, and the first words of his children will be a curse on their father. To arms, therefore, if you are men ; and let the women dig a huge grave in which to bury either our enemies or the Magyar name, Magyar honour, and the Magyar nation." [2]

Kossuth personally repeated this appeal in the south of Hungary, and all classes flocked to the colours in defence of the capital. A last attempt was made to negotiate with Jellacsics. The Archduke Stephen was induced to try to come to terms with him, and offered to

---

[1] Kossuth, *Hirlapja*, September 19 ; Marczali, *A Legujabb Kor Története*, p. 671.

[2] Pulszky, *Életem és Korom*, i., from Kossuth, *Hirlapja*.

meet him on a steamer on Lake Balaton, but the Bán pretended that he was afraid of being kidnapped, and failed to keep the appointment.[1] The Palatine, thereupon, seeing that arms alone could decide the fate of Hungary, left the country, never to return, a broken and discredited man, who, for a time, had conscientiously done his best to fulfil the duties of his position, and to act as mediator between the nation and its King,[2] but lacked the strength of character of his father, who, alone among the Habsburgs, has lasting claims on the gratitude of the Magyar nation.

The camarilla was convinced that no serious opposition could be opposed to Jellacsics, and considered that the time had come to send a commissioner to Hungary to restore order and, as far as possible, to put the country back into the position which it occupied before the March laws were passed. Count Lamberg, a Magyar, who had played a considerable part on the Conservative side, was selected for the post of plenipotentiary and Commander-in-Chief of the Hungarian forces, and was entrusted with the task of proroguing Parliament and re-establishing the connexion with Austria on the basis of the Pragmatic Sanction—that is to say, of the Court's interpretation of that enactment, which involved the destruction of all that

---

[1] Jellacsics wrote to Baron Kulmer, the Austrian Minister, on September 23, "The Archduke plied protestation on protestation, but my officers believed the ship's engines to be stronger than a word of honour . . . besides, what is the use of a lot of haggling? It is not in my nature; three or four days hence bloodshed will decide the matter."—Horváth, *Mag. függ. harcz.* i. 506. See also Eötvös K, *Utazás a Balaton Körul,* 4th ed. pp. 267-288.

[2] It is noticeable that Jellacsics said on the morning of the 24th that he knew the Archduke had fled. At that time no one else knew it. Eötvös, *l.c.* p. 288, says Jellacsics only guessed it, but query. The Hungarian Ministry had previously requested the King to give instructions to the Commandants of fortified towns to take their orders from the Ministry only, and the King complied with the request, but the Archduke Stephen received a hint from Vienna not to send the instructions to their destinations, and secretly recalled them from the post-office. They were found among his papers after his flight. He left behind him a document announcing his resignation, and justifying it on the ground that the King had forbidden him to oppose Jellacsics.—Kossuth, *Schriften aus der Emigration,* ii. 229, 234.

Hungary had gained during the past months.[1] The proclamation announcing Lamberg's appointment was intended to be kept secret till the last possible moment, but Pulszky obtained a copy and sent it to Pest, so its contents were common property before Lamberg arrived. In spite of the usual pretended observance of legal forms, and of the familiar assurance that the King was "unshakably resolved to maintain the integrity of Hungary and its liberties according to law," the intention to abolish the responsible Ministry, and therewith the national independence, was clear. Kossuth, fresh from the scenes of enthusiasm which his journey to the south had produced, declared that Lamberg's nomination abolished by a stroke of the pen all Hungary's constitutional successes and struck Hungary's name out of the list of nations. He pointed out that the appointment was illegal owing to the want of the counter-signature of a responsible Minister, and on September 27, Parliament, which had in the meantime heard that Jellacsics was within two days' march of Pest, unanimously resolved that the "alleged" proclamation was null and void, and forbade obedience to the royal commissioner. The same evening Lamberg arrived at Pest, was recognised by the crowd, and killed as a traitor

[1] Hartig, *Genesis der Revolution*, p. 300, asks whether the King had power to withdraw his sanction of the March laws when once it had been given, and answers the question with a decided affirmative. His misapprehension of the position arises from a failure to comprehend the difference existing between Austria and Hungary. In Austria the Emperor as autocrat could *octroyer* a Constitution and take it away the next moment if he pleased. We have already seen him do so in the early part of the year and will see a repetition of the manœuvre twice in the sixties ; but in Hungary the constitutional monarch, when once a law had been passed by Parliament and had received the royal assent, could no more abolish an Act without reference to Parliament than the latter could do so without the sanction of the King. Law xii. of 1790 is explicit on this point : " Leges *ferendi*, *abrogandi*, *interpretandi potestatem* in Regno hoc Hungariae Partibusque adnexis, salva Art. 8, 1741 (which recognises the immunity of the nobles' lands from taxation) dispositione, *legitime coronato Principi et statibus ac OO. Regni ad Comitia legitime confluentibus communem esse nec extra illa exerceri posse Sua Majestas Sacratissima ultro ac sponte agnoscit.*"

to his country.   One of the murderers, armed with a still
reeking sword and followed by a riotous mob, forced his
way into the House of Parliament and boasted of his
deed to the horrified members, who realised the fact that
the last hope of a peaceful solution of the problems which
confronted Hungary had now disappeared.

Hartig says[1] that before this murderous act was
perpetrated (the only one which sullies the history of the
Hungarian fight for freedom), and until Hungary by
killing Lamberg threw down the glove to Austria,
Ferdinand took no part in the anti-Magyar campaign, but
his statement is incorrect.   In the first place, the Magyars
as a nation were no more responsible for the murder of
Lamberg by an excited mob, than Austria, as a whole,
was answerable for the subsequent murder of Latour, the
Austrian Minister of War.   In the second place, an
intercepted letter from Jellacsics's camp discloses the fact
that "on September 24th (three days before the death
of Lamberg) Count Mensdorff, the Imperial messenger,
arrived at Kiliti, with an autograph letter of the Emperor,
which approved the steps hitherto taken by the Bán and
informed him that all the regiments stationed in Hungary
had been forbidden to fight against the Croatian army
. . . and that those who disobeyed this injunction
would be proclaimed traitors."   The same apologist of
Vienna remarks,[2] that "the fact that Latour's efforts
in many cases could not be in unison with those of
Hungary's Minister of War and Commander is to be
explained by the difference of the aims which they had in
view and does not give rise to a suspicion of treachery
towards the Magyars " ; but the letters of Jellacsics which
fell into Magyar hands remove all possible doubt as to
Latour's complicity in the preparations which Jellacsics
and his Viennese paymasters were making for the ruin of
Hungary, whose suspicions were to be lulled by the issue

[1] Hartig, *Genesis der Revolution*, p. 314.   [2] *Ibid.* p. 298.

of reassuring rescripts until the decisive moment arrived.
On September 23, Jellacsics wrote to Latour: "I am
much obliged by your Excellency's gracious forethought,
and for the remittance of the necessary money which you
have been good enough to make. At the same time I
am compelled humbly to beg for a further supply. . . .
I with my army am now in Hungary, operating on
behalf of the general interests of Austria, and rely, and
am justified in relying, on the assistance of the Imperial
Ministry of War." On the same day he wrote to Baron
Kulmer, his intermediary in Vienna: "You know how
difficult it is to improvise an army . . . . all that is
required is resolution on the part of Vienna, and the good
cause will triumph. My dear friend, they gave me a
practically definite assurance that as soon as my army
arrived in Hungary it should receive regular pay and
allowances from the State. They encouraged me to hope
that they would give me their moral support, and I also
expected to receive a pontoon train and a twelve-pounder
horse battery ; now it is somewhat late." [1] One lot of
supplies sent from Vienna, described as pontoons, was
intercepted by the Magyars, and found to contain guns,[2]
so it is evident that Jellacsics did not ask in vain. When
the Hungarian Government complained to Vienna that
money had been sent to Jellacsics, the reply was sent that
he had, in fact, been supplied with funds from Austria, as
the Hungarian Ministry of Finance had failed to send
him any ;[3] as if it was the business of the Budapest
Ministry to finance the invasion of its own country.
Latour, when the irregularity of his behaviour was pointed
out to him, replied : "Let them abolish their laws
of 1848 and all will be well.[4] As the *Allgemeine*

---

[1] The letters are set out by Horváth, *Mag. függ. harcz.* i. 455 *sq.*

[2] Pulszky, *Életem és Korom*, i. 334.

[3] Kossuth, *Schriften aus der Emigration*, ii. 228.

[4] Deák to Beust.—Beöthy, *o.c.* ii. 527.

Oesterreichische Zeitung said : " The intercepted letters give indubitable proof of the fact that the War-Minister Latour was a party to Jellacsics's plans and assisted him with Austrian money, consequently, *ipso facto*, declared war on Hungary. . . . The Croatian war is the war of reaction, set on foot by the Austrian court-party, not only against the Magyars, but against freedom itself, and Jellacsics is but a tool in their hands." [1]

On September 29, Jellacsics, after Batthyány had once more tried to induce him to abandon his advance on the capital, came into collision with fifteen thousand Magyar troops, consisting chiefly of raw levies and National Guards, under General Móga, and was driven back. A few days later the Croatian reserves, to the number of nine thousand men, were forced to capitulate, and were disarmed and sent home.[2] With the remainder of his forces Jellacsics drew off in the direction of Vienna. The Viennese Government believed that Jellacsics would enter Pest in triumph on or about October 3, and timed the issue of a royal rescript to coincide with his arrival. The King therein complains that Parliament had allowed

[1] Oct. 3, 1848.—Horváth, *o.c.* i. 569 *sq.* See also Jellacsics's intercepted instructions to the Governor of Varasd as to dealing with the guns, ammunition, pistols, etc. sent from Austria.—*Ibid.* i. 457.

[2] These were Slavs of the military frontier organisation. To the reproaches of their officers they replied they saw no reason for fighting their Magyar brothers who had never done them nor their country any harm.—Kossuth, *Schriften aus der Emigration*, ii. 177. Görgei, subsequently Commander-in-Chief of the Magyar forces, was present. He had already made himself notorious by hanging, on Oct. 1, Count Edmund Zichy, one of the leaders of the Conservative party and an ex-"Administrator" of 1844. Copies of Jellacsics's proclamation were found on him, and a store of arms was discovered in his house. According to Görgei (*Mein Leben und Wirken in Ungarn*, i. 28), Zichy's complicity in the Croatian rebellion was clearly established, and Szögyény (*Émlékiratai*, p. 96) says that a free pass from Jellacsics was in his possession, and that he was in close communication with the Slav officers. Beöthy, in his *Magyar Államiság Fejlödése*, etc. iii. 411, says that Görgei hanged Zichy in order to draw attention to himself as a man who would stick at nothing, but the victim's brother Paul shortly afterwards joined Görgei and became his trusted friend, which he would scarcely have done if he thought his brother's fate undeserved.

itself to be led by Kossuth into the paths of illegality, and so had made itself responsible for Lamberg's death. His Majesty consequently was obliged to dissolve Parliament, and to annul all its decisions which had not received the royal assent. The rescript also notified the appointment of Jellacsics as Commander-in-Chief and Governor Pleni-potentiary of Hungary, absolute obedience to whom was enjoined, and the placing of the country under martial law. At the same time, Latour issued an order absolving all troops stationed in Hungary from their oath of allegiance to the Constitution, and sent reinforcements to Jellacsics. War on the Magyars and on their Constitution was thus openly declared.[1] On October 7, Parliament, which still tried to believe that the King was not respon-sible for the hostile acts of the camarilla and of his Ministers, unanimously resolved on Kossuth's motion that the rescript was forged, but that if it should prove to be authentic it was contrary to the laws, to His Majesty's oath, and to the Pragmatic Sanction, and so was revolu-tionary, null, and void of effect.

Kossuth and the Committee of National Defence, formed when the prospects of invasion first necessitated the taking of defensive measures, took the place of the now non-existent Ministry. The time had come either to surrender unconditionally to Vienna, or, with Kossuth as practical Dictator, to fight to the bitter end.

---

[1] " Bezüglich Ungarns gab es nur eine Meinung : es sollte und musste sich die Einordnung in das einheitliche Reich gefallen lassen. Die Rebellion in Ungarn war beklagenswerth, aber sie hatte in den Augen der Machthaber doch das eine Gute, dass man jetzt mit der gefährlichen Verfassung von 1848 reinen Tisch machen konnte. Meinungsverschiedenheiten bestanden nur über den Grad der Autonomie, die dem Lande innerhalb des Einheitsstaates gewährt werden könne."—Friedjung, o.c. i. 135.

CHAPTER XV

The beginning of October witnessed a fresh outbreak of revolutionary disorder in Vienna.[1] The Radicals identified their interests with those of Hungary, knowing that the triumph of reaction in that country would sound the death-knell of constitutionalism in Austria also. Throughout the latter half of September, after the arrival of the news of the Croatian invasion of Hungary, the students and lower classes of the Kaiserstadt gave daily and disorderly proof of their solidarity with the Radicals and with the Magyars. The publication of the Bán's intercepted letters, which proved the complicity of Latour in the plot to.ruin Hungary, poured oil on the fire of public resentment, and confirmed the belief that a *coup d'état* was contemplated for the destruction of the modicum of popular liberty enjoyed by the hereditary provinces. The news of Jellacsics's appointment, and of the establishment of martial law in Hungary, strengthened the conviction that the adoption of similar measures in Austria might be expected at any moment. On October 6, the Reichsrath presented an address to Ferdinand demanding a general amnesty and the withdrawal of the rescript of October 3, to which the Emperor, who had already packed his portmanteau with a view to flight, replied that he would give the matter his most careful attention—in other words, that the petitioners should mind their own

[1] Similar revolutionary outbursts occurred at Gratz, Brünn, and Lemberg.

business. Several regiments, destined for the reinforcement of Jellacsics, refused to obey orders;[1] street fighting began, barricades were erected, and the forces of disorder were everywhere victorious. A mob forced its way into the Ministry of War, killed Latour and hanged his mangled remains on a lamp-post—Vienna's answer to the murder of Lamberg. On the following day the revolutionists seized the arsenal and distributed sixty thousand stand of arms. The capital was clearly too hot for the Kaiser, and he and his family fled to Olmütz. Krauss, the Minister of Finance, alone stuck to his post, with the result that he found himself in the undignified position of having to find pay for the students' legion which was engaged in fighting the troops of his imperial master.

This unfortunate state of affairs prevented the Government from sending the promised reinforcements to Jellacsics, and from giving effect to his appointment as practical Dictator of Hungary till the Kaiserstadt had been reduced to submission. The hopes of the Government were centred in Windischgrätz, who proceeded to collect all available troops, joined hands with Jellacsics, and laid siege to Vienna. On the withdrawal of the Bán the Magyar troops advanced to the frontier; but though a letter had been received from the Committee of the Central Democratic Union of Vienna asking for armed co-operation in the struggle for freedom, a strong feeling existed against the adoption of offensive, as distinguished from defensive, measures dictated by the instinct of national self-preservation. Twice the army crossed the frontier, and twice it returned. Only when it was too late did Kossuth resolve, in spite of the opposition of the majority of the members of the Committee of National Defence, to advance to the relief of the beleaguered Viennese. On October 30 the Magyars attacked Jellacsics at

---

[1] Hübner, *Ein Jahr meines Lebens*, Oct. 6. For the best account of the disorder in Vienna see Reschauer, *Das Jahr 1848, Geschichte der Wiener Revolution*, Vienna, 1872.

Mannwörth, and captured the village at the point of the bayonet ; but at Schwechat a panic occurred in a portion of the troops, which involved the precipitate retreat of the whole force across the border. If they had pressed on and joined hands with the revolutionaries in Vienna, it is more than probable that events would have taken a totally different course to that which they ultimately followed, and that Hungary would have been able to dictate terms of peace in the capital of the Habsburgs ; [1] but that was not to be. The revolutionists, whose hopes were temporarily revived by the news of the Magyar advance, left to their own resources were incapable of prolonged resistance. On November 2 Jellacsics and Windischgrätz entered the town. Militarism was triumphant, thousands of prisoners filled the gaols, and the organisers of revolt were shot or hanged. Revolutionists, and sympathisers with the cause of Magyar independence, were to receive a lesson which would not soon be forgotten, and Windischgrätz's conception of the task which he had undertaken imposed the application to Vienna of the methods which he had successfully employed in Prague.[2] The Reichsrath was removed to Kremsier, near Olmütz, in order that it might be directly under the eye of the Court, and a strong Ministry was appointed. Prince Felix Schwarzenberg, brother-in-law of Windischgrätz, distinguished both as a soldier and as a diplomatist, was made Prime Minister. Animated by the fixed idea of the necessity of reconquering the prestige of which recent events had deprived Austria in the eyes of Europe, he was convinced that the only way to attain the desired object was to establish a single and united Austrian

[1] See Hübner's conversation with Schwarzenberg, *Ein Jahr meines Lebens,* Oct. 9. "L'existence de la monarchie tient à un fil," *sq.*

[2] Helfert, *Geschichte Österreichs vom Ausgange des Wiener Oktoberaufstandes,* iv. 117 *sq.* On the advice of Schwarzenberg, Windischgrätz, to the scandal of Europe, shot Robert Blum, a Radical member of the Frankfort Diet.—Hübner, *Ein Jahr meines Lebens,* November.

Empire by destroying every vestige of Hungarian independence. Windischgrätz, Commander-in-Chief, was not
in the Cabinet, but stipulated that no important step
should be taken without his consent, and practically had
a right of veto in all questions affecting the revision of
the Constitution.[1] An aristocrat of the aristocrats, he is
reported to have expressed the opinion that humanity
begins with barons, and nobility with princes, and to have
entertained the view that the lower orders are fit only to
serve as *chair à canon* and to pay taxes. His ideal was a
return to the benevolent despotism of the age of Maria
Theresa, when the ideas of modern Liberalism were non-
existent. Stadion, the new Minister of the Interior, who
had, as Viceroy of Galicia, got such a hold of the Slavs
that he could do what he liked with them, who utilised
his power to procure the election of ignorant peasants as
members of the Reichsrath, was not in harmony with the
ideas of Windischgrätz and Schwarzenberg, but was convinced of the necessity of Parliamentary government, and
might have done something for his country if he had not
become insane. Bach, ex-Radical and Minister of Justice,
now saw salvation in the autocratic principle and in
uniformity of government, to which Hungary with its
ancient Constitution, its traditions of freedom, and its
responsible Ministry, was the only obstacle. He and
Bruck, the Minister of Commerce, nominally constituted
the Liberal element in the Cabinet, but this fact did
not make them less anti-Magyar than their Conservative
colleagues.

Hungary must be crushed, and the obstacle presented
by the coronation oath and other sacred engagements of
Ferdinand must be brushed aside. The King must make
way for an autocrat whose hands were bound by no
promises to maintain an inconvenient Constitution. The
secret of the intended change, resolved upon in the early

[1] Hübner, *Ein Jahr meines Lebens.*

aays of October,[1] was known only to the Ministry Radetzky, Jellacsics, Windischgrätz, and a few others. Even some of the Archdukes were kept in the dark till the announcement was made to the Reichsrath, on December 2, that Francis Joseph had that day ascended the throne of Austria. The young Emperor can have had but a faint idea of the reasons for his sudden advancement, and, it is to be hoped, did not realise the fact that he was to serve as an instrument for the execution of the cut-and-dried plans of the Ministry which involved the extinction of Magyar liberty in a bath of blood, and the establishment of military and bureaucratic absolutism. The idea that a new King of Hungary was not bound by the promises of his predecessors was an outrage on the most elementary principles of political morality, and, what was worse, it was stupid. An Austrian Emperor could be King of Hungary only in virtue of the Pragmatic Sanction, and of other laws which bound all persons entitled by right of heredity to the Crown of St. Stephen to sign an inaugural diploma guaranteeing the liberties of Hungary, and to swear to maintain the laws and the Constitution. The taking of such an oath was a condition precedent to the right of the person entitled to the throne of Austria to present himself for coronation. Francis Joseph had no claim to the enjoyment of the benefits conferred by the Pragmatic Sanction if he was not prepared to be bound by the obligations which it imposed, and the doctrine that laws or promises lose their binding force on the expiration of the reign during which they were passed or given was a revolutionary innovation completely subversive of the basis of the relations between King and people. Moreover, Francis Joseph had no right to the Hungarian throne, which can become vacant only by the operation of

---

[1] The idea occurred first to the Empress, who often discussed it with Metternich.—Hübner, *Ein Jahr meines Lebens*, December. See especially Helfert, *Geschichte Österreichs*, etc. iii. 342 *sqq.*

nature, or with the consent of the people constitutionally expressed. Even if the abdication of Ferdinand without notification to, and the consent of, the Hungarian Parliament was effective, the position of Francis Joseph was in any case illegal, as the crown must necessarily descend to the eldest male heir of the recent possessor,[1] namely, to the Archduke Francis Charles, father of Francis Joseph ; and nothing but an Act of Parliament could get over this fact. The proclamation announcing Ferdinand's abdication made no reference to Hungary, and only mentioned the fact that the Emperor had thought fit " to abdicate the throne of Austria " and " to renounce the Austrian imperial crown." The question whether the omission was unintentional, or whether the renunciation of the Austrian crown was supposed to make all reference to that of Hungary superfluous, needs no discussion, as, in any case, the latter country could not legally take cognisance of the act of abdication, or regard any person other than Ferdinand as its King. Moreover, as the Austrian Ministry had made up its mind to the effect that Hungary had forfeited its liberties and must henceforth be reduced to the level of a hereditary province,[2] an illegality more or less was of no importance to a monarch selected for the express purpose of pulverising the sacred obligations of his ancestors. The least attempt to approach the Magyars on the basis of a reasonable compromise would have met with instant success on account of the personal popularity of Francis Joseph, and for the reason that a considerable party existed, which comprised such men as Deák, Batthyány,

[1] Law ii. 1687, "descendentium masculorum haeredum primogenitum."

[2] " Die Magyaren haben das geschichtliche Recht des Königreichs Ungarn, die pragmatische Sanktion durch ihre Empörung und insbesondere durch die Akte vom Dezember vorigen Jahres und vom 14. April dieses Jahres selbst vernichtet. Das zur Republik erklärte und von einem Usurpator unter dem Namen eines Souveränen Präsidenten terrorisirten Land muss von seinem legitimen Souverän erobert werden, *und das Gesetz des Siegers ist sein Recht.*"— *Akten des Ministeriums des innern von 1849*, No. 4022, cited by Friedjung, *o.c.* i. 373.

and Wesselényi, who, though just as anxious as Kossuth to maintain the historic rights of their country, did not believe that it could win in the long run, and were ready to make concessions with respect to the control of military, financial, and foreign affairs. But Vienna never gave them a chance to be heard : possibly for the reason that a small Conservative party existed in Hungary which misled the Court as to the true state of Magyar feeling. At the end of November the *Chargé d'Affaires* of the United States offered his mediation to the Committee of National Defence, and Kossuth accepted the offer, declaring in his own and his colleagues' name that the country was ready to accept any honourable peace which would assure the maintenance of its rights and its Constitution ; but the Austrian Government politely told Mr. Stiles to mind his own business.[1]

The proclamation[2] issued by the new Emperor on the day of his succession left no doubt as to his intentions towards Hungary. It confirmed the orders issued to Windischgrätz, on November 6 and 7, instructing him to dissolve Parliament, and proclaiming Kossuth and his followers to be rebels and traitors, and again gave authority to Windischgrätz to reduce Hungary to submission by means of the sword. The determination to seize the opportunity of realising the traditional desire of the Habsburgs to incorporate Hungary in a uniform Austrian Empire was so evident that even the Conservatives had henceforth no justification for dissociating themselves from Kossuth. The summons issued by Windischgrätz to the

[1] See Mr. Stiles's book already referred to, ii. Appendix, p. 402 *sqq.*

[2] Horváth, *Mag. függ. harcz.* i. 163. When Schwarzenberg showed the proclamation to Baron Jósika the latter remarked, "It was only after the battle of White Mountain that Ferdinand II. tore in pieces the charter of Bohemia's liberties. You have not yet conquered Hungary but already assume the right to deal with it as if you had done so."—Hübner, *Ein Jahr meines Lebens,* December. The Ministry was evidently under the impression that the campaign in Hungary would be a mere military promenade. Helfert, *Die Thronbesteigung des Kaisers Franz Joseph,* i. 354 (vol. iii. of his *Geschichte Österreichs,* etc.).

Magyar troops, calling upon them to obey his orders, was naturally disregarded, as his appointment was even less legal than that of Jellacsics had been ; and Parliament made the only possible reply to the manifesto, announcing the change of King, by adopting the correct constitutional attitude, and refusing to take cognisance of a Habsburg family arrangement which could not possibly have any validity in Hungary without the consent, which had not been asked, of the elected representatives of the nation. At the same time, Parliament was still ready to come to terms.   On November 20, Görgei, in a letter to Windischgrätz, insisted on the continued loyalty of the nation to the Throne, and on the 27th Kossuth repeated the assurance of pacific intentions which he had made several months ago.   " We always were, and still are, ready and anxious to hold out a helping hand to smooth away the apparent divergencies between our interests and those of the hereditary provinces, only let us be assured that the sacrifice of our national independence or Con-stitution is not demanded as the price of agreement." Wesselényi used all his influence in favour of the recognition of Francis Joseph, and entreated his country-men not to risk the whole political future of Hungary in a war, the issue of which was at any rate doubtful ; [1] but Kossuth and his party were resolved that a complete recognition of Hungary's historic rights and Constitution must precede the resumption of negotiations.   Kossuth refused to believe that the war could possibly end in the complete discomfiture of his country.   " History," he said, " has shown us Hungary involved in many wars, and surrounded by many adversities, but every single war which she has waged for freedom's sake, has ended not in defeat, but in a bargain." [2]   He was convinced that just as Bocskay,

---

[1] Dec. 6.—Horváth, *Mag. függ. harcz.* ii. 170.   This was Wesselényi's last appearance.   He died a few months later.

[2] Nov. 9.

Bethlen, and Francis Rákóczy had found support in Turkey, France, or in the Protestant nations, so now help would come from abroad. But Napoleon was now master in Paris; Italy was temporarily reduced to impotence; in Germany the revolutionary element had been suppressed, and official England was hypnotised by the idea that only a strong, united, Austrian Empire could guarantee the maintenance of European equilibrium, which the secession of Hungary would necessarily upset. Foreign Governments were made to believe that the war in Hungary was due to the spontaneous revolt of oppressed nationalities against Magyar tyranny, and that Kossuth had stirred up a revolution with the object of breaking all connexion with Austria. In vain Count Ladislaus Teleki and Francis Pulszky, Hungary's representatives in Paris and London, tried to explain the historical basis of Hungary's relations to Austria. The French Government refused to recognise Teleki's *locus standi*, and Palmerston said that the British Government knew Hungary only as a constituent part of the Austrian Empire, a statement which proved the existence of a total misapprehension of the nature of Hungary's connexion with the hereditary provinces of the Habsburgs. No help could therefore be expected from Western Europe, and to the east was Russia, the traditional enemy of Liberalism and freedom.

At the end of November the Magyar forces numbered about 100,000 men, of whom only 16,000 consisted of regular troops, the rest being composed of National Guards and raw levies of all ages and professions. After the fiasco of Schwechat, Kossuth deposed Móga from the office of Commander-in-Chief, and appointed Görgei, an ex-officer of Hussars, in his stead. The want of leaders was severely felt, as many of the officers of the regular troops, in whom the traditions of discipline were stronger than the feeling of patriotism, transferred their

allegiance to Windischgrätz. Their places were taken
by retired army officers, such as Klapka, Damjanics, and
Count Aristides Dessewffy, ex-captains ; Count Leiningen,
cousin of the Queen of England ; and Bem and Dembinsky,
Polish generals who had won great reputations in 1830-31 ;
but for the most part the Magyar officers had to acquire
their experience on the battlefield, and it is therefore not
surprising that the early stages of the war gave but slight
indications of the Magyars' fighting powers, which, later,
evoked the astonishment and admiration of Europe.   On
December 15 Windischgrätz began his advance in the
direction of Pest and met with little resistance.   A last
attempt at negotiation was made by a deputation from the 1849.
Hungarian Government, which included Batthyány, Deák,
and Bishop Lonovics, but Windischgrätz informed them
that he could not recognise the existence of the Parliament
which they represented, and that only " unconditional
submission " could stay his hand.   To this there could
be only one reply.   On January 13 Parliament, which
had in the meantime removed to Debreczen, resolved to
fight to the bitter end.   " What does unconditional submission mean ? " asked Kossuth in his speech of
February 13.   " Does it not mean that Hungary must
cease to be Hungary and become one of the fragmentary
possessions of Austria, deprived of its existence as a nation
and as a State ?   Does it not mean that the nation must
sign its own death-warrant ? "   Parliament answered the
question by unanimously passing a resolution which
declared that : " Whereas the Magyar nation is not
fighting in order to obtain new rights, but has been
compelled to resort to arms by the natural law of self-
preservation, and in defence of its existence as a State
which has lasted a thousand years, and, though guaranteed
by the royal oath, has now in breach of that oath been
made the object of armed attack, the nation will defend
its existence as a State, its independence, its Constitution,

and its nationality to the last man and to the last drop of blood."

On January 5 Windischgrätz occupied Budapest, and both he and the Austrian Government looked upon the war as over, when, in fact, it had hardly begun. Only in Transylvania did matters look tolerably promising for the Magyar cause. At the beginning of October, Puchner, the Austrian General, published a manifesto calling upon the Roumanians to disarm the Magyars, a direct incitement to civil war which resulted in the massacre of hundreds of defenceless persons.[1] The arrival of Bem on the scene early in December soon changed the aspect of affairs, and broke one of the most important links of the chain with which Windischgrätz had intended to crush the ill-organised resistance of the Magyars.[2] The want of organisation and unity of direction was in fact the rock on which the national cause was to suffer shipwreck. Bem, Dembinsky, and Görgei all acted independently of each other and of the Committee of National Defence, which knew little or nothing of what was going on in various parts of the country. At Debreczen the influence of Kossuth was supreme, but there is little evidence to show that he exercised the species of terrorism over dissentients with which his enemies, who wished to throw the whole burden of responsibility for disasters on to his shoulders, subsequently reproached him.[3] At no time was the peace party coerced or exposed to any serious unpleasantness on the part of Kossuth or his supporters, and the very fact of the continuance of discord proves that no undue pressure was put upon the opponents of the policy of the majority. Almost from

[1] See de Bertha, *Magyars et Roumains devant l'histoire*, p. 420. Jancsó Benedek, *Szabadságharczunk és a Dako-Román Törekvések*, 106.

[2] For Bem's campaign see Czetz, *Bem's Feldzug in Siebenbürgen*, Hamburg, 1850.

[3] Kemény, for example, in his pamphlet, *Forradalom után*, for which see Beksics, *Kemény Zsigmond, A Forradalom és a Kiegyezés*, pp. 56-149. For Irányi's refutation, see the Appendix to the same work, p. 331 *sqq*.

the start Görgei severed all connexion with the Committee of National Defence, and, influenced by motives of ambition and of personal hatred of Kossuth, played an insubordinate and almost incomprehensible game, by no means compatible with his duty to the army which trusted him, or to the country which had conferred on him the command of the most important section of the national forces.[1]

Since the transference of the Reichsrath to Kremsier the Government had been occupied by the elaboration of a new Constitution, which should fuse the heterogeneous elements of the dominions of the Habsburgs into a united Austrian Empire in accordance with the manifesto issued by Francis Joseph on his succession, announcing his intention to devote his life to the restoration (*Wiedergeburt*) of the unity of Austria, which, if, as apparently was the case, the term Austria was intended to comprise the dominions of the Hungarian Crown, had in fact never existed. The success of the Austrian arms at Kápolna on February 26, which Windischgrätz magnified into a complete, final victory, led the Court to believe that no further resistance on the part of the Magyars was to be apprehended, and that a suitable moment had arrived for the publication of the new Constitution, for the realisation of the object which Francis Joseph described in his manifesto of March 4 as "the great work of unifying Austria."[2] As the new Constitution of March 4 in fact never had any effective existence, it is unnecessary to do more than refer to those parts of it which concern the Kingdom of Hungary[3] in

[1] He admitted later that he ought to have been shot, under ordinary circumstances, for insubordination.—Marczali, *A Legujabb Kor Története*, p. 703.

[2] The idea of Schwarzenberg, notified by him to the Diet of Frankfurt, was that the united Austrian Empire, the result of the Constitution of March 4, should bodily join the German Confederation, of course as predominant partner. —See Hübner, *Ein Jahr meines Lebens*, March 1849.

[3] For the stillborn Constitution, see Despatch No. 130, *Correspondence*, etc., also Horváth, *Mag függ harcz.* ii. 402, *sqq.* It began with the words, "The source of all power is the people," a somewhat ironical statement, in

order to show the value attached by a constitutional King to the sacred undertakings of his predecessors, and more especially to the Pragmatic Sanction, to which the continued existence of the Habsburg dynasty was due.[1] The Constitution of the Kingdom of Hungary is maintained in so far as its provisions do not interfere with those of the new enactment (sect. 71); in other words, all the characteristics which distinguish it from any petty province of Austria are to be abolished. For this purpose Hungary is to be dismembered by the establishment of a separate Servian Voivodina (sect. 72); by Croatia, Slavonia, Dalmatia, and Fiume being declared a completely independent kingdom (sect. 73); by the severance of Transylvania, the reunion of which with the mother-country, Ferdinand had sanctioned a few months ago; (sect. 74) and by the maintenance of the organisation of the Military Frontiers "which exists for the preservation of the integrity of the Empire."[2] Such were the provisions as far as Hungary was concerned of the new Constitution, which, according to the Emperor's words, was to confer "such identical rights, franchises, and political institutions, as, according to our judgment, are most conducive to the well-being of Austria" and of the "one and indivisible Austrian Empire,"—of Austria, possibly, but certainly not of Hungary. The official *Gazette*, which communicated the contents of the manifesto to the Magyar public, concluded with the words, "the House of Austria has

view of the fact that Vienna and several other large towns were at the moment under martial law, and that an attempt was being made to force Hungary to surrender its constitutional rights. It was formally abrogated in 1851, "as incompatible with the nature and essence of the Austrian Empire."

[1] If Hungary had refused to accept the principle of female succession and had elected its own King, Maria Theresa could never have defended her Austrian provinces against the enemy who robbed her of Silesia, and between the two millstones of Germany and Russia, Austria with its Slav-German population would infallibly have been ground to pieces.—See Deák, Kónyi, iii. p. 41.

[2] Possibly against the Turks, two hundred years ago, but in more recent times as an outpost of Austrian, anti-Magyar, influence.

trampled on law and equity. So be it. Let the sword decide between us, if such is their desire." [1]

The moment selected for the publication of the new Constitution was, as it turned out, particularly inopportune. The tide had turned and the Magyars were everywhere victorious. On March 5 Damjanics obtained the first notable success at Szolnok—the introduction to a series of victorious engagements which culminated in the smashing defeat of the Austrians at Isaszeg on April 6. Windischgrätz, who had been almost uniformly unsuccessful in the field, was relieved of his command, a sign of the nervous depression from which the Court was suffering, and the view was generally entertained in Vienna that the Government's refusal to negotiate with the Magyars when the latter were willing to accept a reasonable compromise would be punished by the total severance of Hungary's connexion with Austria, unless foreign help were quickly obtained. [2] Deák subsequently stated that if the Magyars could have obtained an offer on the morrow of their greatest success at Isaszeg of a settlement on the lines of that arrived at in 1867, they would not have hesitated to accept it. [3] But no such offer was to be made, and compromise had, in fact, been rendered impossible by the premature issue of the imperial proclamation of March 4. It is, therefore, not surprising that the recent victories induced Kossuth to answer that manifesto by taking a step for which he has often been blamed on the ground that his action opened the door to foreign interference, and exposed his country to reprisals which it would otherwise have escaped, though in reality it had no influence on the subsequent course of events. On his return from the camp of the victorious Görgei, Kossuth declared that the time had come for Hungary

[1] March 18, Marczali, *Enchiridion Fontium*, p. 861.
[2] *Correspondence*, etc., Despatch No. 164, Magennis to Palmerston.
[3] Beöthy, *A Magyar Államiság Féjlödése*, etc. i. 561.

to throw off the yoke of the perjured Habsburg dynasty, and to declare its independence. He believed that such a declaration would increase the enthusiasm of the army, and relied on the effect which a *fait accompli* would have on the prospects of European intervention. Francis Rákóczy had also proclaimed the dethronement of the Habsburgs, but in 1707 Louis XIV. of France was ready to help the cause of Hungarian independence, whereas, after the defeat of Victor Emmanuel at Novara, no prospect remained of obtaining foreign assistance, though Kossuth still hoped that its commercial instincts would induce England to interfere, in return for a guarantee of exclusive advantages for British trade in an independent Hungary.[1] Kossuth apparently believed that the final success of the national cause was a certainty,[2] but a considerable party refused to see matters in the same light, and would have opposed the issue of the proposed proclamation had not their leader, Nyáry, insisted on the necessity of apparent unanimity at this crisis in the history of the nation. Many realised the futility of paper thunderbolts which in

[1] Pulszky, *Életem és Korom*.

[2] According to Görgei's account of his interview at Gödöllö with Kossuth, on April 9, Görgei protested on the ground that Hungary was fighting in a just cause which would cease to be just if they fought for separation from Austria ; that they would alienate foreign sympathy by upsetting the balance of power ; that the smallest victory on the field of battle was of greater value than the most self-confident manifesto ; and that battles won in the name of Ferdinand, the legal King, and of the Constitution ratified by him, were the best answer to the dreams of the Viennese Cabinet.— *Mein Leben und Wirken in Ungarn*, Leipzig, 1852, p. 9 *sqq*. It must be remembered that Görgei's account was written two years later, when he had received exceptional treatment at the hands of Francis Joseph and was desirous of justifying himself at the expense of Kossuth, whom he hated, and of whom he was always jealous. Further, in his proclamation to the troops, dated April 10, he called on them ' for still further exertions in order that our beautiful country may be *really free*," and in that of April 29 issued at Komárom, he speaks of freeing the country from "the yoke of a perjured dynasty." These expressions justify the conclusion that Görgei in reality never protested, and had changed his point of view since the issue of his Vácz proclamation of January 5, in which he declared his, and the army's, fidelity to King and Constitution.

no case could strengthen a cause which must depend for its ultimate success on the arbitrament of war, which, by converting a purely defensive campaign (forced on the country by an attempt to deprive it of undeniable historic rights) into a revolutionary struggle, was less likely to conciliate foreign sympathy than to alienate it by giving colour to the statements industriously circulated by Austrian diplomatic agents to the effect that Hungary had all along intended to break away from Austria. But the influence of Kossuth and his stalwarts was too strong for the more moderate minority, and no dissentient voice was raised when a resolution was proposed in favour of the dethronement and perpetual banishment of the Habsburg dynasty. Parliament adjourned to the great Church of Debreczen, and there in the presence of thousands of enthusiastic Magyars the independence of Hungary was solemnly declared. The declaration of independence,[1] published on April 19, was based on the American declaration of 1776. It recited the fact that three hundred years ago the Magyar nation by free vote, and on the basis of a mutually binding contract, had elected the representative of the House of Habsburg to the throne of Hungary. Three centuries of continual suffering was the result. Every Habsburg had tried either forcibly to incorporate the country in the hereditary provinces, or, by paralysing its development, to reduce it to the position of an Austrian colony. Several times Hungary had had to fight to maintain its freedom or its very existence, and on every occasion, when it laid down its arms, fresh guarantees were given only to be violated so soon as an opportunity occurred. From generation to generation the history of the House of Habsburg had been nothing but a record of unintermittent breaches of faith, but in spite of that fact Hungary had faithfully fulfilled its contractual obligations to Austria. If the

[1] Marczali, *Enchiridion Fontium*, p. 864 *sqq.*

Crown leagued itself with the rebellious enemies of the nation, if it attacked its subjects with fire and sword in order to destroy their political existence and the Constitution which the King had sworn to maintain, if it violently dismembered a country the territorial integrity of which it had solemnly guaranteed, if it utilised the armed forces of the foreigner to slay its own subjects and to destroy their legal rights, then at all events was the nation justified in breaking the contract which it had hitherto loyally observed. The Manifesto declared that the House of Habsburg, which had been guilty of every one of these offences, tried to excuse its criminal action by a reference to the laws of 1848 which abolished political inequality, —laws which Ferdinand V. had ratified and confirmed. The Habsburgs were Kings of Hungary in virtue only of the Pragmatic Sanction, which guaranteed the maintenance of the Constitution and the indivisibility of the realms of the Sacred Crown, a fact which had been recognised by every King, with the exception of Joseph II., whose ordinances were consequently void and of no effect. But every King had broken his oath down to Ferdinand V., in whose name the Croatians and others had been incited to kill and murder the Magyars, in whose name race hatred had been engendered, and secret assistance had been given to the rebels until the termination of the Italian campaign allowed the Court to throw off the mask and join openly in the attack on Magyar freedom. The Magyars long believed that all this wickedness perpetrated in the King's name was done without his knowledge, and were anxious to negotiate and ready to crown the new King on receipt of the usual guarantees ; but nothing but the complete destruction of Hungary's historic rights would satisfy the Habsburgs. Therefore, there was no choice but to fight for self-preservation, and to declare that the perjured dynasty was for ever deposed from the throne, that its members were exiled from the Hungarian soil, and that Hungary with Transylvania and the parts annexed took its place in the family of European States, with all of whose members it desired to live on terms of peace and friendship.

Kossuth, now unanimously elected Dictator, has been accused of having ruined his country for the sake of gratifying his personal ambition, and some of his own countrymen repeated the charge in their anxiety to find a scapegoat—to fix the responsibility for their misfortunes on the shoulders of an individual.   The origin of the accusation is to be found in the hatred and jealousy of his opponents and in the disillusionment and disappointment of his supporters.   Kossuth had practically the whole nation at his back, and there is little doubt his refusal to accept the office, for which his overwhelming personality made him the only possible candidate, would have been regarded by the majority of his fellow-countrymen as a worse disaster to the national cause than the loss of many battles.[1]   He had not the slightest desire for a permanent dictatorship ; on the contrary, his one wish was to lay down the burden of his responsibilities at the earliest possible moment.   " I have lived the best of my life," were the words he addressed to Parliament when it unanimously offered him the Dictatorship, " and if I look back on my career, in all those long years there was not one day on which I could say that I was at rest. . . . Let my words be noted in the pages of the Book of Judgment : beyond my earnest desire for the happiness of my country I have no wish save that I may be free to rest. . . . Until the nation is completely assured of its future, so long will I be your Governor and President if such be your will ; but I swear by the living God and my own honour that so soon as the period of uncertainty is over I will be nothing, not even for a single second, but a poor

---

[1] For his influence on the army see Klapka, *Emlékeimből*, Budapest, 1886, 193 *sqq.*, and Beksics, *Kemény Zsigmond*, 126.

and humble private citizen."[1]   Possibly, such words as
these are unconvincing in the mouth of any man who has
raised himself from a comparatively humble station to a
position of pre-eminence. A Cincinnatus is, perhaps, a
rarity, but in any case it is safer to be guided in forming
an estimate of Kossuth's aims and character by the contemporary testimony of those who knew him best than by
the interested malevolence of Görgei, or by the tendentious
criticism of political opponents and foreign detractors.
Kemény[2] and others, who wrote while still under the impression of the bitter days which followed the conclusion
of the war, may describe Kossuth as "the genius of
destruction" and as "a political charlatan," but such
phrases have little weight when compared with the considered judgment of a Deák: "History will connect the
transformation of Hungary with the name of that man
who in 1848 initiated it and carried it through with
unwearied energy. In spite of subsequent events that
part of his work remained and will remain so long as our
country exists. The gratitude of the people will always
be his."[3]

[1] Horváth, *Mag. függ. hartz.* ii. 515. Kossuth repeatedly refused office
in Batthyány's Government, and accepted only when Batthyány told him that
his refusal would make the formation of a Ministry an impossibility.—*Schriften
aus der Emigration*, ii. 290. If he had been ambitious he could have returned
after 1867, and his popularity in the country would have enabled him to carry
all before him.

[2] *A Forradalom után.*

[3] Compare the speech of Count Albert Apponyi, March 23, 1894, when
the news of Kossuth's death was officially announced : "The living are
shrouded in the fog of controversy, in which the transitory opinions of contemporaries are but as feeble, flickering rushlights. Then comes the rough
wind of Death : the mist is dispersed, the petty lamps are extinguished, and
the Sun of History arises. And now in the light of that rising sun we begin
to see what Kossuth was. Let us consider what Hungary was before he put
his hand to the wheel. Was it a nation ? Was it a State ? Was it free ?
Did it belong to the family of European nations ? According to law and
historical tradition, yes. But in reality ? In reality it was torn in pieces by
the contrasts presented by class privilege and servitude. It had no independent
Government. It was a province, which rendered homage to an alien power,
in spite of the futile protests of an impotent Diet. The people was sundered

Unfortunately Kossuth's dictatorship was never really effective, and he could never obtain that concentration of authority which alone could produce unity of action. Not only the Generals in the field, but also members of the Government in the council chamber, developed a mutinous tendency to dispute his supremacy and to play for their own hands.   The declaration of policy of Szemere, the new Minister-President, in which he described the Government as revolutionary and republican, and as determined to resist any attempt to restore the monarchy, a statement which was made without reference to, or consultation with, his colleagues,[1] and to a considerable extent alienated the sympathies of foreign nations, was merely an attempt to curry favour with the extremists and to diminish the prestige of Kossuth,[2] whose acceptance of the Dictatorship, which involved his withdrawal from the scene of his oratorical triumphs, was one of the chief causes of the decline of his authority.   Kossuth has been accused of having ruined his country by having brought

from, and lagged behind, the rest of the civilised world.   The national consciousness was only just waking to life. . . . And to-day ?   To-day, thank God, we are a united nation of free and equal citizens, whose representative assembly is endowed with a decisive influence : a worthy sister-nation of other civilised peoples ; which feels itself to be an independent State, and, imbued with that consciousness, determines its own fate.   The difference between the Hungary of the past and the Hungary of to-day tells us what Louis Kossuth was.   He found the former and created the latter. . . . The historic calling of the Magyar nation and the national development finds its symbol in the name of Louis Kossuth.   That is the secret of the country's feeling for him, that is the measure of our veneration and of our gratitude."—*Apponyi Albert Gróf Beszédei*, Budapest, 1897, ii. 273 *sqq.*

[1] Horváth, who was himself a member of the Government.—*Mag. függ. harcz.* ii. 561.

[2] Kossuth intended, if possible, to find a King abroad.   "I am a republican," he said, "but I love my country more than my political theories. No one can foresee the future, and I consider it my duty as a patriot to declare that in case regard for the independence of our fatherland necessitates the adoption of the monarchical principle I will sacrifice my personal convictions and accept a monarchy, and I believe that every Magyar who loves his country more than himself will act in the same manner.   I propose therefore that we should not declare the establishment of a republic."—*Schriften aus der Emigration*, ii. 293.

about the intervention of Russia, which, so it has been alleged, would not have interfered but for the issue of the Declaration of Independence. The accusation will not bear investigation.

The attention of Russia had been attracted to Hungary in 1831 by the openly-expressed sympathy of the Magyars for the sufferings of the Poles. Two years later the Tsar Nicholas told the Emperor Francis in the presence of Windischgrätz that he was always at the disposal of the Habsburgs, and in 1837 spoke of the possible necessity of armed interference in Hungary to suppress the rising spirit of democracy.[1] In his speech of July 11, 1847, Kossuth called attention to the threatening attitude of the Russian forces assembled in the Danube provinces ; and Palmerston, in an instruction to Sir Stratford Canning, dated November 7, refers to the belief that the presence of those forces "is not wholly unconnected with the events which have been passing in Hungary, and that the Tsar has contemplated the possibility of his being asked by the Austrian Government to restore order in Pest." On the subject of this despatch the British Ambassador wrote to Palmerston stating that he had "little doubt that, should the Austrians receive a severe check in Hungary, the Emperor of Russia would give the most efficient aid to the Emperor of Austria."[2] In January 1849, General Puchner, who had been beaten several times by Bem in Transylvania, entered into communication with General Lüders, Commander of the Russian forces, but did not call upon him for active assistance, as Schwarzenberg hesitated as to the advisability of asking for foreign help. Asked or unasked, on February 1, Generals Engelhardt and Skariatyn occupied Brassó and Nagy Szeben, in order to "stop the threatened invasion of the Magyar and Szekler hordes," only to be ejected by Bem six weeks later.

[1] Marczali, *A Legujabb Kor Története*, p. 720.
[2] Despatch 74, *Correspondence*, etc.

European diplomacy took up the question of Russian interference, and Schwarzenberg made it appear that the towns occupied had themselves called upon the Russians for protection ; but the truth was that the Government of Vienna was beginning to recognise the fact that it must either make terms with the Magyars or call on the Tsar for help [1]—a confession of weakness in which Stadion saw " the grave of Austria's power and reputation." The anti-Liberal ideas of the Tsar, and the fact that Poland was in a state of nervous excitement, and was praying for the success of the Magyars, made him willing, if not anxious, to co-operate with Francis Joseph, to pose in the eyes of Austrian Slavs as the protector of their country, and to acquire a claim to future Austrian assistance in the Balkan Peninsula. Consequently, on April 26, a week before the news of the issue of Kossuth's Declaration of Independence reached Vienna, Nicholas published a manifesto [2] in which he stated that the rising in Hungary had made such progress, and had attained such proportions that Russia could no longer remain an indifferent spectator, but was obliged to accede to the request of the Austrian Emperor, and order the advance of an army to his assistance, " after having invoked the aid, on behalf of so just a cause, of the God of battles who alone can give victory "—the favourite phrase of autocrats preparing to perpetrate an odious act. [3]

[1] See Hübner's account of his conversation with Schwarzenberg. *Ein Jahr meines Lebens*, March 19.

[2] *Correspondence*, etc., Despatch No. 182.

[3] As regards the debated question whether the Austrians called in the Tsar, or Nicholas forced his assistance on Austria, Horváth takes the latter view, but he is clearly wrong. According to Bernhardi, Schwarzenberg brought about Russian intervention by writing to Pashkievitch, playing on his vanity, " *Le sort de l'Europe est entre vos mains*," etc., and saying that the Magyars were trying to bring about a revolution in Poland. Nicholas was made to believe that the Hungarian struggle was in reality a Polish revolution, Schwarzenberg having told him that there were 20,000 Poles in the Magyar army, whereas they never numbered as many as 5000.—Kossuth, *Schriften*, i. 166 ; *A Magyar Nemzet Története*, x. 408, says they did not exceed 1200. The

Nicholas and Francis Joseph met at Warsaw on May 21, and formulated a joint plan of campaign : none too soon for Austria, whose prospects, owing to recent Magyar victories, were anything but encouraging.   The Imperial forces had been dispersed and driven out of Hungary, Komáron had been freed, the Servians had been routed, Transylvania [1] was again in Magyar hands, and Budapest had been recaptured from the enemy.   Unfortunately for the national cause three weeks of precious time had been wasted over the siege of the capital, which, possibly, would have been better employed in an advance on Vienna, where the revolutionary element would have made common cause with the victorious Magyars, with the not improbable result

Wiener Zeitung of Vienna, May 1, 1849, announced that the Emperor Francis Joseph had appealed for assistance to the Tsar, who had promised it "with the most noble goodwill and in the fullest measure." See inclosure in Despatch 168 to Lord Palmerston, *Correspondence*, etc. The Russian official account cited by Beöthy states that Austria asked for help in March.   Subsequently, Austria was ashamed of having had to apply for help to Russia, and tried to make out that the Tsar had forced his assistance on Francis Joseph ; but see the Tsar's proclamation of May 8 (Horváth, *Mag. függ. harcz.* iii. 26), which gives a different version to that of the officious Press of Vienna. Kossuth states that Nicholas, when asked why he sent so many as 200,000 men to Hungary, said : "This expedition is so unpopular in Russia that it must be finished in three months" (*Schriften*, i. 167), a statement borne out by the fact that the Russian officers were particularly friendly to the Magyars, and the reverse to the Austrians.—Görgei, *Mein Leben und Wirken in Ungarn*, ii. In connexion with Austria's invocation of Russian aid, Englishmen should consider what the effect would be on Irish opinion if the British were to have recourse to the German army in order to destroy their Irish fellow-subjects.

[1] The Magyar victories in April, and the recapture of Buda, made the Roumanians begin to think they had put their money on the wrong horse, and Bem encouraged a movement towards reconciliation. Still further victories induced the Roumanian leaders to agree to lay down their arms. On July 21, Szemere introduced a Bill dealing with the Roumanian question, providing for the use of the Roumanian language in schools and law courts in districts in which the Roumanians were in a majority, for a general amnesty, for the appointment of Roumanian officers and Roumanian officials on a footing of equality with the Magyars. Parliament accepted Szemere's proposal, which would no doubt have put an end to discord, but like other just and reasonable proposals, it was nullified by the intervention of the Russians and the temporary destruction of Hungarian liberty. For an account of the reconciliation, see de Bertha, *Magyars et Roumains devant l'histoire*, p. 432 *sq.* ; and especially Jancsó Benedek, *Szabadságharczunk*, etc., 139 *sqq.*, 150 *sqq.*, 159, 160.

that the war would have ended in a compromise providing
for the withdrawal of the Declaration of Independence
and the recognition of Hungarian freedom on the basis
of the Pragmatic Sanction.[1]   Russian intervention entirely
changed the situation.   The Magyars' only chance of success
lay in immediate concentration of their scattered forces,[2]
but the Commanders of the various armies preferred to
earn credit for successful independent action to sharing
the laurels which might be won in combination with other
leaders.   In June, when it was too late, Görgei tried to
induce the Government to order the concentration of all
forces against the real enemy, the Austrians, and to keep
the Russians occupied with negotiations with a view to
obtaining their support against Austria in return for the
offer of the Hungarian crown to the Duke of Leuchtenberg,
the Tsar's son-in-law.[3]   Later, Kossuth wished to concentrate in the south, but the scheme was defeated by the
jealousy and insubordination of Görgei, and by Bem's futile
attempt to create a diversion by invading Moldavia, and
stirring up a revolution there, when he should have joined
hands with the forces operating in the north.   The attempt
failed, and Bem was defeated by a superior Russian force
at Fejéregyház, where the poet Petőfi met his death, and

[1] Kossuth and Görgei (see their letters, March 9 and May 8, Klapka,
National Krieg, 257-387) thought that the Magyar prestige required the
recapture of the capital, and that success there would increase the national
enthusiasm.   Klapka (*Emlékeimből*) denies that Kossuth was responsible, and
that an advance on Vienna could have been made with success (141 *sq.*).   Stiles,
who was in Vienna at the time, was strongly of opinion that the Magyars
could have bivouacked in the Kaiserstadt within two days.—*O.c.* ii. 201.
Irányi was of the same opinion, *Histoire Politique*, etc., ii. 432.

[2] In the middle of May the Magyar forces were distributed thus : Army of
the Danube, 62,640 men ; Army of the Tisza, 16,600; Southern Army, 36,800 ;
in Transylvania, 27,000 ; Reserve, 9500 ; Irregulars, 20,000—total, 172,540
and 498 guns.   The Austrians under Haynau numbered 177,000 and 629 guns ;
the Russians under Pashkievitch, 203,000, and 635 guns. — Horváth, *Mag.
függ. harcz.* iii. 161 *sq.*   Klapka, *Emlékeimből*, 354 *sq.*, says the Magyar forces
amounted to 135,000 men and 400 guns ; the Austro-Russian to 307,000.

[3] Görgei, *Mein Leben*, etc. ii. 375 *sq.* ; Marczaii, *A Legujabb Kor Története*,
725.   Irányi et Chassin, *Histoire Politique*, etc. ii. 568 *sqq.*

again at Szent András on August 9, with the result that
the siege of Temesvár was raised. Görgei, whose army
was still undiminished as regards both numbers and
fighting efficiency, was now confirmed in the opinion which
he had entertained for some time, namely, that there was
no alternative but to save unnecessary bloodshed by
capitulating to the Russians, from whom better terms
could be expected than from Haynau, "the Hyaena of
Brescia,"[1] and from the tender mercies of the Austrian
Government. On August 10, before the result of the
fighting at Temesvár was known, Görgei declared that if
the issue was favourable he would advance against the
Austrians, otherwise he would lay down his arms. The
desire to humiliate Kossuth rather than the necessities of
the situation caused him to insist on the retirement of his
rival from the Dictatorship, and on his own appointment
to the vacant place.[2] Kossuth complied with the demand,
and explained his motives to the nation in a last proclamation. The existing Government, he said, was not only
useless at the present juncture, but was actually injurious
to the interests of the country, for salvation could come
only from the person in actual command of the armed
forces of the nation—a clear indication of the fact that
he never contemplated the possibility of the immediate
abandonment of the struggle. As soon, however, as
Kossuth's back was turned, Görgei issued a manifesto in
which he stated that he could do no more than put a stop

---

[1] So-called from the barbaric brutality with which he treated that town.
"The imperial General who was guilty of these atrocities so disgraceful to the
age, and who publicly avows them in his report to the Government, so far
from being dismissed and dishonoured, was in a few months promoted to a
higher station, and entrusted with the command of all the Austrian troops
engaged at that time in the subjugation of Hungary, where he was enabled
to perpetrate deeds of enormity in comparison with which the treatment of
the Brescians dwindles into comparative insignificance, and which has justly
covered him with the unmitigated execration of the civilised world."—
Stiles, o.c. ii. 274.

[2] Irányi says he intended a *coup d'état militaire*, a military dictatorship.—
Histoire Politique, etc. ii. 492 *sq.*

to useless bloodshed, and entered into negotiations with the Russian General, Rüdiger, with a view to capitulation, in the confident belief that the Tsar would protect his prisoners from the vengeance of Haynau and his masters. On August 12 he led his army to Világos, and not until it had arrived at the position indicated by Rüdiger for the final scene was it apprised of its leader's intentions, the announcement of which was received with furious protests and mutinous despair. On the following day 30,000 men laid down their arms, and Pashkievitch was able to report to the Tsar that, "Hungary lies vanquished at the feet of your Majesty"—a slap in the face for Austria which was not without effect on subsequent history. Görgei's life was spared. He was interned at Klagenfurt, and, according to Horváth, received a pension both from the Emperor and from the Tsar. Whether this is true or not, the exceptional treatment meted out to him gave colour to the suggestion, at first whispered, but later made openly by Kossuth and others, that he was a traitor, and, like Bazaine, had played a selfish game without regard to the interests of his country. According to Kossuth there was no justification for surrender.[1] The road lay open to Komárom, where Görgei's army could have joined hands with a victorious army of 32,000 men under Klapka, and to the parts beyond the Danube where fresh forces could have been raised. General Pashkievitch did not expect surrender. His report on the situation was already on its way to the Tsar, in which he stated that he must temporarily retreat before autumn began, that he was being continually harassed by the Magyar forces, and was surrounded by a hostile population. The fortresses of Komárom, Petervárad, and Arad, were still in Magyar hands, and winter would have brought a fresh accession of strength. Such was Kossuth's view, due, perhaps, in part to the instinct of self-justification, but generally accepted

[1] *Schriften*, ii. 237.

by the nation, which, at the moment of disaster, was not unnaturally disposed to salve the wounds inflicted on its self-respect at the expense of an individual. Dembinski's memoirs [1] would lead one to believe that Görgei was a traitor from start to finish, but the whole history of the war is a refutation of the suggestion that he deliberately betrayed his trust or sought to save his own life at the expense of the nation's interests.[2] The fact is that he was a born soldier who cared little or nothing about his country's constitutional privileges, and entertained the fighter's contempt for hairsplitters and politicians.[3] Rightly or wrongly convinced of the hopelessness of the military situation, he thought it better to put an end to bloodshed than to prolong a useless struggle[4] on the chance of foreign intervention,[5] though he must have known that his decision would tarnish the glory to which his action in the field indubitably entitled him.

On September 27 Klapka surrendered Komárom on terms which guaranteed the personal safety of the officers

[1] Dantzer ed. Budapest, 1874. See also Klapka, *Emlékeimből*, 127 *sq.* For a panegyric on his qualities, see Busbach, *Egy viharos Emberöltö*, Pest, 1898, i. 144 *sq.* Irányi, *Histoire Politique*, takes the same view as Dembinski.

[2] He wrote to Rüdiger : "I tell you solemnly that I am ready to annihilate my army in a battle of despair, no matter how overwhelming the odds may be, rather than lay down my arms unconditionally before the Austrian army."—Horváth, *Mag. függ. harcz.* iii. 488.

[3] See Beöthy (*o.c.* iii. 401) who, though a strong Kossuthite, denies that there was any *dolus premeditatus* in Görgei.

[4] See Görgei's *Mein Leben und Wirken in Ungarn*, ii. 419, etc. Görgei returned to Hungary in 1867 and was cold-shouldered by his countrymen till 1884, when he was whitewashed by a pronouncement signed by Klapka and two hundred and seven officers who took part in the fight for freedom. Public opinion entirely changed, the charge of treason no longer finds support, and full justice is done to his great military talents.

[5] Kossuth still hoped that if Hungary stood out a little longer, England would come to the rescue, and that the Constitution would be restored on the basis of the laws of 1848 under England's guarantee. In his letter to Klapka announcing Görgei's "betrayal of his country," he says : "England's sympathy with us is powerfully demonstrated. If Komárom holds out the country is still saved" (October 2). The war had already cost the lives of 24,000 Magyars.—*A Magyar Nemzet Története*, x. 394.

and men,[1] and the war came to an end. Little doubt
was entertained as to the manner in which Haynau would
use his power. The Tsar appealed to Francis Joseph on
behalf of the Magyars, who had succumbed to Russian,
not to Austrian arms, but in vain. The Emperor replied,
" I have no desire but to find means which would make it
possible to heal the terrible wounds inflicted on unhappy
Hungary—the result of a criminal rebellion, but I must
not forget that I have sacred duties to perform towards
my other peoples, and I must not lose sight of the obligations imposed on me with regard to the general welfare of
my dominions."   The " sacred duties " apparently necessitated the inauguration, by the butcher Haynau, of a reign
of terror and of a system of deliberate brutality which finds
its parallel only in the horrors perpetrated by another
agent of the Habsburgs—Caraffa. On October 16, 1847,
Francis Joseph, on the occasion of the investiture of the
Archduke Stephen with the office of Palatine, said, " I
shall bless the day which gives me the opportunity of
giving public proof of my lively affection for the Magyar
people."   He had such an opportunity on October 6,
1849, when thirteen generals were put to death at Arad
for having done their duty to their country, but refused
to speak the word which would have saved them from the
gallows.[2] On the same day at Pest, Louis Batthyány,
who had taken no part in the revolutionary war, and, as
Prime Minister, had done his utmost to keep his countrymen within the bounds of strict legality, and to find a
peaceful solution of the question at issue, was sacrificed to
the personal spite of Schwarzenberg and the Archduchess
Sophia. Condemned to be hanged like a common criminal,
he attempted suicide, and inflicted a wound on his neck

[1] Klapka, *Emlékeimböl*, 231. Haynau subsequently broke the terms of
capitulation.   See Klapka's letter to him from London, *ibid.* 305 *sq.*
[2] Of the " Martyrs of Arad," Aulich, Damjanics, Alexander Nágy, Count
Vécsey, Török, Láhner, Knezics, Pöltenberg, and Count Leiningen were
hanged. Lázár, Dessewffy, Kiss, and Schweidel were shot.

which made it impossible to execute the sentence. He was shot a few hours later, and the "damned spot" which his murder left on the Imperial Crown of Austria can never be washed away.[1]

In all, forty-nine persons were hanged, sixty-five were shot, and eighteen local courts-martial were busily employed with the hundreds of persons whom services rendered to their country, or private malice, marked out for punishment. The disgust engendered throughout Europe by the brutalities to which the Magyars were subjected reached its highest point when it became known that Haynau had caused women to be stripped and publicly flogged by his soldiers.[2] Leopold I. wreaked a bloody vengeance on Nádasdy and others as part of his scheme to make Hungary first a slave, then a beggar, and then a Catholic; Joseph II. pursued a deliberate policy

[1] For his mock trial and the refusal to allow him to call for the evidence, as to the part he had played, of the late Palatine, the Archduke Stephen, see Friedjung, o.c. i. p. 228 sqq. and Appendix x. "Keiner unter den Blutzeugen für die Freiheit Ungarns verdient grössere Theilname als Graf Ludwig Batthyány. . . . Er hatte sich bis zum letzten Augenblicke in der Vermittlung zwischen dem Hof und der Revolution veizehrt, voll Unwillen über die Leidenschaftlichkeit der er·hier wie dort begegnete. . . . Der gegen ihn angestrengte Prozess gereicht der Regierung zur Schmach. Aus den akten geht ziemlich deutlich hervor dass seine Verurtheilung gegen die bessere Ueberzeugung des Untersuchungsrichters und auf höheren Befehl erfolgt ist. . . . Man sieht dass das Urtheil nichts Beweiskräftiges vorzubringen weiss."

[2] Consul-General Fonblanque to Sir Stratford Canning, Despatch 323, Correspondence, etc. "There may have been technical palliation for the execution of forty or fifty officers; but I can conceive no such excuse for such facts as the arbitrary sentence ori Mme. —— should sweep the streets of Temesvár, or the far more revolting outrage of having caused Mme. —— to be stripped, and in that state flogged by soldiers just after her husband had committed suicide. There are also reports of secret executions and of the sudden disappearance of persons. The Russian agents have, I understand, complained energetically against this cruel system. The Hungarians dread the departure of the Cossacks from the country." A more eloquent testimony to Austrian brutality than this last sentence could not be imagined. The opinion of the British "man in the street" was sufficiently indicated by the fact that when Haynau subsequently visited Barclay and Perkins's brewery in London the employés, as soon as they became aware of his identity, beat him severely.

of forcible germanisation, but he was not bloodthirsty; Haynau, the agent of a later Habsburg, was the willing instrument of a policy which followed that of the former monarch as regards the ferocity of the methods employed, and that of the latter as regards the object to be attained —the extirpation of the spirit of Magyar nationality. If Francis Joseph, after Világos, had employed a statesman instead of a butcher, a permanent system of centralisation might possibly have been established, but organised brutality was answered by dogged passive resistance, and engendered a hatred which only the lapse of many years could eradicate.[1]

And what, after all, was the crime for which Hungary suffered? For having sought to put into practice the rights which it theoretically enjoyed by virtue of its Constitution and its laws, which successive Habsburgs had sworn to observe and had systematically violated. For having drawn the logical conclusion from the Pragmatic Sanction, a contract between a free country and an alien King whose successors claimed to enjoy the benefits derivable from that compact, and disregarded the obligations which it imposed. For having abolished serfdom and put an end to the injustice which imposed the whole burden of taxation on those who were least able to bear it. For having given political rights to all, without regard to racial, religious, or class distinctions,[2] without diminishing the Crown's constitutional authority, or relaxing the bonds

---

[1] It is a question how far Schwarzenberg was responsible for Haynau's brutalities. He is said to have replied to a suggestion that a merciful policy should be adopted with an eye to the future, "That's all very well, but first we want to do a bit of hanging."—Friedjung, o.c. i. 235 n. Wessenberg's criticism of Austria's action is much to the point : "Revolutionen sind moralische Krankheiten die nicht mittels des Schaffots allein geheilt werden können."— Ibid. p. 437.

[2] Out of a population of 11,500,000 (Pauler, A Magyar Nemzet Története Szt Istvánig, p. 130) in 1848 the nobles numbered 675,000, to which must be added 16,000 ecclesiastical voters, the honoratiores, and burgesses of privileged towns.—Apponyi, The Juridical Relations, etc. p. 8 n.

which united Hungary to Austria. For having taken steps to attain to that position of independence which it was entitled to occupy as a "*regnum liberum et relate ad totam legalem regiminis formam independens.*"[1] Kossuth is said by his enemies to have been an armchair revolutionist who stirred up the passions of his coutrymen for the gratification of his own ambition, but no revolutionary measure was ever enacted by him or by his colleagues, and no revolutionary act was committed, until the intention of the Court, finally proved by the manifesto of March 4, became clear and unmistakable. It is absurd to suppose that if he had given way on financial and military questions the Camarilla would have stayed its hand and ceased from collusion with the enemies of Hungary's historic rights. It meant to subdue the Magyars once for all, and to bring about their permanent subordination to the German element in Austria; but it failed, just as Leopold and Joseph, with divergent methods but identical aims, had failed. The ordeal through which the nation passed did but rejuvenate it. Though of Hungary's statesmen some were in exile, some were in prison, and some were in their graves,[2] the spirit of Magyar nationality was again to give proof of that indestructible vitality which had enabled the nation to withstand the open hostility and secret malevolence of which it had been the object throughout the thousand years of its political existence.

[1] Law x. 1790-91.

[2] Kossuth retired to Turkey, whither many followed him. Both Tsar and Emperor demanded that the refugees should be given up, but the Sultan, backed by Sir Stratford Canning and the French Ambassador, refused to surrender them. The more conspicuous of them were therefore hanged in effigy. Horváth, Klapka, and others joined Pulszky in London, whither Kossuth went later to be received with unparalleled enthusiasm.

CHAPTER XVI

THE capitulation of Világos seemed to have realised the fondest aspirations of the reactionaries. The object for the attainment of which successive Habsburgs had striven in vain was apparently within the reach of Francis Joseph. Unhampered by the bonds of an immemorial Constitution, and by the inconvenient oaths of his predecessors, he seemed destined to bring into existence a united and uniform Austrian Empire, in which Hungary would stand on precisely the same footing as any petty principality or countship of the hereditary provinces. For the moment, at all events, the imperial possessions in Italy were secure, and no external complications were to be apprehended from any other quarter. At home Liberal principles were at a hopeless discount, and Vienna, strong in the support of Russia, the arch-reactionary, could devote all its energies to the creation of a new Austria of absolutism, germanisation, and clerical obscurantism. In Hungary, Haynau and martial law reigned supreme. Schwarzenberg cared for nothing but the re-establishment of Austria's position as a Great Power, whose reputation had suffered somewhat owing to recent humiliations; and Francis Joseph, ashamed of owing his Hungarian throne to the intervention of the Tsar, apparently thought it necessary to " save his face " and show the strength of Austria by taking vengeance on the vanquished, and by the inauguration of a military despotism. Oblivious of the fact that the Emperor of Austria could have no rights in Hungary save those conferred upon him by the Constitution, the last vestiges of which he was urged to abolish, he lent a willing ear to the exponents of the bureaucratic idea that the Magyars had long intended to break away from Austria,[1] and, by reason of the issue of the Declaration of Independence, had forfeited all political rights. As a matter of fact, except for a short time, when the country was infuriated by the expression of Francis Joseph's intention to ignore past history and to disregard all dynastic obligations, no one, with the exception of a few extremists, ever contemplated the severance of Hungary's connexion with the Habsburg dynasty ; but the monarch whom the Camarilla had raised to the throne for a specific purpose must necessarily accept the interpretation of past events which suited the views and the aims of the kingmakers, and must attempt the reduction of Hungary to the position of a subordinate province of Austria—a task which history had proved to be impossible. Hungary temporarily suffered, and Austria permanently profited, from the events of the past two years. But for the action of the Magyars Austria would have waited in vain for anything beyond the sham and the shadow of constitutional government which the Schwarzenbergs and the Bachs thought good enough for the hereditary provinces. By widening the franchise, by establishing the principle of ministerial responsibility to Parliament, and, above all, by liberating the peasants, Hungary had made a permanent recurrence to old forms an impossibility, and at the same time had obtained strength to resist the effects of the ensuing period of undiluted despotism. For the mass of the population the so-called revolution had meant neither more nor less than the abolition of feudal subjection, and the name of Louis Kossuth was

---

[1] Pillersdorff, *Handschriftlicher Nachlass*, 1863, p. 325. Somssich refuted this view, *Das legitime Recht Ungarns und seines Königs*, 1850, pp. 1-14 etc. See also Irányi and Chassin, *Histoire Politique*, etc. p. 3.

to be adored for ever, identified, not with the short, bloody ordeal though which his country had passed, but with the lasting work of emancipation.   If Vienna had attempted to interfere with Kossuth's legacy of freedom, every peasant would have risen to massacre landlords and Austrian officials with impartial fury.   If freedom had not been granted in 1848, Bach would have had to deal only with the privileged classes in his task of robbing Hungary of its individuality, and could have won the others to his side by making concessions at the expense of the land-owners.   As matters stood, he found himself face to face with a national solidarity which made the ultimate revival of Magyar independence a certainty.[1]   The very brutality of the Austrian despotism was the cause of its failure. A mild *régime* might have won the support of the Conservatives, who always recognised the importance of the dynasty as the sole tie capable of preserving the connexion between the incohesive elements of Austria and Hungary, and, seeing the destruction wrought by the fight for freedom, would have been glad to accept considerably less than a return to the state of affairs which existed before March 1848.   But for Bach there might have been no Solferino, no Königgrätz, and no Compromise of 1867.[2]   The proclamation, contained in the Constitution of March 4, of religious equality, of the right of free speech and public meeting, of the abolition of the censorship, and of the recognition of the sanctity of private correspondence, found no application in Hungary, but served to throw dust in the eyes of Europe, and as a cloak to cover the nakedness of the tyrannical *régime* which followed the capitulation of Világos.   The Conservatives, who had taken no part in the war, flattered themselves that they would be employed to re-establish the relations which had

[1] "Das Bachsche System war im einzelnen kunstreich gefügt, aber es fehlte ihm jener Tropfen von Weisheit und Milde, ohne den aller Menschenwitz doch nur Vergängliches zu schaffen vermag."—Friedjung, *o.c.* i. 438.
[2] Beksics, *Kémeny Zsigmond*, 158.

existed between their country and Vienna before the Ides
of March, and failed to realise the fact that the triumph
of Austria and Russia would necessarily entail a recurrence
of Josephism, of coercion, centralisation, and germanisation.

Windischgrätz wrote to Count George Apponyi :
" The old Constitution must be modified by the adoption
of such reforms as are in accordance with the requirements
of the age, but its complete abolition is neither advisable
nor desirable. Our task therefore consists in the separation
of the expedient from the inexpedient parts of the Constitution, with a view to bringing Hungary into closer union
with the monarchy as a whole "[1]—a pronouncement which
confirmed the notion of the Conservatives that a recurrence
to the *status quo ante bellum* might be confidently expected.
The appointment of Haynau as Commander-in-Chief, and
the establishment in the following December of a dictatorship, under which Hungary was divided into military
districts under martial law, should have opened their eyes
and made them understand that the modification of the
Constitution referred to by Windischgrätz was a euphemism
for its total destruction. The whole country was practically
in a state of siege. Courts-martial worked incessantly at
the task of purifying the population by the elimination of
unreliable elements. When the gaols were full, Haynau
gave orders that every person who had taken part in the
war should be enrolled in the imperial army, which would
have meant the removal of all working hands, and starvation for innumerable families. About 50,000 were actually
so enrolled before the order was modified by the exemption
of all above the age of thirty-eight, and of those who
were able to pay a fine of 500 florins or to find a substitute.[2] A swarm of foreign officials, Germans, Czechs,
and Galicians, who did not understand the Hungarian
language, descended on the country, and proceeded to
exact by force the payment of taxes from a population

which war had reduced to the verge of starvation. For all Schwarzenberg cared, who devoted all the time he could spare from the gratification of his passions to the consideration of foreign affairs, the state of siege might have continued for ever;[1] but Bach, the Minister of the Interior, who in 1842 had been one of the most violent opponents of Metternich's "shameless" reactionary policy, and was the author of the famous phrase, "The people of Vienna expresses its sovereign will in the easily understood language of the barricade,"[2] was against its continuance as interfering with his scheme of a uniform Austrian Empire. Haynau, therefore, was dismissed in July 1850, and the Archduke Albrecht was appointed Viceroy in his place, as no Magyar could be found to accept office on the terms of "Hungary being reduced to a geographical expression."[3] The Constitution of March 4 was already a dead letter, and under Albrecht the military despotism of Haynau was replaced by civil absolutism, by the so-called provisional government, which lasted till 1853.

The first step was the dismemberment of Hungary. Transylvania and the Banate of Temes were taken from the mother country; the frontier districts again received a special military organisation, and the recognition of the distinctive privileges of the Saxons was promised. Croatia and Slavonia were made into a separate dominion; a Servian Wojwodina was created, and Fiume no longer formed a "*separatum corpus regni Hungariae.*" Hungary, thus maimed and dismembered, was still considered too large and homogeneous. It was therefore split into five districts, each with its separate government and judiciary.

---

[1] According to Emil Dessewffy, Schwarzenberg said that all he knew about Hungary was the existence of one or two pretty women.—*A Mag. Nem. Tört.* x. 464.

[2] Rogge, *Oesterreich von Vildgos bis zur Gegenwart*, i. 276.

[3] It was offered to Baron Nicholas Vay on these terms.—Marczali, *A Legujabb Kor Története*, 849; Levay, *Emléklapok Vajai Báró Vay Miklos Életéből*, Budapest, 1889.

Behind the civil organisation stood a military despotism, which, knowing that but for the bayonet the whole system must collapse, watched with amused contempt the efforts of the bureaucracy to produce a semblance of orderly government. The secret police had every one's *dossier*, and the Black Cabinet controlled all correspondence. All official positions were filled by foreigners dressed in Hungarian national costume and known by the contemptuous designation of Bach's Hussars.[1] The people had to pay taxes as to the purport and justification of which they knew nothing, and had to obey orders couched in a language which they did not understand. Rules and regulations came in showers from Vienna, and increased rather than mitigated the prevailing disorder. Government, and the administration of justice, were practically at a standstill. In many places the peasants turned for a settlement of their disputes to the officials of the old *régime*, who, without pay and without authority, dispensed a kind of rough justice in which the population found greater satisfaction than in the foreign article, until matters became more settled, when, as Hungarians themselves admitted, the administration of justice compared favourably with that of the old local courts. Nothing was done to improve the material wellbeing of the country. The roads were worse than ever, and the projected network of railways never got beyond the paper stage. The collection of taxes gave special opportunity for the exercise of favouritism. A distinction was drawn between districts which were regarded as well disposed towards the Government and those which were supposed to be unreliable. Individuals who enjoyed the protection of the influential got off cheaply, while others, more especially the larger landowners, were at the mercy of collectors who rated them on property which they did not possess. The result was a notable fall in values, as no one knew to what

1 Berzeviczy Albert, *Régi Emlékek*, Budapest, 1907, p. 66 *sqq.*

burdens the land which he proposed to buy might be subject. The land-tax rose from 7½ per cent of the net value of property to 17 per cent, and whereas in 1847 the total cost of local government had been 3,000,000 florins, one year of Bach's *régime* sufficed to raise it to 13,000,000.[1] The crushing burden of taxation increased by 120 per cent, and the loss of feudal dues, the promised compensation for which was not forthcoming, drove the smaller landowners into the arms of the Jews, and completed the ruin which the war had begun.[2] In 1850 a gendarmerie was established as an instrument of oppression, not of protection, for the persecution of political suspects and inconvenient persons, not for the defence of life and property,[3] and an extraordinary system of rewards was introduced—a sliding scale varying according to the severity of the sentence inflicted on the victims of inquisitorial activity. For example, if any person received a sentence of one to three years' imprisonment, the gendarme who had effected his arrest received eight florins. A sentence of fifteen to twenty years brought a bonus of thirty florins, a death sentence one of sixty florins, to the fortunate policeman. There is, therefore, no cause for surprise when we are informed that 342,000 cases were brought before the courts in three months, and that domiciliary visits and arrests totalled more than 800,000 during the same period.[4] The entire population was, in fact, under the permanent supervision

---

[1] *A Mag. Nem. Tört.* x. 436.

[2] "Die Thatsache dass die Robot schon 1848 aufhörte, während die Entschädigung erst einige Jahre später ausgezahlt wurde ; unterdessen waren die Grundbesitzer auf die Aushilfe von Wucherern angewiesen. Als der Übelstand zu drückend wurde, gewährte die Regierung zwar Vorschüsse, verweigerte sie aber denjenigen deren oppositionelle Haltung bekannt war"— in other words, to practically the whole of the "gentry."—Friedjung, *o.c.* i. 352.

[3] "Da es von der Regierung rücksichtslos zu politischen Zwecken, zur Ueberwachung und zur Niederhaltung aller 'Verdächtigen' benützt wurde, so erregte sein Wirken vielfach Erbitterung."—*Ibid.* 324.

[4] *A Mag. Nem. Tört.* x. 440.

of the police, who interfered on the slightest provocation on the ground that the object of their animosity entertained relations with suspect persons. Even the shape of a hat, the wearing of a feather, or the twist of a moustache, were regarded as justifying suspicions of the existence of revolutionary tendencies. With the introduction of the Austrian tobacco monopoly into Hungary in 1850, the unpopularity of the new *régime* among the lower classes reached its highest point. To show their hatred of this new form of governmental interference the peasants broke their pipes and destroyed the tobacco seeds, and were punished in consequence as for a political crime.[1] Like Joseph II., Bach and Count Leo Thun, the Minister of Education, were not satisfied with the establishment of a system of strict centralisation and uniformity, unless it bore the stamp of German origin.[2] The Constitution of March 4 had promised equal privileges to all races and languages, but,[3] as equal language rights were incompatible with complete centralisation, on December 31, 1851, the Constitution was abolished as being "inappropriate as regards its fundamental conceptions to the situation of the Empire and impracticable as a whole." The ground was thus cleared for the compulsory use of the German language even in those parts of Hungary where the Germans formed an insignificant minority, though experience had proved the impossibility of conducting the business of Government solely in the

[1] For the first two years of absolutism, see Zsedenyi, *Ungarns Gegenwart*, Vienna, 1850 ; also *Acht Jahre Amtsleben in Ungarn*, Leipzig, 1861.

[2] "Man versteht die Unterrichtspolitik der Zeit nur dann, wenn man sich in dem widerspruchsvollen Geiste des Kultus-und Unterrichts-Minister Grafen Leo Thun zurechtfindet, der es zuwege brachte liebevolle Förderung wissenschaftlicher Bildung mit Konfessioneller Engherzigkeit, überlaute Theilname an der Wiedergeburt der tschechischen Literatur mit strengen Massregeln zur Germanisierung Ungarns und Galiziens zu vereinigen."—Friedjung, *o.c.* i. 329.

[3] An imperial manifesto of December 2, 1848, contained a similar promise, and for a short time official notices were published in ten languages, but the new departure was soon abandoned in favour of the exclusive use of German (Gumplowitz, *o.c.* p. 105) even in Lombardo-Venetia.—*Ibid.* p. 113.

German language even in Austria, where Czechs and Moravians had successfully resisted the attempted process of germanisation. Schwarzenberg still dreamed of the possibility of creating a German Empire of 70,000,000 inhabitants, which should comprise the German Confederation and all the dominions of the Habsburgs. Early in 1851, at a conference of princes held at Dresden, a scheme was propounded with a view to the utilisation of German numerical preponderance and superiority of culture for the destruction of the individuality of the constituent races of Austria and Hungary, and for the ultimate construction of a solid, uniform, German block in central Europe under Austrian hegemony.[1] The scheme, which provided that any attack on Austria from Hungary or Italy should be regarded as an attack on Germany, to be resisted by the united forces of the Confederation, served only to emphasise the fact of Austria's inherent weakness. The majority of the small German States showed clearly enough that they had no love for Austria; the Government of Turin left no stone unturned in order to defeat the project; Napoleon III. declared that its adoption would be a *casus belli*, and Francis Joseph's patron, the Tsar Nicholas, advised his *protégé* to abandon the idea.[2] So the conference proved abortive, and Austria was left to carry out its germanising policy unaided. At first Thun had allowed the use of other languages as the medium of education in primary and secondary schools, but Bach's influence changed his notions, and, except in the case of the most elementary subjects, the use of German was everywhere made obligatory.

Undisguised reaction was the order of the day. Three imperial rescripts of August 20, 1851, showed a deliberate

[1] Schwarzenberg forgot the fact that the German race never could and never will absorb other nationalities, but that its members, when transplanted from the Fatherland, lose their original nationality more deliberately and completely than those of any other nation.

[2] Kossuth, *Schriften aus der Emigration*, i. 16 *sq.*

intention to recur to the autocratic system of the early part of the century. Ministerial responsibility to Parliament was abolished, and the Reichsrath was reduced to the position of a purely consultative body. All constitutional government came to an end, and the official views of the functions of the Crown and of the people were correctly expressed by Baron Hartig in the phrase, "The Emperor hears, examines, and commands : his subjects desire, speak, and obey."[1] Trial by jury was abolished, and a new penal law was introduced in 1852, providing for the infliction of the severest penalties on persons who should be guilty of doing anything to undermine public confidence in the merits of benevolent despotism. At the same time, a new ordinance not merely muzzled but killed the Press by reintroducing the preliminary censure, and by fixing the forfeitable caution-money at an impossible figure. Independent journalism was defunct, only Governmental organs for the publication of colourless or inspired statements continued to exist.[2] In Hungary General Heyntzl and Protmann started a campaign of almost farcical violence for the suppression of all forms of literary activity.[3] Courts-martial, singularly inappropriate tribunals for the trial of offences against the Press-laws as interpreted by Austrian Generals, and the preliminary censure, were the ineffective instruments of military obscurantism. The public learnt to read between the lines, and the meaning of references to affairs in China or Japan was understood by all, with the exception of the censors. Of the more important journals, the *Magyar Hirlap* made some pretence of

[1] Rogge, *Oesterreich von Vildgos bis zur Gegenwart*, i.

[2] "Von dieser Zeit an wurden die Journale ganz inhaltsleer ; sie schwiegen wenn sie mit der Regierung nicht einverstanden waren, gänzlich, da jedes Wort der Kritik strenge geahndet wurde." "Selbst die harmlosen Witzbolde der Wiener bekamen dies zu fühlen."—Friedjung, *o.c.* i. 462 and *note*.

[3] See Beksics, *Ferencz József és Kora*, ch. v. in vol. x. of *A Mag. Nem. Tört.* The censorship expunged the phrase, "the hussar died for his King," on the ground that he could die with propriety only for his Emperor. See also Szilágyi Sándor, *Rajzok a Forradalom Utáni Időkből*, Budapest, 1876, p. 144 *sq.* and *passim*.

impartiality ; but it was in reality the official organ of the Government, and urged the acceptance of the *fait accompli* and the recognition of the practical absorption of Hungary in Austria. In 1852 it changed its name and its tune, and as the *Budapesti Hirlap* became more and more independent. The *Pesti Napló* also tried to curry favour with the Government, and praised Bach and all his works till 1855, when it transferred its support to the Conservatives. Protmann thereupon persecuted the editor to such an extent that he threw up his job in disgust, and made way for Sigismund Kemény, a journalist who did immense service to his country by backing Deák's programme of historical continuity, though posterity might perhaps be justified in complaining that he was too prone to sacrifice the strict rights of Hungary to Palacky's conception of the necessity of inventing an Austria in the interests of Europe, if one did not already exist.[1]

Hardly a single Magyar in the lower ranks of life could be found to accept even the smallest Government appointment ; consequently, offices had to be filled by foreigners, whose ignorance of the Hungarian language, and insolent determination to treat Hungary as a conquered country, increased the universal hatred of Austrian despotism, and made the realisation of the bureaucratic ideal of union and uniformity an impossibility. In spite of spies and of police restrictions, the exiles kept in close touch with those at home, and with the exception of the Conservatives, few doubted that clouds would eventually break and that Hungary would, sooner or later, come by her own. The natural tendency was to look upon those Conservatives who accepted office at the hands of Vienna as traitors to their country, and as actuated by sordid motives, which certainly were incapable of influencing such men as Baron Jósika or Paul Somssics. One thing,

[1] See for Kemény's influence and policy, Beksics, *Kemény Zsigmond,* especially pp. 159 *sq.*

however, is certain, namely, that the influence of the Conservatives was detrimental to the true interests of Hungary, both before and after Világos. While the war lasted, Jósika and others led the camarilla to believe that the mass of the nation was an unconcerned spectator of the revolutionary efforts of Kossuth and of a few extremists, with the result that the Court failed to recognise the national character of the movement, and refused to negotiate with the moderate Liberals, who at no time were indisposed to compromise. After the war was over, the influence of the Conservatives was equally deleterious, as their desires were limited to a return to the state of affairs which existed before 1848—a compromise which would have involved the abandonment of the principle of legal continuity, and would have had a disastrous effect on the national prospects. Even a politician of the calibre of Paul Somssics, though convinced that Hungary's right to independence was as sacred as the rights of the Crown, in the name of which that independence had been annihilated, was ready to consent to the negation of the possibility of political progress involved by the abolition of the March laws.[1] If even a Liberal like Eötvös, influenced by the apparent hopelessness of the situation, was for a time disposed to recede somewhat from the strictly logical standpoint, it is not surprising that weaker spirits were inclined to sell the national birthright in order to escape from an intolerable situation. In 1850, Baron Jósika, who took office under the Austrian despotism, and had done more than any one to create a false impression in the mind of the Court party as to the extent and nature of the national movement,[2] Count George Apponyi, and many other distinguished Conservatives, addressed a

[1] See his book, *Das legitime Recht Ungarns und seines Königs*, Vienna, 1850, 149 *sq*.

[2] Later he changed his attitude and told Rechberg, the Foreign Minister, that no decent Hungarian would accept office under the Austrian Government, 1859.

petition to Francis Joseph, requesting him to do something to re-establish the confidence which the continuance
of Haynau's tyranny and the multiplication of foreign
officials must permanently destroy.   They assured the
Emperor that future generations would acclaim him as
the renovator of Hungary, and as the author of true
liberty, if he would conciliate present necessities with
past traditions, and so heal the wounds inflicted by the
war.   But the Crown's advisers affected to regard the
Constitution as dead, and as unfit to be resuscitated; and
the only result of the petition was that it confirmed the
mistaken official views that, should resuscitation ultimately
be necessary, Hungary would be glad to accept a mere
shadow of independence.   Count Emil Dessewffy, another
Conservative leader, urged the view that an end must be
put to absolutism, and that a return to the *status quo ante*
1848 must be made in the interests of the monarchy itself,
which otherwise must inevitably collapse in the long run.
Many Austrians agreed with him ; but his opinion had
no weight with Bach, and it is fortunate that it was so,
as otherwise Hungary might have accepted a position of
inferiority and subordination to Austria from which it
could never have emerged.   Deák realised the fact that it
was both useless and impolitic to bombard the Emperor
and his Ministers with petitions and letters, and saw the
true and only remedy in the policy which had proved
its efficacy in the past.   Schmerling, Minister of Justice,
tried to induce him to take part, if not in the actual work
of Government, at all events in a conference to be summoned for the discussion of Hungarian matters ; but he
replied that in the existing position of affairs his co-
operation was impossible, and the publication of his letter
of refusal[1] made the nation understand that thenceforth

---

[1] Kónyi, *Deák F. Beszédei*, ii. 382.   It was published abroad, on account
of the censorship, and thousands of manuscript copies were circulated in
Hungary.

the watchword of all patriots must be "passive resistance." Szögyény, the author of the memoirs to which frequent reference has been made, who took office under the despots, and had been in the camp of Windischgrätz while his country fought for freedom, redeemed himself to some extent in the eyes of his countrymen by championing the rights of the Magyar language against the germanisers, and, like Somssics, proved by his writings that the Conservatives were not necessarily traitors if they served a foreign autocracy.   Eventually, many Magyars were compelled by the force of circumstances to accept minor offices, but the vast majority of the educated would have no dealings with the Government, or, indeed, with the irreconcilables, whose ill-judged and premature attempts to effect a rising in Transylvania gave Vienna an excuse for tightening the bonds of despotism.[1]   Serious people were as convinced of the futility of insurrection without the resolute co-operation of France or Italy, as of the impolicy of a compromise on the lines suggested by the Conservatives, which involved the sacrifice of unquestionable historic rights.

Francis Joseph ·was easily induced to believe that Hungary was flourishing and contented, and his visit to that country in 1852 resembled that of Catherine II. to the Crimea, when Potemkin's merry stage-peasants and painted villages created an impression of non-existent prosperity.   The demonstrations of which the Emperor was the object merely proved his personal popularity and the loyalty of the Magyar populace, which never believed that he was personally responsible for the horrors which marked the end of the war, or for the subsequent period of official tyranny.   The natural obstinacy of Francis

---

[1] The Makk conspiracy, 1852. It was openly talked of in Paris, so Vienna got wind of it, and by the aid of a traitor was enabled to lay most of the conspirators by the heels.   Three were hanged, and forty-eight were sentenced to long terms of imprisonment.

Joseph made it easy for Bach to convince him of the expediency of continuing the policy of germanisation and centralisation, and the negative results of the imperial visit made it clearer than ever that only the pressure of external circumstances could compel recognition of the fact that Hungarian discontent involved the paralysis of Austria, as was proved by the wavering indecision of that country during the Crimean War.

Austria's hesitating and contradictory action in 1854 was due to a multiplicity of causes. On the one hand, the feeling of obligation towards Russia, the knowledge of the fact that the continuance of Austrian domination in northern Italy was dependent on the Tsar's good-will, and the annoyance caused by Turkey's action in refusing to give up Kossuth and his fellow-exiles to the tender mercies of Haynau, dictated co-operation with the Government of St. Petersburg. On the other hand, the fear of a rising in Italy and Hungary,[1] now greatly excited by the prospect of war, the desire to obtain possession of the Danubian principalities, the bankrupt condition of the national finances, and the dislike of perpetual subservience to Russia, intensified by the feeling of humiliation engendered by the circumstances which attended and preceded the capitulation of Világos, pointed to the expediency of an inactive policy.[2] When Austria finally decided to occupy the Danubian principalities, Russia was infuriated by the ingratitude of its *protégé*,[3]

---

[1] Palmerston, aware of the fact that Hungarian discontent made Austrian co-operation against Russia impossible, tried to bring about a compromise between Hungary and the dynasty.—See Beksics, *Kemény Zsigmond*, etc. 169 *sq.*

[2] See Friedjung, *Der Krimkrieg und die österreichische Politik*, Stuttgart, 1907, pp. 3, 4, 9, 11, 22, 39, 60, 109, etc. Also Thouvenel, *Nicholas I. et Napoléon III.*, Paris, 1891, and the *Neun Jahre Erinnerungen*, i. 100 *sq.* of Hübner, the Austrian Ambassador in Paris.

[3] Thouvenel regards the famous sentence ascribed to Schwarzenberg on the subject of astonishing the world by Austria's ingratitude as entirely apocryphal.

and the possibility of obtaining the Tsar's support in the not improbable event of a war with Prussia was lost to Francis Joseph for ever. The end of the war found Austria in a position of complete isolation,[1] hated both by Russia and France instead of by the former only, and despised by England, whose traditional sympathy she had alienated by her vacillation and by the brutality of the despotism in Hungary. Sardinia, on the other hand, by its co-operation with the Western Powers, had greatly strengthened her claims on their goodwill, and brought the unification of Italy within measurable distance.

Long before the meeting of the Congress of Paris it had become evident that Austria must cast about for an ally, and for a new buttress for the shaky fabric of autocracy, which, alone, could neither maintain the European position of the Habsburgs, nor permanently suppress the moral and intellectual forces of discontent. While Schwarzenberg, who fancied himself to be a new Metternich, maintained the prestige of Austria abroad, could restrain the efforts of Prussia towards hegemony in Germany, and, relying on the benevolent neutrality of Russia, could bolster up the antiquated system of Italian disorganisation, the Viennese bureaucracy could indulge its reactionary desires without risk of interference from above or below, from outside or from inside. But when Schwarzenberg died in 1852, the absence of the iron hand and of the energy necessary for the maintenance of bayonet-law was at once felt, and the alliance of Bach and Thun, of the ex-atheist and the sectarian bigot, required to be strengthened by enlisting the aid of the Catholic Church in the sacred cause of obscurantism. The price of Rome's help was, naturally, high. Hitherto even the most pious Habsburgs, even Maria Theresa, had been careful to maintain their supremacy in ecclesiastical matters,

[1] See Friedjung, *Der Kampf um die Vorherrschaft in Deutschland,* 7th ed., Stuttgart, 1907, pp. 10, 11, 13.

and the humiliation of appearing as a suppliant at the foot of the papal throne [1] to entreat the Church's assistance for the maintenance of autocracy, and for the improvement of the secret police by the readmission to Austria of the Society of Jesus, was reserved for Francis Joseph. Even Bach and Thun objected to the acceptance of some of the papal conditions, but the Emperor was prepared to pay any price that Rome demanded, and the negotiations, begun in 1852,[2] culminated in the publication of the Concordat of 1855. An Imperial Patent, dated November 5, explained the motives which actuated Francis Joseph in his surrender of the immemorial privileges of the head of the Catholic Church in Hungary. "Since our accession to the Throne we have laboured unceasingly at the task of renewing and strengthening the moral basis of society and of the public welfare. We consider it to be our sacred duty to bring the relations of the State with the Catholic Church into harmony with the laws of God and with a true conception of the real interests of our realm "— in other words, to utilise religious fanaticism for the abolition of the last vestiges of political liberty, and for the suppression of the Protestants, the born opponents, in Bach's opinion, of all wholesome institutions. The centralisation of religious author ty was to be the precursor of centralisation in all departments of State. The institution of the Placetum Regium was abolished, and all restrictions on the communications of Rome with the Catholic ecclesiastics in Hungary were removed. Article i. confirms the Catholic Church in the perpetual enjoyment of all the rights and privileges which "are in accordance with the will of God and the law of the Church " : that is to say, absolves the bishops from the necessity of obedience

---

[1] The Archduke Ferdinand Max was sent to Rome "to express thanks to His Holiness" for consenting to the Concordat, and it was made clearly to appear that the Pope had conferred a great favour on the Emperor.—Rogge, Österreich von Vildgos bis zur Gegenwart, i. 406.

[2] Krones, Geschichte der Neuzeit Österreichs, 749.

to the civil law if it is in any way in conflict with that of the Church. Articles xiii. and xiv. nominally admit the subjection of the clergy to the jurisdiction of the ordinary courts, but exceptions and conditions, and the recognition of the right of asylum (Article xv.), render the control of the civil authorities completely illusory. In the case of a *causa gravior seu criminalis* in which a bishop is concerned the Pope is to have exclusive jurisdiction. True, a secret agreement provided that in such cases a mixed commission of laymen and ecclesiastics should sit in judgment, but its existence was not discovered till 1869,[1] and the bishops enjoyed the privilege of complete extra-territoriality. Only Catholic teachers are to be admitted to Catholic gymnasia, and the elementary schools are placed under the control of the Church. Article ix. vests the exercise of the censorship in the bishops, who are to have "complete liberty" to indicate what books are "injurious to religion and morality," and the Government undertakes to prevent the circulation of the same. The result of centuries of struggle over the question of mixed marriages, and of the right to change from one religion to another, was wiped out by the establishment of Catholic control in all matrimonial causes in which one party to a marriage is a Catholic, and by the abrogation of all enactments[2] dealing with such matters later than the law of Joseph II. Religious and educational foundations were placed under ecclesiastical control, and their revenues were to be utilised solely for Catholic educational purposes. In a word, Protestantism was to be placed on the same footing as Judaism, to be tolerated but not recognised; and even the interment of Protestant dead in consecrated ground was strictly forbidden.[3] In 1852, the Jesuits, on

[1] By the *Neue Freie Presse.*—Rogge, *Österreich von Világos*, etc. i. 408 *n.* The meaning of this clause is apparently misunderstood by Eisenmann, *Le Compromis Austro-Hongrois*, p. 174.

[2] From xxvi. 1791, *De negotio religionis* onwards.

[3] Rogge, *Österreich von Világos*, etc. i. 413.

whose co-operation Bach specially relied for the attainment of his political aims,[1] obtained readmission to Hungary, and Protestants were ejected to provide for their accommodation.   As Eisenmann puts it, " *le système de Bach est complet. Les quatre armées sur lesquelles il s'appuie sont désormais à son service : les soldats debout, les bureaucrates assis, les prêtres agenouillés, les mouchards rampants.   Ce qui échapperait encore à la police, la censure ecclésiastique l'étouffe.*" The last vestige of Hungarian independence was to be destroyed by putting the Hungarian Church under the domination of Rauscher, the Archbishop of Vienna.[2] History had already proved the fact that an attack on their political liberties invariably silenced all manifestations of religious animosity among the Magyars, and one of the chief results of the Concordat was the intensification of that feeling of national solidarity which Bach was anxious to destroy.

Hungary was supposed to find compensation for the loss of freedom in the promotion of its material interests, and in the abolition of the customs barrier, which had handicapped the country by excluding the possibility of finding a foreign market for the disposal of its surplus products ; but the increase of taxation necessitated by the practical bankruptcy of Austria at the conclusion of the Crimean War, and by the importation of innumerable foreign officials, more than counterbalanced the gains resultant from the increase in the productivity of the country consequent on the abolition of the feudal system, and from the gradual improvement of the means of communication.   In June 1854 a "voluntary" internal loan of 350,000,000 florins was contracted by the Government,

---

[1] "Ungarn," so he declared, "wird in fünfundzwanzig Jahren in eine deutsch-slavische Provinz verwandelt werden.   Der Magyarismus wird blos eine überwundene sporadische Erscheinung bilden."—*Die ungarische Verfassung*, Radó-Rothfeldt, 76.

[2] And by the establishment of a Court of Appeal for the whole "Empire," including Hungary and the Italian provinces (Law of August 7, 1850).

and every tax-payer, every landed proprietor, was compelled to apply for an allotment proportionate to his presumed means.[1] The failure of unwilling subscribers (to an issue which was intended to prove to a wondering Europe the inexhaustibility of the Empire's resources and the confidence reposed in the Government) to pay the due instalments, and the peculation of officials, accounted for the fact that though Austria took no part in the Crimean War the Budget of the following year showed a deficit of 139,000,000 florins, and an increase, since 1849, of 1,092,000,000 in the National Debt.[2] One financial crisis followed another with tedious regularity. Credit was unobtainable; practically all specie was withdrawn from circulation, and paper money stood at an enormous discount; yet the Government affected to be satisfied with its work, and pointed with pride to the signs of material progress discernible in Hungary, which Bach ascribed to the blessings of his rule. In order to justify himself in the eyes of Europe, disgusted with his treatment of the Magyars, and to establish for ever his reputation as a heaven-born statesman, he caused a book[3] to be written by one of his creatures, one Bernard Meyer, a Jewish official in the Ministry of the Interior, which makes it appear as if milk and honey were flowing in Hungary, as if the Magyars now for the first time had become acquainted with the blessings of civilisation, and of material and moral progress resulting from the establishment of a system of enlightened and benevolent despotism. Credit is claimed even for the abolition of the feudal system, with which Francis Joseph and his Ministers had no more to do than the Emperor of China had, and for the regulation of the waterways and other reforms, initiated

---

[1] "Es war das Äusserste, was der Absolutismus bisher gewagt hatte."—Friedjung, *Der Krimkrieg*, etc. p. 61.

[2] *A Mag. Nem. Tört.* x. 532 *sq.*

[3] *Ein Rückblick auf die jüngste Entwickelungsperiode Ungarns*, Vienna, 1857; reprinted 1903.

by Széchenyi and his contemporaries, long before the
"barricade-Minister" had emerged from his native
obscurity. The book removed all doubt as to the intended
permanence of the new *régime*. According to Bach's
mouthpiece, the events of 1848 "smoothed the way for
the attainment of an end which must sooner or later have
been reached in a roundabout manner"—in other words,
for the incorporation of Hungary in Austria. The
introduction of German as the official language is stated
to be due solely to a benevolent desire to enable a
benighted country to enjoy the advantages, and appreciate
the merits, of a higher civilisation and of a superior
literature. The charge of forcible germanisation is refuted
by a reference to the recognition, by the March Constitution, of the equality, as regards rights, of all languages
—a piece of humbug for European consumption which did
not prevent Thun from making German the medium
of instruction in all secondary schools and gymnasia, or
Schmerling from making the use of that language compulsory in the law courts, and for the publication of all
laws and governmental orders. The lying picture of
Hungary's material welfare, and the pharisaical complacency of the apologist of tyranny, provoked a crushing
reply from Széchenyi, who, after years of ill-health and
mental and nervous collapse, made a momentary literary
reappearance before the world, for the purpose of exposing in all its shameless nakedness the despotism of
which his country was the victim.[1] Bach, wrote Széchenyi,
was keeping Francis Joseph in a fool's paradise, and was
deliberately deceiving him by talking of the freedom of
the Press, the equality of all before the law, the contentment and prosperity of Hungary, and the gratitude of
the Magyars for the murder of their brothers, for the
hangman and the turnkeys of Austrian tyranny, and for
the disruption of their old kingdom. Hungary was

[1] See his *Blick auf den anonymen Rückblick*, London, 1859.

only now beginning to be really united, to forget class and political distinctions, and a thousand gallows would fail to compel the Magyars to give up their language, the chief national treasure, or to abandon their hopes. "A lonely, helpless, feeble man may take his own life, if he can help himself in no other way, but nations commit suicide least of all when others attempt to compel them to do so . . . . and no power on earth is capable of tearing out of the heart of a Magyar, or of lessening in the slightest degree, the feeling of love for his nation." According to Bach, the Magyars had "nothing to do but to obey, be silent, tremble . . . . and rejoice," and a refusal to be happy in accordance with his prescription was nothing but a proof of the blindness, stupidity, and malevolence of the nation, and of its inability to appreciate the advantages of Austrian civilisation, as exemplified by the muzzling of the Press, and the destruction of the principle of religious equality. True, the telegraphic system, to which Bach pointed with pride, had been recently developed and extended. Why? Because it was an instrument of centralisation, and tightened the bureaucracy's hold on the country. True, a network of railways had been projected, but, with one exception, the schemes had got no further than the paper stage. Hungary was, in fact, in a backward state, as compared with most European countries, but what was the cause of its stagnation? The obstructive tactics of successive Habsburgs, who, by omitting to summon the Diet, or by prematurely dissolving it, paralysed its legislative activity, and, by their fiscal policy, consistently opposed all efforts to ameliorate the economic condition of the country.

Széchenyi did not overstate the case. The fact was that in Bach's opinion Government and oppression were synonymous, and the inexperience of the imperial autocrat made it easy to convince him that the expression of Hungarian discontent proved the existence of revolutionary, anti-dynastic feeling, whereas in reality it was nothing but the outcome of a natural hatred of the Procrustean system of tyranny, for the continuation of which the innate obstinacy of Francis Joseph was chiefly to blame. The exponents of more liberal views could not obtain a hearing. When, in 1857, the Emperor visited Hungary for the second time, a petition signed by the whole bench of bishops and many leading men was presented to him ; but he refused to receive it, though it made but slight reference to the Constitution, and spoke chiefly of the necessity of preserving the idea of Magyar nationality, of the unfortunate consequences of territorial disintegration, of the abolition of the old counties, and of the exclusion of the Hungarian language from all branches of education and government.[1] The Archduke Albrecht was rebuked for the slackness of his control of the forces of discontent, and Bach was triumphant. "I know," said Francis Joseph, "that the whole thing is a mere empty demonstration, the outcome of continual agitation, which I mean to put down. I know that the nobles are discontented,[2] but the mass of the population is well affected. If I accept the petition, the convocation of county assemblies would immediately follow, and then I could not deny the right of holding similar meetings to my other dominions." On his return to Vienna the Emperor issued a rescript, in which he referred to the signs which he had seen of Hungary's material progress, the result, in his view, of an enlightened and effective administration ; and his declaration to the effect that he was "inflexibly resolved" to maintain the existing form of government was looked upon as a final blow to the hopes which had been raised by his visit. All the same, the dawn of a new era was discernible. A new ally of Hungary appeared in the person of the Empress Eliza-

---

[1] For the text, see Kónyi, *Deák Ferencz Beszédei*, ii. 397 *sqq.*

[2] "*Only* the so-called intelligence keeps itself somewhat apart."—Baron Auguss, cited by Rogge, *Österreich von Világos bis zur Gegenwart*, i. 488.

beth, who had accompanied her husband on his journey, and the grant of an amnesty to numerous exiles[1] and political prisoners is probably to be ascribed to her influence. It was ordained that thenceforward two-thirds of the members of the official body should be Magyars, and that Hungarian documents should be accepted in the law courts; but there the concessions ended, and it was evident that no real move would be made in the direction of the restoration of Hungarian autonomy, except under the compulsion of exterior causes.

1859. Hungary did not have to wait long. The fiasco suffered by the Austrian arms at Magenta and Solferino proved the bankruptcy of the existing system. Austria's national vanity consoled itself for the loss of Lombardy by throwing the blame on the corruption of financiers and army contractors, but it was plain to all but the intentionally blind that Austria was useless as a military power, unless it had the backing of a solid and contented Hungary.[2] Even before the peace of Villafranca was signed, Rechberg, the Minister of Foreign Affairs, sent for Baron Jósika in order to ask his advice, and Jósika told him what he expected to hear, namely, that Hungary must be restored to the position occupied before 1848, which guaranteed the unity of the dual monarchy, the safety of which would otherwise be seriously compromised. The Emperor's manifesto, issued at the end of the war, contained a faint indication of an intention to turn over a new leaf. " My heart rejoices, for the blessings of peace are again assured to my beloved country. To me they are doubly precious, as they give me leisure to concentrate my attention on the execution of my task—the establishment on a firm basis of the internal wellbeing and external

[1] Among others, Count Julius Andrássy, the future Chancellor, returned.

[2] At Solferino the French took 15,000 prisoners, mostly Hungarians. No such thing had ever happened before in the military history of Austria and Hungary. It was evident that the Magyars had no anxiety to be killed in the sacred cause of Austrian tyranny in Italy.

power of the monarchy, by the adoption of suitable means for the development of its moral and material strength, and for the improvement of legislation and administration in accordance with the requirements of the age." As Kossuth points out,[1] in the past ten years there had been about ten weeks of war, and the necessary leisure might have been found a little sooner ; but in any case the dismissal of Bach showed that Francis Joseph was beginning to learn the lesson which Solferino had emphasised, and Königgrätz was finally to drive into his head. The fact, however, that Thun and Bruck still remained in the Ministry proved that only half-measures could be expected, and the Magyars had to console themselves with the conviction that the resumption of hostilities in Italy, and the collapse of autocracy, must follow before long. Great excitement had prevailed in Hungary during the war, especially among the peasant population. Kossuth Lajos was, now as ever, a name to conjure with, and thousands believed that the reappearance of the liberator could not be indefinitely postponed. In England also Kossuth's popularity was enormous ; so much so that it caused him, at one time, to make a false estimate of the effect of his oratory. It is a far cry from dinners and public meetings to official interference in the affairs of a foreign country, and he was unnecessarily surprised when the Government stopped the issue of some millions of paper florins, destined to finance a Hungarian rebellion. Even the peace of Villafranca (partially due to the fear of a revolution in Hungary), in which, in spite of all Louis Napoleon's assurances of his wish to see Hungary free, no mention was made of Hungarian affairs, did not shake Kossuth's belief in the possibility of foreign intervention in some form or other. In any case, his action at this period gave him a double claim on the gratitude of his countrymen ; firstly, for the reason that, though absent,

[1] *Schriften aus der Emigration*, ii. 75.

he prevented them from lapsing into despondency and acquiescence in despotism; secondly, because his refusal to allow the standard of revolt to be raised till either France or Italy had landed an army in Hungary, saved his country from the bloody reprisals of which premature action would undoubtedly have made it the victim.[1]

The first act of the reconstructed Ministry was the issue of an Imperial Patent (September 10) dealing with the religious privileges of between three and four million Hungarian Protestants. It was meant to be conciliatory, but as it was the work of the incorrigible Thun it had precisely the contrary effect to that which the Cabinet anticipated, and the storm it raised caused it to be withdrawn when it had been in force for eight months—a comparatively long life for a Patent of this period. It nominally recognised the validity of the Laws xxvi. of 1791 and iii. of 1844, but subjected the Church to the imperial power in all matters of internal government, and so, in reality, was in direct conflict with the laws which guaranteed ecclesiastical autonomy. The result was a universal outcry on the part of Protestants of all shades. Even the Saxons, who alone derived benefit from the germanising policy of the Government, and were pleased to see their own language exalted at the expense of all other idioms, protested as energetically as any other members of the Reformed Church against interference with the privileges which they had enjoyed in the days of Hungarian freedom. Dogmatic differences were temporarily forgotten, and the Catholics, both priests and laity, strongly supported their Protestant fellow-countrymen[2] on the ground that government by Patent constituted an

---

[1] At his interview with Napoleon, May 5, 1859, he said that he was convinced that Hungary would show its gratitude for intervention by offering the crown to a Bonaparte.—*Schriften aus der Emigration,* i. 240 *sqq.*; also 191, 194, 196; also his letter of Jan. 23, 1861, to Pulszky, in the latter's *Életem és Korom,* ii. 333, *re* his refusal to allow Hungary to be used as a cat's-paw.

[2] Berzeviczy, *o.c.* p. 118.

unjustifiable interference with constitutional rights which could not be abrogated without the consent of the nation. Thus, the question of religious autonomy became identified with that of political liberty, and the Government soon had cause to regret the fact that it had raised a storm which no repressive measures [1] and no concessions in ecclesiastical matters could permanently allay. Every opportunity was taken of emphasising the moral unity of the nation. The national dress was more generally used than ever ; as in Venice so in Hungary, Austrians were cold-shouldered out of society, and a pretended ignorance of the German language increased the efficacy of the social boycott. The festival of the centenary of the birth of Kazinczy, one of the fathers of modern Magyar literature, proved the intensity of the national feeling which autocracy had temporarily driven under the surface, but had entirely failed to destroy. The idea was generally entertained that a word from the exiled Kossuth would suffice to produce an eruption of the slumbering volcano—a fact which possibly accounted for the issue at the end of November of a new press-regulation in Austria's worst style threatening the severest punishment to all who should publish news of a character calculated to weaken the public confidence in the Government. As a matter of fact it was impossible to undermine a non-existent confidence, and the edict, which made the police sole judges of the subversive character of news, merely strengthened the general conviction that the autocracy was gradually becoming conscious of its own impotence. The Government was, in fact, swaying this way and that, in complete uncertainty as to what course it should pursue. Concession and repression, reaction and progress, alternated with the regularity of day and night, but when once the bureaucracy

---

[1] More than a hundred protesters were prosecuted by the Government. *A Mag. Nem. Tört.* x. 527. "Die Leute fingen an sich zu schämen, wenn man sie nicht für gefährlich genug hielt um sie mit Gefängnissstrafen zu belegen."—Rogge, *Österreich von Világos,* etc. ii. 27.

had begun to climb down the ladder it became evident that it would be unable to stop before it had reached the bottom. Though anxious to "save its face," and to continue the pretence of believing in the efficacy of compulsory unification, it could not conceal its fear of the effect which the inevitable final struggle for the possession of Venice would have on Hungary, and on the chronic disorder of Austrian finances. In Austria the Germans rejoiced in their predominance, but wished to see it consecrated by the establishment of parliamentary government—a more reliable preservative than bayonets and sectarian intolerance. In Hungary, the constitutionalists, of whom Deák was the recognised head, had already formulated their plan of campaign, and nothing would satisfy them short of the complete recognition of the validity of the March laws of 1848.

1860.   The autocracy, realising the unavoidability of the approaching collapse, cast about to find something soft on which to fall, and a Patent of March 5, 1860, announced the convocation, in a new form, of the shadowy Reichsrath, a purely consultative body, which, throughout the period of the Bach *régime*, had met from time to time under the presidency of the Archduke Rainer. Hitherto it had consisted entirely of life members nominated by the Emperor, who, from time to time, modified its incompetence by the temporary admixture of reputed specialists. Henceforth it was to be permanently "reinforced" by new blood drawn from all parts of a united Empire, with a view, more especially, to deliberation on financial questions, to the revision of laws, and to the consideration of the expediency of the measures to be passed by the various provincial Diets. Thus strengthened, the Reichsrath was to consist of life-members, archdukes, bishops, and high Government officials nominated by the Crown, and of temporary members, to the number of thirty-eight (of whom six were allotted to Hungary), to be elected for a period of six years by the provincial Diets. That the whole thing was a sham, a sop thrown to public opinion to keep its mouth shut for a time, was shown, firstly, by the fact that the glorified Reichsrath was to deliberate in secret and had no power of initiating legislation ; secondly, by the composition of the nominated section, of which by far the greater half consisted of aristocratic and ecclesiastical reactionaries. With a view to inducing Hungary to take a serious view of the new departure, an edict of April 9 abolished the five districts of the Bach *régime*, and appointed General Benedeck, personally popular with the Magyars, to the position left vacant by the removal of the Archduke Albrecht, with instructions to summon the Diet for the election of representative members of the reinforced Reichsrath. Of those chosen, Andrássy, Majláth and Szécsen refused to allow their presence to be construed as an indication of acquiescence in the *status quo* ; and Nicholas Vay, Somssics, and Eötvös made excuses for non-attendance. The entire value of the reform consisted in the fact that it partially unmuzzled Hungary, now as ever the pivot of the whole situation, to the extent, at all events, of allowing it to proclaim aloud, by the mouths of its representatives, the elementary fact that no modification of the Hungarian Constitution could have any effective reality if it neglected the principle of legal, historical continuity, and did not originate in the harmonious action of the two equal legislative factors, the King of Hungary and the Parliament of Hungary. To a small body of Conservatives, under the leadership of Emil Dessewffy, to whose ideas of a tentative federation, as distorted and emasculated by Rechberg, the Patent was due, the return to constitutional government implied a recurrence to the state of affairs which existed before 1848 ; but they in no sense represented the political convictions of the majority, any more than Eötvös did, whose pamphlet, entitled, *Die Garantien der Macht und*

Einheit Österreichs,[1] had, as will be seen later, considerable influence in Austria, but very little in Hungary. Eötvös started, not from the point of view of the indefeasibility of Hungary's historic rights, but from that of the necessity of binding all the dominions of the Habsburgs together, their unity being essential to the interests, not only of Europe, but of those dominions themselves. He pointed out that unity did not imply territorial or administrative unification, but that, on the contrary, the grant of a limited autonomy to each of the constituent states was essential to the harmonious working of a conglomerate of racially unhomogeneous units. The desired unity could, in his opinion, best be obtained by the grant of self-government to the various provincial factors of the " Gesammtstaat " in such matters as education, religion, ecclesiastical discipline, and the administration of justice ; while military matters, foreign affairs, finance, and trade, were left in the hands of common Ministers of State, responsible only to the Emperor. Such a scheme, which implied the total destruction of the historical, contractual, basis of Hungary's relations with the dynasty, reduced that country, after a thousand years of constitutional government, to the same level as the most insignificant of the autocratically governed hereditary provinces, and converted its Parliament into a glorified County Council, obviously could not satisfy the aspirations revived by the disastrous Italian war, or serve as a substitute for Deák's principle of legal continuity. The issue of such a pamphlet by a politician of recognised authority, such as Eötvös, was particularly inopportune, as it encouraged the Austrian Government in the belief that Hungary would be satisfied with the grant of slight concessions, whereas Deák and the intelligence of the nation would accept nothing short of the rights which a dozen Habsburgs had

[1] Leipsig, 1859.

sworn to maintain. Széchenyi, from his retreat at Döbling, still followed the course of events, but was, to some extent, out of touch with the nation and with Deák, whom he reproached with taking a parochial view of the situation. On March 3, the police visited him and seized his papers, and he relapsed into a state of melancholia, which was heightened by the news of the students' conflict with the police at Pest on the anniversary of the fateful Ides of March, and by that of the death of Baron Jósika, his life-long friend. He ceased to read or write, and continually reproached himself with having ruined his country. Finally, he committed suicide on April 8, and the conclusion that his voluntary death was due to despair of Hungary's future, deepened the impression that in any case would have been caused by the final disappearance of "the greatest of the Magyars." Thenceforth, practically the whole nation looked to Deák for guidance.

The reinforced Reichsrath met on May 31, and it at once became evident that little good could be expected from the elected representatives. A strong minority was frankly in favour of centralisation. The Germans of Transylvania, and the Servians, were well aware of the fact that the continuance of their privileges, newly acquired at the expense of the Magyars, was dependent on the maintenance of a system of veiled autocracy. The Ruthenians and Roumanians saw that for them a choice of system was merely a choice between frying-pan and fire, and took no active part in the proceedings. The Croatians at first sat on the fence, but finally took their stand on the side of federation and local self-government. The representatives of Hungary and Bohemia agreed that any reconstruction must be based on the recognition of historic rights, the only possible foundation for a permanent structure. A committee of twenty-one members, appointed to consider the financial situation, took the opportunity of

condemning the whole system of government, which, since
1849, had vastly increased the burden of taxation, and, at
the same time, had brought the Empire to the verge of
bankruptcy. As usual, the political experience of the
Magyar representatives, the product of centuries of constitutional government, was in marked contrast to the
naïf immaturity of their Cisleithanian colleagues, and
prevented the discussion of legislative proposals, which
would have involved the recognition of the competence
of a heterogeneous body to form a precedent prejudicial
to the principle of Hungarian independence. Szécsen
inside the Reichsrath, and Dessewffy and Eötvös outside
it, exercised an incomparably greater influence than the
official advisers of the wavering, yet obstinate Emperor,
whom circumstances had temporarily convinced that the
days of pure autocracy were numbered, and of the
necessity of finding some solution of the difficulties
which twelve years of despotic government had created
or intensified. Since Világos, the position of Austria as
a great power had become more and more shaky. Signs
of the approaching consummation of Italian unity were
not wanting, and the effectiveness of the army was gravely
compromised by the existence of racial ill-feeling, and by
the necessity, in the event of war, of keeping a large part
of the imperial forces in Hungary for the suppression of
a not improbable revolt. A chronic state of national
bankruptcy was not calculated to induce cosmopolitan
financiers to open their pockets for the sake of bolstering
up an Empire which contained so many explosive elements.
Something required to be done to give a fresh coat of
paint to the *façade* of a rotten edifice, before the meeting
which had been arranged to take place at Warsaw between
the Emperor, the Tsar, and the King of Prussia,[1] in the

---

[1] Andrássy said that but for the ill-advised action of the Conservatives
the Emperor would have been just as ready to sign a document fully restoring
the Hungarian Constitution as to sign the October Diploma.—Kónyi, *Deák
Ferencz Beszédei*, ii. 618.

vain hope of coming to an arrangement in the nature of the Holy Alliance of the halcyon days of despotism. Eötvös's pamphlet and the federalistic ideas of Dessewffy seemed to supply the only possible solution of the problem which confronted Francis Joseph.

An imperial manifesto, dated October 30, and the accompanying Diploma and rescripts,[1] contained the first faint indication of the fact that the bankruptcy of absolutism was beginning to be recognised. The Diploma admits the existence of divergent racial rights and interests which require to be satisfied without infringement of those of the one and indivisible " Austrian Empire," regarded as a political entity of essentially German character, which it never was and never could be. The preamble, by way of justification, refers in the same breath, and with a complete disregard of logic, to the autocratic principle and to the Pragmatic Sanction, which has nothing in common with that principle, and, so far from being in consonance therewith, is, as regards Hungary, a flat negation of its admissibility. The Emperor renounces in perpetuity,[2] on his own and on his successors' behalf, autocracy's assumed right of " passing, amending, and abrogating laws " in favour of the elected representatives of the Empire, oblivious of the fact that Law xii. of 1790, which his predecessors had sworn to observe, had specifically declared that right to be jointly exercisable, as far as Hungary was concerned, by the King and by the Estates and Orders of the realm in Diet assembled, and not otherwise. Henceforward the legislative power is to be shared by the Emperor with the local Diets of the constituent provinces of the Empire (in which Hungary is included), and with the Reichsrath, in which each such province is to be represented by elected members.[3] The control of military

---

[1] For the text, see Kónyi, *Deák Ferencz Beszédei*, ii. 492 *sqq.*

[2] The life of this " perpetual and irrevocable " Constitution lasted just four months. [3] In all one hundred for the whole " Empire."

matters, and the decision of all questions as to the duration and conditions of service, as to customs-tariffs, trade, finance, public loans, railways, post and telegraphs, are reserved to the Reichsrath, as well as the discussion of the Budget and the imposition of new taxes. "All other matters" are left to the decision of the provincial Diets, thus reduced to a position of practical impotence. The Diploma parades the usual high-sounding principles, equality of all before the law, freedom of conscience, admissibility of all to office without racial or class distinction, and lays stress on the condescension of the Crown in sharing its legislative authority with the elected representatives of the people; but in reality it was hardly more than a variation on the theme of the Patent of March 5, with its reinforced Reichsrath; for the new Reichsrath was a purely consultative body, the views of which the Emperor might accept or disregard as he pleased. Moreover, as the Patent was not specifically withdrawn, all deliberations were, presumably, to be conducted in secret. The only concession to Hungary was to be found in the timid recognition of the dualistic principle, of a distinction between Hungarian local affairs, and those of the other dominions which were to some extent controlled by the Reichsrath. Nicholas Vay was appointed Hungarian Chancellor, Szögyény Vice-Chancellor, and with the re-establishment of the Chancery in Vienna, Hungary made a partial return to the bureaucratic government of 1847, the validity of the legislation of 1848 being recognised only so far as the same was not in contradiction with the terms of the Diploma—in other words, so far as recognition was conducive to Austria's interests, to which the abolition of serfdom and of the nobles' exemption from taxation, and the introduction of universal liability to military service, were obviously beneficial. Apart from the encouragement afforded by the nominal abdication of absolutism one satisfactory result followed the publication of the Diploma.

As education was not a "common affair" controlled from
Vienna, Thun's occupation was gone, and he retired,
unregretted, after a career of undiluted maleficence at all
events so far as Hungary was concerned. Questions of
electoral procedure and qualification in Hungary were to
be decided by a special body under the presidency of the
Archbishop ; the old territorial divisions were restored ;
the High Court under the Chief Justice was re-established,
and Hungarian was again made the official language of the
law courts and of the governmental departments. So far
so good ; but to please the Saxons, and for fear lest the
process of climbing down the ladder which led to the
restoration of independence should seem too rapid,
Transylvania was not re-annexed to Hungary, and the
question of the reunion of the Croatians and Servians
was temporarily postponed. Europe was expected to be
amazed by the political wisdom of the new departure,
and for a moment Austria was pleased with the novelty
of the situation ; but it soon discerned the cloven foot
of autocracy beneath the cloak of constitutionalism, and
expressed sullen disgust with the limited nature of its
own privileges, and with the exceptional treatment meted
out to Hungary.

The Magyars said little, hesitating whether to bless or
to curse the Diploma, which, while it drew a distinction
between Hungary and the hereditary provinces, thus
admitting the bankruptcy of the "Verwirkungs-theorie"
of German doctrinaires (of the principle that the revolution had entailed the forfeiture of all political privileges),
at the same time deprived Hungary of its most essential
rights by subjecting it ‧ to the control of a mongrel
Parliament sitting in Vienna. Deák gave the *mot d'ordre*,
recognising the benefits conferred by a partial revival of
constitutional rights, but pointing out that neither the
declared origin (autocratic power), nor the contents, of
the Diploma could satisfy the legitimate aspirations of

the country. Sigismund Kemény, Deák's journalistic lieutenant, fearing lest there might be an inclination to acquiesce in the terms of the Diploma, on the principle that half a loaf is better than no bread, emphasised his leader's pronouncement in the *Pesti Napló* of October 25, and declared that Hungary's only possible answer to the Diploma was a demand for a *restitutio in integrum* of the laws of 1848. His voice was the voice of a united nation. A meeting summoned by the Archbishop of Esztergom on December 18, which Deák's innate consistency would not allow him to attend, clearly showed which way the wind blew. Baron Wenckheim, the first speaker, said that Hungary could, and would, elect deputies to the Diet only on the basis of the laws of 1848 (iv. and v.), and that it would be a farce and an anachronism to return to that of 1608[1] which limited the enjoyment of the franchise to Prelates, Barons, Nobles, and Free Towns. Dessewffy pointed out the absurdity involved by a jump back to a period when the Pragmatic Sanction was non-existent, and the inconsistency of the Government in recognising the validity of certain of the March laws, and not that of all of them, and in treating Transylvania as a separate country, though its reunion with Hungary had received the royal confirmation in 1848, and its Diet had been formally dissolved for ever. A unanimous disinclination was shown to accept, as a concession, a fragment of that which the nation claimed, as of right, in its entirety.

The re-establishment of the organisation of the counties gave the country the desired opportunity of expressing its opinion of the entire situation. Surviving members of the Parliament of 1848 were elected almost without exception. The names of Kossuth and Klapka, even of Garibaldi and Cavour, were included in the list

---

[1] "Quinam Status et Ordines dicantur et qui locum et vota in publicis Diaetis habere debeant."

of successful candidates as a protest against a *régime* which entailed the banishment of the popular heroes. A cry of "dead" greeted the mention of those living, but denationalised, Magyars who had accepted office under Bach's Government—a sufficient indication of the temper of the counties, the majority of which gave unmistakable expression to their feeling in favour of the March laws of 1848, as the only possible basis of reconciliation with Vienna, by refusing to collect or pay taxes pending the restoration of the Constitution. Of the Lords-Lieutenant nominated by the Government, many, among others Count Julius Andrássy, Coloman Tisza, and Melchior Lónyay, refused to accept office, and it soon became evident that Vay and Szécsen were generals without soldiers, and that the Diploma was looked upon merely as an instalment of the nation's dues, and its grant only as an indication of the conscious weakness of the Emperor. Francis Joseph affected to be surprised by the attitude adopted by Hungary, and discerned an antidote to a morbid condition of affairs in the development of purely German influence. The end of December saw Schmerling appointed Prime Minister in the place of Goluchowski the Pole, sacrificed as a peace offering to the Germans, a proof that the days of the "permanent and irrevocable" Diploma, of which Goluchowski was the chief supporter, were already numbered. The new Prime Minister, though by nature a convinced partisan of autocracy, and, consequently, an enemy of Magyar aspirations, realised the fact that absolutism had been weighed in the balance and found wanting, and decided to pose as a Liberal, and to kill by kindness a movement which violence had proved unable to suppress. Francis Joseph was, therefore, induced to begin the new departure by stroking with one hand while he slapped with the other, by attempting to conciliate the Magyars by ordering the abolition of the Servian Vojvodina, and the reincorporation in Hungary

of the Banate of Temes, while he issued a rescript[1]
rebuking the counties for the ill-will evidenced by the
1861. election of Kossuth and other undesirables, and threatened
violent repression of any future manifestations of popular
hostility to the Government. Early in January, Deák
was received by Francis Joseph in private audience, which,
if it served no other purpose, at least satisfied Deák as to
the Emperor's conscientiousness and intimate acquaintance
with the questions at issue, and convinced the latter of
the strength of Deák's convictions and logical faculties,
and of his downright honesty of purpose.[2] Deák insisted
at the interview on the necessity of recognising the
validity of the laws of 1848, but his letter of January 9,[3]
addressed to his brother-in-law, shows that he had little
confidence in the efficacy of his arguments. The four
main obstacles to compromise seemed insurmountable.
The first was the inability of Hungary to bear the burden
of that part of the national debt which Austria wished to
impose on its shoulders. The second was to be found in
the fact that the Emperor and his Austrian advisers were
ready to resort to "extreme measures" rather than
abandon their undivided control of military matters.
Thirdly, there was the question of the fragmentary
nationalities of Hungary which were sure to make inadmissible demands involving the dismemberment of
the kingdom. Lastly, there was the problem of common
(e.g. foreign and financial) affairs, the chief stumbling-
block over which Austria and Hungary had broken
their shins in 1848.

Pseudo-Liberalism was no more capable of effecting
a lasting settlement than the open violence of Bach had
been. It was folly to suppose that a few concessions
could induce the Magyar nation to commit political

[1] January 16, 1861.
[2] See the report of Deák's and the Emperor's conversation with Baron
Vay.—Kónyi, *Deák Ferencz Beszédei*, ii. 532.
[3] *Ibid.* p. 527 *sqq.*

suicide; and Schmerling's statement to the effect that if Hungary failed to see the merits of the existing *régime* he could afford to wait [1] showed a total misapprehension of the situation. The clouds gathering on the international horizon showed that to wait was precisely what Austria could not afford to do. Cavour was not yet dead, and recent events in Italy suggested that the serving of a notice to quit Venice might shortly be expected. In spite of the apparent harmony of the relations which existed between Rechberg and Bismarck, no attempts to foster the interests of the German subjects of Francis Joseph at the expense of other nationalities could conceal the fact that the hegemony in Germany of Austria with its preponderating Slav population was an anachronism and an absurdity, which Prussia, for one, would not tolerate indefinitely. Unless something could be done to restore the financial credit of Austria, the state of military disorganisation disclosed by the recent short Italian campaign must continue to invite disaster. The issue of a revised edition of the sham constitutionalism of the Diploma alone seemed capable of inducing the confiding foreign investor to open his purse to a necessitous Austria. The Diploma must, therefore, be withdrawn; but the temporising, palliative, system was not yet to be abandoned, though it was as clear as daylight that the continuance of Hungarian discontent involved the dislocation of the whole machinery of empire. An imperial Patent of February 26th,[2] the work of Schmerling and Perthaler, convinced champions of the erroneous idea that Austria was an essentially German State, announces the apparent platitude that the function of the Reichsrath is to represent the Empire, and proclaims the nominal conversion of that institution into a Parliament consisting of two Chambers. Of these the Upper is to consist of

---

[1] Krones, *Geschichte der Neuzeit Österreichs*, 769.
[2] For the text see Kónyi, *Deák Ferencz Beszédei*, ii. 589 *sqq.*

members of the imperial family, of high ecclesiastical functionaries, of the heads of noble landowning families selected by the Emperor for the provision of hereditary legislators, and of such life members as the Crown may nominate from time to time, on account of services rendered to the Church, or to science, or to art. The Lower House is to comprise 343 members, of whom 85 are assigned to Hungary proper, 5 to Dalmatia, 9 to Croatia, and 26 to Transylvania (which together form the Hungarian group), and the remaining 220 to the Austrian provinces. A distinction is drawn between the common affairs of the Austrian dominions, which are to be dealt with in the " narrow Reichsrath," *i.e.* in the absence of the members of the Hungarian group, and those which concern both Hungary and the hereditary provinces, and must, consequently, be discussed only when the Reichsrath is rendered " full " by the presence of the members of the above - mentioned section. The competence of the "full Reichsrath" extends to the discussion of all matters enumerated in the third paragraph of the October Diploma, that is to say, of all matters which concern the army, money, note issues, customs, commerce, railways, post and telegraph, and of every question connected with the finances of the Empire, the budget, the " increase " of taxation, and the contracting of new public loans.

The essential vice of the new departure (apart from the fact that Hungary was reduced to practically the same level as Bukovina or Carniola, and that its Diet became a mere provincial council) lay in the fact that the ministers were to be appointed directly by the Crown, and were to be responsible to it alone ; and in Article 13, which provided that " if, when the Reichsrath is not in session, it is urgently necessary to take measures with respect to matters which are within the competence of that body, it is the duty of the Ministry to afford an

explanation of the reasons for, and the consequenc
the measures which it has taken." The effect of th.
provision, which gave the Ministry complete authority to
act behind the back of the Reichsrath, was still further
extended by the interpretation placed upon it by Schmerling, who assumed it to mean that the autocratic power
of the Ministry extended to matters to deal with which
the Reichstag, though actually sitting, was for some reason
or other incompetent.[1] The German population, to
which a position of predominance over all other races was
assured, was temporarily induced to believe that it was at
last to enjoy the blessings of true parliamentary government, but soon found to its disgust that the Patent, as
compared with the Diploma, was retrograde rather than
progressive, and in reality was no more than a cloak
intended to hide the nakedness of absolutism from the
eyes of an inquisitive Europe. The Reichsrath had no
control whatever over foreign affairs or army matters. It
was not within its competence to vote either the annual
contingent of recruits or the money necessary for their
maintenance. Members were not elected directly by the
people, but were nominated by the provincial Diets composed of the representatives of various classes and interests
of the landowners, the towns, the Chambers of Commerce,
and country districts, which latter elected delegates to
whom the ultimate choice of representatives was confided.
The object was to give as much power as possible to the
more conservative classes, and, above all, to the towns, in
which the German element preponderated. A gerry-
mandered franchise and an arbitrary distribution of seats[2]

---

[1] In spite of the protests of the Czechs and Poles the budgets of 1861,
1862, 1863, were discussed and voted in the absence of the Hungarian members. Schmerling admitted that the whole Constitution could be rendered
nugatory by means of clause xiii.—Rogge, *Österreich von Vildgos bis zur
Gegenwart*, ii. 107.

[2] Palacky, quoted by Eisenmann, exposed the swindle as regards Bohemia,
e.g. the towns in which German influence was preponderant returned one repre-

reduced the system of so-called popular representation to a farce, while the attempted perpetuation of German racial supremacy made the unity of Cisleithanian nationalities an impossibility, and so assured the ultimate triumph of the Magyars, who alone knew what they wanted and were determined to have it. The despotism of a foreign bureaucracy[1] smelt no sweeter in Magyar nostrils when disguised by a Patent than when diluted by a Diploma. The old contracts had been broken, and sooner or later must be patched up again, for it was clear that the Patent, and the refusal to grant a responsible Ministry, which Baron Vay had led people to believe would be re-established, had destroyed the last vestige of inclination to acquiesce in any arrangement which would involve the abandonment of the March laws of 1848. It was evident that the resumption of the policy of passive resistance was the only course open to Hungary until a fresh outbreak of war in Italy or elsewhere, and a fresh disaster to the Austrian arms, should finally convince the Emperor of the inability of a house divided against itself to resist the aggression of foreign cupidity.

sentative for 11,666 inhabitants, and the country (Czech) districts one for 49,081. The German town of Reichenberg, with 19,000 inhabitants, had three representatives, while Prague, the capital, with 145,000, had ten. A German village of 500 inhabitants had a representative, though the Slav town of Kladno, with 8000, had none. Such instances could be multiplied indefinitely. Hungary proper had four times as big a population as Transylvania, and was vastly superior in wealth and education, but returned only three times as many members, the object of this "electoral geometry," as it was called, being to favour the Saxons.

[1] The Patent gave full effect to the Austrian bureaucratic ideal of "freie Verfügung über die Armee, die Polizei, die Finanzen und alle Vollzugs-Organe."—Pillersdorf, *Handschriftlicher Nachlass*, p. 240.

CHAPTER XVII

THE Diet met at Buda on April 2, in accordance with the Writ of Summons,[1] which recited the abdication of Ferdinand V. and announced Francis Joseph's intention to have himself crowned, and, in accordance with "the desires of his paternal heart, and with a view to the promotion of the common welfare and happiness of the kingdom, to deliberate with the faithful Estates and Orders on various legislative matters of great moment." The opening speech,[2] read on the Emperor's behalf by Count George Apponyi, expressed regret for the mistrust engendered by the events of the past years, and belief in the loyalty of the nation. It declared that while His Majesty was bound to observe the promises made to the other peoples of his Empire by the October Diploma, which was designed for the better attainment of the objects aimed at by the Pragmatic Sanction, he was anxious not to deprive Hungary of the right of dealing with its own internal affairs, or of the constitutional exercise of influence on the common affairs of the Empire. Such being the case, His Majesty invited the Diet to express its opinion as to the manner in which the constitutional rights of Hungary could be brought into harmony with the necessities of the reorganised Empire. Such a pronouncement, which referred to the Pragmatic Sanction for justification of a total disregard of contractual obligations, the strict

---

[1] Kónyi, *Deák Ferencz Beszédei*, iii. 1.   [2] *Ibid.* iii. 19 *sqq.*

observance of which alone could confer a claim to the crown of St. Stephen, could only increase the resentment generated by years of absolutism, and strengthen the determination to stand firm in defence of inalienable rights. Owing to the long duration of the autocratic *régime*, which gave no opportunities for the acquirement of political experience, the younger members of the Diet, imbued with a feeling of hatred of Austrian oppression, and animated by an excessive belief in the influence of the exiles, and in the prospect of foreign intervention, for the moment desired nothing so much as an opportunity of giving forcible expression to the accumulated grievances of the past years. These formed one party under the leadership of Count Ladislaus Teleki, who, at the end of the previous year, had been handed over by the Government of Saxony to the Austrian police, and had been set at liberty by the Emperor, on condition that he would break off all connexion with the exiled irreconcilables, and would temporarily refrain from all agitation and political activity in Hungary.[1] The other party was that of Deák, Eötvös, and Julius Andrássy, who were not less determined than the followers of Teleki to abandon no part of their country's rights, but were disposed to compromise on minor details which did not affect fundamental principles in order to avoid creating the impression that Hungary was impervious to reason and hopelessly intractable. Between the two parties feeling ran high with respect to the question as to what form the reply to the imperial speech should take—that of an address or that of a resolution. On the principle that it was impossible to address a non-existent king (for up to the present Hungary had no official cognizance of the abdication of Ferdinand, or of the renunciation of his

[1] As he received a letter of summons to the Diet he considered himself absolved from his promise as regards abstention from political life. See his letter, written ten days after his arrest, to Jósika. Kossuth, *Schriften aus der Emigration*, iii. 320 ; also Pulszky, *Életem és Korom*, ii. 311 *sqq.*

rights by Francis Charles, and the formalities essential to
the coronation of a successor had not yet been complied
with), Teleki and his party wished that the Diet should
pass a resolution [1] enumerating the national grievances,
and should then adjourn *sine die*, thus shutting the door
to the possibility of compromise. Deák, on the other
hand, desired that an address should be sent to the
Emperor, the adoption of which by the Diet would imply
neither the abandonment of constitutional rights nor
acquiescence in an intolerable position, but would discourage the idea that nothing but intractable hostility was
to be expected from Hungary. The ultimate victory of
the " Addressists," after a three weeks' debate, was
facilitated by the death of Teleki, who, finding his
position incompatible with the promise [2] given to Francis
Joseph, committed suicide, and so vacated the leadership of
the more irreconcilable party in favour of Coloman Tisza.

The Address, [3] the work of Deák's pen, is an unanswerable presentment of the illegalities which characterised the existing system, and is, at the same time, a
compendium of the constitutional history of Hungary.
The brutalities of absolutism have given place to the
illegalities of a pseudo-constitutionalism. Acquiescence
in the partial restoration of historic rights would amount
to a definite abandonment of the independence guaranteed
by the Pragmatic Sanction and by the laws of 1790,
confirmed by each successive King of Hungary, which
prove the personal nature of the union existing between
that country and the hereditary provinces, the fact of
whose inclusion, formerly in the defunct Romano-
Germanic Empire, and now in the German Confederation,

[1] See Kónyi, *o.c.* iii. 26, and Beksics, Kemény Zsigmond, etc., 254.

[2] Beust, who had given him up to the Austrian police, attributes his
suicide to baffled ambition, but makes no attempt to justify his statement.
Memoirs, ii. 338 *n.*, but see the evidence of Lukács and other contemporaries
quoted by Kónyi, *o.c.* iii. 106 *sqq.*

[3] Kónyi, *o.c.* iii. 36-60.

excludes the possibility of any greater solidarity. The Diet declares its willingness to undertake a larger share of the burdens imposed by the reckless misgovernment of recent times than that of which strict legal obligations require the acceptance, but will discuss the subject with the hereditary provinces only as one free and independent country with another, and will sacrifice the constitutional freedom of Hungary to no considerations of expediency whatever. It refuses to surrender its immemorial right of deciding all questions of taxation, and of the raising of the military forces, and denies the right of the Reichsrath, or any similar body, to legislate on the affairs of Hungary. The Diet protests against the violation of Hungary's territorial integrity, guaranteed not only by the Pragmatic Sanction, but also by the Inaugural Diplomas and Coronation Oaths of successive kings. Until the legislative body is rendered complete by the presence of the representatives of Transylvania and Croatia, it is unable to pass laws or enter into negotiations with respect to the coronation; for while the operation of the old fundamental laws is suspended, it is useless and constitutionally impossible to initiate new legislation. Provided, however, that the illegalities attending the abdication of Ferdinand V. are not allowed to form a precedent, and that proper notification of such abdication, and of the renunciation by the Archduke Francis Charles of his rights of succession, is given, the Diet is prepared to recognise the change of monarch which has *de facto* taken place. The Address concludes by demanding the revocation of sentences of imprisonment and banishment, pronounced by foreign judges in accordance with foreign law, as a condition precedent to the re-establishment of confidence between Hungary and the Crown.

Tisza and Jókai approved Deák's exposition of the meaning and effect of the Pragmatic Sanction, as well as his views on the subject of territorial integrity and of the brutalities of the past twelve years, but objected to the proposed mode of approaching the Emperor on the ground that an address is something in the nature of a petition, while a resolution is a solemn manifestation of the nation's will. Defeated on the main question by a majority of three votes, the Resolutionists obtained a victory on a minor but important point. Deák wished to address the Emperor as " Your Imperial and Royal Majesty," but the opposition of Tisza and his followers succeeded in amending the phrase by the omission of the words " Imperial and Royal," the consequence of which was that the Emperor refused to accept the Address until re-amended in accordance with Deák's formula. The only result, therefore, of Tisza's action was the facilitation of Schmerling's task of persuading Francis Joseph of the irreconcilable hostility of the Diet, and of the necessity of compelling Hungary to comply with the terms of the Patent. Baron Vay, who presented a memorandum to the Emperor urging the advisability of coming to an arrangement with the Magyars on the basis of the recognition of their exceptional position, was curtly dismissed from office [1]—a clear indication of the width and depth of the gulf which still sundered the two individuals on whose co-operation the effectuation of a lasting arrangement depended—Francis Joseph and Francis Deák.

The death of Cavour, who had always been dissatisfied with the peace of Villafranca, negotiated in a hurry behind his back, made the probability of a resumption of an aggressive Franco-Italian policy more remote than had previously been the case. This fact and the unpatriotic intrigues of Count Antony Forgács, who had been in the Russian camp in 1848, while his countrymen were fighting for freedom, and had taken service under the tyrannical government of the Bach *régime*, and those of Count Maurus Eszterházy, a violent anti-Protestant leader of the

[1] July 18. Lévay, *Emléklapok Vajai Báró Vay Miklós Életéből*, p. 35.

Ultramontane party, strengthened the Emperor in his determination to resist the demands of the Magyars. The Rescript of July 21,[1] sent in answer to the Address, is a long disquisition on the theme that the connexion existing between Hungary and the hereditary provinces is a real and effective union, and not a mere personal one, the object of the Pragmatic Sanction being not merely the preservation of Hungary from internal convulsions, liable to arise from a break in the succession to the throne, but also the provision of a "more solid common basis of harmony and union," as proved by the existence of Hungarian legislation admitting the existence of "common affairs" (such as Law xi. of 1741 requesting the admission of Magyar members to the Imperial Ministry),[2] and by the fact of the existence of a common army and of a system of central financial administration.   Oblivious of the fact that the only law which shows the existence of anything more than a personal union was Law iii. of 1848, the Emperor alleges that the legislation of that year consti- tuted an attempt to abolish the real union, and to bring about a separation " productive of all those dangerous convulsions which necessitated the establishment of a form of administration at variance with the constitutional institutions of Hungary."   The recognition demanded by the Diet of the validity of the laws of 1848 is, according to the Rescript, incompatible with the conditions essential to the existence of the Empire ; those laws must, therefore, be revised " in accordance with the spirit of the Pragmatic Sanction, and in the manner required by the common interests of the Empire," before any deliberations on the form which the Inaugural Diploma should assume can take place.   The Diet is therefore "commanded" to submit proposals providing for the repeal of the laws of 1848, as a condition precedent to the settlement of the question of the reincorporation of Transylvania, the union of which

[1] Kónyi, o.c. iii. 193-202.   [2] See supra, p. 47.

with Hungary is alleged to have taken place without the consent of the Roumanian and Saxon nations, and never became effective. The case of Croatia and Slavonia is likewise reserved for future consideration, and all decrees and ordinances having reference to public administration, and to the levying of taxes, are to remain in force until further notice. Thus, though Francis Joseph declares that " the incorporation of the realms of the Crown of St. Stephen is far removed from the intentions of our paternal heart," the Rescript flatly rejects the Diet's demand for a return to constitutional principles, and proposes to perpetuate existing illegalities.

Deák replied in a second Address,[1] the terms of which were accepted unanimously by Tisza and his followers, as well as by the other members of the Diet. He points out the impossibility of negotiation on the basis of the arbitrary suppression of the fundamental laws of Hungary, and of the compulsory acceptance of absolute autocracy — the underlying principle of the Diploma and of the Patent. The autocratic abolition or modification of laws without the consent of the nation is the negation of constitutionalism. If one such action passes unchallenged Hungary's independence is at an end, for what guarantee is there that some successor of His Majesty will not repeat the process ? The assertion contained in the Rescript, that Hungary's control of taxation was always, *de jure* as well as *de facto*, of a limited character, is refuted,[2] as are the imperial deductions from the fact of Hungary's apparent acquiescence in the unity of administration as regards foreign affairs.[3] The laws which prove the Diet's

[1] Kónyi, iii. 220-272.

[2] It is pointed out that the military tax was always fixed and voted by the Diet, and the tax to provide for the expenses of local administration was always assessed and collected by the county organisations. As has been seen, even the price of salt, a royal monopoly, could not be raised without the consent of the Diet, except in the case mentioned by Law xx. of 1790.

[3] See *supra*, p. 46.

control of military matters and the legality of its claim to financial independence, are successively enumerated, and the offer, contained in the first Address, to assist the hereditary provinces without prejudice to the constitutional rights of Hungary, in bearing the heavy burdens imposed by the reckless maladministration of the past twelve years, is repeated.   It is pointed out that the laws of 1848 did not alter the nature of the union resulting from the Pragmatic Sanction, or attempt to confer any new rights on Hungary, but merely gave clearer expression to existing privileges ; and that the "convulsions" alluded to in the Rescript were the result, not of those laws, but of the obstacles thrown by Vienna in the way of their execution.   The absurdity of referring to the laws of 1848 by way of justification for the introduction of absolutism is shown by the fact that Croatia, which was in no sense responsible for the passing of those laws and fought on the imperial side, has also been deprived of its constitutional rights.   The use of a phrase to the effect that the Emperor will conditionally restore the Constitution, " by the exercise of royal absolute power," makes the re-establishment of confidence impossible ; for the royal absolute power in the field of legislation is unknown to the Pragmatic Sanction, and the Diet cannot recognise the legality of one-sided arbitrary action, when the law expressly declares that legislative functions can be exercised only by the King and the Diet acting together.   The international position of a State does not depend exclusively on the number of its regular soldiers, and a compulsory unity can give no strength to the Empire.   Austria was a great power at the time when Hungary enjoyed the attributes of an independent State, and could always rely on the cordial co-operation of the Magyars.   The maintenance of Hungarian independence involves no risk to the safety of the Empire, while the mutilation of political rights must

undermine the feeling of solidarity with the hereditary
provinces, and destroy all confidence in a monarchy
which is unable to guarantee even the material prosperity
of its subjects.   The Rescript states that His Majesty has
given validity to some of the laws of 1848, but never
did, and never will, recognise the rest of them ; but as
King of Hungary, His Majesty has no power to repeal
laws without the consent of the nation, or to draw
distinctions between one law and another as regards the
question of validity.   The Diet is prepared to consider
the modification of certain of the laws, but is not
competent to do so until completed by the attendance of
the representatives of all the constituent elements of the
nation.   Only existent laws can be modified or repealed,
and His Majesty, by requiring the Diet to modify or
repeal the laws of 1848, *ipso facto*, acknowledges their
existence, while refusing to allow them to be put into
force.   If the statement contained in the Rescript, to
the effect that His Majesty does not consider himself
personally bound to recognise those laws, is allowed to
pass unchallenged, what constitutional guarantee remains ?
For if the principle of the " continuity of obligation "
is wiped out, every Constitution, and the political
security of every State, become the sport of circumstance.
" Should Croatia wish to separate herself definitely from
us, to include herself among the number of Austrian
provinces, and to subject herself to the government and
legislature of the latter, a hypothesis which, in our belief,
the constitutional feelings of the Croatians cannot allow to
be realised, we shall make no attempt to raise any
obstacles, though, on the other hand, we cannot give our
consent, for the reason that we have no power to assent to
the dismemberment of the realms of the Crown of
St. Stephen."   In the meanwhile, inasmuch as His Majesty
claims the benefits, but repudiates the obligations resulting
from the Pragmatic Sanction, and demands to be crowned,

but refuses to restore more than isolated fragments of the Constitution, Hungary must refuse to send representatives to the Reichsrath, which, in direct violation of the Pragmatic Sanction, and of Law x. of 1790, presumes to legislate on matters which are beyond the limits of its competence ; and the Diet must declare with regret that, in consequence of the Rescript, it is compelled to regard the thread of negotiation as broken off. The Address concludes with the words :—

It may be that hard times are again in store for our country, but we cannot avert them at the expense of our duty as citizens. The constitutional liberty of Hungary is no chattel of which we can freely dispose ; the nation has intrusted it to us, and we are responsible to our country and to our own consciences for its safe-keeping. The nation is prepared to suffer, if necessary, in order to be able to hand down to future generations that constitutional liberty which it inherited from its forefathers. It will suffer, but it will not despair, just as our ancestors endured and suffered in defence of the national rights ; for what might and power take away, time and favouring circumstance may be able to restore ; but the recovery of that which a nation abandons of its own accord for fear of suffering is ever a matter of difficulty and un-certainty. The nation will endure in the hope of a better future, and relying on the justice of its cause.

Deák was quite aware that he exposed his country to the risk of a further period of tyrannical violence, but was determined that it should not permanently abandon sacred rights for considerations of temporary convenience. How right he was in the view he entertained of the intentions of Vienna, in spite of the pseudo-constitutional spirit breathed by the Rescript, was proved by Schmerling's speech, delivered in the Reichsrath on August 23, which declared that " the Constitution of Hungary has not merely been destroyed by revolutionary violence, but has been forfeited *as of right*, and is in fact abolished "—in other words, that Francis Joseph was irrevocably determined to reduce Hungary to the position of a province of the

Austrian Empire.   By way of reply to the second Address the Emperor ordered the dissolution of the Diet by military force.   The county assemblies followed the lead of the Diet, protested against the violation of the Constitution, and exhorted the people to stand firm. Schmerling consequently dissolved the organisation of the counties,[1] and Count Forgács was entrusted with the task of restoring order, or rather of breaking down resistance to illegality.   A refusal to pay taxes, which had not been voted by the Diet in accordance with constitutional usage, brought Austrian soldiers into play, and led to a repetition of the scenes of violence with which the country was already familiar.   In spite of the protests of the Chief Justice and of the Court of Appeal, martial law was again established, with a view to a complete recurrence to Bach's system of absolutism and oppression, which, in Schmerling's opinion, was bound in the long-run to force the Magyars to give way, and to produce the desired incorporation of Hungary in the Austrian Empire.

Even Kossuth, who had always complained of Deák's " parochial views," and of his tendency to sit with folded hands waiting till the pressure of external circumstances should compel compliance with Hungary's demands, though forced to admit the effectiveness of Deák's second Address from the point of view of pure constitutionalism, was disposed to attach greater importance to other weapons than those provided by logic and knowledge of constitutional history.   Only a few months after the conclusion of the Peace of Villafranca Italy was again seething with discontent ; and in September 1860, Pulszky, Kossuth's representative, was able to come to an arrangement with the Government of Turin, providing that in the event of a resumption of hostilities between Italy and Austria, Victor Emmanuel would send troops to Hungary, and would bind himself not to make peace till the

[1] Rescript of March 5.

independence of that country had been assured. A Hungarian legion was to be formed, and a rising was to take place in Hungary as soon as war was declared. The plan was adopted with enthusiasm by the emigrants, and many young Mágyars left their country for Italy to join the legion, which, under the command of Garibaldi, Klapka, and General Türr, was to form the nucleus of the national forces. In spite of the negative results of the recent Italian war, the number was still considerable of those who were dissatisfied with the idea of playing a waiting game, and were convinced that salvation could come only from Kossuth, and from the proper utilisation of the opportunity for armed revolt which European complications were sure, sooner or later, to afford. To the enthusiasm of these militant patriots the publication of Kossuth's immature scheme for the establishment of a confederation of Danubian States was a deadly blow.

As early as 1851 Kossuth had come to the conclusion that Hungary could never hope to stand in splendid isolation between the devil and the deep sea, represented respectively by Austria and Russia,[1] but apparently he formed no definite scheme till the death of Cavour, the dissolution of the Magyar legion, and the *rapprochement* between Austria and France consequent on the acceptance of the crown of Mexico by the Archduke Maximilian, had made the probability of an Austro-Italian war comparatively remote. The prospect of the Eastern Question being the next matter to occupy the attention of Europe, convinced him of the necessity of having some cut-and-dried plan which would obviate the possibility of Hungary being 1862. regarded as a *quantité négligeable* either at the beginning or at the end of a new episode in the history of the Balkan Peninsula. On the advice of Pulszky,[2] Canini, an Italian newspaper reporter, visited Kossuth, and discussed with him the possibility of a confederation of Hungary,

---

[1] *Schriften aus der Emigration*, iii. 707.   [2] *Életem és Korom*, ii. 351 *sqq.*

Transylvania, Croatia, Servia, and Moldo-Wallachia, which should supply the European necessity of a strong Power in the basin of the Danube.   Kossuth's ideas were put on paper and signed by him without any intention that they should be made public, which they promptly were in the columns of the *Alleanza*,[1] with the result that public opinion in Hungary was greatly incensed against the ex-dictator, and that his reputation as a serious statesman received a blow from which it never entirely recovered. Instead of explaining that the statement published in the *Alleanza* was only a draft, and never intended for the public eye, Kossuth attempted to defend his immature scheme—the outcome of a blind hatred, which would rather split Hungary into three parts, and sacrifice Magyar interests to those of a mongrel Southern Slav confedera-tion, than maintain any connexion with the House of Habsburg.   The "common affairs" of the proposed confederation were to comprise not only military matters and foreign affairs, but all matters connected with customs-tariffs and commercial policy.   The representation of the various States was to be proportionate to the population of each constituent factor of the confederation, and the executive power was to be vested, not in the Hungarian Government, but in a Senate composed for the most part of non-Magyar representatives.   Hungary would scarcely have occupied the position of *prima inter pares*. The common legislative body was to decide what was to be the official language, and in Parliament each repre-sentative was to be allowed to use his native idiom.   A more complete surrender of the historic rights, for which Hungary had fought and bled for centuries, could hardly be imagined than this scheme which involved the dis-memberment of the realms of St. Stephen, and the abandonment of Magyar predominance, in return for the

---

[1] For the text as published see Jancsó Benedek, *Szabadságharczunk és a Dako-Román Törekvések*, pp. 304-308.

questionable benefits to be derived from association on equal terms with fragmentary, non-cohesive nationalities; an association which, owing to the wide divergence of social and religious interests, must necessarily be inharmonious. Kossuth was far from being the only one who disbelieved in the efficacy of a policy of passive resistance, as was proved by the arrest and trial, in 1864, of Paul Almássy, Stephen Nedeczky, and many other conspirators belonging to well-known families; but the vast majority was on the side of Deák, and the opinion that freedom must soon come to those who knew how to wait was general, not only in Hungary, but in all Europe as well.

The refusal of Hungary to send representatives to the Reichsrath was the death-knell of the February Constitution. The disgust of the Croatians and Servians, who found that the gratitude of a dynasty, which their efforts in 1848 had helped to save, found expression in a germanising policy and in a total disregard of the national aspirations of the Southern Slavs,[1] gave final proof of the fatuity of Bach and of his successors, who failed to see the uselessness of attempting the final destruction of Hungarian independence without providing the subordinate races with a satisfactory substitute for

---

[1] "Auch in Kroatien wurde 1852 die freie Wahl der Gemeinderäthe bis auf weiteres aufgehoben; überall trat Willkur an die Stelle des alten Rechtes. . . . Kroatien war ebenso eine Provinz wie irgend eines der fünf Verwaltungsgebiete des rebellischen Ungarn."—Friedjung, *Österreich von 1848 bis 1860*, i. 426-427. "Hier aber wurde ein verhängnissvoller Fehler begangen, denn die Centralisation und Germanisation machten vor keiner Nationalität Halt: man wollte alle unterschiedslos beugen, Kroaten und Serben, Slowaken und Rumänen so gut wie die Magyaren, und selbst die Treuesten der Treuen, die Siebenburger Sachsen, wurden durch Zerstörung ihrer uralten Selbstverwaltung tief gekränkt . . . sie all der Rechte verlustig wurden, die sie durch Jahrhunderte geübt hatten. Damit war auch ihre lokale Selbstverwaltung vernichtet, nachdem zuerst ihre politische Autonomie aufgehoben worden war. Der Sachsengraf und die Nationsuniversität waren Antiquitäten geworden. So übles wie jetzt durch die Kaiserliche Regierung war ihnen unter keiner anderen Herrschaft zugefügt worden."—*Ibid.* 413-420.

the privileges which they had enjoyed as members of a constitutionally governed Hungary. Magyars and Slavs were equally determined to refuse to be incorporated in a new-fangled Austrian Empire. Only in Transylvania 1864 did the Government meet with some measure of success, for the Saxons and Roumanians finally decided to send representatives to the Reichsrath, in spite of the protests and abstention of the Magyars and the Szeklers, who maintained the validity of the reunion with Hungary pronounced in 1848. The attendance of Transylvanian deputies to some extent justified Schmerling's pretence that the Reichsrath was "full," *i.e.* was representative of the Empire as a whole, and could now deal with affairs which it was otherwise incompetent to treat, such as the Hungarian budget, and other financial matters hitherto dealt with by the Government in exercise of the extraordinary powers conferred by Clause xiii., to which reference has been made. But the position and authority of the Reichsrath was hopelessly shaken. Bohemia and Galicia saw clearly that the new Constitution was no more than a veiled continuation of the Bach system. For two years the Czechs took part in the proceedings of the Reichsrath, chiefly for the reason that they were anxious not to break with the Poles and Moravians, though they were often tempted to secede in a body when the germanising tendencies of the Government became too naked and unashamed. Finally, in 1863, they followed the Magyar lead, and notified the Reichsrath that they would take no further part in its deliberations, and only the German landowners and manufacturers were left to misrepresent Bohemia in the councils of the Empire.

Nothing shows more clearly the essential difference between Czechs and Magyars than this episode. As regards the claim to independence, the rights of the two nations are, possibly, theoretically indistinguishable. In the case of the former, independence was permanently destroyed by the battle of White Mountain, and the Czechs now once again recognised and acquiesced in the accomplished fact by explaining their abstention merely by a reference to the unfairness of the franchise and to the inequality of electoral divisions.   In the case of the latter, historic rights were only temporarily suspended by the capitulation of Világos ; and the refusal to take part in a central Parliament was justified on the ground of the indestructibility of an ancient Constitution.   In the case of the Czechs, the lapse of two centuries did but tighten the bonds of German domination ; in the case of the Magyars, five years of passive resistance sufficed to prove to an obstinate autocrat the fact that Hungarian discontent involved the paralysis of Austria, and to compel surrender to the demands of a united and homogeneous nation.   Even the Slováks, who, in 1848, had been on the Austrian side, and had demanded the establishment of an autonomous "Slovákia,"[1] within a year refused to have anything to do with the Reichsrath, and expressed their anxiety for the re-establishment of the Hungarian Constitution and the formation of separate federalised States for each of the constituent nationalities of Hungary.   But, for the moment, no fresh alterations of the "permanent and irrevocable" could be expected, for the Court considered Schmerling, the arch-centraliser, indispensable to the execution of its German policy.   The failure of that policy, and the conviction that Austria had pulled the chestnuts out of the fire for Prussia's benefit in the Schleswig-Holstein campaign, and must eventually abandon the cherished hope of recovering its hegemony in Germany, satisfied the Liberals of Vienna that there was no alternative but to effect the permanent pacification of Hungary, not by force, but by recognising its exceptional historical position.

---

[1] See their petition.—Despatch 332, Ponsonby to Palmerston. *Correspondence,* etc.

As early as 1861 a body of opinion had begun to form in Vienna in favour of compromise on the basis of dualism [1] involving the establishment of a responsible Ministry in both countries, and of a common Ministry for the management of common affairs. Dualism was to be the first step in the direction of substantial unity,[2] which the existing system had proved its inability to effectuate. What proved to be the last session of the Reichsrath began in November 1864, and was characterised by a series of wrangles, the outcome of the disgust generated by the excessive use of Clause 13, which, as the Deputies now realised, reduced the Reichsrath to the level of a debating society.[3] The feeling became general that the existing state of affairs could not last, and that some kind of compromise must be made with Hungary to enable the monarchy to settle down to business. The close of the Reichsrath was followed by the dismissal of Schmerling whom the Emperor had supported in the belief that his system of centralisation would consolidate the Empire, and enable it to play a commanding part in European politics. Like Bach, Schmerling had proved to be a broken reed, and his place was given to Count Belcredi, the popular governor of Bohemia, a strong Catholic with pronounced federalistic views, and therefore, theoretically, an enemy of the dualistic principle. The appointment was satisfactory to Catholic Austria (for the reason that it was considered to be conducive to the establishment of a counterpoise to Protestant Prussia), and to Bohemia, which prided itself on the theoretical equality of its rights with those of Hungary, and expected the recognition of its exceptional position should Belcredi bring federalism into fashion. But now as ever Hungarian opinion was the one thing that mattered.

[1] *Zur Losung der Ungarischen Frage*, 1861, Fischhof und Unger.
[2] *Zur Einigung Österreichs*, 1862, Friedman.
[3] " Schmerlingstheater " was the current nickname for the "narrow" Reichsrath. Krones, *Geschichte der Neuzeit Österreichs*, 769.

Diplomas and Patents, palliatives which might be tried with
impunity on the hereditary provinces, had proved to be
inflammatory rather than sedative when applied to
Hungary, yet official believers in the efficacy, and official
partisans of the " Verwirkungstheorie," who affected to
regard Hungary as a fit subject for the experimental
prescriptions of autocracy, were still to be found.[1]
Lustkandl, ex-tutor of Rechberg's children and the father
of the Tezners and Springers of to-day, undertook the
task of destroying the historical basis of the Hungarian
Constitution, and proving that a real union had existed
between Hungary and Austria both before and after the
Pragmatic Sanction.[2]   He tried to prove that the February
Patent with its Clause 13 was more liberal in the true
sense of the word than the Hungarian Constitution, and
that the Magyars with their passion for parliamentary
government should have accepted it with joy.[3]   He
denied the legality of the laws of 1848 chiefly on the
ground that Ferdinand had been coerced, and, that " as
the principle of constitutionalism had been openly proclaimed," could no longer treat with Hungary without
reference to the representatives of Austria, or behave as
" absoluter Herr "[4]—an argument which, if well founded,
would be fatal to the validity of the February Patent of

[1] "Ungarn freilich war das grosse Fragezeichen, denn wenn hier auch
Deutsche, Slawen und Rumänen zu gewinnen waren, so lag der Schwerpunkt
doch in den Magyaren ; und sie waren einig in dem Kampfe gegen den
Zentralismus, der Ungarn zu einer von Wien regierten Provinz herabdrückte.
Ob man in Ungarn einen oder fünf Landtage nach den neuen Verwaltungs-
bezirken berief : immer waren diese Körperschaften der Herd einer unversöhn-
lichen Opposition."—Friedjung, *Österreich von 1848 bis 1860*, i. 290.

[2] *Das Ungarisch-Österreichische Staatsrecht.*   Vienna, 1863.   See *supra*,
p. 35 *sqq.*

[3] See Schmerling's speech in the Reichsrath, August 23, 1862, in which
he asserts that Hungary's rights are observed, and its privileges have been
restored *subject only to the condition* that all matters connected with military
service, finance, foreign affairs, and national economics are referred to the
Reichsrath, and that the Constitution is "purged of superannuated relics."

[4] *Ibid.* pp. 7 and 389 *sqq.*

which Lustkandl urged the grateful acceptance.   The
book which suffers from the fact that its arguments are
largely founded on misquotations and intentional omission of
inconvenient facts, served a useful purpose in that it provided
Deák with an opportunity of making a contribution [1] (to
which frequent reference has already been made) of
inestimable value to the history of Hungary's constitutional 1865.
development.   He shows that, apart from the fact that
the Pragmatic Sanction was a contract made, not with
Austria, but with its Emperor, in 1848, there was no
Austrian Constitution limiting the autocrat's power of
negotiation with Hungary, even though the old heads of
departments were rebaptized as ministers.   He points
out that Francis Charles and Francis Joseph were both
present on the occasion of the ratification of the laws of
1848, a fact which was justly taken as indicative of their
consent—an answer to Lustkandl, who asserted, but without a shadow of constitutional justification, that the
consent of the next heirs was essential to the validity of
the March laws.   To the suggestion that ratification was
extorted by force of circumstances, and consequently was
invalid, Deák replies that all laws have been the result of
the force of circumstances from Magna Charta onwards,
and asks whether only those which have been passed
without regard to contemporary conditions are to be
considered as endowed with permanent validity.

Deák utilised his unsurpassed knowledge of his country's
constitutional history, not merely for the purposes of destructive criticism, but to indicate the only direction in which
a possibility of reconciliation of conflicting interests was
discernible.   In an article which appeared in the *Pesti
Napló* of April 16, 1865,[2] he pointed out that since 1680
the monarch had more than once appeared as a *deus ex*

---

[1] *Adalék a Magyar Közjoghoz*, also in German, *Ein Beitrag zum
Ungarischen Staatsrecht*.   Pest, 1865.

[2] Set out in full by Kónyi, *o.c.* iii. 401 *sqq.*

machine, when the action of ill-advised or malevolent Ministers had brought matters to a deadlock.   He denied that the Magyars were animated by separatistic desires, or wished for anything which would threaten the existence of the monarchy.   On the contrary, Hungary, which had ever been a convinced adherent of the monarchical principle, while it took its stand on the Pragmatic Sanction, was prepared to bring its laws and institutions into harmony with those required by the interests of the monarchy as a whole, and had no wish whatever to stand in the way of the constitutional development of the Austrian provinces. The article, which Francis Joseph learnt with pleasure was from the pen of Deák, was not without effect.   On the 30th of the same month the Emperor attended the races at Pressburg without military escort, and a week later went on to Budapest, abolished the courts-martial, re-established the Council of Lieutenancy, and promised that the Diet should soon be convened.   The successor of Count Forgács, Count Hermann Zichy, who was chiefly celebrated for the fact that at a banquet given by the Mayor of Vienna he had pronounced himself as un-compromisingly in favour of the abandonment of Hungary's constitutional rights, retired from the office of Hungarian Chancellor, and Count George Mailáth was appointed in his stead.   Finally, the issue on September 20 of an Imperial edict which suspended the February Constitution, removed the chief obstacle to agreement, and opened the door to the possibility of an arrangement.

For three hundred years the struggle had continued almost without intermission between Austria, trying to incorporate Hungary in a uniform Empire, and Hungary fighting in defence of its liberty.   At last it seemed as if both parties were convinced of the necessity of a compromise on the basis of the recognition of actual historical facts.   One of the causes of the war of 1848 had been the failure to make proper provision for the handling of affairs of common interest, and the definition of such affairs was still the chief obstacle to agreement. Count George Apponyi was prepared to abandon Hungary's right of interference in questions of foreign policy, and, what would have been far more fatal, to leave all matters connected with Hungary's military contingent to the uncontrolled discretion of the Crown.[1] But even these concessions to Austria were insufficient, in the opinion of his former allies, the Conservatives, and feeling the impossibility of his attitude, "with one foot on the laws of 1848 and the other on the October Diploma," he gradually drifted into the camp of Deák, who occupied a position midway between the opportunism of Apponyi's memorandum and the uncompromising disinclination to make any concession to Vienna which characterised Tisza and the stalwarts of the Extreme Left. The ultimate compromise, the germ of which is to be found in the "Easter Article" of the *Pesti Napló*, to which reference has already been made, may be said to date from the appearance in the *Debatte* of Vienna of three articles,[2] inspired if not actually dictated by Deák. Taking his stand on the Pragmatic Sanction, the basis of the contractual relations existing between Hungary and the Austrian monarch, Deák deduces therefrom the necessity of admitting the existence of "common affairs," resulting from the recognised obligation of mutual defence in time of peace as well as in time of war. Both diplomacy and military matters must, consequently, be regarded as "common," more especially as the Diplomatic Service can only represent the monarch, who himself is "common."[3] But the admission of the "common" nature of defence does not imply the abandonment by Hungary of its

[1] See his Memorandum presented to the Emperor in 1863.—Kónyi, *o.c.* iii. 302 *sqq.*

[2] May 1865. Text in Kónyi, *o.c.* iii. 422 *sqq.*

[3] This is not strictly accurate. The monarch is identical, but not "common."

historic right to determine the numbers of its military contingent, the conditions of service, and the manner in which the necessary recruits are to be provided. Defence being common, it necessarily follows that finance, so far as the cost of military and diplomatic matters are concerned, must also be regarded as common. The proportion, therefore, in which the two countries must contribute requires to be settled by mutual agreement, and the funds so provided must be dealt with by a common Minister of Finance. Further, unless a customs barrier is again erected between Hungary and Austria, tariff questions, and commercial policy in general, require unity of treatment. Thus, the whole principle which ultimately developed into the Ausgleich, or Compromise, embodied in the law of 1867, is to be found in the above-mentioned articles. The foundation for subsequent agreement was provided, but endless opportunity remained for quarrelling over the nature of the superstructure.

In the state of affairs which followed the dissolution of the Diet and of the county organisation it was difficult for public opinion either to form or to express itself. The Hungarian Press was muzzled, and writers like Jókai, in whose opinion the opportunism of Apponyi and the conciliatory moderation of Deák alike involved a cowardly betrayal of the country's interests, were thrown into prison. A general refusal to pay taxes, the payment of which was rendered impossible, in many cases, by the droughts of the two preceding years, brought the soldier tax-collector on the scene; and it was only the want of a favourable opportunity which prevented a violent explosion of the pent-up forces of discontent from taking place. A safety-valve was provided by the convocation of the Diet, and the suspension of the Constitution of February 1861, by Patent dated September 20, removed the chief obstacle to compromise. But the true meaning of the history of the past sixteen years was not yet fully appreciated by Francis

Joseph, though the pseudo-constitutional centralisation of Schmerling had proved to be just as great a failure as the undisguised despotism of Bach.   The object of both had been the consolidation and strengthening of the Austrian Empire ; the result was the creation of a cancerous sore in the body politic on which the successive Patents and Diplomas of autocracy had acted as so many irritants.   The contrast presented by the Austria-Hungary of 1847 and the Austrian Empire of 1865 should have sufficed to emphasise the obvious fact, that Magyar discontent entailed the paralysis of the Habsburg monarchy. The responsibility for Solferino rested chiefly with Bach, and failure to recognise the futility of Schmerling made Königgrätz inevitable.

CHAPTER XVIII

1865. "LET them make their programmes in Hungary if they like, we can revise them in Vienna."[1] Such was the comment of Schmerling's organ on a situation of the seriousness of which no Austrian statesman, with the exception of Francis Joseph himself, seems to have had more than the vaguest conception. Though the uselessness of attempting even a veiled incorporation of Hungary in the Austrian Empire should have been patent to all, Schmerling still believed in the possibility of compelling consent to some form of representation in a central Reichsrath, the composition and legislative competence of which could be so arranged and defined as, practically, to reduce the Hungarian Parliament to the level of a provincial Diet.[2] The Emperor alone seems to have realised the necessity of restoring the Hungarian Constitution ; but, unfortunately, in his view restoration meant the issue of a new edition, revised and expurgated, at a moment when no variation of the original was capable of satisfying the requirements of a nation which knew that time was on its side, that the greater the delay in yielding to its demands the greater the certainty of its ultimate triumph, though few, if any, realised the fact that Deák's arguments would so soon be reinforced and emphasised by the Prussian needle-gun.

The opening of the Diet on December 14, 1865,

[1] *A Mag. Nem. Tört*, x. 631.
[2] For his view see Fröbel, *Ein Lebenslauf*, ii. 375 *sqq.*

showed that Deák was supported by a compact majority
of one hundred and eighty members. Ninety-four, under
the leadership of Tisza, Ghyczy, and Nyáry, formed the
Left Centre, the root of whose dissidence was distrust of
what they styled the opportunism of Deák and Andrássy,
and belief in the necessity of insistence on a strict interpretation of the Pragmatic Sanction, which imposed no
obligation on their country save that which resulted from
the personal identity of King and Emperor. Twenty
extremists, who represented the views of Kossuth and of
the exiled " bitterenders," saw salvation only in the severance of the last link which bound Hungary to Austria,
and nothing but disgrace and disaster in the recognition
of the possibility of compromise. A like number under
Apponyi's leadership, desirous of office rather than devoted to principles,[1] were ready to accept almost any
settlement of the questions at issue which would preserve
the influence of the Habsburg monarchy in the councils
of Europe, and would put an, even temporary, end to
an intolerable situation. Unfortunately, as in earlier days,
the existence of such a party led the Emperor to believe
that Hungary was ready for the sake of peace to accept
terms involving a practical recurrence to the state of
affairs which existed before the passing of the March
laws, and increased the difficulties which confronted the
representatives of the common-sense of the nation.

The width of the gulf which separated Francis Joseph
and Deák became apparent on the day of the opening of the
Diet. The Emperor's speech[2] recognised the Pragmatic
Sanction as the basis of the relations of Hungary and
Austria, and as the starting-point for negotiation on the

---

[1] Letter of Eötvös to Andrássy, Aug. 1, 1865.—Kónyi, o.c. iii. 441.
They considered the laws of 1848 to be incompatible with the maintenance
of Austria's position as a great Power. At the same time they wished for
a recurrence to the pre-1848 system of local government.—Beksics, *Kemény
Zsigmond*, p. 320.

[2] See Kónyi, o.c. iii. 503 *sqq.*

subject of common affairs, but insisted on the revision
and amendment of the March laws, on the ground of
their inconsistency with the royal prerogatives, as a condition precedent to the restoration of the Constitution.
Insistence on such a condition was necessarily fatal to the
possibility of agreement, in that it amounted to the negation of the principle of legal continuity, the abandonment
of which must shatter the whole fabric of the Constitution.   Though the Emperor admitted the ineptitude of
the theory that Hungary had forfeited all constitutional
privileges as a basis for the reconstruction of the
monarchy, the assumption that Hungary could be induced to accept the grant of a new or modified Constitution as a compensation for the abandonment of
unquestionable rights, showed a total misconception of
the juridical relations of Hungary and Austria, of the
temper of the former country, and of the essential mean-
1866. ing of Deák's contentions.   The Address [1] voted in reply
to the King's speech respectfully pointed out the absurdity
of a one-sided reference to the Pragmatic Sanction, of
appealing to a contract for a justification of a total disregard of the obligations which it imposed.   The consideration for Hungary's renunciation of its elective rights
was the recognition of the inviolability of the Constitution
as a whole, and of the indivisibility of the realms of the
sacred Crown.   A partial inviolability is a contradiction
in terms ; a denial of the principle of continuity of
obligation would be fatal to the claims of the House of
Habsburg-Lorraine to the throne of Hungary, as it would
involve the excision of the fundamental condition of the
" *pactum bilaterale* " contained in the laws of 1723.   The
Magyars, said the Address, rejoiced at the announcement
of His Majesty's decision to grant a form of constitutional
government to the hereditary provinces, for they saw

[1] See Kónyi, *o.c.* iii. 545-561 ; also Deák's speech of 22nd Feb. 1866,
ibid, p. 578 *sqq.*

therein an earnest of an intention to restore the inalienable rights of their country; but joy was turned to mourning when the production of the October Diploma proved the inability of the monarch to recognise the difference which existed between his Austrian possessions, hitherto subject to autocracy, and the kingdom of Hungary, whose Constitution did not owe its existence to a royal grant or charter, but was part and parcel of the life of the nation, and was subject to modification only with the consent of two parties of equal competence—King and Parliament. The Diet expressed its readiness to proceed to consider the question of the revision of the laws of 1848 so soon as the restoration of Hungary's constitutional independence and territorial integrity was an accomplished fact; at the same time it pointed out that no legislative proposal could possibly have the binding force of law until the ceremony of coronation, which alone gave the King the necessary powers of ratification, had taken place. But it could not take place unless and until the person entitled to the throne had signed an Inaugural Diploma, and had taken an oath to maintain the Constitution and to observe the laws which his predecessors had confirmed. The Address concluded with a demand for the restoration of the old-established autonomy of the counties, and with a reference to the lessons of past history which proved that the security of the throne is proportionate to the attachment evinced by its subjects to their constitutional privileges.

As Deák reminded his countrymen, the hungry Esau sold his birthright for a mess of pottage, but though he received the stipulated consideration an intensified hatred was the result of the transaction. Hungary was no place for the opportunist politician. The Diet preferred a continuance of despotism and distress to the, even temporary, abandonment of the rights of which it was the trustee. How little effect the Address had on the

Emperor's intentions was shown by the terms of the reply,[1] received on March 3, in which Francis Joseph indicated those of the laws of 1848 which, in his opinion, were incompatible with the maintenance of the royal authority and with the proper management of affairs of common interest to Austria and Hungary. The authority conferred on the Palatine requires modification ; the limitations imposed on the royal power of dissolving Parliament must be abolished ; the whole question of local government needs reconsideration ; and Law xxii., which provides for the establishment of a national defensive force, must be repealed prior to the re-establishment of a constitutional *régime*. The effect of the peremptory nature of this Rescript is distinctly discernible in the determined tone adopted by the Diet in its reply,[2] which points out the inconsistency of asking the nation to exercise its legislative functions while denying the binding force of existing laws, and more especially of that fundamental law which alone gave the House of Habsburg a *locus standi* to interfere in the affairs of Hungary. Until the coronation takes place in accordance with immemorial ceremony one of the necessary parties to the revision of laws is, constitutionally, non-existent, and there is no means of effecting any alteration in the legislation which has been expressly confirmed by the predecessors of the person entitled to the throne.[3] The Diet therefore demands the *restitutio in integrum* of the constitutional

---

[1] Kónyi, *o.c.* iii. 608 *sqq.*　　　　　[2] *Ibid.* iii. 626 *sqq.*

[3] It is advisable that the reader should remember the words of the *Diploma inaugurale* signed by Kings of Hungary before coronation : "Quod praeter ab antiquo deductam haereditariam Regiam successionem Coronationemque, in reliquo universas et singulas communes istius Regni Hungariae Partiumque eidem adnexarum libertates, immunitates, privilegia, *statuta communia, jura, leges, et consuetudines* a divis quondam Hungariae regibus, et gloriosissimae memoriae praedecessoribus nostris, hactenus *concessas et confirmatas in futurumque condendas et per nos confirmandas* . . . *in omnibus suis punctis, articulis et clausulis* . . . *firmiter et sancte observabimus, per aliosque omnes et singulos inviolabiliter observari faciemus.*"

rights of the country as an essential preliminary to the consideration of, possibly necessary, amendments of the laws of 1848.[1] Too much blood had flowed in defence of those laws for it to be possible to return to the state of affairs which had existed before their passing, and the daily increasing probability of an Austro-Prussian war made a national surrender more unthinkable than ever. But Vienna was still blind to the real position of affairs, and amused itself with plans for the reconstruction of the governmental institutions of Hungary which involved the abolition of the essentials of independence, even of the title "Minister," and gave to Austria the undivided control of foreign military, commercial, and financial affairs.[2]

Hungary was better occupied. On March 1, to show its readiness to meet all reasonable requirements, and as an indication of its belief in the goodness of Francis Joseph's intentions, the Diet had appointed a committee, on Deák's motion, to consider the whole question of common affairs. The Committee, which consisted of sixty-seven members, fifteen of whom formed a sub-committee on which practically the whole work devolved, met for the first time on March 22 under the presidency of Count Julius Andrássy. The object of its labours, as defined by Deák, was to decide what matters should be considered as coming within the category of common affairs, and to what extent they were common ; what steps were necessary to provide for the expedient handling of such affairs, and for the necessary expenses ; in what manner and to what extent

---

[1] These laws were on precisely the same footing as any other laws passed since the time of St. Andrew, and could be abrogated or amended only in accordance with Law xii. of 1790-91 : " Leges ferendi, abrogandi, interpretandi potestatem in Regno Hungariae Partibusque adnexis legitime coronato Principi et Statibus ac Ordinibus regni ad comitia legitime confluentibus communen esse, nec extra illa exerceri posse, sua Majestas sacratissima ultro ac sponte agnoscit." As Kemény pointed out, if the laws of 1848 were invalid, Law iii. of that year, the only law in existence which recognised the existence of common affairs, would disappear from the statute-book.—Beksics, o.c. p. 269.

[2] Stephen Gorove's Diary, April 16, 1866 ; see Kónyi, o.c. iii. 651.

the representatives of the two countries should, from time to time, come in contact for the purpose of giving effect to any arrangement that might be adopted ; and, lastly, to indicate what amendments of existing laws might be necessary for the purposes above referred to.[1] Of the members of the sub-committee, Tisza, Ghyczy, and Nyáry were, throughout the period of discussion, always in more or less violent opposition to the majority which represented Deák's views. The difference between the two parties lay in the fact that whereas the former was indisposed to budge from the strictly constitutional position (the foundation of which was the limitation of Hungary's political contact with Austria to that which necessarily resulted from the identity of King and Emperor, and from the sole obligation imposed on the former country by the Pragmatic Sanction, viz. the obligation of defending the Austrian dominions of its King), the Deákists were ready to give a wider meaning to the phrase " common affairs " than was properly deducible from existing legislation, and to make greater concessions, with a view to the expedient handling of such affairs, than could be justified by a strict interpretation of the essential principle of Hungarian independence. Tisza and his followers wished that the Hungarian army should be entirely distinct from the Austrian, save in so far as the identity of the Commander-in-Chief of both was concerned. Deák also desired military separation,[2] but was afraid lest negotiations might break down over this point,[3] and therefore contented himself with the maintenance of Hungary's ancient right of voting men and money for an army which had, in fact, been " common " ever since 1714, though no constitutional justification for such community is to be found either in the laws of 1723, which gave effect to the Pragmatic Sanction,

[1] Kónyi, *o.c.* iii. 688, citing Ernest Hollán, one of the members of the sub-committee.

[2] Lónyay's *Diary*, May 7, 1866 ; see Kónyi, *o.c.* iii. 692.

[3] *Ibid.* May 8.

or in subsequent legislation. As will be seen hereafter when we come to consider the effect of Law xii. of 1867, which incorporated the results of the deliberations of the sub-committee, it is more than questionable whether Deák's undoubted intention finds expression in that enactment, an acquaintance with which is essential to a comprehension of the relations of Austria and Hungary. As regards the relative merits of Deák's and Tisza's points of view, it will suffice for the moment to recall the fact that as the Pragmatic Sanction, the sole basis of the negotiations which culminated in the passing of Law xii. of 1867, does not even mention the obligation of common defence, it obviously cannot make the organs of defence common ; further, that the possibility of such community was excluded by the fact that Austria, as a German Power, was subject to military obligations with which Hungary, which never was a member of the German Confederation, was in no way concerned.

The whole history of the sub-committee is the story of the conflict of two irreconcilable principles, championed respectively by Tisza and Deák ; of the struggle of strict consistency in the interpretation of Hungary's obligations with considerations of expediency. Though victory temporarily rested with the latter, in reality the result was a drawn battle, the renewal of which was only a question of time. As regards common affairs Tisza took his stand on the fact that the dual control had hitherto been vested in the absolute ruler of the hereditary provinces on the one hand, and in the Hungarian Diet on the other ; and that Hungary's obligations were obligations towards Austria's Emperor and not towards Austria, between which, as a despotically governed country, and Hungary there never was any privity of contract.[1] Such being the case, it would have been a mistake, in Tisza's opinion, to make a new departure in the direction of an agreement

---

[1] See the minority report of the sub-committee.—Kónyi, *o.c.* iii. 749 *sqq.*

with the hereditary provinces as distinguished from their monarch ; for though the latter had expressed his intention of conferring a Constitution on his Austrian possessions there was nothing to prevent his withdrawing at any time the concession intended to be made, and awkward complications might ensue if one of the parties to a contract to be entered into by two constitutionally governed countries again became subject to autocratic control, in spite of the fact that the abolition of parliamentary government in Austria could not affect Hungary's constitutional position. Any new arrangement with respect to common affairs required, in Tisza's view, to be made between Hungary and the Emperor, without regard to third parties, the importation of whom into the contract would change its whole character by converting it from a guarantee of the minimum rights of Hungary into a definition of its maximum rights. Tisza insisted that Hungary must retain its power of altering at any time, by agreement between the two equal legislative factors— King and Parliament—any arrangement which present expediency might dictate, and the interposition of a third party could only tend to limit Hungary's freedom of action. Deák, on the other hand, was convinced that the strongest guarantee of Hungarian independence was to be found in the conclusion of a contract, not between Hungary and an Austrian autocrat, but between two equal, constitutionally governed countries, whose identical institutions and community of interests would be the best protection against possible autocratic encroachment. That Tisza's contention was neither idle nor captious was proved by the subsequent political history of Austria, by the fact that the practical collapse of parliamentary government in that country, which might have made the compromise of 1867 unworkable if it had borne, as Deák intended it should, the character of a contract between Austria and Hungary, did not dislocate the whole machinery of State.

That the conflict of principles found a comparatively faint echo outside the committee-room was due to the confidence which Deák inspired in the mass of his countrymen, and nothing shows the greatness of his influence so well as the fact that the battle of Königgrätz did not cause the nation to make a unanimous and irresistible demand for the rejection of a compromise which the great majority of the Magyars would have accepted with joy on the eve of the outbreak of hostilities.

War was declared by Prussia and Italy on June 18, before the sub-committee had finished its work. That Hungary's immediate future depended on the issue of the campaign was obvious to all. It was generally anticipated that in the event of Austrian success the military party in Vienna would obtain the upper hand, and that the patient labour of the past years would be thrown away. If, on the other hand, a series of disasters should befall the Austrian arms, there was reason to fear a revival of the dormant revolutionary spirit which Kossuth and other exiles had done their best to keep alive.[1] The sub-committee was hastily summoned, Deák's draft report was accepted without discussion and immediately published, not only in order to prove to Vienna, at a critical moment, the good faith of the political leaders of the nation, but that Hungary might have the means of judging what there was to gain and what to lose, might stop to think before it allowed itself to be carried away by some hasty impulse, and exposed itself to reprisals at the hands of an infuriated Austria.[2] The same day the news arrived of the defeat of the Italians at Custozza, and twenty-four hours later the Emperor prorogued the Diet—a fair indication of what Hungary might expect if the fortune

[1] Gorove's *Diary*, June 19, Kónyi, iii. 679, 683-684.
[2] Deák feared that Francis Joseph might make a hasty peace with Prussia and Italy, and let loose his army of 300,000 men on Hungary.—Friedjung, *Der Kampf um die Vorherrschaft in Deutschland*, Stuttgart, 1908, ii. 379.

of war should continue to be favourable to Francis Joseph. Fair treatment and a conciliatory policy were obviously not to be expected from a victorious autocrat.[1] Continued success meant the consignment of the sub-committee's report to the imperial waste-paper basket, and the indefinite postponement of the re-establishment of constitutional government. Fortunately for all concerned, the war was of short duration, and the revolutionary party had little or no opportunity for effective action. " Austria is very tough," wrote Moltke, " and can lose two or three battles without great danger, but the outbreak of revolution in Hungary will put an end to the whole business." [2] Von Usedom, the Prussian envoy in Florence, convinced of the necessity of " striking Austria in the heart " in order to assure the final evacuation of Venice,[3] was in close communication with the exiles ; and Bismarck, resolved in the event of a prolongation of hostilities " to make an appeal to the Magyar nationality," [4] took steps to obtain the co-operation of a Hungarian legion under the command of General Klapka, one of the heroes of the fight for freedom in 1848.[5] But Bismarck mistook the meaning of Hungary's outspoken enthusiasm for Italy and Garibaldi, and did not realise the extent of the dislike with which Germany, and Austria's connexion with Germany, was regarded. The Empress Elizabeth went to Budapest in order to see which way the wind was blowing, and the chivalrous manner in which she was received showed plainly enough that Hungary would not rise in arms to

[1] Even Friedjung admits that victory for Austria would have meant the rejection of Hungary's demands, o.c. p. 399.

[2] Marczali, *A Legujabb Kor Története*, p. 866.

[3] Friedjung, *Der Kampf*, etc. i. 400.

[4] *Reflexions and Reminiscences*, ii. 37, 38. Bismarck " hielt es für notwendig Österreich das Schreckbild der Revolutionierung Ungarns vorzuhalten."— Friedjung, o.c. ii. 538.

[5] Klapka did in fact invade Austrian Silesia with less than 2000 men, who were to form the nucleus of a Magyar army, but the expedition ended in a complete fiasco.—See Friedjung, o.c. ii. 536-541.

please a Hohenzollern. At the same time the Magyars had no wish to risk their lives unnecessarily in the cause of Austrian domination in Italy and Germany, more especially as they knew that the maintenance of such domination would be fatal to their own prospects of liberty, and Austria's defeat at Königgrätz on July 3 was generally regarded as equivalent to a victory for Hungary. It was evident that, ejected from Germany, the house of Habsburg would be obliged to come to terms with the Magyars, if it did not wish to see the monarchy reduced to the level of a second-rate power. Bach and Schmerling, by making Hungary discontented, had weakened Austria, and disaster was the inevitable consequence. A Königgrätz was required to convince Francis Joseph and his advisers of the futility of absolutism, and of the rottenness of a system the essence of which was at one time the exploitation of Hungary as a colony, at another its treatment as a conquered country. Until Austrian hegemony in Germany was a thing of the past, no lasting peace with Hungary could be expected ; and without such peace Austria could never hope to consolidate its position in order to be able to stand up to Bismarck and the new Prussia.

On July 18, Francis Joseph received Deák in secret audience and asked him straight out what Hungary wanted and what was to be done. Deák could, probably, have insisted on the unconditional restoration of the Hungarian Constitution on the basis of the laws of 1848 or of a strict interpretation of the Pragmatic Sanction, but apparently he felt that to extort better terms for his country than those which he had already formulated would be to sow the seeds of future strife, and replied that Hungary asked for no more after Königgrätz than it had demanded before the war began. Deák, no doubt, acted like a magnanimous gentleman, to whom it is impossible to kick an adversary when he is down ; but the rules of politics differ from those of honour or of the prize-ring, and in the light of subsequent history it would seem that he made a mistake in letting slip the opportunity of putting the relations of his country with Austria once for all on a satisfactory footing. Francis Joseph subsequently complained that Deák viewed the Austro-Hungarian problem from the purely juridical standpoint, and was incapable of appreciating the needs of the monarchy as a whole,[1] but the moderation of Deák's demands, more especially as regards the question of the military independence of Hungary, is a sufficient refutation of the charge of inability or unwillingness to understand the exigencies of the international situation. The Emperor was still smarting from the beating inflicted by Prussia and dreamed of revenge, whereas the last thing that Hungary wished to see was a revival of Habsburg ambitions with respect to Germany ; no wonder, therefore, if Francis Joseph and the Hungarian statesman, though both desired a settlement of the questions at issue, approached those questions from opposite points of the compass. All difficulties and dangers had not been removed from Deák's path by the defeat of Austria. His task consisted in enforcing the recognition of the absolute parity of the two countries, and several obstacles still required to be surmounted. The first was the obstinacy of the Emperor with his fixed idea as to the necessity of military union and uniformity for the maintenance of the monarchy's character as a great Power and for the recovery of lost prestige. The second was the natural objection of the Viennese bureaucracy to the prospective loss of place and profit, its inveterate jealousy of the Magyars, and its desire to keep its hold on Hungarian purse-strings. Thirdly, there was the danger to be apprehended from Belcredi's encouragement of Czech pretensions, from Slav expectations of coming federalism, and from the belief that, expelled from Germany, the Emperor must necessarily throw himself into the arms of

[1] Lónyay's *Diary*, Aug. 31, Kónyi, *o.c.* iv. 44.

the non-German element in Austria.[1] For a time Francis
Joseph failed to see that his defeat by Germany could be
compensated only by a defeat by Hungary, and his German
subjects to understand the obvious fact that their position
of predominance in Austria could be maintained, in view
of Slav numerical preponderance, only by the frank acceptance of the dualistic principle. The Magyars' only
allies across the border were the irresistible logic of history
and the Empress Elizabeth, and the fact that the course of
the *negotiations ran as smoothly as it did is possibly
ascribable to the influence of the latter.

The first definite indication of coming triumph for the
Magyar cause was the appointment to the post of Foreign
Minister of Count Beust [2] (formerly Minister of King John
of Saxony), whose appeal to Napoleon III. at the end of the
late war, and steady support of Habsburg interests, had
earned him the special dislike of Bismarck, and compelled
the transference of his services from Saxony to Austria.
His dislike of Prussia made him realise the fact that nothing
but the preservation of their influence in Cisleithania
could prevent the Germans of Austria from turning their
eyes to Berlin, and that dualism alone could give a new lease
of life to the somewhat dilapidated monarchy. A fortunate
ignorance of Hungarian affairs enabled him to break away
from the traditions of the governing caste of Vienna, and
to disregard the bureaucrats' reading of the copy-book
maxim, according to which compulsory union necessarily meant strength. Possibly a desire for revenge on
Bismarck, with French assistance, was the mainspring of his
action ; [3] he denies it, but the whole course of his policy

[1] See Lónyay's account of his and Andrássy's conference with Belcredi and
Hübner, August 21. Belcredi said that the Germans in Vienna were in favour
of compromise on the lines of the sub-committee's report, for the reason that
they foresaw that it would result in hopeless confusion, and so, ultimately, to
a return to strict centralisation.—Kónyi, o.c. iv. 24.

[2] October 30.

[3] Bismarck calls him "that Saxon Minister in a bad temper."—*Reflexions
and Reminiscences*, ii. 58.

down to 1870, when Magyar influence prevented the Franco-German war from developing into a general European conflagration, throws doubt on the value of the denial.[1] His enemies, and he had many, for the appointment of a foreigner and a Protestant was, naturally, unpopular in Vienna, complained of his weak-kneed attitude towards Magyar pretensions, and that he surrendered all along the line.   He did surrender, but the fact of his having done so was a proof of strength of character rather than of weakness.   It would have been easy for him to make a greater show of resistance to the irresistible, to have continued the interminable series of argumentative Rescripts so much in favour with his predecessors, but he was strong enough to be able to recognise the logic of accomplished facts, and to abandon a position which he knew to be untenable.   A diplomat said of him : " He has buried Saxony, he has buried the German Confederation, and now he will bury Austria " —a phrase which fairly indicated the opinion entertained by jealous Austrian bureaucrats of an imported statesman, who, in their view, must necessarily be handicapped by the fact that he had not been trained in the musty atmosphere of Vienna archives ; but in estimating the value of his services to Austria it is safer to be guided by the considered judgment of Friedjung than by the malevolent criticisms of the Saxon Minister's disillusioned contemporaries. " The Compromise," says the most objective of modern historians, " though of over-hasty construction as regards the financial part, and disadvantageous to Austria from the point of view of external policy, resulted in the rejuvenescence of the monarchy.   That race which, animated by a proud consciousness of national individuality, had given only unwilling service to the Empire in 1859 and 1866, became thenceforth one of the strongest pillars of its might." [2]   In other words, the reconciliation with the Magyars, to the effectuation of which Beust's recognition

---

[1] See his *Aus drei Vierteljahrhunderten*, ii. 26 *sqq.*   [2] *Der Kampf*, etc. ii. 570.

of the inevitable largely contributed, restored, and alone was capable of restoring, to the Habsburgs the influence in Europe which the ineptitude of their policy towards Hungary had caused them to forfeit.

The Diet was summoned to meet on November 17th. The imperial Rescript [1] which was read on the opening day was not of a nature to satisfy the expectations of Deák and his party. Though the Rescript accepted in principle the results of the deliberations of the sub-committee, and announced the intention of establishing a " system of responsible government " in Austria as well as in Hungary, the ambiguity of a reference to the necessity of proceeding to a revision of the March laws seemed to give the lie to the statement that the Kingdom " stood on the threshold of the realisation of its desires," which nothing but the unconditional restoration of the Constitution was capable of satisfying. Tisza proposed the appointment of a committee for the purpose of drawing up a reply to the effect that the Diet refused to proceed to business until such unconditional restoration was an accomplished fact —an ultimatum to Francis Joseph, which, like that of the Resolutionists of 1861, might have shut the door to the possibility of further negotiation. One hundred and seven members voted in favour of the motion, an indication of the change which had come over public opinion since the meeting of the Diet in December 1865, of the weariness and disgust generated by the haggling and procrastinating tactics of Vienna. Any sign of weakness on Deák's part, of an inclination to compromise with his political conscience for the sake of peace, would have inflicted a fatal blow on his authority, and, consequently, on the prospects of the nation. Any indication of unreasoned hostility, such as that of which Tisza's ultimatum would have conveyed the impression, might have justified Francis Joseph in following the prompting of his native obstinacy which recent events

[1] Kónyi, o.c. iv. 80 sqq.

had temporarily mitigated. The Address,[1] ultimately voted on Deák's motion, answered all requirements. Its firmness was of a nature to satisfy all but the irreconcilables, and the moderation of its tone was such that no offence could be given to imperial susceptibility. It declared afresh that no lasting and satisfactory compromise is possible between absolutism and a nation which has been deprived of its constitutional liberties. A conditional restoration of a Constitution is a contradiction in terms, a negation of the principle of continuity, abandonment of which would be subversive of the whole foundation of constitutional government. Unless and until a complete restoration has taken place no representative body is competent to undertake the revision of existing, or the enactment of new, legislation. In the meanwhile it is impossible to consider the observations which His Majesty has thought fit to make on the result of the labours of the sub-committee, which requires to be submitted, first of all, to the original Committee of sixty-seven members, whose report will be considered by the elected representatives of the nation so soon as the restoration of the Constitution has invested them with the necessary competence.

The result of the respectful firmness of the Address was soon apparent. On December 19, by the Emperor's instructions,[2] Beust started for Budapest in order to see Deák, and to inform himself on the spot of the true position of affairs. He came, saw, and was conquered. His great antagonist refused to shift his ground, to modify his demand for the complete restoration of the Constitution as a condition precedent to the revision of the March laws ; and Beust, if he had the wish, had not the means to drive him from his position. The Austrian Government produced draft terms of compromise,[3] based on the report of the Hungarian sub-committee, and closely

1867.

---

[1] See Kónyi, o.c. iv. 124 sqq.   [2] Beust, Aus drei Vierteljahrhunderten, ii. 84.
[3] See Kónyi, o.c. iv. 163 sqq.

resembling it in form, though widely differing from it in certain important details.   It accepted the Pragmatic Sanction as the foundation of the relations of the two countries, and the principle of complete parity as regards the management of common affairs.   Like its prototype it provided for the appointment of common Ministers and of two Delegations invested with the control of the actions of such Ministers ; but its attempt to extend the functions of the Delegations at the expense of Parliament,—to create, in fact, something in the nature of a common legislat: e body, the existence of which would have implied Hungary's recognition of a much closer union with Austria than could be justified by a reference to the Pragmatic Sanction,—made its acceptance impossible.   Beust and Andrássy finally agreed that 'the report of the sub-committee should be accepted as the basis of negotiation, but that certain modifications should be introduced with a view to the more accurate definition of Hungary's military relations with the Austrian Empire, to the maintenance of the " constitutional " rights of the King as supreme war-lord, and to the adoption of identical principles as regards the management of matters which, though they could not be regarded as coming within the category of common affairs, were of common interest to both countries.   It was further agreed that, in the event of the acceptance of the proposed modification by the full Committee, the appointment of the responsible Hungarian Ministry should be delayed no longer.[1]

The Committee resumed its labours on February 28, with a view to the amendment of the original draft in accordance with the alterations introduced by Deák into the text as settled by Beust and Andrássy.   The minority report, signed by Tisza and by those members of the sub-committee who supported him, was withdrawn, but the fact of its withdrawal did not imply the abandonment of hostility to the suggested terms of compromise by those

---

[1] Beust, *Aus drei Vierteljahrhunderten*, ii. 86.

who took their stand on the principle the essence of which
was the limitation of Hungary's obligations to those strictly
deducible from the terms. of the Pragmatic Sanction, and
objected to everything in the nature of common institutions as derogatory, if not fatal, to the principle of
Hungarian sovereignty and independence.[1]   A certain
amount of acrimony characterised the debates which ensued.
Deák suggested that the opposition was of a disingenuous
character, and that its authors would be the first to regret
the failure of negotiations which aimed at restoring happiness and tranquillity to a distracted country.[2]   In his turn
Tisza contrasted the strictly constitutional attitude adopted
by Deák in 1861 with that which he now assumed, and
accused him of inconsistency—an accusation which is easily
substantiated in the case of any politician who is not too
young to have had the opportunity of making mistakes,
or too foolish to be able to recognise them when made.
Absolute consistency implies the possession of an omniscience which Deák was far too modest to claim, or an
inability to profit by experience which no one could lay
to his charge.   The fact was that the strain and worry of
the past years had begun to tell upon the "old gentleman,"
as he was affectionately called.   He had missed the golden
opportunity which Königgrätz had, apparently, offered of
exacting full recognition of the constitutional rights ot
Hungary, and now, fearing the responsibility of exposing
his country to a further period of alien rule, agreed to a
compromise which involved the partial abandonment of a
still defensible position.   The prompt conclusion of an
arrangement which might deprive Hungary of the undivided control of the expenditure of its blood and treasure
seemed preferable to the continuance of a thinly disguised
absolutism, or to the attainment of a victory so complete

---

[1] For these objections see Tisza's speeches of January 30, and that of
Ghyczy, January 28.—Kónyi, o.c. pp. 219 sqq. and 253 sqq.

[2] Kónyi, o.c. iv. 298.

that its memory must perpetuate the friction which he hoped and believed was shortly to cease for ever.

On February 6 the report of the Committee, as amended, was finally approved, and twelve days later an imperial Rescript announced the restoration of the Constitution. Deák, to whom Francis Joseph had offered the post of Prime Minister, felt that he had earned the right to rest, and that the task of reorganising the Government of the country should be entrusted to younger hands. Count Julius Andrássy, "the providential man," as Deák called him, the originator of the scheme which provided for the appointment of an Austrian and a Hungarian Delegation to control the actions of the common Ministers,[1] undertook the formation of Hungary's second responsible Ministry, in which Eötvös, as Minister of Education, formed the connecting link between the new Government and the coalition Cabinet of 1848.[2] On March 9 the result of the deliberations of the Committee came before Parliament in the shape of a Government Bill, which was finally passed on May 29, by 289 votes to 89, practically in the same form as that in which it had left the hands of the sub-committee. The end had not been reached without a severe struggle, though the Deákists had been strengthened by the adhesion of a section of the Conservatives, which had abjured its heretical views as to the incompatibility of true parliamentary government with the interests of the monarchy as a whole, for fear lest its abstention should make possible the advent to power of Tisza and

[1] Andrássy originated the scheme, but was not responsible for the way in which the details were worked out. He strongly objected to the joint meeting for the purpose of voting on matters on which the Delegations might fail to agree, but he was overruled by Deák.—*Gróf Andrássy Gyula Beszédei*, ed. Lederer Béla, i. 152.

[2] The new Cabinet consisted of Andrássy, Eötvös, Wenckheim (Interior), Horvát (Justice), Lónyay (Finance), Gorove (Commerce), Mikó (Communications and Public Works), and Festetics, the Minister in attendance on the person of the Sovereign.

his adherents, who persisted in continuing the unequal fight both in Parliament and in the Press. Before the final vote had been taken, the exiled Kossuth made an eleventh-hour attempt to prevent the ratification of the terms of settlement, but without success. An open letter to Deák,[1] published broadcast in leaflets and in the newspapers, expressed astonishment at the fact that Königgrätz had resulted in the diminution, rather than in the increase, of the demands put forward by the acknowledged leader of the nation ; reproached him with digging the grave of Hungarian independence, and entreated him to reflect once more before taking an irrevocable step. The letter concluded with the words, " If I cannot carry with me to the grave the tranquillising consciousness of success, at least let me be accompanied by hope for the future of my country. I know that Cassandra's rôle was a thankless one, but remember that she was a true prophetess."[2] Deák wisely refused to be drawn into a newspaper controversy, and left to others the task of defending the policy of expediency, with the adoption of which Kossuth reproached him. Sigismund Kemény, Deák's chief journalistic lieutenant,[3] and Francis Pulszky,[4] took up the challenge which Kossuth had thrown down, and had little difficulty in proving that Kossuth's own plan for the formation of a confederacy of Danube States involved far more serious consequences to the cause of Hungarian independence, and of Magyar hegemony in Hungary, than a compromise based on the principle of absolute parity with Austria, for which the exiled leader's *pronunciamento* offered no alternative proposition. Kossuth's bombshell, intended to break the thread of negotiation

[1] See Kónyi, *o.c.* v. 1-8.

[2] Compare the letter of the exiled Rákóczy, who also had proclaimed the deposition of the Habsburgs, written at the eleventh hour to prevent the ratification of the peace of Szatmár arranged by Károlyi in 1711, *supra* i. 172.

[3] See Beksics, *Kemény Zsigmond*, p. 324 *sqq.*

[4] See his letter, Kónyi, *o.c.* v. 74, 75.

with Vienna, failed to attain its object. Few were to be found, even in the ranks of the exiles,[1] who wished to sever all connexion with Austria, or were prepared to stake the nation's future on the recurrence of European complications of such a kind as to afford a fresh opportunity of limiting Hungary's obligations to the minimum consistent with the due performance of its duty to defend the Austrian possessions of its King against foreign aggression.[2]

It needed no ill-considered intervention of Kossuth to show that the accepted terms of compromise contained the germ of future misunderstanding and discord, as was proved by Tisza's insistence on the necessity of retaining the right to modify by agreement between King and Parliament, without reference to third parties, any arrangement which considerations of temporary expediency might dictate.[3] Deák was wrong in believing in the possibility of effecting a permanent settlement of all controversial questions. His "gran' rifiuto" on the morrow of Königgrätz was the outcome of a fear of the perpetuation of international jealousy and dislike, and of an exaggerated estimate of Habsburg ability to break with the traditions of the past. He at least acted with absolute good faith. Not so official Vienna, which believed it saw in the compromise the possibility of effecting in a roundabout way what it had failed to accomplish by direct means.[4] The triumph of the dualistic principle was, in fact, complete. Pangermanism in its modern form had not yet been invented. Panslavism was not dead but sleeping. Serious opposition to the proposed terms of compromise was to be apprehended only in Bohemia, which saw in the final acceptance of dualism no more and no less than the

[1] When the grant of an amnesty permitted return to Hungary, most of the exiles became Deákists.

[2] Foreign diplomacy, said Andrássy, resembled the Roman people in the amphitheatre, which applauded the Christians if they made a good fight of it with the wild beasts, but never lifted a finger to help them.—*Beszédei*, ed. Lederer, i. 133. [3] See Kónyi, *o.c.* iv. 219. [4] See *infra*, pp. 254, 261, 262.

destruction of the expectations which Belcredi's known federalistic leanings had generated, and the loss of all hope of differentiation from the other hereditary provinces. The mutual jealousies of Pole and Ruthene, and the refusal of the Czechs to take part in a Parliament of Cisleithania, a geographical expression with which they were not acquainted, the existence of which they declined to recognise, did but facilitate the task of Beust and Andrássy. The dissentient nationalities lost sight of the fact that Königgrätz could not fail to produce a tendency to *rapprochement* between Austrian Germans and the Magyars, which Slav hostility could only accentuate.

The Reichsrath met, but it was hard to say what its functions were, or what it represented, for the Constitution of 1861 had been abolished nearly two years ago, and nobody knew whether the elected representatives of the constituent nationalities had the right to discuss and amend the terms of compromise, or if they were summoned merely for the purpose of registering a formal assent. Belcredi, who wished to give the widest scope to their deliberations, realising, at last, the impossibility of further resistance to the demands of the Magyars, resigned his office on February 7, and made way for Beust.[1] Influenced by Andrássy, and aware of the Emperor's anxiety to get the matter settled as quickly as possible, the new Prime Minister made up his mind to throw the ready-made Compromise at the Reichsrath's head, with an intimation to the effect that it could take it or leave it. It took it, for it could not do otherwise, and a practically unanimous vote at the end of a debate, of the futility of which no one was more painfully conscious than the Reichsrath itself, gave final consecration to the dualistic principle, the principle of absolute parity, which to-day forms the basis of the relations of Austria and Hungary.

1 See Wullersdorf, Minister of Commerce, in Kónyi, *o.c.* iv. 304 *sqq.*

The failure of the document of December 2, 1848, in which Ferdinand announced his abdication of the Austrian throne, to make any mention of Hungary, was remedied by a special law, which recited the fact of the abdication of Ferdinand and of Francis Charles, and declared, once for all, that for the future no such renunciation could be valid as regards the Sacred Crown, unless and until Hungary had expressed its consent in proper constitutional form.[1]   Early in June Francis Joseph signed the Inaugural Diploma, and took the oath in the Hungarian language to maintain all the rights and privileges of Hungary, to observe the laws passed and to be passed by the elected representatives of the nation in Parliament assembled, and to cause all others to do so likewise.   A complete amnesty was granted to all political prisoners and exiles, and the coronation took place on June 8, in accordance with the ceremonies prescribed by immemorial tradition, amid scenes of unparalleled rejoicing, which reached its culminating point when announcement was made of the King's intention to devote the coronation gift of 100,000 florins to the widows and orphans of those who had fallen in Hungary's fight for freedom.   And so the long struggle ended.   The troubled relations which had existed between Hungary and the Habsburgs ever since the importation of the dynasty had been due, in early days, to the intentional misconception of successive kings of their constitutional position, and at a later period to an attempt to read into the Pragmatic Sanction, and the explanatory law of 1790, a meaning which they could not possibly bear. Law iii. of 1848, on the abolition of which, as a condition precedent to the restoration of the Constitution, Francis Joseph had vainly insisted, contained the first clear recognition of the existence of common affairs which required the joint management of the Hungarian

[1] See *Gróf Andrássy Gyula Beszédei*, ed. Lederer, i. 233.

Parliament and of the Austrian Emperor acting through the responsible Hungarian Minister in attendance on his person. Unfortunately, the absence from that law (which in reality increased rather than diminished the strict constitutional rights of the Sovereign) of a clear definition of what came within the category of common affairs led to misunderstanding and to war.

Altered circumstances and the proposed establishment of constitutional government in the hereditary provinces —a concession on the part of the imperial autocrat on which Hungary insisted as a condition precedent to its acceptance of the terms of the Compromise—necessitated the modification of the laws of 1848. In view of the existence of a responsible Ministry, a Palatine was no longer required to protect the constitutional rights of the country, and to act as a mediator between King and nation. That part, therefore, of Law iii. of 1848 which had reference to the Nádor's powers of representing the King was repealed, and the election to the office was postponed pending the passing of legislation with a view to a new definition of the limits of the Palatine's functions and authority.[1] Section 12 of the same law, which provided that the Prime Minister should submit the names of his colleagues to the King for " confirmation," was modified by an enactment to the effect that the Crown "appoints" the members of the Cabinet on the "proposal" of the Prime Minister.[2] Section 6 of Law iv. of 1848 forbade the prorogation or dissolution of Parliament before the adoption of the accounts for the past twelve months, and of the estimates for the ensuing period. Law x. of 1867 contains no such restriction, but provides that in the event of dissolution or prorogation Parliament must be summoned again in time to allow the accounts and estimates to be passed before the end of the current year—a provision which prevents a dissolu-

---

[1] Law vii. 1867.   [2] Law viii. 1867.

tion from taking place after the middle of November. Law xi. suspends the operation of Law xxii. of 1848 (which established a National Guard) pending the intro- duction of a measure dealing with the whole question of the reorganisation of national defence. The fact that no further modifications of the laws of 1848 were required to enable the relations of Hungary with the rest of the monarchy to be regularised in accordance with the widest possible interpretation of the Pragmatic Sanction, shows plainly enough how little justification existed for stigmatising the work of Kossuth and his contemporary legislators as unconstitutional and revolu- tionary. The sin of those legislators—if, in fact, any can be laid to their charge—was one of omission, not of commission. The sole objection that could fairly be raised to the March laws was that, though they admitted the existence of common affairs, they failed to provide either a clear definition of such affairs, or the necessary machinery for dealing with them. No doubt the omission could and would have been supplied if Ferdinand and his advisers had given the Hungarian Parliament time to settle down to business, but they preferred to cut the knot, though the process of untying it would, as it turned out, have been far less detrimental to the interests of autocracy.

The victory of Hungary's policy of passive resistance was also a victory for the hereditary provinces, which, but for the Magyars, would have asked in vain for anything more than the shadow of constitutional government.[1]

[1] Belcredi asked Andrássy during the progress of the negotiations with Hungary : "Wenn die Forderungen Ungarns bewilligt werden, dann können wir Österreich doch so einrichten, wie wir es für richtig halten ?" Andrássy answered: "Nein, das ist Ungarn nicht gleichgültig, denn Ungarn muss wünschen, dass Österreich *ein* Staat bleibe . . . Ungarn müsse wünschen, dass die Deut- schen die Führung des Österreichischen Staates haben . . . wir bestehen auf einer einheitlichen Verfassung und Verwaltung für Österreich."—Rudolf Springer, *Grundlagen und Entwicklungsziele der österreichisch-ungarischen Monarchie*, Vienna, 1906, p. 46.

Deák's insistence on the grant of such government to
Cisleithania necessitated the elaboration of a definition of
common affairs, in the absence of which from the March
laws despotism affected to find a justification of the unjustifiable.   Such definition is supplied by Law xii. of
1867.   The sole basis of the relations of Hungary and
Austria is to be found in the Pragmatic Sanction, the
essential consideration for the acceptance of which, as the
preamble to Law xii. states, was the maintenance of the
complete constitutional independence of the former
country, of the indivisibility of the provinces of the latter,
and of the security of both from foreign attack.   Hungary, says Law xii., was at all times ready in the past,
and always will be ready in the future, to do all that is
indispensably required in accordance with the Pragmatic
Sanction for the defence and maintenance of the common
security, but will accept no obligation which is not
unavoidably necessary for the purpose of such defence and
maintenance (sect. 4).   Hitherto all matters connected
with the political relations of Hungary and Austria were
managed without the intervention of any third party, by
agreement between the Hungarian Diet on the one hand,
and the Hungarian King, who was at the same time
absolute autocrat in the hereditary provinces, on the other ;
since, however, His Majesty has expressed his intention of
conferring a Constitution on those provinces, he can no
longer have unlimited power of representation, but must
admit their constitutional influence on common affairs
(sect. 5).   As to what matters come within the category
of common affairs the Pragmatic Sanction is the sole
criterion (sect. 6).   The monarch is common,[1] inasmuch
as the Hungarian Crown belongs to the person who is
entitled to that of Austria, but it does not follow that the
Court expenses are necessarily common ; on the contrary,

---

[1] As has already been pointed out, this is not strictly accurate. The
Monarch is identical, but not " common."

they require a separate vote of the Hungarian Parliament (sect. 7). The expedient management of foreign affairs is one of the means of common and united defence, the necessity of which flows from the Pragmatic Sanction. Such management demands community of action in all such matters as *jointly* interest *all* the States under His Majesty's rule; consequently, questions connected with diplomatic and commercial representation, and with international treaties, come within the province of the common Minister of Foreign Affairs, acting in concert and in agreement with the Austrian and Hungarian Ministries, whose duty it is to communicate international treaties to their respective Parliaments.[1] Hungary, therefore, admits the community of such matters, and will contribute to the expense of their management to an extent to be subsequently determined (sect. 8).

The other organ of common defence is the army, as regards the community of which the following principles, subject to those already enunciated,[2] are laid down. *As the result of the constitutional rights* of the monarch in relation to military affairs, the management of all that has reference to the unity of command, leadership, and internal organisation of the *Hungarian army*, as a complementary part of the *whole* army, is recognised as belonging to His Majesty's province (sects. 9, 10, 11). On the other hand Hungary retains the right of legislative and executive control, *on the basis of existing legislation*, of all matters connected with the supply of recruits, the conditions of such supply, the fixing of the period of service, the distribution and provisioning of the troops. As far as Hungary is concerned, the organisation or reorganisation of the system of defence at all times requires the assent of the Hungarian Parliament ; as, however, such organisation

[1] See *infra*, p. 257.
[2] *I.e.* Hungary's obligations are qualified by the essential principles and object of the Pragmatic Sanction, as defined above, and by the words "*indispensably required*" and "*unavoidably necessary*" in sect. 4.

or reorganisation can be expediently effected only on the basis of similar[1] principles, the two Ministries will lay legislative proposals embodying such principles before their respective Parliaments, which, in the possible event of disagreement, will communicate with each other through the medium of deputations, with a view to the settlement of such disagreement (sect. 13). As regards the civic relations of all members of the Hungarian army, the Hungarian Legislature retains complete control (sect. 14). Military expenses are common to Austria and Hungary to the extent that the proportion in which Hungary will contribute to such expenses is to be settled by mutual agreement in the manner hereinafter provided (sect. 15).[2]

Financial matters are common so far as such expenses are concerned as have reference to the matters the community of which has been expressly recognised, but the assessment and collection of the sum necessary to enable Hungary to pay its share of such expenses belong exclusively to the province of the Hungarian Parliament and responsible Ministry (sect. 16) ; as do all matters connected with other branches of State expenditure and taxation, to the complete exclusion of foreign (Austrian) interference (sect. 17). For the purpose of ascertaining the proportion in which Hungary should contribute to the expense of those matters, the community of which admittedly results from the Pragmatic Sanction, each legislative body will appoint a deputation from among its own members which will assess the quota or proportion in which such expense should be borne by Austria and Hungary respectively, and will submit the result of their deliberations for discussion by the respective legislative bodies. Should the two deputations fail to arrive at an agreement, the opinion of both shall be submitted to both Parliaments, which, if they cannot agree, will submit the matter to His Majesty for final decision

[1] Lit. "equal."   [2] See *infra*, pp. 268 *sq.* 289.

on the basis of the data supplied to him. The assessment shall remain in force for a fixed period only, on the expiration of which the same process must be adopted for the purpose of arriving at a fresh agreement (sects. 18-22).

As regards the method of handling such affairs as have been defined as common, though the Pragmatic Sanction does not necessitate community of management, the change of circumstances resulting from the grant of constitutional government to Austria makes such community expedient, and the Hungarian Parliament expresses its *willingness* to be brought in contact with the non-Hungarian realms of His Majesty in their character of constitutionally governed countries subject to the maintenance of the independence of both parties. It follows, therefore, that one of the *fundamental conditions* of Hungary's consent to the present arrangement with respect to common affairs and their management is the *maintenance of the Hungarian Constitution* (sects. 23, 24). The second fundamental condition is that *true constitutional government* shall be brought into existence in the hereditary provinces, for Hungary can be brought into contact for the purpose of common affairs, of whatever nature they may be, only with the constitutional representatives of such provinces (sect. 25). A common Ministry must therefore be established for the purpose of dealing with specifically common affairs, which said Ministry will exercise its functions within the strict limits of such affairs, and will exert no influence on the Government either of Hungary or of Austria. Hungary does not admit the expediency of establishing a central or common Parliament *of any kind whatever*,[1] and will not agree to its establishment, but adheres to the principle of the separation and complete equality of the realms of the Hungarian Crown on the one hand, and of the hereditary provinces on the other. Consequently, *complete parity* is an in-

[1] See *infra*, pp. 254, 255.

dispensable condition as regards the management of common affairs (sect. 28).

In pursuance of this principle of parity the Hungarian Parliament and the Legislative Assembly of the hereditary provinces will each elect, from among the members of its own body, a Commission (Delegatio), consisting in each case of not more than sixty members, elected for one year, or for one session, at the expiration of either of which their functions entirely cease (sects. 29, 30). These Delegations will be summoned to meet at a fixed date, at the place of residence of His Majesty, but the Hungarian Parliament desires that their sittings should take place alternately at Pest and at Vienna (sect. 32). Each Delegation will deliberate separately, the result of its deliberations will be decided by vote, and the decision so arrived at will be regarded as the decision of the Delegation as a whole. The two Delegations may not deliberate together, but each will communicate its views and decisions in writing to the other, each in its own language, together with an official translation. If after these exchanges of messages the two Delegations are unable to agree, either of them may demand a joint sitting for the purpose of settling the matter at issue by a joint vote. As the maintenance of absolute parity is of essential importance, if, for any reason, any of the members of either Delegation are absent, the other Delegation will reduce its numbers proportionately by drawing lots. Numerical equality having been thus obtained, the question at issue will be decided in accordance with the vote of the majority (sects. 33-36). The functions of the Delegations are limited to those affairs which are specifically referred to them as common, and the Delegations cannot interfere in matters which are included in the competence of the Hungarian Parliament and Government. Within the limits of its authority, the Hungarian Delegation represents the Hungarian Parliament, vis-à-vis the hereditary provinces, and is not to be bound by preliminary instructions (sects. 37, 38). It is the right of the members of the common Ministry, and its duty, if summoned, to appear before the two Delegations, and to answer questions and afford necessary information, either verbally or in writing (sect. 39). The most important part of the duties of the Delegations is the preparation of the annual estimates of the cost of common affairs. The common Ministry prepares such estimates in conjunction with[1] the two separate responsible Ministries, for separate discussion by the two Delegations, which, failing agreement, decide the question at issue by a joint vote in the manner above provided. The estimates so arrived at cannot thereafter be made the subject of discussion by either country, but each must bear its share of the cost of the estimated expenditure in the proportion fixed by the Quota-Deputations. The *question of amount* cannot be debated, but the assessment and collection of the necessary taxation belong exclusively to the competence of the Hungarian Parliament and the responsible Hungarian Ministry. The amount of Hungary's contribution to the payment of common expenses is to be handed in monthly instalments by the Hungarian Ministry of Finance to the common Finance Minister, who will be responsible for the application thereof to the proper objects. The monthly instalments so to be handed over are to bear the same proportion to Hungary's national expenses as those expenses bear to the expenses of common affairs. The auditing of the accounts of the common Finance Minister forms part of the duties of the Delegations (sects. 40-42). All proceedings of the Delegations are to be conducted on the same lines as those above indicated. Such of their resolutions which require to be submitted to His Majesty for confirmation are invested, when confirmed, with binding force, but require to be notified by His Majesty to

[1] Lit. "under the influence of."

both legislative assemblies through the medium of the respective responsible Ministries. The duty of giving effect to such resolutions devolves, as regards Hungary, solely on the Hungarian Ministry, as well as that of assessing and collecting the taxation rendered necessary by such resolutions, and by the Budget as passed by Parliament (sect. 43). The Delegations' powers of initiative are strictly confined to those common affairs to which its competence, as herein defined, extends (sect. 44). The dissolution of Parliament necessitates the election of a new Deputation by the new Parliament (sect. 44).[1]

In addition to the common affairs described above, which, inasmuch as they derive from the Pragmatic Sanction, require common management, there are other important matters which, though not common within the meaning of the Pragmatic Sanction, from considerations of policy, or in consequence of the identity of interests of the two countries, can be more expediently managed by common agreement than by strict separation of control. As regards the public debt, though Hungary, in consequence of its constitutional position, is, strictly, under no obligation to accept responsibility for any debts which have been contracted without the consent legally expressed of that country, Parliament has, nevertheless, expressed its willingness, in consideration of a complete restoration of constitutional government in Hungary, and of the grant of a Constitution to the hereditary provinces, and from considerations of policy and equity, to do what it can, without prejudice to the Kingdom's independence and constitutional rights, to prevent the monarchy from collapsing under the burden of accumulated debt, and to ward off the consequences of the recent period of autocratic government. The Kingdom is, therefore, ready to enter into negotiation with the hereditary provinces *as one*

[1] Sects. 47-51 deal with the immunity from arrest, liability to indictment, and other cognate matters.

free country with another with a view to Hungary's acceptance of a part of that burden.   For the future, however,
no loan is to be contracted on the joint credit of Austria
and Hungary without the legally expressed consent of the
Hungarian Parliament, which also requires to be consulted
as to the employment of the proceeds and the terms of
repayment (sects. 52-57).

It does not follow from the Pragmatic Sanction that
commercial matters are common, for, according to the
meaning of that enactment, the realms of the Hungarian
Crown are juridically independent of the other realms of
the Monarch, and are entitled to manage such matters
through their own responsible Ministry and Legislature,
and to regulate their commercial affairs by means of
customs barriers.   As, however, there are numerous and
important points at which the interests of Hungary and
those of His Majesty's other dominions come in contact,
Parliament is prepared to enter from *time to time* into a
customs and commercial alliance with such dominions for
the regulation of those questions which have reference to
commerce, and in order to settle the method of handling
commercial affairs.   Such alliance shall be arrived at by
negotiation *as between two juridically independent* States.
The two responsible Ministries, acting in agreement, shall
prepare a Bill embodying the details of the proposed
alliance, and shall submit the same to their respective
Parliaments, and the resolution arrived at by the two
legislative bodies shall be submitted to His Majesty for his
sanction.   The effect of commercial treaties hitherto made
with foreign countries will, in consequence of such alliance,
be extended to Hungary (sects. 58-63).   On the formation of such an alliance, such rules may be adopted with
respect to indirect taxation, its nature, proportion, and
handling, as will exclude the possibility of either of the
two responsible Governments or Legislatures adopting such
a mode of procedure as would involve the crippling of the

resources of the other. At the same time a basis may be fixed with a view to concerted action as regards future reform of such taxation by both Legislatures, as well as with a view to uniformity of management and control of the customs barrier as a whole. The revenue resulting from customs duties is to be applied in the first instance to the payment of the expenses of common affairs (sects. 63, 64).[1]

With a view to the promotion of trade interests an agreement may be come to, at the time of the formation of a commercial and customs alliance, as to what railways require community of management, and as to the extent of such community. The management of all other railways shall be a matter exclusively for the Ministry and Legislature of that country through whose territory such railways run (sect. 65). It is not only desirable, but necessary in the interests of both countries, that the coinage and monetary basis of both should be equal; an agreement must therefore be come to with respect to these matters on the occasion of the formation of the above-mentioned alliance. Should any subsequent modification or rearrangement of the coinage and monetary basis be necessary or expedient, it must take place by agreement between, and with the approval of, the two legislative bodies. It is self-understood that the privileges of the Magyar King with respect to the minting and issue of coinage are maintained in full force. The amount of Hungary's annual contribution in connexion with the public debt will be determined by free negotiation at the time when the quota (or rate in which Hungary contributes to the cost of common affairs) is fixed, and the customs and commercial alliance is entered into. *It is self-understood that if and so far as no agreement can be arrived at with respect to the matters enumerated in sections 58 to 67, Hungary retains its independent legal right of*

[1] See *infra*, pp. 272-282.

dealing with the same, and that all its rights with respect thereto remain unimpaired (sect. 68). The extent to which the other dominions of the Hungarian Crown will take part in the Delegation will be subsequently determined. The above resolutions will become law so soon as they have received the royal sanction, but those sections thereof which refer to the handling of common affairs will come into force only so soon as the realms of His Majesty which do not belong to the Hungarian Crown have expressed their adherence to the terms thereof in constitutional manner (sect. 69).[1]

Though Hungary was under no obligation to accept any responsibility for Austria's public debt, which had not been contracted with Hungary's consent or for its benefit, it undertook (Law xv. of 1867) to contribute 29,188,000 florins annually to the interest and sinking fund,[2] subject to the reservation that no future loan should be contracted on the joint credit of Hungary and Austria without the consent of the Hungarian Parliament. Should such consent be given Hungary undertakes to contribute to the interest and sinking fund of the new loan in the same proportion as that in which it contributes, at the moment of issue of such loan, to the cost of common affairs as defined by Law xii. The ratio of Hungary's contribution to the cost of such affairs was fixed at 30 per cent for the ensuing ten years by Law xiv., which also provided that the net proceeds of the customs duties should be applied in the first instance to the payment of drawbacks, and that the balance should be applied in reduction of the common expenses.

By Law xliii. of 1868 Transylvania was reincorporated in Hungary ; and Law xxx. of the same year regularises the relations of the latter country with Croatia and Slavonia. The Diet of 1861 had recognised the importance

---

[1] For the corresponding inaccurate Austrian law see *infra*, pp. 263 *sq.* 293, 294.

[2] *I.e.* about 21 per cent of the total, see *Gróf Andrássy Gyula Beszédei*, ed. Lederer, i. 281 *sqq.*

of coming to terms with Croatia,[1] which dreamed of the possibility of a separate existence, of a dissolution of the immemorial connexion with the Crown of St. Stephen. Königgrätz resulted in a temporary revival of Panslav aspirations, but as soon as the terms of the compromise were settled, and it became evident that no encouragement for separatistic tendencies could be expected from Vienna, the party in favour of reunion with Hungary obtained the upper hand. Two committees were appointed for the purpose of settling debatable questions, one by the Hungarian Parliament, one by the Croatian Diet, and Law xxx. of 1868 was the result of their deliberations. The unity of the realms of the Sacred Crown is, in principle, fully maintained, and the theory of Croatian independence is negatived by the preamble to the law, which states that "Croatia and Slavonia, both juridically and in fact, have belonged for centuries to the Crown of St. Stephen," and that the inseparability of the realms of that Crown has been declared by the Pragmatic Sanction. Slavonia, which, up to 1848, had received direct representation in the Hungarian Diet, was now joined to Croatia, while Dalmatia, its right to demand the incorporation of which Hungary has never abandoned, was left under Austrian control.

Hungary and Croatia-Slavonia form, vis-à-vis the other dominions of the Monarch, a single political entity, and crowning with the Sacred Crown of Hungary is all that is required to invest the King with authority over Croatia-Slavonia (sects. 1, 2). It follows, therefore, that as regards matters which are common, or of common interest to the realms of the Sacred Crown and to the hereditary provinces of Austria, in accordance with the terms of Laws xii., xiv., xv., xvi. of 1867, Hungary and Croatia-Slavonia must be jointly

---

[1] It was Paul Somssics who originated the famous phrase as to the necessity of keeping a "clean page" for Croatia in the book of the Hungarian Constitution.

represented by a common Legislature and Executive. The fact that the effect of the said laws extends to Croatia-Slavonia is expressly recognised, on the understanding that, for the future, no similar fundamental statutes or agreements shall be enacted or made without the legal intervention of that country (sects. 3, 4). Affairs of common interest to Hungary and Croatia-Slavonia, which require to be dealt with by the common Legislature and Government, comprise the vote for the expenses of the Court, the vote of the annual contingent of recruits, the organisation of defence, and legislation with respect to the obligation to perform military service, and the quartering and provisioning of the troops (sects. 5, 6, 7). Finance is common as regards the whole system of taxation, the imposition of direct and indirect taxes, their assessment, collection, and handling, the vote of the expenses of common affairs, the issue of new State loans, and the conversion of existing ones. These, and all other matters connected with the common financial affairs of all the realms of the Sacred Crown, require to be controlled by the common Legislature. Coinage and the monetary basis also constitute common affairs, as do the consideration and approval of commercial treaties which are of common interest to all the realms of St. Stephen's Crown ; matters relating to banking and insurance ; weights and measures ; and, in general, all affairs connected with commerce, customs duties, posts and telegraphs, railways, ports, navigation, and such State roads and rivers which are of joint interest to Hungary and Croatia-Slavonia. Common affairs also comprise questions relating to the control of foreigners, citizenship, and naturalisation (sects. 8-10). Croatia-Slavonia recognises the obligation of contributing to the expenses of the common affairs of Austria and Hungary, and of Hungary and Croatia-Slavonia. As regards the first category, the share of Croatia-Slavonia is fixed for the ensuing ten years at 6.44 per cent, but Hungary agrees that during that period a sum of 2,200,000 florins shall first of all be deducted from the revenues of Croatia-Slavonia, and shall be applied in payment of the cost of the internal government of that country, which sum shall be provided by setting apart 45 per cent of the revenues. The balance of 55 per cent shall be paid into the common Treasury (sects. 11-17). The executive control of the direct or indirect taxation, revenues, stamps, etc., of Croatia-Slavonia, is vested in the Hungarian Minister of Finance, who will exercise the same through the financial administration to be appointed in Agram. If the 45 per cent above referred to proves insufficient in any year to meet the expenses of the internal government of Croatia-Slavonia, Hungary will advance the balance required. If it is more than sufficient, the surplus is to be applied to the payment of the cost of common affairs (sects. 22, 25, 26).

The legislative control of all matters which are common to the realms of the Hungarian Crown and the other dominions of His Majesty, as well as of those matters which, as hereinbefore provided, are common to the realms of the Hungarian Crown, is vested in the common Parliament which will sit in Pest every year. In that Parliament Croatia-Slavonia will be represented by twenty-nine deputies chosen by the Diet of Croatia-Slavonia from among its own members. If the number of Hungarian Members of Parliament is subsequently increased, the number of the representatives of Croatia-Slavonia will be increased in the same proportion, regard being had to the relative numbers of the population of Hungary and Croatia-Slavonia (sects. 31, 32).[1] The representatives of Croatia-Dalmatia shall have the same rights of speaking and voting as the other members of

[1] On the reincorporation of the frontier districts the number of Croato-Slavonian representatives was increased to forty.—Law xxxiv. of 1873.

the common Parliament *as regards all those matters which are hereinbefore recognised as common* (sect. 35). In the Hungarian Upper House Croatia-Slavonia will be represented by two deputies chosen by the Diet (sect. 36). In the Delegation to be appointed, in accordance with clause 28 *sqq.* of Law xii. of 1867, Croatia-Slavonia will be proportionately represented, that is to say, by four of their representatives in the Lower House, and by one from the Upper House. The executive control of all matters which are defined by Law xii. of 1867 as common to the realms of the Hungarian Crown and to the other dominions of His Majesty, as well as of all those matters which, as hereinbefore provided, are common to the realms of the Sacred Crown, is vested in the central Government residing in Budapest (sects. 40, 41, 43). A Minister without portfolio will be appointed to represent the interests of Croatia-Slavonia, and to represent the connexion between His Majesty and Croatia-Slavonia. Such Minister will be a member of the common Cabinet, will be entitled to vote as such, and will be *responsible to the common Parliament* (sect. 44). The central Government will endeavour to act as regards Croatia-Slavonia in accord with the separate Government of those countries, but will be responsible only to the common Parliament in which Croatia-Slavonia is represented (sect. 45). The central Government will, as far as possible, and having due regard to efficiency, appoint Croato-Slavonians to official positions in Croatia-Slavonia (sect. 46).

As regards all matters the control of which is not expressly reserved to the common Parliament and central Government, Croatia-Slavonia enjoys complete legislative and executive autonomy. Its autonomous rights, therefore, include the legislative and executive control of local Government and of religious, educational, and judicial matters (sects. 47, 48). The head of the autonomous Government is the Bán, who is responsible to the Croato-

Slavonian Diet, and will be appointed by His Majesty on the nomination of the Hungarian Prime Minister, whose counter-signature such appointment will bear. Henceforth the Bán will not exercise military functions (sects. 50, 51, 52). The organisation of the autonomous Government will be determined by the Diet of Croatia-Slavonia, and the details will be submitted by the Bán to His Majesty for approval (sect. 54). In Croatia-Slavonia the official language of the Legislature, administration, and judicature, is the Croatian, as is that of the organs of the central Government employed in those countries. Reports and presentments from Croatia-Slavonia to the common Ministry, and the replies thereto, will be couched in the Croatian language. It is further provided that the deputies of Croatia-Slavonia, as representatives of a political nation which possesses a separate territory, and, *as regards internal affairs*, its own Legislature and Government, may use Croatian *also*,[1] in the common Parliament and in the Delegation (sects. 56-59). In connexion with internal affairs the Croato-Slavonian flag and arms may be used, as regards the latter, below the Crown of St. Stephen. During the discussion of common affairs the Hungarian and Croato-Slavonian flags will be hoisted side by side on the House of Parliament (sects. 61, 63, 64). The law concludes with a declaration to the effect that, after it has received the royal assent, it is to be incorporated in the Statute-book both of Hungary and of Croatia-Slavonia as a common fundamental law, into which no change can be imported without the concurrence of all the factors which brought it into existence (sect. 70).[2]

[1] *I.e.* as well as the official language of State, the Magyar language. This clause must obviously be read subject to clause 35, which gives the Croatian representatives the right of speaking and voting in the Hungarian Parliament on matters which are defined as common and on no others. They have not the right to speak on purely Hungarian matters in Croatian or in any language, much less to use the Croatian dialect solely for obstructive purposes in connexion, for example, with the revision of the rules of the House.

[2] See *infra*, p. 312.

The difference between this law and Law xii. of 1867 is sufficiently obvious.   The object of the latter was the affirmation of Hungarian sovereignty and independence, and the definite establishment of the dualistic principle, whereas the essence of the former was the reaffirmation of the indivisibility of the realms of the Sacred Crown (which, *vis-à-vis* the other possessions of the Monarch and the rest of the world, form a single political entity), and the grant of autonomy, within strictly defined limits, to Croatia and Slavonia, which are thus converted from " subject or annexed parts " of the Hungarian Kingdom into a single associated State for the purpose of local self-government.   The autonomous rights conferred by Law xxx. must be interpreted in the light of the clear statement which it contains of this principle of indivisibility, and no matter how extensive the right of self-government may seem to be, the cardinal fact remains that the King of Hungary is necessarily and *ipse facto* King of Croatia-Slavonia, that crowning with the Sacred Crown is all that is required to give him regal authority in that part of his Hungarian dominions, and that the competence of the Croatian Diet is practically limited to matters connected with religious worship, education, and the administration, of justice.   Save in so far as these matters are concerned, the authority of the Hungarian Parliament, in which Croatia-Slavonia is directly represented, is maintained, and the outward and visible sign of that authority is the Bán, who is appointed by the King on the nomination of the Hungarian Prime Minister, whose counter-signature is necessary to give validity to the appointment.   As will be seen below,[1] the Croatians, oblivious of the fact that there is, juridically, no such thing as Croatian, as opposed to or distinct from Hungarian citizenship, affect to see in Law xxx. an affirmation of the independence of their country and a

[1] See *infra*, p. 309 *sqq.*

limitation of their connexion with Hungary to that which necessarily results from the identity of the Monarch. A study of the terms of the law summarised above will enable the reader to form an opinion as to the extent to which Croatia's claim to have converted dualism into trialism is justified by the facts of the case.

For the *de facto* restoration of historic dualism Austria should be grateful to the Magyars, whose wise insistence thereon put an end to the sham constitutionalism of Schmerling and compelled the establishment in Vienna of a responsible Ministry, and of that which, but for the existence of Clause 14 of the fundamental law of 1867,[1] would be true parliamentary government. Apart from that clause it is, of course, obvious that the Constitution granted, conceded, *octroyé*, by an autocrat to his hereditary provinces cannot be compared with that of Hungary, of which the Compromise expressly acknowledged the legal, historical continuity. As far as the latter country was concerned, the net result of the legislation of 1867, " the primordial fact, is an independent Kingdom of Hungary, which has allied itself for certain purposes and under certain conditions to the equally independent and distinct Empire of Austria by an act of sovereign free-will, without ever having abdicated the smallest particle of its sovereignty as an independent nation, though it has con-

---

[1] Clause 14 : "If at a moment when the Reichsrath is not sitting there appears to be pressing necessity for the adoption of measures for which its consent is necessary according to the Constitution, such measures may be taken on the responsibility of the Ministry as a whole by Imperial Order, provided that their object is not a modification of the fundamental laws of the State, and that they do not entail either the imposition of a permanent burden on the State Treasury or the alienation of State property. Such Imperial Orders have provisionally the force of law if they are signed by all the Ministers, and are published with special reference to the provisions of the fundamental law. They lose the force of law if the Minister concerned omits to submit them for the approval of the Reichsrath at its first meeting after the promulgation of such orders, in the first instance to the Chamber of Deputies, within the first four weeks of the session, or if such orders fail to obtain the approval of either of the two Chambers of the Reichsrath."

sented to exercise a small part of its governmental functions through executive organs common with Austria."[1]

'For the first time since the accession of Ferdinand I., Hungary obtained an effective acknowledgment of its indubitable right to influence the management of the foreign affairs of the monarchy as a whole, and to an independent fiscal policy of its own. On the management of common affairs it secured an influence equal to that exercised by the hereditary provinces, though, nominally at all events, it bore only 30 per cent of the cost of those affairs.[2]   The fundamental rights of the nation are what they were in the days which preceded the importation of the Habsburgs—permanent and inalienable ; those of the Crown are delegated, and therefore modifiable. In Austria, on the other hand, the laws of 1867 brought into existence a Constitution which, based on a revision of the October Diploma of 1860 and of the February Patent of 1861, can, apparently, be revoked by some future Emperor, just as its "irrevocable" predecessors were abolished by Francis Joseph. True, the Emperor is bound to take an oath to maintain the Constitution, but what if he declines to do so ? In Hungary there is no King until the person entitled to the throne has given the necessary constitutional guarantees,—the essential preliminaries of coronation,—whereas in Austria there is no power to compel the Emperor, who is necessarily placed in full enjoyment of imperial authority by the mere fact of the death or abdication of his predecessor, either to take the prescribed oath or to observe it when taken. Further, there is nothing to prevent him from proroguing the Reichsrath at any moment for the purpose of bringing Clause 14 into play, to the practical destruction

---

[1] Count Albert Apponyi, *The Juridical Nature of the Relations between Austria and Hungary*. An address delivered at St. Louis, 1904, p. 2.

[2] On the question whether Hungary's contribution was not, in fact, increased by the payment of a hidden tribute, the result of the commercial alliance, see the next chapter, p. 274 *sqq.*

of the vaunted institution of parliamentary government. But in spite of these drawbacks, which justify the existence of a doubt as to whether one of the conditions precedent to Hungary's acceptance of the terms of the Compromise has been fulfilled, and notwithstanding the fact that those terms proved to be incapable of putting an end to all possibility of friction and misunderstanding, Austria was to be congratulated on the results obtained for her by the wisdom of Deák and of his Magyar coadjutors, on the settlement of a question the non-solution of which had destroyed her prestige by reducing her to a state of impotence during and after the Crimean War,[1] had brought her to the verge of bankruptcy, and had made her ultimate ejection from Italy and Germany a certainty.[2]

[1] "Mehr als einmal erklärte Rechberg und bestätigte der Kaiser dem preussischen Unterhändler (Manteuffel), dass Österreich vor dem Ausgleich mit Ungarn nicht in der Lage sei, einen grossen Krieg zu führen, ja, dass es schwierig sein würde, auch nur dem Armeecorps in Schleswig einige Verstärkung nachzusenden." — Von Sybel, *Begründung des Deutschen Reiches*, Munich, 1889, iii. 258.

[2] Freiherr von Lichtenfels said to Francis Joseph in 1867 : "I could have understood it if we had made this compromise before the war with Prussia. Denn wenn mir die Reichseinheit auch als ein hohes Gut gilt, so sehe ich ein, dass es notwendig gewesen wäre, Ungarn zu versöhnen, um unterstützt durch die öffentliche Meinung Ungarns in den Krieg zu gehen, der über die Zukunft Österreichs entscheiden könnte."—Rudolf Springer, *Grundlagen und Entwickelungsziele*, etc., p. 43.

CHAPTER XIX

THE war of 1848 was partly due to the failure of the March laws to define and to regulate the management of common affairs and affairs of common interest to Austria and Hungary. The Compromise of 1867 corrects some errors, and supplies some deficiencies which marred the great work with which the name of Kossuth is closely connected. Up to April 1848 Kossuth was as loyal and moderate as Deák, and the Compromise is but the logical development of the principles enunciated by him before that date. "I maintain," he said, in November 1847, "that he who asserts and strives to spread the opinion that the legal rights of our country are necessarily in conflict with those of Austria, does a bad service to the reigning house. I flatly deny the assertion, and repeat with heartfelt conviction the words used by the Estates and Orders in 1844, to the effect that the complete development of the constitutional life of Hungary side by side with the hereditary provinces is possible ; and maintain that if difficulties arise, and if our interests here and there seem to be in conflict, such difficulties and conflicts do not originate in the nature of the relations existing between Hungary and the allied provinces, but in the divergent nature of the governmental institutions of the two countries." Kossuth was clearly right. The parties to the "mixed marriage" could not be expected to live in lasting harmony so long as such dissimilar political conditions existed.   It was not likely that Austria with its autocratic government could entertain any feeling but one of jealousy and dislike for a sister nation, with a thousand years of constitutional life behind it.   Austria, next to Russia, the most retrograde country in Europe, had first to learn the lesson which the year 1848 had taught the rest of the Continent.   Hungary, on the other hand, had to recognise the fact that for the maintenance of the essentials of independence some slight sacrifice must be made.   It was before all things necessary that Hungary, the point of contact of East and West, should be strong enough to avoid becoming the blind instrument of others' ambitions, reduced to the position occupied by small Balkan States, "whose existence depends on the goodwill and mutual jealousies of their neighbours." [1] The Bocskays and Rákóczys always required foreign assistance.   Insufficiently strong to stand alone after Mohács, Hungary turned to its neighbour ; and its natural ally in 1526 was its natural ally in 1867, in spite of the Caraffas and Haynaus, the Bachs and the Schmerlings.   Kossuth's unfortunate plan for the federation of the Balkan provinces was only a proof that he too recognised the necessity of alliances, to prevent Hungary from falling victim to the exigencies of some European complication. [2]   His hatred of Austria made him ready to depart from the tradition established by St. Stephen, to turn to the East instead of to the West, and to abandon, for the sake of an alliance with Servia and Roumania, the characteristics of sovereignty, with the abandonment of which he reproached Deák, though his own plan involved a far greater sacrifice.   Defence, foreign policy, diplomatic

---

[1] Andrássy Gyula, *Az 1867-iki Kiegyezésről*, Budapest, 1896, p. 21.   An acquaintance with this book is essential to a comprehension of the antecedents and results of the Compromise.

[2] "By itself Hungary would vegetate as a second-rate Power.   It can become a great European Power only in alliance with others."—Kossuth, cited by Horváth János, *Az 1867-évi Kiegyezés*, Budapest, 1895.

representation, commercial and fiscal policy and legislation, would all have been common to the confederate States; even the territorial integrity of the realms of St. Stephen would not have been respected. The confederation could have continued to exist "only if Russia had given it her blessing," [1] so in all probability would have served only to bring the triumph of Panslavism within measurable distance. The whole episode was a proof of the necessity of some form of Austro-Hungarian union from the point of view of Hungary, of Austria recently ejected from Germany, and of the Balkan States, of whose independence of Russia a contented and powerful Hungary, the "wedge" driven between the northern and southern Slavs, was the best guarantee. It was not Kossuth who laid the foundations of the Compromise, but centuries of slow constitutional development. Deák built the superstructure in haste while still under the impression of the period of absolutism. The following pages may help to the formation of an opinion as to whether he might have produced a more stable and satisfactory edifice.

The Compromise does not mark the introduction of any new principle. It does no more than provide a fresh definition of the meaning of the Pragmatic Sanction, as adopted and explained by the Hungarian laws of 1723 and 1790, and a fresh guarantee of Hungary's sovereignty and independence. It neither creates nor recognises anything which can be construed as binding Austria and Hungary into a single Empire; it merely brings a limited common organisation into existence for reasons of expediency and convenience. Hungary and Austria are two perfectly distinct entities—a fact which is continually being obscured by the loose English fashion of speaking of Austria as if it included Hungary, of an Austro-Hungarian Empire, and of the Trans- and Cisleithanian halves of the monarchy. Francis Joseph's order to Beust of November 14, 1868,

[1] Andrássy, *o.c.* p. 41.

to the effect that the lands and kingdoms constitutionally united under his rule should be styled alternately Austro-Hungarian Monarchy and Austro-Hungarian Kingdom, tended to perpetuate an inaccurate conception of the relations existing between the two countries. Strictly speaking, not even the obligation of common defence is to be found in the Pragmatic Sanction, but it necessarily follows, from the identity of the Monarch of the two countries, that the King of Hungary cannot fail to defend the Emperor of Austria and *vice versa*. As Kossuth wrote in his own Journal, July 4, 1848, "The tie of the Pragmatic Sanction binds us to Austria, the meaning of which is that our friends are common and our enemies are common." Here the necessary connexion between the two countries begins and ends, for the sole object of the law of 1723 was, as it clearly states, the preservation of the two countries from foreign attack, and the maintenance of domestic tranquillity, *i.e.* of the tranquillity which was always liable to be disturbed by uncertainty as to the succession to the throne.[1] At the most there is a limited community of interests, and Austria is for Hungary a foreign empire, allied, just as any other country might be, for purposes of defence and fiscal policy. There is no common territory, common citizenship, common legislative body, common judicature, or common monarch. There is a, conceivably only temporary, identity of the King of Hungary and the Emperor of Austria so long as legitimate, Catholic, descendants of certain specified Habsburgs continue to exist, and no longer—a fact which itself provides a sufficient answer to Lustkandl and his disciples, who maintain the existence of a "real union" between the two countries,[2] oblivious of the essential

[1] The corresponding Transylvanian Law iii., 1744, also defines its object as "*mutua et reciproca defensio.*"

[2] Gumplowicz states the true fact when he says : "Die heutige staatsrechtliche Gestaltung Österreich-Ungarns ist das Resultat seiner eigenartigen historischen Entwickelung . . . . dies Verhältniss kann nicht mit einem

differences which make such a union an impossibility. On
the one side is Austria, a conglomerate of "kingdoms and
states represented in the Reichsrath,"—to use its legal
definition,—fragments of greater nations, united in a " real
union " with each other, and for the purposes of the
Compromise forming a nominally constitutional country,
the Constitution being made up of scraps of the October
Diploma and of the February Patent, with an incorrect
version of the provisions of Hungary's Law xii. of 1867
to leaven the lump. The Constitution is not the product
of historical continuity as in Hungary, for the simple
reason that there was nothing to continue except the
limited rights conceded by autocracy which can to-day
withdraw the concessions it has made, in the same way as
it withdrew the "irrevocable" Constitutions of the past.
Formed of scraps of Italy and Poland, of fragmentary
Slav races with a German admixture, nothing but the
monarchical principle and the fear of dissolution into its
constituent elements to the profit of its greater neighbours
can keep it together. On the other hand is Hungary,
with a Constitution which was not conferred by any
charter, but is partly based on immemorial custom, and
partly to be found in the Corpus Juris, every law of
which is of equal binding force, which was not made, but
grew, and is still growing, and knows no obstacle to
prevent its further growth. Between such a country,
where " His Majesty recognises the fact that the right of
legislation, of the interpretation and abrogation of laws,
belongs jointly to the lawfully crowned King, and to the
Estates and Orders in Diet assembled, and must not be exercised outside that assembly,"[1] and Austria, where Clause 14

doctrinären Terminus bezeichnet, es kann nur aus der Betrachtung des in
diesem Gezetze zum Ausdruck gelangten Compromisses zwischen den
entscheidenden Machtfaktoren Österreichs und Ungarns dargelegt werden."
Ferdinand I. by will divided his possessions, consequently there was not even
a complete personal union between all the realms of Austria and Hungary.
Only the dynasty was common or identical at the end of the sixteenth century.

[1] Law xii., 1790-1.

of the fundamental law enables the Emperor to treat the
Reichsrath as a nonentity, there can be no more than a
personal union resulting from the identity of the Monarch.

The events of 1866 gave conclusive proof of the
necessity of coming to terms with Hungary. Königgrätz
finally taught Francis Joseph the lesson that unless he
gave contentment to the Magyars, Austria must cease to
be a great Power. The ejection of Austria from Germany
was a necessary antecedent to the final abandonment of
the Habsburg ideal of centralisation and germanisation,
though history had shown, over and over again, the folly
of attempting to strengthen Austria by weakening
Hungary, and of sacrificing true union for the outward
semblance of unification. A dissatisfied Hungary would
probably have fought on the Turkish side against Russia,
with the result of producing a general European conflagration. If Austria had not regained its strength by coming
to terms with the Magyars, the Berlin Congress, the
occupation of Bosnia and Herzegovina, and the formation
of the Triple Alliance, would not have taken place.[1] No
more foolish doctrine was ever propounded than that of
Schmerling, to the effect that Hungary, by its action in
1848, had forfeited its independence and Constitution,
and that Austria (in consequence of the success of Russian
arms) could deal with it as she pleased by right of
conquest. The acceptance of such a theory would
necessarily have justified Hungary in aspiring to break
away from Austria so soon as it was strong enough to do
so, and would have perpetuated the discord which had
paralysed the latter country during the Crimean War, and
ensured its expulsion from Italy and Germany. Hungary
had to be satisfied by the restoration of its independence,
and at the same time to be converted into an equal partner
in a great European Power, assured of the influence on
the management of common affairs which was its due.

[1] Andrássy, o.c. p. 146.

There had always been common affairs ever since Mohács. They lay hidden in the terms of the Pragmatic Sanction and emerge, though ill-defined, in the March laws of 1848. They came into existence with the establishment by Ferdinand I. of the Privy Council and War Council in Vienna, and misuse of power soon forged a stronger chain to bind the two countries together than was provided by the identity of King and Archduke. The Pragmatic Sanction, subsequently interpreted by Law x. of 1790-91, defined, for the first time, the true nature of the relations existing between Austria and Hungary, and reaffirmed the principle of Magyar sovereignty. The law of 1867 further develops that principle, gives a clearer definition of the nature of common affairs than was hitherto to be found in the Corpus Juris, and provides the novel method of handling them necessitated by the birth of constitutionalism in Austria.[1] The minority in the committee of 1867 based its opposition to Deák's proposals on the doctrine of the purely personal nature of the union resulting from the Pragmatic Sanction, and alleged that he was sacrificing national rights from motives of opportunism for which there could be no place after Königgrätz. It urged that Hungary was being unnecessarily deprived of the undivided control of the expenditure of its own blood and treasure, and was thus smoothing the way for complete amalgamation with Austria. Deák replied that common affairs were not the invention of to-day, but had always existed, and that the Delegations, so far from lessening Hungary's control of essentials, actually enabled it to make a decisive voice heard on matters on which it had hitherto exerted little or no influence.[2] In view of the difference which existed ever

[1] See Deák's speech of March 28, 1867. Kónyi, o.c. iv. 447 sqq.

[2] "Hungary always had affairs in common with the whole monarchy ; the only difference is that before 1867 others managed them without us and against our interests, while now we manage them in common with the other parties concerned. If any one prefers the former state of affairs it is a matter

252 THE POLITICAL EVOLUTION

since 1526 between Hungary's theoretical independence
and *de facto* subordination to Austria's interests,[1] the
answer was as satisfactory as any reply can be which
depends for its justification on the principle that half a
loaf is better than no bread, but judged by the light of
subsequent events it would seem that in some respects
the criticisms of the minority were not ill-founded. In
all matters not specifically described as common affairs
the Hungarian laws and constitutional rights are completely unaltered and unimpaired, but the fact remains
that a wider definition was given to such affairs than was
strictly justifiable, and the continued existence of sores
in the body politic must be ascribed, in some measure, to
Deák's refusal to profit by the opportunity seemingly
afforded by Königgrätz of removing all removable causes
of future friction and irritation, by limiting Hungary's
contact with Austria to the minimum consistent with the
due observance of the obligations resulting from the
Pragmatic Sanction.

Affairs which are often loosely spoken of as common
affairs are not in fact common. The only absolutely
common matter is the common obligation of defence
which continues to exist whether Austria has a constitutional government or is subject to absolutism. The
question how provision is to be made in men and money
to satisfy this obligation is left entirely to Hungary. In
addition to the above there are matters requiring common
management, for the purposes of which the Delegations
and common Ministers have been invented, but these
matters can maintain their common character only so long
as Austria is a constitutionally governed country, for the
grant of a Constitution to the hereditary provinces was
a condition precedent to Hungary's consent to the

of taste."—Count Julius Andrássy, Jan. 14, 1869, *Gróf Andrássy Gyula
Beszédei*, ii. 13. Lederer ed.

[1] See *supra*, pp. 35-50; Andrássy, *o.c.* 192-95; Horváth János, *Az 1867
évi Kiegyezés*, chaps. i.-iii.

Compromise.[1]   A third class is formed by matters which
considerations of expediency suggest should be managed
by mutual consent on similar principles, with which, if
no understanding is arrived at, Hungary can deal as it
pleases.   Thus, as regards the first two classes, if no agreement is come to as to their management, if the Delegations cannot, for some reason or other, perform their
functions, if no decision can be reached as to the quota,
or relative proportion in which the cost of common organs
has to be borne, the existence of such common affairs
would not be affected.   It would merely mean that a new
method would have to be found of dealing with them—
in other words, there would have to be a recurrence to
the pre-1848 position, when common affairs were a matter
for settlement by agreement between the King and the
Hungarian Diet of the one part and the Emperor of
Austria of the other.   The same course would necessarily
have to be adopted in the event of the abolition of constitutional government in Austria.   On the other hand,
failure to come to an agreement on matters which are not
common, but are managed on similar or identical lines
by mutual agreement, for the sake of convenience, not
for the purpose of satisfying any obligation, puts an end
to such matters, and each country is free to make its own
arrangements.[2]   It should be noted that Bosnia and
Herzegovina do not constitute a common affair or a
common possession.   They could not be attached to
either Austria or Hungary, and there is no composite
Austro-Hungarian Empire or monarchy of which they
could form a part.   They belong to the Sultan, and their
inhabitants are therefore neither Austrian nor Hungarian
subjects.   The Hungarian law regards the occupation of
these provinces as temporary, like the British occupation
of Egypt, and for the purposes of control agreed to the

[1] *Supra*, p. 229.
[2] *E.g.* as to customs, commercial matters, money, and railways.

extension of the functions of the common Minister of
Finance, for the reason, presumably, that he has less work
to do than his colleagues.   The Delegations have no
locus standi to interfere in the management, nor has
Parliament, unless and until national financial interests are
adversely affected, or a change is made in the relations of
the provinces to the monarchy.   Law vi. of 1880, sect. 5,
provided that no such change should take place without
the consent of both Parliament and Reichsrath.   Should,
however, both legislatures agree to a permanent annexation,
the future of Bosnia-Herzegovina must, apparently, depend
on the uncontrolled decision of the Hungarian Parliament,
as both coronation oath and inaugural diploma oblige the
King to reincorporate in Hungary any territories which
formerly belonged to the Sacred Crown, and both provinces
come within that category.

Save for the exception provided by the case of Bosnia
and Herzegovina, the common Ministers of War, Finance,
and Foreign Affairs are strictly limited to the management
of strictly common affairs.   They have no right whatever
to interfere with the affairs of either country.   The
common Minister of War has no control of the territorial
army of either, and the common Minister of Finance has
nothing to do but to prepare the estimates of the cost
of the common army and of common diplomatic representation.   Apparently Francis Joseph and his advisers
believed in 1867 that the common Ministers would be
superior to the Ministers of Austria and the Ministers of
Hungary, and would be "Ministers of the Empire"—
a designation which might be construed to imply a non-
existent union ; but Hungary rightly objected to the
proposed title, and, in fact, the common Ministers are
inferior to their Austrian and Hungarian colleagues if only
for the reason that they can take no part in legislative
work.   If there were a real union there would necessarily
be a common Legislature ; hence the efforts of some to

prove that the Delegations are not Delegations, but are a body endowed with a form of legislative authority.[1] As a matter of fact they do not in the smallest degree constitute a common legislative organ.[2] Each Delegation consists of a commission of sixty members (forty from the Lower, twenty from the Upper House) chosen for one year, or one session of Parliament as the case may be. The two Delegations cannot even meet for discussion, only for voting, after three fruitless exchanges of messages.[3] Each Delegation represents only the Parliament or Reichsrath from which it issues, and its duty is clearly confined to the control of the actions of the common Ministers, and to the fixing of the amount of the budget of common affairs which has to be found by the two countries in the proportions determined by the quota-deputations. Parliament cannot alter the amount so arrived at, but is entirely free as regards the method of finding such amount. Thus, the Delegations exist to perform a strictly limited function, and it is only within the specified limits of their authority that they have a free hand. Their decisions are binding only when ratified by the Hungarian Parliament, which can refuse to pass the budget as a whole, and so

[1] See Dantscher von Kollesberg, *Der staatsrechtliche Charakter der Delegationen*, Vienna, 1903. The author sees an embryonic federation in the Delegations, and denies them their generally recognised character of commissions appointed for a special purpose, pp. 6 *sqq.* and 54 *sqq.* and *passim*. For the opposite view see Jellinek, *Die Lehre von den Staatenverbindungen*, Vienna, 1882, pp. 245, 246.

[2] See Rudolph Springer's *Grundlagen und Entwickelungsziele der österreichisch-ungarischen Monarchie*, Vienna, 1906, p. 154. "Es kann sein, dass die österreichische und die ungarische Delegationen ursprünglich beide als eins und als ein Gesetzgeber gedacht waren, und darauf deutet der Umstand hin, dass sie in einem praktischseltenen möglichen Fall rechtlich befugt sind, eine *Abstimmungs Pantomime* aufzuführen. Tatsächlich aber hat das ungarische Parlament ohne kompetenten Widerspruch seine Delegation als simplen Spezialausschuss behandelt."—See section 28 of Law xii., *supra*, p. 229.

[3] The reason why the Committee of 1867 would not allow meeting for discussion was that German would necessarily have been the language employed, and this fact might have been taken to imply a certain degree of subordination of Hungary to Austria.

can nullify the action of the two commissions. In Austria, on the other hand, the decisions of the Delegations have the force of law and need no confirmation—a fact which alone suffices to refute the theory as to the existence of something in the nature of a legislative assembly common to Austria and Hungary. Andrássy did not wish the Delegations to meet even for the purpose of voting together, fearing the result of the possible defection of a Croatian or Saxon member, but he was overruled by Deák, and as a matter of fact his fears have proved to be unfounded, as the practically homogeneous Hungarian body is necessarily more than a match for its Austrian counterpart, in which racial and local jealousies are liable to be destructive of solidarity.[1]

The unity of the diplomatic representation of Austria and Hungary has, perhaps more than anything else, helped to give rise to a false idea of political unity. The laws of 1848 regarded the management of foreign affairs as the exclusive privilege of the King, for Deák's evidence proves that the functions of the Minister *a latere* were not considered or intended to extend to interference in such matters ; consequently, the law of 1867 marks a considerable advance from Hungary's point of view. Clause 8 of Law xii., as originally drafted by Deák, clearly shows that he did not intend all foreign affairs to be regarded as common. "The suitable conduct of foreign affairs is one of the instruments of common and united defence, the obligation of which derives from the Pragmatic Sanction. Such suitable conduct demands that such foreign affairs should be treated in common as *interest jointly all* the States which are under His Majesty's rule." This phrase was, unfortunately, amplified by the committee in such a way as to include diplomatic and consular representation and commercial treaties, thus justifying to

---

[1] As a matter of fact the Delegations have held a joint sitting only on four occasions since their invention.

some extent the idea that such matters were necessarily common, which they clearly are not. The test of community is supplied by the words of the law as finally adopted, " instruments of common and united defence " ; consequently, the conduct of foreign affairs is necessarily common only so far as it deals with matters affecting Austria and Hungary jointly, and only so far as matters are concerned which affect the obligation of mutual defence. The clause must be interpreted in the light of the words quoted above, and though the law refers to commercial matters as coming within the purview of the common Foreign Minister, they are not strictly common affairs. Save in so far as diplomatic representation is concerned with the defence of the two countries, Hungary is entitled to negotiate separately with foreign nations ; and in fact the common Minister does not control Hungary's external relations, but is the intermediary through whose diplomatic agents negotiations are conducted. Foreign treaties require Hungary's acceptance and incorporation in a special law to give them binding force.[1] An attempt was made by Austria to restrict the right of Parliament by interpreting the law to mean that the common Foreign Minister has merely to communicate the fact of a treaty having been concluded, not to lay it before Parliament for acceptance ; but the attempt was defeated, and Parliament's right of interference was established.[2] As a matter of fact, Hungary's influence on the conduct of foreign affairs, at present limited to that exercised by the Hungarian Delegation to whom the common Foreign Minister is responsible, and by the Prime Minister who is responsible to Parliament, has been enormously increased by the Compromise. It is hardly too much to say that Hungary alone counts, as Francis Joseph, though still, thanks to Clause 14, an autocrat in Austria, in

[1] *E.g.* the Treaty of Berlin, 1879, negotiated by Counts Andrássy and Károlyi communicated to Parliament and embodied in Law viii. of that year.

[2] Beksics, *A Dualismus Története*, Budapest, 1892, p. 117.

Hungary is but the equal of Parliament, and it is fairly safe to predict that the foreign policy of Austria and Hungary will always depend on the attitude adopted by the latter country.   Beust,[1] ejected from Germany, wished for revenge after Königgrätz with the help of France, but the last thing that Hungary wished to see was a revival of Austrian ambitions of hegemony in Germany.   Thanks to the Magyars, Beust had to retire, and the Dual Monarchy maintained an attitude of neutrality in 1870.   It is a true saying that the road to Constantinople lies through Vienna.[2] Fortunately for Europe it also passes through Budapest.

The termination of the Customs Union between Hungary and Austria must necessarily put an end to the community of commercial representation.   In any case, as the consular service is not an "instrument of common and united defence" essential to the fulfilment of obligations resulting from the Pragmatic Sanction, there is no reason whatever why Hungary should not have separate representation.   On the contrary, there is every reason why it should have it, as Austrian and Hungarian trade interests are neither identical nor impartially represented. The diplomatic service is possibly on a different footing. If an ambassador theoretically represents only the monarch who signs what may be called his power of attorney, it might seem absurd that one and the same person, though he has two distinct personalities as King and Emperor, should have two accredited representatives.   But through the King the ambassador represents his country, and questions may easily arise, of international railway policy for instance, in which the interests of Austria and Hungary may be widely divergent and need separate representation.

The choice of an ambassador is a matter for the Crown's discretion, subject to the provision that Hungarians must be employed equally with Austrians ; at the same time it

[1] "That Saxon Minister in a bad temper," as Bismarck calls him.—*Reflexions and Reminiscences*, ii. 58.

[2] Ascribed to Pashkievitch.   Friedjung, *Krimkrieg*, p. 65.

must be remembered that the King has no privilege of any kind which he did not receive directly from the nation. The people divested itself of certain rights in his favour, and the exercise of royal privileges is subject to the control of the nation which gave them. The supreme authority is vested in the legislative body which can confer rights on the King, but can receive none from him [1]; and in the case of a conflict as to the limitations of royal authority the presumption must always be against the Crown. Consequently, the Compromise arrived at by King and nation cannot be extended by implication or treated in any way as a new departure ; it must be construed strictly by the light of previous legislation and in accordance with the principle of legal continuity. The rights of the nation are the only permanent rights ; those of the Crown are delegated, and therefore liable to modification. It is entirely conceivable that in the future, as in the past, the nation should abolish, or modify, certain royal privileges on the accession of a new King, without in any way doing violence to the Constitution. The heir apparent does not *ipso facto* become King on the death of his predecessor. True, he possesses an exclusive right to the throne, but it is the ceremony of coronation, to which the taking of an oath and the signing of a diploma guaranteeing the maintenance of the laws and liberties of Hungary are necessary antecedents, which gives him his authority. Oath and diploma embody the terms of the contract between him and the nation, and a contract necessarily implies consent, consent implies the possibility of disagreement and the consequent necessity of negotiation. Constitutionally there is nothing to prevent the nation from exacting whatever conditions it pleases to exact as the price of its consent. The King is bound by law to be crowned within six months of the death of his predecessor,[2] and it is a question what would be the result of failure to comply

[1] "The King does not confer rights on the people, the people confer rights on the King, for the people is the source of all rights"—Deák, cited by Kmety, *o.c.* p. 163. [2] 1790, iii.

with the law. Presumably Hungary would not tolerate a second "hatted King," and his right would ultimately be treated as having lapsed, for, according to Verbóczy, no obedience is due save to the lawfully crowned monarch. An uncrowned one can summon Parliament only for the purpose of his own coronation ; no taxes or recruits could be voted, and the whole machinery of government would come to a standstill. In Austria, on the other hand, the heir becomes Emperor immediately on the death of his predecessor, unless excluded by the operation of a Hausgesetz, which has no binding force in Hungary. Parliament, as a matter of fact, accepted the Hausgesetz of 1899, excluding the possible direct heir from the throne, but there was no obligation to do so.[1] Abdication of the Austrian throne does not mean abdication of that of Hungary ; a separate act is required by Law vii. of 1867. The origin and nature of the monarch's authority is perfectly distinct in the two countries ; the Emperor is a stranger in Hungary, and he is no more fused with the King of Hungary than the Emperor of China would be were there a treaty in existence between Hungary and the Celestial Empire providing for common defence and the management of certain affairs of common interest. In Hungary the King acts solely by virtue of his kingship, and the consent or concurrence of Austria or of the Emperor of Austria is not required. The distinction between the two monarchs, identical but not "common," is emphasised by Law xii. of 1867, which declares that the expenses of the Court are not to be borne in common by Austria and Hungary, but require a separate vote of the Hungarian Parliament.[2] Unfortunately, the Emperor is a stranger to Hungary in more senses than one. For centuries the successors of St. Stephen were the titular heads of the German race, and never lost sight of the fact, and Francis Joseph has consistently shown that

[1] *Kossuth Ferencz Harmincz Parlamenti Beszéde*, ed. Szatmári Mór, p. 228 sq.

[2] Hungary provides £455,000 per annum, and not unnaturally complains of the spending of that sum outside the country of origin.

he is no more able to forget that he is an Austrian than his predecessors were able to forget their purely German ambitions.   It is characteristic of the British to take more interest in the details of the intimate life of crowned heads than in the essentials of public conduct.   How and to what extent Francis Joseph has fulfilled his duties to his Magyar subjects is a matter of indifference to the majority of Englishmen, who allow their judgment of the King of Hungary to be obscured by their enthusiasm for descriptions of the simple life of the Emperor of Austria, of his fidelity to ancient connexions, of what he has for breakfast, and where, and with whom.   They forget Louis Batthyány and Arad, Bach, and the long years of tyranny, the partiality, and the neglect which have been the Magyars' reward for centuries of excessive loyalty to the reigning House.

Can the Compromise be mended or ended ? whose consent is necessary for its alteration or abolition ?   Count Julius Andrássy said in his speech in the Upper House on April 5, 1888, that the Compromise was not a temporary arrangement, but was " intended to settle matters for all time."   His son in his masterly book says that " nothing was further from the intention of the Legislature in 1867 than merely to establish fundamental principles " [1] to be developed subsequently in accordance with the necessities of the times.   But no eternal settlement is ever possible.   To regard Deák's work as unalterable would be to shut the door to the possibility of progress ; new conditions must necessarily arise from time to time, new phases of commercial and political development must appear, and new generations arise which see matters through other spectacles than those of 1867. [2]   Fundamental principles based on the Pragmatic Sanction remain,

[1] *Az 1867-iki Kiegyezésről*, p. 330.

[2] Eisenmann, *o.c.* p. 656, rightly says, " Ces paragraphes n'enferment pas la Hongrie dans une infranchissable barrière, ils ne fixent pas le maximum de ses droits, ils lui en assurent le minimum ; ils lui donnent une base d'opérations pour les étendre et les agrandir."

but the method of giving effect to them must change. Community of defence remains, but the method of satisfying the obligations which it imposes must be a matter for the legislation of each independent country.   It is clear that the Austrian politicians of 1867 did not regard the Compromise as a final, irrevocable settlement ; why, therefore, should Hungary do so ?   Austria regarded it as a temporary measure necessitated by circumstances, or rather as a new starting-point for, or a new stage in the development of a uniform Austrian Empire.   Schmerling distinctly stated that he viewed it only as a step towards the representation of all the dominions of the Habsburgs in a common Parliament ; and Beust evidently entertained the same opinion.[1]   The carrying out of Count Hohenwart's programme of tentative federalisation would have destroyed the whole basis of the Compromise, and would have converted dualism into trialism.   Law xii. 5, 1867, recites the fact that hitherto common affairs had been settled by the Magyar King and Magyar Legislature on the one hand, and by the absolute monarch of Austria on the other, and goes on to state that as the Emperor had decided to grant a Constitution to the hereditary provinces he could no longer act autocratically—that is to say, that a new method must be found of managing common affairs.   No change was imported into the relations established by the Pragmatic Sanction (which remain the same perpetually unless and until the elective rights of Hungary revive), only into the method of dealing with the consequences of such relations.   As there is no Parliament common to Austria and Hungary, for, as we have seen, the Delegations are merely temporary commissions and in no sense a common legislative body, obviously there can be no common legislation.   Law xii. is, therefore, a purely Hungarian Law passed with the sanction of the Magyar King, invested with no more and no less sanctity

[1] See Andrássy, o.c. p. 346.

than any other law in the Corpus Juris, and subject to
modification and abrogation at the hands of the two
parties to its birth.   There was no third party, and the
consent of Austria is therefore not required.[1]   If there
was anything in the nature of a treaty with the hereditary
provinces, it amounted to no more than a temporary
arrangement for the treatment of the results of principles
which long pre-existed the birth of a constitutional
Austria.   As the law says, the provisions dealing with
the handling of common affairs were to become effective
only so soon as Austria expressed its adherence in a
constitutional manner.   If Austria had not expressed its
adherence, it would have made no difference to the
common affairs, only to the method of handling them.

The validity of the Compromise is dependent on the
observance of certain essential conditions.   Firstly, the
maintenance of the identity of the King of Hungary
and the Emperor of Austria.   Secondly, that Hungary
and the parts annexed, Croatia, Slavonia, and Dalmatia
continue to form the one and indivisible Kingdom of the
Sacred Crown.   Thirdly, that the Hungarian Constitution is maintained intact.   Fourthly, that the connexion
between the hereditary provinces of Austria, the indivisible possessions of the House of Habsburg, remains
the same as it was in 1867.   Lastly, the maintenance
of constitutional government in Austria, "for Hungary
can deal only with the constitutional representatives of
His Majesty's other realms and possessions with respect
to mutual relations of whatever nature."[2]   Any attempted
disintegration of Hungary or conversion of dualism into
trialism would not only be fatal to the continuance of the
Compromise, but would absolve Hungary from the conditional obligations deriving from the laws which gave effect
to the Pragmatic Sanction.   It is incorrect to speak of an
Austro-Hungarian Ausgleich or Compromise ; there is

[1] See Kmety, *Közjog*, 468, *n*.   [2] xii. 1867, section 25.

no Austro-Hungarian law, but there are two non-simultaneous, independent, non-identical laws the provisions of which are sufficiently similar to enable common affairs to be handled in accordance therewith. That there is no contract between Austria and Hungary is proved by, *inter alia*, the fact that the Austrian law of December 21, 1867, is not identical in terms with the Hungarian Law xii., and fails to give expression to the constitutional independence of Hungary and to the limited nature of the King's authority which condition all the provisions of the Compromise. The attempt to treat the two countries as two equal contracting parties when there is no contract and no equality is obvious. The Austrian law is entitled "Gesetz betreffend die *allen Ländern des österreichischen Monarchie gemeinsamen Angelegenheiten* und die Art ihrer Behandlung"—an attempt to smuggle into the law an expression which would imply the inclusion of Hungary in the Austrian Monarchy. "Das Kriegswesen des Heeres" is described as "common to the kingdoms and lands represented in the Reichsrath and to the lands of the Hungarian Crown, and the command and inner organisation of the forces as a matter for the sole decision of the Kaiser"— an unqualified statement which ignores the principle of legal continuity and the limitations imposed by the Hungarian Constitution on the royal power. Further, "das Finanzwesen," so far as it is concerned with the expenses to be borne in common, and with the Budget and verification of accounts connected with such expenses, is declared without reservation to be common, and no mention is made of the constitutional influence expressly reserved to the Hungarian Ministry by the fortieth section of Law xii.[1] Moreover, the establishment of complete

---

[1] The principle of perfect parity is obscured by the Austrian law, and is not observed. It was the Austrian idea that common affairs were in reality to be Austrian affairs. The Austrian law does not bring out the fact that the Pragmatic Sanction is the sole basis of the relations between the two countries, nor the fact that the maintenance of the Hungarian Constitution

constitutionalism in Austria was a condition precedent
to Hungary's acceptance of the Compromise ; but true
constitutional government cannot be said to exist when
section 14 of the Austrian law enables the Emperor to
rule the country autocratically without reference to the
Reichsrath.   It is a question, therefore, whether Hungary,
which refused to be brought into contact with Austria
save as a free country with another free country, would
not be justified in regarding one of the fundamental
conditions of compromise as unfulfilled, and in refusing,
were it disposed to do so, to give effect to any provisions
which have reference to the method of handling common
affairs and tend to limit Magyar sovereignty.   It seems
strange that neither Deák nor Count Julius Andrássy
entered a contemporaneous protest against a misrepresentation of the relative positions of Austria and Hungary
which must necessarily tend to blind Europe to the true
nature of the Compromise.   Presumably their energy
was temporarily exhausted by the long struggle for the
recovery of the national independence, and they were
indisposed to fight over details which they regarded
as possessing no intrinsic importance, for the reason that
no inaccuracies or misstatement in an Austrian law can
affect the pre-existing rights of Hungary.

The matter of primary importance was the consolidation of Hungary's position rather than the insistence
on strict historical right. Though the Compromise had
restored the relations between Hungary and Austria to a
more normal condition, it had not put an end to the
hostility of the Viennese bureaucracy, which viewed with
malicious pleasure the difficulties, the result of its own

and of true parliamentary government in Austria is an essential condition of
the Compromise. The Austrian object was to produce the impression that
there is a united Empire which includes Hungary. The Austrian law does
not even refer to the fact that failing agreement Hungary's rights with respect
to the management of affairs of joint interest are unimpaired. The object was
to give the appearance of permanence to a temporary arrangement.

mismanagement of affairs during the past eighteen years, which confronted the Hungarian Government. It hoped that unavoidable financial difficulties would ensure the collapse of the new order of things, and that a broken and contrite Hungary would soon be obliged to have recourse to Austria, which would then be able to dictate very different terms than those embodied in the law of 1867.[1] Hungary itself was far from being unanimous as to the merits of that enactment. The more reactionary of the Conservatives believed that its inevitable result would be the disruption of the Habsburg monarchy, while several counties, encouraged by the exiled Kossuth, who saw in the Compromise the grave of Hungarian independence, made no concealment of their dislike of the new definition of common affairs, and of the method of handling them. Fortunately, the overwhelming weight of public opinion was on Deák's side ; consequently, the strife of parties in the early stages of the new *régime* never reached such an acute phase as to be dangerous to the stability of the work of reconstruction. It is, perhaps, not unfair to assume that the avowed hostility of the extremists was partly assumed for electioneering purposes, with the object of securing the votes of ignorant peasants, who looked on Kossuth as on the sole author of their freedom, and were ready to give unquestioning credence to his assertions as to the betrayal by Deák of the nation's interests. In any case the fact remains, that down to the death of Deák in 1876 the main characteristic of the early period of restored parliamentary government was fidelity to the terms of the Compromise. Apart from minor subdivisions, there always were two main parties : one, which may be called the Party of 1867, which was convinced that by effecting the Compromise Hungary had abandoned no right, and in fact had obtained such influence on affairs in general as it had never, *de facto*, before possessed ; and another, which

[1] Coloman Tisza, speech of September 2, 1904.

may be called the Party of 1848, which saw nothing but an abandonment of the essentials of independence, to the reattainment of which all effort must be directed, and accused their opponents of readiness to sacrifice the nation's interests for the sake of power. Of these two main divisions the former was for a long time more than a match for the latter. Both were doctrinaire rather than constructive, and failed to shake themselves free from the hypnotic influence of their divergent dogmas. Designations have changed from time to time, new sections have formed and disappeared in consequence of temporary exigencies, but essentials have remained, and nearly every development of party politics may be traced back to the same original source—to the division of the country into two camps by the doctrines of 1848 and 1867. The opportunism of Tisza, who originally occupied a position midway between Kossuth and Deák, and subsequently abandoned the attitude which he adopted at the time of the negotiation of the Compromise, produced a reaction in the direction of the principles of 1848, and a desire for a larger measure of national independence, the necessary result of the demand for the development of national, Magyar, culture formulated by Count Albert Apponyi,[1] who, though an adherent of the principles of 1867, regarded the Compromise not as a perfect creation, but as a foundation for a satisfactory superstructure. He travelled by another route, but in the same direction as the Party of Independence, which aimed at the gradual realisation of the principles of the Party of 1848, its direct progenitor. The result was the adoption of a constructive policy which does not imply the alteration of the Compromise by the importation of new clauses, but the giving of the proper meaning to Law xii., and the carrying of the provisions of that enactment to

---

[1] See *Apponyi Albert Gróf Beszédei*, Budapest, 1897, *Speech on the Army Bill, 1889*, p. 561 *sqq*.

their logical conclusion, the essence of which is independence of economic control, and the abolition of the emblems of military subordination to Austria. Few comprehensive programmes can be realised at once, and in their entirety, but everything points to the ultimate triumph of the principles of 1848, which in fact meet with far more general acceptance now than at any period since the inception of the so-called Revolution. Francis Kossuth revives the principles of the old Party of Independence; Count Andrássy represents all that is best in the "gentry," the backbone of Tisza's *régime*; Count Zichy the conservative, clerical element; Count Albert Apponyi the national conception of the essentiality of distinctive Magyar culture, the Magyar idea. The existence of such a combination is an object lesson in patriotism, enlightened or mistaken, and a proof of the intensity of the national conviction that the time has come to give the Compromise its correct interpretation with a view to placing Hungary on a footing of complete military and economic equality with Austria, and of giving her her proper place in the family of European nations. It is for Hungary, and Hungary's King, to decide whether such revision would diminish rather than increase her ability to answer the requirements of the sole obligation imposed on her by the Pragmatic Sanction. Austria also complains of the Compromise, and the fact that she does so shows that she was not actuated by good faith at the time of its acceptance, that she intended it to lead to the practical absorption of Hungary, and believed that the institution of the common Ministers and Delegations would give her a veiled but complete control. If she complains that she bears 70 per cent of the cost, and has only 30 per cent of the influence on common affairs, let her withdraw her opposition to the dissolution of the limited partnership into which she entered with the intention that, for Hungary, the "parity" referred to in the contract should mean inequality as regards rights and equality as regards the sharing of financial burdens.

As matters now stand, finance is common only so far as it is concerned with the question of the relative proportions in which each country bears the expenses of such military and foreign affairs as are treated as common. How Hungary's share of such expenses is to be met is a question for the decision of the Hungarian Parliament, without the consent of which no foreign loan can be contracted on the joint credit of the two countries.[1] The quota or ratio of contribution is decided by two deputations from Parliament and the Reichsrath respectively, hitherto consisting of fifteen members, ten from the Lower and five from the Upper House. If the deputations cannot agree, each communicates its own conclusions to its own Legislative Assembly, and failing agreement between Parliament and Reichsrath, the decision of the question at issue is left to the King-Emperor as umpire, whose award, according to Austrian law, fixes the quota for twelve months only, whereas the quota-laws of 1867, 1878, and 1887 fixed it in each case for a period of ten years. In 1867 Austria naturally did its best to make Hungary pay dearly for independence. Of the two commissions appointed for the purpose of fixing the quota, the Hungarian proposed that the taxable capacity of the two countries, as shown by the relative percentage of revenue produced by each during the past six years, should be adopted as the basis for assessment, the result of which would have been that Hungary would have borne 28 per cent of the common expenses. Though it may safely be presumed that Hungary had been taxed by Austria up to the limits of its capacity during the period of subordination, the Austrian commission began by demanding 38 per cent, but finally agreed to fix the respective proportions at 70 and 30 per cent for the

[1] xii. 1867, sections 53, 57.

ensuing ten years.[1]   At that period the common expenses, after deduction of customs receipts, amounted to 77,000,000 florins,[2] consequently, the difference to Hungary between 28 per cent and 30 per cent was 1,500,000 florins per annum, a difference which was largely increased as the common expenses grew.   In 1879 the proportions were assessed at 68.5 and 31.4 respectively.   In 1898, as the two parties failed to agree, Francis Joseph fixed the quota at $66\frac{4}{19}$ and $33\frac{3}{19}$, to which latter figure must be added a proportionate part of 2 per cent, by which Hungary's share was increased, in accordance with Law iv. of 1872, on account of the reincorporation of the frontier districts, raising Hungary's percentage to 34.4 of the common expenses.[3]   These latter, as provided by Sect. 64 of Law xii. of 1867, have to be paid in the first instance out of the proceeds of the common customs receipts[4] (so long as a customs alliance exists between the two countries), from which all drawbacks have also to be deducted.   The balance required has to be made up by the two countries in the proportions fixed by the quota-deputations, or by the umpire, as the case may be. The unfairness of the system is patent, as each country has to bear the burden of the payments of drawbacks not to an extent proportionate to its export trade in a given article, but to an amount proportionate to the ratio in which it contributes to the common expenses.   Drawbacks should have been paid from the first either by the exporting country or from the common fund, by debiting each country with an amount proportionate to the total drawbacks payable in respect of its own export trade; but this would not have suited Austria.   The result of a one-sided arrangement was that Austria, which produces

[1] Law xiv. 1867.
[2] Ság Manó, *Austridhozvaló Gazdasdgi Viszonyunk. 1526-tól napjainkig*, Budapest, 1907, p. 36.
[3] From 1907, 36.4 per cent; see below, p. 289.
[4] These provide for about one-third of the common expenses.

beer and sugar to a large extent specially for export purposes, while Hungary produces chiefly for home consumption, was largely benefited by the drawback system at the expense of Hungary, which contributed annually a large sum in excess of its proper proportion for the encouragement of a branch of Austrian trade which was already far more highly developed than the corresponding Hungarian industry.[1]

It is a common saying that Hungary is not a manufacturing country, and therefore is not interested in, or entitled to make its voice heard on, economic questions to the same extent as Austria ; but those who presume to settle a complicated question by an offhand pronouncement of this nature do not take the trouble to inquire why Hungary has not yet attained the same degree of commercial development as Austria, which ever since the days of Charles III.[2] deliberately defeated Hungary's attempts to emerge from a condition of commercial subordination, and to cease to depend for its existence on the production of raw materials for the benefit of the Austrian manufacturer.   But for this deliberate policy of suppression there is no apparent reason why Hungarian manufacture should not have developed to the same extent, and on the same lines, as that of Austria.   In Maria Theresa's reign, goods imported from abroad into Hungary paid a 30 per cent duty unless imported through an Austrian middleman (in which case a 5 per cent rebate was allowed), while those imported into Austria paid one of 5 to 20 per cent.   Vienna forbade

----

[1] In 1894, of the total amount of beer *exported*, Hungary's proportion was 3.8 per cent ; Austria's was 96.2 per cent.   Of sugar the proportions were : Hungary, 11.5 per cent ; Austria, 88.5 per cent.   Hungary's relative *production* was far greater.—Mudrony Soma, *A Vámkérdés Megoldása,* Budapest, 1896, p. 43 ; Ság Manó, *o.c.* pp. 37, 46.

[2] At the Peace of Passarowitz, 1718, he made a commercial treaty with the Sultan facilitating the import of Turkish raw material into Austria, so as to knock down the price of the Hungarian product.   The Diet protested in vain.

the export of Hungarian cattle except *via* Styria or Carinthia, for transit through which countries heavy duties were imposed. Joseph II. prohibited the direct importation from abroad into Hungary of any goods which could be produced by Austria. Such as were imported through that country paid both customs and transit duty to Austria, which paid nothing on goods intended for re-export, whereas Hungary paid a double export duty. Some slight concessions were obtained in 1807 by the abolition of the scandal which required Hungarian exporters of wine to export an equal quantity of the Austrian product, and of the double import duty ; but the step-motherly treatment to which Hungary was subjected continued practically unabated down to 1848. Some Magyar statesmen, Stephen Széchenyi for example, urged the abolition of the customs barrier erected between the two countries ; others, among whom was Ladislaus Szalay, saw salvation only in the adhesion of Hungary to the German Zollverein ; Kossuth, more far-seeing than his contemporaries, insisted on the necessity of economic independence — an essential part of the independence guaranteed by the Pragmatic Sanction and by Law x. of 1790-91. During the period of absolutism which preceded the birth of the Compromise, Hungary had no opportunity of making her voice heard, and in 1867 no special stress was laid on the economic question. Deák and his coadjutors were statesmen first and political economists afterwards, and data were wanting for the formation of a considered judgment. The result was that the customs barrier fell in the interests of a fatal conception of the merits of uniformity without equality.

"It does not result," says section 58 of Law xii., "from the Pragmatic Sanction that commercial affairs are common affairs, for according to the meaning of the said Pragmatic Sanction the realms of the Hungarian Crown are, by virtue of their juridical severance from the other dominions of the Monarch, entitled to manage their commercial affairs through their responsible Government or Legislature, and to regulate the same by means of customs barriers ; as, however, there are numerous and important points at which the interests of Hungary and those of His Majesty's other dominions come in contact, the Hungarian Parliament is prepared to come to an agreement with respect to commercial matters with a view to the establishment of a customs and commercial alliance from time to time between Hungary on the one hand and the other dominions of His Majesty on the other " (sect. 59). Section 61 provides that such temporary alliance is to be formed on the basis of negotiation in the same way as similar agreements are arrived at by other independent countries. In consequence of this arrangement the effect of commercial agreements already formed by Austria with foreign countries was extended to Hungary, and certain railways which traverse both it and Austria were to be managed on identical principles. Identity of coinage and of the monetary basis was declared to be " not only desirable in the interests of the two parties, but also necessary " ; it was, therefore, provided that on the occasion of the formation of the proposed commercial and customs alliance an agreement should be come to on these matters. Hence, identity of coinage and of the monetary basis is temporary, as is the commercial and customs alliance, and the law declares it to be self-understood that if and so far as no agreement is come to on the above matters, " Hungary retains its right of independent legal control thereof, and all its rights in connexion therewith remain unimpaired." The customs alliance concluded in pursuance of the above in 1867 for ten years was not renewed in 1897, and Hungary became entitled to complete freedom of action. As, however, it declared itself ready to prolong existing arrangements, a prolongation to the end of 1907 was agreed to. Many ideas have

changed since 1867. Within the limits of these pages it
is impossible to do more than give some slight indication
of the circumstances which in the eyes of many necessitate
a change in the economic relations of Hungary and
Austria ; to express a definite opinion on the question
would be presumptuous, at all events on the part of any
Englishman the value of whose views on the fiscal question
in his own country is open to doubt.

Hungary, which in 1867 was, for a variety of reasons,
an almost entirely agricultural country, has since that date
made great strides in the manufacturing line, and agriculture has made an almost equal headway ;[1] but he
would be a bold man who would assert that the progress
discernible is the result of the abolition of the customs
barrier between Austria and Hungary in 1850, and of the
subsequent commercial and fiscal alliance. As a matter of
fact a very short time sufficed to prove the divergent
nature of the commercial interests of the two countries,
and that Hungary, by agreeing to a customs union, had
deprived itself of its only weapon of defence. Want of
money and credit facilities soon caused the resuscitation
of the old question as to the necessity of establishing a
separate national bank. Deficit followed deficit,[2] and the

---

[1] In the ten years ending 1905 the number of hands engaged in manufacturing increased 13.78 per cent in Austria and 26 per cent in Hungary, but
the total number so engaged was 2.73 times as great in the former as in the
latter country. The value of the exports of Hungary was 892,900,000 kronen
in 1882, and of the imports 875,100,000. Twenty years later the figures were :
exports 1,352,600,000, imports 1,215,300,000, an increase of 51.5 per cent and
38.8 per cent. In 1906 the figures were 1,508,800,000 and 1,555,600,000
respectively.—A Magyar K. Kormány, etc. Statistikai Évkönyv, 1907, p. 273.
From 1870 to 1900 the land under cultivation increased 22 per cent. From
1890 to 1900 agricultural produce increased by 23 per cent, the output of iron,
machinery, and metal goods increased 48.4 per cent in the same period, and
that of chemicals, in England a test of prosperity, by 87.6 per cent. Money
invested in banking and kindred institutions amounted to 21,538,000 florins
in 1867, and in 1903 to 654,506,000. In 1867 there were 2285 kilometres
of railway in Hungary ; in 1903 there were 17,703.—Matlekowitz, Közös
Vámterulet, pp. 6, 17, 18, 25, 34, 48 sq.

[2] The budget deficit reached its highest point, 180,000,000 crowns, in 1873.

fact could not long escape attention that Hungary, as an importer of manufactured articles, should derive a large revenue from import duties which increased the cost to the consumer by 8,582,000 florins in 1867, by 12,803,400 in 1868, and by 13,677,500 in 1869,[1] and, if directed into the Hungarian treasury instead of into the pockets of Austrian producers, would vastly improve the financial condition of the country.   It gradually became evident that fiscal uniformity was an expensive luxury, as owing to the protective duties imposed on foreign manufactures for Austria's benefit Hungary could neither buy in the cheapest market nor find an outlet for its own surplus raw materials, for the sale of which it had to compete with the foreigner in the Austrian market, where duties on such produce were either non-existent or insufficiently high to prevent foreign competition.   Hungary began to complain of a fiscal system which was destructive to her growing industry, for the reason that it supplied Austria with cheap raw materials for the production of manufactured articles with which to flood the Hungarian market, one result of which was that Hungary paid the wages of Austria's workmen instead of finding employment for its own population, compelled, in consequence, to emigrate, since agriculture finds work only for a limited number of hands and at certain seasons only.

The result, shortly stated, of tariff uniformity was that Austria had a monopoly in Hungary for its manufactured goods while Hungary had none in Austria for its raw produce, and that the volume of imports from Austria was growing more rapidly than the exports to that country, so the balance in Austria's favour was always on

A surplus was shown for the first time in 1880.   In 1867 a 5 per cent loan cost 8.07 per cent, including sinking fund, to issue, and the whole was not placed.   In 1873 a 6 per cent loan of 153,000,000 with sinking fund cost 10.89 per cent.   Of the 4 per cent conversion loan of 1880 the cost of issuing was 5.39 per cent.—Matlekowitz, o.c. p. 18 sq.

[1] Mudrony Soma, o.c. p. 8.

the increase.[1] In 1894, 348,000,000 florins worth of protected articles were imported by Hungary from Austria, which took similar goods to the value of 55,000,000 florins from Hungary.[2] The balance in Austria's favour was therefore 293,000,000 florins, and as the average duty was 20 per cent, Hungary lost 58,600,000 florins as the result of a protective system maintained for the benefit of the Austrian manufacturer. To take an instance : if 10 per cent was the average duty on cotton goods, it meant that Hungary paid the Austrian manufacturer for the 148,000,000 crowns worth imported from Austria 14,800,000 crowns more than it would have had to pay to the foreigner for similar, and possibly better goods, if there had been no protective duties. If, on the other hand, there were a customs barrier between Austria and Hungary, the importer would pay the extra 10 per cent to the Hungarian Treasury instead of making a present of it to the Austrian producer, the hidden tribute paid to whom, reckoned on the basis of the statistics of 1893, amounted to something between 62,300,000 and 69,500,000 florins.[3] The amount which Hungary would now receive every year from Austria in the shape of duties, if an end were put to the customs union, has been estimated at 150,000,000 crowns ;[4] moreover, the country would benefit by the partial exclusion of Austrian manufactures in consequence of

[1] In 1906, of the total imports into Hungary 76.8 per cent, as regards value, came from Austria, i.e. goods to the value of 1,195,100,000 crowns. Of Hungary's exports 71.1 per cent went to Austria, i.e., goods to the value of 1,072,900,000 crowns.—A Magyar K. Kormány, etc. Statistikai Évkönyv, p. 280.

[2] Mudrony Soma, o.c. p. 22.

[3] Mudrony Soma, o.c. p. 22. In 1872 the hidden tribute was estimated at 25,000,000 to 30,000,000 florins, from which Hungary benefited as regards its share of the customs proceeds to the extent of 5,000,000. Net loss, 20,000,000 to 25,000,000, p. 9. Francis Kossuth estimated the hidden tribute paid in 1898 at 89,656,000 crowns.—K. F. Harmincz Parlamenti Beszéde, p. 205.

[4] Pap David, Kvota, Vámszövetség, Bank.

the impulse which would be given to home industries and by the increased employment of native labour.

The tax on goods imported from abroad is paid by the purchaser in the necessarily enhanced prices paid for such goods, and the price of the protected goods imported from Austria is increased beyond the normal almost by the full amount of the protective duty. If the protective system is effective, foreign competitive products are partially or wholly excluded ; the result therefore is that it is the Austrian manufacturer who is benefited, not the common customs receipts, and Hungary receives comparatively little countervailing advantage in the way of reduced taxation, or of protection for its own produce, of which in the great majority of cases the supply exceeds the home demand, and thus renders protection unnecessary. Forty years ago Hungary's surplus cereals had no protective duties to face in foreign markets, but since 1867 higher and higher duties have been imposed by western nations on agricultural produce. Hungary has now no free market for its produce, save England and Austria (where it is insufficiently protected), and owing to its customs union with the latter country is unable to make its own commercial treaties for the protection of its own interests or to retaliate against unfair competition. Hungary nominally has the right to make its voice heard in the matter of commercial treaties with foreign countries, but to say the least, excessive zeal for the protection of Hungarian interests has not hitherto been a characteristic of the existing system of joint diplomatic representation.

A further grievance was to be found in the fact that down to 1899 the excise or consumption tax on beer and sugar was collected in the producing instead of in the consuming country ; consequently, the Hungarian consumer paid the taxes by which the price of such articles of consumption was increased, not to his own but to the Austrian treasury, which in 1894 received from beer and sugar alone nearly 2,750,000 florins,[1] which should fairly have gone in reduction of Hungarian taxation. If the concealed tribute paid to Austrian manufacturers amounts to no more than 60,000,000 florins per annum, a minimum figure according to some authorities, ten years of compound interest gives a total loss of 750,000,000 florins incurred by Hungary[2] solely for the purpose of increasing the cost of all branches of home production, of making competition with Austria impossible, and of preventing the rearrangement of the basis of taxation which could be effected if even half only of the profits which now go to Austrian pockets were diverted into the Hungarian Treasury. Recent legislation has done little to improve Hungary's economic position. Tisza's new arrangement (1878, xxi.) raised the protective duty on goods which Austria could produce by 50 to 100 per cent, and provided for the payment of duties in gold instead of in silver as formerly. Consequently, Hungary, as the consumer of such goods, had to pay at least 100,000,000 florins more than hitherto, as was shown by, inter alia, the fact that the balance of the common customs receipts, after deducting expenses and drawbacks, jumped from 22,000,000 florins in 1879 to 47,000,000 in 1884.[3] Count Albert Apponyi denounced the new arrangement, and pointed out that the collection of duties in gold instead of in silver meant an average increase on the cost of all goods of 15 per cent, and that the increase in the tariff applied specially to such essential articles as textiles and woollen goods, the duty on which was raised by 50, 100, and even 300 per cent.[4] Thus, the revised Compromise was, economically, even more disastrous than the first edition. Ten years later a new commercial treaty was concluded with Germany, as the result of which the customs tariff on manufactured goods was again raised

---

[1] Mudrony Soma, o.c. p. 42.   [2] Ibid. p. 29.
[3] Ság Manó, o.c. pp. 53-54.   [4] Apponyi Albert Gróf Beszédei, i. 59 sq.

by 15 to 20 per cent to the benefit of the Austrian manufacturer and to the loss of the Hungarian consumer. At the same time a tax was imposed on Hungarian corn, rye, and flour, imported into Germany, which had hitherto entered duty free. Hungary was consoled with the statement that the raising of the tariff was essential to the protection of her nascent industries against foreign competition, but to protect her on one side while the other was left unguarded against the far more highly developed manufacturing industries of Austria was a useless precaution, more especially when competition with that country was rendered still more difficult than it would otherwise have been by the absence of credit facilities, the result of having no National Bank, and by railway rates designed to favour Austrian trade.

1898 was the year of the Bánffy-Badeni negotiations for the renewal of the customs alliance, but parliamentary obstruction, which prevented the passing of the estimates, caused them to be dropped, and the Government resigned. Coloman Szél formed a new Ministry, and he and Dr. Körber resumed negotiations, with the result that Hungary received some compensation for the raising of the quota to 34.4 per cent of the common expenses. Law xv. of 1894 had already provided for the application of the right principle as regards the excise or consumption tax, viz., that the proceeds of the tax on spirits should go to the consuming instead of to the producing country—a reform with which Hungary would willingly have dispensed, as it exported more spirits, the only article to which the new arrangement applied, to Austria than it received from that country. Some compensation for previous injustice was now afforded by the extension of the principle to beer and sugar,[1] and by throwing obstacles in the way of the favourite device of Austrian producers of marking wines and other produce as " made in Hungary," when in reality

---

[1] 1899, xvii. and xxx.

Austria was the country of their origin. A further consideration for the Szél-Körber agreement was the undertaking to revise the system of railway rates in operation, which dated from the period of absolutism, and was obviously detrimental to the interests of Hungarian trade. Unfortunately, promise is not always followed by performance.

Law xii. of 1867 provides for the making from time to time of a commercial and customs alliance between Austria and Hungary to be arrived at by negotiation as between two equal and independent countries, and that as regards indirect taxes, their nature, proportions, and handling, such rules shall be adopted as shall exclude the possibility of one country crippling the resources of the other (sects. 59 and 63). On the other hand, the law declares that the imposition, collection, and handling of taxation is a matter solely for the Hungarian Government, and that, so far as no agreement is come to from time to time with respect to the matters enumerated in sections 58 to 67, Hungary's sovereign rights are unimpaired. Hungary's economic independence is therefore legally complete, subject to the condition already mentioned as to the avoidance of measures calculated to injure the interests of the allied country. It would seem to be a counsel of perfection to prescribe the invention of an economic policy capable of promoting the interests of one country without injury to those of its neighbour. Unquestionably Austria has hitherto failed, for want of ingenuity or goodwill, to devise such a fiscal scheme ; therefore it cannot be a matter for astonishment that Hungary should consider that the time has come to utilise what the law has given it—freedom to work out its own economic salvation on its own lines. On the question of expediency and method Hungary alone has a right to be heard.

Three modes of effecting the desired change naturally suggest themselves—the complete economic separation of

Austria and Hungary; complete separation modified by the assurance of preferential treatment ; maintenance of the alliance for the purpose of negotiation with foreign nations, and separation of the two countries by the re-erection of the customs barrier.   The first alternative would seem to offer the simplest and most satisfactory solution.   Hungary would be free to negotiate its own commercial treaties, without reference to Austria—a freedom which would necessitate separate diplomatic representation, in any case as regards commercial matters, as the interests of the two countries would no longer be, even theoretically, identical. The tribute now paid by Hungary to Austrian manu-facturers would be lost to them, but as Austria denies the fact of payment of such tribute, it would not be entitled to object to its abolition.[1]   The fear that economic separa-tion would injure the interests of Hungarian agriculture would seem to be unfounded, as either the two countries will agree to give each other preferential treatment as against other nations, in which case Hungarian cereals will hold the field in Austria against foreign competition ; or they will not so agree, in which case, as Austria must import agricultural produce, the consumer must pay the full price plus the duty, and, apart from the question of quality, as the freight is less from Hungary to Austria than from elsewhere, the latter must necessarily take its supplies from the former.   If, on the other hand, com-plete separation modified by preferential treatment were effected, matters might be complicated by the attitude which foreign countries might adopt on the strength of the most - favoured - nation clause.   Would they

[1] "It is unquestionable that, except for the Bohemian and Moravian agrarians, no one (in Austria) desires or could tolerate customs separation. For Galicia and Bukovina it is, economically, a matter of indifference ; for the Alpine districts it is dangerous ; for the industry and manufacture of Austria it spells ruin."—Springer, *Grundlagen*, etc. p. 219. The same writer admits that the Hungarian peasantry, who, one might suppose, would fear the loss of the Austrian market, "is heart and soul on the side of the party of Inde-pendence," *o.c.* p. 214.

acquiesce in the new situation or would they demand treatment for their products similar to that accorded by Austria and Hungary to each other's exports? The whole matter is further complicated by the peculiar position of Bosnia and Herzegovina. Are they to become a separate entity for fiscal purposes, or are they to be joined with Dalmatia (which properly belongs to the Magyar Crown) to Hungary, or are they to form a neutral territory to which both Austria and Hungary can send their goods duty free? But, in the first place, Dalmatia forms *de facto*, though not *de jure* part of Austria, which apparently has no intention of relinquishing her hold; in the second place, Austrian goods destined for Bosnia-Herzegovina would have to pass over the Hungarian railways; consequently, unless carried for little or nothing, and free of transit duty, they would have no chance of competing with Hungarian exports. The third alternative, the nominal continuation of the economic union subject to the erection of a customs barrier between Austria and Hungary, might conceivably surmount some at least of the above-mentioned difficulties, but would not remedy the disadvantages under which Hungary labours as regards foreign nations. Hungary might lose such advantages as it now possesses in the Austrian market, and would not be able to compensate the loss, if any, by the independent conclusion of favourable treaties with other countries.

Whichever of the above alternatives is ultimately adopted, one thing seems certain, namely, that no modification of economic relations can be satisfactory to Hungary which does not provide for the establishment of a separate Hungarian National Bank. The notes of the Banks established in Austria by Maria Theresa were circulated in Hungary without the consent of the Diet, but without protest, though the exploitation of the country and the flow of specie to Austria were greatly facilitated by acquiescence in the new departure. Not till 1811 was any objection raised by the Legislature to the continuation of a state of affairs for which no justification could be deduced either from the laws which gave effect to the Pragmatic Sanction, or from any other enactment to be found in the *Corpus Juris*. In that year the Diet passed a resolution enunciating the obvious fact that " the King of Hungary possesses neither the power nor the privilege, either by virtue of any *jus reservatum*, or for any other reason, of issuing notes in Hungary or of putting them into circulation . . . without the consent of the Diet," and discussed the question of establishing a National Hungarian Bank ;[1] but nothing was done, and Austrian notes continued to circulate in Hungary with disastrous results, as we have already seen,[2] to the trader and the taxpayer.

In 1848 the Twelve Points of Pest demanded the establishment of a national banking institution, and in 1867 the question was again mooted, only to be dropped for the reason that insistence on Hungary's undoubted right would have necessitated the grant of a banking monopoly to foreigners for a long term of years, owing to the insufficiency of cash at the disposal of the Government. Temporarily, the country has deprived itself of its liberty of action by granting an exclusive privilege to the Austro-Hungarian Bank, but the privilege lapses in December 1910, and it seems scarcely conceivable that Hungary should again allow its hands to be tied for any considerable period, in view of the fact that a far-reaching reform of the fiscal policy would be incapable of execution without the assistance of a National Bank of issue. In 1907, in order to bring pressure to bear on Hungary with a view to a long term extension of the commercial alliance and to the increase of Hungary's percentage of the common expenditure, Austria threatened to withdraw from an

---

[1] Kmety, *Közjog*, 506, *n*.   [2] *Supra*, i. 250, 257, 258.

arrangement which, so it alleged, is maintained for the benefit of its partner rather than for its own profit. To what extent the allegation is justified is open to question. Presumably the reason for the existence of a National Bank should differ from that for the establishment of a private institution : for whereas the latter exists solely for the purpose of making a profit, the primary object of the former should be the promotion of the commercial and general development of the country by the extension of credit facilities. If this view is correct, we can form an opinion as to the expediency of prolonging an exclusive privilege only by ascertaining the extent to which the common institution, judged from Hungary's point of view, fulfils essential conditions. A recent publication[1] shows, in a tabulated form, the result of the operations of twenty-two branch establishments opened in Hungary and Austria respectively, eleven in each, from 1900 to 1902, from which it appears that those operating in the former country had an average annual turnover of -9,280,000 crowns, while those opened in Austria had an average of only 15,300,000. It shows that in Hungary five branches worked at a loss in 1900, four in 1903, two in 1904, none in 1905, and none in 1906 ; whereas in Austria the corresponding figures were fourteen, fifteen, twenty-one, twenty-two, eighteen, seventeen, and fourteen. In 1906, of the thirty-four Hungarian branches thirty-two earned over 20,000 crowns profit ; of the forty-six Austrian establishments only nineteen could show a similar result. True, the total profit of the Austrian section was larger than that of the Hungarian by 3,100,379 crowns, but the Viennese establishment earned 3,249,464 crowns more than the corresponding institution in Budapest, which shows that, excluding the two capitals, the country and urban branch banks of Hungary have a greater earning capacity than those of Austria, though the former are far

[1] Rózsa Károly, *Magyar Nemzeti Bank*, Budapest, 1907, pp. 18, 20.

less numerous than the latter. It seems not unfair to draw the conclusion from the above figures that the object has been to open branches in Hungary only in places where they would be practically assured of a profit, whereas in Austria the object was the provision of credit facilities and the development of industry, rather than the acquisition of profitable business. Judged, therefore, by the test suggested above, the Austro-Hungarian Bank fulfils its proper functions in Austria, but fails to do so in Hungary.

In the event of a dissolution of partnership taking place, on the basis of the 1905 balance-sheet, Hungary's share of the assets would amount to 346,153,000 crowns in gold and 100,397,000 in silver. In that year the Austro-Hungarian Bank had notes in circulation to the average amount of 1,756,000,000 crowns, and Hungary's share in the total turnover amounted to 35.5 per cent. Therefore, in order to continue to do the same volume of business, Hungary would require a note issue of only 605,000,000 crowns, whereas the amount receivable on the dissolution of partnership would provide a metallic reserve justifying a note issue of roughly 1,000,000,000, without the necessity of having recourse to the public or to foreign sources.[1] When the Austro-Hungarian Bank was established in 1878 the charter provided that of the profits, after 5 per cent had been paid to the shareholders, 10 per cent should be carried to reserve, and that after the payment of a further 2 per cent, making the total dividend 7 per cent, surplus profits should be divided between the two countries in the proportion of seventy to thirty. This arrangement was clearly unfair to Hungary, as each country should have shared in the surplus, either according to the proportion in which it contributed to the earning of a profit, or it should have received a share corresponding to the proportion in which it contributed to the expense of common affairs. The adoption of either

1 Rózsa Károly, *Magyar Nemzeti Bank*, p. 46 *sq.*

principle of distribution would have materially increased Hungary's percentage. Hungary was also unfairly treated by the provision that no more than 50,000,000 florins should be applied to loan and discount purposes, though, on the average, notes to the amount of nearly 330,000,000 florins were in circulation in that country.[1] This limitation was, in fact, removed by Law xxxvii. of 1899, which declared that it is the Bank's duty to promote the interests of traders and agriculturists—a declaration which affords confirmatory evidence of the view that the common Bank had not hitherto served the essential object of its establishment.

Hungary's right to have its own Bank is undisputed. It is clearly implied by Law xii. of 1867 (the Compromise), and was expressly affirmed by Law xxv. of 1878, at the time of the establishment of the common institution. The question of expediency is another matter. It awaits the decision of the Hungarian Parliament, the only competent tribunal, the result of whose solution of the problem presented by the economic relations of Austria and Hungary is of importance to the whole of Europe, for the possible failure to arrive at a satisfactory arrangement is the one dangerous element in the situation. So long as one country tries to keep the other in a position of economic subordination harmony is impossible. Here, it seems, is a case where union is not necessarily strength, where separation alone is capable of removing the chief cause of dissension, and of producing a friendly union, for the attainment of which the sacrifice of outward uniformity would be a small price to pay. It is sometimes suggested that the Magyars should acquiesce in the existing situation for fear of weakening Austria's feeling of solidarity with a sister nation, and of risking disintegration of the Habsburg monarchy ; but why should Hungary buy Austria's goodwill by sacrificing its own vital interests ? In the first place, dualism and commercial union have nothing in

[1] Ság Manó, o.c. pp. 52, 53.

common ; in the second place, no sacrifice will buy the affection of the Luegers, Schönerers, and Pan-Germans.

The reader will form his own opinion as to the expediency of economic separation ; the object of the foregoing pages will have been attained if they have convinced him of the erroneousness of the view not infrequently expressed in England, that the wish for such separation is merely the product of Magyar chauvinism and megalomania. Hungary's right to a separate customs territory was expressed in recent years by Law xxx. of 1899, and by Law iii. of 1906, which established a separate customs tariff ; but the former law was a one-sided expression of independence recognised by Austria only by the medium of an imperial ordinance, and the latter amounted to no more than a theoretic gain, as the independent tariff was identical in all respects with the Austrian one. By the new Compromise negotiated with Austria at the close of 1907, Hungary obtains complete recognition of its right to economic independence, and attains a position *vis-à-vis* Austria and the rest of the world which, whatever its strict constitutional rights may have been, it in fact never occupied since Mohács. The customs alliance (Zoll und Handels-Bündniss, Vám-szövetség) is replaced by a customs treaty (Zollvertrag, Vámszerzódés) such as might exist between any two completely distinct and independent countries, and Hungary's autonomous tariff receives formal confirmation. Hungary's hands are still tied to some extent by the fact that commercial treaties with the most important foreign nations do not expire till December 31, 1917, and thus exclude the possibility of complete separation till their expiry, and necessitate the continuance of reciprocity between Austria and Hungary for a further period of ten years. After 1917 Hungary will obtain entire liberty to negotiate its own commercial treaties without reference to Austria. Treaties which expire before December 31,

1917, can be renewed only for the period which intervenes between their expiry and that date.   In the case of such renewal taking place Hungary will play the part of an independent contractant, and the treaties will be drawn up in the French, German, and Magyar languages.   Henceforth such treaties will be made in the names of the two countries, Austria and Hungary, not only in the name of Francis Joseph on behalf of a single customs territory.[1] They will still be signed by the common Minister of Foreign Affairs, but in order to give expression to the independence of Hungary they will also be signed by a Hungarian as well as by an Austrian representative. Questions arising out of the economic relations of the two countries will be decided by a Court of Arbitration, half the members of which will be appointed by Hungary and half by Austria.   The Court, the President of which will be chosen by lot, will sit alternately in Vienna and Budapest, and will be guided by rules based on those adopted at the first meeting of the Hague Conference. No question can be submitted to it which affects the sovereignty or juridical relations of the two parties to the new arrangement, which thus stand on precisely the same footing as regards each other as any two completely independent nations which have adopted the principle of arbitration for the settlement of possible disputes.   The Bank necessarily continues to be a joint institution, in accordance with Law xxxvi. of 1899, but only till December 31, 1910, after which date Hungary's freedom of action is regained.   Should the Government decide to prolong the existing privilege of the Austro-Hungarian Bank, the unity of coinage and the monetary basis will necessarily be maintained ; if the privilege is not prolonged, the possibility of inconvenience as regards the free exchange of coinage and the maintenance of relative values is

[1] Hitherto, with the exception of the Brussels Sugar Convention of 1902 and the commercial treaty with Switzerland 1906, such treaties had been signed only by the common Minister of Foreign Affairs.

obviated by fixing the value of the gold crown as the medium of exchange for the purpose of all matters in which the two countries come in financial contact.[1]

Other practical as well as theoretical gains result to Hungary from the revised Compromise of 1907. The consumption tax is henceforth a matter solely for Hungary, which is no longer under an obligation to consult Austria's convenience, or to act on identical lines with that country. After 1910 Austrian and Hungarian flour will be placed on an equal footing in Dalmatia, where hitherto the consumption tax was levied chiefly on the Hungarian product. An end will now be put to the fraudulent marking of Austrian goods with Hungarian names in order to deceive the purchaser as to the country of origin, and to Austrian falsification of Hungarian wines. Henceforward foreigners will be able to obtain protection for trade-marks and designs in Hungary without reference to Austria, whereas hitherto such protection could be obtained in the former country only if it was also afforded in the latter. With respect to the Post and Telegraph service Hungary obtains complete independence as regards both internal matters and international negotiation. Against these gains, which, taken as a whole, amount to unconditional recognition of Hungary's right to economic independence, must be set the fact that Hungary agreed to the raising of the quota or proportion in which it contributes to the common expenses by 2 per cent, making its share of such expenses for the next ten years 36.4 as against the 63.6 payable by Austria.

For the present it is idle to speculate as to what will happen after the expiry of that period. For the moment it suffices to indicate the fact that the objections of the party of Independence to the new assessment are based, not so much on the relative proportion of Hungary's

[1] See the Prime Minister's (Wekerle's) speech, Oct. 16, 1907, *Budapesti Hirlap*.

share, as on the fundamental fact of the continued existence
of relations which necessitate the negotiation of such
assessment.[1] Economic separation in no way affects the
principle of dualism.   Neither the Pragmatic Sanction
nor the Compromise of 1867 imposes any limitation on
Hungary's right to financial independence save that resulting from the necessity of making provision for the
military protection of the King's other dominions.   The
law of 1867 makes no essential change in the obligation of
mutual defence necessarily arising from, though not
expressly mentioned by, the law of 1723.   The problem
confronting the authors of the Compromise was the
discovery of some solution of the questions at issue which
would involve no infringement of Hungary's rights as a
sovereign State, and at the same time would avoid the
risk of weakening the military forces of the monarchy.
After Königgrätz Deák could, it may be, have compelled Francis Joseph to consent to the establishment of a
completely separate Hungarian army, but he did not do
so, his object being to effect a settlement for all time, and
to leave no loophole for the readmission of international
hostility and complications.   Even the so-called revolutionary laws of 1848 did not contemplate anything
approaching complete military separation, though had
they done so no constitutional objection could have been
raised.   According to Law iii. of that year the employment
of the Hungarian army and the making of military
appointments were matters for the King's decision, subject
to the countersignature, not of the Hungarian Minister
of War, who was only Minister of Home Defence, but of
the Minister in attendance on the royal person, who,

---

[1] See the speech of Francis Kossuth, October 17, 1907.   He estimates the
amount of the additional burden placed on Hungary at 4,800,000 crowns, to
which must be added 350,000 loss on the abolition of the tax on Austrian
shipping.   Total on the debit side, 5,150,000 crowns per annum.   The gains
he calculates at 5,530,000, including the annual saving effected by the arrangement which provides for the conversion of the so-called Hungarian Block, i.e.
Hungary's share of the Joint Debt.

according to section 13, was entrusted with the representation of Hungary's interests in common affairs, the existence of which thus received express recognition. Deák's speech of August 3, 1868,[1] clearly shows that he at all events never contemplated the establishment of a separate army. In his view, Law viii. of 1715, "a bad law for Hungary," had made the army a "common" institution, and he thought it wise to be satisfied with the maintenance of Hungary's ancient right of voting money and recruits for the Hungarian army, or regiments, which ever since 1715 had, practically if not theoretically, always formed a complementary part of the whole Austro-Hungarian forces. Deák's intention is clear, but it is doubtful whether Law xii., strictly interpreted, bears the meaning which he intended should be assigned to it. It is equally clear that the Committee deliberately accepted Deák's interpretation,[2] at the expense of the strict constitutional rights of the country ; for, in view of the fact that the Pragmatic Sanction was, and was expressed to be, the sole basis of the Compromise, there can be no doubt that Tisza was right in insisting on the fact that the law of 1723 had made the obligation of defence " common," but not the organs of defence.

From the earliest times the Constitution recognised the necessity of vesting the chief command of the national forces in the King, whose rights as War-Lord were derived from the law, and could be exercised only in accordance with the law under the constitutional control afforded by the exclusive right of the Diet as regards the voting of money and recruits. As we have seen, the King had no *jus reservatum* different or superior to the rights of the nation : only a delegated right, conferred by custom or by law, and, consequently, capable of being abrogated or modified by legislative enactment of the

---

[1] Kónyi, *Deák Ferencz Beszédei*, v. 447 *sqq.* See also vol. iv. 693 *sqq.* for his and Tisza's views.

[2] See Count Julius Andrássy's speech in the Upper House, April 5, 1888.

two, for this purpose equal, factors—King and Nation. As all laws duly enacted by those two factors are of equal binding force, and maintain their validity until abrogated by subsequent express enactment or necessary implication, the whole of Law xii. of 1867 must be interpreted by the light of previous unrepealed legislation, bearing in mind the fact that the right of leadership of the Hungarian forces was originally conferred, not on the Archduke of Austria, or on the Holy Roman Emperor, but on the Magyar King ; and that if at the present day there is a "common" army, it is at all events not a common Austrian army, but is a "whole" army made up of two distinct factors, each of which is commanded by a person who derives his authority from two entirely distinct sources. Further, it must be remembered that the obligation of common defence deriving from the Pragmatic Sanction is conditional on the complete maintenance of Hungary's constitutional independence, and that as the King's right to command the Hungarian forces exists solely by virtue of his constitutional kingship, his rights as War-Lord are necessarily subject to the limitations imposed by unrepealed legislation, and by the fact that the royal prerogative is defined as "constitutional" by Law xii.[1] *i.e.* limited by law and custom, and by Law ii. of 1867, which incorporates the coronation oath by which Francis Joseph swore to maintain all Hungary's privileges, legal customs, and laws, passed and to be passed by Parliament. Consequently, the royal right of command and the control of the internal organisation of the Hungarian forces, re-affirmed but not created by Law xii. of 1867, implies no more than that the King is Commander-in-Chief in war and in peace, can delegate his authority as such to another, and has the exclusive right of appointing to military offices. The limited nature of his authority is shown by the fact that though the right of regulating disciplinary

---

[1] Sect. 11.

punishment would appear to be a necessary corollary of the prerogative of supreme command, such is not the case, as Parliament has maintained its right of interference in matters of internal organisation, as is proved by the abolition of corporal punishment by Law xl. of 1868,[1] as well as by the necessity of obtaining the counter-signature of the responsible Minister of War to give validity to the exercise of royal authority.

By Clause 2 of Law xii. it is provided that the "common security" is to be maintained by the "united" forces of the two countries, and by Clause 4 Hungary undertakes to do what is "unavoidably required" for the maintenance of the common security, but refuses to undertake any obligation the acceptance of which is not essential to the attainment of the object in view. The test, therefore, of Hungary's obligations was essentiality for the purposes of the common defence of Austria and Hungary, and where no essential modifications of the rights of the King and nation were deemed to be required, and were effected by Law xii., previous legislation retains its validity. The Hungarian forces are described by Law xii. as the Magyar army, not as forming part of a "common army," but as a complementary part of the "whole army,"[2] and as such are subject to the Hungarian laws and the Hungarian Government (Clause 14), save in so far as the latter has abandoned its rights in favour of the King. In this, as in other particulars, the Austrian law of December 21, 1867, is an incorrect version of the corresponding Hungarian law, for it fails to give expression to the constitutional independence of Hungary, the maintenance of which was a condition precedent to the adoption of the Compromise. "Das Kriegswesen des Heeres" is declared to be common to the kingdoms and lands represented in

---

[1] Kmety, Közjog, p. 225.

[2] The wrong expression "common army" first appears in a ministerial order of January 30, 1870. It first appears in a Law in 1875 (li.), and is repeated by vi. 1889.

the Reichsrath, and to the lands of the Hungarian Crown
—a general and misleading statement which implies that
Hungary, as regards military matters, is on precisely the
same footing as the hereditary provinces. The command
and inner organisation of the army are expressed to be a
matter for the Kaiser only, whereas, in reality, as regards
Hungary, they are a matter for the King, whose powers
are subject to entirely different limitations to those
imposed on the Kaiser of a pseudo-constitutional country.
The attempt to misconstrue the phrase "whole army"
as "common army" was the last manifestation of the
traditional policy, the object of which was to produce the
appearance, at least, of something more than a personal
union, and to justify the deliberate austrianisation of the
army[1] by insistence on the use of a Habsburg flag and
of the German language of command.

As regards the latter, from the purely legal point of
view the Magyars occupy an unassailable position. No
law has ever declared that German shall be the language
of the Hungarian forces; on the contrary, in Law xvi.
of 1790-91, "*de non introducenda pro negotiis quibuscunque
lingua peregrina*" (*i.e.* German), "His Majesty assures
the Estates and Orders that a foreign language shall not
be introduced in any governmental business of any nature
whatsoever," and this law and others of a like character
have never been repealed.[2] The question of the language

---

[1] Down to October 17, 1889, the army was incorrectly styled *Kaiserliche-
Königliche*, when Hungary insisted that it should be *Kaiserliche und Königliche*—apparently a trifling distinction, but one which gave expression to an
important principle.

[2] See 1807, i. sect. 9, *re* the difficulty of obtaining recruits because of the
non-Hungarian-speaking officers. His Majesty undertakes to appoint only
such officers as can speak the national language. 1808, ii. sect. 20 enacts that
Hungarian is to be the language of command in the special regiments then
voted. 1808, vi. sect. 5, recruits are under no pretext to be assigned to other
than Hungarian regiments. The Royal Order of August 6, 1868, provided
that Hungarian officers are to be appointed to Hungarian regiments, a confirmation of the validity of the Law of 1840 already referred to.—See Kmety,
o.c. p. 464 *sq.*; see also *supra*, ii. 44.

of command is therefore purely a question for the Hungarian Parliament and the King of Hungary, and neither Reichsrath, Delegations, nor common Ministers have any *locus standi* to make their voice heard in the matter; for it is a question merely of expediency, and an alteration of the existing system would import no change into the common affairs arising out of the Pragmatic Sanction, but only into the method of dealing with such affairs. The reply is commonly made that Hungary has denuded itself of the right to interfere in matters affecting the internal organisation of the army, but this is not so. Hungary has given certain defined rights to the Hungarian King, who, as a constitutional monarch, can exercise such rights only in accordance with unrepealed laws and immemorial practice; and both law and practice are unimpeachable witnesses in favour of Parliament's right to interfere in practically all matters of internal organisation,[1] except the supreme command and the appointment of officers. Neither directly nor by implication has Parliament renounced its control either of civil or military education.[2] There is not a word on the subject of military education, or of education in general, in the law of 1867, and everything which has not been expressly made a common affair, or an affair of common interest, is necessarily a purely Hungarian affair.

Englishmen, who are in general incapable of realising the meaning of the phrase " a nation in arms," or the

[1] Ever since the establishment of a regular army in 1715 the Diet exercised the right of interfering in its internal organisation. See *supra*, ii. 42-45, and Kmety, *o.c.* p. 226, *re* vote of recruits, conditions, and period of service, the fixing of the relative numbers of cavalry and infantry, the civic rights and obligations of men serving with the colours, and the provisioning of the troops. See also previous note. Section 12 of xii. 1867, reserves to Hungary its old right of voting the annual contingent *under such conditions* as it may choose to impose. Obviously it could refuse the vote if dissatisfied as to the language of command, flag, etc. Further, an alteration of the existing system of defence can take place only with the consent of the Hungarian Legislature, sect. 13.

[2] Law vii. of 1808, *re* the Ludoviceum or Military Academy, shows that the Diet had not abandoned its right of interference.

effect of universal service on the national character, are necessarily disposed to take a narrow view of the question of military education, and to condemn the Magyars off hand for desiring to prevent the possible denationalisation of the younger generation by training in a foreign language in non-Magyar surroundings. It was no narrow chauvinism which prompted Count Albert Apponyi[1] to emphasise the necessity of magyarising military instruction, and of providing facilities for higher military education in Hungary in order to prevent the diminution of attachment to the Magyar idea. There is as little justification for the germanisation of Hungarian military education as there would be for the magyarisation of that of the German-speaking population of Austria.[2] The nationalities of Hungary should fairly be instructed in the language of the Magyar State, and not in that of the Germans of Austria, who, by insisting on the continuation of German military instruction, contribute to the difficulties which lie in the way of the

[1] See his speech on the Army Bill of 1889, already referred to.—*Beszédei*, i. 470 *sqq.*, 561 *sqq.*

[2] If German were the language of the majority of the population of the two countries it would be another matter, but it is the language of not more than 20 per cent of the population—a dwindling minority. German was justifiably the language of command at a time when there was a long-service army (ten years or more with the colours gave time to acquire a proper knowledge) but not in the days of short service of two or three years. As half the German-speaking soldiers are in exclusively German-speaking regiments, the rest forms an inconsiderable fraction of the rank and file of the other regiments to which it is desired to give a purely German character. Only 24 per cent of the army is German ; 22 per cent is Hungarian. It seems idle to the layman to suggest that the use of different words of command by the lower grade officers of different regiments would impair the fighting efficiency of the troops in view of the fact that in actual fighting signals of bugle or whistle to a great extent are substitutes for spoken words. The impossibility of maintaining the exclusive use of German is shown by the fact that it is now no longer necessary to know that language to become a non-commissioned officer. Of the Hungarian soldiers 55 per cent are Magyar, and 70 per cent can speak Hungarian. The question of the language of command is temporarily in abeyance by agreement between the King and the leaders of the Coalition (April 15th, 1906) pending the election of a new Parliament on the basis of universal suffrage.

magyarisation of the subordinate races of Hungary. The question of the practical result of having two separate armies, the officers of which would command their men in Hungarian or in German as the case might be, must be left to the judgment of those who are competent to form an opinion, which, to be of value, requires a knowledge, to which the writer of this book can make no claim, of past military history, and of the present practice in armies composed of soldiers of diverse nationalities. It is often suggested in England that if Hungary had a separate army, Bohemia also would be entitled to have one ; and that if Hungarian were the language of command for the Hungarian forces, all the small nationalities of Hungary would want to be commanded in their own tongue, with the result that half a dozen languages would require to be used for the command of a single regiment. The answer is obvious. In the first place, Bohemia is an integral part of the hereditary provinces of Austria, not an independent sovereign State like Hungary ; in the second place, apart from the impossibility of splitting the Hungarian regiments into companies and half companies composed solely of the members of subordinate nationalities, the State is Hungary, the land of the Magyars, and Magyar is the language of State. Hungary as such has no technical corps, no general staff, and those aspiring to higher commands must go to a Staff College where the language of instruction is German and the *esprit de corps* is Austrian, and necessarily destructive of the feeling of distinctive Magyar nationality.[1] The germ of

---

[1] There are more than 3000 Austrian officers in Hungarian regiments. There are fifteen military schools in Austria, and only seven in Hungary, and those are not in the essentially Magyar centres. The result is that some thousand Hungarian cadets go to Austria for their military education. See *Budapesti Hirlap*, December 22, 1907. It is suggested that the insufficiency of Magyar officers and the dislike for military service in time of peace would disappear if there were a distinctively Hungarian army and distinctively Magyar military education. Hungarian regiments could be so organised as to consist of 70 per cent of Magyar-speaking soldiers. Hungarian regi-

a separate army already exists in the Honvéd, or army of home defence, which is far more than the Landwehr of other countries, for it is not a mere reserve formed of those who have served their time with the colours, but an independent force kept on foot by the incorporation of a fixed annual contingent of recruits. This body cannot be called upon to serve outside Hungary, except with the consent of Parliament, or, should Parliament not be sitting, by an order signed by the whole Ministry, and requiring subsequent ratification by Parliament. The flag and the language of command are Hungarian, and the connexion with the common army consists only in the King's right of supreme command, which gives him no authority to compel Hungarians to fight under an Austrian flag, a symbol of non-existent unity, as Law xxi. of 1848 provided for the use of the national colours, and that has never been repealed. The development of this germ into a separate army with its own flag, corps of engineers and artillery, and general staff, is a question of expediency, and one for the decision only of the Hungarian people and its King. Clause 2 of the law of 1867 clearly indicates that the King's right of supreme command is derived, not from that law, but from previous legislation with which Austria had nothing to do, and section 13 says no more than that it is expedient, not imperative, that similar principles should be observed in both countries. Even if Law xii. had *expressis verbis* made the army common, it could cease

men s would be quartered only in Hungary, and would be commanded only by Magyar-speaking officers. It is often said that as Hungary provides only 41 per cent of the recruits for the whole army, and as its share of common expenses is 36 4 per cent, Austria bears an excessive share of the military burden. The answer is that in proportion to the relative wealth of the two countries Hungary still pays too much. With separation of the army into two distinct forces, Austrian and Hungarian, Hungary's expenses would be increased, but the extra cost involved would be more than recouped by the gain resulting from customs separation, and by the fact that Hungary would spend its own money at home instead of in Austria.

to be so at any moment by agreement between King and nation, and Austria would have no right to object : for the Compromise of 1867 was made between the Magyars and their King, not between the Magyars and Austria. The possibility of arriving at such an agreement is another matter, for the case of General Janszky [1] and the army order of Chlopy [2] are incidents which clearly show what Francis Joseph's feelings are. At the same time they prove that public opinion can compel his withdrawal from an indefensible position, and can force the tardy concession of an ell where the prompt concession of an inch might allay the feeling of resentment generated by Francis Joseph's inability, or unwillingness, to cease to subordinate the Hungarian King to the Austrian Emperor.

[1] On the anniversary of the recapture of Buda by the Magyars from the Austrians under General Hentzi, General Janszky took the opportunity of making an anti-Magyar demonstration by ostentatiously, in company with his officers, visiting the burial-place of Hentzi (whose statue in Buda was for many years a national eyesore and reminder of the period of Austrian tyranny) and laying a wreath on his grave. Tisza protested against the tactless act, and excitement increased when General Edelsheim Gyulai, who objected to Janszky's action, was retired from the service and Janszky was promoted. Francis Joseph had to write and explain that the motive of the retirement and promotion was misinterpreted, but the incident left a bad feeling, and gave Count Albert Apponyi a good opportunity for insistence on the necessity of magyarising military education to prevent the denationalisation of the younger generations.—See his speech, *Apponyi Albert Gróf Beszédei*, i. 459 *sqq.*

[2] September 14, 1903, when Francis Joseph expressed himself as firmly resolved to allow nothing to interfere with the indivisibility of the common army, "though the bonds of union are threatened by one-sided aspirations which fail to comprehend the exalted nature of the mission fulfilled by the army for the welfare of both countries." Five months later he was compelled to recede from his previous uncompromising attitude, and to make concessions on military questions to Hungary.

CHAPTER XX

THE army question constitutes a problem for the jurist, as well as for the authority on military matters, and can no more be settled by the *obiter dicta* of foreign critics than the problem presented by the existence of fragmentary nationalities can be settled by the ill-considered intervention of foreign celebrities of the magnitude of Björnson and Tolstoi, whose *a priori* condemnation of British action in South Africa should make Englishmen hesitate to attach undue importance to his criticisms of an Anglophil nation. British public opinion has, apparently, arrived at the conclusion that the Magyars are consistently guilty of the employment of methods of barbarism in their treatment of subordinate races. Trial by newspaper, condemnation without investigation, are such labour-saving processes that their employment is naturally popular, more especially when the means of forming a considered opinion are not easily accessible. The Magyars are themselves largely to blame for the fact that judgment has been allowed to be passed on them on the *ex parte* statements of self-interested agitators and of humanitarian philosophers, and that they are left to console themselves with the conviction that the abuse of which they are made the target is begotten of ignorance of actual facts, of past history, and of the vital considerations of national expediency. The problem presented by the persistence of minor nationalities is not confined to Hungary, but affects a large part of Europe, from Ireland to Bessarabia, and the measure of the abuse lavished by the spectator of the process of absorption, which is going on as slowly and as surely now as in the past, is in inverse proportion to the magnitude of the absorbing nation. What Russia does, and has done with impunity, would have evoked the thunders of Exeter Hall if perpetrated by a weaker country. Wreschen passes almost unperceived,[1] while a petty Slovák village earns European notoriety through the disturbances resulting from the dismissal of a disorderly priest.[2] The Irishman and the Pole has a recent historical basis for their claims to independent existence, as well as the justification of antiquity, which is wanting in the case of the fragmentary nationalities of Hungary.

The aboriginal population of what is now Hungary— scattered, incohesive tribes incapable of resisting Magyar arms, or, later Magyar civilisation—died out or was absorbed by the superior race. The process of civilisation was purely Magyar. The development of governmental institutions proceeded along purely Magyar lines, and bore hardly a trace of either Slav, or, save for the fact that Latin was the literary medium, of Western influence. As we have seen, the mass of the existing nationalities was imported, or filtered into, the country long after it had received a permanent Magyar stamp—desirable or undesirable aliens, who, in most cases, repaid the hospitality they received by lending themselves to the disruptive policy of the Habsburgs. The disappearance or absorption of the aborigines was due, not to fire or sword or violent compulsion, but to

[1] It must not be forgotten that the Poles in Germany number only about 3,000,000 out of over 61,000,000, consequently the Polish question is not a question of life and death for the dominant race as the question of nationalities is in Hungary.

[2] For the true version of the events of which Csernova was the scene, the English reader should see Count Joseph's Mailáth's article in the *Contemporary Review*, August, 1908, p. 218 *sqq.*

the essential superiority of the Magyar nation, so convinced of that superiority that it never saw the necessity of magyarising races which, in early days, having no conscious feeling of individuality, would have been as wax to receive the permanent impress of Magyar nationality. The gates were opened wide to European culture from the time of St. Stephen, whose maxim, "*regnum unius linguae uniusque moris debile et imbecille*, shows his recognition of the fact that the only language and civilisation which had hitherto counted for anything in Hungary was the Magyar, as well as his appreciation of the benefits derivable from contact with the West. There is no approximately pure race in Europe except the Basques, the Jews, and the Gipsies, but there are many countries in which the factors have existed which produce the fusion of heterogeneous elements into a single nation[1]—common recollection of dangers surmounted, common history, common religion, and common civilisation. Such factors were largely wanting in Hungary. The dangers surmounted were surmounted by the Magyars, who alone did the fighting, the bearing of arms in defence of the fatherland being the privilege of the nobility. There was no common history, for history was made solely by the Magyars. There was no community of religion, as St. Stephen turned to Rome for the national religion instead of to the Eastern Church, thereby, in all probability, saving the Magyars from degeneration to the level of the Balkan races, and from ultimate absorption in the ocean of Slavdom. Civilisation, such as it was, was purely Magyar, and all governmental institutions were directly developed from the germ evolved by the Magyar national genius before the great migration westwards. The races imported into Hungary at a later date arrived too late to alter accomplished facts

[1] British critics commonly suggest that there are no Magyars. It would be as reasonable to say that there are no English, in fact more so, as the English race is more composite. But future generations will probably agree in regarding Edward VII. and Benjamin Disraeli as Englishmen.

even if they had possessed a far higher degree of civilisation
than any of them had in fact attained.   What they chiefly
cared for was freedom to exercise their various religions,
and such freedom they received at the hands of Hungary,
the land *par excellence* of religious tolerance.   The better
class aliens received the rights of nobility or became fused
in the Magyar nation.   The inferior elements remained
apart, in a condition neither better nor worse than that of
the great mass of Magyar peasants, and had little or no
consciousness of distinctive nationality, or power to resist a
deliberate policy of magyarisation, had such a policy ever
entered the heads of the predominant race, which, unfortunately, it never did.[1]   Unfortunately, for the reason that
successive Habsburgs were enabled to utilise the forces of
ignorance for the purposes of their traditional policy of
divide ut imperes—of centralisation and absolutism.   For
the existence of hostility to the Magyar idea, tentative and
embryonic before 1848, the Magyars have to thank, in the
first place, their own consciousness of a superiority which
made deliberate magyarisation superfluous, and, in the
second place, the Habsburg connexion.[2]   There never has

---

[1] The nationalities were never interfered with as regards their language and
habits, and for eight centuries " never for a moment ceased to be Hungarians."
Their numbers were too small, and their geographical distribution was not of a
nature to allow them to aspire to an independent existence.   Only the unity of
the Hungarian Kingdom formed a shield to protect them from destruction.—
Eötvös, *A Nemzetiségi Kérdés*, 1903 ed. pp. 17, 20, 26.   Nationalities never
fought as such, but members of the different races from the time of John
Zápolya onward were divided just as the Magyars were on political and
religious questions, and were to be found fighting on both sides.—*Ibid.* p. 155.

[2] After 1848 "begann auch in Ungarn unter dem Vorwand der Durch-
führung des Gleichberechtigungs-Princips theils eine stramme Germanisation,
theils antimagyarische Nationalitätenhetze."—Gumplowicz, *Das Recht der
Nationalitäten und Sprachen in Österreich-Ungarn*, Innsbruck, 1879, p. 110.
After 1861 "wieder einmal also nahm das unbedingt centralisirende und
germanisirende System die Nationalitätsrechte der Slaven (in Ungarn ebenso
wie in Triest) und der Rumänen, zum Vorwande, um den Ansprüchen der
mächtigeren Nationalitäten entgegenzutreten, *und das that dasselbe System,
welches in Böhmen und Galizien zu den gegründetsten Klagen über Bedrückung
ihrer Nationalität und Sprache Anlass gab*."—*ibid.* p. 160.   The "Schreck-

been any recognised citizenship in Hungary but Magyar citizenship. Though from time to time the Habsburgs encouraged the separatistic tendencies of the Serb, the Croat, the Saxon, and the Slovák, the fact remains that from the time of St. Stephen to the present day there has been and is no territory in Hungary but the territory of the Sacred Crown, and no political rights save those conferred by membership of that Crown. Austria made a last attempt to produce a mongrel federalism in Hungary in 1861, and now itself suffers from the poison of particularism and nationalistic antagonism which the Habsburgs so long tried to infuse into Hungary for their own purposes.

Nothing can be more misleading than the majority of the maps which purport to show the geographical distribution of the constituent races of Hungary. The broad, uniform smudges of colour which indicate that this part is Magyar, this Roumanian, this Servian, this Slovák, and so on, and serve as a text for the disquisitions of the prophets of federalism, obscure the fact that the various races are so intermingled in all parts of the country, and so interspersed with Magyars, that it is impossible to effect clear-cut geographical subdivisions for federalistic purposes such as are possible in Bohemia, where the country is peopled by only two races, the Germans and the Czechs, between whom the lines of demarcation are comparatively easily drawn. A glance at the map appended to the recent book of Mr. Ernest Baloghy[1] would do more to disperse erroneous notions as to racial distribution than many pages of statistics. Minute squares of colour, showing the interpenetration of the nationalities, replace the familiar broad smudges, and the result bears as much resemblance to the ordinary ethnographical map of Hungary as a pheasant's plumage does to the tricolour. The great central plain of

gespenst" of federalisation was to drive the Magyars into the Reichsrath.—Gumplowicz, *ibid.* 171, citing Rogge.

[1] *A Magyar Kultura és a Nemzetiségek*, Budapest, 1908.

the Danube and the Tisza is almost solidly Magyar, as is
the eastern part of Transylvania; elsewhere, except in the
Serbo-Croatian district south of the Száva, the patchwork
diversity of colour points an unmistakable moral—the
impossibility of a territorial subdivision for purposes of
local autonomy, which would not result in the subjection
of Magyar and German intelligence to inferior types, whose
sole claim to political differentiation lies in the fact that
they speak a bastard variety of the languages of more
important races. The Magyar element is wanting in not
one of 413 electoral divisions; the German only in 37.
Slováks are absent from 211, Roumanians from 235,
Croatians from 344, Servians from 351. Ruthenes are to
be found in 57 divisions, and fragments of other races in
no less than 360.[1] As regards the eighteen divisions of
what Brote and other agitators regard as *Roumania irredenta*
—Transylvania and Hungary up to the Tisza, the
Roumanians are in an actual majority in only eleven;
Magyars and Germans form over 37 per cent of the
population; and in no single district in which the
Roumanians are in the majority is there an admixture of
less than eleven per cent of other nationalities. Though
the Magyars constitute no more than $54\frac{1}{4}$ per cent of the
whole population of Hungary proper, they are more than
three times as numerous as the numerically strongest
nationality,[2] whereas the German population of Austria
forms no more than $38\frac{1}{3}$ per cent of the inhabitants of the
hereditary provinces.[3] Between the subordinate races there

[1] Baloghy, *o.c.* p. 61, citing Baloghy Pál.
[2] According to the census of 1900 the figures were: Magyar, 8,742,000;
Roumanian, 2,799,000; Slovák, 2,019,000; German, 2,135,000; Servian,
1,062,000; Ruthenian, 384,000; Croatian, 1,563,000.—*A M. Kir. Kormány
1906 évi . . . Statistikai Évkönyv*, Part II. 20. The Magyar percentage in
Hungary and Croatia has increased from 42.8 in 1890 to 47.6 in 1907. In
1900 the Magyar-speaking population numbered 8,742,000, or 52.8 per cent
of the total. In 1906 it formed 59.7 per cent of the male, and 56.8 per cent of
the female population.—*Ibid.* pp. 20, 44.
[3] *Österreichisches statistisches Handbuch*, Vienna, 1903. The percentage of
the German population was the same in 1850, in fact it was a fraction higher.

is no cohesion or solidarity ; the Magyar is the only binding element. Panslavism, Pangermanism, and Panroumanism, have alternated from time to time, and in every case the source of agitation was to be found outside the limits of Hungary. Roumanians and Slováks have nothing in common. The Roumanian hates the Servian, and the Servian the Roumanian. The German settlements are too scattered for it to be possible to carve out a characteristically German territory not permeated with Magyar, or Slovák, or Roumanian elements, are too far removed from Germany to dream of union therewith, and too good Hungarian citizens to wish such union were possible in spite of the prognostications of M. Cheradame.[1] The Germans of Zips fought in Rákóczy's army, stood side by side with the Magyars in the fight for freedom in 1848, and prayed for the restoration of the Hungarian Constitution—the sole guarantee of their liberties. The Transylvanian Germans are less disposed than those of Zips to forget their origin, but considerations of self-preservation must compel them to ally themselves with the Magyars against the numerically preponderant, but

On the other hand the Czechs and Moravians from 1850 to 1900 increased from 22.8 per cent to 23.24 per cent, and the Poles from 12.4 per cent to 16.6 per cent.

[1] *L'Europe et la question d'Autriche.* As a German member of the Delegation publicly declared in 1904 : "The Saxons are Hungarian patriots, and their fate is irrevocably bound to that of Hungary." Of the 2,135,000 Germans in Hungary 450,000 live in the Tisza-Máros district among Roumanians and Serbs, 230,000 in Transylvania among Roumanians, 200,000 in Croatia, 300,000 among the Slováks and Ruthens, 190,000 among the Serbs, 300,000 in the essentially Magyar districts. According to the fancy maps of the Pan-Germans, Roumania will some day receive the so-called Roumanian districts of Transylvania and Hungary, and the Saxon part will become a Markgrafschaft Siébenbürgen. The centre of Hungary will be converted into a Magyar Markgrafschaft in which a knowledge of the German language will be a condition precedent to the possession of civic rights, and the Magyar landowners who are not friendly to the idea of German domination will be expropriated like the Prussian Poles. On the subject of Pangermanism in Hungary see Herczeg Ferencz, *National Review*, September 1903.

educationally inferior, Roumanians. Eisenmann[1] and others suggest that the Magyars might take a hint from the cantonal system of Switzerland, but Switzerland is populated by three equally civilised races, the geographical demarcation of which is natural and distinct.

An inferior civilisation cannot swallow up a superior one. The Slováks in the north-western part of Hungary are more compact than most of the nationalities, but they are on too low a plane to be able to stand alone. In the north-east they are mixed up with Magyars and Germans who would never submit to the domination of an inferior race which has never done anything for its adopted country or for itself. According to Hunfalvy,[2] the great authority on the nationalities of Hungary, the Slováks, so far from being aboriginal inhabitants, are of Czech-Moravian origin and wandered into Hungary in the fifteenth century. They had no conception of a separate national existence before 1848, when, as the author of the petition to Francis Joseph stated, they awoke from their sleep of nine hundred years' duration. There was no Slovák language, only a Czech *patois*.[3] Not until 1850 was there a Slovák Grammar. In 1862 a society, the Matica Slovenska, was formed for the purpose of fostering the Slovák literature and promoting the use of the Slovák language[4] — a task which was complicated by the fact that both literature and language had first to be invented. Discontented with the proverbial blessedness enjoyed by races which have no history, the Matica also invented the absurdity of an independent Slovák Duchy, alleged to have existed prior to the arrival of the Magyars, and to have continued down to the time of St.

[1] *O.c.* p. 680.
[2] *Magyarország Ethnographidja*, Budapest, 1876.
[3] See *A Czeh-Tót Nemzetegység Multja, Jelene es Jövöje.* Czambel Samu. Túrócz-Szt-Márton, 1902, pp. 12 *sqq.* 23 *sqq.*
[4] See *A Tót Nemzetiségi Mozgalmak Fejlödésének Története.* Dugovich Titus. Túrócz-Szt-Márton, 1903, pp. 50 *sq.* 60 *sqq.*

Stephen.[1] So far Slovák literature has nothing to boast
of save a third-rate poet or two and a few translations.
There are no scientific Slovák writings, and even the
books in use in 326 schools in which the language of
instruction is Slovák are Czech. The creation of an
independent Slovakia is unthinkable, and Slovák autonomy,
implying the subordination of Magyar and German
intelligence to mere numerical superiority, would be
intolerable. Such Slováks as wish for a change desire
fusion with the Czechs[2] or are tarred with the brush of
Panslavism. The very existence of a Slovák question, of
a Slovák nationality, is a proof that the Magyars have
not been guilty of undue interference with the natural
development of subordinate races whose separatistic
tendencies, devoid of historical justification, are the artificial production of the traditional Habsburg policy, and
of the times in which we live. Servian autonomy is
equally inconceivable. The Serbs of Hungary proper,
less than half a million strong, are to be found in
considerable numbers only in four counties.[3] Elsewhere
they are numerically unimportant, and provided that their
ecclesiastical autonomy is respected, have no more wish for
a separate political existence than they have for reunion
with the inferior civilisation of their congeners in Servia,
the limits of whose capacity for orderly self-government
are sufficiently notorious.[4]

The Croatians stand on an altogether different footing,
especially since the passing of Law xxx. of 1865, which
confirmed and greatly extended the autonomous rights,

[1] "Von einer Slovakischen (Nationalität) wusste leider die Geschichte und
das Europäische Bewusstsein nichts."—Gumplowicz, o.c. p. 59.

[2] For the propaganda of the Česko-Slovanská Jednota (Czech-Slav union
Society) see Czambel Samu, o.c. pp. 1 sq. and 6-8. For the, originally purely
Czech, origin of the movement see ibid. pp. 34, 37, 38, 77.

[3] According to the census of 1900 the total Servian population was
1,062,000. For their origin see supra, i. 164.

[4] The story of the member of the Skupstchina who asked, "Who is this
Mr. Budget of whom they talk so much?" is presumably well known.

the limits of which were concisely defined by Verbőczy over three hundred years ago. As we have seen, in 1848 'Croatia fought nominally in defence of the unity of the realms of the Habsburgs, but the address presented by its Diet to the Crown on June 5th of that year puts a different complexion on the matter. "The triple Kingdom of Croatia, Slavonia, and Dalmatia reserves to itself the right to unite not only the sister races now living under Austrian domination in Styria, Carinthia, Carniola, Istria, Görz, and the islands, but also in connexion with the districts belonging to Turkey, should these be recovered, to found a southern Slav Kingdom." There, in a nutshell, is the essence of Croatia's action in the past and of its ambitions for the future. After Világos, Croatia was not slow to discover the fact that it had put its money on the wrong horse, and complained, not without justification, that it received as a reward for its efforts on behalf of the Habsburgs no more and no less than Hungary received as a punishment. It soon recognised the folly of having exchanged the liberties it enjoyed under Magyar supremacy for the despotism of Bach and his successors, and on the occasion of the presentation of an address to Francis Joseph on September 24, 1861, stress was laid on the fact that "closer political connexion with Hungary is the best guarantee of the Constitution ; for a union of forces enables a more successful resistance to be offered to the encroachments of Austria's policy of absolutism." Consequently, when in 1868 an arrangement was come to between the Magyars and the Croatians, it was hoped and believed that the latter would abandon Panslavism and "Illyrian" ideas for ever. The hope was doomed to disappointment, and almost from the start the Croatians never lost an opportunity of taking sides against the authors of their limited independence. From time to time attempts were made to lull Magyar susceptibilities

with assurances of attachment to the Hungarian connexion, and by declaring that hostility hereto was to be
found only in the sparse ranks of an extremist party ;
but no reliance could be placed on such protestations.
Croatians will never abandon the idea of a great southern
Slav kingdom. To satisfy their megalomania Dalmatia
must be annexed to Croatia, dualism must become
trialism, and Hungary must be deprived of the essential
condition of vitality, the control of its access to the sea.
As a matter of fact, far greater concessions were made to
Croatia in 1868 than it was historically entitled to claim.
Law xxx. gave it a measure of independence very different to that with which it was contented in the days
when Gáj and Illyrism had not been born or thought
of. Then Croatia was a nation, in the sense in which the
Saxons of Transylvania constituted a nation before the
Act of Union ; now it claims to possess all the attributes
of independence.[1] It has its own coat of arms surmounted
by the crown of St. Stephen, and its own flag, which is
hoisted alongside that of Hungary when Parliament is
occupied with the discussion of Hungarian-Croatian
common affairs (Law xxx., sect. 63), a fact which is
calculated to produce the erroneous impression that

[1] Marczali points out (*Az 1790-1 Országgyűlés*, i. 376) that Croatia never
claimed to be an allied State on an equal footing with Hungary till 1790, and
that the use of the expression "annexed" instead of "subject parts" was due
partly to the Roman Church, which wished to curry favour with Catholic
Croatia, and partly to the Court of Vienna, which foresaw the possibility of
utilising Croatian aspirations to combat those of the Magyars. Deák's words,
to be found in the first Address of the Diet of 1861 (Kónyi, *o.c.* iii. 47),
"Croatia possesses its own territory, occupies a distinct position, and never was
incorporated in Hungary, but was united to us, and was a partner in our
rights and obligations, our prosperity and adversity," have been utilised to
prove the independence in Deák's view of Croatia, but the phrase in question
must be read in connexion with others to be found in the same and in the
second Address, both of which insist on the impossibility of consenting to the
dismemberment of the kingdom by the severance of Transylvania and Croatia.
Deák clearly meant no more than that Croatia was an "annexed part" enjoying
a certain degree of self-government, and so differing from the rest of Hungary.
For the second Address see Kónyi, iii. 261.

Croatia possesses a separate existence, different from and superior to that which it enjoys as a member of the Sacred Crown — an impression which is strengthened by the second section of the governing Act, which requires the Diploma Inaugurale to be published in Croatian as well as in Hungarian, and to contain a guarantee of Croatia's territorial integrity and Constitution.[1] Croatia now has its own appellate jurisdiction, and its penal laws are not identical with those of Hungary. It deals with its own budget, and has independent legislative powers as regards internal, local, matters, including religion and education. The official language is Croatian, and all communications addressed to Hungarian Government officials must be replied to in that idiom. Croatian deputies to the Hungarian Parliament may *also* use their own language in addition to the Magyar, a concession in which racial malevolence affects to find a justification for ignorance, real or feigned, of the official language of Parliament, and for deliberate obstruction of the course of purely Hungarian business.[2]

It is a far cry from local autonomy to complete independence under a Croatian King, from subordination to the Sacred Crown to the substitution of a bastard trialism for the dualism of to-day. Croatia claims to occupy the

[1] If Croatia ever had been absolutely independent of Hungary, it clearly could no longer claim to be so since the passing of Law xxx. of 1868, the preamble of which says : "Croatia and Slavonia having belonged for centuries *de jure* and *de facto* to the Crown of St. Stephen, and as the Pragmatic Sanction declares that the realms of the Magyar Crown are inseparable, the following agreement has been made *on the foregoing basis* between Hungary of the one part and Croatia and Slavonia of the other part." Hungary made a mistake from the constitutional point of view in allowing the agreement to be incorporated in two laws, Hungarian and Croatian, instead of in one Hungarian law ; for the existence of a corresponding Croatian law (i. 1868), in which Croatia is described as the Kingdoms of Croatia and Slavonia, gives some colour to the contention that Croatia and Hungary came to an arrangement as two equal contracting nations in spite of the preamble above referred to, and of sect. 1, which enunciates the fact that Hungary, Croatia, and Slavonia form one single kingdom *vis-à-vis* Austria and other countries.

[2] See *supra*, p. 240.

same position with respect to Hungary as Hungary does towards Austria; in other words, to be an independent kingdom with no connexion save such as results from the identity of the Monarch and from the existence of common affairs and affairs of common interest. But an independent Croatia is an historical absurdity. Never since Croatia's union with Hungary took place has there been a Croatian King. The Habsburg who is crowned King of Hungary, *ipso facto* becomes King of Croatia [1] —an indivisible part of the realms of the Sacred Crown, so expressed by the laws of 1723 and 1868. The Bán does not come in direct contact with the King, as he would necessarily do if he were the chief official of an independent State, but communicates with the Crown though the Croatian member of the Hungarian Ministry, who is responsible to the Hungarian Parliament, whose countersignature is necessary to give validity to the countersignature of the Bán of official nominations and other royal acts. Further, the Bán is himself nominated by the Magyar Prime Minister, who countersigns the royal appointment made in pursuance of such nomination. There are no Croatian or Hungaro-Croatian Ministers or Parliament within the realms of St. Stephen. Parliament is Hungarian, and the Ministers are Hungarian servants of an indivisible State of which Croatia-Slavonia forms an integral part. There is no Croatian citizenship or nationality. As a member of the Sacred Crown Croatia was affected by the results of the Compromise of 1867, and as such member would have no power of independent action should the law of that year be abrogated or modified, save in so far as it is entitled and enabled to make its voice heard through its delegates to the Hungarian Parliament should a revision of the Compromise affect its local or common interests, or necessitate an alteration

[1] Abdication of the Hungarian throne involves abdication of all rights with respect to Croatia and Slavonia; no separate act of abdication is required.

of financial relations with Hungary on whom Croatia's insolvent autonomy lays a considerable burden.[1]   As Baron Beck, the Austrian Prime Minister, said in his speech in the Reichsrath on October 29, 1907, the Austrian Government and Parliament, in accordance with the sixth section of the Law of December 21, 1867, in questions affecting common affairs as defined by the Compromise of that year, "can take only the Hungarian Parliament into consideration, not the Croatian Diet."[2]   Such is the view of official Austria, based on the only possible interpretation of the laws of 1867 and 1868, and necessarily distasteful to the would-be creators of a greater Croatia,[3] whom nothing will satisfy short of severance of the last link which binds them to Hungary. The Magyarisation of Croatia which they affect to fear has been rendered impossible by the establishment of Croatian as the official language, and as the language of instruction in the schools.   Obstacles to instruction in the Hungarian tongue are thrown in the way even of the children of the Magyar population, though in Hungary proper Croatian schools, in which Hungarian is only a subject, not the medium, of instruction, are supported by the Hungarian Government.   Even the language of command of the territorial forces of Croatia is not, as it

[1] Croatia bears only a trifling percentage of the common expenses, 7.93 per cent as against 92.07 borne by the rest of Hungary.   Though 44 per cent of Croatia's revenue is set apart for its separate internal expenditure, it is insufficient, and Hungary has to find the balance required, an annual irrecoverable advance of a few million florins from which Hungary derives no benefit.

[2] See the *Budapesti Hirlap* of Oct. 30, 1907, for the speech.

[3] The "Croatian Nation," it should be remembered, consisted in 1905 of just over one and a half million souls, or 61 per cent of the population of Croatia. The Servians form 25 per cent, the Magyars 4.20 per cent, the Germans 5.80 per cent.   In the, historically strictly Magyar, district between the Száva and Dráva there are more than 103,000 Magyars.—See the *Budapesti Hirlap*, Sept. 18, 1908.   "Croatien und Slavonien staatsrechtlich sind nichts anderes als eine wenn auch mit sehr weitgehende und überdies nur mit seiner Einwilligung abzuändernder Autonomie ausgerüstete Ungarische Provinz."—Jellinek, *Die Lehre von den Staatenverbindungen*, Vienna, 1882, p. 76, *n*.

should be, the language of the indivisible Hungarian State. With the exception of the Bán, the one outward and visible sign of Hungarian political unity and of Hungarian sovereignty in Croatia is the State railway, the control of which, its only means of communication with the sea, is a matter of life and death to the Magyar nation. It is hatred of the symbol of Magyar hegemony, not considerations of convenience, which dictates Croatian action, and suggests the argument that as Croatian has been made the official language of the governmental organs in Croatia by clause 57 of the Law of 1868, it should necessarily be the official language of that part of the State railway which runs through Croatia. The Hungarians reply to this contention that the railway is not a governmental department within the meaning of the Act,[1] and is, and always has been, subject to the control of the Hungarian Ministry of Commerce and Communications, which alone is responsible, for the proper working of a commercial undertaking, the management of which, in the interest of the State as a whole, has been entrusted to its care. Apart from commercial considerations it is essential for military reasons that all employees should be acquainted with the Hungarian language, otherwise in time of war the mobilisation of troops might be seriously hampered by the inability of stationmasters and other officials to understand the instructions of the central authority. The Hungarian Government has no objection to the use of the Croatian language in all communications between the Croatian authorities and the railway officials, but it rightly requires a knowledge of the language of State from candidates for employment on a railway which is maintained at the State's expense for military as well as for commercial reasons. Croatian convenience is sufficiently studied if, as is the case, an

---

[1] Moreover, railways constitute a common affair, and as such come under the control of the Hungarian Parliament, 1868, xxx. sect. 9.

acquaintance with the Croatian idiom is demanded of all railway officials employed within the limits of Croatia. The fact that Croatian malcontents demand still further concessions would seem to justify the inference that they are actuated, not by regard for the interests of the travelling public, or for the effective working of the railway, but by a desire to destroy the last vestiges of political union, and to deprive Hungary of the control of its one means of access to the outer world, in the interest of the great southern Slav State of Croatian dreamers.

The realisation of Croatian ambitions would be as distasteful to the Servian population of Croatia as the success of the Home Rule agitation would be to Ulster. Relations always have been, and always will be, strained between Croatian Catholics and the orthodox Servians. The prospect of a forced racial and ecclesiastical subordination to the Croatians causes the Servians to look for protection to the Magyars, just as local Servian oppression as regards the use of their language, and Servian religious intolerance, is gradually forcing the Roumanians to the conclusion that the Magyars are their natural allies and protectors against Slav pretensions.   But the foreign public listens only to the propagandists who earn cheap martyrdom by treasonable agitation such as no European nation but England would be foolish enough to let pass unpunished.[1] The Magyars have made a mistake in neglecting to inform Europe as to the nature, origin, and object of Roumanian intrigue, and in allowing public opinion to be formed chiefly by voluntary exiles who have left their country in order to escape an insufficient punishment.

For centuries the Roumanians of Hungary had no notion that they could boast a Roman origin.   Not until they turned to Roman Catholicism did they conceive the

---

[1] The recent prosecutions of persons guilty of seditious utterances in India, which England won by the sword and holds by the sword, show that England also realises the fact that there is a point at which freedom of speech begins to constitute a danger to the interests of the paramount race.

idea that they were anything but what they are—Balkan Slavs whose remote ancestor were more or less Latinised by contact with the Roman colonial forces.[1] It would indeed be remarkable if a Roman army of occupation had left no illegitimate mementoes of its stay in the country, but what percentage of Roman blood is likely to be traceable in its descendants after a nomad existence of over a thousand years in the Balkan Peninsula? There is not a particle of evidence to show that the Roumanians were already domiciled in Transylvania when the Magyars arrived there. As we have seen, the theory of a settled political existence in a permanently Romanised Dacia is a late invention of Sinkai and his followers. The idea of a uniform, united, Roumanian nation never occurred to anyone before 1848, and even after that date the ideas of Bishop Siaguna,[2] the prophet of Roumanian union, went no further than a demand of local self-government and of ecclesiastical autonomy for the Roumanians of Transylvania. The notion of a greater Roumania was not yet conceived. Majorescu, the chief of Siaguna's immediate followers and imitators, went a step further and demanded the union of all Roumanians in Transylvania, Bessarabia, and Bukovina under Austrian hegemony, and with the benevolent support of the German Confederation. By the peace of Paris, Russia's protectorate over Moldavia and Wallachia came to an end, and part of Bessarabia was incorporated in Moldavia. Later, the Roumanians were rewarded for their action in saving Russia from a fiasco at Plevna by the creation of a Roumanian Kingdom and by the loss of Bessarabia. The aim of the modern Sinkais and Siagunas, of Brote and his school of agitators, is the creation (they would call it reconstitution) of Dako-Roumania, including Bessarabia, Bukovina, Transylvania, Hungary up to the

---

[1] See Hunfalvy, *Magyarország Ethnographiája*, p. 479 *sqq.* Beksics Gustav, *A Roman Kérdés és a fajok harcza*, Budapest, 1895, p. 22 *sq.* See *supra*, i. 92-95.
[2] See his petition to Francis Joseph, February 25, 1849.

Tisza, and the parts of Servia which border on the Danube. Thus united, the ten million or so, theoretically homogeneous, descendants of Trajan's legionaries, are to be the arbiters of the fate of the Balkan provinces. From the point of view of Roumania proper this is the justification for Roumano-Transylvanian irredentism in Hungary. Abuse of the Magyars is merely the first stage of a campaign, the ultimate object of which is the union of all Roumanians.[1] The irredentist agitation might just as well be begun in Bessarabia instead of in Hungary, except for the fact that Russia has a short way of dealing with inconvenient propagandists, and that the Magyars err on the side of excessive tolerance. The Roumanians see a justification and an example in Italy's struggle for union,[2] oblivious of the fact that in that case the fight was for *re*-union; whereas there never was a greater Roumania, united or disunited, that the scattered Roumanians never conceived the idea of a common origin till a few years ago, and that the country has yet to be discovered which can boast with certainty of being the cradle of the Moldavo-Wallachians or Transylvanian Vlachs. The demand for the reorganisation of Hungary on a federalistic basis, for its subdivision into autonomous districts on purely arbitrary lines, has as its object the aggrandisement of Roumania. For whose ultimate benefit? Of Germany (which has its Hohenzollern on the Roumanian throne) to which the propagandists of greater Roumania look as to their future patron and protector, or of Russia, the sight of whose tender mercies

[1] See the resolution passed at the national conference of 1890, which, while denying the existence of Dako-Roumanian tendencies, says: "We are and feel ourselves to be members of a great Roumanian family of more than eleven million souls. As members of such family we strive for the material and cultured development of the Roumanian race and to defend our people from all foreign influence."—Brote, *o.c.* Appendix 38.

[2] See the speech of Count Kalnoky, Austro-Hungarian Minister of Foreign Affairs, September 18, 1894, and that of Demeter Sturdza, leader of the National Liberal Party in Roumania, December 9, 1893, as to the absurdity of the comparison with Italy.—Brote, *o.c.* Appendix 42.

to their congeners in Bessarabia should discourage feelings
of attachment to the idea of a Russian protectorate? In
every development of the Eastern question Roumania must
be a considerable factor, and its fate depends on its choice
of an ally. Should it side with a victorious Russia it
would hope to receive Transylvania as its reward. Allied
with Germany, or with Germany, Austria, and Hungary,
it would expect to be recompensed at Russia's expense in
Bessarabia ; a temporary recompense in either event, for it
is impossible to imagine that the future masters of the
Balkan peninsula would long permit the retention of the
keys of the Carpathians and the Balkans in Roumanian
hands.[1] In any case the fate of Roumania, which lies
across the road to Constantinople, is intimately connected
with that of the whole of south-eastern Europe ;
consequently, the primary manifestations of Roumanian
irredentism, of which Hungary is the scene, are of far
more than merely local interest.

The Roumanian agitators from time to time demand :
(1) the separation from Hungary of Transylvania and of
the parts beyond the Tisza—a modest request, compliance
with which would involve the dismemberment of Hungary,
the infraction of the coronation oath of Francis Joseph,
the disregard of the lessons of past history, and the
destruction of Austrian influence in the Balkan Peninsula ;
or (2) Transylvanian autonomy, i.e. the right of the
ignorant majority to dominate their superiors in wealth and
education ; or (3) the formation of units of self-government in Transylvania by drawing arbitrary lines which
should divide the country into linguistically homogeneous
sections when no absolute homogeneity exists. There is
no justification for any one of these demands ; no recurrence to a past of Roumanian unity [2] based on common

---

[1] Austria could in no case tolerate the sight of the Carpathians in the hands
of a possible enemy, Roumania, which would be a certain enemy if it saw the
possibility of laying hands on Bukovina.

[2] The programme of the Roumanian National Party, drawn up at a

history, on distinctive civilisation, or on the right of prior occupation. As Beksics says,[1] an Italian claim to Provence and a Russian claim to Brandenburg and Berlin on the ground that they were once occupied by Slavs would be no more absurd from the historical point of view. As regards the demand for Roumanian control of Transylvania and of Hungary up to the Tisza, it is to be observed that the Roumanians are in an actual minority, forming about 40 per cent of the population ; so whatever justification it may possess from other points of view, it has none from that of mere numbers.[2] With respect to the suggested *Sonderstellung* of Transylvania the position is somewhat different. Of a population of 2,250,000 the 1,276,000 Roumanians form 56 per cent, whereas the Magyars number only 698,000 and the Saxons 217,000 ; but, as will be seen hereafter, it would be not merely tyrannical to give rights of predomianace to a Roumanian majority, but it would be absurd, as no one can suppose that Transylvanian autonomy could long remain Roumanian autonomy when the preponderance of wealth and education is on the side of the minority. As regards the third alternative proposed, the *specifically Roumanian* territory, made up according to Brote's recipe, contains 4,116,000 inhabitants, of whom 2,370,000 (57.55 per cent) are Roumanians, over a million are Magyars, and half a million are Germans. Only in two counties does the Roumanian percentage reach 80, while in some it sinks

conference held in May 1881 (confirmed in 1887), demanded the reacquisition of Transylvanian autonomy ; but at the time when Transylvania was autonomous the Roumanians had no political rights whatever. The programme also demands the official use of the Roumanian language in all districts inhabited by Roumanians, no matter what proportion they bear to the other races, and that no officials shall be appointed who are not acquainted with that language and with Roumanian customs. For this programme see Brote, *Die rumänische Frage*, Appendix 35.   [1] *A Román Kérdés*, pp. 52, 54.

[2] Beksics, *o.c.* p. 78 *sq.*, gives the figures for 1895 (the Magyar proportion is now relatively greater), Roumanians, less than 2,600,000 ; Magyars, 2,250,000 ; Germans, 780,000. Total population of all races, 6,228,500.

as low as 33. As has been already mentioned, only in eleven of the eighteen electoral divisions of Transylvania and Hungary up to the Tisza are the Roumanians in an actual majority, and in no preponderatingly Roumanian district is there less than an 11 per cent admixture of other races. The towns are almost entirely Magyar, and when not Magyar are German, so even in the parts to which Brote points as distinctively Roumanian, wealth and civilisation are entirely non-Roumanian.[1]

But history, wealth, and education are of no importance in the eyes of separatistic agitators. As regards education, the Roumanians of Hungary are on a lower plane than any constituent race. In 1890, of Roumanian males, only 19.89 per cent could read and write their own language ; of females, only 8·19.[2] According to Baloghy,[3] in 1907, 86 per cent were entirely illiterate, and it is absurd to suggest that such a race is fit for autonomy, or could be politically self-sufficient. The agitators would reply that the low percentage of literates is due to Magyar oppression and obscurantism. Let us examine this allegation. In 1880, 5.71 per cent of Roumanians could speak the Magyar language ; in 1890 the figure had risen to 6.95, an increase of $1\frac{1}{4}$ per cent in ten years, which hardly bears out the statement that the Roumanians are being robbed of their language and compulsorily magyarised.[4] According to a favourite lie, intended for foreign consumption, Law xviii. of 1879, which made Magyar a compulsory *subject* of instruction, made it the compulsory *medium* of instruction

---

[1] In the eighteen chief towns, out of a population of 316,000, 180,000 are Magyars, and 231,500 are Magyar speaking. See the table in Beksics, *o.c.* p. 87 and preceding pages.

[2] See Beksics, *o.c.* pp. 95-99, as compared with 60.20 and 46.49 per cent, the general average of Hungary, and the 74 per cent of the Magyars.

[3] *A Magyar Kultura*, etc., pp. 120, 121.

[4] See the speech of Dr. Wekerle, the Hungarian Prime Minister, August 5, 1894, in which he challenges any one to produce a specimen of the alleged forcibly magyarised Roumanians.

in all schools, and the Roumanians were consequently deprived of the means of learning their own language. What are the facts? In 1881 there were 2781 elementary schools in which Roumanian was the sole language of instruction, and only 322 in which both Roumanian and Magyar teaching was given. In 1892 the number of purely Roumanian schools had risen to 3289,[1] and the Magyar-Roumanian to 364—a 9 per cent increase in favour of the Roumanian language. The fact should be noted that though the Roumanians of Hungary are on a lower educational level than any other nationality, there is one place where the darkness is still more intense than in Transylvania, namely, the Mecca of the irredentists, Roumania proper, where only 13 per cent of the population can read and write, and only 18 per cent of the children of the age of instruction go to school. The Magyars are to blame, not for robbing the nationalities of their language, but for not properly carrying out the law of 1879. So recently as 1897, of 3000 Roumanian teachers, more than 500 were ignorant of the language of the State;[2] and to-day, for more than one-quarter of the schools of Hungary, the Magyar is a non-existent idiom.[3] Darkest Hungary is that part of the country to which Brote assigns an essentially Roumanian character. The commercial capacity of the inhabitants is such as might be expected—it is commensurate with their intellectual abilities. But for the existence of trifling cottage industries, it might be said that the manufacturing arts are unknown to the Roumanians. According to the official return of 1890, there was not one Roumanian manufacturer in all Hungary who gave employment to as many as twenty workmen. The taxable capacity of the Roumanians is smaller than that of any race in Hungary, which would have the pleasure of paying for Roumanian autonomy, unable to finance

---

[1] Beksics, *o.c.* p. 99.   [2] *Ibid.* p. 164.   [3] Baloghy, *o.c.* p. 221.

itself except by putting the whole burden of the expense of government on the shoulders of the Magyar and German inhabitants of the "Roumanian" autonomous districts. In 1894, out of one hundred million florins of direct taxation, Transylvania paid eight millions, and almost the whole of that sum was paid by the Magyar and German population. Budapest alone pays nearly as much in taxation as Transylvania, Croatia, and the Slovák districts put together.[1] Under the circumstances, it would not be surprising if the tax-paying Magyar and German were favoured in the matter of the Parliamentary franchise at the expense of the Roumanians, but such is not the case. No doubt, as in England, and still more so in Ireland, there are districts which are more fully represented than their population entitles them to be, which would disappear from the list of constituencies if a new and reasonable scheme of redistribution were adopted;[2] but on the whole, the Roumanians in Translyvania are over rather than under-represented, for the qualification is considerably lower there than in other parts of Hungary, so the Roumanians, who form the majority of the population, are actually favoured at the expense of better educated races which have a far larger stake in the country. If the qualification were placed on a uniform basis throughout Hungary

---

[1] Beksics, *o.c.* pp. 170, 172, 175.

[2] The average is one member to 35,000 to 40,000 inhabitants. In Budapest there is one to 70,000. The average number of voters is 2400 per constituency. In Transylvania it is about 1500. In 2 constituencies there are less than 200 voters ; in 47 less than 1000 ; in 91 less than 2000 ; in 162 less than 3000 ; in 72 less than 4000 ; in 27 less than 5000 ; in 12 under 10,000 ; in 2 under 13,000. Of the voters, 637,000 are qualified as landed proprietors, 42,000 as householders, 201,000 on an income basis ; for 75,000 the qualification is an educational one—engineers, schoolmasters, lawyers, etc. Twenty-seven per cent of all males of over twenty years have the vote.— Kmety, *Közjog*, 207 *n.* Beksics, *o.c.* p. 108, compares the electorate of 55 divisions of Hungary in which Magyars preponderate with that of 44 in which the Roumanians are in a majority. In the former there is one member to 47,881 inhabitants ; in the latter one to 40,695. In Transylvania there is one to 30,000 ; in the rest of Hungary the average is one to 38,000.

and Transylvania thousands of Roumanians would be disqualified to whom exceptional treatment now assures the enjoyment of the franchise. If ability to read and write were an essential qualification the Roumanians would be in an absolute majority only in thirty-five divisions instead of in fifty-seven. If there were a uniform property qualification their preponderance would be limited to forty-four divisions. The Magyar figures would, in either case, increase proportionately, wealth and education being on the side of the predominant race, the difference in this respect between the other races and the Magyar tending to become more pronounced every year.[1]   In the

[1] Taking the whole of Hungary, about 1,100,000 have hitherto possessed the franchise. The proposed reform will increase the number of voters to something over 2,500,000. Austria's object in forcing Hungary to follow its lead and to introduce universal suffrage was the destruction of Magyar supremacy. The widening of the franchise in Austria has increased rather than diminished the manifestations of race hatred and jealousy. If the Magyars commit political suicide by walking open-eyed into the trap laid for them it will be a great misfortune for Europe. It is to be hoped that the new law will not place all power in the hands of the most ignorant and most anti-Magyar element. Presumably the qualifying age will be fixed at twenty-four as in Austria. Ability to read and write will undoubtedly be a condition precedent to the possession of the franchise. The question is what ability to read and write implies. Surely not merely the ability to write one's name and read that of the candidate for whom one intends to vote. It is to be hoped that proof of having attained a certain standard of elementary education in the recognised schools will be insisted on. In the case of urban voters it would seem to be advisable to insist on proof of ability to read and write the Magyar language, and after the lapse of a certain period, say ten years, no one should acquire the right to vote who does not know the language of State, ignorance of which after that period should be regarded as proof of unworthiness to enjoy the privileges of Hungarian citizenship, or of such a low level of intelligence as should naturally disqualify. As a certain percentage of those who now possess the vote would be disqualified by insistence on a certain educational standard, and as the object in view is the increase, not the restriction of the ranks of the enfranchised, it would be fair to allow those who now vote on a property qualification to continue to do so as long as they live, provided they continue to hold the qualification; just as in 1848 Parliament did not disqualify those who had the right to vote in virtue of possessing rights of nobility and no other qualification. It is to be presumed that redistribution of seats will take place simultaneously with the enlargement of the number of voters, and that the anomaly will be abolished, the result of which is that the richer and better educated districts of central and western Hungary receive less representation than the more sparsely populated, poorer, and more ignorant

Middle Ages all European countries were more or less polyglot, but eventually the language of the towns became the
language of the nation. In Hungary this was not so. In
old days the towns were chiefly German while the country
was Magyar, but now the towns are yearly becoming more
and more deeply impressed with the Magyar stamp. Of
the urban [1] population 68 per cent are born Magyars, over
80 per cent are Magyar speaking, and only 3 per cent are
of Roumanian origin. From 1880 to 1890 the Magyar
proportion increased by 23.80 per cent, the Roumanian
by 1.54.[2] The tortoise is not invariably successful in the
race ; the Magyar has established a strong lead, and
seems to be in no danger of losing it through inadvertence.

Roumanian centres, disseminators of distinctive Rou-
non-Magyar and non-German districts. According to the *Budapesti Hirlap,*
August 19, 1908, of the present voters 56.2 per cent are Magyar, 12.7 per cent
German, 11.4 per cent Slovák, 11.2 per cent Roumanian. On the reading
and writing basis the percentages would be—Magyar, 61.4 ; German, 14.8 ;
Slovák, 11.5 ; Roumanian, 7.2. The higher the educational standard the
more certain the preservation of the Magyar character of Hungary.

[1] "Urban manufacturing industry and trade which were in the hands of the
Germans (nearly all Hungarian towns, before all Pest and Ofen, were overwhelmingly German), and were managed by German Jews, went with flying
colours into the camp of constitutionalism and religious toleration. Nationality was willingly abandoned for the sake of ardently desired political and
religious toleration."—Springer, *Grundlagen,* etc., p. 51.

[2] In 1821 Budapest had 87,700 inhabitants, of which less than 2000 were
Magyars. In 1890, out of 491,938, 326,395 were Magyars. In 1900, the
population was 716,476, of which 79.3 per cent were Magyars, and 91.3 per
cent spoke Magyar.—*A M. K. Kormány Stat. Évkönyv,* 13.20. The same
process of natural Magyarisation is taking place in the large county towns.—
Beksics, *o.c.* 221. According to the same authority, throughout Hungary the
Magyars increased over 54 per cent in the fifty years from 1840 to 1890 ; the
Roumanians by less than 18 per cent. The latter occupy the twenty-fifth
place in order of reproductivity, the former the fourth. According to Beksics
(*Magyarország Jövője,* Budapest, 1900, 8; 11, 12, 51), there is no nationalities
question where the Magyar population reaches or exceeds 50 per cent. There
the non-Magyar population feels itself to be practically Magyar, and final
assimilation is assured. Such is the case in twenty-eight counties in which
the percentage varies from 50 to 99. At the present rate of increase in 1940
the population of Hungary without Croatia will be 24,600,000, and the Magyars will form 72 per cent of the total. Then there will no more be a
nationalities question than there is in Russia, where only 70 per cent are
Russians, including the White Russians and Little Russians.

manian civilisation in Hungary, may be searched for with a magnifying glass, but the search would be vain. Distinctive language without distinctive culture confers no claim to special consideration. As Gumplowicz says, a distinction must be drawn between the purely political conception indicated by the word " people," and the implication of a special form of civilisation contained in the word " nation." [1] To the uneducated mass a common language is the badge of local, ethnical, or religious fellowship, not the expression of a characteristic, distinctive culture, without which no guest-nationality is justified in claiming to possess the characteristics of a " nation," as distinguished from a " people," and to territorial separation in virtue thereof. Judged by this standard a demand for the political " Sonderstellung" of the Roumanians, who stand on a lower plane as regards education and civilisation than any of the constituent races of Hungary, requires a better justification than that supplied by language and origin, which, as Mancini has pointed out, are no more than the raw materials for the construction of a nation. Mr. Louis Mocsáry [2] combats the view that the nationalities entertain a desire for territorial separation, and fail to recognise the fact that the protection which a strong Hungary alone can give to the Roumanians against Russia and the Slavs in general, and to the Slavs who hate the Germans of Austria as well as those of the German empire, is of far greater value than the benefits to be derived from the disruption of the Magyar State or from an exaggerated form of local autonomy. If the Roumanians do, in fact, realise the obvious advantages conferred by membership of a united Hungarian monarchy they have hitherto been grossly misrepresented by the would-be formers of nationalistic public opinion, both within and without the limits of Transylvania. [3]

[1] *Das Recht der Nationalitäten und Sprachen in Österreich-Ungarn.* Innsbruck, 1879, 6, 298.   [2] *A Válság,* Eger, 1905.

[3] See the speech of Count Kalnoky, already referred to, as to the " Profes-

What were the sins of which the Magyars were
guilty towards the Roumanians which justified the actions
of the latter in 1848 ? To have admitted them to a
footing of religious equality, and to have put them on the
same level as regards political rights and the right to own
land as Magyars themselves. Before that date the
Roumanian common people were no worse off than the
vast majority of the dominant race which had no political
rights and could not own real property. Unfit for freedom, it was not until they were free that they rose against
their liberators. The idea of territorial separation is
foolish, as it affords justification for the use of repressive
measures.[1] It was Roman Catholicism which originally
aroused and now maintains racial feeling among the
Roumanians, but the Magyars have never followed the
example of Russia, who attacks the Catholic Church in
Poland, knowing that it is the strongest agent for the
maintenance of nationalistic feeling. As in Ireland, so in
Hungary, but for the priests and professional politicians,
political, separatistic agitation would die a natural death.[2]

soren-politik "in Roumania, and the use, which still continues, in Roumanian
schools of maps from which Hungary disappears, and in which Roumania
includes Transylvania and Hungary up to the Tisza.

[1] See the speech of Mr. Charles Hieronymi, formerly Minister of the
Interior, July 19, 1894, and Schwicker, Die nationalpolitischen Ansprüche der
Rumanen in Ungarn, in Westöstliche Rundschau, 1894, p. 212. The
Roumanian Memorandum of 1892 complains that an attempt is made to make
a united Hungarian nation, and to consolidate the position of Hungarian as
the language of State, and in the same breath complains that the Nationalities
law is not carried out ; but that law declares plainly that there is only one
nation in Hungary, the Hungarian, of which all, no matter of what origin, are
members, and makes Hungarian the State language of that nation.

[2] The peasants are influenced by economical, not by political questions.
The political agitation is solely due to a fraction of the numerically trifling
middle class which at the outside numbers 8000 persons, including all the
clergy and all school teachers, i.e. less than ⅜ per cent of the Roumanian
population. As in 1848 the ignorant peasants are led to believe that their
economic difficulties are due to the Magyars, who should be driven out of the
country by a species of Irish land-league terrorism. The poverty of the
peasants is in reality largely due to the economic tyranny of their own middle-
class co-nationalists. See Farkas Pál, Az Oláh Kérdésről, pp. 9-11, 18-22, 30

Deák regarded the regularisation of Hungary's position as regards the nationalities as almost as important as the regularisation of its relations with Austria. Hungary, he said, was "determined to do everything that could be done to remove misunderstanding short of territorial disintegration and the sacrifice of independence," and to produce a fusion of interests and a feeling of solidarity between all Hungarian citizens whatever their origin might be.   Law xliv. of 1868 was an honest attempt to satisfy the legitimate desires of the nationalities, even at the risk of infringing the rights of the paramount race. As usual the Magyars erred by taking insufficient care of their own interests.   The fundamental error of Deák, and of the law of 1868, was that it protected alien dialects, but failed to protect the rights of the language of the Magyar State.   It would have been more reasonable if the Legislature, instead of making weak concessions to the nationalities in the hope that they would the more appreciate the privileges of Hungarian citizenship, had made a knowledge of the language of State a condition precedent to the enjoyment of civic rights.   If this had been done, and if the Magyar language had been made an obligatory subject of instruction in all schools in 1868, its use would have become general in the present, second, generation.[1]   The law declares that all inhabitants of

sqq., 45-47. The remark of Eötvös is as true now as half a century ago : "Wir sehen, dass so sehr diejenigen, die an der Spitze nationaler Bewegungen stehen, auch abmühen mögen, so laut sie ihre Ansprüche im Namen des Volkes erheben, doch der Begriff dem Volke selbst noch fremd geblieben ist." —*Einfluss der herschenden Ideen*, p. 79.

[1] Section 14 of xliv., 1868, states that it is essential to the success of elementary education that the nationa ities should be instructed in their own languages up to the point where "higher academic education begins." xxvi. and xxvii. of 1907 take a step in the right direction by providing that where at least half the scholars are Magyars, Magyar shall be the medium of instruction, but steps may also be taken to give the non-Magyars instruction in their own language. In schools in which the language of instruction is non-Magyar, Magyar is to be a daily subject of instruction, with a view to the non-Magyars being able to express themselves in the language of the State both in speech and writing at the end of the fourth year of instruction. In 1904-5, the

Hungary, no matter of what nationality, form the one and indivisible Magyar nation, and as such enjoy equal rights. Concessions are made as regards the use of the various languages, as far as it is possible to do so without infringing the essential principle of national unity, and as far as is compatible with the proper working of the organs of central and local government. The law contains concessions which are not compatible with the above conditions, are impracticable, and make the strict carrying out of the law impossible. It can be and is carried out as regards equality of political rights, but cannot be as regards equality of language. When there are two or even three languages in use in a country it may be unnecessary to differentiate between them, but it is a different matter in the case of half a dozen. The work of legislation, central and local government, must be seriously hampered, and as the country, *i.e.* the predominant race which has given its name to the country, gives all its citizens the requisite facilities for learning the State language,[1] it would be only reasonable to insist on its use in all governmental and judicial matters. No doubt it is advisable that officials

language of instruction was entirely German in 272 schools, Slovák in 326, Roumanian in 2433, Ruthenian in 46, Servian in 156. In all there were 3248 schools in which Magyar was not the medium of instruction. For more than one-fourth of the total number of schools the State language practically did not exist!—Baloghy, *o.c.* p. 221. See also *A M. Kormány* 1906 *Statistikai Évkönyv*, pp. 322, 326 ; Part ii. p. 346.

[1] Law xviii. of 1879 : object, according to the preamble, to give every child the opportunity of learning the State language. Sufficient time to be given to instruction in that language that at the end of the instructional period all pupils may be able to read and write Magyar (sect. 1). After the lapse of three years a knowledge of the State language to be demanded of those desirous of obtaining a teacher's diploma (sect. 2). Those who are already teachers are required to learn the language in four years. In filling teachers' places the preference to be given to those who know the language. Sections 58 of law xxxviii. of 1868, and 13 of xxxvii. of 1876, to be strictly observed, *i.e.* every pupil is to be taught in his own language if that language is in general use in the Commune. Consequently teachers are to be provided who know the languages in general use and can teach them. In Communes of mixed languages assistant teachers for the different languages are to be provided as far as means allow.

should be acquainted with all the languages of the district
in which they are employed, and a recent order of Count
Andrássy provides for this desideratum in order to give
effect to the law of 1868, which allows the nationalities to
use their various idioms in law courts and in their
intercourse with the Executive ;[1] but this will not satisfy
the agitators, who demand territorial separation, oblivious
of the fact that the nationalities never were and never
could be nations, and that the Slavs and Roumanians of
Hungary possess civic and political rights as members of
the one and indivisible Hungarian nation, as subjects of
the Sacred Crown, and not otherwise.

If the modern creators of nationalistic public opinion
would direct their energies, not to the perpetuation of
racial antagonism, but to the task of imbuing the various
races with a proper conception of the meaning of the
phrase *Civis Hungaricus sum*, of the privileges and
obligations conferred and imposed by membership of an
indivisible Hungarian State, the preservation of which is
a matter of vital importance to every member, no matter
what his origin or language may be,[2] the Magyars would

[1] The records of the organs of local government are to be kept in the
Hungarian language, but to protect the rights of minorities can be kept also
in any language, the use of which is demanded by at least one-fifth of the
representative members (sect. 2). At the general meetings any language may
be used (sect. 3). The business language of local government officials is the
Hungarian, but if necessary they can also use one of the languages used in
accordance with the provisions of sect. 2 (sect. 5), and as far as possible they
must use the language of the various Communes and private individuals with
whom they come in official contact (sect. 6). The Communal assemblies
choose their own language for official purposes, but the records must be kept
also in any language demanded by one-fifth of the members entitled to vote
(sect. 20). Communal officials are bound to use the language of the various
members of the Commune in their dealings with such members (sect. 21).
Every one can address the Government and the local government in his own
language (sect. 23). In the Court of his own Commune every one may use his
own language ; in the Courts of his own district any language which may be
in official use in accordance with sect. 2, and in Courts of other Communes or
Districts the official language of such Commune or District (sect. 7).

[2] The Swiss is a Swiss, and feels himself to be such, though of French,
German, or Italian origin. The Belgian feels himself to be Belgian, though

have no reason for trying to hasten the natural process of magyarisation which their enemies accuse them of attempting to do. Each constituent race could be encouraged to develop its own idiom and its own special form of civilisation, if it has one, and the existing form of local government could be revised and improved, possibly in the direction of territorial subdivision with a view to safeguarding the interests of minorities, without risk of danger to the State as a whole. Under present conditions, in view of the existence of exaggerated centrifugal tendencies, anything in the nature of further decentralisation is impossible, if Hungary is to continue to be Hungary. It is usual for foreign critics to exhort the Magyars to return to the principles of Deák and Eötvös, taking it for granted that if those statesmen could return to earth they would necessarily condemn the actions of their successors. It is true that Deák warned his country against attempting to " magyarise the nationalities at all costs," and pointed to the necessity of respecting their rights ; but in the same breath he defined the nature of those rights in a phrase which earned the applause of the representatives of the nationalities in 1872, but certainly would fail to do so in the twentieth century.[1] Every nationality, he said, has the right to facilities for the education of its children in its own language—a right respect for which is carried to an absurd length in the Hungary of to-day, which spends 65 per cent of the sum annually spent on primary education on schools in which the language of instruction is not the language of the State.[2] Deák was against everything which would

the constituent elements of the nation are of diverse origin. In the United States there is no question of having more than one language of State, yet how many thousand Germans there are who, in spite of their origin and language, feel themselves to be American citizens, and resent the imputation of being German though they can hardly speak English.

[1] January 12, 1872.—Kónyi, *Deák Ferencz Beszédei*, vi. 339.

[2] In 1905-6 there were 3154 elementary schools in which the language of instruction was not Magyar. In 14.73 per cent of the total number

tend to impair the unity of the governmental system or interfere with the natural rights of the official language,[1] and Eötvös took the same line. The latter insisted that " the demands of the linguistically diverse nationalities can be satisfied only if the unity of the Kingdom and its existence as a State are guaranteed, and that the Magyars should oppose the demands of the various races only so far as the interests of the State make opposition unavoidable."[2]   He never contemplated the serious development of separatistic tendencies, and was convinced that among the various nationalities there was " not one which would not feel itself deeply injured in its most sacred feelings if anything took place which would injuriously affect the constitutional independence of the common fatherland."[3]   He pointed out the obvious fact that territorial subdivision for purposes of local government is possible " where two or three nationalities live side by side in compact masses, but is incapable of effectuation in Hungary where the nationalities are so intermingled that their geographical demarcation is out of the question," and that the result of such subdivision would be that every nationality would consider itself to be oppressed in every district in which it did not constitute the majority of the population.[4]   " It requires," he said, "an unusual degree of optimism to suppose that the territorial separation of the nationalities would permanently satisfy their demands " ; and the result would necessarily be that they

of such schools it was Roumanian. — *A M. Kormány* 1906 *Statistikai Évkönyv, l.c.* Compare this with Prussian Poland, where Polish children are obliged to go to schools in which they do not hear a single word of their own language, where children were beaten for refusing to say their catechism in German, and their mothers were fined and imprisoned for intervening. See René Henry, *Questions d'Autriche-Hongrie*, p. 147.   The *Times* of July 10, 1907, stated that the teaching of French had been recently suppressed in Lorraine, though at Thionville, for instance, of 660 children only 190 were of German origin.

[1] November 12, 1868.—Kónyi, *o.c.* vi. 101, 102.
[2] *A Nemzetiségi Kérdés*, 1903 edition, pp. 34, 41.
[3] *Ibid.* p. 44.   [4] *Ibid.* pp. 68, 71.

would ultimately aspire to be united with their congeners across the border to the destruction of the Hungarian State. Instead of putting an end to friction it would end in the destruction of personal and political liberty, and would be fatal to those very objects for the attainment of which the idea of territorial subdivision was originally conceived.[1] Eötvös was so far from anticipating the recrudescence of the racial antagonism for the existence of which the Habsburgs were primarily responsible, that he believed that every nationality would realise the necessity of having a single language of State, and would agree that that language should be Magyar.[2] If ever there was a convinced partisan of centralisation it was Eötvös, as is shown by his book, *Reform*, already referred to, which emphasised the necessity of modifying the existing system of county organisation for the reason that it was destructive to the possibility of true parliamentary government. All his chief political writings which touch on the question of the nationalities proceed from the point of view of the necessity of maintaining the territorial integrity of the Kingdom, and Magyar predominance—essentials which, in his opinion, must be kept steadfastly in mind in con-

[1] *A Nemzetiségi Kérdés*, pp. 78, 89.

[2] *Ibid.* p. 102. Even Palacky, the originator of the idea of Austrian federation, pointed out the necessity of a single language of State. He even suggested that it should be a "neutral" language, French or Latin.—*Gedankenblätter*, p. 202. "Jedes Naturvolk hat ein Recht auf seine natürliche Existenz, somit insbesondere ein Recht seine Sprache zu reden. . . . Aus diesem Prinzip folgt aber nicht, dass es in den Staatsangelegenheiten nicht eine bevorzugte Staatssprache geben dürfe, mit Ausschluss aller übrigen Volkssprachen. So weit es sich nicht um das blosse natürliche Volksleben, sondern um das Staatsleben handelt, da kann das Interesse des gesammten Staatsvolkes die Einheit der Sprache erfordern. So wird im englischen Parlament mit recht nur Englisch, nicht auch Irisch noch Galisch, gesprochen ; in den französischen Staatsbehörden nur Französisch, nicht auch Deutsch noch Keltisch."—Bluntschli, *Allgemeine Staatsrecht*, 2nd ed. i. 71. The Roumanians demand the use of their own language in Parliament. See the pamphlet drawn up by the Roumanian Committee in 1872.—Brote, *o.c.* Appendix 31. Popovici would allow all the nationalities to use their own language in the new tower of Babel, his Central Parliament.

sidering the possibility of making concessions to the subordinate races, more especially in view of the fact that the union of Germany, which could not be postponed indefinitely, and the possible fusion with that country of the German provinces of Austria, would change the whole position of affairs in Eastern Europe.[1] The anticipations of Eötvös as regards Germany have been realised, in part at all events, and the fact of their realisation would but have deepened his conviction of the necessity of the unity of the Hungarian State and of the preservation of its Magyar character. Nothing can hold Hungary together but the Magyar idea and the development of Magyar culture. Magyars created Hungary, formerly the "bulwark and shield of Christendom," and none but Magyars can preserve it. It was, therefore, a mistake to contribute to the survival of the bastard idioms of inferior races who may be capable of destroying a civilisation but certainly have shown no ability to create one. Europe, or in any case England, has no use for a Hungary that is not Magyar. England's traditional policy favours the existence of a strong power in Eastern Europe, and Dako-Roumanism, and other separatistic or federalistic fads, can only tend to threaten the existence or undermine the influence of that necessary power.

The protagonists of the federalistic principle are not yet agreed as to the precise form which disruption should take, whether it should be organised on a geographical or on a linguistic basis. Palacky, the originator of the idea of Austro-Hungarian reorganisation on federalistic lines, was a partisan of the geographical principle, and required the splitting up of the monarchy into eight provinces without regard to the interpenetration of the constituent

[1] *Die Sonderstellung Ungarns vom Standpunkte der Einheit Deutschlands*, Leipzig, 1860. See also his letter of May 5, 1865, explaining the meaning of his book, *A Nemzetiségi Kérdés*, as to his views on the necessity of resisting disintegration, maintaining Magyar supremacy, and of the utilisation by the nationalities of the opportunity given them of learning the language of State.

races. Popovici,[1] realising apparently the difficulties resulting from such interpenetration, increases the number of autonomous States to fifteen. Why not to fifty, if any regard is to be had for the rights of sparse minorities? His idea is based, not on the exigencies of local irredentism, but on the ideal of a "Gross-Österreich," the prototype of which he sees in the United States of America, and, strange to say, in the Australian Commonwealth, where there is not only unity of origin, but unity of language, the absence of which factors in Austria and Hungary is the sole cause of a state of affairs which, according to Popovici, necessitates the adoption of the federalistic principle. The Federalists are, in fact, guilty of the error of which de Sismondi has pointed out the fundamental character—of creating States for the purpose of union, instead of creating union for existing States.[2] Each of Popovici's sixteen creations would choose its own official language for the purpose of local self-government, while the official "international" language of communication would be German, as would be that of all branches of the central Government residing in Vienna, and of the army, though the German element in Austria, and German influence, are continually decreasing. Springer recognises the fact that the territorial principle, the essence of which is the subordination of possibly wealthier and more civilised minorities to a merely numerically preponderant section, must be fatal to the possibility of racial harmony. The result must be the same whether the territorial divisions are eight or eighty in number, more especially in Hungary, Transylvania, and the coast districts, where "ethnographic mosaics" exist, the arbitrary subdivision of which " would produce ridiculous results."[3] Springer suggests the division of the monarchy into small sections

[1] *Die vereinigten Staaten Gross-Österreichs*, Leipzig, 1906.
[2] *Études sur les constitutions des peuples libres*, Brussels, 1839, p. 289.
[3] *Grundlagen und Entwickelungsziele der österreichisch - ungarischen Monarchie*, Vienna, 1906, pp. 60, 195, 197.

for purposes of local self-government, and, where the carving out of racially homogeneous districts is impossible, the creation of "Mischkreise," in the government of which each nationality would be proportionately represented. That he does not regard his own recipe as a panacea for all forms of racial discontent is evident from the fact that his scheme provides for the constitution of a Court of Arbitration for the settlement of "international disputes." Federation is to be a "federation of two dimensions," providing for local self-government of a kind that will give the control to the numerically preponderant race of each arbitrarily constituted federal unit, and for the formation, without regard to geographical position, of "Nationsuniversitäten," corresponding in number to the various constituent nationalities of the monarchy. Both federalistic principles, geographical and racial, would be represented in the central Parliament of an Austrian Empire, which would thus become "a democratic Switzerland with a monarchical apex." So far as Hungary, and the nationalities of Hungary are concerned, the best criticism of Springer's scheme is to be found in his own words : "Hungary is geographically the most concentrated of lands—it is an ideal of concentration which will mock all attempts at political subdivision." [1] "Every nationality which tries to carve out a separate national State for itself will immediately have all the other seven nationalities against it." [2]   As the *Pester Lloyd* said some years ago, "Irish Home-Rule is as lemonade to nitric acid compared with the form of autonomy which the modern programme demands for our

[1] *Grundlagen und Entwickelungsziele der österreichisch - ungarischen Monarchie*, p. 169.

[2] *Ibid.* p. 186. Springer here speaks of Austria, but his words are still more applicable to Hungary than to the hereditary provinces. He admits that "eine widersinnige Föderation ist der Todt Österreichs, der gewisse Untergang."—*Der Kampf*, etc., p. 79. In Hungary it must be "widersinnig," as it is impossible to carve out homogeneous States.

various nations. Hungary would literally be torn to tatters."[1] For whose benefit? Not for that of the Germans of Austria, whose only hope of preserving their influence lies in the maintenance of the dualistic principle ; who, together with the Magyars, would have to finance an experiment, the object of which is their own destruction.[2] Not for that of Croatia, which enjoys a form of independence vastly more attractive than that which would be symbolised by the nomination of three out of the forty-two members of the central Council of "Great-Austria," federalised according to Popovici's prescription.[3] What guarantee is there that a plan which provides for the grant of autonomy even to the scattered Jews of Austria and Hungary would diminish rather than intensify racial hatred?[4] Popovici recognises the impossibility of getting any Parliament, Austrian or Hungarian, to agree to the adoption of his scheme of reconstruction ; it is therefore to be brought about by a revolution from above, by the Emperor's "Machtwort"; but it has been well said that no one ever attempted the task of breaking Parliament with any other result than that Parliament broke him, and it is unlikely that the future occupants of the Habsburg throne will form exceptions to the rule.

[1] August 10, 1905. Quoted by Popovici, *o.c.* p. 53.

[2] Popovici's real object is clear : "also nur ein kräftiges Dazwischenfahren und mit dem ganzen magyarischen Spuk ist Kehraus gemacht," *o.c.* p. 332. Let Austria perish if need be, provided Hungary is destroyed to please the Roumanians.

[3] The functions of the Federal Government would include all foreign affairs, including diplomatic and commercial representation, all military and fiscal matters, legislation regarding general political rights and judicial matters. Finance so far as federal, apart from local, receipts and expenditure are concerned. All questions of naturalisation, trade, trade-marks, patents, coinage, sanitary and veterinary police, etc., *o.c.* p. 318. If we compare the present position of the Croatian Diet with that which it would occupy as a member of an Austrian Empire federalised in accordance with Popovici's or Springer's recipes, we can hardly doubt what Croatia's opinion would be as to the merits of federalism.

[4] "Auch der gesammten Judenschaft des Reiches könnte man eine Nationalautonomie gewahren," *o.c.* p. 310.

Russia saved Austria in 1848, and Bismarck did not dismember it in 1866 for one and the same reason. Napoleon III. and Cavour both wanted Magyar aid against Austria, but neither wished permanently to weaken or destroy the only force which could maintain the balance of power in Central and Eastern Europe. Circumstances have changed to some extent since 1867, for the nationalities of the hereditary provinces have developed notions which are inconsistent with the idea of a strong and united empire. The grant of pseudo-constitutional government has only served to emphasise the fact that the component races have little or no conception of the existence of permanent Austrian national interests, different and superior to temporary local considerations.[1] The nationalities of Austria are like the trees in the adage, so numerous that it is impossible to see the forest. It has become more and more evident that the future of the realms of the Habsburgs depends on the only homogeneous race, the only nation, which they contain ; that the Magyars are almost alone in possessing something higher than a parish patriotism, and alone possess the constitutional, parliamentary instinct, allied with a feeling of attachment to the ruling dynasty, which is capable of preserving for the Habsburgs their importance in the eyes of Europe.[2] It is, therefore, a matter of general interest that nothing should take place which might tend to the weakening or dismemberment of Hungary. It seems that Palacky's much-quoted phrase requires re-editing. If there were no Hungary it would be necessary to invent one, were it possible to do so. Absolutism failed to produce a uniform, united Austrian

[1] Eötvös, *Ueber die Gleichberechtigung der Nationalitäten*, Leipzig, 1859, ch. ix.

[2] "Consciente ou inconsciente l'Autriche n'est en Orient que l'avant-garde de l'Allemagne. Elle continue, suivant une tradition inéluctable, à travailler pour le Roi de Prusse."—Leger, *La Save, le Danube et le Balkan*, Paris, 1884, p. 219.

Empire ; federalism was tried and found wanting ; and if it failed after the Magyar idea had suffered the crushing blow of Világos, it can hardly succeed when Hungary has become the predominant partner in the dual monarchy. Success could only be brought about by another '48, by a second interference of some alien giant, who would expect some recompense for his intervention, some more decisive proof of gratitude than Russia received in the early fifties ; and where would then be the strong central Power to keep the balance even between the only possible competitors for supremacy ?

Federalism may possibly be applicable to Austria, every constituent nationality of which is a fragment of some greater nation, but not to Hungary, where its application would involve the neglect of all the lessons taught by past history, where there is a homogeneous Magyar nation, which has, for a thousand years, maintained its hegemony in spite of internal and external enemies, of mutinous subordinates, and autocratic Habsburgs. The Germans of Austria were to be compensated for the loss of their control of Hungary by the strengthening of their position of predominance in Austria, but time has proved the impossibility of concentrating all power in the hands of the minority ; and though universal franchise was to create a new heaven and a new earth, the Reichsrath is so fully occupied with questions affecting the divergent interests of discontented nationalities, that it necessarily loses sight of Austria as a whole.[1]   The Germans, some

---

[1] The Reichsrath, elected by universal suffrage, contains the following parties and some minor subdivisions : Social Democrats, Christian Socialists, German Clericals, German Popular Party, German Progressives, German Agrarians, Pan-Germans, Independent Pan-Germans, Polish Club, Polish Radicals, Polish Socialists, Ruthenians, Old Czechs, Young Czechs, Czech Agrarians, Czech Clericals, Czech Realists, Czech Radicals, Slovene Liberals, Slovene Clericals, Italian Liberals, Croatians, Servians, Roumanians, and Zionists. The Christian Socialists and German Clericals combined hold 96 seats, the Social Democrats, 90. As far as Hungary is concerned, there are two main tendencies in Austria, that of the Jews, Pan-Germans, and many

of whom have the conception of an Austria, of an entity superior to its constituent elements, can never agree with Slavs who have no such conception, who interpret the racial equality proclaimed by Article 19 of the fundamental law to mean inequality of opportunity for the Germans. German racial and educational superiority makes absolute political equality an impossibility,[1] and produces the impression of an unjust monopoly of

German Liberals, to get "los von Ungarn" as the necessary first step in the direction of incorporation of German Austria in the German Empire ; and the "Grossz-Österreich" tendencies—the desire to incorporate Hungary and Croatia in a federated uniform Empire. This is the ideal of a strong party of anti-Semitic clericals. The Ruthenes hate the Poles worse than ever since the introduction of universal suffrage, for the reason that 3,500,000 of them return only 33 members, while 4,500,000 Poles return 81. See *The Times*, Dec. 17, 1907. As regards the standing quarrel of the Czechs and Germans, Popovici (*o.c.* p. 31 *sq.*) has pointed out the erroneousness of the supposition that a settlement of the language question would put an end to it. There are bloody fights from time to time in Innsbruck and Trieste, just as in Cracow and Prague, between the different nationalities. In spite of language ordinances the Czechs are more discontented than ever. The Slovenes want the creation of a separate Slovene autonomous district. The Croatians in Istria and Dalmatia want to be joined to Croatia-Slavonia. The Ruthenes want to cast off the Polish yoke and self-government. The Italians want autonomy for the Trentino. Under the circumstances the title of Popovici's book, *The United States of Great Austria*, sounds somewhat ironical. He was right in prophesying that the introduction of universal suffrage would accentuate rather than allay racial antagonism and discontent, *o.c.* p. 39. There are not only racial divisions, but political subdivisions among the representatives of every nationality. Even in the case of the smallest there are three such fractions. The Poles being Catholics, can conceivably join hands with the Clerical-Conservative landed proprietors, especially in view of their hatred of Protestant Prussia and of Russia, both of which persecute Catholic Poles. Where the Germans are in a minority they demand protection ; where they form the majority of the population they demand the rights which numerical preponderance confers, and object to the establishment of Czech schools — Springer, *Der Kampf*, etc. p. 41 *sqq.* For the extent to which race-hatred has permeated the working and even the professional classes, see the same author's *Grundlagen und Entwicklungsziele*, p. 53. What can be the future of Austria in such conditions ? Probably the proletariat will become conscious of its strength, and international socialism will put an end to all that makes Austria Austria. The only hope is the maintenance of German hegemony, which is unthinkable if Magyar preponderance in Hungary becomes a thing of the past.

[1] Der Deutschösterreicher war einmal der herschende Stamm in Österreich ; mit der Herrschaft hat es ein Ende, aber das *führende* Volk wird er

influence ; consequently, a temporary parliamentary truce has to be bought by appointing superfluous Slavs to ministerial posts.   The educated Czechs will never aban-, don the hope of converting dualism into trialism, even after a passive acquiescence in Austrian domination for nearly three centuries.   In 1871 Francis Joseph was ready to give way for the sake of peace, commissioned Count Hohenwart to negotiate with Prague, issued a rescript in which he recognised the historic rights of Bohemia, and announced his willingness to confirm them by oath on coronation as King of Bohemia.   But neither Hungary nor Germany could remain passive spectators of the new departure ; the former, for the reason that the whole basis of the Compromise would be destroyed, as well as one of the essential considerations for the passing of the laws of 1723 ; the latter, for the reason that Germany, disposed to regard itself as the heir of the Habsburgs, could not view with indifference the prospect of the diminution of German supremacy in Austria— the necessary result of Slav development.   Language ordinances, withdrawn almost as soon as given, cannot buy Bohemian affection, nor can exceptional treatment for Galicia, intended to wean the population from a possible attachment to Russia, win permanent peace for the Austrian Reichsrath, or destroy the feeling of Pan-Polish solidarity.   The pro-Italian sympathies of the Trentino, of Istria, and Trieste, are notorious ; the Ruthenians quarrel with the Poles, and the Slovenes entertain an impartial hatred for Italians and Germans alike.   But Austria is Austria still,—an artificial geographical expression justified by the existence of an Austrian aristocracy, bureaucracy, and military hierarchy, of an unusual degree of religious unity, of an unusual loyalty

immer sein.   Und besser ist es sieben Nationen zu führen als ein Hinterland der Hohenzollern zu bildern.—Springer, *Der Kampf der österreichischen Nationen,* p. 170.

to the Throne, and of an Austrian patriotism, the chief, if not the only exponents of which, outside the limits of the aristocracy, are Austrian Germans. Pangermanism was made in Germany, not in Austria,[1] of the German population of which, over eight millions strong, less than a third can be accused of Pan-German leanings. The bugbear of Panslavism is apparently temporarily laid. The spectacle presented by the treatment of the Poles, whether by Russia or by Prussia, is not sufficiently attractive to induce Czechs, Ruthenians, or Poles, to wish to give themselves up to the tender mercies of either of their great neighbours. The only uncertain factor, the only disruptive element, would seem to be discernible in a German section whose pocket interests incorporation in the German Zollverein could not possibly suit, but whose pride might be flattered by the idea of contributing to form a still greater Germany. To the picture of a possible future drawn by M. Cheradame (to whose work[2] the reader should refer for information on a subject which is outside the scope of this book), and by others who have made a study of Pan-German pretensions and intrigues, the reply is commonly made that Germany, a Protestant Power, would never willingly abandon its Protestant character by increasing its Catholic population to over twenty-six millions by the incorporation of the Catholics of Austria; but it is more than doubtful

---

[1] Schwarzenberg, with his idea of a greater Germany of 70,000,000 inhabitants, was in a way the founder of modern Pangermanism in Austria, but his object was the maintenance of Austrian supremacy, not the incorporation of Austrian provinces in Germany under Prussian hegemony.

[2] *L'Europe et la question d'Autriche.* See also Weil, *Le Pan-Germanisme en Autriche,* and René Henry, *Questions d'Autriche-Hongrie.* Of German publications the reader should refer to *Österreichs Zusammenbruch und Wiederaufbau,* Munich, 1899; *Gross-Deutschland und mittel Europa um das Jahr 1950,* Berlin, 1895; *Gross-Deutschland,* Munich, 1900; Dr. Hassé's *Deutsche Weltpolitik,* 1897; *Deutschland bei Beginn des 20. Jahrhunderts; Ein Deutsches Weltreich,* 1892, etc., especially the publications of the Odin Verlag, Munich. Both Weil and Henry deny the possibility of success to Pan-German aspirations.

whether in the twentieth century religion would weigh heavily in the balance if the possibility of a German Trieste, an all-German Danube, and a direct connexion between Hamburg and the Black Sea were in the other scale. The Pan-Germans encourage the separatistic tendencies of the Roumanians of Transylvania solely for the reason that they are in favour of anything which would tend to weaken Hungary ; the rights and wrongs of Slavs and Roumanians are a matter of perfect in-difference, and the Habsburgs are tolerable only so long as they serve to maintain the preponderance of German influence.[1] Hungary lies across Germany's path, there-fore the Magyars, the undermining of whose predominance is of essential importance to the Pan-Germans, are fit subjects for execration. That the Luegers and Schönerers, in fact, the Germans of Austria in general, make no concealment of their hatred of the Magyars, is not sur-prising. It is partly the tribute paid by jealousy to superior political genius, partly the outcome of the fact that, as Tacitus says, " *humanae naturae proprium est odisse quos laeseris.*" [2]

[1] See the speech of Deputy Iro at Salsburg, May 24th, 1907, Cheradame, *o.c.* p. 135 : " We require the reunion of the Austrian Empire with Germany. Austria will become a confederated province like the other German provinces. The Emperor will continue to style himself Emperor if he likes, but as far as we are concerned, we rely on our Mother Germany, who will not abandon her children in Austria." Also the speech of Karel Türk in the Reichsrath, Oct. 25th, 1899, *o.c.* p. 136 : " The German hereditary provinces must lean on the German Empire. . . . An economic customs-union with Germany would be the first step. . . . We Germans are ready for anything. Bring about a civil war between the Germans and the Czechs in Bohemia, Moravia, and Silesia, and you will see how the German armies of Prussia will make you dance." " The Slavs all hate us, as they know that our exaltation means death to them " (P. de Lagarde, *Deutsche Schriften*).

[2] Burgermaster Lueger's speech to the Viennese mob, June 10, 1906, his abuse of the " Judaeo-Magyars," and the cry, " los von Ungarn," " los von Galizien," " los von Böhmen," etc., is the cry of despair of the Germans, who see the end of their predominance approaching. " Das Vaterland muss *kleiner sein* " is their reading of the song. They are not concerned with the Pragmatic Sanction and the indivisibility of the " kingdoms and States represented in the Reichsrath." It is hard to imagine a more shameless confession than

Possibly it is the fate of Austria to become a conglomerate of loosely federated States ;[1] it can become such only with the consent of Magyar Hungary, the price of whose consent must necessarily be complete independence, *i.e.*, the limitation of its connexion with Austria to the obligation of mutual defence resulting from the identity of the Emperor of Austria and the King of Hungary. Let the faddists of federation at least keep their hands off Hungary, for it is scarcely an exaggeration to say that the fate of Europe depends on the proper interpretation of, and the giving of due effect to, the Pragmatic Sanction and the dualistic principle. For the present, official Germany has no desire to see the break-up of Austria, the disruption or slavisation of which means war ; for it is impossible to believe that the former country could resist the cry, " Come over and help us, we are of your own flesh and blood," addressed to it by Austrian Germans threatened with absorption in the ocean of Slavdom. Germany could no more tolerate the possession of Trieste by any Power other than a friendly Austria than Italy could tolerate the annexation of that port to the German Empire. The maintenance of the *status quo* in the Adriatic is of vital importance if a conflict is to be avoided, which, for magnitude, would be comparable only to the wars of the Napoleonic era. Trieste may be said to be the crux of a situation which will change only with the collapse of dualism—the sole guarantee of the peaceful maintenance of German influence

that of Rudolph Springer, to the effect that if Hungary had to fight Servia and Roumania, " *dankbare Schadenfreude ist alles, was Österreich als lachender Dritter beistellen wird,*" if it did not actually take a hand against Hungary, *o.c.* p. 235.

[1] Le problème fédéraliste n'existe qu'en Autriche . . .; bien que le Royaume de Hongrie comprenne des races diverses, il est un État un, historiquement centralisé, des plus vigoureux. Au contraire l'Autriche est un agglomérat d'états comme de nations, et le problème du fédéralisme, ou, si l'on veut, de la décentralisation progressive, est en train d'y être résolu."—René Henry, *Questions d'Autriche-Hongrie*, p. 73.

in Austria, and at the same time the chief obstacle to the realisation of the dreams of Pan-German and other megalomaniacs. Germany could not be an indifferent spectator of the creation of a characteristically Slav Federation in Austria and Hungary, the tendency of which would necessarily be to range itself on the Russian side against Germany. The federalisation of the monarchy must infallibly drive the Germans of Austria into the arms of the German Empire. Germany and Russia would be brought face to face, and the result must be either a general conflagration, or a compromise between those two countries (which the rest of the Continent would be powerless to prevent), providing for the division of Eastern Europe. With Trieste in German, Constantinople in Russian hands, it will be easy to forecast the fate of the minor nationalities.

It is not true that the Magyars wish to break the connexion with Austria, or misinterpret the nature of their obligations to the House of Habsburg. Two of Hungary's foremost statesmen have expressed themselves in no ambiguous terms on the subject of their country's conception of its duty, and, as compared with their pronouncements, the interested malignity of the Jews and Pan-Germans of Vienna and Berlin is undeserving of consideration. "My strong insistence, my whole country's strong insistence, on her national independence does not in the least imply a will or a wish to break from Austria. We mean to keep faith to the reigning dynasty, and no nation in its dominions is more absolutely reliable in that respect. We mean loyally to fulfil our compact of mutual defence with Austria ; in a word, what our forefathers agreed to as being obligations freely accepted by Hungary we mean to adhere to as honest men should."[1] "To-day divergencies of political opinion exist among us.

[1] Count Albert Apponyi, *The Juridical Nature of the Relations between Austria and Hungary*, p. 24.

There are some who think a separate army, and separate diplomatic representation, to be more expedient, and strive to attain them ; but there is no one who resembles the insurgents of old, who preferred to see the victory of a foreign enemy than to contribute blood and treasure to the maintenance of an illegal situation. To-day there may be some who believe that victory would be more easily obtained with two armies than with one, and agitate in favour of military separation ; but there is not one who does not desire the success of the united forces of Austria and Hungary, and would not promote the same to the best of his abilities. There may be, in fact there is, diversity of opinion among us, but there is no diversity as regards reliability and readiness for sacrifice." [1]

There is a much-quoted saying to the effect that the Magyar is blind to everything that he does not wish to see.[2] "Damn it, sir," said Nelson at Copenhagen, as he put his telescope to his sightless eye in order to be able to say that he had not seen the signal of recall, "a man has a right to be blind sometimes"—and most of all when the future of his nation is at stake. It is also said that the hegemony of the Magyars is maintained, and can be maintained, only by artificial means. It is untrue. Beksics has justly remarked that the Magyars might well despair if national unity depended on grammatical unity. It is divergence of civilisation, not grammatical differences, which prevents the coalescence into a nation of hetero-geneous elements. The history of centuries is the history of the abortive attempt to impress the German stamp on Hungary, in which there has been, and is, only one absorbent civilisation — the Magyar. The rebirth of the Magyar idea in some respects dates only from the day when, some seventy-five years ago, Stephen Széchenyi first addressed the Diet in its proper language ; but what

---

[1] Count Julius Andrássy, *Az 1867-Ki Kiegyezésről*, p. 135.
[2] Auct. Laveleye.

a change in the relative positions of Hungary and Austria those few years have brought about, in spite of intervening Világos! Three-quarters of a century are but as one day in the history of the development of a nation. In Guizot's words : "Quelle est dans la vie des peuples la grande cause qui n'a pas éprouvé de cruels revers, passé par de tristes alternatives et mis des siècles à triompher ? Dieu vend cher aux hommes le progrés et le succés. . . . Que n'en a-t-il pas coûté à l'Angleterre ? Que de révolutions et de réactions ! que de temps, de sang, et de travail ! " The Magyars also have paid the price of progress and success in labour and in blood.

INDEX

THE END

Printed by R. & R. CLARK, LIMITED, *Edinburgh.*